Exploring Jewish Literature

of the Second Temple Period

A Guide for
New Testament
Students

LARRY R. HELYER

IVP Academic

An imprint of InterVarsity Press
Downers Grove, Illinois

InterVarsity Press
P.O. Box 1400, Downers Grove, IL 60515-1426
World Wide Web: www.ivpress.com
Email: email@ivpress.com

InterVarsity Press® is the book-publishing division of InterVarsity Christian Fellowship/USA®, a movement of students and faculty active on campus at hundreds of universities, colleges and schools of nursing in the United States of America, and a member movement of the International Fellowship of Evangelical Students. For information about local and regional activities, write Public Relations Dept., InterVarsity Christian Fellowship/USA, 6400 Schroeder Rd., P.O. Box 7895, Madison, WI 53707-7895, or visit the IVCF website at <www.intervarsity.org>.

Scripture quotations, unless otherwise noted, are from the New Revised Standard Version of the Bible, copyright 1989 by the Division of Christian Education of the National Council of the Churches of Christ in the USA. Used by permission. All rights reserved.

Quotations from the Mishnah are reprinted by permission of the publisher from Jacob Neusner, The Mishnah: A New Translation, New Haven, Conn.: Yale University Press, copyright ©1988 by Yale University Press.

Quotations from the Bar Kochba letters are reprinted by permission of the publisher from Joseph A. Fitzmyer and Daniel J. Harrington, A Manual of Palestinian Aramaic Texts (Biblica et Orientalia 34), Rome: Editrice Pontificio Instituto Biblico, 1978.

Quotations from the Dead Sea Scrolls: The Dead Sea Scrolls: A New Translation by Michael Wise, Martin Abegg, Jr. & Edward Cook. Copyright © 1996 by Michael Wise, Martin Abegg, Jr. and Edward Cook. Reprinted by permission of HarperCollins Publishers Inc.

Quotations from the Letter of Aristeas to Philocrates: The Old Testament Pseudepigrapha by James H. Charlesworth, copyright © 1983, 1985 by James H. Charlesworth. Used by permission of Doubleday, a division of Random House, Inc.

Quotations from the pseudepigrapha: Translations © Oxford University Press 1984. Reprinted from The Apocryphal Old Testament edited by H. F. D. Sparks (1984) by permission of Oxford University Press.

Cover images: Tova Teitelbaum/iStockphoto
            Peter Zelei/iStockphoto

ISBN 978-0-8308-2678-0

Printed in the United States of America ∞

Library of Congress Cataloging-in-Publication Data

Helyer, Larry R.
   Exploring Jewish literature of the Second Temple period: a guide for New Testament students / Larry R. Helyer.
      p. c.m.
   Includes bibliographical references.
   ISBN 0-8308-2678-5 (pbk. : alk. paper)
      1. Bible. O.T. Apocrypha—Criticism, interpretation, etc. 2. Apocryphal books—Criticism interpretation,etc. 3. Dead Sea scrolls—Criticism, interpretation, etc. 4. Greek literature—Jewish authors—History and criticism. 5. Judaism—History—Post-exilic period, 586 B.C.-210 A.D. 6. Bible. N.T.—Criticism, interpretation, etc. I. Title.
BS1700 .H43 2002
296.1—dc21

2002019703

P 23   22   21   20   19   18   17   16   15   14   13   12   11   10   9   8   7   6   5
Y 27   26   25   24   23   22   21   20   19   18   17   16   15   14

To my beloved wife, Joyce,
who like Judith is
"beautiful in appearance, and . . . very lovely to behold. . . .
No one [speaks] ill of her,
for she [fears] God with great devotion."
(Judith 8:7-8).

Contents

Preface

This book is written primarily for undergraduates, seminary students, pastors and interested lay persons as an introduction to a large corpus of primarily Jewish writings essential for a full-orbed understanding of the New Testament. Included are selections from Apocrypha, Pseudepigrapha, Dead Sea Scrolls, Josephus, Philo, Bar Kochba Letters, Mishnah and excerpts from a few Apostolic Fathers. The selections are comprehensive but not exhaustive.

A primary objective has been to immerse the student in the texts themselves. I have provided just enough introductory matter to make sense of the individual pieces. Secondary literature at the end of each chapter generally consists of easily accessible sources in English. Footnotes occasionally direct the student to more specialized sources. I should emphasize that this book is written not for specialists but for students, though I hope specialists will appreciate some of the synthetic insights offered. As a teacher of the New Testament, my debt to specialists is enormous, as I am not a specialist in any of the above-mentioned literatures.

The classroom birthed this book. Over the years I have taught a course on the Jewish literature of the Second Temple. George Nickelsburg's introductory text *Jewish Literature Between the Bible and the Mishnah* has been a mainstay. Gradually the conviction arose that there was a need for a comparable book written from an evangelical perspective. After having devoted seven years to the project, I am more convinced than ever of the importance of this material for understanding the New Testament.

My approach is to treat the respective works, as much as is possible, chronologically. In this way one can more readily appreciate each individual piece within its own time and setting. As will be quickly discovered, however, dating these documents is not an exact science, and for some works considerable difference of opinion exists as to the time of composition. I have tried to make the best judgments possible.

I gratefully acknowledge the assistance and encouragement of several institutions and individuals. Taylor University, where I have been privileged to teach for twenty-three years, granted me a sabbatical for the fall semester of 1995. The encouragement of the Provost and Vice President for Academic Affairs, Dr. Dwight Jessup, and my congenial colleagues in the Department of Biblical Studies, Christian Education, and Philosophy has been greatly appreciated. Thanks also go to the library staff at Taylor, who expeditiously fulfilled many requests for interlibrary loans. The faculty and staff of Regent's Park College, Oxford, are also gratefully acknowledged for accommodations and assistance during a delightful stay doing research. Special mention goes to Dr. Larry Kreitzer, Fellow and Tutor for Graduates at Regent's Park College, who took an interest in my project and spent a number of hours discussing various issues relating to it. I am also greatly indebted to Dr. SeJin Koh, President of Jerusalem University College, Jerusalem, Israel, for his assistance in my research and to the École Biblique library in Jerusalem, one of the world's truly great libraries for biblical studies. Special thanks go to Daniel Reid, senior editor of reference and academic books at InterVarsity Press. His patient, unflagging support and wise counsel are deeply appreciated. Mention must also be made of my copyeditor, Robert Buller, whose eagle-eyed attention to detail and accuracy is extraordinary.

A special word of thanks, however, goes to those for whom the book was initially written. I am indebted to my students over the years who took this course and provided feedback on early editions of the book. Their comments proved to be invaluable. So many contributed that I hesitate to name some for fear of leaving out others. Nonetheless, I must single out Mr. Edward Cyzewski. Ed did yeoman work by carefully proofreading the entire work and coming up with the "Questions for Further Discussion" at the ends of the chapters. Finally, I want to express deep appreciation to Dr. Martin Abegg Jr. for his invaluable assistance in reading the chapters on the Dead Sea Scrolls and correcting errors. His expertise is truly remarkable.

I hope this book will accomplish two things: open up an entirely new perspective on the New Testament by showing its indebtedness to Second Temple Judaism and create a more appreciative attitude toward this Jewish heritage and its ongoing development in modern Judaism.

As this project comes to an end during the Christmas season, I am reminded once again that the New Testament centers on Jesus, "who was descended from David according to the flesh" (Rom 1:4).

Larry R. Helyer
Shamrock Lakes
Hartford City, Indiana
December 26, 2001

Abbreviations

Periodicals, Reference Works, Serials and General

AB	Anchor Bible
ABD	*Anchor Bible Dictionary.* Edited by D. N. Freedman. 6 vols. New York: Doubleday, 1992.
ABRL	Anchor Bible Reference Library
AGJU	Arbeiten zur Geschichte des antiken Judentums und des Urchristentums
AnBib	Analecta biblica
ANET	*Ancient Near Eastern Texts Relating to the Old Testament.* Edited by J. B. Pritchard. 3d ed. Princeton, N.J.: Princeton University Press, 1969.
ANF	The Ante-Nicene Fathers. Edited by Alexander Roberts and James Donaldson. 10 vols. 1885-1887; reprint, Peabody, Mass.: Hendrickson, 1994.
AOT	*The Apocryphal Old Testament.* Edited by H. F. D. Sparks. Oxford: Clarendon Press, 1985.
APOT	*The Apocrypha and Pseudepigrapha of the Old Testament.* Edited by R. H. Charles. 2 vols. Oxford: Clarendon Press, 1913.
BA	*Biblical Archaeologist*
BAR	*Biblical Archaeology Review*
BBR	*Bulletin for Biblical Research*
BJS	Brown Judaic Studies
BRev	*Bible Review*

CBC	Cambridge Bible Commentary
CBQMS	Catholic Biblical Quarterly Monograph Series
CCWJCW	Cambridge Commentaries on Writings of the Jewish and Christian World, 200 B.C. to A.D. 200
CJA	Christianity and Judaism in Antiquity
CRINT	Compendia rerum iudaicarum ad Novum Testamentum
DJG	*Dictionary of Jesus and the Gospels.* Edited by Joel B. Green, Scot McKnight and I. Howard Marshall. Downers Grove, Ill.: InterVarsity Press, 1992.
DLNTD	*Dictionary of the Later New Testament and Its Developments.* Edited by Ralph P. Martin and Peter H. Davids. Downers Grove, Ill.: InterVarsity Press, 1997.
DNTB	*Dictionary of New Testament Background.* Edited by Craig A. Evans and Stanley E. Porter. Downers Grove, Ill.: InterVarsity Press, 2000.
DPL	*Dictionary of Paul and His Letters.* Edited by Gerald F. Hawthorne, Ralph P. Martin and Daniel G. Reid. Downers Grove, Ill.: InterVarsity Press, 1993.
DSD	*Dead Sea Discoveries*
DSS	Dead Sea Scrolls
EBC	*The Expositor's Bible Commentary.* Edited by Frank E. Gaebelein. 12 vols. Grand Rapids, Mich.: Zondervan, 1976-1992.
EDSS	*Encyclopedia of the Dead Sea Scrolls.* Edited by Lawrence H. Schiffman and James C. VanderKam. 2 vols. Oxford: Oxford University Press, 2000.
EncJud	*Encyclopaedia Judaica.* Edited by Cecil Roth. 16 vols. Jerusalem: Encyclopedia Judaica,1972.
ExpTim	*Expository Times*
frag(s).	fragment(s)
Gk	Greek language
HBC	*Harper's Bible Commentary.* Edited by James L. Mays. San Francisco: HarperCollins,1988.
HBD	*HarperCollins Bible Dictionary.* Edited by P. J. Achtemeier et al. 2nd ed. San Francisco: HarperCollins,1996.
HDR	Harvard Dissertations in Religion

Heb	Hebrew language, New Testament book of Hebrews
HR	*History of Religions*
HSM	Harvard Semitic Monographs
IDB	*The Interpreter's Dictionary of the Bible.* Edited by G. A. Buttrick. 4 vols. Nashville: Abingdon, 1962.
IDBSup	*Interpreter's Dictionary of the Bible: Supplementary Volume.* Edited by K. Crim. Nashville: Abingdon, 1976.
IEJ	*Israel Exploration Journal*
Int	*Interpretation*
ISBE	*International Standard Bible Encyclopedia.* Edited by G. W. Bromiley. 4 vols. Grand Rapids, Mich.: Eerdmans,1979-1988.
JAL	Jewish Apocryphal Literature
JDS	Judean Desert Studies
JETS	*Journal of the Evangelical Theological Society*
JQR	*Jewish Quarterly Review*
JSNTSup	Journal for the Study of the New Testament: Supplement Series
JSPSup	Journal for the Study of the Pseudepigrapha: Supplement Series
LCL	Loeb Classical Library
LEC	Library of Early Christianity
MS(S)	manuscript(s)
MT	Masoretic Text
NASB	New American Standard Bible
NBD	*New Bible Dictionary.* Edited by I. Howard Marshall, A. R. Millard, J. I. Packer and D. J. Wiseman. 3d ed. Downers Grove, Ill.: InterVarsity Press, 1996.
NIDNTT	*New International Dictionary of New Testament Theology.* Edited by C. Brown. 4 vols. Grand Rapids, Mich.: Zondervan,1975-1985.
NIV	New International Version
NRSV	New Revised Standard Version
NT	New Testament
NTS	*New Testament Studies*

OCD	*Oxford Classical Dictionary.* Edited by S. Hornblower and A. Spawforth. 3d ed. Oxford: Oxford University Press,1996.
OT	Old Testament
OTP	*The Old Testament Pseudepigrapha.* Edited by J. H. Charlesworth. 2 vols. Garden City, N.Y.: Doubleday, 1983.
par.	parallels
QC	*Qumran Chronicle*
RB	*Revue biblique*
RevQ	*Revue de Qumran*
SBLMS	Society of Biblical Literature Monograph Series
SBLSBS	Society of Biblical Literature Sources for Biblical Study
SBLSCS	Society of Biblical Literature Septuagint and Cognate Studies
ScrHier	Scripta hierosolymitana
SNTSMS	Society for New Testament Studies Monograph Series
SVTP	Studia in Veteris Testamenti pseudepigraphica
TDNT	*Theological Dictionary of the New Testament.* Edited by G. Kittel and G. Friedrich. Translated by G. W. Bromiley. 10 vols. Grand Rapids, Mich.: Eerdmans, 1964-1976.
TS	*Theological Studies*
TynB	*Tyndale Bulletin*
UBS[4]	*The Greek New Testament,* United Bible Societies, 4th ed.
VT	*Vetus Testamentum*
ZPEB	*Zondervan Pictorial Encyclopedia of the Bible.* Edited by M. C. Tenney. 5 vols. Grand Rapids, Mich.: Zondervan, 1975.

Ancient Sources

Ag. Ap.	Josephus, *Against Apion*
Ant.	Josephus, *Jewish Antiquities*
As. Mos.	*Assumption of Moses*
b.	Babylonian Talmud
B. Meṣiʿa	*Baba Meṣiʿa*
Bar.	Baruch

Barn.	*Barnabas*
Bel	Bel and the Dragon
Ber.	*Berakot*
CD	Cairo Genizah copy of the *Damascus Document*
Contempl. Life	Philo, *On the Contemplative Life*
Dial.	Justin Martyr, *Dialogue with Trypho*
Did.	*Didache*
Diogn.	*Diognetus*
1 En.	*1 Enoch*
ʿErub.	*ʿErubin*
Flacc.	Philo, *Against Flaccus*
Gen. Rab.	*Genesis Rabbah*
Giṭ.	*Giṭṭin*
Good Person	Philo, *That Every Good Person Is Free*
Hist. eccl.	Eusebius, *Ecclesiastical History*
Ign. *Magn.*	Ignatius, *To the Magnesians*
Ign. *Phld.*	Ignatius, *To the Philadelphians*
J.W.	Josephus, *Jewish War*
Ketub.	*Ketubbot*
Let Jer	Letter of Jeremiah
Lev. Rab.	*Leviticus Rabbah*
Life	Josephus, *The Life*
m.	Mishnah
Meg.	*Megillah*
Menaḥ.	*Menaḥot*
Mid.	*Middot*
Miqw.	*Miqwaʾot*
Nat.	Pliny the Elder, *Natural History*
Num. Rab.	*Numbers Rabbah*
Od.	Homer, *Odyssey*
Pan.	Epiphanius, *Refutation of All Heresies (Panarion)*
Pesaḥ.	*Pesaḥim*

Pesiq. Rab.	*Pesiqta Rabbati*
Pss. Sol.	*Psalms of Soloman*
QG	Philo, *Questions and Answers on Genesis*
Qidd.	*Qiddušin*
Šabb.	*Šabbat*
Sanh.	*Sanhedrin*
Song of Thr	Song of the Three Young Men
Sus	Susanna
t.	Tosefta
Ta ʿan.	*Ta ʿanit*
Tg. Ps.-J.	*Targum Pseudo-Jonathan*
Tob	Tobit
y.	Jerusalem Talmud
Yad.	*Yadayim*
Yebam.	*Yebamot*
Zebaḥ.	*Zebaḥim*

Introduction

Importance

The Second Temple, standing on the same site as Solomon's great edifice, the First Temple, endured from 516 B.C. to A.D. 70. According to Jewish tradition, this was the same site as Mount Moriah, where Abraham nearly sacrificed his son Isaac (2 Chron 3:1; cf. *b. Sanh.* 89b). Of course, the structure dedicated in the time of Zerubbabel was but a pale shadow of Solomon's (cf. Ezra 3:12; Hag 2:3). In time, however, it grew to eclipse even that building in grandeur and splendor. Herod the Great began a tremendous renovation project (c. 20-19 B.C.) that resulted in the Second Temple taking its place among the great wonders of the ancient world. During Jesus' ministry, the courtyards surrounding the temple were still under construction (cf. Jn 2:20) and were finished only a few short years before its destruction by the Romans in A.D. 70.

Our interest, however, lies not primarily in the Second Temple per se but in the time span designated as the Second Temple period (586 B.C.-A.D. 135). This era was one of immense importance for Jews and Christians. The roots of both Christianity and rabbinic Judaism reach back into the soil of the various expressions of Second Temple Judaism. It was a time of crisis, transition and creativity.[1] For the most part, Christians are unacquainted with this era, which is unfortunate, because the New Testament (hereafter NT) Scriptures did not spring into existence out of a vacuum. Rather, Jewish Christians, who were heirs of this rich culture and tradition spanning more than five hundred years, wrote most of what the church now calls the NT. When one studies the NT against the backdrop of the Second Temple period, a new understanding

---

[1] I am indebted for this phraseology to George W. E. Nickelsburg, *Jewish Literature Between the Bible and the Mishnah: A Historical and Literary Introduction* (Philadelphia: Fortress, 1981), p. 1.

emerges. Christianity now appears as a sister faith, alongside rabbinic Judaism, both of whom are greatly indebted to their mother, namely, Second Temple Judaism, itself a development of the ancestral faith rooted in the Hebrew Bible. Despite common roots, Christianity and rabbinic Judaism struck out in decidedly different directions. But the kinship is unmistakable. The heart of this study lies in demonstrating the indebtedness of Christianity to the Judaism of the Second Temple period. We think the reader will find the process of rediscovering the Jewish roots of Christianity an enriching experience.

Protestant Christians have been accustomed to label the approximately four hundred years between Malachi (the last OT prophet) and the NT the "silent years." From a Protestant perspective, divine inspiration temporarily ceased after Malachi; the voice of prophecy fell silent and did not resume until John the Baptist began preaching in the Jordan Valley about A.D. 26/27 (Lk 3:1-3). But Jews were not silent, nor did they cease to reflect upon God and his ways with human beings—far from it! As our study will amply demonstrate, a sizable body of literature was composed during the period between 586 B.C. and A.D. 200. This literature, while not part of the Protestant Bible, illuminates the thought of the NT, and many portions edify one's soul. In short, there is profit in its study.[2]

Crises That Shaped the Jewish People During the Second Temple Period

The Destruction of the First Commonwealth and the First Temple (586 B.C.)

Like devastating earthquakes or volcanic eruptions, five great events reshaped the landscape in which Jews lived during this era. The first of these was the invasion of Judah by the Babylonian forces of Nebuchadnezzar and the ensuing destruction of Jerusalem with its centerpiece, Solomon's temple (587/586 B.C.). Thousands perished in the fighting; other thousands were deported hundreds of miles away to resettlement camps along the Euphrates River; thousands more fled to nearby countries as refugees. Some few thousand, the poorest of the land, remained among the ruins barely managing to eke out a living. This catastrophe was the Lord's long-threatened covenant sanction of expulsion from the land for failing to obey the stipulations of the Sinai Covenant (Ex 24; Lev 26:14-39; Deut 28:15-68; cf. Amos 4:2-3; 6:7; 7:11, 17; 9:9). The northern tribes had already been swept away by Assyrian invasions in 734-721. The long exile had begun. It left a deep scar upon the collec-

---

[2]See Martin Luther's preface to the Apocrypha in his German translation of the Bible: "books which are not held equal to the Holy Scriptures, and yet are profitable and good to read" (cited in Bruce M. Metzger, *An Introduction to the Apocrypha* [New York: Oxford University Press, 1957], p. 183).

tive memory of the Jewish people and prompted many soul-searching questions: Had God abandoned Israel forever? Would he return and be gracious, and if so, under what conditions? The literature of the Second Temple period ponders these questions and offers various responses.

The Collapse of the Persian Empire in the Wake of Alexander the Great's Invasion

The ruthless foreign policy of wholesale destruction and deportation practiced by the Assyrians and Babylonians gave way under the Persian Empire to a more lenient policy. The various ethnic groups who wished to rebuild their religious shrines in their ancestral homelands—demolished by the Neo-Babylonian depredations—were permitted to do so. Some ethnic groups were even allowed to emigrate back home—provided, of course, that they submitted to the political hegemony of the Persian Empire (cf. Ezra 1:1-4). Most Jews opted *not* to emigrate. Instead, they settled down and became participants in a vast political and commercial network. A few Jews even rose to high ranks in government (cf. Neh 1:1; 2:1; 5:14; Esther 2:5, 19-23; 3:2; Dan 1—6). For the most part, however, they were small farmers, herders, traders, merchants and artisans. On the whole they flourished, all the while continuing to hold fast to the ancestral faith. This relatively tranquil state of affairs lasted for some two centuries.

The calm was shattered by a conqueror. Racing across the Middle East (cf. Dan 8:5-8) and settling an old feud with the Persians, Alexander the Great rapidly became the master of the Near East by 331 B.C. His conquest was not, however, merely military and political; it was nothing short of a cultural revolution. Hellenistic ideals became the measure of all things. Hellenism would last for a millennium and was Alexander's greatest legacy to Western civilization. Jews now had to contend with a cultural imperialism unlike anything they had ever faced before. Our literature reflects the varied responses of Jews to this cultural phenomenon that seemed to brook no rival. The question now became, How can Jews be a part of this larger world and still remain true to the Mosaic traditions?

Persecution by Antiochus IV Epiphanes (Beginning in 175 B.C.)

One of the Seleucids, a successor dynasty carved out of the empire of Alexander after his death in 323 B.C., etched his name deeply within Jewish memory. It is not of blessed memory! Antiochus IV sought to unify his diverse kingdom by a thoroughgoing hellenization program. Unfortunately, Jews and Judaism did not fit into his grand scheme. Antiochus IV mandated that all Jews become good Greeks. This crisis prompted one of the greatest resistance movements of all time, led by the sons of Mattathias and known by the nickname the Maccabees.

Several literary works bear the unmistakable imprint of those hard times when Jews literally had to decide if their faith was worth dying for. After a protracted struggle, the Maccabee family, also known as the Hasmoneans, established an independent Jewish state that lasted from 141 to 63 B.C. We shall later read two versions of the heroic struggle that forged this political reality.

Domination by Rome (Beginning in 63 B.C.)
A new and powerful player assumed center stage in Middle East politics in 63 B.C. Rome ended the relatively short period of Jewish autonomy during the Second Commonwealth. Now Judea became an occupied province of the mighty Roman Empire. The Romans ruled Judea by either native, client kings or directly appointed Roman governors. Resentment seethed and hopes for independence waxed and waned according to living conditions under the occupation. Once again there were varied responses by the Jewish people. Some harked back to the glory days of the Maccabees and called for violent resistance. Others insisted that the people must wait for the Messiah, the promised scion of the house of David, to lead the liberation movement. Still others counseled accommodation with imperial Rome. The question now became, What are the legitimate means by which to realize the messianic prophecies of Israel's future glory? Those with vested interests tried to keep the lid on a simmering pot.

Roman Destruction of the Jewish State and Temple (A.D. 66-74)
The pot finally boiled over. After a succession of incredibly inept governors, the boiling point was reached and the country erupted into open rebellion. The Roman response was brutal and devastating. The rebels were systematically annihilated as Jewish centers of resistance one by one came under siege. Jerusalem and its splendid temple went up in smoke in A.D. 70. It was one of the darkest days in Jewish history, ironically occurring on the same calendar day (the ninth of Ab) as the destruction of the First Temple. Human losses were so great that one marvels how the Jewish people survived as a distinct entity. Not only did they survive, but they also continue to this very day. We will conclude our study of the Second Temple period by briefly noting how they reorganized and redefined themselves in the wake of this disaster and in the ensuing controversy with the new claimants to the title of "Israel," namely, the Palestinian Jesus movement.[3]

---

[3]This descriptive term for the early followers of Jesus is borrowed from James H. Charlesworth, "The Dead Sea Scrolls and the Jewishness of Jesus" (public lecture delivered at the Twentieth Forum on Jewish/Christian Relations: Judaisms, Jesus, John and the Dead Sea Scrolls, Christian Theological Seminary, Indianapolis, Ind., April 2, 2001).

Each of these crises produced great trauma and required Jews to adapt to new circumstances. It is a testament to their indomitable spirit and to God's faithfulness that they did persevere. They are survivors.

The Corpus

The Jewish literature of the Second Temple period is a sizable corpus—considerably larger than the Bible. It is also a bit daunting because no anthology brings all these diverse strands together. First, one must acquire a copy of the Apocrypha (unless one has an edition of the Bible that includes it, such as the NRSV). Second, one needs a copy of the even larger Pseudepigrapha (the editions of R. H. Charles and James H. Charlesworth extend to nearly two thousand pages each). Finally, one needs to secure an edition of the Dead Sea Scrolls (approximately four hundred pages), an edition of Philo (running to about nine hundred pages) and an edition of Josephus (another nine hundred pages). This is no small investment!

This book will delve into portions of the five distinct blocks enumerated in the above paragraph. For now we will briefly define each of these blocks. As we proceed, more detailed introductions will be provided for the individual writings under discussion.

The first block of writings is designated the Apocrypha. This derives from the Greek word ἀπόκρυφος *(apokryphos)*, which means "hidden." In the neuter plural, it means "hidden things" or, in our particular context, "hidden books." This term is not the best, but since it has been in use since the time of Jerome in the fourth century A.D., we must make do with it. Simply stated, the Apocrypha refers to those books or parts of books not found in the Hebrew Bible but included in the Greek translation of the Hebrew Bible called the Septuagint (abbreviated LXX). Matters are not, however, quite so simple. We will later discuss the formation of the LXX and its important role for both Jews and Christians. Scholars variously date the individual works from as early as the fourth century B.C. down to about A.D. 90.

The second block of material goes under the title of Pseudepigrapha. The Greek neuter plural ψευδεπίγραφα *(pseudepigrapha)* literally means "falsely ascribed." It designates Jewish literature written between 200 B.C. and A.D. 200 and spuriously ascribed to various prophets, kings and ancient worthies mentioned in the Hebrew Scriptures. Once again, this is not the best term to describe the diverse contents of this material, but the designation is long-standing and traditional. It actually encompasses a variety of genres, such as apocalypse, testament, hymn, narrative fiction and so forth. None of this material is found in the Hebrew Scriptures or, for that matter, in the LXX. Thus, it does not appear in English Bibles and, for the most part, is even more unexplored territory than the Apocrypha. I think the reader will have a mixed reaction reading this literature. The apocalyptic writings are at times quite fascinating, especially since they stand in some relationship to the apocalyptic visions of the end times found in both the OT and NT. Other sections are frankly quite tedious: lengthy descriptions of the supposed inner workings of the movement of heavenly bodies and atmospheric conditions generate little enthusiasm! But one cannot fail to be impressed by expressions of sincere piety and unquenchable faith encountered in this literature.

The Dead Sea Scrolls have received much more publicity than the previous two blocks of material, in part because they precipitated fierce scholarly debates over their interpretation, provenance and significance for Judaism and Christianity. But even more sensational have been the fantastic conspiracy theories alleging that their contents were deliberately withheld from the public because they undermined key doctrines of Christianity. As we shall see, there is no basis for such charges. These writings (mostly fragments of works, not complete manuscripts) from the caves of Qumran are perhaps the single most important archaeological discovery of the twentieth century. We may generally date the Qumran library to the period circa 140 B.C.-A.D. 68. Like the Pseudepigrapha, the Dead Sea Scrolls encompass a wide range of literary genres. Probably the most significant for understanding the ethos of this group are the community rules—expositions dealing with standards of behavior and penalties for violations, ritual purity laws, and affirmations of belief. The Dead Sea Scrolls reveal a movement with a degree of commitment rarely matched in Christendom. Some of the hymns produced by this community are deeply moving and spiritually uplifting. The parallels between this community and the early Christian movement will, of course, be of utmost interest.

The Jewish writer Philo, from Alexandria, Egypt (c. 20 B.C.-A.D. 50), has bequeathed to Western civilization a voluminous collection of commentaries on the Bible, along with a number of philosophical treatises. His importance lies in offering us a glimpse into the world of highly educated Jews quite at home in the Hellenistic culture at the end of the first century B.C. and in the first half of the first century A.D. In other words, we have a near contemporary of both Jesus and Paul, but one who continues, in his own mind at least, to adhere faithfully to the traditions handed down from Moses. Philo affords a prime example of how an acculturated Jew harmonized and integrated his faith with the intellectual tradition of the Hellenistic world. It is a fascinating result. Philo's exegetical and hermeneutical techniques influenced Jews, and especially Christians, for centuries. In a sense, his legacy still lives on.

The importance of Flavius Josephus (c. A.D. 37-100) for understanding the history of early Judaism and early Christianity can scarcely be overemphasized. He fills a huge gap in our knowledge of the Second Temple period. Josephus was a Jewish historian who wrote for a cultured Roman audience.

Two of his works are of special importance: *Jewish War* and *Antiquities of the Jews*. In both we find a survey of our period. The latter work is much broader in scope, being a sort of paraphrase or running commentary on biblical history as found in the Hebrew Bible (and supplemented by traditional Jewish interpretation—with perhaps a dash of Josephus's own creativity thrown in!). *Antiquities* leaves off on the eve of the outbreak of the first revolt against Rome. *Jewish War* starts with the conquests of Alexander the Great and traces Jewish history up to the end of the war against Rome. Readers will enjoy the works of Josephus, since he knows how to tell a good story, and the story itself is quite amazing. If Josephus stretches the truth a bit here and there— well, so be it! We sample another of his works, *Against Apion*, because it is an apologetic work defending Judaism against anti-Judaic slanders and phobias. Listening in on this spirited reply will throw light on a larger and ubiquitous problem that continues to this very hour: the plague of anti-Semitism.

To round out our excursion into the Jewish literature of the Second Temple, we will read some private letters and documents recovered by archaeologists from the period of Bar Kokhba, the second revolt against Rome in A.D. 132-135. Reading these pieces clothes with humanity the people mentioned in the correspondence. In spite of war and death, life went on and people made decisions about all sorts of matters, such as marriage and divorce, buying and selling, and the nitty-gritty details of life. We will also briefly introduce the immense world of Mishnah. This demonstrates how Jews transformed themselves and maintained their identity in the centuries following the collapse of the Second Commonwealth. Rabbinic Judaism ushered in, for more than fifteen hundred years, an era of uniformity within Judaism. Only the intellectual earthquake called the Haskalah (the Jewish Enlightenment of the eighteenth century A.D.) eventually unravels the unified, symbolic worldview that rabbinic Judaism fashioned at the end of the Second Temple period.

Finally, it should not be forgotten that the NT itself is a product of Second Temple Judaism.[4] As Christians, we all too often forget the larger context in which it emerged. Thus we will at numerous points refer to NT documents as they supplement, amplify or challenge various views and positions staked out by the various groups or individuals within the larger arena of Second Temple Judaism.

We conclude this section by drawing attention to Jacob Neusner's helpful

---

[4]As J. Julius Scott Jr. reminds us in *Customs and Controversies: Intertestamental Jewish Backgrounds of the New Testament* (Grand Rapids, Mich.: Baker, 1995), p. 32. Bruce Chilton and Jacob Neusner argue that we really should speak about *"the* Judaism *of* the New Testament" (*Judaism in the New Testament: Practices and Beliefs* [New York: Routledge, 1995], p. 8 [italics theirs]). See pp. xii-18 for their full arguments.

analysis of Judaism and its developments.[5] Neusner posits four Judaic systems that have appeared in history:

1. The age of diversity (586 B.C.-A.D. 70)
2. The formative age of Judaism (A.D. 70-640)
3. The classical period of Judaism (A.D. 640-1787)
4. The modern age—the second age of diversity (A.D. 1787-present)

From this outline it is evident that the Second Temple period was the first great age of diversity. Why did this diversity occur? What factors led to such schism within the Jewish people? These and other questions will be better answered at the conclusion of our study. Working through this era will prompt similar questions for Christians. Why are we so diverse today? What factors have led to such schism? In some respects Jews and Christians are mirror images of each other. I hope that this excursion into a Judaism now long past will provide some light on our own spiritual pilgrimage.

---

[5]Neusner has set this out in numerous works. For a lucid discussion, see his *Self-Fulfilling Prophecy: Exile and Return in the History of Judaism* (Boston: Beacon, 1987), pp. 5-17.

For Further Reading

Craig A. Evans, *Noncanonical Writings and New Testament Interpretation* (Peabody, Mass.: Hendrickson, 1992), pp. ix-8. An evangelical scholar's brief overview of an even larger corpus of related literature.

Bruce M. Metzger, *An Introduction to the Apocrypha* (New York: Oxford University Press, 1957), pp. vii-10, 175-247. A standard overview of the contents and influence of the Apocrypha.

George W. E. Nickelsburg, *Jewish Literature Between the Bible and the Mishnah: A Historical and Literary Introduction* (Philadelphia: Fortress, 1981), pp. ix-7. A useful survey of both the method of study and the corpus of Second Temple Judaism by a recognized authority on the subject.

Stephen F. Noll, *The Intertestamental Period: A Study Guide,* TSF-IBR Bibliographic Study Guides (Downers Grove, Ill.: InterVarsity Press, 1985). An overview of areas of study and bibliographic resources. For a more current bibliography, see the entry by Chapman and Köstenberger below under Advanced Reading.

Lawrence H. Schiffman, *From Text to Tradition: A History of Second Temple and Rabbinic Judaism* (Hoboken, N.J.: Ktav, 1991). A survey of the era by an internationally recognized Jewish scholar.

————, *Texts and Traditions: A Source Reader for the Study of Second Temple and Rabbinic Judaism* (Hoboken, N.J.: Ktav, 1998), pp. 1-5.

J. Julius Scott Jr., *Customs and Controversies: Intertestamental Jewish Backgrounds of the New Testament* (Grand Rapids, Mich.: Baker, 1995), pp. 17-39. A good survey of the period and literature by an evangelical scholar.

Michael E. Stone, *Scriptures, Sects and Visions: A Profile of Judaism from Ezra to the Jewish Revolts* (Philadelphia: Fortress, 1980), pp. 1-25. A succinct discussion of the period and literature by an internationally recognized Jewish scholar.

James C. VanderKam, *An Introduction to Early Judaism* (Grand Rapids, Mich.:

Eerdmans, 2001), pp. xi-52. A good survey of the period by an internationally recognized scholar.

Advanced Reading

Richard Bauckham, "The Relevance of Extra-Canonical Jewish Texts to New Testament Study," in *Hearing the New Testament: Strategies for Interpretation*, ed. Joel B. Green (Grand Rapids, Mich.: Eerdmans, 1995), pp. 90-108.

Gabriele Boccaccini, *Middle Judaism: Jewish Thought, 300 B.C.E. to 200 C.E.* (Minneapolis: Fortress, 1991), pp. xiii-xix, 1-25.

David W. Chapman and Andreas J. Köstenberger, "Jewish Intertestamental and Early Rabbinic Literature: An Annotated Bibliographic Resource," *JETS* 43 (2000): 577-618.

Bruce Chilton and Jacob Neusner, *Judaism in the New Testament: Practices and Beliefs* (New York: Routledge, 1995), pp. xii-18.

Isaiah Gafni, "The Historical Background," in *Jewish Writings of the Second Temple Period: Apocrypha, Pseudepigrapha, Qumran Sectarian Writings, Philo, Josephus*, ed. Michael E. Stone, CRINT 2 (Assen: Van Gorcum; Philadelphia: Fortress, 1984), pp. 1-31.

Michael E. Stone, "Introduction," in *Jewish Writings of the Second Temple Period: Apocrypha, Pseudepigrapha, Qumran Sectarian Writings, Philo, Josephus*, ed. Michael E. Stone, CRINT 2 (Assen: Van Gorcum; Philadelphia: Fortress, 1984), pp. xvii-xxii.

One

The Rise of the
Second Commonwealth

In our introduction we surveyed the landmark events that shaped the era of the Second Temple. We begin our journey through the literature of the Second Temple by first reviewing the biblical description of the collapse of the First Commonwealth.

Destruction and Exile

Second Kings 25 concludes a work (1 and 2 Kings) surveying the kings (and occasionally queens) of Israel and Judah from a theological and religious point of view. Each is evaluated on the basis of adherence to the Mosaic covenant made at Sinai. With the reign of the notorious Manasseh, the sacred historian editorializes that the limit to God's patience and grace had been reached (2 Kings 21:10-16). The violations of covenant loyalty were too many and too flagrant. The day of reckoning was at hand, and even the godly Josiah could not stave off the inevitable (2 Kings 23:26-27). Thus 2 Kings 25 narrates the tragic moment when the ultimate covenant sanction, expulsion from the land (cf. Lev 26:14-39; Deut 28:15-46), was finally enacted.

As we pick up the story, the last king of Judah, Zedekiah, has made a fatal political decision: attempting to rebel against the Neo-Babylonian Empire of Nebuchadnezzar. The historian narrates the swift response: in late December 589 or early January 588 B.C., Nebuchadnezzar's army invaded the city and settled in for a long siege.

Siege warfare was not a subtle strategy; it amounted to a grim process of allowing deprivation to take its toll upon the defenders inside a city. Malnutrition and disease militated against the besieged; the besiegers had to fight off boredom and maintain an absolutely tight blockade, permitting nothing in or out. The length of time required for the process depended, of course, upon the provisions available to the besieged. In this case the siege lasted two and a half years, until July 586 B.C.[1] According to the sacred historian, "the famine became so severe in the city that there was no food for the people of the land" (2 Kings 25:3). Now was the time for an all-out assault on selected points of the walls judged to be most vulnerable to the battering rams. With the defenders demoralized and weakened, the outcome was not surprising: "Then a breach was made in the city wall" (2 Kings 25:4). The king of Judah and his army made a desperate bid to escape eastward to the ancient kingdoms of Ammon and Moab (today the Hashemite Kingdom of Jordan), but the fleet cavalry of Nebuchadnezzar headed them off before they could cross the frontier of the Jordan River. Ironically, near the ancient site of Jericho, where Israel's national history in the Promised Land had begun so gloriously under Joshua centuries before (cf. Josh 5—6), the kingdom of Judah suffered its final defeat. Judah was no more.

The historian rapidly summarizes the dismantling of all semblance of statehood. Survivors of any standing or consequence were either executed or deported to Babylon. Only the peasants were left in the ruined countryside and rubble to fend for themselves. A Judean governor was placed over the region, directly answerable to the Babylonian government. Of primary importance for the narrator is the description of the burning of the temple and the looting of its last remaining treasures and utensils. Psalm 74:3-8 probably describes this tragic occasion:

> Direct your steps to the perpetual ruins; the enemy has destroyed everything in the sanctuary. Your foes have roared within your holy place; they set up their emblems there. At the upper entrance they hacked the wooden trellis with axes. And then, with hatchets and hammers, they smashed all its carved work. They set your sanctuary on fire; they desecrated the dwelling place of your name, bringing it to the ground. They said to themselves, "We will utterly subdue them"; they burned all the meeting places of God in the land.

According to Jewish tradition (*t. Ta'an.* 4:10; *b. Ta'an.* 29a), the temple's destruction occurred on the ninth of Ab (July). The temple treasures, furniture and utensils were toted off to Babylon to grace Nebuchadnezzar's palace and temples. Some of it, no doubt, was melted down and minted in order to

---

[1]Some scholars date the fall of Jerusalem to the summer of 587 B.C., with a siege lasting eighteen months.

finance the huge costs of waging war. The historian laconically concludes: "So Judah went into exile out of its land" (2 Kings 25:21b).

The long narrative of Kings does not, however, end on this melancholy note. Remarkably, we learn that back in the capital of the Neo-Babylonian Empire a change of fortune occurred. Jehoiachin, who preceded Zedekiah and who had been deported to serve a life sentence in prison, probably for treason (2 Kings 24:8-12; cf. Jer 52:31-33), found favor in the eyes of Evil-merodach, a successor of Nebuchadnezzar, and was released from prison. Not only so, he was elevated to the level of a pensioner, regularly dining at the king's court.[2] This extraordinary turn of event signaled in a small way that God had not totally abandoned his people. There was still hope for the Davidic dynasty.

In the meantime, the exiles somehow had to put their lives together and carve out a new living in a strange and foreign land. We possess only a few, but highly valuable, glimpses of this dispersed community. The meager sources at our disposal demonstrate the lasting trauma inflicted by the destruction of Judah and Jerusalem. One of the most poignant of these is the book of Lamentations. Written not long after the great disaster, these communal laments reflect back with deep sadness on what had been.[3] In the first chapter (arranged as an acrostic; i.e., each stanza begins with a different letter of the twenty-two-letter Hebrew alphabet), the reader is swept along in a funeral procession as if accompanying a bier to the grave. The grief is nearly inexpressible: "How lonely sits the city. . . . How like a widow she has become. . . . She weeps bitterly in the night, with tears on her cheeks; . . . she has no one to comfort her . . . and finds no resting place" (Lam 1:1-3). The passage personifies Jerusalem as a widow left with no support and consolation in the world. This must have seemed like the plight of all who survived the harrowing trek across the desert to their encampments along the Euphrates River.

How would they be able to make new lives for themselves and yet maintain their identity as a people? Several pieces of evidence provide some answers. The book of Lamentations supplies what is doubtless the most important. The human spirit can overcome incredible adversity when there is determination. But determination requires hope and a sense of purpose, which, for the most part, was not lacking among the Jewish people. On the contrary, there was an enduring conviction that God was not finished with them yet, that the last

[2] Archaeological excavations have confirmed this detail. See the note in *The New Oxford Annotated Bible: New Revised Standard Version,* ed. Bruce M. Metzger and Roland E. Murphy (New York: Oxford University Press, 1991), OT 502, note on 25:27-30. Chits were discovered listing rations to various individuals, one of whom is none other than *Ia-ku-ú-ki-nu* (Jehoiachin), son of the king of *Ia-ku-du* (Judah). For text, see *ANET,* p. 308c.
[3] For specifics, see *New Oxford Annotated Bible,* OT 1047.

chapter had yet to be written. Lamentations 3:19-24 underscores this conviction. The exiles fell back on the unchanging character of God in the midst of
daunting circumstances: "great is your faithfulness" (Lam 3:23b). Christians
may recognize that this passage serves as the text for one of the most beloved
of all Christian hymns. The Diaspora community rallied around the notion that
the kingdom of God was still intact, in spite of the fact that their national existence had come to a crashing end. Out of the ashes, like a phoenix, arose the
confession: "But you, O LORD, reign forever; your throne endures to all generations" (Lam 5:19). This, by the way, is the same confession that had launched
Israel's theocratic history at the exodus (cf. Ex 15:18).

As for Jerusalem, its place in the history of Israel would always be kept
alive in Jewish memory. "If I forget you, O Jerusalem, let my right hand
wither! Let my tongue cling to the roof of my mouth, if I do not remember
you, if I do not set Jerusalem above my highest joy" (Ps 137:5-6).[4] In a foreign
land the deportees faced the taunts of the haughty Babylonians. "For there
our captors asked us for songs, and our tormentors asked for mirth, saying,
'Sing us one of the songs of Zion!' " (Ps 137:3). The initial response of the Jewish survivors was understandable: "By the rivers of Babylon—there we sat
down and there we wept when we remembered Zion" (Ps 137:1). But one can
weep just so long. Life must go on, and so it did.

Two prophets, Ezekiel and Jeremiah, lived through this traumatic era,
though in quite different circumstances. They afford further glimpses into
those early years of exile and help us understand how this people survived.
Ezekiel was deported to Babylon in 597 B.C., well before the destruction of
Jerusalem in 586 B.C. (cf. 2 Kings 24:14). Four years later (593 B.C.) the Lord
called Ezekiel as a prophet (Ezek 1:1). From his book we glean information
about the status and condition of these deportees. According to Ezekiel 1:1,
he was settled along a canal, the Chebar, that flowed southeastward from the
Euphrates at the bend near Babylon and then rejoined the Euphrates further
south in the region of Erech. One of the settlement towns along the Chebar
was called Tel-abib (Ezek 3:15), located in the Nippur region.[5] The Babylonians probably settled Jews in areas that the government wished to

---

[4]The significance of Jerusalem in Jewish history can hardly be overemphasized. In modern times the capture of East Jerusalem, and especially access to the Western Wall (the
remnants of Herod the Great's retaining wall for the temple platform), touched a deep
chord within the hearts of many Jews. A moving poem by Chaim Chefer, "The Paratroop-
ers Weep" (in Hebrew), recalls the emotional moment in June 1967 when Israeli para-
troopers forced their way through the narrow streets of Old Jerusalem to this ancient wall
whose access had been denied by the Jordanian government since 1948.

[5]One should mention here that the name Tel-abib, or Tel Aviv, as it is pronounced in modern Hebrew, lives on in the modern Israeli city of that name along the Mediterranean
coast. This was the first modern city built by Jews at the end of the nineteenth century.

develop.[6] One can be sure the locations were not initially well-appointed neighborhoods! The homes were made of the mud brick so typical even today of this region of the world (cf. Ezek 4:1; 8:1). Ezra supplements this information by providing the names of several towns from which Jews emigrated when they returned to Judah (Ezra 2:59; 8:17). We know from archaeological evidence that Jews lived in at least twenty-eight towns out of a total of about two hundred in the Nippur region.[7] The Ezra narratives imply that Jews were permitted a measure of self-governance under the direction of "family heads." Ezekiel mentions a group consisting of "the elders of Judah" and certain "elders of Israel" who seem to have functioned as a sort of council (cf. Ezek 8:1; 14:1). This limited autonomy concerned matters of personal status, such as marriage, divorce and religious questions. Even today in the modern state of Israel the various recognized religious communities adjudicate matters of personal status. This system, called "Millet," derives from the Ottoman Empire (beginning in the fourteenth century A.D.) but may have roots reaching back into the Babylonian and Persian eras. One of the reasons the Jews survived as a distinct ethnic-religious community lay in their ability to maintain, over the centuries, some form of internal governance, direction, advice and encouragement for the various Diaspora communities.[8]

In addition to the Jews who were deported to Babylon, there were substantial numbers who fled to neighboring countries at the time of the Babylonian invasion: Ammon, Moab, Edom and especially Egypt (Jer 40:11-12; 41:15; 42:1—44:30; cf. Obad 14, 20). From the Elephantine papyri we learn of a Jewish community in Elephantine, Egypt (about 550 miles south of Cairo at the Aswân Dam), during the Persian period. This community probably had its origins in the aftermath of the Babylonian invasion of Nebuchadnezzar.[9] There is reason to believe that these isolated communities did have some contact with one another throughout the exilic and postexilic periods.

The book of Jeremiah adds another important component. Jeremiah lived through the horrors of the final siege of Jerusalem by Nebuchadnezzar (cf. Jer 39:1—40:6). Before the total collapse of Judah in 586, Jeremiah communi-

---

[6]For a hypothetical reconstruction of Babylonian policy during this era, see Jon L. Berquist, *Judaism in Persia's Shadow: A Social and Historical Approach* (Minneapolis: Fortress, 1995), pp. 15-17.

[7]See Elias J. Bickerman, "The Babylonian Captivity," in *The Cambridge History of Judaism,* vol. 1: *Introduction; The Persian Period,* ed. W. D. Davies and L. Finkelstein (Cambridge: Cambridge University Press, 1984), p. 346 and n. 2.

[8]For a fascinating account of how modern Zionists were able to capitalize upon their political skills in the fashioning of a new Jewish state, see Kenneth W. Stein, *The Land Question in Palestine, 1917-1939* (Chapel Hill: University of North Carolina Press, 1984).

[9]See further R. K. Harrison, "Elephantine Papyri," *ISBE* 2:58-61. For a translation of two of these papyri, see *ANET,* pp. 222-23.

cated by letter to the exilic community in Babylon. He urged the exiles to settle down and set about the business of earning a livelihood:

> Thus says the LORD of hosts, the God of Israel, to all the exiles whom I have sent into exile from Jerusalem to Babylon: Build houses and live in them; plant gardens and eat what they produce. Take wives and have sons and daughters; . . . multiply there, and do not decrease. But seek the welfare of the city where I have sent you into exile, and pray to the LORD on its behalf, for in its welfare you will find your welfare. (Jer 29:4-7)

This exhortation was taken seriously, with the result that Jews soon contributed to the vast Babylonian and Persian empires. They became small farmers, shepherds, irrigation experts, estate managers, skilled artisans and merchants. The discovery in the Nippur region of commercial documents mentioning a Jewish family, the Murashu family, confirms the involvement of Jews in the economy of the late Babylonian period.[10] Some Jews, as attested in books such as Daniel and Esther, even rose to positions of great political influence and power. It seems reasonable that the Babylonians (and later the Persians) would capitalize on the bureaucratic expertise of deported Jews who had served in the Judean government.[11] This was not, however, typical of most Jews. Some, serving as government purchasing agents, plied the caravan routes radiating across the Middle East and extending even to the Far East. There is no evidence of any Jewish involvement in business and finance during the Babylonian captivity, something that would later become a hallmark of Jewish ethnic identity.[12]

Both Jeremiah and Ezekiel allude to communication between Jews living in Judah and the exiles in Babylon. Even after the destruction of Jerusalem, some contact was maintained between the remnant in Jerusalem and the Diaspora communities (cf. Neh 1:1-3; Ezek 33:21-22). While it is true that from 586 B.C. to this day a majority of Jews have lived in Diaspora rather than in the land of Israel, never has there been a complete break between the Diaspora and the Holy Land.[13] This strong sense of connection between the

---

[10]For an English translation of a tax receipt from one of the Murashu family members, see *ANET,* p. 221d. See n. 75 for the source to consult for all the business documents that were discovered.

[11]See Berquist, *Judaism in Persia's Shadow,* pp. 15-17.

[12]Bickerman pointedly observes: "The modern idea, expressed originally by Voltaire, that the Jews became tradesmen and usurers in the Babylonian captivity, belongs to the professional mythology" ("Babylonian Captivity," p. 348).

[13]The Jewish population of the State of Israel has grown to some 5.3 million. In the United States alone there are some 5 million Jews. Whether a majority will eventually live in Israel depends upon further Russian Jewish immigration and the large American Jewish community.

ancestral homeland and the Diaspora has undoubtedly been a factor in the continuance of the Jewish people as a distinct ethnic-religious community. The last line of the Passover Seder recited annually to commemorate the exodus from Egypt gives voice to this connection: "Next year in Jerusalem!"

Return and Restoration

With Cyrus the Great's decree in 538 B.C. allowing Jews to return to their ancestral home and to rebuild their temple in Jerusalem, a new optimism surged through the collective hearts of the Diaspora.[14] One senses this newfound hope in the majestic poetry of Isaiah 40—55.[15] "Get you up to a high mountain, O Zion, herald of good tidings; lift up your voice with strength, . . . lift it up, do not fear; say to the cities of Judah, 'Here is your God!' " (Is 40:9; cf. 43:1-7, 14-21; 44:21-28). The key player who prompted this enthusiasm was Cyrus the Great. Though personally unaware of it, he performed the bidding of the Lord, the God and King of Israel: "Thus says the LORD . . . who says of Jerusalem, 'It shall be inhabited,' and of the cities of Judah, 'They shall be rebuilt, and I will raise up their ruins'; . . . who says of Cyrus, 'He is my shepherd, and he shall carry out all my purpose'; and who says of Jerusalem, 'It shall be rebuilt,' and of the temple, 'Your foundation shall be laid' " (Is 44:24-28; cf. 45:13; 48:14-15, 20-21; 49:8-23).

According to the book of Ezra, God also stirred up the hearts of family heads in the tribes of Judah and Benjamin and of priests and Levites to go back and rebuild the temple (Ezra 1:5). In this endeavor there was financial support by those who elected not to go back to Judah—apparently the sizable majority of exiles. The return seems to have taken place in stages. The first wave (537 B.C.?) was under the leadership of Sheshbazzar (Ezra 1:8), possibly a son of Jehoiachin and thus a Davidide who might reasonably be expected to assume leadership under Persian auspices. For some reason he disappears from the record, and we can only speculate why. Zerubbabel, a nephew of Jehoiachin, and the high priest Jeshua became key players in the second wave of immigration back to the ancestral homeland: a census from this immigration tallies 49,897 persons (Ezra 2:64-65; Neh 7:66-67). The Persian government appointed Zerubbabel governor of the province Yehud (the Aramaic equivalent of Judah). Yehud was a very small province (Esther 1:1 says there were a total of 127 such provinces in the days of Xerxes I [485-464 B.C.])

---

[14]For a Persian historical text recounting Cyrus's defeat of Babylon and his permission for exiles to return and rebuild their sanctuaries, see *ANET,* pp. 315-16.

[15]On the difficult issue of dating this section, see William Sanford LaSor, David Allan Hubbard and Frederic William Bush, *Old Testament Survey: The Message, Form, and Background of the Old Testament* (Grand Rapids, Mich.: Eerdmans, 1982), pp. 371-78.

that was part of a much larger administrative unit, a satrapy called "Beyond the River" (Cf. Ezra 5:3, 6; 6:6). This satrapy stretched all the way from the Euphrates River at Tiphsah to Gaza on the Mediterranean coast. Archaeological finds from this period in the land of Israel include jar handles and coins with the name "Yehud" either impressed or inscribed on them. These artifacts occur only in areas of ancient Judah that the biblical sources indicate were inhabited by Jews during the restoration.[16] The high priest Jeshua, a descendant of the great Zadok of Solomonic times, assumed leadership in religious and cultic matters. This dual type of leadership—civil and cultic—characterized much of Jewish life in the postexilic era and became, at times, a source of conflict, as we shall see in later chapters.

Alongside these leaders were prophets who criticized and cajoled the returnees in their endeavors and who were more than a little responsible for the rise of the Second Commonwealth. The prophets Haggai, Zechariah and Malachi throw welcome light on conditions during these difficult years of rebuilding. Haggai captured the hard times in these words: "You have sown much, and harvested little; you eat, but you never have enough; you drink, but you never have your fill; you clothe yourselves, but no one is warm; and you that earn wages earn wages to put them into a bag with holes" (Hag 1:6; cf. Zech 8:10). Haggai and Zechariah, however, laid the blame for these conditions squarely at the feet of the returnees. They had put their own welfare above that of God and his house and had not faithfully observed the moral and ritual requirements of the law (Hag 2:11-14; Zech 1:4-6). Both prophets insisted that when priorities are right, God's blessing will flow and glory will return (Hag 2:6-9, 19; Zech 2:8-13; 8:3-8).

Of course, towering above all the key figures thus far mentioned are two heroes of the period: Ezra and Nehemiah. Without their dogged persistence and unbending convictions, it is doubtful that the restoration would have succeeded.

Ezra the scribe was a priestly reformer. Empowered by Artaxerxes I, he set off for Yehud with some 1,500 returnees (Ezra 8:1-20) as an official envoy of Persia, arriving there in 458 B.C. (Ezra 7:8). Once there he reacted strongly against mixed marriages with the neighboring peoples.[17] All such unions were

---

[16]See Yohanan Aharoni and Michael Avi-Yonah, *The Macmillan Bible Atlas*, 3d ed., ed. Anson F. Rainey and Ze'ev Safrai (New York: Macmillan, 1993), p. 130.

[17]The *NIV Study Bible* suggests that "one of the reasons for such intermarriages may have been the shortage of returning Jewish women who were available. What happened to a Jewish community that was lax concerning intermarriage can be seen in the example of the Elephantine settlement in Egypt, which was contemporary with Ezra and Nehemiah. There the Jews who married pagan spouses expressed their devotion to pagan gods in addition to the Lord. The Elephantine community was gradually assimilated and disappeared" (Kenneth Barker et al., eds., *The NIV Study Bible* [Grand Rapids, Mich.: Zondervan, 1985], p. 688, note on Ezra 9:1).

dissolved and vows taken that none would be contracted in the future (Ezra 9—10). One of the most memorable events of Ezra's tenure is recorded in Nehemiah 8. Ezra assembled the people in the square before the house of the Lord and read to them from the law "from early morning until midday" (Neh 8:1-8; cf. 9:3). Commitment to the Mosaic law as its basic constitution characterized postexilic Judaism. Controversy over the law would arise, but it would always be a question of the *interpretation* of the law, not its binding authority.

That other doughty leader, Nehemiah, was also a highly placed official in the Persian government. Bearing the title "cupbearer," a close confidant and attendant of the king (Neh 1:11), Nehemiah obtained permission from Artaxerxes I in about 445 B.C. to return for a specified time to rebuild Jerusalem's walls.[18] These had apparently been in ruins since the destruction by Nebuchadnezzar's army. In an extraordinary operation lasting two months, Nehemiah mobilized the Jewish population of Yehud and repaired the breaches in the wall. Archaeological evidence indicates that Nehemiah also considerably reduced the area enclosed by the new walls. All of this was accomplished in the face of overt and covert opposition by the neighboring peoples, especially their leaders, whose self-interests were threatened by an emerging Jewish entity in their midst (Neh 6:15-16; cf. 4:1-23; 6:1-19). Nehemiah served his first term as governor of Yehud for twelve years (Neh 5:14). Besides providing for the security and viability of a Jewish community within the walled city of Jerusalem, Nehemiah vigorously instituted economic reforms designed to alleviate injustices and the oppression of the poor by the more wealthy Jewish citizens (Neh 5).[19] Later he returned again (Neh 13:6-7), but we cannot be sure when or how long he served. During his second tenure in Yehud, laxness in sabbath observance and a recurrence of intermarriage, even among priestly families, again required stern measures (Neh 13:15-31).

What becomes evident in all this is that Yehud survived because of the timely appearance of courageous leaders who were prepared to make the necessary sacrifices and hard decisions that ensured the preservation of the restored community. The parallels between this period and the founding of the modern State of Israel are striking.[20] Both Ezra and Nehemiah, however,

---

[18]The dating of Ezra and Nehemiah is disputed by modern scholars. For a different chronology, see *New Oxford Annotated Bible,* OT 581.

[19]Berquist makes much of a supposed tension between the immigrant elites, who had served in the Babylonian government, and the native population, who had never been deported (*Judaism in Persia's Shadow,* pp. 26-29).

[20]For a survey of the strong, and often competing, leaders in the early years of Zionism and the creation of the State of Israel, see David J. Goldberg, *To the Promised Land: A History of Zionist Thought from Its Origins to the Modern State of Israel* (New York: Penguin, 1996).

would mention another and, to them, much more important reason for their success—the eye and gracious hand of God was upon them (Ezra 5:5; 7:6, 9, 28; 8:18, 22, 31; Neh 2:8, 18; cf. 6:16). Though neither man is directly mentioned in the NT, we wonder if the writer to the Hebrews had them in mind when he referred to those who "administered justice, obtained promises" (Heb 11:33). Certainly they qualify to be listed in the "Hall of Faith."

Sociological and Religious Changes in the Old Covenant People of God

Needless to say, the Jewish people underwent significant changes throughout the period of exile and return, changes both sociological and religious in nature.[21] Failure to distinguish clearly between the earlier period of the biblical traditions and the era of the Second Temple leads to faulty readings of the later NT documents.

Sociological Changes

The first change is the least important in the total picture, but it helps us avoid confusion. This has to do with the new name of this people. Henceforth they were known as "Jews." This term first came into use just before the exilic period (cf. Jer 32:12; 40:11). Earlier they had been known as "Hebrews," "children/people/men of Israel," "Israelites," "people/men of Judah" or "Judeans" (the people of the southern kingdom). During the period of the Second Temple they were generally called "Jews," a shortened form of Judah.

A second, more significant, change involved a shift from an essentially rural to an urban way of life. With this came a move from a primarily agrarian-based economy to a primarily commercial and craft-based economy. Whereas before the exile most Jews lived in small towns and villages, after the exile they resided primarily in the great cities of the reigning empires. This observation is true even today. In the United States, the great majority of Jewish people dwell in the largest cities, such as New York, Los Angeles, Miami and Chicago. A number of factors are responsible for this situation, and it is beyond our scope to go into this in detail.[22] We should, however, at least mention that, throughout the Middle Ages, Jews were not allowed to own property and often were confined to specific sections of the cities called *ghettos*.

Hebrew, a member of the Semitic languages, was not spoken by the surrounding nations. Dispersed Jews, therefore, necessarily learned new languages, as they became an integrated part of the social and economic fabric

[21]For further discussion, see Larry R. Helyer, *Yesterday, Today and Forever: The Continuing Relevance of the Old Testament* (Salem, Wis.: Sheffield, 1996), pp. 251-54.
[22]The interested reader will find a good starting point in Richard E. Gade, *A Historical Survey of Anti-Semitism* (Grand Rapids, Mich.: Baker, 1981), pp. 33-38.

of their new homes. Throughout the Persian period (c. 586-330 B.C.), Aramaic became the most commonly spoken language of the Near East and thus the primary language of most Jews. Hebrew still maintained its place as the language of worship and scholarship, but it fell out of use as a mother tongue for most Jews. In fact, Jewish scholars paraphrased the Hebrew Bible into Aramaic to facilitate understanding of the sacred Scriptures. These Aramaic paraphrases were called targumim (from Aramaic *targûm*, "translation," "interpretation"). Because of their dispersion among the nations, Jews typically became conversant in more than one language. Today, in the modern State of Israel, Hebrew is the official language. Still, one encounters many of the modern European languages, with English and Arabic widely spoken and understood.

Religious Changes

The worship of Israel also underwent significant development. With the destruction of the First Temple and the dispersion of most Jews, a new center of worship was imperative. To be sure, as we have already seen, a rebuilt temple did arise (completed in 516/515 B.C.). In fact, this temple stood until the first century A.D. The reality, however, was that most Jews could afford to make but one pilgrimage to Jerusalem in their lifetimes.[23] What, then, was to be done in the various regions where Jews lived? The answer was the synagogue. The Hebrew phrase *bêt kᵉneset* means literally "a house of gathering." Readers may know that the modern Israeli parliament building in Jerusalem is called the Knesset. The Greek word *synagōgē*, from which we get our English transliteration "synagogue," likewise means "a bringing together, an assembling or assembly."

The synagogue became the focal point for Jewish life. Although there is considerable scholarly debate about the origins of this institution, there are good reasons to think that the synagogue arose as early as the Babylonian period.[24] The felt need to meet together and perpetuate the ancestral traditions may have prompted a spontaneous development of synagogue worship. Be that as it may, by the first century B.C., the synagogue was a fixed feature of Jewish life.[25]

---

[23]See E. P. Sanders, *Judaism: Practice and Belief 63 BCE-66 CE* (London: SCM Press; Philadelphia: Trinity Press International, 1992), p. 130.

[24]See W. White Jr., "Synagogue," *ZPEB* 5:555; W. S. LaSor and T. C. Eskenazi, "Synagogue," *ISBE* 4:677-78; Sanders, *Judaism*, pp. 198-200; B. Chilton and E. Yamauchi, "Synagogues," *DNTB*, pp. 1145-53; and Lee I. Levine, "Synagogues," *EDSS* 2:905-8.

[25]Ehud Netzer now claims he has discovered at Jericho the oldest known synagogue in Israel, dating to the early part of the first century B.C. Previously, only synagogues dating to the first century A.D. had been uncovered at Gamala, Masada and Herodium. Furthermore, Virgilio Corbo and Stanislao Loffreda also claim to have discovered a synagogue of

The synagogue served not only as a place of worship but also as a social center for Jewish life. Here the rites of passage unfolded: boys were circumcised, children attended school, decisions affecting family status were adjudicated—even a market was held during the week! Of course the sabbath services took pride of place. The reading and exposition of Scripture conferred upon the synagogue the epithet *bêt hammidrāš*, "house of instruction." Prayers and praises were also offered up to the God of Israel. It was thus a *bêt t^epillâ*, a "house of prayer." The essential features of a synagogue service left an enduring influence upon Christian worship, since the early church was born in the cradle of Judaism. The glimpses of worship in the NT reveal unmistakably a strong Jewish influence.[26]

As one reads the literature of the Second Temple Period, theological differences from the canonical Scriptures begin to surface in both emphasis and perspective. Since the majority of Jews were unable to participate regularly in the cultic activity of the Second Temple, almsgiving and charity substituted for animal sacrifice. Observing the *miṣwôt* (commandments) took on an atoning function. This is reflected, for example, in Tobit, an apocryphal work dating to the third or second century B.C., which we will read in the next chapter (cf. Tob 4:11; 12:8-9).

In this literature we discern a new understanding of how one pleases God and obtains his favor. The inevitable question of the exilic community was, Why did God punish us in this way? The answer was not hard to find. They had violated the Sinai Covenant and the Lord had requited them for disloyalty (cf. Neh 1:5-11; Dan 9:4-19). On the basis of this recognition, the exilic religious leaders set about rectifying the situation. If Israel was ever again to experience God's favor nationally, there had to be a concerted effort to observe all the covenant stipulations. This raised a serious problem. Many of the stipulations were addressed to a people living a pastoral-agrarian lifestyle in the land of Canaan. How could Jews keep these particular regulations living in cities in the far-flung Diaspora?

This dilemma generated one of the most remarkable responses in the history of religion. Jewish scholars set about adapting and amplifying the 613 commandments, negative and positive, found in the Pentateuch.[27] Since the

---

approximately the same date as the alleged Jericho synagogue at Migdal (Magadala) in Galilee. The problem is that the respective claimants deny the other's claim! For Netzer's arguments in favor of his find and against that of Corbo and Loffreda, see Hershel Shanks, "Is It or Isn't It—A Synagogue?" *BAR* 27, no. 6 (2001): 51-57. Footnotes cite the technical articles by the respective archaeologists reporting their discoveries.

[26]See Ralph P. Martin, *Worship in the Early Church* (London: Marshall, Morgan & Scott, 1964), pp. 18-27.

[27]This process will be explored in more detail in chapter thirteen.

aim was to achieve as much compliance as was humanly possible, these scholars sought to make it difficult to break a *miṣwâ*. This they did by "hedging the law," by gradually devising other commandments to surround and protect the original ones. Obviously, the 613 grew rapidly into an ever-increasing number of regulations. These new rulings were not written down but taught orally. Hence they became known as the "Oral Torah" or the "tradition of the elders (fathers)" (cf. Mt 15:2; Gal 1:14).

In the process of time, the Oral Torah acquired legitimacy by being ascribed to Moses himself.[28] The tradition arose that on Mount Sinai two Torahs were delivered to Moses: the *tôrâ kᵉtûb* (Written Torah) and the *tôrâ šebbᵉᶜalpeh* (the Oral Torah, lit. "Torah by means of mouth"). Both were equally authoritative. This concept of the dual Torah became the hallmark of Pharisaism and is still fundamental for Orthodox Judaism. Eventually much of this legal material was written down in what is called the Mishnah (ca. A.D. 200). This body of literature was commented on and expanded over several centuries and eventually codified in the Talmud (ca. A.D. 600).[29] For Orthodox or traditional Jews today, the Talmud constitutes the basis for religious authority.

What we see in this long process is a shift in emphasis. While it would be unfair and inaccurate to label postbiblical Judaism as a religion of works and not of grace, a tendency toward ritualism and legalism did appear.[30] In much of the literature that we read from the Second Temple period, stress falls upon the performance of deeds and ritual as the means to atone for sins and gain eternal life. Jesus criticized the Pharisaic version of this approach as being superficial (cf. Mt 5:21-48), hypocritical and unnecessarily burdensome (Mt 6:1-18; 15:1-20; 23:1-31). Most of Jesus' quarrels with the Pharisees revolved around his rejection of their interpretations of the pentateuchal laws. In some cases, according to Jesus, the real intent of the law was subverted by Pharisaic casuistry. "You have a fine way of rejecting the command-

---

[28]See *m. 'Abot* 1:1-5.

[29]This oversimplifies the situation, since there were actually two Talmuds: *Talmud Yerushalmi* (ca. A.D. 400) and *Talmud Bavli* (ca. A.D. 500). The latter, the Babylonian Talmud, is considered the more authoritative and is the one usually intended. See Jacob Neusner, "Talmud," *ISBE* 4:717-24.

[30]This is a highly charged and debated issue. Christian scholars have too easily dismissed Judaism (both of the Second Temple period and modern developments) as a religion of works that ignores the notion of God's grace. For a critique of past scholarship, see E. P. Sanders, *Paul and Palestinian Judaism: A Comparison of Patterns of Religions* (Philadelphia: Fortress, 1977). On the other hand, legalism does appear in postbiblical Jewish literature. For evidence, see Donald A. Hagner, "Paul and Judaism: The Jewish Matrix of Early Christianity: Issues in the Current Debate," *BBR* 3 (1993): 117-19; and Thomas R. Schreiner, *The Law and Its Fulfillment: A Pauline Theology of Law* (Grand Rapids, Mich.: Baker, 1993), pp. 114-21.

ment of God in order to keep your tradition!" (Mk 7:9). Thus the Oral Torah appears to have been a primary bone of contention between Jesus and the Pharisees. In contrast to the Pharisaic traditions, which were called "the yoke of the Torah" by the later rabbis (*m. 'Abot* 3:6; but see already Sir 51:26), Jesus offered his own: "Come to me, all you that are weary and are carrying heavy burdens, and I will give you rest. *Take my yoke upon you,* and learn from me; for I am gentle and humble in heart, and you will find rest for your souls. *For my yoke is easy,* and my burden is light" (Mt 11:28-30; italics added).

But in the end, Jesus' criticism went much deeper than specific religious practices, which are ineffectual to deal with the real problem facing humanity (Mk 7:20-23). Already Mark's Gospel preserves a saying of Jesus that points in a different direction: "For the Son of Man came not to be served but to serve, and to give his life a ransom for many" (Mk 10:45; cf. Mt 20:28). The NT presentation of Jesus' death as an atonement for the sins of the world (cf. Jn 3:16; Rom 3:25; Gal 1:3-4; 1 Jn 2:2) differs sharply from all other expressions of Judaism during the Second Temple period. It insists that acceptance before God is received as a gift *through faith in Jesus Christ alone.* In theological terms, salvation is rooted in Christology (i.e., the person and work of Christ).[31] Good works are not unimportant for Christians; rather, good works demonstrate the genuineness of one's faith in Jesus Christ (Rom 3:21-26; Gal 2:16; 5:3-6; cf. Eph 2:8-10). For Judaism generally, observing the works of Torah maintains one's position in the covenant community, a status graciously granted by the Lord's election of Israel to be his special people (cf. Deut 7:6-11). Such an approach has been designated as covenantal nomism.[32] But this stands in stark contrast to the NT gospel, and this fundamental difference in perspective between Christians and Jews led ultimately to a parting of the ways (sometime between A.D. 70-135) and a clear demarcation between Christianity and Judaism.[33] The centrality and finality of Jesus Christ remains the major obstacle to reconciliation between these two religions to this day.

For Further Discussion

1. How did Jews respond to the exile?

2. What changes occurred among the Jewish people as a result of the exile?

---

[31]Donald A. Hagner expresses this nicely in an epigrammatic summary: "Paul's Christianity is christocentric, not nomocentric" ("The Law of Moses in Matthew and Paul," *Int 51* [1997]: 27). His entire article is a good discussion of this issue.

[32]See Sanders, *Judaism.*

[33]We will say more about this later in chapter fourteen, "The Partings of the Ways."

3. How did some of the religious changes during the Second Temple period assist the rise of Christianity? Did any hinder?

4. What are some parallels you see in Christianity to the Pharisaic concept of "hedging the law"?

5. What role do you think the Babylonian captivity played in God's plan of redemption?

For Further Reading

Elias J. Bickerman, "The Babylonian Captivity," in *The Cambridge History of Judaism,* vol. 1: *Introduction; The Persian Period,* ed. W. D. Davies and L. Finkelstein (Cambridge: Cambridge University Press, 1984), pp. 346-48.

Lester L. Grabbe, "Jewish History: Persian Period," *DNTB,* pp. 574-76.

T. R. Hatina, "Exile," *DNTB,* pp. 348-49.

George W. E. Nickelsburg, *Jewish Literature Between the Bible and the Mishnah: A Historical and Literary Introduction* (Philadelphia: Fortress, 1981), pp. 9-18.

C. F. Pfeiffer, "Israel, History of the People of," *ISBE* 2:918-22.

J. Julius Scott Jr., *Customs and Controversies: Intertestamental Jewish Backgrounds of the New Testament* (Grand Rapids, Mich.: Baker, 1995), pp. 73-78, 107-12.

Michael Edward Stone, *Scriptures, Sects and Visions* (Philadelphia: Fortress, 1980), pp. 1-25.

P. R. Trebilco and C. A. Evans, "Diaspora Judaism," *DNTB,* pp. 281-96.

Edwin Yamauchi, *Persia and the Bible* (Grand Rapids, Mich.: Baker, 1990).

Advanced Reading

Jon L. Berquist, *Judaism in Persia's Shadow: A Social and Historical Approach* (Minneapolis: Fortress, 1995), pp. 3-127.

Lester L. Grabbe, *Judaism from Cyrus to Hadrian,* vol. 1: *The Persian and Greek Periods* (Minneapolis: Fortress, 1992), pp. 27-145.

Two

Tales from the Diaspora

The basic text for the Apocrypha in this study is The New Oxford Annotated Bible: New Revised Standard Version, *ed. Bruce M. Metzger and Roland E. Murphy (New York: Oxford University Press, 1991). The third edition of this work has now appeared and could also be used, although the page numbers do not correspond with the 1991 edition used in this book* (The New Oxford Annotated Bible Third Edition: New Revised Standard Version with the Apocrypha, *ed. Michael D. Coogan [Oxford: Oxford University Press, 2001]). This work numbers the Apocrypha separately from the canonical books and uses the abbreviation AP. See page xxvii for a list of abbreviations for the books of the Bible and the Apocrypha, since we will use these abbreviations throughout. For this chapter you will need to read the following pages of the Apocrypha (AP): Tob, 1-19; Let Jer, 169-72; Song of Thr, 173-78; Sus, 179-82; Bel, 183-85. One may also consult the New American Bible translation in* The Catholic Study Bible, *ed. Donald Senior (New York: Oxford University Press, 1990), pp. 503-19, 1031-33 [= Bar 6], 1091-93 [= Dan 3:24-90], 1105-7 [= Dan 13], 1107-8 [= Dan 14]; or* The Oxford Study Bible: Revised English Bible with the Apocrypha, *ed. M. Jack Suggs, Katharine Doob Sakenfeld and James R. Mueller (New York: Oxford University Press, 1992), pp. 1058-70, 1184-86, 1187-89, 1190-92, 1193-94).*

Introduction

We begin our discussion of these tales from the Diaspora by briefly surveying their content and introductory matters relating to historical and literary issues.

Tobit

Genre

Tobit is a fictional story about the problem of unmerited suffering.[1] In classical literary terms, it is a comedy, since it has a happy ending and treats the story with lighthearted humor. God sends an angel to deliver Tobit and Sarah from their afflictions. Even though the author informs the reader of the felicitous outcome near the beginning of the story (Tob 3:16-17), interest is sustained by melodramatic flourishes and delightful irony. The characters are arranged in a triadic pattern as follows:

- ☐ Tobit (principal character), Tobias (Tobit's son) and Anna (Tobit's wife)
- ☐ Raguel (Tobit's relative), Sarah (Raguel's daughter) and Edna (Raguel's wife)
- ☐ God (the real hero), Raphael (an angel sent to assist Tobit and Sarah) and Asmodeus (an evil spirit who haunts Sarah)

The plot centers primarily on the trials and tribulations of pious Tobit. Ironically, this man, whose name means "goodness," suffers because of his good deeds shown to unfortunate and indigent Jews, especially those deprived of proper burial. The author incorporates a subplot involving the harassment of beautiful Sarah, the object of lustful envy by an evil spirit. Seven grooms in succession perish on their wedding night, slain by the evil Asmodeus before they consummate their marriage to Sarah. The plights of Tobit and Sarah are mirror images of each other. We read first of Tobit's troubles leading to his petition to die because of his misery, then of the ill-starred Sarah and her prayer for deliverance by death from an intolerable situation. Interwoven into these two plots is a third: the recovery of money deposited by Tobit from a relative in far-off Rages. The three subplots intertwine, and resolution is achieved by divine intervention in the person of an angel in disguise, namely, Raphael, whose name means "God heals." In terms of the basic movements of the story, we have a joining of the two families in marriage and an exorcism of Asmodeus through the means provided by Raphael. Thus at the conclusion of this well-told story, Tobit recovers his sight, Sarah marries Tobias, and Tobias inherits both Tobit and Raguel's wealth.

Sources

A number of scholars argue that the basic plot of Tobit derives from one or more secular folktales: "The Grateful Dead" (reward for providing proper burial), "The Bride of the Monster" (demon-haunted woman) and "The Tale of

---

[1] This material is adapted from Larry R. Helyer, "Tobit," *DNTB*, pp. 1238-41.

Ahiqar" (an ancient Semitic story—existing already in a fifth-century B.C. Aramaic version—about a betrayed and ultimately vindicated courtier). Ahiqar briefly appears in our story as Tobit's nephew and benefactor (Tob 1:21-22; 14:10) but serves more as window dressing than as a leading character, although final vindication is important to the plot of Tobit. Another possible source is an Egyptian tale called "The Tractate of Khons," which deals with the exorcism of a woman. This proposal is generally linked to an Egyptian provenance for Tobit.

Many scholars draw attention to the Hebrew Bible as a major factor in the story. Some would minimize or even deny the influence of the secular folktales. The patriarchal stories of the angelic visitors (Gen 18—19), the quest for a bride (Isaac in Gen 24; Jacob in Gen 29), the Joseph story (Gen 37—48) and the story of Job are close at hand to provide the basic plot and substructure of Tobit. Tobit's prayer, prophesying Israel's restoration (Tob 13:16-17), draws freely from Isaianic passages (cf. Is 54:11-12; 60:1-22). Attention has been drawn to the distinctly Deuteronomic theology of retribution underlying the basic premise of the story. Especially noteworthy are the allusions to Deuteronomy 31—32 in Tobit 12—13. In addition, two biblical prophets, Amos and Nahum, are actually cited (Tob 2:6 cf. Amos 8:10; Tob 14:4 cf. Nahum 1:1; 2:8-10, 13; 3:18-19). The tales of a wise courtier in Daniel 1—6 and Esther are also germane to the Tobit story. Finally, there are echoes of sapiential (wisdom) teaching as found in the book of Proverbs (see esp. Tob 4:5-19). Clearly, the influence of the Hebrew Bible is paramount in Tobit.

Purpose

This story does more than simply entertain the reader. Beneath the ostensible plot lurks a very real and disturbing problem: the people of Israel are in exile. Tobit and Sarah represent an oppressed minority within a largely hostile culture. The author inserts three passages (Tob 4:3-21; 12:6-10; 14:8-11) that function paraenetically (i.e., giving moral, ethical and ritual exhortation and advice) as guidelines for correct behavior. Furthermore, the leading characters, while not perfect or famous, nonetheless serve as role models. Here are ordinary people who live out their lives in faithfulness to the Torah with steadfast faith that the God of Israel will ultimately vindicate and restore them. Through the lens of this story the anonymous author offers encouragement to Diaspora Jews. "God will again have mercy" (Tob 14:5) is the fervent conviction resonating in the climax to the story. An eloquent hymn celebrates God's certain restoration of the temple, Jerusalem and the Jewish people. Even the Gentiles will convert to the God of Israel. Seen in this light, Tobit is fundamentally a theodicy (a vindication of divine justice in spite of evil).

Composition

The author was a pious, observant Jew. Beyond that, consensus evaporates. Identification with any particular sect seems ruled out by the probable date of writing. The book expresses the sentiments of a Jew committed to Torah and temple and concerned that Jews remain loyal to both. No consensus exists on the provenance, whether in Palestine or the Diaspora. Perhaps a slight nod may be given to the assumed setting of the story, namely, the eastern Diaspora.

Internal evidence for dating the book consists of the following: dependence upon the Hebrew Prophets, no reflection of the turbulent times of Antiochus IV (175-164 B.C.) and the Maccabean revolt (167 B.C.), and no awareness of Herod's greatly expanded and beautified temple (work on this beginning in 20-19 B.C.). Since the canonization of the Prophets is usually placed in the middle of the third century B.C., this would provide outside limits of roughly 250-175 B.C. A few scholars push the date back into the fourth century B.C., but this is a minority position. A date in the first century B.C. is rendered unlikely by the external evidence from Qumran, namely, Aramaic and Hebrew fragments of Tobit dating from the first century B.C.[2]

The Additions to Daniel

What is the relationship of the book of Daniel to its three additions, namely, Susanna, Bel and the Dragon, and The Prayer of Azariah and the Song of the Three Young Men? These additions are found in the Septuagint (LXX) but not the Masoretic Text of the Hebrew Bible (MT). To complicate matters further, another Greek translation, *Theodotion,* has a slightly more fulsome account of Susanna than does the LXX.[3] George Nickelsburg summarizes the most likely literary relationship between canonical Daniel and the additions as follows:

> Stories about Daniel and his friends were part of a living body of tradition. Although they were quite possibly of diverse origin they crystallized as a collection in what we call Daniel 1—6. Around 166-165 B.C.E. this collection was supplemented by a cycle of visions ascribed to Daniel (chaps. 7—12), and together they were issued as a single book. . . . Less than a century after its compilation Daniel 1—12 was itself expanded. The ancient Greek translations of the book

---

[2]See further Daniel J. Harrington, *Invitation to the Apocrypha* (Grand Rapids, Mich.: Eerdmans, 1999), p. 12; and James C. VanderKam, *An Introduction to Early Judaism* (Grand Rapids, Mich.: Eerdmans, 2001), pp. 69-70.

[3]See the discussion of this textual question in *The New Oxford Annotated Bible: New Revised Standard Version,* ed. Bruce M. Metzger and Roland E. Murphy (New York: Oxford University Press, 1991), AP 173.

included three lengthy additions which served to enrich and enhance the cycle of stories about Daniel and the three young men.[4]

We turn our attention to these three additions, each of which illuminates the life of Jews in Diaspora.

Susanna

Susanna is a skillfully told short story with a moralistic purpose, employing the motif of the innocent victim accused of a crime but vindicated at the last possible moment. Bruce Metzger describes Susanna as "one of the best short stories in the world's literature."[5] I think the reader will agree. It also owns the distinction of being "among the earliest detective stories ever written."[6] With the sparest economy of words (only 114 lines of Greek text) the author spins his tale. Like a good Mozart composition, it has neither too many nor too few words—just the right number! With increasing suspense we are drawn into the seemingly hopeless plight of the virtuous Susanna. Then suddenly, in the nick of time, Daniel, like a modern Perry Mason, challenges the verdict, cross-examines the two lecherous villains, and succeeds in reversing the decision.

Purpose. So what is the purpose of Susanna? Is it simply a morality tale inculcating traditional Jewish piety? Some scholars have suggested that Susanna is a tale alluding to the demise of the two false prophets, Ahab and Zedekiah, who were guilty of adultery in the days of Jeremiah (Jer 29:21-23). Thus the story of Susanna warns Jews that judgment is inevitable for such an offense. While there may be a possible allusion to those miscreants referred to in Jeremiah, one should note that in Susanna the two elders were judges, not prophets. Other scholars have sought a more specific agenda behind the tale. A rather popular view suggests that the tale reflects a polemic between Pharisees and Sadducees during the first century B.C. over the correct procedure to be followed in the courtroom. The specific issue concerns the manner in which cross-examination was to be conducted and the penalty for false

---

[4]George Nickelsburg, *Jewish Literature Between the Bible and the Mishnah: A Historical and Literary Introduction* (Philadelphia: Fortress, 1981), p. 25. On the dating of canonical Daniel, see Peter C. Craigie, *The Old Testament: Its Background, Growth, and Content* (Nashville: Abingdon, 1986), pp. 244-49; John Goldingay, *Daniel*, WBC 30 (Dallas: Word, 1989), pp. 326-29; and William Sanford LaSor, David Allan Hubbard and Frederic William Bush, *Old Testament Survey: The Message, Form, and Background of the Old Testament* (Grand Rapids, Mich.: Eerdmans, 1982), pp. 665-68.

[5]Bruce M. Metzger, *An Introduction to the Apocrypha* (New York: Oxford University Press, 1957), p. 107. *New Oxford Annotated Bible* says that the story is "one of the most engaging short stories in world literature" (AP 179). Similar accolades could be multiplied.

[6]Metzger, *Introduction to the Apocrypha*, p. 107. Dorothy Sayers included it in one of her mystery novels. See ibid., n. 2.

accusations.[7] I think this reads too much into a story having a rather transparent purpose. Nickelsburg is more likely correct when he says that the purpose was to encourage "obedience to God in the midst of the temptations and pressures that arise in the Jewish community."[8]

Let us examine this a bit further. Susanna must bear calumny and disgrace with not a word in defense from even her husband or family. Her name means "lily" and symbolizes her purity and innocence, highlighting this outrageous miscarriage of justice. Does it not seem that our anonymous author sketches the portrait of Susanna as a paradigm for Jews who might find themselves, from time to time, falsely accused and with no defense in a hostile, even life-threatening situation? One thinks again of the story of Tobit. The reality was that family members could do virtually nothing to help in such circumstances; hence the surprising, and to most readers, shocking silence in the face of the malicious accusations. One suspects that Holocaust survivors have more understanding of this part of the story than the rest of us do. The moral and ethical point of the story lies in Susanna's courageous decision: "I choose not to do it: I will fall into your hands, rather than sin in the sight of the Lord" (Sus 23). The critical point in the story becomes the turning point: "The Lord heard her cry" (Sus 44). This line recalls the ancient story of bondage in Egypt: "God heard their groaning, and God remembered his covenant with Abraham, Isaac, and Jacob. God looked upon the Israelites, and God took notice of them" (Ex 2:24-25). The point of the story is clear: the God of the patriarchs is still there; he will be the mainstay of Jews in exile.

Susanna is the real hero of this literary gem. She takes her place alongside Queen Esther, the virtuous Sarah and the pious Judith, about whom we shall read in chapter five, as leading female figures in Second Temple literature who serve as positive role models, not only for Jewish women, but also for Jewish men. Each of the three women, however, lives out her Judaism in a distinctly different way. Unfortunately, we will discover that women were not always held in such high regard in Second Temple literature, as our next chapter demonstrates.

Composition. The unknown author sets the story in Babylon, but its actual provenance is unknown. What we can say is that the story reflects life in exile for Jews. There is internal evidence that Susanna was originally written in either Aramaic or Hebrew, even though to date no Semitic *Vorlage* (prototype) has been discovered.[9]

---

[7] For a discussion of the precise points in dispute, see Michal Dayagi Mendels, "Susanna, Book of," *ABD* 6:246-47.

[8] Nickelsburg, *Jewish Literature,* p. 26.

[9] For the linguistic arguments, see Mendels, "Susanna," 6:247; and Carey A. Moore, *Daniel, Esther and Jeremiah: The Additions,* AB 44 (Garden City, N.Y.: Doubleday, 1987), pp. 81-84.

Sources. Earlier German scholarship imagined that behind the Jewish story of Susanna lay an old pagan myth about the virgin Phryne, a goddess attended by two slaves who were later put to death. Similar pagan variations of this myth were also suggested. One hardly need go so far afield to find the probable background of our story. Susanna reminds us of the story of Joseph and Potiphar's wife in Genesis 39:1—41:45, except that it is the woman who is virtuous and not the male! There is, of course, the connection to the court tales in Daniel 1—6, in that we have Daniel himself suddenly appearing on the scene just in time to rescue the damsel in distress. But even more telling is the observation that there are numerous links to the Pentateuch, especially in regard to civil and legal matters.[10] In short, the story gives every indication of stemming from pious Jewish circles.

Bel and the Dragon

Written as a farce, employing deliberate sarcasm, ridicule and humor, Bel and the Dragon once again features Daniel, who outwits the pagan priests of the god Bel and thoroughly discomfits the grotesque dragon. This work, like Susanna, represents one of the earliest detective stories in world literature.

Plot. The story is set in the time of Cyrus the Persian and unfolds in three segments. The first, in verses 1-22, involves Daniel's exposé of fraudulent claims by the priesthood of the god Bel. The great idol called Bel was alleged to consume huge amounts of food daily (Bel 3). Daniel, like an earlier version of "Columbo," demonstrated that it was the priests and their families who surreptitiously dined during the night in the temple precincts.

The second, in verses 23-39, is a hilarious account detailing how Daniel "burst the bubble" of belief in the deity of a great dragon (or snake) by means of a "homemade hairball" (Bel 27). In retaliation, the Babylonians charged the king with having become a Jew (Bel 28) and forced him to consign Daniel to the dreaded lions' den (Bel 27-32).

Into these dire straits came a most unlikely rescuer: Habakkuk the prophet. Why has our author selected this relatively obscure prophet to assist Daniel? There is a thematic connection: Habakkuk's prophecy deals with the problem of why the Lord allowed pagan Babylon to destroy Judah and prophesies judgment for her violent crimes (cf. Hab 1:12-13; 2:2-17). The insertion of Habakkuk into our story thus subtly alludes to the demise of this empire with all its pretensions to grandeur. But even more relevant to our story is the denunciation of idol worship in Habakkuk 2:18-19, with its triumphant conclusion: "See, it is gold and silver plated, and there is no breath in it at all." Jewish readers of Bel and the Dragon doubtless made these connections.

---

[10]Mendels, "Susanna," 6:247.

Again and again in the literature of the Second Temple we hear echoes of Scripture utilized in creative ways.

In one of the really funny lines of the story, Habakkuk protests to the angel who has ordered him to take his freshly made stew and bread to Daniel: "Sir, I have never seen Babylon, and I know nothing about the den" (Bel 35). This is probably a deliberate put-down similar to Genesis 11:5, where the Lord has to come down to see the great tower of Babel, which its builders described as having "its top in the heavens." Recall that this episode is set in the plain of Shinar, which, according to Daniel 1:2, was where Babylon was located. At any rate, Habakkuk is immediately airlifted over the den, courtesy of the angel, who carries him by the crown of his head, so he can deliver Daniel's lunch to him (Bel 36-39).

A third, short segment in verses 40-42 describes Daniel's preservation from the voracious lions for six days, after which time the king rescues Daniel and throws Daniel's opponents into the lions' den, where they are instantly eaten.

Purpose. The purpose of Bel and the Dragon lies closer to the surface than in Susanna. What we see is an example of Jewish response to idolatry in the Second Temple period. Polemic against idolatry hardly originated in this era; one has only to turn to the Hebrew prophets of the eighth through the sixth centuries for some classic examples of invective and ridicule directed toward pagan idolatry (cf. Is 40:19-22; 41:6-7; 42:17; 44:9-20; 45:16, 20; Jer 10:1-10).

Clearly our author aimed to reinforce steadfast refusal to participate in and embrace the idolatrous rites of the surrounding pagan neighbors (Bel 3-4).[11] In spite of difficulties or even threats to life itself, those remaining loyal to the God of Israel, "the living God" (Bel 25), will be protected. Hence the felt need, as a distinct minority, to reinforce the religious and theological boundaries between the ancestral faith of Israel and polytheism. "Oppressed folk often ridicule what their malefactors hold dear, and satire is an antidote for the suffering endured."[12]

Genre and sources. Bel and the Dragon incorporates at least two different genres: stories about a wise courtier and stories about court conflict (as in Dan 1—6 and Ahiqar). But in addition our author seems aware of an ancient Semitic creation myth involving a sea serpent, Tiamat. The Babylonian epic called *Enuma Elish* features the national god Marduk, who defeated the chaos monster of the sea (Tiamat) and fashioned the world out of her remains.[13] Bel

---

[11]See *New Oxford Annotated Bible,* AP 183.

[12]Ibid.

[13]See *ANET,* pp. 60-72, for translation; and Larry R. Helyer, *Yesterday, Today and Forever: The Continuing Relevance of the Old Testament* (Salem, Wis.: Sheffield Publishing, 1996), pp. 44-48, for further discussion.

is a reflex of Marduk, and the great dragon derives from Tiamat. Metzger helpfully draws attention to the persistence of this ancient myth in both Jewish and Christian writings, including the NT (cf. Rev 12:3-9; 20:2).[14]

Finally, one should also note that biblical traditions are evident in this story. Obviously canonical Daniel has played some role in the drafting of this story (Dan 6; cf. Ezek 8:3). In addition, Nickelsburg draws attention to the influence of Isaiah 45—46, suggesting that our work may even have been conceived as a commentary on these chapters.[15] We have already mentioned the relevance of the prophet Habakkuk for the story.

Composition. Once again the identity of the author is unknown. The most likely time for composition lies in the second century B.C., though some would date it to the first century B.C. The language was probably either Hebrew or Aramaic. As to the place of composition, "virtually every major Jewish settlement has been suggested."[16] The fact, however, that fragments identified as Pseudo-Daniel have turned up at Qumran points to Palestine as the probable location.[17]

The Prayer of Azariah and the Song of the Three Jews

Whereas Susanna and Bel and the Dragon are quite extraneous to MT Daniel, The Prayer of Azariah and the Song of the Three Jews is at least relevant to the plot of MT Daniel. To be sure, the placement of verses 3-22, a national confession of sin, right after Daniel 3:23, the point at which the three young men are cast into the fiery furnace, is a bit disruptive. But the prose narrative in verses 23-28 does identify the fourth person seen walking about in the fiery furnace (cf. Dan 3:25) as the angel of the Lord, who protects the young men from the intense heat (Song of Thr 26-27). Furthermore, the three young men are exhorted to bless the Lord in verse 66 in light of their deliverance from the "burning fiery furnace."

Structure and content. The Prayer of Azariah and the Song of the Three Jews actually consists of three discrete compositions: the prayer (Song of Thr 1-22), a short prose narrative (Song of Thr 23-28) and a hymn (Song of Thr 29-68). From a literary standpoint, each unit has little intrinsic connection to the other or, for that matter, to MT Daniel. This suggests that the prayer and hymn originated independently of canonical Daniel and were inserted by a later editor along with the narrative elaboration of the fiery furnace.

The prayer of Azariah strikes a note similar to Tobit's penitential prayer

---

[14]Metzger, *Introduction to the Apocrypha*, pp. 119-22.
[15]Nickelsburg, *Jewish Literature*, p. 27.
[16]Moore, *Daniel, Esther and Jeremiah*, p. 128.
[17]See Florentino García Martínez, *The Dead Sea Scrolls Translated: The Qumran Texts in English*, 2nd ed. (Leiden: E. J. Brill; Grand Rapids, Mich.: Eerdmans, 1996), pp. 288-89.

(Tob 3:4-5). Azariah, however, does not beseech the Lord for personal deliverance but rather confesses the righteous dealings of the Lord with erring Israel, as in Tobit 13:1-6. The covenant promise to Abraham (Song of Thr 12) provides the basis for the confidence that forgiveness and deliverance will be forthcoming so long as there is heartfelt repentance (Song of Thr 16-17).

The hymn (The Song of the Three Jews) is a litany showing much indebtedness to Psalms 136 and 148, in terms of both content and liturgical refrains. Though a single composition, the hymn actually comprises two separate parts: an ode, identified by the introductory phrase "Blessed are you . . ." (Song of Thr 29-34), and a psalm in which each exhortation begins with the words: "Bless the Lord . . ." (Song of Thr 35-68). The ode in particular has strong links to Second Temple liturgical language.[18] As we will discover in chapter seven, the Qumran community also excelled in crafting hymns in imitation of the canonical Psalms. Like the prayer of Azariah, this hymn is more communal in orientation than personal. Verse 66 looks like an editorial insertion into the hymn in order to connect it to the narrative setting of Daniel.[19] Everything else in the hymn, however, suggests a liturgical setting, perhaps even the Jerusalem Temple liturgy.[20]

Composition. There are some clues in The Prayer of Azariah suggesting a time of writing in the late second century B.C. Especially important is verse 9: "You have handed us over to our enemies, lawless and hateful rebels, and to an unjust king, the most wicked in all the world." Whereas Herod the Great (reigned 40-4 B.C.) would certainly qualify for this opprobrious epithet in the view of many of his contemporaries, one is probably on surer ground identifying this king with the archenemy, Antiochus IV Epiphanes. Verse 5 seems to reflect the havoc wreaked upon Jerusalem during Antiochus's reign of terror, and verse 15 seemingly describes the situation after Antiochus forbade sacrifices offered according to the requirements of the Torah. We shall have much more to say about him in chapters four and five. Since Antiochus IV persecuted Jews faithful to Torah in the era 167-163 B.C., this would provide the earliest possible date (unless, of course, Song of Thr 9 is a later insertion). The Prayer of Azariah obviously postdates canonical Daniel, so we are led to a time of writing near the end of the second century B.C.

---

[18]See further David Flusser, "Psalms, Hymns and Prayers," in *Jewish Writings of the Second Temple Period: Apocrypha, Pseudepigrapha, Qumran Sectarian Writings, Philo, Josephus,* ed. Michael E. Stone, CRINT 2 (Assen: Van Gorcum; Philadelphia: Fortress, 1984), p. 554.

[19]Nickelsburg, *Jewish Literature,* p. 29.

[20]In this regard, it is interesting that The Song of the Three Jews has passed into the Christian liturgical tradition as well. See Metzger, *Introduction to the Apocrypha,* pp. 104-5.

Purpose. One must admit to considerable uncertainty in assessing the purpose. We have already mentioned the reason for this. An unknown editor inserted the prayer, narrative and hymn into canonical Daniel, making it difficult to say precisely how it originally functioned. We can only observe how the additions now function when read as a part of the Daniel story. As such, they encourage and exhort to faithfulness by means of well-known liturgical and confessional material. As Nickelsburg puts it: "The poems convert the story from mere narrative to quasi-liturgical drama, eliciting the involvement of an audience attuned to such liturgical tradition."[21]

The Letter of Jeremiah

This piece has little of the appeal displayed in the previous works. Fortunately, it is not long. Ostensibly written as a letter, it strikes a keynote, namely, avoidance of idolatry, and relentlessly hammers it home. *The New Oxford Annotated Bible* aptly styles it "an impassioned sermon against idol worship and polytheism."[22]

Purpose

The inspiration for this work is not hard to find. According to Jeremiah 29, to which we referred earlier in chapter one, Jeremiah sent a letter to the exiles in Babylon. Our anonymous author pens another letter under the name of Jeremiah. In so doing, he picks up on Jeremiah's tirade against idolatry in Jeremiah 10, epitomized in verse 11: "The gods, who did not make the heavens and the earth, shall perish from the earth, and from beneath the heavens." This "new" letter falls neatly into ten sections, each of which concludes with a common refrain: "From this it is evident [or a similar phrase] that they are not gods; so do not fear them" (Let Jer 16, 23, 29, 40, 44, 52, 65, 69, 72).[23] The purpose is transparent.

Composition

The work was probably composed before 100 B.C., since 2 Maccabees 2:1-3 apparently alludes to it, and 2 Maccabees dates rather securely to between 104 and 63 B.C.[24] This is strengthened by the discovery of a Greek fragment of the Letter of Jeremiah in Qumran Cave 7 dating to approximately 100 B.C. On the other hand, if one takes Letter of Jeremiah 3 at face value, it dates to

---

[21]Nickelsburg, *Jewish Literature,* p. 30.
[22]AP 169. Nickelsburg calls it a "tractate" (*Jewish Literature,* p. 35), and Metzger, a "pamphlet" (*Introduction to the Apocrypha,* p. 95).
[23]For more discussion of the structure, see Nickelsburg, *Jewish Literature,* p. 36.
[24]But see VanderKam, *Introduction to Early Judaism,* p. 135: "One cannot be sure his source was the Letter of Jeremiah."

around 317 B.C. Most scholars, however, opt for a date in the second century B.C. At any rate, the letter most likely comes from the Hellenistic period. This dating has led some scholars to conclude that the work was written originally in Greek. Like the other writings we have thus far considered, however, the Letter of Jeremiah may well go back to a Semitic *Vorlage*. In this connection, it is worth noting that Jeremiah 10:11, central to the main thesis of our author, is, in fact, written in Aramaic in Jeremiah—the only such instance in the book.

We cannot be certain about the place of writing. Whereas the author shows some familiarity with ritual prostitution as practiced in Mesopotamia (Let Jer 42-43), someone in other parts of the Diaspora or the land of Israel could also have been aware of this feature.[25]

Life in Exile

These stories and writings afford an opportunity to reconstruct, to some extent, the Jewish experience in exile. Most North Americans, who have never experienced displacement from their homeland, will need to exercise some creative imagination in order to enter into the psyche of a people who are always viewed as foreigners and displaced persons. By means of these writings, we revisit the world of Diaspora Jews in the period of approximately 200-100 B.C.

Social and Economic Conditions

The story of Susanna reflects life in the Diaspora. Joakim, husband of the virtuous Susanna, is described as "very rich" (Sus 1:4). As Jeremiah had earlier urged his Jewish compatriots (Jer 29:5), Joakim, whose name means "the Lord will establish," had indeed established himself in Babylon, complete with a fine house and garden. But one gets the impression that Joakim's economic status was not typical of all Jews. We read that "the Jews used to come to him because he was the most honored of them all" (Sus 4). His house served as the Jewish court where questions of religious and family matters were adjudicated. In the imperialistic age of the ancient Near East, matters of personal status were left to the various ethnic-religious communities making up the far-flung empires.[26]

The suggestion that only a few Jews acquired great wealth in the Diaspora is strengthened by the fictional story of Tobit. Tobit had the good fortune of being one of the purchasing agents of the king of Assyria (the reference to

---

[25]See George W. E. Nickelsburg, "The Bible Rewritten and Expanded," in *Jewish Writings of the Second Temple Period,* p. 148.

[26]See above chap. 1, p. 31.

Assyria is an anachronism). He is pictured as plying the trade routes eastward in what is today Iran. This role as traveling merchant and purchasing agent became a fixed feature of Jewish economic life for centuries, well into modern times. Jewish life in America features a significant number of Jews eking out a living on the edges of the frontier as peddlers and merchants, then later as store owners and wholesalers. Jews established major department stores in America, such as Bloomingdales, Lazarus, Strauss, R. H. Macy and Sachs. Nearly any town in the Midwest can document one or two stores founded by Jews in the period of westward expansion.[27]

The story of Tobit portrays a pious man performing many acts of charity for unfortunate Jews in his city. Most notable was his commitment to a proper burial for even the least of his brothers and sisters. Evidently Tobit was not typical of his kin in being well to do. Most Jews did not enjoy significant economic power and status. A majority were probably small farmers, day laborers (cf. Mt 20:1-16), semi-skilled artisans and owners of small businesses. Though it is much later in time, the musical *Fiddler on the Roof*, set in czarist Russia in the 1880s, depicts the Jewish citizens of Anatevka as barely self-sufficient Jews.[28] This is probably not far from the situation of most Jews in the Diaspora during the fourth to the first centuries B.C.

Notice that Tobit sent his son Tobias out into the streets to bring in any destitute Jews to share in the bounty during the Festival of Pentecost (Tob 2:1-3). The story implies that there might well have been impoverished Jews in Diaspora cities. After his blindness, Tobit was himself poverty-stricken and relied upon relatives and the good graces of Ahiqar, a fellow Jew and advisor to the king, to care for his family. Tobit's wife, Anna, helped provide some income by selling garments she made in her home. This little detail in the story is almost prophetic, in that Jews often found the garment industry to be a major source of livelihood, even in modern times. Jewish workers significantly populated the garment district of New York City in the period of 1880-1940.

One can thus conclude that, while a few Jews did become wealthy and, like an Ahiqar, Mordecai, Daniel or Nehemiah, rise to political power, the economic and political status of most Jews in Diaspora or Palestine was precarious, to say the least. We draw attention to this observation because one of the long-lived anti-Semitic stereotypes, still much in evidence today, is that Jews

---

[27]Thus in the city in which I reside, Hartford City, Indiana, two Jewish families, the Steins and the Mulhollands, operated clothing stores. The garment industry and clothing retailing have always played a big role in the economic life of American Jewry.

[28]The movie is based on the stories of Sholem Aleichem. For an English translation of some of these, see *The Old Country*, trans. Julius and Frances Butwin (New York: Crown, 1946).

are greedy, dishonest in business and control much of the wealth and bank-ing in the world.[29]

Persecution and Assimilation

The plot of Tobit also includes an incident in which Tobit incurs the wrath of Sennacherib for burying the bodies of Jews killed by the king. When Tobit flees imminent arrest and execution, his property is confiscated (Tob 1:20). This little detail became an all-too-frequent part of life in exile. Throughout Jewish history, jealousy against Jews periodically resulted in the confiscation of their property. Especially during the medieval period, confiscation of prop-erty and expulsion from their countries disrupted Jewish life.[30] One senses from the story of Tobit that life among the Gentiles could be threatening.

These stories all share a deeply felt concern: they are designed to rein-force Jewish identity in the midst of pagan culture. The intention of the authors, therefore, was to instill hope in the God of Israel and pride in their heritage as his chosen people. In spite of their lowly estate and loss of politi-cal autonomy, they must never forget this lesson: if Jews are faithful to the covenant, God will at last reward and restore them.

The ever-present danger lurking just beneath the surface of the text is assimilation into the pagan culture. Assimilation refers to the process whereby a minority group gradually adopts the values and characteristics of the majority culture. For Jews this would have involved a turning away from the distinctive lifestyle called for by the Mosaic covenant and, most impor-tantly, from the basic creed of Israel: "Hear, O Israel: The LORD is our God, the LORD alone" (Deut 6:4). We must read these tales from the dispersion in such a way that the leading characters are viewed as a lens through which a pattern or model is projected for the reading and listening audience. Tobit and Tobias are models of faithful Jews, as is the vexed Sarah. Susanna is a par-agon of virtue who chooses to die, if need be, rather than compromise her commitment to the standards of Torah (cf. Sus 3, 23, 62).[31] The three young men are likewise examples of faithful, covenant-keeping Jews (cf. Song of

---

[29]For a study of Jewish stereotypes among Christians, see Charles Y. Glock and Rodney Stark, *Christian Beliefs and Anti-Semitism* (New York: Harper & Row, 1966), chap. 7. For a flagrant example of an evangelical anti-Semite, see Theodore Winston Pike, *Israel: Our Duty . . . Our Dilemma* (Oregon City, Ore.: Big Sky Press, 1984). For a helpful survey of evangelicals and anti-Semitism, with a generally positive assessment, see David A. Rausch, *Fundamentalist-Evangelicals and Anti-Semitism* (Valley Forge, Penn.: Trinity Press International, 1993).

[30]For examples, see Richard E. Gade, *A Historical Survey of Anti-Semitism* (Grand Rapids, Mich.: Baker, 1981), pp. 33-38.

[31]Nickelsburg says concerning the story of Susanna: "This is basically a story about life in the Jewish community" (*Jewish Literature*, p. 26).

Thr 18). Young Daniel, a shrewd detective and defense attorney, or the older
Daniel, a loyal public servant falsely accused of treason, triumphs as a faithful Jew (cf. Sus 44-45, 64; Bel 4-5, 25, 41). The Letter of Jeremiah warns of the
grave dangers of idol worship and polytheism. Thus the real issue in these
stories goes well beyond the individual, personal suffering of Jews and looks
at the plight of the entire community. Nickelsburg correctly calls our attention to this feature:

> Although our analysis may suggest that Tobit is a treatise on the suffering right-
> eous person not totally dissimilar from the book of Job, we may note one impor-
> tant substantive difference. Whereas the book of Job confines its treatment to an
> individual, the fate of the nation is of great concern to the author of Tobit, and
> he speaks almost exclusively of it in the last two chapters.[32]

Notice how the stories emphasize continuance in the ancestral traditions.
In the book of Tobit, we find a scene in which Tobit sends his son off to
retrieve the family fortune. Tobit gives a long, impassioned exhortation to
young Tobias. We overhear the concerns of many Jewish parents in this section: "those who act in accordance with truth will prosper in all their activities. . . . For none of the nations has understanding. . . . You have great wealth
if you fear God and flee from every sin and do what is good in the sight of the
Lord your God" (Tob 4:6, 19, 21).

The motivation for faithfulness in these stories becomes apparent in the last
two chapters of Tobit (Tob 13—14). Here we have a glowing picture of a
restored Jerusalem and a regathered and reconstituted Jewish state. In George
W. E. Nickelsburg's words: "For the author of Tobit, God's dealings with the suffering righteous person are paradigmatic of his dealings with Israel."[33] In language recalling the book of Deuteronomy, the author urges patience in
suffering and repentance in order to ensure the future restoration. This section
is addressed to the Jewish Diaspora. The hope of return to Zion is an enduring
motif of Jewish literature and liturgy throughout the centuries.

Customs, Traditions and Superstitions
These stories of the dispersion also afford glimpses into the daily life of Jews
in *gālût* (Hebrew word for exile or Diaspora).[34] One of the things we notice is

---

[32]Ibid., p. 33.
[33]"Stories of Biblical and Early Post-Biblical Times," in *Jewish Writings of the Second Temple Period,* p. 43. See the note in *New Oxford Annotated Bible,* AP 16. In contrast to those scholars who see these chapters as later additions, I follow Nickelsburg (ibid., pp. 40-46, esp. n. 55; *Jewish Literature,* p. 40 n. 39) in seeing these chapters as integral to the entire work.
[34]As Metzger observes, "Nowhere else is there preserved so complete and beautiful a pic-
ture of the domestic life of the Jews after the return from the Babylonian Exile" (*Introduction to the Apocrypha,* p. 37).

the sudden appearance of new customs and beliefs not mentioned in the OT. Especially noteworthy in this regard are demonology, magic and superstition. The tale of Tobit is a good example. The plot involves demonic influence and a strange concoction calculated to ward off their baneful activity. As Azariah (really Raphael the angel) explains to Tobias:

> As for the fish's heart and liver, you must burn them to make a smoke in the presence of a man or woman afflicted by a demon or evil spirit, and every affliction will flee away and never remain with that person any longer. (Tob 6:8)

Tobias does indeed perform this ritual before consummating his marriage and thus exorcises the jealous demon Asmodeus to Egypt, the traditional haunt of magic, demons and witchcraft.[35]

The influence of pagan culture is evident throughout this period. Persian influence is especially prominent. The name of the demon, Asmodeus, probably reflects the Persian demon Aeshma Daeva.[36] This illustrates a problem common to both Judaism and Christianity: the problem of being in the world but not being a part of the world. In the story of Tobit, only he among his relatives continued to observe the dietary laws as commanded in the Pentateuch (Tob 1:10-20). Clearly the author holds Tobit up as a role model for all Jews. Likewise, Susanna and Daniel were virtuous Jews who remained steadfastly committed to the faith of Israel. As we will demonstrate, Christianity adopted some of the same strategies as Judaism in order to protect against assimilation.

Importance for the New Testament

General Background of the New Testament

These tales from the dispersion are invaluable for understanding the Jewish culture from which the NT documents emerged. This often overlooked or simply unknown fact results in readings of the NT that are divorced from its larger context. What we want to do now is to show how these Jewish tales provide insight into the thought world presupposed by NT writers.

We begin by calling attention to the condition of world Jewry assumed by the stories we have just read. All these stories presuppose the tragedy of the destruction of the First Temple and the dispersion of the majority of Jews among the Gentiles. Likewise, to read the NT sympathetically and with more insight, one must presuppose this continuing reality: Israel was *still* in exile and, thus, in a real sense, *still* under God's judgment.[37] The majority of Jews

---

[35]See *New Oxford Annotated Bible,* AP 11, note on v. 3.

[36]*New Oxford Annotated Bible,* AP 5, note on v. 8.

[37]See N. T. Wright, *The Climax of the Covenant: Christ and the Law in Pauline Theology* (Minneapolis: Fortress, 1991), pp. 137-56.

resided outside the ancestral homeland. Just how extensive the Diaspora was may be grasped by Luke's description of the Jewish pilgrims who were present on the Day of Pentecost (Acts 2:8-11). But even the minority who lived in the Holy Land did so under the domination of a foreign power and thus under exilic conditions.

To be sure, not all Jews would have viewed the situation in quite the same way. For example, the Sadducees, with their vested interest in the temple and its rituals, were probably not as acutely conscious of the continuing dispersion as the Pharisees, Essenes and, certainly, the Zealots—the most extreme nationalists of the time.[38] Nonetheless, most Jews were concerned with this stubborn fact. The brief period of independence during the Hasmonean dynasty (ca. 141-63 B.C.) had been brutally terminated by the intervention of Rome into the Middle East.[39] The Holy Land was under the ultimate jurisdiction of a pagan overlord who ruled by means of client kings or directly appointed governors. To add to the humiliation, Rome also stationed legionnaires at Caesarea, the major seaport of Palestine, and at the Tower of Antonia, guarding and overlooking the sacred temple precincts.

Both the Pharisees and Essenes diagnosed the political problem in religious terms: God would restore Israel only when Israel was obedient to Torah (cf. Tob 13:6). The Pharisees had a mission to instill the requisite obedience in all Jews. This helps us understand the Pharisees' fierce opposition toward Jesus. Since he did not endorse all of their interpretations of Torah, Jesus would have been, in their estimation, contributing to the continuing *gālût*. Thus we read Jesus' criticism of the Pharisees in Mark 7:9: "You have a fine way of rejecting the commandment of God in order to keep your tradition!" We will elaborate on the Pharisaic doctrine of the dual Torah and Jesus' stance toward it later.

This also throws light on Saul of Tarsus. He viewed the sect of "the Way" with hatred because it undermined the place of the law in the scheme of things. Saul the Pharisee was committed to the mission of bringing all Israel into compliance with the twofold Torah. Thus, if Israel were to experience its prophesied destiny, the new sect must be eradicated. No wonder Paul the Christian could say later: "I was violently persecuting the church of God and was trying to destroy it" (Gal 1:13).

The Essenes were not optimistic that the majority of Jews would become serious about keeping Torah, so they withdrew into their own communities. There they awaited the eschatological day of God's wrath upon all sinners,

[38]The *ZPEB* articles by Donald A. Hagner, "Pharisees" (4:745-52) and "Sadducees" (5:211-16); R. K. Harrison, "Essenes" (2:365-74); and J. H. Bratt, "Zealots" (5:1036-37), are helpful in providing further background on these various sects of Judaism.
[39]See chapter one for background; also *New Oxford Annotated Bible,* AP 415-18, for a historical summary of this time.

whether Jewish or Gentile. We will have much more to say about this sect of Judaism in chapters six and seven.

The Gospels must be read against the backdrop of a strong expectation that God would soon act to reestablish the Davidic dynasty.[40] Already Tobit depicts this glowing future. The regathering of all Israel and the restoration of the kingdom and temple are vividly portrayed in Tobit 13—14. The writer of the book of Revelation envisions the New Jerusalem in terms similar to that of Tobit (cf. Tob 13:16-17 with Rev 21:9—22:5).

The preaching of John the Baptist in the wilderness of Judah attracted large crowds from all other the country (cf. Mt 3:5; Mk 1:5; Lk 3:7). Why? The people thought it was the prelude to the coming of the Messiah, which featured the regathering and restoration of Israel (cf. Is 11:10-16). This is most clear in the report that "the people were filled with expectation, and all were questioning in their hearts concerning John, whether he might be the Messiah" (Lk 3:15).

In fact, it is the Gospel of Luke that features this strong nationalistic under-current most dramatically. In the first two chapters Luke narrates, in diptych style (i.e., like two photographs hinged together and facing the viewer), the births of John and Jesus. The atmosphere recalls the stories of the patriarchs in Genesis 12—50 and their familiar theme of the barren matriarch and the need for a male heir. Gabriel, an angel of the Lord, announced to Zechariah, in the holy place of the temple, the good news that he would have a son. The destiny of this son sounded the note of messianic hope: "He will turn many of the people of Israel to the Lord their God. With the spirit and power of Elijah he will go before him, to turn the hearts of parents to their children, and the disobedient to the wisdom of the righteous, to make ready a people prepared for the Lord" (Lk 1:16-17). Gabriel likewise visited the virgin Mary and announced the destiny of her son: "He will be great, and will be called the Son of the Most High, and the Lord God will give to him the throne of his ancestor David. He will reign over the house of Jacob forever, and of his kingdom there will be no end" (Lk 1:32-33). The note of nationalism can scarcely be missed in this announcement.

John's role in redemptive history fulfilled the words of the last canonical prophet, Malachi (see Mal 3:1; 4:5), who predicted the coming of Elijah before the Day of the Lord. Jewish literature of the Second Temple kept alive the tra-dition of Elijah's return (see Sir 48:1, 10). The NT itself reflects the fact that an expectation of Elijah's return was current. After the transfiguration (Mt 17:1-8; Mk 9:2-8; Lk 9:28-36), Mark and Matthew record a question three disci-ples put to Jesus: "Why do the scribes say that Elijah must come first?" (Mk

[40]For a discussion of Jewish nationalism between 200 B.C. and A.D. 135, see Doron Men-dels, *The Rise and Fall of Jewish Nationalism,* rev. ed. (Grand Rapids, Mich.: Eerdmans, 1997), pp. 1-9.

9:11; cf. Mt 17:10). Jesus appears to have held that John the Baptist fulfilled
the prophecy of Elijah's return (Mt 17:12). The Mishnah (a codification of the
traditional oral law compiled about A.D. 200) likewise elaborates upon the
role of Elijah in the eschatological drama.[41] At any rate, we better understand
the excitement surrounding the appearance of John the Baptist, who was
preaching a baptism of repentance and dressed in the garb of Elijah himself
(Mk 1:6; cf. 2 Kings 1:8). In the minds of the crowds, if John were Elijah, the
Messiah could not be far behind.

But even more to the point, the Spirit-inspired prayers and prophecies of
the key actors of the drama draw attention to the national longings for
redemption. Notice Zechariah's prophecy at the naming of his son. Twice
Zechariah mentions being saved or rescued from enemies (Lk 1:71, 74) and
the raising up of a savior in the house of David. The spiritual and national
dimensions of deliverance are tightly woven together and founded upon
God's promise to Abraham and the covenant between God and Israel. Two
individuals at Jesus' dedication offered up praises for the fulfillment of God's
promise to Israel. Luke describes Simeon as "righteous and devout, looking
forward to the consolation of Israel, and the Holy Spirit rested on him" (Lk
2:25). The expression "consolation of Israel" carries nationalistic overtones in
Jewish literature of this period.[42] Anna, a prophetess, likewise added her
praises on that occasion and, according to Luke, began "to speak about the
child to all who were looking for the *redemption of Jerusalem*" (Lk 2:38, italics
added). This expression, too, highlights the political aspect.

This hope for national restoration does not disappear in Luke's Gospel and
its sequel, the book of Acts.[43] After the resurrection, the two disciples on the
way to Emmaus expressed their disappointment: "But we had hoped that he
was the one to redeem Israel" (Lk 24:21). To this Jesus replied: "Oh, how foolish you are, and how slow of heart to believe all that the prophets have
declared! Was it not necessary that the Messiah should suffer these things
and then enter into his glory?" (Lk 24:25-26; cf. Tob 14:3-4). The disciples
must have connected "his glory" with the full restoration of Israel, because,
according to Acts 1:6, the very last question they put to Jesus before his

---

[41]See further on this J. H. Stek, "Elijah," *ISBE* 2:68. In addition, we know from Passover
haggadot (books containing the story of the exodus and the ritual of the Passover Seder)
that the expectation of Elijah's return before the coming of the Messiah was kept alive.
An empty chair and place setting with a glass of wine were set out in case he should
appear at the Passover Seder, the most fitting time for his coming. While one cannot be
certain, it is possible that this tradition already was a part of the Seder during Jesus' time.
[42]See John W. DeHoog, "Comfort; Consolation," *ISBE* 1:735; and Walter Liefeld, "Luke," *EBC*
8:840.
[43]For a full defense of this position, see Larry R. Helyer, "Luke and the Restoration of
Israel," *JETS* 36 (1993): 317-29.

ascension was: "Lord, is this the time when you will restore the kingdom to Israel?" Significantly, this question follows a period of forty days in which Jesus instructed them about the kingdom of God (Acts 1:3). Jesus' reply is hardly a rejection of the notion but a refocusing of their attention on the immediate objective of giving witness to the resurrection. When the time set by the Father comes, the kingdom will be restored to Israel. Peter's sermon in Solomon's Portico likewise holds out the prospect of this future restoration.

> Repent therefore, and turn to God so that your sins may be wiped out, so that times of refreshing may come from the presence of the Lord, and that he may send the Messiah appointed for you, that is, Jesus, who must remain in heaven until the time of universal restoration that God announced long ago through his holy prophets. (Acts 3:19-21)

One other episode from the Gospels underscores the point being made. All four Gospels record the miracle of the feeding of the five thousand (Mt 14:13-21; Mk 6:32-44; Lk 9:10-17; Jn 6:1-15), but John makes clear the reason why Jesus abruptly left when the people became aware of what had happened: "When Jesus realized that they were about to come and take him by force *to make him king,* he withdrew again to the mountain by himself" (Jn 6:15, italics added). The crowds were filled with nationalistic fervor and saw in Jesus one who could drive out the hated Romans with their client kings and puppet government.[44] If Jesus could multiply loaves and fishes, think what he could do militarily! This was not, however, the kind of kingdom Jesus came to establish. As he would later say to Pilate: "My kingdom is not from this world. If my kingdom were from this world, my followers would be fighting to keep me from being handed over to the Jews. But as it is, my kingdom is not from here" (Jn 18:36).

As we read the Gospels, we must be aware of this strong nationalistic fervor. This probably explains why Jesus never used the title "Messiah" of himself when preaching and teaching in a Jewish setting. The only time he ever clearly identified himself as such before his trial (cf. Mk 14:62) was to a Samaritan woman in a private conversation (Jn 4:26). The term "Messiah" had such political connotations that Jesus chose not to call himself this or to allow his followers to do so (cf. Mk 8:29-30; Lk 9:20-22). It would have precipitated a clash with the Roman authorities.

Patriotic nationalism is also a probable reason for Judas's betrayal. When it finally became clear to Judas that Jesus was not going to restore the Davidic dynasty and drive out the Romans, Judas was bitterly disappointed and, in anger, decided to turn Jesus over to the authorities. The prospect of reigning

---

[44]See *New Oxford Annotated Bible,* note on Jn 6:15.

with Jesus over a restored Israel also explains the wrangling and jealousy among the disciples. The mother of the Zebedee brothers (John and James) even requested of Jesus that they might sit on either side of him when the kingdom was established (Mt 20:20-28). This led to anger on the part of the others, jealous, no doubt, that they had not requested this honor first! According to Luke, even on the night of the Last Supper a dispute broke out among the disciples as to which of them was the greatest (Lk 22:24).

The literature of the Second Temple leaves no doubt that there was an intense longing by many Jews for national liberation. This desire is also discernible in NT literature. Later we will see that the movement for national liberation led to disaster for the Jewish people.

This is not, however, the only significance of the exile for reading the NT documents. The earliest Christians transposed the theme of exile into a different key and utilized it as a means of self-identity. That is, Christians viewed themselves as foreigners and aliens living under the conditions of exile. Peter addressed a primarily Gentile Christian audience as "exiles of the Dispersion" (1 Pet 1:1), and James, addressing a Jewish Christian group, referred to them as "the twelve tribes in the Dispersion" (Jas 1:1). The letter to the Hebrews features as a major motif the pilgrim people of God. Like the OT worthies (Heb 11:13-16), believers are depicted as undertaking a long trek through the wilderness en route to the Promised Land: "For here we have no lasting city, but we are looking for the city that is to come" (Heb 13:14). This world, under the malign influence of the "god of this world," is no longer the true home of Christians. In Paul's words, Christians need to remember that "the present form of this world is passing away" (1 Cor 7:31b) and that "our citizenship is in heaven, and it is from there that we are expecting a Savior, the Lord Jesus Christ" (Phil 3:20). Like their Jewish counterparts, Christians yearn for a New Jerusalem; for Christians, however, it is no longer historic Mount Zion but the heavenly Mount Zion (Gal 4:26; Heb 12:22).

Not surprisingly, just like Jews living in Diaspora, Christians are exhorted to be separate from the world, to avoid the compromise and contamination so much a concern of the tales of the Diaspora we have just read. Peter exhorts his flock, "Beloved, I urge you as aliens and exiles to abstain from the desires of the flesh that wage war against the soul. Conduct yourselves honorably among the Gentiles" (1 Pet 2:11-12). In 2 Corinthians 6:14—7:1, Paul calls for separation from this world and quotes the OT in support: "Therefore come out from them, and be separate from them, says the Lord, and touch nothing unclean; then I will welcome you" (2 Cor 6:17; cf. Is 52:11). Paul reminds his colleague Titus, "For the grace of God has appeared, bringing salvation to all, training us to renounce impiety and worldly passions, and in the present age to live lives that are self-controlled, upright, and godly" (Tit 2:11-12). This emphasis in Christian epistolary literature leads us into our next consideration.

Christian Paraenesis (Moral Exhortation)

One of the distinctive features of NT letters is the presence of sections urging believers to follow a certain course of action. In Paul's letters, for example, he typically concentrates his advice on holy living in the concluding section (see, e.g., Rom 12:1–15:13; Gal 5:1–6:10; Eph 4:1–6:20; Col 3:1–4:6; 1 Thess 4:1–5:22). What may not be as readily apparent is the Jewish background and shaping of this material. Paul's Pharisaic background provided much of the form and content of his paraenesis (moral and ethical exhortation). This is not to deny, of course, that Paul's paraenesis was profoundly altered by his experience with Christ. These observations apply to the General Epistles as well, most notably, the Petrine letters and James. But let us now look at some of the parallels between the literature we have just read and NT paraenesis, whether Pauline or non-Pauline.

Polemic against idolatry. As we saw earlier, the Letter of Jeremiah is a sustained sermon against the evils of idol worship and polytheism. The author announces his theme in verses 4-7:

> Now in Babylon you will see gods made of silver and gold and wood, which people carry on their shoulders, and which cause the heathen to fear. So beware of becoming at all like the foreigners or of letting fear for these gods possess you when you see the multitude before and behind them worshiping them. But say in your heart, "It is you, O Lord, whom we must worship." For my angel is with you, and he is watching over your lives.

Likewise, Bel and the Dragon ridicules idolatry by means of a detective story and the Prayer of Azariah extols the one, true and living God. This concern about the dangers and evils of idolatry permeates the NT writings, the Gospels excepted. The reason for its virtual absence in the Gospels is that the ministry of Jesus unfolded in a Jewish context where idolatry was anathema. When, however, the gospel extended beyond the boundaries of Judaism and began making an impact among Gentiles (cf. Acts 10–15), the issue of idolatry became urgent. The epistolary literature and Luke's narrative of the growth of the early church in the book of Acts display considerable concern over this issue, as does the final book, the Apocalypse (see Rev 2:14, 20; 9:20; 21:8; 22:15).

We turn first to the book of Acts. On Paul's first missionary journey to the interior of Asia Minor, in the Roman province of Galatia, an incident occurred illustrating the problem of Gentile idolatry. When Paul healed a man who was crippled from birth, this induced such amazement that the locals cried out: "The gods have come down to us in human form!" (Acts 14:11). Barnabas was identified as Zeus and Paul as Hermes, gods of the Greek pantheon. Furthermore, the inhabitants were about to offer sacrifice and worship them. Once Paul and Barnabas realized what was happening—they did not speak the Lycaonian language and must have had someone translate for them into Greek—they expressed their shock and protest in the strongest actions and language possible. Tearing their clothes as a sign of horror and dismay, they cried out, "Friends, why are you doing this? We are mortals just like you, and we bring you good news, *that you should turn from these worthless things to the living God,* who made the heaven and the earth and the sea and all that is in them" (Acts 14:15, italics added).[45] This description of idolatry recalls the denunciations of the OT prophets (e.g., Is 40:18-20; 41:7; 42:17; 44:9-20; 45:16, 20; Jer 10:1-16) and the literature we have just read.

Later, at the Jerusalem Council (Acts 15), the issue of Gentile admission into the church sparked a vigorous debate. The advocates of Gentile freedom from the demands of the law carried the day, but not without a compromise. After hearing all the parties involved, James rendered a decision. Gentiles would not be required to be circumcised or to observe the dietary laws in order to be admitted, but they would be requested to observe the Noahic prohibitions, understood by Jews of the Second Temple period to be binding on all Gentiles (Gen 9:1-6). The rabbis included in these prohibitions eating food offered to idols.[46] James's rationale appears to have been that Jewish sensibilities had to be respected if Jewish and Gentile Christians were to worship and fellowship together. Thus the more lenient party on Gentile freedom was expected to avoid offending the more strict (Pharisaic) party by completely avoiding food that had been offered to idols (cf. Acts 15:21).[47] The literature we have just read helps us understand how repugnant anything connected to idolatry was to observant Jews. This is reflected, for example, in Paul's letter to the Romans, where he directs his remarks to non-Christian Jews whom he characterizes as those who "abhor idols" (Rom 2:22).

Paul's ministry in Athens illustrates Jewish-Christian revulsion toward idolatry. While awaiting the arrival of Silas and Timothy from Beroea, Paul "was deeply distressed to see that the city was full of idols" (Acts 17:16). This led to a two-pronged evangelistic effort in the synagogue and the marketplace. Paul's preaching soon elicited mild interest on the part of Epicurean and Stoic philosophers. Invited to address them at the Areopagus, Paul sought

---

[45]See the helpful background comments of Craig S. Keener, *The IVP Bible Background Commentary: New Testament* (Downers Grove, Ill.: InterVarsity Press, 1993), p. 362.

[46]See *New Oxford Annotated Bible,* p. 12 note on Gen 9:1-17.

[47]See further on this passage Keener, *IVP Bible Background Commentary,* p. 365.

common ground as a prelude to the kerygma (proclamation of the gospel). The presence of an altar dedicated to an unknown god provided just what he needed. He presented the message of Christ as a revelation of that unknown god now made manifest. Notice that in his message, idolatry is exposed as erroneous and unsatisfying. Paul's preaching sounds much like the language of Bel and the Dragon and the Letter of Jeremiah. "[The Lord of heaven and earth is not] served by human hands, as though he needed anything . . . [and] we ought not to think that the deity is like gold, or silver, or stone, an image formed by the art and imagination of mortals" (Acts 17:25, 29).

The book of Acts also highlights the dangers of preaching monotheism in a polytheistic environment. During his more than two years in Ephesus, Paul's preaching made deep inroads among the Gentiles, so much so that the local silversmiths noticed a sharp decline in revenue from sales of their Artemis shrines.[48] This prompted Demetrius to instigate a riot against Paul as a protest (Acts 19:23—20:1). Providentially, the rioters did not discover Paul, nor did his friends and some savvy officials allow him to respond to his adversaries in the great theater at Ephesus, which could have been hazardous to his health! The confident and easy triumphs over idolatry by the heroes and heroines of the Apocrypha reflect the fantasies and desires of pious Jews rather than the harsh realities confronted by the apostle Paul.

In light of the foregoing, it is no surprise that Paul, the apostle to the Gentiles, encountered problems in this area during his church-planting efforts. The book of 1 Thessalonians preserves what may be Paul's earliest letter (ca. A.D. 50-51) and presents us with a primarily Gentile church. Paul summarizes his evangelistic message and the Thessalonians' response to the gospel. "For the people of those regions report about us what kind of welcome we had among you, and *how you turned to God from idols, to serve a living and true God*" (1 Thess 1:9, italics added; cf. above on Acts 14:15). But that turning to God was not always decisive, and the strong attraction of ingrained habits was a continuing temptation for some. For example, in 1 Corinthians Paul warns the congregation that certain behaviors, if persisted in, would result in exclusion from the kingdom of God. Included among the vices is idolatry (1 Cor 6:9). The seduction of idolatry and its associated practices was no small force to be reckoned with: "You know that when you were pagans, *you were enticed and led astray to idols that could not speak*" (1 Cor 12:2, italics added). Compare this also with Peter's comment relating to Gentile Christians' past behavior: "You have already spent enough time in doing what the Gentiles like to do, living in licentiousness, passions, drunkenness, revels, carousing, and *lawless idolatry*" (1 Pet 4:3,

---

[48]See note in *New Oxford Annotated Bible,* NT 190.

italics added). Paul notes that idolatry is a consequence of faulty thinking stemming from a failure to acknowledge God and give him thanks (Rom 1:21-25). This in turn leads to a downward spiral into the depths of depravity (Rom 1:26-32), a line of argumentation unmistakably bearing the earmarks of Hellenistic Judaism.

The issue of food offered to idols surfaces several times in the NT. In 1 Corinthians 8—10, Paul gives directives on the various aspects of this problem. What is seldom recognized is that this section has the earmarks of Jewish halakic (pertaining to legal prescriptions) rulings much like those of the rabbis in the Mishnah.[49] The difference is, of course, that Paul gives his counsel from the new-covenant perspective of being "in Christ." Paul prefaces his rulings with the admonition "my dear friends, flee from the worship of idols" (1 Cor 10:14). The rulings themselves may be summarized: food offered to idols and then sold in the market may, in principle, be eaten by Christians (1 Cor 10:25). If invited to the home of an unbeliever and served meat that had first been offered to idols, the Christian may also, in principle, eat it without asking questions (1 Cor 10:27). The exception to the two above rulings is when a fellow Christian raises objections. Paul explains, "some have become so accustomed to idols until now, they still think of the food they eat as food offered to an idol; and their conscience, being weak, is defiled" (1 Cor 8:7). This must have been a frequent problem, and the church at Corinth was deeply divided by controversy over whether Christians should eat meat offered to idols. The problem could scarcely be avoided, since virtually all meat for public consumption in a Greco-Roman city had first been offered up to idols.[50] The third ruling was emphatic: no Christian may participate in banquets held in pagan temples *as part of a religious ritual*. The reason appears to be demonic influence (1 Cor 10:14-21): "You cannot drink the cup of the Lord and the cup of demons. You cannot partake of the table of the Lord and the table of demons" (1 Cor 10:21).

Finally, note that this entire discussion is undergirded by a theological confession (1 Cor 8:4-6). Paul combines the Shema (the fundamental creed of Israel affirming the oneness and uniqueness of God based upon Deut 6:4) of biblical and postbiblical Judaism with a distinctively Christian modification of monotheism. For Paul, "there is one God, the Father, from whom are all things and for whom we exist, and one Lord, Jesus Christ, through whom are

---

[49]The halakah is the legal part of talmudic literature, an interpretation of the laws of the Scriptures. See further J. Neusner, "Talmud," *ISBE* 4:717-24. See also Peter J. Tomson, *Paul and the Jewish Law: Halakha in the Letters of the Apostle to the Gentiles* (Minneapolis: Fortress, 1990). We will discuss halakah and Mishnah in more detail in chapter thirteen.

[50]For further background on this issue, see B. B. Blue, "Food Offered to Idols and Jewish Food Laws," *DPL*, pp. 306-10.

all things and through whom we exist" (1 Cor 8:6).[51]

The foundation and shape of Christian opposition to idolatry grew unmistakably out of Jewish soil. The tales from the Diaspora help us recognize how intensely conditioned Jews of the first century A.D. were against idols and idolatry. Standard descriptions and denigration of idolatry in this literature reappear in the NT. We are not arguing that there is direct dependence; rather, the tales from the Diaspora reflect Jewish attitudes that continued in NT literature. Knowing that idolatry had been a major reason for the exile and the continuing oppression under Roman occupation, pious Jews, certainly the Pharisees, sought to eradicate idolatry from world Jewry.[52] Likewise, early Jewish Christians shared this disgust with idolatry and strongly attacked its evils in their mission to the Gentiles. In the words of the elder statesman, John the apostle, "Little children, keep yourselves from idols" (1 Jn 5:21).

The practice of piety. Another area in which our literature helps us better understand the NT concerns ideals of piety (reverence, devotion and godliness). In this regard Tobit takes pride of place. Once again, we see parallels to Christian paraenesis. The virtues extolled and the vices excoriated in the NT are similar to those in Tobit and the other tales from dispersion.

Let us first place the teachings of Jesus alongside the book of Tobit. Tobit 12:8 is a nice summary of the "three pillars of Judaism—prayer, fasting and almsgiving."[53] Remarkably, and seldom realized by Christian readers, when Jesus turns his attention to the topic of "practicing your piety before others" (Mt 6:1), the first three items he elaborates on are almsgiving, prayer and fasting (Mt 6:1-21). It is worth noting that Tobit accords almsgiving the greatest worth: "Prayer with fasting is good, but better than both is almsgiving with righteousness" (Tob 12:8). To be sure, Jesus does not, like Tobit, assign any redemptive efficacy to the performance of almsgiving. Tobit says:

> To all those who practice righteousness give alms from your possessions. . . . So you will be laying up a good treasure for yourself against the day of necessity. For almsgiving delivers from death and keeps you from going into the Darkness. Indeed, almsgiving, for all who practice it, is an excellent offering in the presence of the Most High. . . . For almsgiving saves from death and purges away every sin. Those who give alms will enjoy a full life, but those who commit sin and do wrong are their own worst enemies. (Tob 4:6b-7a, 9-11; 12:9-10).

---

[51]On this Christian modification of monotheism, see Larry Hurtado, *One God, One Lord: Early Christian Devotion and Ancient Jewish Monotheism* (Philadelphia: Fortress, 1988).

[52]For a slightly different perspective on Jewish opposition to idolatry, see B. W. R. Pearson, "Idolatry, Jewish Conception of," *DNTB*, pp. 526-29.

[53]See also Metzger, *Introduction to the Apocrypha*, pp. 38, 39.

Jesus' concern in the Sermon on the Mount, however, is over-ostentation and hypocrisy in the practice of piety. But he does endorse all three acts of piety, so long as they are heartfelt concerns and not mere outward displays. He even uses the expression "store up for yourselves treasures" (Mt 6:19-20). Even more startling, we find the negative form of the golden rule already stated two centuries before Jesus: "And what you hate, do not do to anyone" (Tob 4:15; cf. Mt 7:12). To be sure, Jesus' positive statement of the golden rule requires a more radical display of love than do Tobit and later rabbinic writings, but it is still thoroughly at home in a Jewish milieu.

The Sermon on the Mount also radically differs from Tobit on how one obtains eternal life. For Jesus it all hinges upon a personal relationship with him: "On that day many will say to me, 'Lord, Lord, did we not prophesy in your name, and cast out demons in your name, and do many deeds of power in your name?' Then I will declare to them, 'I never knew you; go away from me, you evildoers' " (Mt 7:22-23). This is the decisive test whether one "does the will of [the] Father in heaven" (Mt 7:21). Obedience to the teaching of Jesus is another way of expressing this same truth (Mt 7:24-27). Still, one cannot help sensing the Jewishness of Jesus' ethical teaching and its congruence with the moral and ethical concerns of Tobit.

Another prominent feature of the book of Tobit is concern for a proper burial. It is a sacred duty to provide this when the deceased's family, for whatever reasons, has not. Indeed, this strong sense of duty to provide proper burial functions in the author's plot to bring about the low point in Tobit's life, raising the classic problem of evil: "when bad things happen to good people." Notice that all four Gospels reflect this typically Jewish concern for proper burial. Joseph of Arimathea (a man of means) and Nicodemus (a man of position and prestige) take considerable risks in asking for the body of Jesus from Pilate the Roman governor (Mt 27:57; Mk 15:43; Lk 23:51; Jn 19:38-39).

Perhaps the best way to illustrate the Jewish influence upon NT literature in the area of acceptable behavior and piety is to compare Tobit with sections of Pauline letters in which he exhorts his Christian readers to live a life "holy and acceptable to God" (Rom 12:1). Table 2.1 shows phrases from Tobit set alongside comparable expressions in Pauline epistolary paraenesis. We could, in fact, multiply examples, not only from Paul, but also from other NT writers. Once again, our point here is not to argue that Paul or any other NT author is literarily dependent upon Tobit but rather that Christian paraenesis reflects and is indebted to a Jewish background.

Angelology

Many NT readers are unaware of doctrinal developments that may be traced to Jewish sources other than the OT. Yet a cursory reading of the NT demonstrates

Table 2.1. Acceptable behavior and piety according to Tobit and Paul

Tobit	Paul
"Honor your mother and do not abandon her all the days of her life. . . . Remember her, my son, because she faced many dangers for you while you were in her womb" (4:3a, 4a).	"'Honor your father and mother'—this is the first commandment with a promise" (Eph 6:2; cf. Col 3:20; 1 Tim 4:3). "If a widow has children or grandchildren, they should first learn their religious duty to their own family and make some repayment to their parents" (1 Tim 5:4).
"Revere the Lord all your days" (4:5a).	"perfecting holiness out of reverence for God" (2 Cor 7:1 NIV).
"Live uprightly all the days of your life, and do not walk in the ways of wrongdoing" (4:5b).	"Live lives that are self-controlled, upright, and godly" (Tit 2:12).
"Do not turn your face away from anyone who is poor, and the face of God will not be turned away from you" (4:7b).	"They asked only one thing, that we remember the poor, which was actually what I was eager to do" (Gal 2:10).
"If you have many possessions, make your gift from them in proportion; if few, do not be afraid to give according to the little you have" (4:8).	"They voluntarily gave according to their means, and even beyond their means. . . . The gift is acceptable according to what one has—not according to what one does not have" (2 Cor 8:3, 12).
"Watch yourself, my son, in everything you do, and discipline yourself in all your conduct" (4:14b).	"Train yourself in godliness. . . . Pay close attention to yourself and to your teaching" (1 Tim 4:7, 16a).
"Do not drink wine to excess or let drunkenness go with you on your way" (4:15b).	"Do not get drunk with wine" (Eph 5:18a).
"Beware, my son, of every kind of fornication" (4:12a).	"Shun fornication!" (1 Cor 6:18a).
"At all times bless the Lord God, and ask him that . . . all your paths and plans may prosper" (4:19a).	"I desire, then, that in every place the men should pray" (1 Tim 2:8a). "Pray in the Spirit at all times in every prayer and supplication" (Eph 6:18a). "Devote yourselves to prayer, keeping alert in it with thanksgiving" (Col 4:2).

that certain ideas and assumptions about reality do not stem directly from the OT but are mediated by the literature between the Testaments. One such area is angelology, the branch of theology having to do with angels and demons.

The book of Tobit is a classic example of the development of angelology in the centuries prior to the birth of Christ. In this delightful story we are introduced to Raphael, an angel of God, who poses as Azariah, a shirttail relation to Tobit. But Raphael is no mere angel; he is an archangel, one of seven such beings "who stand ready and enter before the glory of the Lord" (Tob 12:15). The OT knows of no such category of angelic beings, and certainly not of seven archangels in the presence of God. To be sure, there is the notion of the divine council where angelic beings surround the throne (see 1 Kings 22:19-23; Job 1−2; Dan 7:10; Zech 3:1-7), but no mention of seven archangels who are distinct from this larger host. The book of Daniel presents the most developed angelology in the OT, and indeed, many scholars would date it close in time to the book of Tobit. Thus, for example, Daniel informs us of the names of two powerful angels: Gabriel (Dan 8:16; 9:21-23) and Michael (Dan 10:13, 21; 12:1). But we do not learn that Gabriel and Michael are among the seven archangels until we read it in *1 Enoch* 9:1; 54:6 and *2 Enoch* 8:1−10:1 (we discuss this material in more detail in the next chapter). The spelling of the names of the seven varies in our sources, but we may list them as following: Uriel, Raphael, Raguel, Michael, Saraqael, Gabriel and Vreveil (see *2 Enoch* 10:1). Sure enough, Raphael is within this circle of privileged and powerful angelic beings.

Of course, readers of the NT already know the names of two of the seven: Gabriel, entrusted with the birth announcements to Zechariah and Mary (Lk 1:19, 26), and Michael, mentioned in the book of Jude as contending with Satan over the body of Moses (Jude 9). We will have more to say about this incident later. Our point here is to observe that the theological development of the intertestamental era is carried forward and taken up by the NT.

Armed with this information, we may be able to resolve an interesting exegetical question in the book of Revelation. In Revelation 4 John is raptured into heaven and views the awesome throne room of God. Surrounding the throne in ever-widening concentric circles are various categories of angelic beings. Note how John describes one group: "in front of the throne burn seven flaming torches, which are the seven spirits of God" (Rev 4:5). Already in the salutation of 1:4 we have greetings from these seven spirits. Who are they? Many commentators opt for a symbolic designation of the Holy Spirit.[54] Understood in this way, one has a trinitarian formulation: "him who is and who was and who is to come" is God the Father, "the seven spirits" are the manifold energies of the Holy Spirit, and, of course, the faithful witness is Jesus Christ. The seven spirits are often linked to the sevenfold manifestation of the Spirit of the Lord in Isaiah 11:2. But may they not be the seven archangels of the intertestamental literature? Going further, may not the angels (guardians) of the seven churches of Asia in fact be the archangels? If so, then they may also be the executors of divine judg-

---

[54]See, e.g., Robert Mounce, *Revelation,* NICNT (Grand Rapids, Mich.: Eerdmans, 1977), pp. 69-70.

ment upon the earth, as in the seven trumpets (Rev 8:2) and seven bowls (cf. Rev 7:1; 16:1; 17:1; 21:9). On this reading, there is a consistency of role and function for the archangels in the book of Revelation and in apocalyptic literature generally. We will say more about this in the next chapter.

We also call attention to the intertestamental development of demonology. Again, Tobit is our star witness. The evil demon Asmodeus reflects a fascination with "the dark side," possibly as a result of Jewish encounters with Babylonian and Persian religions during the exile.[55] At any rate, our literature shows an amazing variety of names and descriptions of evil angelic or demonic beings. In the Song of the Three Jews we have a reference to "all . . . powers," referring to angelic beings (Song of Thr 39; cf. Eph 1:21; Col 2:10). Coupled with this elaborate angelology and demonology are superstitions and rituals designed to evade and exorcise demons. For example, Tobias is instructed to concoct a disagreeable odor in order to banish Asmodeus back to his lair in Egypt!

The NT takes seriously the reality of the demonic and even incorporates some of the names for the leader of the powers of darkness.[56] One recalls that the Pharisees explained Jesus' remarkable healing abilities by claiming he was in league with Satan, styled as "Beelzebul, the ruler of the demons" (Mt 12:24; cf. Lk 11:15). For his part, Jesus viewed his exorcisms as clear signs of his kingdom authority: "But if it is by the Spirit of God that I cast out demons, then the kingdom of God has come to you" (Mt 12:28).[57] There can be no doubt that Jesus viewed the realm of the demonic as real. A related title for Satan, Beliar (NIV Belial), crops up in passing in Paul's letter to the Corinthians: "What agreement does Christ have with Beliar?" (2 Cor 6:15). This title for Satan occurs already in *Jubilees* (see chapter four below). Furthermore, Paul accepts the notion, widespread in our literature, of a hierarchy of angelic and demonic beings (cf. Rom 8:38). Indeed, he envisions the Christian life as primarily a struggle with these spirit beings: "For our struggle is not against enemies of blood and flesh, but against the rulers, against the authorities, against the cosmic powers of this present darkness, against the spiritual forces of evil in the heavenly places" (Eph 6:12; cf. 1 Cor 2:8 [?]; 10:20-21; Eph 1:21; 2:2; Col 1:16; 2:8 [?], 15). Enough evidence has been marshaled to conclude that the NT displays indebtedness to the Jewish literature of the Sec-

---

[55] *New Oxford Annotated Bible* discusses the fact that behind Bel and the Dragon stands the mythical figures of Marduk and Tiamat, deities of the ancient Near East (AP 183).

[56] The NT reports the practice of exorcism by Jews in the Gospels and Acts. See Mt 12:27; Mk 9:38; Lk 11:19; Acts 19:13-14.

[57] For a treatment of the relationship of Jesus' ministry of exorcism to his messianic claims, see George E. Ladd, *A Theology of the New Testament*, rev. ed., ed. Donald A. Hagner (Grand Rapids, Mich.: Eerdmans, 1993), pp. 46-51.

ond Temple for its conception of angelology and demonology. If for no other reason than that, it is mandatory reading for a full understanding of the NT.

We conclude this chapter by drawing attention to several assorted parallels, either verbal or conceptual, between the tales of the dispersion we have just read and NT literature. Table 2.2 features an assortment of these parallels.

Summary

We have shown in this chapter that an acquaintance with these tales from the Diaspora throws welcome light on the NT writings. This can be summarized as follows:

1. We become more aware of the intense longings for national liberation lying just below the surface of the Gospels. Details recorded in the Gospels are now seen in a new light. We can understand better how Jesus had to refocus the priorities of his disciples (cf. Acts 1:7-8).

2. We can better appreciate the strong antipathy of Jewish-Christian missionaries, like the apostle Paul, toward idolatry and its associated practices. Jewish-Christian missionaries sought to warn and fortify new converts against lapsing back into their former way of life.

3. The early Christians transposed the fact of Jewish exile into a new key. Christians viewed themselves as exiles looking forward to the New Jerusalem: "For here we have no lasting city, but we are looking for the city that is to come" (Heb 13:14; cf. Jas 1:1; 1 Pet 1:1). An important aspect of early Christian paraenesis turns on the importance of realizing one's resident-alien status: "But our citizenship is in heaven, and it is from there that we are expecting a Savior" (Phil 3:20).

4. Christians, like Jews, faced recurring temptations to assimilate, to compromise with the surrounding culture. Thus, alongside warnings about failing to persevere, NT literature, like the tales from Diaspora, holds out bright hope for the future. Like Tobit 13—14, the book of Revelation radiates with a heavenly vision. But it is only available "to everyone who conquers."

5. Finally, we learn to appreciate how thoroughly Jewish the NT literature really is. Language, diction, imagery, concepts and ideas are influenced and shaped by the Judaism of the first two pre-Christian centuries and the first Christian century.[58] In short, we recover an essential part of the context within which to read the NT.

---

[58]For a stimulating book arguing that Christianity is really a species of Judaism, see Bruce Chilton and Jacob Neusner, *Judaism in the New Testament: Practices and Beliefs* (New York: Routledge, 1995), pp. xii-18. They remark: "Hence the proper title of this book should be '*the* Judaism *of* the New Testament' " (p. 8).

Table 2.2. Specific points of comparison between the Apocrypha and the New Testament

Apocrypha	NT	Nature of parallel
Tob 4:6	Jn 3:21	This is a typically Jewish way of describing the upright: "those who act in accordance with truth."
Tob 5:15	Mt 20:2	Reference is made to the typical daily wage (one drachma = one denarius; the former is the Gk coinage; the latter, the Roman).
Tob 7:17	Mt 11:25	"Lord of heaven" or "Lord of heaven and earth" is a typically Jewish way of referring to God.
Tob 13:7, 11	Rev 15:3	Both doxologies are indebted to the Song of Moses (Deut 32) and the Song of the Sea (Ex 15:1-18), but the formulation in Rev 15:3 is verbally closer to Tobit than to the OT.
Tob 14:4	Lk 24:44	Jesus' conviction concerning the necessity of prophetic fulfillment recalls the sentiment expressed in Tobit.
Tob 14:5	Lk 21:24	The expressions "when the times of fulfillment shall come" and "until the times of the Gentiles are fulfilled" reflect a similar understanding that the eschatological fulfillment lies beyond an indefinite time of exile and oppression. (This will be developed in more detail later on.)
Song Thr 4	Rev 16:7; 19:2	Christian churches took over and adapted liturgical language from the synagogue, such as "your judgments are true and just."
Song Thr 11-13	Rom 11:28-29	The doctrine of the irrevocable election of Israel was still held by Paul, the apostle to the Gentiles.
Sus 9	Lk 15:18	"Heaven" is used as a circumlocution (roundabout expression) for the name of God. This simply reflects a Jewish aversion to pronouncing God's name lest one inadvertently transgress the third commandment (Ex 20:7; see *New Oxford Annotated Bible*, AP 180, note on v. 9).
Sus 42	Heb 4:13	The two verses have a similar formulation of the doctrine of God's omniscience. The author of Hebrews was almost certainly a Jewish Christian.
Let Jer 67	Mt 16:1; 1 Cor 1:22	This reflects the interest of Jews in signs as indicators of God's will and activity.
Tob 13:4	Mt 6:9	This reflects the fact that in the intertestamental period, God was on occasion referred to as "our Father." Jesus was the first, however, to directly address God as "my Father" or simply "Father" (see G. W. Bromiley, "God the Father," *ISBE* 2:510).
Tob 5:4-14; 12:11-22	Heb 13:2	The author of Hebrews doubtless had the Abraham incident in mind (Gen 18), but the theme is one that is at home in Judaism.

For Further Discussion

1. What are some of the key concepts and phrases that the NT carries over from the apocryphal works studied in this chapter?

2. How was nationalism a burden to Jesus' ministry? What are some modern preconceived notions about Jesus that obscure one's perception of him?

3. Compare and contrast Second Temple Judaism's polemic against idolatry with the NT polemic against idolatry.

4. How does one account for the many parallels between Tobit and Paul's writings?

5. How crucial is the issue of assimilation for Christians today?

For Further Reading

Robert Doran, "Narrative Literature," in *Early Judaism and Its Modern Interpreters,* ed. Robert A. Kraft and George W. E. Nickelsburg (Philadelphia: Fortress; Atlanta: Scholars Press, 1986), pp. 287-310.

D. Flusser, "Psalms, Hymns and Prayers," in *Jewish Writings of the Second Temple Period: Apocrypha, Pseudepigrapha, Qumran Sectarian Writings, Philo, Josephus,* ed. Michael E. Stone, CRINT 2 (Assen: Van Gorcum; Philadelphia: Fortress, 1984), pp. 553-54.

Daniel J. Harrington, *Invitation to the Apocrypha* (Grand Rapids, Mich.: Eerdmans, 1999), pp. 109-21.

Larry R. Helyer, "Tobit," *DNTB*, pp. 1238-41.

J. Jarick, "Daniel, Esther and Jeremiah, Additions to," *DNTB*, pp. 250-52.

Bruce M. Metzger, *An Introduction to the Apocrypha* (New York: Oxford University Press, 1957), pp. 31-42, 95-122.

Carey A. Moore, *Daniel, Esther and Jeremiah: The Additions: A New Translation with Introduction and Commentary,* AB 44 (Garden City, N.Y.: Doubleday, 1977).

———, *Tobit: A New Translation with Introduction and Commentary,* AB 40A (New York: Doubleday, 1996).

George W. E. Nickelsburg, "The Bible Rewritten and Expanded," in *Jewish Writings of the Second Temple Period: Apocrypha, Pseudepigrapha, Qumran Sectarian Writings, Philo, Josephus,* ed. Michael E. Stone, CRINT 2 (Assen: Van Gorcum; Philadelphia: Fortress, 1984), pp. 146-52.

———, "Stories of Biblical and Early Post-Biblical Times," in *Jewish Writings of the Second Temple Period: Apocrypha, Pseudepigrapha, Qumran Sectarian Writings, Philo, Josephus,* ed. Michael E. Stone, CRINT 2 (Assen: Van Gorcum; Philadelphia: Fortress, 1984), pp. 33-44.

———, "Tales of the Dispersion," in *Jewish Literature Between the Bible and the Mishnah: A Historical and Literary Introduction* (Philadelphia: Fortress, 1981), pp. 19-42.

James C. VanderKam, *An Introduction to Early Judaism* (Grand Rapids, Mich.: Eerdmans, 2001), pp. 69-71, 75-78, 135-37.

Three

Hellenism Invades
the Middle East

*F**or the English translation of* 1 Enoch *1—36; 72—82 we use H. F. D. Sparks,*
ed., The Apocryphal Old Testament *(Oxford: Clarendon Press, 1985), pp. 184-221,*
257-274. One may also consult J. H. Charlesworth, ed., The Old Testament
Pseudepigrapha, *2 vols. (Garden City, N.Y.: Doubleday, 1983), 1:13-29, 50-61; and*
the older work of R. H. Charles, ed., The Apocrypha and Pseudepigrapha of the
Old Testament, *2 vols. (Oxford: Clarendon Press, 1913), 2:163-208, 237-48. We use*
Sparks's edition because it is less expensive and bulky for the student. Sirach is eas-
ily accessible in The New Oxford Annotated Bible: New Revised Standard Ver-
sion, *ed. Bruce M. Metzger and Roland E. Murphy (New York: Oxford University*
Press, 1991), AP 86-160; The Catholic Study Bible, *ed. Donald Senior (New York:*
Oxford University Press, 1990), pp. 822-76; and The Oxford Study Bible: Revised
English Bible with the Apocrypha, *ed. M. Jack Suggs, Katharine Doob Sakenfeld,*
and James R. Mueller (New York: Oxford University Press, 1992), pp. 1116-76.

Introduction

Ancient (or early) Judaism (the period between the sixth and third centuries
B.C.)[1] confronted one of its most dangerous challengers in the wake of Alexander the Great's conquests of the Middle East (333-323 B.C.). That challenger

---

[1]Gabriele Boccaccini prefers the designation "Middle Judaism" for this era (*Middle Judaism:
Jewish Thought, 300 B.C.E. to 200 C.E.* [Minneapolis: Fortress, 1991], pp.18-25). Terminol-

was Hellenism. Alexander the Great was not merely a military leader of extraordinary ability; he was also an ardent lover of Greek culture. He envisioned himself as destined to bring the known world under the influence of the Greek language and culture. Alexander brought about what is known as the Hellenistic age, lasting from his death in 323 B.C. down to 31 B.C. Wherever he went, he established Greek cities in which the Greek language, culture and institutions were superimposed upon the native populations.[2] Alexander's successors continued the process throughout their far-flung kingdoms.[3]

Palestine was not exempt from this process. In this region alone, some thirty Greek cities were founded along the Mediterranean coast, in Galilee and Samaria, and in Transjordan.[4] One league of Hellenistic cities constituted the district known as the Decapolis in NT times.[5] Excluded from this development was the old tribal territory of Judah, the most conservative and resistant to change. We should also note, however, that the various ethnic populations in the villages and rural settlements, even in regions where Hellenistic cities were founded, were not impacted by Hellenism as much as earlier scholars had assumed.[6] Still, even Judah could not escape the pervasive influence of the Greek culture, as we will see.[7] It was this meshing of cul-

---

ogy for this period is currently under debate. Charlesworth prefers "early Judaism," as does Nickelsburg. See ibid, p. xviii; and George W. E. Nickelsburg, *Jewish Literature Between the Bible and the Mishnah: A Historical and Literary Introduction* (Philadelphia: Fortress, 1981), pp. 2-3.

[2]See J. E. H. Thomson, "Alexander the Great," *ISBE* 1:87-89 and map xiii, for some appreciation of the extent and impact of Alexander's conquests. See also Yohanan Aharoni and Michael Avi-Yonah, *The Macmillan Bible Atlas*, 3rd ed., ed. Anson F. Rainey and Ze'ev Safrai (New York: Macmillan, 1993), nos. 172-74. For a popular treatment, see Frank Holt, "Alexander in the East," *Odyssey* 4 (2001): 14-23, 58.

[3]"Geography, History and Archaeology," in *The New Oxford Annotated Bible: New Revised Standard Version*, ed. Bruce M. Metzger and Roland E. Murphy (New York: Oxford University Press, 1991), NT 416-17, provides a brief overview of this turbulent period. See also Nickelsburg, *Jewish Literature*, pp. 43-46; J. Julius Scott Jr., *Customs and Controversies: Intertestamental Jewish Backgrounds of the New Testament* (Grand Rapids, Mich.: Baker, 1995), pp. 112-20; Lee I. Levine, *Judaism and Hellenism in Antiquity: Conflict or Confluence?* (Peabody, Mass.: Hendrickson, 1998), chaps. 1-2; and the essays in John J. Collins and Gregory E. Sterling, eds., *Hellenism in the Land of Israel* (Notre Dame, Ind.: University of Notre Dame Press, 2001).

[4]For map and description of these cities, see Aharoni and Avi-Yonah, *Macmillan Bible Atlas*, no. 181.

[5]The Decapolis was a confederation of ten cities located in the northeastern part of Palestine. It was established in 62 B.C. and governed directly by Rome. See ibid., no. 231, for map.

[6]On this see Eric M. Meyers, "The Challenge of Hellenism for Early Judaism and Christianity," *BA* 287 (1992): 84-91 and bibliography.

[7]See Martin Hengel, "Judaism and Hellenism Revisited," in *Hellenism in the Land of Israel*, ed. John Collins and Gregory E. Sterling, CJA 13 (Notre Dame, Ind.: University of Notre Dame Press, 2001), pp. 6-37; and John Collins, "Cult and Culture: The Limits of Hellenization in Judea," in *Hellenism in the Land of Israel*, pp. 38-61.

tures that shaped so much of the literature of the Second Temple period.

The encounter with Hellenism prompted differing responses by the Jewish people. Some resisted this alien, pagan system mightily and sought to build a hedge against its influence. Others embraced it fervently as an escape from outdated traditions that were out of touch with the times. Still others adopted a middle road. They absorbed some aspects of Hellenism and adapted others without abandoning the essentials of their Hebraic heritage. Probably a majority of Jews followed this "third way."[8]

Our task in this chapter is to explore some Jewish literature written during this era in order to gain an insight into how Hellenism shaped the way Jews understood their place in the world. The literature consists of (1) two segments of an apocalyptic document, a composite work, dating from the third and second centuries B.C., and (2) a fine example of wisdom literature also dating to the second century B.C. The first two pieces, *1 Enoch* 72–82 and 1–36, are generally designated as part of the Pseudepigrapha, whereas the latter, Ecclesiasticus, or the Wisdom of Jesus Son of Sirach, is part of the Apocrypha.

The Book of Enoch

A rather sizable body of literature grew up around the figure of Enoch. The reasons for this may be found in the fascinating account recorded in Genesis 5:24: "Enoch walked with God; then he was no more, because God took him." Two essentials qualified Enoch to become a legendary figure: he was a righteous man in the midst of an unrighteous generation, and he was raptured into the presence of God. Since Enoch was caught up to the celestial realms, he provided the perfect informant on matters cosmic and celestial. Anonymous Jewish authors used Enoch as the mediator of such esoteric knowledge. In reality, the figure of Enoch simply served to legitimate various Jewish reflections concerning how the cosmos operates and the divine decrees relating to the end of the world.

The compositional history of *1 Enoch* is uncertain; the majority view holds that we have five independent pieces spliced to form one lengthy work featuring the revelations of Enoch.[9] Sparks draws attention to the fact that a five-fold division recalls both the Pentateuch and the Psalter and suggests the

---

[8]See further on this Scott, *Customs and Controversies,* pp. 112-27.

[9]Read Sparks's introduction to the Enoch literature (*AOT,* pp. 169-79), noting especially page 173, where the five books of the entire work are outlined. So also Michael E. Stone, "Apocalyptic Literature," in *Jewish Writings of the Second Temple Period: Apocrypha, Pseudepigrapha, Qumran Sectarian Writings, Philo, Josephus,* ed. Michael E. Stone, CRINT 2 (Assen: Van Gorcum; Philadelphia: Fortress, 1984), p. 396; Martin Rist, "Enoch, Book of," *IDB* 2:103-5. Nickelsburg apparently divides the work into nine different component parts in "Enoch, First Book of," *ABD* 2:508-16.

designation of our work as an "Enochic Pentateuch."[10]

The dating of the various "books" varies considerably from scholar to scholar. As Sparks points out, we simply do not know when the book (or its supposed separate books) was composed in Hebrew or Aramaic and translated into Greek and then, much later, into Ethiopic.[11] Nickelsburg offers a span from the third to the first centuries B.C. for all the component parts.[12] At any rate, the Astronomical Book (*1 En.* 72—82) is considered to be the oldest and is attested already among the Qumran writings. On paleographic grounds, the fragments at Qumran are dated to the period 200-150 B.C.[13]

1 Enoch 72—82, The Astronomical Book

The contents of *1 Enoch* 72—82 can be outlined as follows:

I.   Introduction to the Astronomical Book (72:1-2)
    A. Explanation: the rules and regulations for the lights
    B. Expositor: Uriel ("God is my light") as the informant
    C. Extent: the regulations last until the new creation
II. Rationale for a 364-day year (72:3—75:9)
    A. Regulations of the sun (72:3-37)
       1. Its twelve gates
       2. Its course across the sky and the increase and decrease of light and darkness throughout the year
       3. The year equals exactly 364 days (a solar calendar)
    B. Regulations of the moon and phases of the moon (73:1—74:17)
    C. The importance of the four intercalated days and summary of heavenly regulations (75:1-9)
III. A cosmological and geographical gazetteer: the twelve gates of the winds and the four quarters of the heavens (76:1—78:17)
    A. Effects of the winds upon the earth (76:1-14)
    B. The four quarters of the heavens, the seven high mountains of the earth, the seven great rivers and the seven great islands (77:1-9)
    C. Names of sun and moon and phases of the moon (78:1-17)
IV. The preservation and legitimation of the revelation (79:1—81:10)

---

[10]Stone, however, cautions that the fivefold nature of *1 Enoch* in its Semitic original, after the analogy of the Mosaic Pentateuch, may be accidental rather than intentional ("Apocalyptic Literature," p. 398 and notes).

[11]*AOT,* p. 177.

[12]In fact, in his most recent evaluation he says it was composed between the fourth century B.C. and the turn of the era. This pushes its earliest material (*1 En.* 72—82) even further back ("Enoch, First Book of," 2:508).

[13]Nickelsburg, *Jewish Literature,* p. 47; see also his "Enoch, Book of," *IDBSup,* p. 266.

("And now my son Methuselah" frames the section: 79:1; 82:1)
- A. Summary of the whole law of luminaries (79:1-6)
- B. Prophecy of end times and the changing of the times (80:1-8)
- C. Book of destiny revealed (81:1-10)
  Enoch given only one year to strengthen his family before his rapture to heaven
V. Admonitions to the righteous (82:1-20)
- A. Enoch inspired by Uriel
- B. Angels of the four seasons

This section of *1 Enoch* is not the most interesting reading. In fact, for most readers, it will seem tedious and monotonous.[14] On the face of it, the Astronomical Book (hereafter AB) describes the mechanics of how the sun and moon and stars run their appointed courses in a 364-day solar year. The sun and moon rise and set in "gates," six on the east and six on the west. In addition, the winds issue from twelve different gates, resulting in differing effects upon the earth.

The reader may well ask, What is the point of this rather boring recital of "sunrise, sunset, quickly go the days"? We suggest the following answer: it is extremely important for our author to validate the fact that there are precisely 364 days in the year and that this has been the case from creation and will last until the new creation (cf. *1 En.* 72:1). And why should this be thought so crucial? Chapters 74—75 and 80 contain the clues that point us to the answer. In 74—75 the author informs us that the number of days for the moon to fulfill its yearly cycle "falls behind" that of the sun. Thus the lunar calendar has 360 days, as compared to the solar calendar of 364. The author solemnly informs us: "And because of them men go wrong in them, for these lights really serve in the stations of the world . . . and the exact harmony of the course of the world is completed in the separate three hundred and sixty four stations of the world" (*1 En.* 75:2). This hint becomes explicit in chapter 80:

> And in those days Uriel answered me and said to me, Behold I have shown you everything, O Enoch, and have revealed everything to you, that you may see this sun, and this moon, and those who lead the stars of heaven, and all those

---

[14]Two earlier researchers on *1 Enoch* give their impressions about the impact of the book on those who pick it up for the first time. F. Crawford Burkitt notes: "I think that those of you who have tried to read 'Enoch' will agree that the first impression it leaves is that of words with very little sense" (*Jewish and Christian Apocalypses,* The Schweich Lectures 1913 (London: Humphrey Milford, Oxford University Press, 1914], p. 21). R. H. Charles concurs: "The reader who comes to peruse the Book of Enoch, for the first time will find much that appears to him strange and unattractive" (*The Book of Enoch* [New York: Macmillan, 1935], p. xix).

who turn them, their tasks, and their times and their rising. But in the days of the sinners the years will become shorter, and their seed will be late on their land and on their fields, and all things on the earth will change, and will not appear at their proper time. And the rain will be withheld, and heaven will retain it. And in those times the fruits of the earth will be late and will not grow at their proper time, and the fruits of the trees will be withheld at their proper time. And the moon will change its customary practice, and will not appear at its proper time. . . . And many heads of the stars in command will go astray, and these will change their courses and their activities, and will not appear at the times which have been prescribed for them. And the entire law of the stars will be closed to the sinners, and the thoughts of those who dwell upon the earth will go astray over them, and they will turn from all their ways, and will go astray, and will think them gods. And many evils will overtake them, and punishment will come upon them to destroy them all.

It appears that our author is in dispute with an unnamed group or custom that follows a lunar calendar. According to our author and the community he represents, this is an error of grave proportions. For pious Jews, who are committed to the entire keeping of the pentateuchal legislation, performing ritual worship on the prescribed days is absolutely essential. But if the proper calendar is not observed, then the ritual is performed on the wrong day and it is presumably ineffectual at best and sacrilegious at worst.

"Calendrical correctness" is also a major issue in the Qumran writings. For now we simply call attention to the fact that in the library of Qumran, no fewer than eleven manuscripts of *1 Enoch* have been recovered. Of these manuscripts, four were of *1 Enoch* 72—82. This tells us that the Qumran community must have valued this book and shared at least its view on the correct calendar. We will take this up later in chapters six and seven.

Still, one wonders why it was necessary to delineate in such detail and repetition the circuit of the heavenly bodies in order to make the point about the calendar. The evidence at Qumran even indicates that AB in its Aramaic form was considerably longer than the version from which our Ethiopic translation was made. Whence this sudden interest in the "how" of the heavenly bodies? This is a very complex issue, and a complete discussion is beyond our scope. We can, however, offer a few suggestions.

Fascination with the mechanics of the cosmos is not indigenous to the Hebrew Scriptures. To be sure, there is the majestic account of creation in Genesis 1 in which the works of creation are assigned to the various days of the week. But this account hardly displays a captivation with the detailed workings of the universe. On the contrary, it reflects the simple observation of basic life forms from a pastoral, agrarian perspective.

Nonetheless, the author(s) of AB had at hand some traditions in the

Hebrew Bible with regard to the heavenly bodies.[15] Genesis 1:14-19 narrates the creation of the greater light (the sun) and the lesser light (the moon) on the fourth "day" of creation. These two lights were to rule over the day and night and were for "signs and for seasons and for days and years" (Gen 1:14). This is a point of great importance for the Enochic tradition. The pentateuchal legislation emphasizes a yearly cycle of ritual observances, all established at set times (cf. Ex 23:12-17; 34:18-26; Lev 23:1-44; Deut 16:1-17). The flood story (Gen 6—8) makes reference to "the windows of the heavens" (Gen 7:11). But perhaps most suggestive of all is the splendid Psalm 19, in which the sun is depicted as a bridegroom or strong man running from his wedding canopy to pursue his course across the circuit of the heavens. In Job one finds reference to the full moon, the boundary between light and darkness, the pillars of heaven (Job 26:9-11), the paths of darkness, the storehouses of snow and hail, channels for the rain and thunderbolts, various constellations (Pleides, Orion and the Bear), the ordinances of the heavens and their rule on the earth (Job 38:20-33). There are also a few brief passages that allude to the stars and even the planets in the prophetic texts (Jer 7:18; 8:2; 10:2; 19:13; 44:17-19; Amos 5:26). But nothing extant in the Hebrew Bible really parallels the AB's focus upon the "mechanics" of the celestial bodies. We must turn to other possible sources.

References to astronomical observations occur already in the Kassite period of Babylonian history (ca. 1650-1175 B.C.), and astrological texts for the purpose of divination existed by the reign of Ashurbanipal of Assyria (668-633 B.C.).[16] The Hebrews must have known a good bit of this lore, as we may infer from texts such as Amos 5:26 (which probably refers to the planet Saturn) and Jeremiah 7:18; 44:17-19 (which denounce the worship of the Queen of Heaven, most likely the planet Venus).

Remember that Nebuchadnezzar's Neo-Babylonian juggernaut destroyed Judah in 586 B.C. The surviving nobility, artisans and leaders of the Jewish

---

[15]Of course, it is widely recognized that these traditions reflect a Mesopotamian background. See, e.g., Kenneth Barker et al., eds., *The NIV Study Bible* (Grand Rapids, Mich.: Zondervan, 1985), p. 1.

[16]See J. S. Wright, "Astrology," *ISBE* 1:341-44, esp. p. 342. The Akkadian epic *Enuma Elish*, considered by most scholars to go back to the first part of the second millennium B.C., has striking similarities to Genesis 1. See both E. A. Speiser's (*ANET*, pp. 67-68) and A. K. Grayson's (*ANET*, pp. 501-3) translations. In a work entitled "The Duties and Powers of the Gods: Inscriptions on the Statue of King Kurigalzu" (c. 1500 B.C.), we read of the gods (Igigi) whose responsibility concerns the performance of certain rituals at set times. We read, for example, of "the great Igigi who *parade in* the sky, whose brilliance, like fire . . . s the *evening* and the black night, did not at all enlarge the . . . As *for* Belitili who crosses the sky, in the earth . . . , from the district(s) of the sky" (*ANET*, p. 59; the gaps in the translation are lucunae or breaks in the tablets).

community were exiled to Babylon, leaving only the poorest to forage from the remains of the desolated land. In Babylon, exiled Jews lived among polytheistic pagans who already had a long tradition of astrology and what could even be called astronomy. Some of the Babylonian achievements by 400 B.C. included "a zodiac as a reference for solar and planetary motion, a fixed lunisolar calendar, basic period relationships for the moon and planets, a knowledge of the variation in the length of day and night, and a numerical method that could be used in astronomical calculations."[17]

The Hebrews, of course, did not accept the reality of the "gods," but in a work such as *1 Enoch* they did ascribe to angelic beings duties similar to those carried out by the Igigi (gods) of the Babylonian literature (cf. *1 En.* 82:11-20). Persia, the successor to Neo-Babylonia, likewise focused considerable attention upon the heavenly spheres, and Babylonian studies of astronomy and astrology continued apace. We recall here the books of Daniel, Esther, Ezra, Nehemiah and portions of Isaiah (Is 40—66), which feature the Persian period as their background. For some scholars, Iranian religion provided a stimulus that prompted Jews to reflect upon the vastness and orderliness of the heavens above.[18]

It is worth noting that AB may have been composed just before or during the Seleucid era (ca. 198-164 B.C.), the time when Babylonian astronomy reached its greatest development. That is to say, during the Hellenistic Age, Babylonian astrology and astronomy were introduced to Greek scholars.[19] In

---

[17]J. M. Everts, "Astronomy," *ISBE* 1:346.

[18]Older scholars postulated the strong influence of Zoroastrianism upon *1 Enoch*. See, e.g., James Hope Moulton, *Early Zoroastrianism* (London: Williams & Norgate, 1913). John J. Collins ("Genre, Ideology and Social Movements in Jewish Apocalypticism. Appendix: A New Proposal on Apocalyptic Origins," in *Mysteries and Revelations: Apocalyptic Studies Since the Uppsala Colloquium*, ed. J. J. Collins and J. H. Charlesworth, JSPSup 9 [Sheffield: Sheffield Academic Press, 1991], pp. 11-25 and appendixes 25-32) notes that more recent scholarship has tended to dismiss it as too late (p. 8). David Winton ("The Iranian Component in the Bible, Apocrypha, and Qumran: A Review of the Evidence," *HR* 5 [1965]: 183-216) evaluates the evidence and argues that there was Iranian penetration into Qumran (pp. 186-87). See further M. Dandamayev, "The Diaspora: A. Babylonia in the Persian Age," in *The Cambridge History of Judaism*, vol. 1: *Introduction: The Persian Period*, ed. W. D. Davies and Louis Finkelstein (Cambridge: Cambridge University Press, 1984), pp. 326-42, esp. pp. 337-38.

[19]According to Herodotus, Berossus, a Babylonian priest, transmitted this lore to the Greeks. Burkitt believed that the closest parallel to *1 Enoch* 72—82 was the Greek philosopher Posidonius (b. ca. 135 B.C. and d. 51 B.C.): "Both alike are interested in the Universe as a whole. . . . He was interested in all natural phenomena, but, as with Enoch, his special interest was in the heavens, the heavens above us, in which the Sun and Moon have their course. And below the Moon, in the sublunary sphere, to Posidonius as to Enoch, the air was full of demons, beings whose substance was lighter than flesh and blood, but yet too gross to ascend into the empyrean" (*Jewish and Christian Apocalypses*, p. 31). However, Burkitt recognized that there was a complete difference between the two in basic worldview (see pp. 31-32).

this Babylonian material of the Seleucid age, two types of texts were extant: procedure texts and the ephemerides. The latter consisted of quite accurate tables of celestial phenomena, including lunar eclipses. By contrast, the astronomy of AB is rather archaic and unsophisticated.[20]

The Jews did not adopt Babylonian astronomy and astrology lock, stock and barrel; in fact, Isaiah 47:13 ridicules the futility of astrology for prediction. Rather, Jews, confronted by a culture that emphasized the movements of the heavenly bodies, found that they could incorporate this interest into their received traditions without undermining the sovereignty of Yahweh. From a monotheistic framework, AB provides an explanation for the mechanical regularity of the created order. In short, we have an enrichment of the Hebrew traditions, prompted by advances in astronomical knowledge during the Hellenistic age.[21]

1 Enoch 1—36, The Book of the Watchers

We turn now to *1 Enoch* 1—36, the Book of the Watchers (hereafter BW). While not being particularly scintillating reading either, it does provide a story line of some interest and grapples with a theological problem of perennial concern, the problem of evil.

Outline of contents. BW, as we now have it, falls into fairly recognizable

---

[20]"By the standards of contemporary Hellenistic astronomy, that of Enoch is archaic" (Stone, "Apocalyptic Literature," p. 404 n. 113).

[21]Zoroastrianism, the religion of ancient Persia, has roots antedating those of postexilic Israel, in fact, nearly contemporaneous with Moses (ca. 1500 B.C.). There was a form of Zoroastrianism extant during the Persian Empire, the time when large numbers of Jews resided in this huge kingdom. Zoroaster himself should probably be dated to the era 569-492 B.C. Note that this is shortly after the destruction of the First Temple and the ministries of Ezra and Nehemiah in Jerusalem. Some scholars, however, date Zoroaster as early as 1000 or even 1400 B.C. At any rate, scholars have detected parallels between Zoroastrian thought and the Hebrew Bible.

We can start with a fairly certain parallel, discussed earlier with reference to the book of Tobit. The demon Asmodeus is certainly to be connected to Aeshma. The problem with the cosmological texts of Zoroastrianism, our special interest with regard to *1 Enoch* 72—82, is the fact that we cannot be sure they date as early as the end of the third and the second century B.C., the time of AB. We may not, however, rule out the influence of this religious thought on the thinking of Jews during the Persian era.

Of course, we have another possible source to consider. The Hellenistic age continued an interest in the cosmic order, indeed, according to some historians of human thought, inaugurated one of the most important revolutions in the history of humankind. The pre-Socratics, Plato and Aristotle introduced a rational approach to explain the universe. The thought of Aristotle, however, moves in quite a different direction from that of *1 Enoch*. Furthermore, we learn that Berossus, a Babylonian priest, introduced astrology to the Greeks when he established a school on the island of Cos. Thus, despite the claim by Greek historians that they invented the discipline, it would appear that they were really dependent upon the Babylonians.

units. We may lay them out as follows:

I. An introduction in the form of a testamentary blessing; summarizes the occasion and essential message of the visionary experience of Enoch (1)

II. A call to contemplate the moral order of creation as opposed to the lack of order among humanity; basically an admonition and warning (2—5)

III. A retelling and expansion of Genesis 6, the angelic rebellion and subversion of humankind (6—8)

IV. Divine response to moral corruption and Enoch's revelation of divine punishment for the Watchers (9—11)

V. Enoch's rapture into the heavenlies and reading of the irreversible divine sentence against the angelic rebels (12—16)

VI. Enoch's recounting of his heavenly journeys and revelations of reward and retribution (17—36)[22]

BW is much absorbed in the problem of the origin of evil. Evidently at least two different accounts for the origin of evil have been combined in these chapters, one of which traces it back to the angel Semyaza and the other to the angel Azazel. For our purposes, however, it is sufficient to note that in either case evil is traced back to an angelic rebellion. This is a major burden of BW. For our author, evil is of such magnitude that it cannot be attributed to a misuse of human freedom alone—there must be a more cosmic and sinister explanation. As we will see in our discussion of apocalyptic literature, this is a keynote of the apocalyptic movement. Evil is bigger than humanity and has consequences beyond one's comprehension. Evil has invaded the earth from the heavenly realms.

A second feature dominates the section: the revelation of heavenly secrets and decrees to the righteous scribe Enoch. We have an account of an ascent to the very throne of God as well as descriptions of the various compartments for the punishment of the wicked and the reward of the righteous. The viewpoint of our document is very much otherworldly. The purpose for which these descriptions are designed becomes clear: to comfort and fortify the righteous. Eternal retribution is certain for the wicked, as is eternal felicity for the righteous. BW displays indications that it was intended to "buck up" a community feeling great pressure from external forces. It has characteristics of a group undergoing persecution for their faith or at least experiencing great hardships.

The attribution of these revelations to Enoch makes sense in terms of the information Genesis offers about Enoch. There we learn of his righteous behavior and his apparent rapture into the presence of God (Gen 5:21-24).

---

[22]Several other ways of analyzing the section may be compared. See, e.g., Nickelsburg, *Jewish Literature*, p. 48.

Thus our author has adroitly attributed his revelatory information to the first person raptured to heaven. Not only so, but the form of the BW deliberately evokes the prophetic tradition of the divine commissioning (cf. Num 23:4; Is 6:1-13; Ezek 1:1-28). In short, this establishes the authority of the revelations—the author presents his work as being inspired.

Can we locate the *Sitz im Leben* (life setting) of this work? Nickelsburg's suggestion that the wars of the Diadochi (successors to Alexander the Great) provide the setting makes good sense of the writing.[23] During this period repeated invasions and depredations wracked Palestine. To pious Jews living then it must have seemed like the preflood generation all over again. "If the foundations are destroyed, what can the righteous do" (Ps 11:3)? The answer is that the righteous must "hunker down"[24] and endure to the end. The BW helps the righteous do precisely that by establishing a typology between God's judgment in the days of Noah and his certain intervention and judgment of the wicked in the future.

Background and influences. We have already indicated that our author has a snippet of information about Enoch from the Hebrew Bible. Was this the only source for his work? Probably not, though it must be confessed that this type of investigation is always tentative at best.

Several features mentioned in BW have a long prehistory in the ancient Near East. The figure of Enoch in the Hebrew Bible itself shows some similarities to figures mentioned in Sumerian and Babylonian mythology. James VanderKam draws attention to parallels between Enoch in our literature and Enmeduranki of the Sumerian King List. Enmeduranki, the seventh in the list (cf. Gen 5:21-24 and the note on Gen 5:24 in *The New Oxford Annotated Bible*), was credited with being the founder of a guild of diviners and received heavenly revelations. Even more significant, he was taken up into the divine assembly and shown the tablets of the gods (cf. *1 En.* 81).[25] Furthermore, one may note that in the Gilgamesh Epic, Utnapishtim, the survivor of the great flood, was taken to live with the gods. John Collins makes this connection:

All of this suggests that the figure of Enoch as revealer of heavenly mysteries

---

[23]Ibid., p. 52. VanderKam suggests that "it may be another third century text" (James C. VanderKam, *An Introduction to Early Judaism* [Grand Rapids, Mich.: Eerdmans, 2001], p. 91).

[24]This was President Lyndon Johnson's expression for his personal response during the late 1960s, when protests against his Vietnam War policies began to rise to a fever pitch.

[25]For the Sumerian King List, see *ANET,* p. 265. For other details, see James VanderKam, *Enoch and the Growth of an Apocalyptic Tradition,* CBQMS 16 (Washington, D.C.: Catholic Biblical Association, 1984). D. S. Russell (*The Old Testament Pseudepigrapha: Patriarchs and Prophets in Early Judaism* [London: SCM Press, 1987], pp. 37-43) accepts VanderKam's thesis, as does Collins ("Genre, Ideology and Social Movements," p. 21).

was developed as a Jewish counterpart to Babylonian mythological heroes. The most natural setting for such a development, at least in its earliest stages, was in the Exile or subsequent eastern Diaspora.[26]

We should not, however, overlook the Greek parallels to BW. As Nickelsburg points out, Enoch's journeys to the place of the dead and their punishment have closer contacts with Greek models than with Babylonian.[27] Particularly telling in this regard is Nickelsburg's observation that the fiery river (*1 En.* 17:5) is unknown in extant Babylonian literature but is found in the *Odyssey* under the name *Pyriphlegethon*.[28] Furthermore, the description of the places Enoch visited seems indebted to popular Greek geography.[29]

We conclude that BW is a creative synthesis drawing upon a number of traditions available to our author. The Hellenistic age was a time of remarkable intellectual ferment, a period, many would say, that witnessed the greatest intellectual advances in human history.[30] In this crucial era, the author of BW appeals to a particular faith community, a community that maintains the traditions of the Hebrew Bible. He does so, however, whether consciously or unconsciously, in terms that reflect his own awareness of the larger Hellenistic world. The predominant attitude of this work, however, is *against* the culture of the day. Hope resides not in this world but in the heavenly world, a world that is both above and future. We will return to this point in the next chapter.

Significance for the New Testament

General significance. The importance of the Enoch literature for the interpretation of the NT can scarcely be overemphasized. R. H. Charles, early twentieth-century scholar of Second Temple period literature, put it this way:

> Nearly all the writers of the New Testament were familiar with it, and were more or less influenced by it in thought and diction. . . . [It] is for the history of theological development the most important pseudepigraph of the first two centuries B.C. . . . In fact the history of the development of the higher theology during the two centuries before the Christian era could not be written without the Book of Enoch.[31]

---

[26]"Genre, Ideology and Social Movements," p. 26.
[27]See, e.g., *Od.* 11.
[28]Ibid., 10.513.
[29]Nickelsburg, *Jewish Literature*, p. 52 and p. 66 n. 27.
[30]See, e.g., W. T. Jones, *A History of Western Philosophy* (New York: Harcourt, Brace & World, 1952), 1:253-54.
[31]*APOT* 1:163.

At the beginning of the twenty-first century, Charles's assessment still stands. Why? In the first place, the worldview of AB and BW is clearly that of the NT. This common ground takes its starting point in the doctrines of God and creation. All things have their origin in the will of the one true and living God. One may object that we have nothing more than that already taught in the Hebrew Bible. To be sure, the OT is foundational for both the Enoch literature and the NT. But AB and BW, along with the NT, transcend the OT perspective. There is a spatial dualism between the heavenly and earthly spheres that is only adumbrated in the OT.[32]

Second, as we already saw in Tobit, angelology and demonology are much more developed in comparison with the OT.[33] In fact, the heavens are alive with spiritual beings in AB and BW. The heavenly bodies are orchestrated by angelic beings who operate according to the rules and regulations established by the Creator. The evil in the cosmos is traced to an angelic revolt. A satanic ringleader, with his host of malevolent, demonic beings, dominates the present world. The same perspective appears in the NT, as discussed earlier in chapter two. Paul's letters allude to this aspect of reality; namely, the heavenlies constitute a sphere of divine warfare (cf. 1 Cor 2:8 [?]; 4:9; 6:3; 11:10; 13:1; 15:24; 2 Cor 11:14; Gal 1:8; 3:19; 4:3 [?], 14; Eph 1:21; 6:12; Col 1:16; 2:10, 15, 18; 2 Thess 1:7; 1 Tim 3:16; 5:21). In this he is simply following the common Jewish viewpoint shared by Jesus and his apostles (cf. Mt 4:1-11; 16:23; Mk 1:12-13; Lk 4:1-13; Jas 4:7; 1 Pet 5:8).

According to Matthew and Luke, the birth of John the Baptist and Jesus was attended by angelic visitations and announcements; indeed, Luke informs us that Gabriel was the heavenly informant. Furthermore, angels play a role throughout the Gospel narratives and are assumed by Jesus to be vital participants in salvation history (Lk 1:19; cf. 1:26; 2:9, 13; 12:9; 15:10; 16:22; 20:36; 22:43; Mt 1:20; 2:13, 19; 4:11; 13:39-49; 16:27; 18:10; 22:30; 24:31, 36; 25:31, 41; 26:53; 28:1, 5). In this regard, Jesus' apparent acceptance of the notion that there are guardian angels is especially significant (Mt 18:10). Luke's second volume, the book of Acts, features angelic interventions in several well-known episodes (Acts 5:19; 8:26; 10:3-22; 12:7-11, 15, 23; 27:23). Par-

---

[32]For example, in the narrative of the Sinai theophany (Ex 19—40), Moses is instructed to make the tabernacle and its furnishings "in accordance with all that I show you concerning the pattern of the tabernacle and of all its furniture" (Ex 25:9). However, when one compares what the author of Hebrews does with this text in terms of a vertical dualism, we must acknowledge a considerable advance in thought (cf. Heb 8—10). See further George W. E. Nickelsburg, "The Apocalyptic Construction of Reality in 1 Enoch," in *Mysteries and Revelations*, pp. 54-60.

[33]Here one's view of the date of the final composition of Daniel enters the picture. Still, even allowing Daniel to have been written in the sixth century B.C., one can detect considerable development in the angelology and demonology of Enoch vis-à-vis Daniel.

ticularly striking is the narrative of Peter's release from prison in Acts 12:1-17, in which the fearful believers thought that Peter's angel was standing outside the door and knocking (Acts 12:15)![34]

Another piece of common ground between the worldview of the Enoch literature and the NT resides in the doctrine of the two ages. The fundamental dualism of Second Temple period Judaism and the NT is a horizontal or temporal dualism. God's plan for the cosmos unfolds in two ages. "This age" stretches from creation to the mighty intervention of God and his holy angels at the great Day of the Lord. This introduces a completely new era, "the age to come." The fall (or angelic rebellion, as in BW) is the reason for the necessity of a new age. Resurrection or the conferring of immortality must overcome death, one of the consequences of the introduction of sin.[35] The age to come is a return to paradise, an age of unending glory on a renewed earth; it is, in short, a new creation. Note in *1 Enoch* 72:1 that the regulations for the heavenly luminaries last "until the new creation shall be made which will last forever." In BW the age to come is referred to several times (cf. *1 En.* 1:3-9; 5:6-9; 10:7; 10:16—11:2; 25:3-7).

The NT accepts this basic dualism with one very important qualification: the age to come has already begun for believers in Jesus the Messiah. Already the Holy Spirit has been poured out on all believers, both men and women (Acts 2:14-39); already the powers of the age to come are exerting their force in the lives of believers (cf. Heb 1:1; 6:5); already the age of resurrection has begun with the resurrection of Jesus (cf. 1 Cor 15:20-28). Of course, the NT maintains a reservation here. The powers of the age to come are already at work, but by no means has the age to come arrived in all its fullness. That awaits the parousia (Greek word meaning "presence, coming or arrival") of Jesus Christ at the Day of the Lord (see esp. Paul's ironic rebuke of Corinthian "over-realized eschatology" in 1 Cor 4:8; cf. Rom 13:11-14; 1 Cor 15:20-28; Phil 1:10; 3:20-21; Col 3:4; 1 Thess 4:13-17; 2 Thess 1:9-10; 2:1-12; 2 Tim 4:1; Heb 12:25-29; Jas 4:7-9; 1 Pet 1:5; 4:5-7; 5:4; 2 Pet 3:3-13; 1 Jn 2:18; 3:2-3; Jude 21, 24; and throughout Revela-

---

[34]The suggestion here of Parsi influence is interesting but not fully convincing. See Moulton, *Early Zoroastrianism,* pp. 324-25. More recently Winton has argued for a "strong probability for an Iranian penetration into Qumran" ("The Iranian Component in the Bible," 183-216). But Winton also significantly qualifies this penetration: "The Iranian impact, however, seems to have been along the periphery of Judaism only. The Qumran sect was certainly not a part of the mainstream (the same may be said of the apocryphal literature), and the Persian elements in the rabbinic literature are essentially confined to demonology and eschatology" (p. 210).

[35]As we will discover, our sources during the Second Temple period do not agree on the final state of the righteous. Do they possess resurrected bodies, and if so, are they essentially the same or reconstituted? Or do they exist as spirits?

tion).[36] The upshot is that for the NT we have a "now but not yet" tension between this age and the age to come. There is a sort of overlap between the ages.[37] This understanding is crucial for reading the NT.

There is a noticeable difference, however, between the emphasis of AB and BW and that of the NT. The NT generally does not take an interest in the workings of the cosmos. Nowhere do we have sustained reflection upon the created order. Paul may refer to creation as under a curse, passing away or destined to be renewed (Rom 8:19-22), but clearly, for Paul the really important thing is the cross of Christ (cf. 1 Cor 2:1-2). Although he is quite aware that Christ is the creator of the cosmos (cf. Col 1:15-16), what really counts is a new creation in Christ (cf. 2 Cor 5:17; Gal 6:15).[38]

The origin of sin. On the question of the origin of sin, we have a fascinating comparison between BW and the NT. Whereas BW mutes the importance of individual responsibility, the NT emphasizes human culpability without denying that there is a demonic dimension. Let us consider several NT passages on this point.

Jesus took seriously the Enochian conviction that demons infest the earthly regions (cf. *1 En.* 15:8-12 with Mt 12:43-45; Lk 11:24-26). In fact, Jesus explicitly drew attention to his exorcisms as signs of his messianic mission (Mt 12:27-28; Lk 11:19-20). In the Synoptic Gospels one finds repeated mention of Jesus casting out demons by his own authority, and several stories describe graphically the harm and malignancy of demonic possession and influence. In the Matthean account of the Gerasene demoniac (Mt 8:28-34), the demons plead with Jesus not to be tormented "before the time." Luke's Gospel adds this passage: "They begged him not to order them to go back into the abyss" (Lk 8:31), recalling Enoch's description of this fearful prison house for demons (*1 En.* 10:6; 18:11-16: 21:7-10).

In John's Gospel, the metaphor of darkness has broad implications for a doctrine of demonology (cf., e.g., Jn 1:5). Jesus styles Satan as the "ruler of this world" (Jn 14:30). In dispute with the religious leaders, Jesus describes the devil as "a murderer from the beginning" and one who "does not stand in the truth, because there is no truth in him. When he lies, he speaks

---

[36]See further L. J. Kreitzer, "Eschatology," *DPL*, pp. 256-57.

[37]For a helpful discussion of this concept of "now but not yet," see C. Marvin Pate, *The End of the Age Has Come: The Theology of Paul* (Grand Rapids, Mich.: Zondervan, 1995), pp. 22-70. See also the seminal work of George E. Ladd, *A Theology of the New Testament*, rev. ed., ed. Donald Hagner (Grand Rapids, Mich.: Eerdmans, 1993). Also helpful is the treatment by Scott, *Customs and Controversies*, pp. 269-72, 283-95.

[38]We may say generally that for Paul soteriology is of utmost importance as compared to cosmology. This is not to say, however, that Paul has no cosmic understandings of the work of Christ. See further Larry R. Helyer, "Cosmic Christology and Col 1:15-20," *JETS* 37 (1994): 235-46.

according to this own nature, for he is a liar and the father of lies" (Jn 8:44). This seems to presuppose the angelic revolt as elaborated in BW. However, the Gospel traditions do not have a saying of Jesus in which he describes "the original sin." Nor do we have in Jesus' sayings any suggestion that humans are merely pawns in the hands of demons or Satan. Though not as strong as their opponents, human beings are responsible to act morally and resist the influences and machinations of the demonic realm. Jesus stresses the human heart as the source of evil and sin (Mt 5:28; 12:34-35; 13:15; 15:18-19; Lk 6:45). In this regard he indicates that none are without sin (Mt 7:1; Lk 11:13). John's Gospel locates ultimate responsibility for sin in the individual (Jn 3:19-21).

Paul offers a theological reflection upon the origin of human sin and its consequences in Romans. Whereas Romans 1:18-32 highlights human responsibility for sin, Romans 5:12-21 speaks to the question of the origin of sin in humanity (cf. 1 Cor 15:21-22). This highly disputed section—especially concerning the mode of transmission—links Adam's transgression and disobedience to the spread of sin and death in all humanity.[39] Paul does not mention Satan in this context; however, in two other places he does refer to the temptation story in Genesis 3 (2 Cor 11:3; 1 Tim 2:14). Although nowhere in the Pauline corpus does he explicitly refer to the angelic revolt, he is aware of the Jewish story of Satan transforming himself into an angel of light when he tempted Eve (cf. 2 Cor 11:14 and *Adam and Eve* 9:1 [see *AOT,* p. 148]). Consequently, it seems probable that he also knew and accepted the view that the "original sin" was Satan's rebellion, especially since Paul does not call the Adamic transgression "the original sin."

Do other NT writers accept the story of the angelic rebellion? The answer seems clearly to be yes. Peter and Jude directly refer to such an event:

> For if God did not spare the angels when they sinned, but cast them into hell and committed them to chains of deepest darkness to be kept until the judgment. . . . (2 Pet 2:4)
>
> And the angels who did not keep their own position, but left their proper dwelling, he has kept in eternal chains in deepest darkness for the judgment of the great Day. (Jude 6)

These two passages are unmistakably similar to BW. Possibly 1 Peter 3:19-20 and 4:6 allude to the same event, but their interpretation is uncertain. Attempts to explain the 2 Peter and Jude passages as being interpretations of Genesis 6, Isaiah 14 and Ezekiel 28 without recourse to *1 Enoch* are not convincing. There are simply too many points of contact here to assume inde-

---

[39]See L. J. Kreitzer, "Adam and Christ," *DPL,* pp. 12-13.

pendent exegesis.[40] Rather, what we have is an example of how the NT took up and incorporated Jewish traditions that we first encounter in pseudepigraphic writings.[41]

Specific points of comparison. Table 3.1 concludes this section with a listing of similarities between *1 Enoch* 1—36, 72—82 and the NT. Once again we emphasize that we are not here arguing for literary dependence; rather, these parallels simply illustrate the Jewish background of the NT writings.

Table 3.1. Parallels between *1 Enoch* and the New Testament

1 Enoch	NT
"And I heard everything from them, and I understood what I saw, but not for this generation, but for a distant generation which will come" (1:2).	"It was revealed to them that they were serving not themselves but you, in regard to the things that have now been announced to you" (1 Pet 1:12).
"And behold! He comes with ten thousand holy ones to execute judgement upon them and to destroy the impious, and to contend with all flesh concerning everything which the sinners and the impious have done and wrought against him" (1:9).	"It was also about these that Enoch, in the seventh generation from Adam, prophesied saying, 'See, the Lord is coming with ten thousands of his holy ones, to execute judgment on all, and to convict everyone of all the deeds of ungodliness that they have committed in such an ungodly way, and of all the harsh things that ungodly sinners have spoken against him'" (Jude 14-15); this appears to be a direct quote.
"The King, Lord of Lords, God of Gods, King of Kings!" (9:4).	"For he is Lord of lords and King of kings" (Rev 17:14; cf. 15:3; 19:16; 1 Tim 6:15).
"And everything is uncovered and open before you, and you see everything, and there is nothing which can be hidden from you" (9:5).	"And before him no creature is hidden, but all are naked and laid bare to the eyes of the one to whom we must render an account" (Heb 4:13).
"They will not again do wrong, and they will not be judged all the days of their life" (5:9).	"But with me it is a very small thing that I should be judged by you or by any human court. I do not even judge myself. I am not aware of anything against myself, but I am not thereby acquitted. It is the Lord who judges me. Therefore do not pronounce judgment before the time" (1 Cor 4:3-5).

---

[40]See further J. D. Charles, "Noncanonical Writings, Citations in the General Epistles," *DLNTD*, pp. 817-19.

[41]See Craig S. Keener, *The IVP Bible Background Commentary: New Testament* (Downers Grove, Ill.: InterVarsity Press, 1993), pp. 728, 754.

Table 3.1.—*Continued*

1 Enoch	NT
"For the chosen there will be light and joy and peace, and they will inherit the earth" (5:7).	"Blessed are the meek, for they will inherit the earth" (Mt 5:5).
"There was a righteous man whose eyes were opened by the Lord. . . . And I heard everything from them and I understood" (1:2).	Note that the apostle Paul alternates between third-person and first-person narration of his visionary experience (2 Cor 12:1-13).
"And you were spiritual, holy, living an eternal life, but you became unclean upon the women, and begat children through the blood of flesh" (15:4).	"Who were born, not of blood or of the will of the flesh or of the will of man, but of God" (Jn 1:13). This is an interesting contrast whereby believers in Christ move from fleshly to spiritual. Both authors, however, share a common view of human procreation.
"And I saw the spirits of the sons of men who were dead, and their voice reached heaven and complained" (22:5).	"I saw under the altar the souls of those who had been slaughtered. . . . They cried out with a loud voice, 'Sovereign Lord, holy and true, how long will it be before you judge and avenge our blood. . . ?' " (Rev 6:9-10).
"And here their souls will be separated for this great torment, until the great day of judgement and punishment and torment for those who curse forever" (22:11).	"In Hades, where he was being tormented, he looked up and saw Abraham. . . . 'Besides all this, between you and us a great chasm has been fixed, so that those who might want to pass from here to you cannot do so, and no one can cross from there to us' " (Lk 16:23, 26).
"Bind Azazel by his hands and his feet, and throw him into the darkness. . . . And cover him with darkness . . . that he may not see light, and that on the great day of judgement he may be hurled into the fire" (10:4-6; cf. 10:10-15).	"He has kept in eternal chains in deepest darkness for the judgment of the great Day" (Jude 6). "[God] committed them to chains of deepest darkness to be kept until the judgment" (2 Pet 2:4). "Then I saw an angel coming down from heaven, holding in his hand the key to the bottomless pit and a great chain. He seized the dragon . . . and bound him . . . and threw him into the pit. . . . And the devil . . . was thrown into the lake of fire and sulfur" (Rev 20:1-3, 10).
"Go, inform the Watchers of heaven who have left the high heaven and the holy eternal place, and have corrupted themselves with the women" (12:4).	"And the angels who did not keep their own position, but left their proper dwelling . . ." (Jude 6). "For if God did not spare the angels when they sinned . . ." (2 Pet 2:4).

Ecclesiasticus, or the Wisdom of Jesus Son of Sirach
(Wisdom of Ben Sira)

Introduction

Our second piece of literature illustrating how Jews responded to the incursion of Hellenism is a fine example of the continuation of the Hebrew wisdom tradition. Readers familiar with the OT books of Proverbs or Ecclesiastes will feel more at home reading Sirach than *1 Enoch*. Here we have the wise sayings of a sage often couched in pithy, memorable language.

There is much in Sirach that is just good common sense, and there is much that is spiritually uplifting. Our author has a good grasp of the Hebrew Scriptures and represents a conservative, pious Judaism that seeks to come to grips intellectually with the Hellenistic world.

Bruce Metzger and Roland Murphy provide a brief introduction to Sirach in *The New Oxford Annotated Bible*. This introduction discusses the transmission of the text, a sketch of the author and his translator grandson and the leading characteristics of the work itself. We will expand just a bit on the second and third items.

The Author

Sirach forms an exception to all the other works in the Apocrypha and Pseudepigrapha in that it is not anonymous or pseudonymous. In Sirach 50:27 we read: "Instruction in understanding and knowledge I have written in this book, Jesus son of Eleazar son of Sirach of Jerusalem." But just who was this Jesus Ben Sira? This is the Hebrew form of "Jesus Son of Sirach," and we will use the shortened form Ben Sira to refer to the author. No other sources refer to him as an individual, so we are limited to his work itself for any clues.

Clearly Ben Sira was a Jerusalemite and probably the headmaster of a school or academy (cf. Sir 51:23). From his favorable reference to the profession of scribe (cf. Sir 10:5; 38:24—39:11), we may surmise that this was his chosen occupation, which he parlayed by setting up a school for young men. Furthermore, his obvious love for the priestly rituals of the temple, his glowing description of Simon the high priest and his failure to mention the great national hero Ezra reflect tendencies that would later crystallize into the party of the Sadducees. We should not, however, impute all the positions of this later development to Ben Sira.[42] We also gather that Ben Sira had traveled widely, since he makes reference to his experiences, some of them rather unsavory (cf. Sir 29:21-28; 39:4). He presents himself in his *magnum opus* as a man of extensive worldly experience but also as a pious and committed Jew.

---

[42]See note 67 below.

Date of Sirach

Ben Sira's grandson (and translator) provides some information that helps place the work in its historical setting. According to the grandson (who never gives his name), "I came to Egypt in the thirty-eighth year of the reign of Euergetes" (prologue). The Euergetes referred to is taken by most scholars as Ptolemy VIII, who ruled from 170 to 117 B.C.[43] This would mean that in 132 B.C. the grandson came to Egypt and then proceeded to translate his grandfather's work. From this we may infer that Ben Sira himself was born sometime in the era between 250 and 210 B.C. The date 180 B.C. seems close to the time of original publication. At any rate, it must have been before the tumultuous times of the Maccabean revolt (167 B.C.), since there is no indication whatsoever of such times reflected in the book, nor is there any hint of the strife that befell the priestly family of Simon (when Antiochus IV Epiphanes deposed Onias III and replaced him by a Benjaminite, Menelaus).[44]

Literary Genre and Structure

Sirach is most akin to the book of Proverbs. As a conscious continuation of the Hebrew wisdom traditions, this work features several characteristic types of wisdom utterance. Of basic importance to the composition is the *māšāl*, that is, a proverb or proverblike saying. In addition, one finds hymns of praise, prayers of petition, autobiographical narratives, lists *(onomastika)* and didactic narratives. Nickelsburg calls attention to the fact that Ben Sira is fond of linking proverbs by means of identical formulas or by word association or catchword.[45] As an example, note the following verses (italics added):

> For the Lord *honors* a father (3:2)
> Those who *honor* their father (3:3)
> And those who *respect* their mother (3:4)
> Those who *honor* their father (3:5)
> Those who *respect* their father (3:6)
> *Honor* your father (3:8)

Ben Sira arranges his material for the most part in bicola, that is, two balanced, matching lines of poetry, or couplets, as may be seen as one begins reading Sirach 1. But he shows considerable variation in the way these couplets are fashioned, and sometimes he has a tricolon.[46] We do notice, in con-

---

[43]See R. C. Van Leeuwen, "Sirach," *ISBE* 4:529.

[44]For further discussion of this question, see Robert H. Pfeiffer, *History of New Testament Times with an Introduction to the Apocrypha* (New York: Harper, 1949), pp. 364-67.

[45]*Jewish Literature*, p. 57.

[46]For a more in-depth study of Ben Sira's poetic technique, see P. W. Skehan and A. A. Di Lella, *The Wisdom of Ben Sira*, AB 39 (New York: Doubleday, 1987), pp. 63-74.

trast to canonical Proverbs, that Ben Sira's observations form more connected wholes. It is almost like a series of short essays on various topics dealing with behavior and ethics. The wide variety of material leads John Snaith to describe the contents as "the life-time scrap-book of a lecturer or teacher."[47] The present writer can certainly identify with that apt characterization! According to Nickelsburg, the end result "is a more polished literary product than is found in many analogous collections in Proverbs."[48]

Is there an overall structure to these fifty-one chapters?[49] Like Proverbs, Sirach seems to have no apparent logical structure. However, there is a discernible arrangement into two primary sections.[50] Note that each of the two "books" is introduced by a poem in praise of wisdom:

  1:1—23:28 (1:1-20 in praise of wisdom)
  24:1—51:30 (24:1-34 in praise of wisdom)

It is interesting that just as Proverbs concludes with an alphabetic acrostic placed in an appendix, so does Sirach (Sir 51:13-30). Clearly Proverbs, more than any other canonical book, has shaped the work of Ben Sira.

Purpose

What was Ben Sira trying to accomplish in this the lengthiest work of Second Temple Judaism? What motivated him to put in writing what appears to be the essence of his lectures to his students in Jerusalem? What audience did he intend to reach? Locating Ben Sira's teaching career at the end of the third and the beginning of the second century B.C., in Jerusalem, we can reconstruct to some degree the life setting of this masterpiece:

> It was a Hellenistic world—a world dominated by Greek ideas and ideals, customs and values, art and excellence; a world in which the Jews of Palestine were not politically free but subject to Egyptian or Syrian kings who fought many wars against each other to gain or maintain control of that strategically significant land.[51]

If we want to know how Ben Sira felt about all this, no more eloquent response may be read in his work than the following:

---

[47] *Ecclesiasticus, Or the Wisdom of Jesus Son of Sirach,* CBC (Cambridge: Cambridge University Press, 1974), p. 3.

[48] *Jewish Literature,* p. 57.

[49] For discussion of whether Ben Sira does in fact have an organizational plan, see Pfeiffer, *History of New Testament Times,* pp. 353-54; M. Gilbert, "Wisdom Literature," in *Jewish Writings of the Second Temple Period,* pp. 292-93.

[50] Some scholars suggest that Ben Sira actually published the two parts as separate works but then later joined them together in their present shape (see Pfeiffer, *History of New Testament Times,* p. 353).

[51] Skehan and Di Lella, *Wisdom of Ben Sira,* p. 12.

Have mercy upon us, O God of all, and put all the nations in fear of you. Lift up your hand against foreign nations and let them see your might. As you have used us to show your holiness to them, so use them to show your glory to us. Then they will know, as we have known, that there is no God but you, O Lord. Give new signs, and work other wonders; make your hand and right arm glorious. Rouse your anger and pour out your wrath; destroy the adversary and wipe out the enemy. Hasten the day, and remember the appointed time, and let people recount your mighty deeds. Let survivors be consumed in the fiery wrath, and may those who harm your people meet destruction. Crush the heads of hostile rulers who say, "There is no one but ourselves." Gather all the tribes of Jacob, and give them their inheritance, as at the beginning. Have mercy, O Lord, on the people called by your name, on Israel, whom you have named your firstborn. Have pity on the city of your sanctuary, Jerusalem, the place of your dwelling. Fill Zion with your majesty, and your temple with your glory. Bear witness to those whom you created in the beginning, and fulfill the prophecies spoken in your name. Reward those who wait for you and let your prophets be found trustworthy. Hear, O Lord, the prayer of your servants, according to your goodwill toward your people, and all who are on the earth will know that you are the Lord, the God of the ages. (Sir 36:1-22)

This passage provides the key for unlocking the motivation of Ben Sira. Hellenism, with all that it entailed, presented a grave threat to the well-being of the ancestral faith. Ben Sira is deeply concerned to preserve the Hebrew traditions based upon the sacred Scriptures of Israel. But our author is not a narrow fundamentalist. He knows that the answer is not to retreat into a ghetto of intellectual isolation, pretending that Hellenism does not exist. On the contrary, Ben Sira is able to appreciate that not all in Hellenism is bad. He himself has clearly absorbed some aspects of Hellenism. He is not simply a Hebrew like his ancestors who wrote Proverbs but a hellenized Jew who is intensely aware that the Hebrew traditions are at risk.[52] In short, he has been able to appropriate that which is useful and helpful, but not in contradiction to the Scriptures. He is fearful, however, that Hellenism may seduce young Jewish men by its seeming sophistication and trappings of grandeur.[53] To this end he points the way: Torah, not Hellenism, is the fountain of all wisdom; Torah is the guiding star that leads to life.

Noteworthy Topics
Worldly wisdom. The bulk of Sirach deals with the very practical matter of liv-

---

[52]For a useful survey of scholarly opinion as to the degree of indebtedness to Hellenism there is in Ben Sira, see Burton L. Mack and Roland E. Murphy, "Wisdom Literature," in *Early Judaism and Its Modern Interpreters,* ed. Robert A. Kraft and George W. E. Nickelsburg (Philadelphia: Fortress; Atlanta: Scholars Press, 1986), pp. 371-77.

[53]See further Skehan and Di Lella, *Wisdom of Ben Sira,* pp. 8-16.

ing successfully, an undertaking that combines a reverence for God and obedience to the Torah with the tested experience of someone such as Ben Sira. "The authority of years and experience is evident enough in all parts of the book."[54] The range of experiences is considerable. Metzger gives a concise overview of the types of sound advice served up by the venerable Ben Sira:

> Whether it is upon the subject of behavior at table, or a father's treatment of a headstrong daughter, or the need of keeping guard over one's tongue, or recommendations concerning the relationship between husband and wife, or the folly of a fool, or the delights of a banquet, or whether the author is dealing with self-control, borrowing, loose women, diet, slander, the miser, the spendthrift, the hypocrite, the parasite, keeping secrets, giving alms, standing surety, mourning for the dead—these and a host of other subjects give us a valuable picture of many aspects of the Judaism of Palestine during the second century BC.[55]

The result is a veritable "handbook of moral behavior or code of ethics that a Jew of the early second century B.C. was expected to observe."[56]

Women. North American and European readers of Ben Sira soon sense that he had a problem with women. As many have pointed out, he lets us know more of his likes and dislikes than any other writer in the Apocrypha. And there can be no mistaking it: he has a deep distrust of females. Let us explore this a bit more.

There is a tension in the thought of Ben Sira with regard to women. On the one hand, he has nothing but praise for a good wife: "Do not dismiss a wise and good wife, for her charm is worth more than gold" (Sir 7:19). "I take pleasure in three things, and they are beautiful in the sight of God and of mortals: . . . a wife and a husband who live in harmony" (Sir 25:1). "Happy is the husband of a good wife; the number of his days will be doubled. A loyal wife brings joy to her husband, and he will complete his years in peace. A good wife is a great blessing; she will be granted among the blessings of the man who fears the Lord" (Sir 26:1-3).

On the other hand, Ben Sira has some very jaundiced opinions of women in general and wives and daughters in particular. Apparently one is very fortunate to get a sensible wife: "Happy the man who lives with a sensible wife" (Sir 25:8). If one does not, says Ben Sira, beware of trusting her (Sir 7:26). If a wife interferes with money, lock everything up (Sir 42:6). Never deed a wife property before you die nor give her what we would call today power of attorney (Sir 33:20). If a wife will not obey, get rid of her (Sir 25:26). Women in general

---

[54]Charles Cutler Torrey, *The Apocryphal Literature: A Brief Introduction* (Hamden, Conn.: Archon, 1963 [1945]), p. 95.
[55]Metzger, *Introduction to the Apocrypha*, p. 81.
[56]Skehan and Di Lella, *Wisdom of Ben Sira*, p. 4.

present a grave temptation, according to Ben Sira, and a man is well-advised not even to look at other women and certainly not to dine with another man's wife (Sir 9:1-9). With regard to harlots, Ben Sira continues the wisdom tradition's constant warning about succumbing to their wiles. As Kenneth Bailey observes, prostitutes are "mud puddles to be avoided."[57] The perspective of Ben Sira, in keeping with his culture, assumes that the fault lies in the very nature of women. The image of a woman as a seductress permeates Sirach.

Daughters are a constant source of anxiety for fathers. While a daughter is at home and unmarried, the danger of becoming pregnant before marriage is a recurring specter; yet the danger of remaining unmarried and dependent is even more worrisome! But alas, even after marriage a father has no real respite, says Ben Sira. She may act unfaithfully and bring shame on the family, or, equally shameful and disappointing, she may remain childless. Thus the birth of a daughter is considered a liability in that she constantly threatens to bring shame upon the family, something dreaded by that culture.[58] As Kenneth Bailey observes, "middle-eastern customs still require one to offer condolences when a girl is born."[59]

Ben Sira's bitterest invective, however, is poured out upon wives who talk, drink, nag and boss too much, thus making life miserable for husbands—especially scholars! One is inclined to think that Ben Sira's marriage was unhappy and that he considered most marriages to be like his own.

How shall we evaluate his advice to young men? It is important first of all to place him in his time and culture. Ben Sira lived in a time when women in general were not held as equals. In fact, a line from his book gives us the needed historical perspective: "He who acquires a wife gets his best possession, a helper fit for him and a pillar of support" (Sir 36:29). In the period of Ben Sira, as with the Bible as a whole, patriarchy was the social pattern. Wives were considered to be chattel, that is, personal property. They were "purchased" and could be divorced rather easily if one was displeased. While this may seem deplorable to moderns, if we are to enter sympathetically into the world of Ben Sira, we at least need to understand the cultural patterns and attitudes that shaped his thought. Furthermore, as demeaning as some of his statements about women are, the broader Hellenistic culture of that time was even worse.[60]

---

[57]Kenneth E. Bailey, "Women in Ben Sira and in the New Testament," in *For Me to Live*, ed. Robert A. Coughenour (Cleveland: Dillon/Liederbach, 1972), p. 59.

[58]On the importance of honor and shame as core values, see Joseph Plevnik, "Honor/Shame," in *Biblical Social Values and Their Meaning: A Handbook*, ed. John J. Pilch and Bruce Malina (Peabody, Mass.: Hendrickson, 1993), pp. 95-98.

[59]Bailey, "Women in Ben Sira," p. 71 n. 4.

[60]See Skehan and Di Lella, *Wisdom of Ben Sira*, pp. 90-92.

Torah. Sirach demonstrates the development of an idea that we first encounter in canonical Proverbs. In Proverbs we observe the personification of God's wisdom as a virtuous woman who calls out to be heeded. This technique of personification rises to its height in a magnificent section of Proverbs 8. Here Lady Wisdom makes her appeal to all her listeners: "To you, O people, I call, and my cry is to all that live" (Prov 8:4). Especially noteworthy is Proverbs 8:22-36, where Dame Wisdom is likened to a master worker (Prov 8:30), the first of all created beings (Prov 8:22), who takes a leading role in creation. One's well-being and destiny are dependent upon a right relationship to Wisdom (Prov 8:35-36).

We have already indicated that the book of Proverbs is the single most important source for Ben Sira's lectures. Sirach 24 is a case in point, clearly indebted to Proverbs 8. But Sirach 24 goes well beyond Proverbs 8 in one very important regard: Ben Sira explicitly identifies Wisdom with the Torah. "All this is the book of the covenant of the Most High God, the law that Moses commanded us as an inheritance for the congregations of Jacob" (Sir 24:23). This identification becomes well nigh normative for the various Judaisms thereafter. Thus the Torah is a preexistent entity involved in the creation of the world and determinative for the salvation of humankind. As Pfeiffer points out:

> Sirach marks the transition from the Bible to the Talmud, from the authority of inspiration (which he still claims [Sir 24:33], although the rabbis denied it) to the authority of learning. The two phases of this study, wisdom and Law, remained basic in Judaism after Sirach and are called, respectively, *Haggadah,* aiming at "religious and moral instruction and edification" (G. F. Moore, *Judaism,* vol. 1, p. 162), and *Halakah,* formulating juristically the rules of the traditional law and connecting them through ingenious exegesis with the revealed Law (cf. Moore, ibid., p. 161).[61]

The Literary Craft of Ben Sira

We can only touch on a few of the noteworthy features of Ben Sira's masterwork. Any assessment of his work must, however, include words of admiration for his literary gifts. Ben Sira can write eloquently. We pick out a few representative passages.

Sirach 42:15—43:33 is justly famous for its magnificent portrayal of God the great Creator, initiated by the line, "I will now call to mind the works of the Lord" (Sir 42:15). One may readily discern similarities to Job 38—41, and to Proverbs 30:15-16, 18-20, 24-31, as well as many verbal links to passages in Psalms and Ecclesiastes. Note also the interest in seasons and festivals, a con-

---

[61]Pfeiffer, *History of New Testament Times,* pp. 369-70.

cern of the Astronomical Book of *1 Enoch* 72–82. Ben Sira, however, follows a lunar calendar, not the solar one defended so emphatically in *1 Enoch*. Thus he accepts the temple calendar of the Jerusalem priesthood, championed by the later Sadducees, rather than the astronomical calendar of the Enoch traditions and the Qumran community.

The themes of the Lord's omnipotence, omniscience and omnipresence rise like introits from Ben Sira's finely tuned poetry. He tries to do justice to the greatness of God, but the task is overwhelming: "We could say more but could never say enough; let the final word be: 'He is the all' " (Sir 43:27). Ben Sira's exhortation still strikes a responsive chord in the heartstrings of earnest worshipers: "Glorify the Lord and exalt him as much as you can, for he surpasses even that. When you exalt him, summon all your strength, and do not grow weary, for you cannot praise him enough" (Sir 43:30).

There is something interesting about Ben Sira's observation that "All things come in pairs, one opposite the other, and he has made nothing incomplete" (Sir 42:24). While it may remind one of the determinations of time in Ecclesiastes 3, we suggest that it goes well beyond Ecclesiastes 3 and reflects Hellenistic speculation about the cosmos. Its presence in Ben Sira's meditation testifies to the subtle influence of Hellenistic thought upon a devout sage of Israel.

The Torah, wisdom and salvation history. Perhaps the best-known passage from Sirach is the section in praise of famous men (Sir 44–50). Here Ben Sira celebrates the qualities and exploits of the heroes of the faith. The list is fascinating for several reasons. Not least is the observation that the canonical wisdom tradition (Proverbs, Ecclesiastes, Job) conspicuously lacks reference to the Lord's saving acts in Israel's history. Ben Sira makes up for this by integrating salvation history with wisdom, the quintessential expression of which is the Torah.[62] The hymn in praise of the ancestors begins by describing them as "wise in their words of instruction" (Sir 44:4).

We also should note that two individuals are especially singled out in terms of length of description: Aaron and Simon (Simon II son of Onias [ca. 219-196 B.C.]), both high priests. Ben Sira is enamored with the priestly office and ritual. His description of Simon's officiating reads like an eyewitness account and thus affords a valuable window into temple worship in the second century B.C.[63] Feel the obvious delight with which Ben Sira describes Simon's exit from the holy of holies on the Day of Atonement:

> How glorious he was, surrounded by the people, as he came out of the house of the curtain. Like the morning star among the clouds, like the full moon at the

---

[62]See further on this M. Gilbert, "Wisdom Literature," pp. 296-97.
[63]For details, see Skehan and Di Lella, *Wisdom of Ben Sira*, pp. 550-55.

festal season; like the sun shining on the temple of the Most High, like the rainbow gleaming in splendid clouds. (Sir 50:5-7)

Finally, Ben Sira's list of worthies does not hesitate to assign fault or to delete some figures that others might well have included. Solomon's folly ties in with Ben Sira's repeated warnings about the evil influence of women (Sir 47:19). Rehoboam and Jeroboam are castigated for their folly and wickedness (Sir 47:23-25). In fact, only David, Hezekiah and Josiah of the Davidic dynasty are excluded from Ben Sira's censure of "great sinners" (Sir 49:4). How surprising that, whereas Nehemiah's memory is lasting, there is nary a mention of Ezra, the priest-scribe. This omission is hard to account for unless, as Metzger suggests, this reflects Ben Sira's allegiance to the group that later became the Sadducees.[64]

In praise of the physician. Ben Sira offers some sound advice for those who are ailing. First, he says, pray and confess your sins (Sir 38:9-10). Second, offer a sacrifice to demonstrate your contrition (Sir 38:11), then consult a physician (Sir 38:12). This last step should be one not of desperation but of trust in God. Why? Because the Lord has included doctors among his good gifts to humankind, and they too seek his direction as they practice the healing arts. This balanced position contrasts markedly with some modern cultic groups who view seeking professional help as a lack of faith! We might also point out that the apostle Paul saw no contradiction between faith and physicians, since one of his most valued colleagues was "Luke, the beloved physician" (cf. Col 4:14).

Significance for the New Testament

How, then, does Sirach contribute to a better understanding of the NT? There are several dimensions to this question.

Wisdom Christology. In the first place, Ben Sira's treatment of Wisdom and Torah is of great significance for understanding NT Christology, that is, the study of the person and work of Jesus Christ. We are so bold to claim that Paul, John and the author of Hebrews, in setting forth their understanding of Jesus, incorporated and adapted concepts found in the wisdom tradition of Israel, of which Sirach is a prime example.[65] Particularly in formulating Jesus' relationship to the created order, NT writers reflect indebtedness to Ben Sira's thought.

---

[64]Metzger, *Introduction to the Apocrypha*, p. 87. But see note 67 below.

[65]Nickelsburg says: "The Wisdom of Jesus the Son of Sirach is the earliest datable work in our literature that discusses the relationship of Wisdom and Torah in detail and in theory" (*Jewish Literature*, p. 59; see further pp. 59-62; and Skehan and Di Lella, *Wisdom of Ben Sira*, pp. 75-80).

This is a claim requiring validation. For the moment we will simply lay out some ideas in Sirach that are paralleled in some sense by NT christological texts. We postpone a more detailed analysis until after we have read Baruch and Wisdom of Solomon. Here are some relevant affirmations made by Ben Sira concerning Wisdom:

1. Wisdom is a preexistent entity (Sir 1:4; 24:9).
2. Wisdom reflects the very being and character of God (Sir 24:3).
3. Wisdom played a role in creation (Sir 24:3, 6; cf. 1:9).
4. Wisdom became embodied in the people of Israel (Sir 24:7-8, 12).
5. One's destiny is determined by a positive response to and acceptance of Wisdom (Sir 1:13; 4:13; cf. 19:20).[66]

The alert NT reader immediately recognizes that if we make the identification that Wisdom equals Jesus, we have clear parallels (cf., e.g., Jn 1:1-14; Phil 2:5-10; Col 1:15-20; Heb 1:1-3). Our point is simply to show that NT authors had at hand, from their Jewish traditions, categories with which to fashion statements about the person and work of Jesus Christ. Unlike Ben Sira, however, the NT authors affirm that *Jesus,* not Torah, is Wisdom. Wisdom, according to the NT, is incarnated and embodied in a person, not inscribed in a book. Torah is fulfilled in Christ and, in a certain sense, superseded (cf. Mt 5:17). Furthermore, the distinctive Christian doctrine of the cross as the means of reconciliation finds no analogue in either Proverbs or Sirach.

While it might be argued that Paul, Hebrews and John were simply reflecting upon Proverbs 8 without regard to Sirach, it is hard to believe that an honored teacher in Jerusalem whose work was highly regarded by the Essenes, for example, was not also studied by Pharisaic students such as Saul of Tarsus or the eloquent author of Hebrews (Apollos?).[67] Yes, Proverbs 8 is the groundwork of wisdom Christology, but it has been taken further by Ben Sira and brought to a radically new formulation in the NT. It is this identification of Wisdom with Jesus Christ that contributes to the uniqueness of the NT message.[68]

---

[66]Sirach 19:20 is important here because Ben Sira makes explicit the equation that runs through his work, namely, that piety, wisdom and the law are essentially the same. With this identification, we have the broadening of the concept of wisdom as found earlier in Proverbs. See further on this Pfeiffer, *History of New Testament Times,* pp. 381-86.

[67]Scholarship some twenty years ago or so was inclined to view Ben Sira as a proto-Sadducee. See, e.g., Metzger, *Introduction to the Apocrypha,* p. 87. On this understanding, one could argue that Pharisees would not have valued Ben Sira's work. This equation, however, is now viewed as unlikely. In fact, Ben Sira has points of contact with Pharisaism, such as the evil impulse *(yēṣer hārā').*

[68]For further arguments in support of this position, see E. J. Schnabel, "Wisdom," *DPL,* pp. 967-73; A. G. Patzia, "Wisdom," *DLNTD,* pp. 1200-1204; and F. W. Burnett, "Wisdom," *DJG,* pp. 876-77.

The canon of Jesus and the apostles. Ben Sira's grandson, besides putting us in his debt by translating his grandfather's work, throws an intriguing ray of light on the question of the canon of Scripture used by NT writers.[69] In the prologue the grandson writes: "So my grandfather Jesus, who had devoted himself especially to the reading of the Law and the Prophets and the other books of our ancestors. . . ." Then a bit later in the same prologue he adds: "Not only this book, but even the Law itself, the Prophecies, and the rest of the books differ not a little when read in the original." What stands out here is the threefold division of the Scriptures, a division that Jesus of Nazareth recognizes as well.[70] In Luke's Gospel, we have Jesus saying to his disciples following his resurrection: " 'Everything written about me in the law of Moses, the prophets, and the psalms must be fulfilled.' Then he opened their minds to understand the scriptures" (Lk 24:44-45). Since Psalms was the first book in the third section (the Ketubim or "Writings"), it could be used as a reference to the entire section, what the prologue to Sirach calls "the rest of the books." Most scholars conclude from this that by the first century A.D. there was a recognizable collection of sacred books, consisting of three divisions and being nearly identical to the later canon acknowledged by rabbinic Judaism.[71] Sirach thus witnesses to a stage in which the canon was already virtually complete (by 132 B.C., the approximate date of the grandson's translation, if not already by 180 B.C.).

Conceptual parallels. One can also identify certain conceptual parallels between Sirach and the NT, both in the Gospels as well as in the Epistles and Revelation.

With regard to the thought of Ben Sira, we find some rather close parallels in the teaching of Jesus as transmitted by the Synoptic Evangelists. Modern scholarship has produced quite varied portraits of the historical Jesus—some of them stretching credulity![72] One facet of the historical Jesus, however, is

---

[69]Fragments of the Hebrew text have been found at Qumran and Masada, but we are still dependent on the Greek for the bulk of the book. For discussion, see Skehan and Di Lella, *Wisdom of Ben Sira,* pp. 51-62.

[70]It now appears that the famous 4QMMT (see chapter six for background on Qumran) also refers to a threefold division of Scripture [". . . the book of Moses [and the words of the pro]phets and of David [and the annals] [of eac]h generation" (lines 95-96; see Florentino García Martínez, *The Dead Sea Scrolls Translated: The Qumran Texts in English* [Leiden: E. J. Brill, 1994], p. 79). We take it that "David and the annals" refers to Psalms and 1 and 2 Chronicles, both being in the Ketubim ("Writings"), the third division of the Hebrew Bible.

[71]For particulars on this issue, see Lee MacDonald, *The Formation of the Christian Biblical Canon,* rev. and expanded ed. (Peabody, Mass.: Hendrickson, 1995).

[72]The Jesus Seminar has been a highly visible organization attempting to correct the traditional views of Jesus with a "scientifically" based reconstruction. Their methodology is set out in *The Five Gospels: The Search for the Authentic Words of Jesus: New Translation and*

rather widely acknowledged: the picture of Jesus as a sage.[73] The picture that emerges from the Matthew, Mark and Luke is that Jesus, like Ben Sira, gathered around himself students or disciples. One thinks here of Ben Sira's invitation to come and study under him in light of a similar call by Jesus:

> Draw near to me, you who are uneducated, and lodge in the house of instruction . . . . Put your neck under her yoke, and let your souls receive instruction; it is to be found close by. (Sir 51:23, 26)
>
> Come to me, all you that are weary and are carrying heavy burdens, and I will give you rest. Take my yoke upon you, and learn from me; for I am gentle and humble in heart, and you will find rest for your souls. For my yoke is easy, and my burden is light. (Mt 11:28-30)

To be sure, there is an important difference here: Jesus says "my yoke" (teaching centered in him), not "her yoke" (i.e., instruction embodied in the Torah). But the picture of Jesus as a sage in the tradition of a Ben Sira is striking. Not surprisingly, it is in Matthew, the most Jewish of the Gospels, in which this portrait most clearly emerges. In fact, in a verse that may be taken as a key to the purpose of Matthew's Gospel, we have Jesus' stated objectives for his students in this memorable saying: "Therefore every scribe who has been trained for the kingdom of heaven is like the master of a household who brings out of his treasure what is new and what is old" (Mt 13:52).[74] Ben Sira is also a scribal master (*grammateus;* cf. Sir 38:24) seeking to instruct pupils in the treasures of Torah.

Several of Jesus' sayings are reminiscent of Ben Sira's observations. In Luke 12:16-21 Jesus tells a parable about a rich man who builds bigger barns for his abundant crops. The man says to himself,

> "Soul, you have ample goods laid up for many years; relax, eat, drink, be merry." But God said to him, "You fool! This very night your life is being demanded of you. And the things you have prepared, whose will they be?" So it is with those who store up treasures for themselves but are not rich toward God.

Note how similar this is to a passage from Sirach:

Commentary, ed. Robert W. Funk, Roy W. Hoover and the Jesus Seminar (New York: Macmillan, 1993). For critiques of their methodology and presuppositions, see R. Hays, "The Corrected Jesus," *First Things* (May 1994): 43-48; N. T. Wright, "The New, Unimproved Jesus," *Christianity Today* (September 13, 1993): 22-26; and Ben Witherington III, *The Jesus Quest: The Third Search for the Jew of Nazareth* (Downers Grove, Ill.: InterVarsity Press, 1995).

[73]See Witherington, *Jesus Quest.*

[74]On the importance of Matthew 13:52 as a pointer to Matthew's purpose, see Glenn W. Barker, William L. Lane and J. Ramsey Michaels, *The New Testament Speaks* (New York: Harper & Row, 1969), pp. 260-71.

One becomes rich through diligence and self-denial, and the reward allotted to him is this: when he says, "I have found rest, and now I shall feast on my goods!" he does not know how long it will be until he leaves them to others and dies. (Sir 11:18-19)

Luke seems to place Jesus' parable in a Jerusalem setting (cf. Lk 10:38). If so, the appropriateness of an adapted saying of a famous Jerusalem sage becomes clear. Certainly, Jesus sharpened the issue in his version.

Two petitions of the so-called Lord's Prayer also find close conceptual parallels in Sirach: "And forgive us our debts, as we also have forgiven our debtors. And do not bring us to the time of trial, but rescue us from the evil one" (Mt 6:12-13). Ben Sira writes, "Forgive your neighbor the wrong he has done, and then your sins will be pardoned when you pray" (Sir 28:2); "O Lord, Father and Master of my life, do not abandon me to their designs, and do not let me fall because of them!" (Sir 23:1; cf. 33:1). One should also note that in Sirach we have God addressed as Father, just as Jesus taught his disciples (Sir 23:1; cf. Mt 6:9: "Our Father in heaven").

Again, Ben Sira makes this observation: "Its fruit discloses the cultivation of a tree; so a person's speech discloses the cultivation of his mind" (Sir 27:6). With this we compare Jesus: "You will know them by their fruits. Are grapes gathered from thorns, or figs from thistles?" (Mt 7:16). To be sure, this is a truism and doubtless not confined to Palestinian Jewish teachers. But taken together with the other passages, it strengthens our suggestion that Jesus knew the writings of Ben Sira and could adapt them to his own teaching. Complete originality is neither required nor desirable in order to affirm the uniqueness of Jesus' teaching. As has been pointed out many times, it is the focus upon his own person and the rearrangement of traditional Jewish teaching that sets apart Jesus' message.[75]

In another context Jesus says to a certain ruler: "There is still one thing lacking. Sell all that you own and distribute the money to the poor, and you will have treasure in heaven; then come, follow me" (Lk 18:22; cf. Mt 6:20). Ben Sira had earlier exhorted his students: "Lay up your treasure according to the commandments of the Most High, and it will profit you more than gold" (Sir 29:11). The notion of treasure in heaven is a shared concept.[76]

One more reference to the Synoptic Gospels is interesting. In Sirach 48:1-11 Ben Sira celebrates the life of Elijah. This is part of his famous section in praise of famous men. In this connection he says: "At the appointed

---

[75]Of great help here is Robert Stein, *The Method and Message of Jesus' Teachings* (Philadelphia: Westminster, 1978), pp. 109-11. See also Ladd, *Theology of the New Testament*, pp. 118-32.

[76]On the notion of laying up treasure, see chapter two (p. 67) above.

time, it is written, you are destined to calm the wrath of God before it breaks out in fury, to turn the hearts of parents to their children, and to restore the tribes of Jacob" (Sir 48:10). Mark's Gospel records a question Peter, James and John put to Jesus with regard to Elijah. This question was no doubt precipitated by the transfiguration experience in which Elijah had momentarily appeared with Jesus on the mount: " 'Why do the scribes say that Elijah must come first?' He said to them, 'Elijah is indeed coming first to restore all things. . . . But I tell you that Elijah has come, and they did to him whatever they pleased, as it is written about him' " (Mk 9:11-13). Jesus linked this prophecy with the ministry of John the Baptist. Thus the disciples already knew a scribal tradition, based upon Malachi 4:5-6 and going back at least to Ben Sira in the second century B.C., in which Elijah would return to restore Israel.

In addition to conceptual parallels between Jesus and Ben Sira, in Paul's letters we detect a few phrases reminiscent of Sirach. This, too, is not surprising, given that fact that Paul was a student under Gamaliel at Jerusalem. Ben Sira probably lived before a distinctive Pharisaic party arose. Even though he does not espouse Pharisaic teachings, such as a bodily resurrection and the twofold Torah, it seems likely that his teaching would have been studied and valued. Ben Sira's unequivocal assertion of recompense on the basis of deeds—"Everyone receives in accordance with one's deeds" (Sir 16:14)—finds an echo in Paul's theology as a Christian: "For he will repay according to each one's deeds" (Rom 2:6).

In 1 Corinthians 6:12 Paul appears to be quoting a slogan from the libertine party at Corinth.[77] His rejoinder, "but not all things are beneficial," resembles an observation of Sirach: "For not everything is good for everyone, and no one enjoys everything" (Sir 37:28). The points being made in the respective contexts are not quite the same, but the general ideas are comparable.[78]

Perhaps the clearest parallel to any NT writing is Sirach 44—50, the "hymn in honor of our ancestors." This recital of worthies from Israel's history finds a counterpart in Hebrews, with its famous "hall of faith" (Heb 11). Both authors begin their panegyric with a prologue. Ben Sira's is considerably longer and consists of twelve categories of great men, exemplified in what follows (Sir 44:3-6), whereas Hebrews provides an initial definition of faith illustrated by each worthy mentioned.[79] Note, however, that Ben Sira has no

---

[77]See the footnotes in *New Oxford Annotated Bible,* NT 235; and Gordon Fee, *The First Epistle to the Corinthians,* NICNT (Grand Rapids, Mich.: Eerdmans, 1987), pp. 249-66.

[78]Several other allusions or verbal parallels are listed in the index to the UBS[4] on pp. 900-901.

[79]See Skehan and Di Lella, *Wisdom of Ben Sira,* p. 500. If one includes an allusion to Joshua (Heb 11:30) and lumps together those mentioned in 11:32, Hebrews has twelve different examples of heroes of the faith. The significance of twelve in OT history is obvious.

women in his list, whereas Hebrews has three such references. Ben Sira begins his narration with Enoch, Hebrews with Abel. The former brings his list down to Simon the high priest (Simon II, c. 219-196 B.C.); the latter seems to bring his down to the time of the Hasmonean martyrs (cf. Heb 11:34-36, 37b-38). The respective authors have different agendas and perspectives, but the precedent set by Ben Sira seems likely to have prompted the writer of Hebrews to provide his Christian readers with a list of heroes of the faith, although space restraints necessitated a shorter listing. Table 3.2 reveals possible allusions and parallels from James, 1 Peter and Revelation.

Table 3.2. Possible allusions and parallels from James, 1 Peter and Revelation

Sirach	NT
"There is but one who is wise, greatly to be feared, seated upon his throne—the Lord" (Sir 1:8).	"Fall on us and hide us from the face of the one seated on the throne" (Rev 6:16; cf. 4:2, 10; 5:1, 7, 13; 7:10, 15; 19:4; 21:5).
"Be quick to hear, but deliberate in answering" (Sir 5:11).	"Let everyone be quick to listen, slow to speak, slow to anger" (Jas 1:19).
"Do not say, 'It was the Lord's doing that I fell away'; for he does not do what he hates. Do not say, 'It was he who led me astray'; for he has no need of the sinful" (Sir 15:11-12).	"No one when tempted, should say, 'I am being tempted by God'; for God cannot be tempted by evil and he himself tempts no one" (Jas 1:13; the two allusions to James fit nicely the portrait of James in Acts as a leader of the Jerusalem church).
"O Lord, Father and God of my life, do not give me haughty eyes, and remove evil desire from me" (Sir 23:4-5).	"If you invoke as Father the one who judges all people impartially according to their deeds, live in reverent fear during the time of your exile" (1 Pet 1:17).

Summary

1. In this chapter we have explored the impact of Hellenism upon Jews, especially Palestinian Jewry. The works of *1 Enoch* 72—82 (AB), *1 Enoch* 1—36 (BW) and Sirach demonstrate, each in its own way, the pervasive influence of this cultural invasion.

2. AB reflects a more sophisticated way of viewing the universe. Though by no means a scientific treatise in the modern sense, it nonetheless gives evidence of awareness of Hellenistic science during the Seleucid era. The author or community behind AB is not directly engaging Hellenistic science but, in defense of its solar calendar, has made use of current views.

3. BW indirectly witnesses to the turmoil of the era. The wars of the Dia-

dochi and the struggles between the Seleucids and Ptolemies washed across the ancient lands of Israel like a flood tide. How could pious Jews reconcile such evil with the covenant promises of sacred Scripture? How could one explain such unmitigated evil? The problem of evil dominates the thought of this, at times, bizarre composition. Evil has dimensions far transcending the sphere of individual choices. BW, picking up on the sons of God motif of Genesis 6, develops an elaborate demonology, a concept having precedents in the ancient Near Eastern and in the Hellenistic traditions. The author(s) of BW sounds an alarm about abandoning the ancestral traditions. Faithfulness is called for; moreover, a sense of imminent judgment gives force to calls for steadfast perseverance, since God will soon destroy the kingdoms of this world and inaugurate the promised age to come. Hellenism as a worldview and way of life is simply not an option for faithful Jews.

3. Sirach provides a welcome window into a relatively calm era just before the storm of the Antiochian persecution and Hasmonean revolt broke out. How does Ben Sira view Hellenism? He is deeply concerned about its inroads, especially among the young, well-off Jews of Jerusalem and its environs. Is he opposed to all that Hellenism stands for? Clearly not. In some respects he himself has adopted and accepted aspects of Hellenism. He is a cultured, urbane figure who can comfortably move in Hellenistic circles. But he does not assimilate, nor does he think this a viable option. His academy in Jerusalem is a bastion of conservatism for young Jewish students. While they must adapt to certain features of their day, this does not entail an abandonment of the core of the ancestral faith. For Ben Sira the Torah is the crown jewel of the Israelite tradition. Nothing in Hellenism can supplant this. Success in life hinges upon adherence to its teaching. What we have in Ben Sira, then, is a restrained accommodation to Hellenism.

4. How do these pieces help us understand the NT better? They are instructive for Christian readers. In the struggles of pious Jews to come to grips with the reigning worldview of their day, we have a mirror image of NT Christian responses to the larger Greco-Roman world. The NT writings reveal the same diversity as our three selections from Jewish literature. The cultured and urbane Paul displays a considerable amount of accommodation to the Greco-Roman world of his time. He does, however, indicate clear limits. In this regard 1 Corinthians is most instructive as Paul deals with issues such as lawsuits, sexual morality, food offered to idols and veiling of women in worship, among others. The book of Revelation, similar in many respects to BW, paints a more ominous portrait of the world system. While some apparently were succumbing to moral and ethical compromise, the Apocalypse sounds a call for purity and separation. In fact, the Johannine literature in general (the

Gospel of John and the three epistles) presents a more pronounced world-denying leitmotif.

5. The Enoch literature draws attention to a characteristic ethical dualism found throughout NT literature. Furthermore, the NT depiction of evil as having cosmic, transcendental dimensions does not spring out of a vacuum. As we have already seen in the previous chapter, eschatological dualism, along with its demonology and angelology, developed considerably during the Second Temple period. The NT documents reflect this same basic understanding of reality.

6. Of major importance for NT thought is the personification of Wisdom in the writing of Ben Sira. His equation of Wisdom with Torah pointed toward a way of proclaiming the person and work of Jesus Christ. Most notably, the writings of Paul, Hebrews and the Gospel of John display indebtedness to this Wisdom trajectory.

7. As was the case in the previous chapter, we uncovered a pervasive Jewish cast to the foundational Christian documents. Old themes, categories and notions are infused with a new, christological content, but the Jewish contours remain. This rediscovery of Jewishness, meeting us on page after page of the NT, is vital for a full appreciation of Christianity. Certainly in this exercise we can profit from the earnest appeals to devotion and commitment found in the Enoch literature and the common sense still to be discerned in the wisdom of Ben Sira.

For Further Discussion

1. What was it about the ancient worthy Enoch that appealed to Jews of the Second Temple era?

2. We see from *1 Enoch* that Jews were influenced by the surrounding Babylonian-Persian culture. In what ways has modern culture influenced Christianity?

3. Compare and contrast the explanation for the origin of evil in the NT with that of AB and BW.

4. How did Ben Sira's identification of Wisdom with Torah provide assistance to early Christians in their understanding of who Jesus was?

5. What evidence is there that Jesus of Nazareth knew and probably borrowed some of the teachings of Ben Sira? Is anything at stake in this admission?

6. How does Ben Sira handle the problem of Hellenism? What can modern Christians learn from this?

For Further Reading

Historical Background

John J. Collins and Gregory E. Sterling, eds., *Hellenism in the Land of Israel* (Notre

Dame, Ind.: University of Notre Dame Press, 2001).

I. Gafni, "The Hellenistic Period," in *Jewish Writings of the Second Temple Period: Apocrypha, Pseudepigrapha, Qumran Sectarian Writings, Philo, Josephus,* ed. Michael E. Stone, CRINT 2 (Assen: Van Gorcum; Philadelphia: Fortress, 1984), pp. 3-9.

Lester L. Grabbe, *Judaism from Cyrus to Hadrian,* vol. 1: *The Persian and Greek Periods* (Minneapolis: Fortress, 1992), pp. 147-311.

John H. Hayes and Sara R. Mandell, *The Jewish People in Classical Antiquity: From Alexander to Bar Kochba* (Louisville: Westminster John Knox, 1998), pp. 13-59.

Lee I. Levine, *Judaism and Hellenism in Antiquity: Conflict or Confluence?* (Peabody, Mass.: Hendrickson, 1999), pp. 3-32.

George W. E. Nickelsburg, *Jewish Literature Between the Bible and the Mishnah: A Historical and Literary Introduction* (Philadelphia: Fortress, 1981), pp. 43-46.

F. E. Peters, "Hellenism," *IDBSup,* pp. 395-98.

J. Julius Scott Jr., *Customs and Controversies: Intertestamental Jewish Backgrounds of the New Testament* (Grand Rapids, Mich.: Baker, 1995), pp. 78-82.

G. R. Stanton, "Hellenism," *DNTB,* pp. 464-73.

Michael Stone, *Scriptures, Sects and Visions* (Philadelphia: Fortress, 1980), pp. 87-98.

James C. VanderKam, *An Introduction to Early Judaism* (Grand Rapids, Mich.: Eerdmans, 2001), pp. 11-31.

W. T. Wilson, "Hellenistic Judaism," *DNTB,* pp. 477-82.

Edwin M. Yamauchi, "Hellenism," *DPL,* pp. 383-88.

Literature

R. H. Charles, "1 Enoch," in *The Apocrypha and Pseudepigrapha of the Old Testament,* ed. R. H. Charles, 2 vols. (Oxford: Clarendon Press, 1913), 2:163-281.

James H. Charlesworth, *The Old Testament Pseudepigrapha and the New Testament,* new ed. (Harrisburg, Penn.: Trinity Press International, 1998), pp. 70-80.

R. J. Coggins, *Sirach* (Sheffield: Sheffield Academic Press, 1998).

John J. Collins, "Apocalyptic Literature," in *Early Judaism and Its Modern Interpreters,* ed. Robert A. Kraft and George W. E. Nickelsburg (Philadelphia: Fortress; Atlanta: Scholars Press, 1986), pp. 345-70.

————, "Enoch, Books of," *DNTB,* pp. 314-15.

————, *Jewish Wisdom in the Hellenistic Age* (Louisville: Westminster John Knox, 1997).

John J. Collins and Gregory E. Sterling, eds., *Hellenism in the Land of Israel,* CJA 13 (Notre Dame, Ind.: University of Notre Dame Press, 2001).

D. A. deSilva, "Sirach," *DNTB,* pp. 1116-24.

A. A. Di Lella, "Wisdom of Ben Sira," *ABD* 6:931-45.

M. Gilbert, "Wisdom Literature," in *Jewish Writings of the Second Temple Period: Apocrypha, Pseudepigrapha, Qumran Sectarian Writings, Philo, Josephus,* ed.

Michael E. Stone, CRINT 2 (Assen: Van Gorcum; Philadelphia: Fortress, 1984), pp. 290-301.

Daniel J. Harrington, *Invitation to the Apocrypha* (Grand Rapids, Mich.: Eerdmans, 1999), pp. 78-91.

E. Isaac, "Apocalyptic Literature and Related Works," in *The Old Testament Pseudepigrapha,* ed. J. H. Charlesworth, 2 vols. (Garden City, N.Y.: Doubleday, 1983), 1:5-89.

M. A. Knibb, "1 Enoch," in *The Apocryphal Old Testament,* ed. H. F. D. Sparks (Oxford: Clarendon Press, 1985), pp. 169-220, 257-74.

Burton L. Mack and Roland E. Murphy, "Wisdom Literature," in *Early Judaism and Its Modern Interpreters,* ed. Robert A. Kraft and George W. E. Nickelsburg (Philadelphia: Fortress; Atlanta: Scholars Press, 1986), pp. 371-78.

H. McKeating, "Jesus ben Sira's Attitude to Women," *ExpTim* 85 (1973-1974): 85-87.

Bruce M. Metzger, *An Introduction to the Apocrypha* (New York: Oxford University Press, 1957), pp. 77-88.

George W. E. Nickelsburg, "The Bible Rewritten and Expanded," in *Jewish Writings of the Second Temple Period: Apocrypha, Pseudepigrapha, Qumran Sectarian Writings, Philo, Josephus,* ed. Michael E. Stone, CRINT 2 (Assen: Van Gorcum; Philadelphia: Fortress, 1984), pp. 90-97.

—————, *Jewish Literature Between the Bible and the Mishnah: A Historical and Literary Introduction* (Philadelphia: Fortress, 1981), pp. 55-69.

P. W. Skehan and A. A. Di Lella, *The Wisdom of Ben Sira,* AB 39 (New York: Doubleday, 1987).

J. G. Snaith, *Ecclesiasticus, Or the Wisdom of Jesus Son of Sirach,* CBC (Cambridge: Cambridge University Press, 1974).

Warren Trenchard, *Ben Sira's View of Women: A Literary Analysis* (Chico, Calif.: Scholars Press, 1982).

James C. VanderKam, *An Introduction to Early Judaism* (Grand Rapids, Mich.: Eerdmans, 2001), pp. 88-94.

Four

Apocalypticism

Hope for Hard Times

*F*or an English translation of Jubilees *(with introduction) see H. F. D. Sparks, ed., The Apocryphal Old Testament (Oxford: Clarendon Press, 1985), pp. 1-139; J. H. Charlesworth, ed.,* The Old Testament Pseudepigrapha, *2 vols. (Garden City, N.Y.: Doubleday, 1983), 2:35-142; R. H. Charles, ed., The Apocrypha and Pseudepigrapha of the Old Testament, 2 vols. (Oxford: Clarendon Press, 1913), 2:1-82; or R. H. Charles, The Book of Jubilees or the Little Genesis (London: Adam & Charles Black, 1902). For* 1 Enoch *83—90, see Sparks, ed., Apocryphal Old Testament, pp. 274-91; Charlesworth, ed., Old Testament Pseudepigrapha, 1:61-72; Michael A. Knibb, The Ethiopic Book of Enoch: A New Edition in the Light of the Aramaic Dead Sea Fragments (Oxford: Clarendon Press, 1978); Charles, ed., Apocrypha and Pseudepigrapha of the Old Testament, 2:248-60. For* Testament/Assumption of Moses *(with introduction), see Sparks, ed., Apocryphal Old Testament, pp. 601-16; Charlesworth, ed., Old Testament Pseudepigrapha, 1:919-34; Charles, ed., Apocrypha and Pseudepigrapha of the Old Testament, 2:407-24; or R. H. Charles, The Assumption of Moses (London: Black, 1897).*

Introduction

This chapter provides essential background for understanding the world of early Judaism and Christianity. In it we trace the events leading up to the Maccabean revolt (ca. 167 B.C.). This was a watershed in Jewish history, a time during which many Jews had to make a life-or-death decision. The Hebraic traditions anchored in the Sinai covenant were at stake. A despotic version of Hellenism forced the Jewish community to make a choice: either abandon the ancestral traditions and be thoroughly integrated into Hellenistic culture, or die. This crisis drove a wedge through the Jewish community and created fractures—fractures that never completely healed until the aftermath of two devastating wars against Rome (A.D. 66-73 and 132-135).

One of the responses to this crisis appears in Jewish literature bearing the name "apocalyptic." Apocalypticism, really more a movement and mindset than a distinct genre, is the focus of our readings in this chapter. We examine three works that illustrate an apocalyptic worldview. This outlook characterized a sizable number of Jews during the first two pre-Christian centuries and the first two Christian centuries as well. Of special interest to us is the impact this way of thinking had on early Christianity. A number of modern scholars agree that "apocalyptic is the mother of Christianity."[1] This claim must be taken seriously and has considerable implications for a correct understanding of the NT.

Three selections are the focus of our investigation in this chapter: *Jubilees*, *1 Enoch* 83—90 and the *Testament of Moses*. In these works we sense an intense longing for deliverance and vindication. The circles that produced this literature clung to such an expectation tenaciously, and the upshot was a remarkable perseverance of the human spirit in the face of dire threat and tribulation. Parallels in Christian history will help us understand and appreciate better the attitudes and behavior of people living in similar circumstances. Indeed, as modern Christians, we still share with those Jewish stalwarts some very important common ground.

A Sketch of the Times

In order to place these three writings in their historical milieu, we provide a brief sketch of the turbulent times out of which they emerged.[2] We pick up

---

[1]See already R. H. Charles, who says that "apocalyptic . . . was the source of the higher theology in Judaism, and subsequently was the parent of Christianity" (*APOT* 2:1). See also Ernst Käsemann, "On the Subject of Primitive Christian Apocalyptic," in *New Testament Questions of Today* (Philadelphia: Fortress, 1969), pp. 108-37.

[2]For helpful surveys of this period, see V. Tcherikover, *Hellenistic Civilization and the Jews* (Peabody, Mass.: Hendrickson, 1999 [1961]), chap. 5; George W. E. Nickelsburg, *Jewish Literature Between the Bible and the Mishnah: A Historical and Literary Introduction* (Philadelphia: Fortress, 1981), pp. 71-73; I. Gafni, "The Historical Background," in *Jewish Writings of the Second Temple Period: Apocrypha, Pseudepigrapha, Qumran Sectarian Writings, Philo, Josephus,* ed. Michael E. Stone, CRINT 2 (Assen: Van Gorcum; Philadelphia: Fortress, 1984), pp. 6-13; and J. Julius Scott Jr., *Customs and Controversies: Intertestamental Jewish Backgrounds of the New Testament* (Grand Rapids, Mich.: Baker, 1995), pp. 80-84.

the earlier threads of the story already traced during the spread of Hellenism following the conquests of Alexander the Great.[3]

The protracted struggle between the Ptolemies and the Seleucids for the control of Palestine climaxed with Antiochus III's decisive victory over the Ptolemies at Panias, at the foot of Mount Hermon, in 198 B.C. At first Seleucid hegemony seemed benign enough. Antiochus III extended to Jews many benefits, which included the right to maintain their ancestral traditions and laws and the reduction of taxes. He even allowed Jews a measure of internal autonomy by conferring civil as well as religious authority on the Jewish high priest in Jerusalem. Under this arrangement the Torah assumed the status of constitution and Judea was governed as a theocratic state. Such an outcome was better than many could have hoped for. We recall the almost rapturous praise of Ben Sira for the high priest Simon son of Onias during these peaceful days (Sir 50:1-21). But the honeymoon was short-lived.

This relatively happy condition for Jews might have been longer-lived had not an international power struggle ensued that swept up little Judea in its backwash. The problem was the collision between two different dreams of nationalistic expansion: that of the Seleucids in the Middle East and that of Rome to the west. The eastern Mediterranean was increasingly feeling a Roman presence. Antiochus III sought to shore up his kingdom by conquering Asia Minor and Greece. The latter venture, like that of the Persians before him, failed in a military defeat at the hands of the Romans. Scipio Africanus pursued him into Asia Minor and inflicted an even more decisive defeat at Magnesia in 190 B.C. As victors, the Romans levied upon Antiochus III a crushing indemnity and, to provide even more leverage, forcibly removed one of his sons to Rome as a hostage. This adverse turn of events precipitated Antiochus III's assassination and elevated to power another of his sons, Seleucus IV, with little prospect for improvement.

As a means of scraping up enough money to pay the compensation due Rome, the Seleucid regime resorted to looting sanctuaries. Heliodorus was dispatched to the Jerusalem temple in order to confiscate the rather sizable sums that were collected there. This event is doubtless the one referred to in Daniel 11:20: "Then shall arise in his place one who shall send an official for the glory of the kingdom; but within a few days he shall be broken, though not in anger or in battle"[4] (cf. also 2 Macc 3).

This was a harbinger of things to come. In 175 Antiochus IV, who had been held hostage in Rome since 189 B.C., succeeded his brother as regent. With his

---

[3]For a concise review, see Scott, *Customs and Controversies,* pp. 78-82.
[4]See *The New Oxford Annotated Bible: New Revised Standard Version,* ed. Bruce M. Metzger and Roland E. Murphy (New York: Oxford University Press, 1991), note on Dan 11:20.

eye on the Roman menace to the west, he sought to unify his diverse king-dom for the continuing struggle with Rome. One ethnic-religious group stood out like a sore thumb: the Jews (cf. Esther 3:8). They persisted in their ances-tral traditions and resisted the enticements to assimilate thoroughly to a Hel-lenistic way of life. Antiochus IV viewed this as a weakness in his position, given that Palestine was the crossroads of the Middle East.

First Antiochus IV tried the carrot: he offered the status of Antiochene cit-izen to all inhabitants of the empire who were prepared to adopt a Greek way of life. In this gambit he was not lacking help from the Jewish side. Already a small but influential number of Jews advocated Hellenism and abandoned many of the ancestral ways. Among these was none other than Jason, a brother of Onias III, the high priest.[5] Jason secured the high priesthood by bribing Antiochus, with the assurance that he would bring the Jewish people fully into the fold of imperial ideology. To this end Jason undertook the trans-formation of Jerusalem into a veritable Greek *polis* (city). Greek schools, a *gymnasion* and *ephēbeion* (places for physical exercise and athletic training), and an official roll of citizenry were established. Athletic games were spon-sored in which even priests clamored to take part. Some Jews, embarrassed at their circumcision (Greek athletic contests were conducted in the nude), sought to have an operation reversing that outward sign (cf. 1 Macc 1:11-15; the Greek word for this was *epispasmos*). There seemed to be a popular tide toward the Greek way of life. But this was not a grass-roots movement; it appealed primarily to the upper classes and the more aristocratic elements within Jewish Palestinian society.[6]

Meanwhile, Menelaus entered the arena by bribing Antiochus even more generously and, as a consequence, secured for himself the office of high priest. Predictably, this incited a bloody clash between the partisans of the two claimants to the high priesthood.

At this point, in 170-169 B.C., another showdown between the Seleucids and Rome occurred when Antiochus invaded Egypt. Rome viewed Egypt as vital to its national interests, since it provided much-needed grain for the bur-geoning populace of Rome and its empire. Consequently, Rome promptly countered this move. The Roman senate sent a delegate to Egypt with a dire threat directed at Antiochus. According to one version of the encounter, the legate, Popilius Laenas, drew a circle around Antiochus and told him to make his decision before his stepped out of it: either withdraw immediately from

---

[5]In what follows, see Josephus, *Ant.* 12.5.2; 1 Macc 1:11-15; 2 Macc 4:7-15.

[6]On the whole question of the degree of hellenization that took place in Palestine at this time, see Lee I. Levine, *Judaism and Hellenism in Antiquity: Conflict or Confluence?* (Pea-body, Mass.: Hendrickson, 1999), pp. 3-95; and Scott, *Customs and Controversies,* pp. 116-20.

Egypt or face a declaration of war by Rome. He withdrew.

In a foul mood, Antiochus retreated north toward Palestine. Back in Jerusalem rumors spread that he was dead. This prompted Jason to invade Jerusalem from across the Jordan, where he had been biding his time. The partisans of Jason and Menelaus squared off against each other, and a third group opposed to both entered the fray. Into this general melee, Antiochus suddenly appeared before the walls of Jerusalem with a sizable military force. He stormed the divided city and massacred many Jews. Menelaus was recognized as legitimate high priest, and Philip the Phrygian remained in the city to maintain order.

Order did not prevail, however. In response to further disturbances by Jews opposed to hellenization, Antiochus dispatched Apollonius to Jerusalem. Apollonius attacked the city on a sabbath—at this point in time, Jews would not fight on the sabbath—and massacred many of the inhabitants. In the vicinity of the temple, a fortress called the Akra was garrisoned with troops. This military installation would continue for some twenty-six years under the control of the Seleucid regime.[7]

Antiochus IV then struck at the very heart of Judaism. He forbade the observance of the Torah—all copies of it were to be burned—and decreed the death penalty for all who failed to comply. If mothers had their infant sons circumcised, the sons were killed and hung around their mothers' necks. Jews were forced to eat pork, which, of course, was forbidden by the law (cf. Lev 11:7; Deut 14:8). In Jerusalem itself the temple was transformed into a pagan cult center with the altar now dedicated to Zeus. On the fifteenth of Chislev (December) 167 B.C., a sow was offered up on the great altar in front of the Jerusalem temple. This is almost certainly the outrageous act referred to in 1 Maccabees 1:54-55:

> Now on the fifteenth day of Chislev, in the one hundred forty-fifth year, they erected a desolating sacrilege on the altar of burnt offering. They also built altars in the surrounding towns of Judah, and offered incense at the doors of the houses and in the streets (cf. also Dan 8:11-14; 9:27; 11:36-39; 12:11).

Under this onslaught many Jews abandoned the ancestral faith and complied with the edicts of Antiochus. Others, however, resisted. This meant either certain death or flight to wilderness caves and hideouts. Against this bleak scenario appeared one of the greatest resistance movements of all time. The Hasmonean family, a priestly family living at Modein in Judah, rose up in righteous indignation against these atrocities. The aged priest Mattathias urged his five sons to take up armed resistance against the cultural imperial-

---

[7]For an illustrated discussion, see Leen Ritmyer, "Locating the Original Temple Mount," *BAR* 18, no. 2 (1992): 24-45, 64-65.

ism of Antiochus IV. This they did with amazing and unexpected success. Waging guerrilla warfare against Seleucid mercenaries and terrorism against apostate Jews, the Maccabee brothers, over about a fifteen-year period, eventually carved out an independent Jewish state that lasted from 142-63 B.C.

We will describe the dynastic achievements of the Hasmoneans in a later chapter. For now we break off the historical narrative and turn to the three writings under discussion inasmuch as they reflect the terrible persecution of Jews during Antiochus IV's despotic reign. Antiochus styled himself "Epiphanes"—"the manifestation [of God]." Jews had a different title for him: "Epimanes"—"the madman"! In each piece we examine, there will be discernible allusions to this notorious monarch and his maniacal efforts to destroy Judaism.

Apocalyptic Literature

Apocalyptic literature flourished between 200 B.C. and A.D. 200. Several features characterize this literature.[8]

1. All of the apocalyptic writings, except the NT book of Revelation, are pseudonymous, that is, falsely attributed to some ancient worthy, such as Adam, Enoch, Abraham, Moses, Elijah, Daniel, Isaiah and so forth. The three works we consider in this chapter are ascribed to Enoch and Moses. The reason for pseudonymity probably springs from a crisis in authority: since there was general recognition that prophecy had ceased (cf. 1 Macc 4:46), there was a need to legitimize the revelation given. This authority came in the form of a traditional figure possessing the status of a prophet. Thus the writing was viewed as having been written and hidden away in earlier times, but only now made known to the elect.

2. The primary mode of revelation in apocalyptic literature is visionary. That is, much of this material consists of descriptions of visions beheld by the ancient worthies. We may assume that these were not, for the most part, mere fabrications by our unknown authors, but rather actual visionary experiences, which were then attributed to great figures of the past. Troubled times tend to produce visionary activity. Viewed in purely psychological terms, one might be tempted to dismiss such responses as coping mechanisms. It is a way of dealing with forces beyond one's control. We should not,

---

[8]The literature on this topic is enormous. See surveys in D. E. Aune, T. J. Geddert and C. A. Evans, "Apocalypticism," *DNTB*, pp. 45-58; J. J. Collins, "Apocalyptic Literature," in *Early Judaism and Its Modern Interpreters,* ed. Robert A. Kraft and George W. E. Nickelsburg (Philadelphia: Fortress; Atlanta: Scholars Press, 1986), pp. 345-70, as well as his, "Apocalyptic Literature," *DNTB*, pp. 40-45; Michael E. Stone, "Apocalyptic Literature," in *Jewish Writings of the Second Temple Period,* pp. 383-94; and G. E. Ladd, "Apocalyptic Literature," *ISBE* 1:151-61.

however, deny out of hand any positive benefits and theological value to visionary experiences. Quite the contrary. Christianity owes much to visionary experience emerging out of hard times. Only a rather rigid Christian rationalism has no room for the visionary in its inn! We will say more of this later in the chapter.

3. The actual content of these visions focuses on the transcendental world and the end times. By "transcendental" we mean the otherworldly, supernatural realm. Of foremost importance to the apocalypticists was the throne room of God, but fascination with the workings of the exalted spheres above included such supramundane matters as the movements of the heavenly bodies and the forces of nature, such as wind, rain, ice and snow. We have already encountered this in our reading in *1 Enoch*, especially chapters 72—82.

4. The visionaries typically describe mystical journeys into the heavens and secrets revealed to them by angelic guides. The angelic hosts are of great interest in these visionary ascents, as is the mobile throne chariot of God (Heb *merkābâ*) described in Ezekiel 1. Later Jewish literature, known as the *Hekhalot* (Heb "palaces"), elaborates even more on this theme.[9] As we will see in chapters six and seven, already in the first two centuries B.C. there were Jewish groups who ascribed great importance to angelic worship and liturgy; indeed, they viewed their own worship as a mirror image of the heavenly entourage.

5. All of this reflects the conviction that earthly realities are counterparts of the heavenly. Thus we have a heavenly temple that serves as the pattern for the earthly temple. Furthermore, flesh-and-blood rulers on the plane of history are subject to the influence and control of heavenly principalities and powers, that is, angelic and demonic beings. A strong sense of the heavenly sphere impinging upon the affairs of earth characterizes apocalyptic thought and its literary expression.

6. Apocalyptic writers discerned patterns whereby the end times recapitulate beginnings. To put it another way, they see in the end times a return to the pristine times of the primeval world. The apocalyptic vision of the future entails a return to the Garden of Eden. As we will discover in the Qumran literature, apocalyptic thought is characterized by the notion that the present world is about to pass away and the current generation is living in the end times—or at least the end times are imminent. Before the end can arrive, however, the righteous must endure a time of great distress. The end times are times of cosmic disturbance and conflict. Given the turmoil surrounding the Hasmonean revolt, it is no wonder that many thought such a time had arrived.

---

[9]This refers to a "tradition in Jewish mysticism centering on mystical journeys through the heavenly spheres and palaces to the Divine Chariot" (Gershom Scholem, "Kabbalah (J. Mysticism)," *EncJud on CD-ROM* [Judaica Multimedia, version 1.0, 1997]).

7. In apocalyptic literature we discover differing views as to the agent of God's deliverance in the end times. Sometimes it is God himself who supernaturally intervenes to terminate human history. Other times it is a supernatural agent such as an archangel—Michael is a prominent player in many scenarios—or a messianic figure such as the Davidic scion or a transcendent figure such as the "son of man" found in Daniel 7:13-14. Some Jews expected more than one messianic figure, as we will discover in our reading of *Jubilees* and the Qumran literature.

8. The eschatological expectations of apocalyptic writers varied. For some, the future was essentially a restoration of the Davidic dynasty in a restored kingdom of Israel. In other words, the old prophetic hopes of a renewed Davidic kingdom were maintained (cf. Is 2:1-5; 11:1-16; Amos 9:11-15). The future hope was cast in very concrete, earthly terms. For others, this was simply inadequate. Evil was so monstrous and entrenched that a mere restoration was not sufficient. Nothing short of transformation could eradicate the damage done. This expectation, too, had its roots in the OT. Isaiah speaks of "new heavens and a new earth" (cf. Is 65:17; 66:22), the transformation of the animal kingdom (Is 11:6-9; 65:25), the complete destruction of the earth (Is 24:1-6, 17-20) and the abolition of death (Is 25:7-8). In Daniel this transformation is taken even further and features the righteous, no longer in Jerusalem, but shining "like the brightness of the sky" (Dan 12:3). Our literature speaks of the translation of souls into Paradise, where they enjoy mystic communion with God and the angels. Sometimes we sense that these two visions of the future—a restored earthly kingdom and a transformed utopia—are melded into one unified vision.

9. Finally, we should mention that apocalypticism was not the unique preserve of any particular Jewish group of the Second Temple period. Apocalyptic seems to have been a mindset or way of looking at reality that crossed traditional party lines. Out of the diverse scenarios for the future, there are nonetheless some common denominators. Hope in God's intervention to reward the righteous and punish the wicked remains a constant. We also sense that the majority of Jews in this era thought the end times were imminent. Perhaps only the group later called the Sadducees, with their vested interest in the ongoing temple ritual, displayed little or no enthusiasm for eschatological speculation.

Jubilees

Introduction

At first sight, *Jubilees* does not fit the above description of apocalyptic, since it retells the story of Genesis 1—Exodus 19. It is not, however, a mere retelling but a creative and expansive retelling. In short, there are embellishments to the familiar biblical stories. Moreover, the perspective throughout is recast in the form of a secret revelation transmitted by the angels of the presence to Moses when he was on the summit of Mount Sinai. It is this feature that connects it to apocalypticism. Furthermore, there is a section (*Jub.* 23:13-31) that is eschatologically oriented and possesses features characteristic of apocalyptic. For this reason we include it in our discussion of apocalypticism.

This reuse of traditional, biblical material is an early example of a developing tradition within Judaism and later Christianity. The anonymous author of *Jubilees* must be seen as standing at the very fountainhead of what is now a venerable tradition of commenting on the Bible. Its importance for this reason alone justifies its inclusion into our study of the literature of the Second Temple period.[10]

Dating and Composition

There are several compelling reasons for dating the composition of *Jubilees* to the period of about 175 B.C. to no later than 100 B.C. For one thing, the internal evidence points to the period sketched out above, namely, the time of Hellenistic reform. In *Jubilees* 3:31, for example, we have this statement: "That is why it is prescribed on the heavenly tablets that all those familiar with the provisions of the law should cover their shame and not uncover themselves as the Gentiles uncover themselves." One thinks of the eagerness of some, notably the priests, to engage in the athletic contests held in Jerusalem and in the Greek fashion of complete nudity. *Jubilees* 15:34 warns of the consequences of failing to circumcise sons, a counterblast to Jewish families who were prepared to forsake this sign of the covenant with Abraham. There are other allusions to that time when the hellenizers aggressively pushed their reform agenda (cf. *Jub.* 6:12-14, 35; 7:30; 20:4, 7-9; 21:6; 22:16-18, 20; 25:1; 27:10; 30:1-15).

Second, the connections between the ideas found in *Jubilees* and the Qumran literature are quite close.[11] This helps us to locate the general time period of *Jubilees*. But even more important, *Damascus Document* 16:3-4 (hereafter CD) quotes from *Jubilees*. Since CD is dated to around 100 B.C., this establishes at least a *terminus post quem* for *Jubilees*.[12]

Third, the Qumran manuscripts of *Jubilees* are dated on paleographical grounds to about 100 B.C. Thus the original composition, almost certainly in

---

[10]See James C. VanderKam, "Jubilees," *DNTB*, p. 602.

[11]Ibid., pp. 600-601.

[12]R. H. Charles, before the discovery of the Dead Sea Scrolls, had argued for a rather precise date between 109 and 105 B.C. He theorized that the destruction of Shechem recorded in *Jubilees* 30:4-6 mirrors the destruction of Samaria by John Hyrcanus c. 109 B.C. The Dead Sea Scrolls render such a dating virtually impossible.

Hebrew, would have been somewhat earlier, since the Qumran manuscripts are copies, not the original.

Nickelsburg argues that we should date the book's composition to about 168 B.C. (the "high date"), since there is no mention either of the Hasmonean high priesthood (c. 142 B.C.) or of the abomination of Antiochus IV (c. 167 B.C.). Given the temper of the author and his concerns, this may be hard to reconcile, if in fact the book were written after these events.[13] Arguments from silence are precarious, but the evidence suggests that the book was composed in the middle or second half of the second century B.C.[14]

There is general agreement that the work is a unified composition. It also seems reasonable to assume that its author was of priestly connections.[15]

Outline of the Composition
The following serves as a convenient outline of the contents of *Jubilees*:
I.   Introduction (*Jub.* 1)
II. Creation and Adam stories (*Jub.* 2—4)
III. Noah stories (*Jub.* 5—10)
IV. Abraham stories (*Jub.* 11—23)
V.   Jacob and his family (*Jub.* 24—45)
VI. Moses stories (*Jub.* 46—50)[16]

Approach to the Biblical Text
The author's approach to the biblical text is instructive. Rather often he simply reproduces the biblical text. On other occasions, however, he deletes material found in the Bible. Some of these deletions are probably on account of passages not easily explained from the sectarian viewpoint of *Jubilees* or as reflecting negatively on the character of the patriarchs.[17] As an example of

---

[13]James C. VanderKam, however, thinks that there are "some reflections of events in Maccabaean wars in the author's descriptions of Jacob's battles with his enemies (e.g., 38:1-14)," but he admits that "this is highly uncertain" ("The Book of Jubilees," in *Outside the Old Testament,* ed. M. De Jonge, CCWJCW [New York: Cambridge University Press, 1985], p. 116). See further Nickelsburg, *Jewish Literature,* pp. 78-79; George W. E. Nickelsburg, "The Bible Rewritten and Expanded," in *Jewish Writings of the Second Temple Period,* pp. 101-4. Sparks simply notes that some scholars have opted for a dating as early as the fifth century, but with "most preferring a date about 100 BC" (*AOT,* p. 5)
[14]VanderKam concludes that "in view of all the evidence, . . . the author composed *Jubilees* in the period between 160-150 BCE" (*The Book of Jubilees* [Sheffield: Sheffield Academic Press, 2001], p. 21).
[15]See VanderKam, "Book of Jubilees," p. 116.
[16]After Craig A. Evans, *Noncanonical Writings and New Testament Interpretation* (Peabody, Mass.: Hendrickson, 1992), p. 31. His outline is a slight adaptation of Wintermute's in *OTP* 2:35.
[17]VanderKam, "Jubilees," p. 602.

the latter, *Jubilees* does not narrate Abraham's or Isaac's deception about their wives when they were in threatening situations involving powerful Gentiles (Gen 12:10-20; 20:1-18; 26:6-11). The author says of Abraham's sojourn in Egypt: "his wife was torn away from him" (*Jub.* 13:11; cf. 17:17)! The episode concerning Abimelech is not even narrated.

Typically, the author of *Jubilees* expands upon or refashions the biblical narrative in line with the special interests and concerns of the community he represents. We provide several examples to illustrate the point.

The creation account (*Jub.* 2:1-33) provides some fascinating additions. The author tells us that there were seven great works created on the first day (*Jub.* 2:2-4). What Genesis does not tell us our author does, namely, that all the angelic beings were also created on the first day. These beings are classified in accordance with their area of responsibility or supervision, just as we saw in *1 Enoch* 72—82, the Astronomical Book.

Jubilees calls attention to the fact that there were a total of twenty-two different kinds that God created in the six creative days. This tallies if one starts with seven things created on day one. The number twenty-two happily correlates with the twenty-two patriarchs from Adam to Jacob (*Jub.* 2:23). It is worth noting in this regard that there are also twenty-two letters in the Hebrew alphabet, a point made by Josephus when he discusses the creation narrative.

Not surprisingly, the seventh day receives extended treatment. Here we have halakic (from Heb *hᵃlākâ,* the Jewish oral laws explaining the laws of the OT) material more rigorous in its prohibitions than that which gained currency in later Mishnaic literature (*Jub.* 2:29-33).[18] This is relevant for identifying the circles from which the author emanated.

Because Enoch is important among the patriarchal figures revered by *Jubilees,* the biblical passage mentioning him is greatly augmented (*Jub.* 4:16-26). This expansion shows its indebtedness to the traditions we have already read in *1 Enoch* and provides another link with the Qumran community, about whom we will say more in chapters six and seven.

The most revealing of the expansions in *Jubilees* are those passages where Abraham already observes the rituals of the law of Moses. This is clearly an important point for our author. He adds this notice after narrating Abraham's death: "For Abraham was perfect in all his dealings with the Lord and gained favour by his righteousness throughout his life" (*Jub.* 23:10).

Several expansions reflect negatively upon the character of Esau. This seems to be a thinly veiled expression of the hostility and hatred of Jews toward the Idumeans (the biblical Edomites, descendants of Esau according to

---

[18]See chapter thirteen for further discussion of the Mishnah.

Genesis), who had slowly infiltrated into Judean territory during the centuries following the Babylonian captivity. As we will see in our reading of 1 Maccabees, this hostility expressed itself in bloody conflicts between these two related peoples throughout the Second Temple period. The book of Obadiah in the Bible already provides some historical background for this bitter enmity.

The author of *Jubilees* describes Esau as "ruthless" (*Jub.* 19:14). Furthermore, in the account of Jacob's purchase of Esau's birthright, our author adds, "And thus Jacob became the elder, and Esau was demoted" (*Jub.* 24:7). Jacob is portrayed as telling his mother, Rebecca, that Esau had been pressuring him for twenty-two years to marry one of the sisters of his wives (*Jub.* 25:8).

An especially interesting addition to the biblical story is Rebecca's blessing upon Jacob (*Jub.* 15:13-14). Perhaps we already see here the development of the tradition whereby Jewishness is traced to the mother rather than the father. Note that the author of *Jubilees* puts in Rebecca's mouth this statement: "[the Lord] has given me Jacob as a pure son and a holy offspring" (*Jub.* 25:12). Later she complains to Isaac about Esau: "for you know Esau's disposition, how savage he has been from his youth up, and there is nothing good about him, and he is only waiting for your death to kill Jacob. . . . He deliberately left us and has done us evil: he has appropriated your flocks and stripped you of all your possessions" (*Jub.* 35:9-10). On the other hand, Jacob is "your perfect and upright son; for in Jacob there is nothing evil, but only what is good" (*Jub.* 35:12).

At this point even Isaac agrees with Rebecca's assessment and delivers the ultimate malediction: "neither he [Esau] nor his descendants will be saved, for they are destined to perish from the earth and be uprooted from under heaven" (*Jub.* 35:14). The notion of predestination to everlasting destruction should be filed away in memory and recalled when we read about the Qumran community in chapters six and seven. Here is another striking similarity between *Jubilees* and the sectarian literature from Qumran.

This rewriting of the Jacob-Esau story hits its apogee in the narration of a war of Esau and his sons against Jacob and his sons in which Jacob kills Esau with his sword (*Jub.* 37–38). Of course, Genesis narrates no such war. But a comparison with 1 Maccabees makes it likely that we have a reflex of the Hasmonean conflicts with these ancient foes and the surrounding neighbors (cf. *Jub.* 37:6, where Aram, Philistia, Moab and Ammon are also mentioned). Clearly Jewish animosity toward the Idumeans has colored the retelling of the familiar biblical story.

The reworking of the episode at Shechem, when Simeon and Levi massacred the inhabitants, is especially startling. The author inserts this moral dictum into the account: "And let no Israelite girl ever be defiled in this way again; for judgement was ordained in heaven against them—that all the

Shechemites should perish by the sword, because they had committed an outrage in Israel" (*Jub.* 30:4-5). This is followed by an eternal commandment that no Israelite should permit his daughter or son to marry a Gentile (*Jub.* 30:13). Finally, the author blatantly changes the moral standpoint from which the biblical story was told. "And on the day when Jacob's sons killed Shechem, it was recorded in their favour in heaven that they had executed righteousness and justice and vengeance on the sinners; and it was written as a blessing" (*Jub.* 30:23).

Some scholars think that this episode reflects the destruction of Shechem by the Hasmonean Hyrcanus. In effect, the author is justifying a savage military operation against the Samaritans. Of course, the correctness of this supposition rests upon the dating of the document. Hyrcanus did not destroy Shechem until 128 B.C. Clearly one would have to abandon a "high date" of 168 B.C. for such a correlation. We are not sure if the internal evidence is strong enough to consider this likely. What the passage does demonstrate is a strong aversion to the Samaritans and a clear demarcation between Jews and Gentiles in terms of sexual relations and ritual purity.

This refashioning has led some scholars to suggest that we have an early example of midrash, a form of biblical paraphrase that later appears in the rabbinic exegetical tradition (ca. A.D. 200-600). But an even earlier biblical parallel is the work of the so-called Chronicler (i.e., 1-2 Chronicles and possibly Ezra-Nehemiah). Scholars have long noticed how the Chronicler used Samuel-Kings as his primary source, which was rewritten from his own particular viewpoint and interests. The additions and deletions observed in comparing the "primary history" with the Chronicler's version afford some instructive parallels in the way the author of *Jubilees* has rewritten the well-known biblical stories in Genesis 1—Exodus 19.[19]

Purpose

Judging from the disproportionate amount of space devoted to the patriarchs, we conclude that they figure prominently in the overall purposes of the author. Indeed, it would appear that a primary concern was to establish the fact that the patriarchs already observed the law of Moses. This no doubt reflects the conviction of the author and his circle that the interpretation of the law considered "orthodox" stemmed from the great lawgiver himself and, furthermore, that this interpretation even went back to the founding fathers of Israel. Indeed, the Torah, according to our author, is eternal and immutable. Thus when the angel of the presence dictated to Moses the law and commandments, these were the selfsame law and commandments that had

---

[19]See further on this Ralph W. Klein, "Chronicles, Book of 1-2," *ABD* 1:993-98.

already been inscribed on heavenly tablets, observed and faithfully handed down by the patriarch Enoch. As was the case with Ben Sira, so also our author views the Torah as eternal. Of course, the particular interpretations of the Torah espoused by the author are also included in the notion of Torah.

The upshot of such a view is to define rather sharply who the "true" Israel really is and to enforce a separation from the Gentiles and their "abominations." Clearly, we are overhearing a fierce argument within Judaism itself.[20] It is this observation that is part of the evidence for placing *Jubilees* close in time to the Hellenistic crisis just preceding the Hasmonean revolt.

Another purpose of *Jubilees* must surely be to argue for the eternal validity of the solar calendar over against a lunar one. The calendar followed by our author is based upon twelve months divided into thirty days each. This is intercalated with an extra day at the beginning of every fourth month in order to arrive at a year containing exactly 364 days. With such a calendar, the feasts always fall on the same calendar day each year. Such a scheme is very important to our author and reminds one of the same insistence in *1 Enoch* 72–82 and, as we shall see, the Qumran sectaries.

The work begins with a prologue in which the author sets out the organizing principle for the ensuing narration: the year-weeks and their Jubilees. Thus God's creation of the world in one week provides the fundamental unit for all time reckoning. Events are placed in their proper sequence of year-weeks and Jubilees, the latter being a unit of forty-nine years.[21] Thus beginning with creation and proceeding through Exodus 19, each event is placed in its proper time frame.

Features of the Book

In the prologue there is an interesting section that speaks of the future hopes of our author. This follows a passage in which the exile of Israel is "predicted" because Israel has forgotten the law and commandments:

> And after this they will turn to me from among the Gentiles with all their heart and with all their soul and with all their strength: and I will gather them from among all the Gentiles, and they will seek me, and I will let them find me. And when they seek me with all their heart and with all their soul, I will grant them an age of peace and righteousness and set them apart as an upright plant, with all my heart and with all my soul: and they shall be a blessing and not a curse, the head and not the tail. And I will build my sanctuary in their midst, and I will

---

[20]See further Sparks, *AOT,* pp. 2-3; Ladd, "Apocalyptic Literature," 1:157; Wintermute, *OTP* 2:37-38.

[21]The Jubilee was originally a special time of liberation and redemption of property every fiftieth year (cf. Lev 25:10-12). Our author adapts it to serve as a time period of forty-nine years. See Sparks, *AOT,* p. 4.

dwell with them and be their God, and they shall be my people in truth and righteousness. And I will not forsake them nor fail them; for I am the Lord their God. (*Jub.* 1:15-18)

Several things that we have previously read reappear: the importance of law-keeping for Israel's restoration; the rebuilding of a temple; and the national prominence of end-time Israel.[22] These constitute common ground for most Jews of the period. The differences between various groups centered on the specifics of *how* the laws were to be interpreted and *how* the temple rituals should be observed and implemented. In chapters six and seven we will delve more into the differences that emerged. Here we simply call attention to the core items that most Jews subscribed to.

Notice that our author incorporates themes and phrases from Deuteronomy, Jeremiah and Ezekiel into his prophecy of future restoration. Especially noteworthy is the notion of a circumcision of the heart and a holy spirit created within repentant Israel (*Jub.* 1:23-24; cf. Rom 2:25-29; 8:1-27).

The angelology of *Jubilees* reflects the same conceptual framework as *1 Enoch* 72–82. The different categories of angelic beings perform specific supervisory functions over the various terrestrial and extraterrestrial realms. The same interest in natural phenomena as found in *1 Enoch* 72–82 surfaces in *Jubilees* 2:1-15. These phenomena, however, are explained from a religious perspective.

As indicated in our introductory remarks, an especially intriguing section in *Jubilees* 23 can be labeled "apocalyptic." Following the death of Abraham, the author incorporates an angelic revelation to Moses surveying the course of the age up to and including a golden age at the end of human history. But this prophecy has the earmarks of being *vaticinium ex eventu* ("prophecy or prediction made after the event"); that is, it narrates history under the guise of prediction. Let us see if we can unravel this revelation.

The death of Abraham (*Jub.* 23:8-10), who is extolled for his perfection and righteousness, provides the beginning point for the unveiling of the future. After Abraham's death, the human life span is limited to two Jubilees maximum, though for most, seventy years is all that can be expected. This shortening of the life span is attributed to an increase in wickedness and a lessening of the perfect observance of the law exemplified by Abraham. In a passage reminiscent of the Olivet Discourse by Jesus (cf. Mt 24; Mk 13; Lk 21), the author of *Jubilees* sketches out the downward spiral of the unfolding age:

For calamity follows on calamity, and wound on wound, and tribulation on tribulation, and bad news on bad news, and illness on illness, and all such painful punishments as these, one after another—illness, and disaster, and snow, and

---

[22]See above, chapter two, especially Tobit.

frost, and ice, and fever, and chills, and torpor, and famine, and death, and sword, and captivity, and all kinds of calamities and pains. And all these will come on an evil generation that transgresses on the earth and practices unclean-ness and fornication and pollution and abominations. (*Jub.* 23:13-15)

But, in spite of this bleak prospect, we next read of "sons [who will] convict their fathers and their elders of sin and unrighteousness" (*Jub.* 23:16). Could this be an oblique reference to the religious community represented by the book of *Jubilees?* We think that it is and that, in the mind of the author, his movement would spearhead a reformation marked, of course, by the proper observance of the Torah. Note, however, that the message of the "sons" is not widely accepted: "And they will quarrel with one another . . . because of the law and the covenant" (*Jub.* 23:19). The disagreement is intense. One is inclined to see here the clash between the Hasideans and the enthusiastic Hellenistic reformers, especially the priestly families and agents such as Jason and Menelaus.

Dissension erupts into violence: "And some among them will take their stand with bows and swords and other weapons of war to restore their kins-men to the accustomed path; but they will not return until much blood has been shed on the earth on either side" (*Jub.* 23:20). This certainly correlates well with the Hasmonean revolt led by the sons of Mattathias, the priest of Modein. However, it seems to me that the author is not a great admirer of the Hasmonean dynasty by what he next narrates (all under the guise of an angelic revelation). Those who had begun to do righteousness failed. The description of their regime is telling:

And those who have escaped will not return from their wickedness to the path of righteousness; but they will all attempt to enrich themselves by dishonest means and filch all they can from their neighbours, and they will call them-selves by the great name, but not in truth and not in righteousness, and they will defile the holy of holies with their uncleanness and the corruption of their pollution. (*Jub.* 23:21)

As we will see in the next two chapters, this sounds very similar to the strong objections that the Essenes lodged against the Hasmonean priest-kings.

At any rate, this corruption of the priestly leadership brings on, in good Deuteronomic fashion, the retribution of God by means of the Gentiles (*Jub.* 23:23). The question here is whether this punishment should be viewed as that endured under Antiochus IV Epiphanes or as the battles of the Maccabee brothers and their heirs against the various Seleucid armies and the neighbor-ing kingdoms such as the Idumeans, Philistines, Ammonites and Samaritans. What should not be missed, however, is the author's insistence that this will be a time of unprecedented suffering and affliction (*Jub.* 23:24-25). We seem to have a description of the end times.

This period of great tribulation gives way, however, to a golden age of peace and renewal. The transition occurs when "the children begin to study the laws, and seek the commandments" (*Jub.* 23:26). Note that we do not have a form of holy war waged by the faithful against the wicked but instead a peaceful transition ushered in by spiritual renewal. This differs markedly from the *War Scroll* that we shall read about at Qumran. The attitude of our author appears to be one of pacifism rather than militaristic activism.

The new age is marked by longevity of life until the life spans "approach a thousand" (*Jub.* 23:27). R. H. Charles thought this passage was the earliest reference (in post-OT Jewish literature) to a temporary messianic kingdom. I tend to agree with him, though many modern scholars do not.[23] Certainly our author has drawn upon the pictures of the New Jerusalem found in Isaiah 65–66. However, *Jubilees* adds the explicit notice—not found in the Isaiah passages—that "there will be no Satan" (*Jub.* 23:29), an idea also found in the NT book of Revelation (Rev 20:10).

The new age of righteousness climaxes with a description of the righteous enjoying their blessedness all the while viewing the punishments of the wicked. Then we read that "their bones shall rest in the earth, and their spirits shall have much joy" (*Jub.* 23:31), a verse that has prompted much discussion. At face value, it would seem that the author believed in the immortality of the souls of the righteous, but not the doctrine of bodily resurrection, so important to the stance of the Pharisees who came into existence at about this period of time.[24] On the other hand, this text does not rule out completely a doctrine of bodily resurrection. There is now some evidence that the Essenes did indeed hold to bodily resurrection.[25] Perhaps our author is simply giving emphasis to the great spiritual joy of the righteous. We leave this as an open question.

One last question: Did this community believe in a Messiah from Judah? Charles held that they did, based upon the blessing given to Judah (*Jub.* 31:18-20).[26] I agree with him and would compare that to the Dead Sea Scrolls, where

---

[23]See Charles, *APOT* 2:9. For a careful study of the relevant passages in *Jubilees* and a negative verdict on the temporal kingdom idea, see Larry J. Kreitzer, *Jesus and God in Paul's Eschatology,* JSNTSup 19 (Sheffield: JSOT Press, 1987), pp. 37-41.

[24]Charles says: "In our text all hope of a resurrection of the body is abandoned. The souls of the righteous will enjoy a blessed immortality after death (XXIII.31). This is the earliest attested instance of this expectation in the last two centuries B.C." (*APOT* 2:9-10).

[25]See James C. VanderKam, *The Dead Sea Scrolls Today* (Grand Rapids, Mich.: Eerdmans, 1997), pp. 78-81. The specific text is 4Q521. This point will be discussed further in chapters six and seven.

[26]Charles, *APOT* 2:61.

we have the doctrine of two messiahs, one from the house of David and the other, more important, messiah from the tribe of Levi.[27] Though Davidic messianism plays little role in *Jubilees,* it likely was a part of the author's convictions.

Relationship to the New Testament

R. H. Charles considered *Jubilees* of great importance for understanding the background of the NT.[28] The most important contribution, according to Charles, centered on the focal point of this chapter, namely, apocalyptic. In his words, "apocalyptic . . . was the source of the higher theology of Judaism, and subsequently was the parent of Christianity."[29] We shall elaborate on this claim further. Before we do that, however, there is another contribution this work makes to our understanding of NT literature.

In the first place, we inquire whether we have anything similar in NT literature in terms of genre. Do we have examples of a creative rewriting of OT narratives or the oral traditions about Jesus? This is a difficult issue and must be approached carefully, since it touches upon the relationship of faith and history.

At the outset we may safely say that none of the NT genres, in broad terms, set out to retell the familiar OT stories. We have in our NT canon four examples of the genre Gospel, one of a highly selective history of the Christian movement (Acts), nineteen letters, two theological treatises or written sermons (Hebrews; 1 John) and one good example of a Christian apocalypse. But in no case do we have a sustained retelling of OT narrative passages.

While this is highly controversial within evangelical circles, a case has been made that we do have examples of Christian midrashic interpretation within the larger genres of NT literature. In particular, it has been impressively argued that the Gospels incorporate midrashic techniques.[30]

Let us first provide a little background. A common assumption in the scholarly study of the Gospels is that Mark is the earliest Gospel and that Matthew and Luke used Mark as one of their sources. This is called the Markan Priority and Two-Document Hypothesis.[31] Accepting this hypothesis for

---

[27]Not all scholars agree that there was an expectation of two messiahs at Qumran. We will discuss this in more detail in chapters six and seven. For arguments and evidence that they did, see VanderKam, *Dead Sea Scrolls Today,* pp. 117-18, 177-80; and C. A. Evans, "Messianism," *DNTB,* pp. 701-3.

[28]*APOT* 2:1.

[29]Ibid. See also Käsemann's assessment in "On the Subject of Primitive Christian Apocalyptic," pp. 108-37.

[30]See Craig Evans, "Midrash," *DJG,* pp. 544-48 and the extensive bibliography. Cf. also Robert H. Gundry, *Matthew: A Commentary on His Literary and Theological Art* (Grand Rapids, Mich.: Eerdmans, 1982), pp. 627-33.

[31]For description and arguments in favor and against this hypothesis, see R. H. Stein, "Synoptic Problem," *DJG,* pp. 784-92.

the sake of argument, one may then compare Matthew and Luke against Mark for additions, deletions and reinterpretations, much the same as we did with *Jubilees*. This discipline, called redaction criticism, leads to some interesting observations.

Why is it, for example, that Matthew begins his Gospel with a genealogy that is artificially constructed so that each section has exactly fourteen names? That it is artificial (i.e., there are deliberate omissions) is easily verified by comparing it with 1 Chronicles 1—4. We have already noted the importance of the seven-year schema for the author of *Jubilees*. Thus we have the weeks (a period of seven years) making up the larger units of Jubilee periods (forty-nine years). Daniel spoke of seventy sevens (i.e., 490 years) as the time frame for the consummation of God's kingdom. Is Matthew implying something similar by the arrangement of his genealogy into multiples of seven?

Or could the explanation be rooted in Matthew's concern to demonstrate that Jesus is truly the great Son of David? The connection is that David's name in Hebrew totals fourteen when one adds up the value of the letters (4 [d] + 6 [w] + 4 [d] = 14). The Hebrew text during this time was written without vowels, so only consonants are taken into account. Thus the genealogy is an example of Jewish gematria, a number game in which each letter is assigned a numerical value. We know that later Jewish midrashim (homiletical commentaries on the Bible) feature gematria. Probably it was already practiced during the NT era. Remember how already in *Jubilees* the author fastened upon the significance of twenty-two in the creation account. For audiences familiar with such exegetical procedures in homilies, this would have appeal.[32]

Matthew's infancy narrative gives evidence of several midrashic techniques, especially his handling of OT citations, the so-called formula quotations.[33] But some commentators extend Matthew's midrashic approach to the actual narrative portions of the Gospel itself. Robert Gundry raised eyebrows in evangelical circles when he argued that Matthew did in fact embellish the traditions about Jesus in his Gospel. In a meticulous comparison of Mat-

---

[32]Donald A. Hagner does not think there is an intentional connection between the numerical value of David's name in Hebrew and the obvious grouping of the genealogy into three segments of fourteen names each. He notes that "the Book of Matthew, it should be remembered, is written in Greek, and the numerology of the Hebrew name would not at all be evident to Greek readers without explanation. That David's name in Hebrew is equal to fourteen may well be only a coincidence; it can hardly be determinative in a Greek text" (*Matthew 1—13*, WBC 33A [Dallas: Word, 1993], p. 7). But we think Gundry has a good point when he observes: "Readers limited to Greek may not have caught the point, but Matthew himself probably intended it and might well have expected Jewish addressees to understand. Otherwise the correspondence between the repetitious genealogical fourteen and David's name seems too unlikely" (Gundry, *Matthew*, p. 19).

[33]For examples, see Evans, "Midrash," p. 546.

thew's use of Mark and isolation of typical Matthean diction, he argued that Matthew does occasionally introduce nonhistorical details and incidents in his retelling of the story of Jesus.[34] Needless to say, this has generated an ongoing debate in conservative circles.[35]

Let us consider a few examples. First of all, only Matthew tells us about the visit of the mysterious magi. How do these Eastern astrologers figure in the story? The answer may lie in Matthew's stress on the mission to the Gentiles. Already his genealogy begins with Abraham (Mt 1:1-2), to whom the promise had been given: "in you all the families of the earth shall be blessed" (Gen 12:3b). In light of Matthew's emphasis upon the gospel reaching out to the Gentiles (cf. Mt 8:11-12; 13:37-38; 21:41, 43; 24:14; 25:32-33), he may have deliberately foreshadowed the Great Commission in 28:19-20 by narrating the visit of the magi.

Why is it that Matthew twice says there were two individuals (cf. Mt 8:28 with Mk 5:1-20; Lk 8:26-39; and Mt 20:29-34 with Mk 10:46-52; Lk 18:35-43) or, in one instance, two animals (cf. Mt 21:6-7 with Mk 11:7) involved in an episode, whereas Mark and Luke only have one? Attempts to harmonize the accounts (there were really two, but Mark and Luke chose to mention only one) seem forced.

Perhaps a better explanation lies in an OT requirement for criminal cases: "A single witness shall not suffice to convict a person of any crime or wrongdoing in connection with any offense that may be committed. Only on the evidence of two or three witnesses shall a charge be sustained" (Deut 19:15).[36] Given the highly polemical purpose of Matthew vis-à-vis the unbelieving Jewish community, one wonders if the consistent "doubling" is an aspect of Matthew's brief against the synagogue. Thus Matthew's point may be that Jesus' claims are not based upon solitary witnesses, but multiple witnesses. This may not seem very convincing to modern readers, but it had its own compelling logic for those who were reared in a Jewish environment and who took with utmost seriousness the sacred texts.

Another instance of a unique Matthean addition is the account of Peter walking on the water (Mt 14:28-33; cf. Mk 6:45-52; Jn 6:15-21). Gundry does not call in question the historicity of Jesus' miracles in general, nor is he averse to the supernatural.[37] For him it is a literary question: this Matthean

---

[34]See Gundry, *Matthew*, especially pp. 623-31.

[35]For a brief critique of Gundry's position, see Hagner, *Matthew 1—13*, pp. lvii-lix.

[36]In this regard note that Matthew has Jesus appeal to this very text when disputes arise in the future church (Mt 18:15-17). Paul also appealed to this same text as a requirement for bringing accusations against elders in his churches (1 Tim 5:19).

[37]See B. L. Blackburn, "Miracles and Miracle Stories," *DJG*, pp. 549-60, for a discussion of the historicity of Jesus' miracles. Curiously, he omits discussion of this particular miracle!

insertion has the earmarks of an ad hoc pastoral admonition designed to encourage believers to keep their eyes on Jesus in the midst of the storms of life. By itself, this would hardly be enough to deny its historicity. When, however, one considers the episode in light of Matthew's overall literary techniques, questions do arise, especially given Mark's silence on this point. Mark has traditionally been viewed as dependent upon Peter for his basic material, and one wonders why Mark would have omitted to tell such a dramatic episode in the life of his mentor. This is especially puzzling because Mark's narrative of Peter's denial of Jesus at the trial does figure prominently in his Gospel.[38] In other words, Mark is not reluctant to use Peter as a negative example. We confess that we are in the realm of conjecture and lack hard evidence to settle the matter one way or the other. As is often the case, one's prior understanding of what is entailed in the doctrine of the inspiration of Scripture is the determining factor in how one handles such texts.

Virtually all scholars agree that each Evangelist selects and shapes the Jesus traditions in accord with his particular purpose and focus. The more controversial question is whether we also find episodes or events that are not, strictly speaking, historical. Some evangelical scholars think so and regard such instances as reflections of Jewish midrash such as we see in *Jubilees*. One thing is certain: this will continue to be a hotly debated topic.

We do have a passage in the NT that covers in survey fashion a large block of biblical narrative. This is in the so-called hall of faith in Hebrews 11. What is fascinating here is the uncontested fact that the biblical author, in commenting briefly on the lives of OT worthies, adds material not found in the OT text itself. This is very close to the procedure witnessed in *Jubilees*.

For example, it is no surprise that the book of Hebrews, probably written by a Jewish Christian to Jewish Christians, like *Jubiliees* also highlights Abraham's importance in salvation history.[39] Note that in Hebrews 11:10 the author imputes to Abraham a view that could be inferred from the narrative in Genesis but is nowhere explicitly stated as it is here: "For he looked forward to the city that has foundations, whose architect and builder is God." Thus Abraham becomes a prime example of the kind of faith (cf. Heb 11:1) that the author of Hebrews was seeking to instill in his readers.

Another example from the life of Abraham is the offering up of Isaac (Heb 11:17-19). The author provides an explanation for Abraham's ability to reconcile God's command to sacrifice Isaac with his prior promises: "He considered

---

[38]One could, of course, argue that it simply did not fit Mark's purpose or that modesty prompted Peter to urge its omission. See Gundry, *Matthew,* pp. 299-300, for further discussion of this point.
[39]See William Lane, *Hebrews 9–13,* WBC 47B (Dallas: Word, 1991).

the fact that God is able even to raise someone from the dead—and figuratively speaking, he did receive him back" (Heb 11:19). Once again, this may well be a legitimate inference one might draw from the Genesis text. The point is that the author of Hebrews, by this interpretive addition, makes such an inference explicit.

The retelling of the Moses story also contains a significant interpretive addition. In light of the pastoral purpose of the author to warn his readers against apostasy, he makes explicit why Moses decided to cast his lot with his own people: "[He chose] rather to share ill-treatment with the people of God than to enjoy the fleeting pleasures of sin. He considered abuse suffered for the Christ to be greater wealth than the treasures of Egypt, for he was looking ahead to the reward" (Heb 11:25-26). The explanation reflects a clear Christian reading of the OT text with a special eye to the pastoral problem as our author perceived it.

An even clearer parallel to *Jubilees* occurs in Hebrews 12:16-17. Here Esau is characterized as an "immoral and godless person, who sold his birthright for a single meal. You know that later, when he wanted to inherit the blessing, he was rejected, for he found no chance to repent, even though he sought the blessing with tears." Since this description of Esau as an "immoral and godless person" is not explicit in Genesis, it is hard to resist the conclusion that the author shared the same Jewish interpretive tradition as *Jubilees* that casts Esau in a negative light (*Jub.* 19:13-15; 25:1-2, 8-10). We emphasize that this view of Esau's character is an inference one might come to in reading the Genesis stories, but not a necessary one. One could, in fact, argue for a much more positive assessment of Esau as to his final disposition than that found in either *Jubilees* or Hebrews.

We give one more example of an NT expansion of an OT text. This is especially fascinating because it proceeds in an entirely different direction from *Jubilees*. In 2 Peter 2:7-8, Lot functions as a paradigm for how God rescues the righteous. But in retelling the story of Lot's rescue, 2 Peter presents Lot in a much more favorable light than either Genesis 18—19 or *Jubilees*: "for that righteous man, living among them day after day, was tormented in his righteous soul by their lawless deeds that he saw and heard" (2 Pet 2:8; cf. Jub 16:7-9). While this is a possible inference from Genesis, we should recognize it as an interpretive addition and not an explicit statement of the OT text.

Just like their Jewish counterparts, NT writers occasionally engaged in creative retellings of OT narratives. Intertextuality—the influence by, reuse of and adaptation of earlier sacred texts—is an important dimension in the task of interpreting the NT. Though midrash may not be the most accurate word for this kind of creative retelling of the OT occurring here and there in the NT, it does usefully serve our purposes to describe the process of contemporizing sacred texts.

Preachers have for years done much the same in their sermons. A perusal of popular commentaries and sermons by leading preachers would quickly produce some fascinating examples of interpretive expansions and additions to the biblical text, a fair number of which one might dispute on grammatical-historical grounds![40] Nonetheless, the believing community is edified and no essential teaching of the church is denied. Within reasonable limits, such creative retellings of the biblical text can have positive benefits.

We return to Charles's observation about the importance of apocalyptic for Christianity. Although most of *Jubilees* is a narrative, it is cast in the framework of an angelic revelation to Moses on Mount Sinai. The one NT document adopting a similar framework is the Apocalypse, or Revelation. The book of Revelation unfolds within the framework of an unveiling of Jesus and his coming kingdom given to John by means of visionary experience and angelic messengers. As such, it represents a much more developed form of an apocalypse, more akin to *1 Enoch,* portions of which we have already read, and even more closely the works of *4 Ezra* and *2 Baruch,* which we shall take up later. Still, there are many specific points of commonality shared between Revelation and *Jubilees.*[41]

Only *Jubilees* 23, however, exhibits the eschatological dimension of apocalyptic in which we have the future unveiled under the guise of prophecy. Comparable to this section, one notes Jesus' well-known Olivet Discourse recorded in three narrative works: Matthew, Mark and Luke (Mt 24; Mk 13; Lk 21). We cannot enter into a detailed commentary on this discourse here but must content ourselves with several general observations on the similarities to *Jubilees* 23.

First, the Olivet Discourse, like *Jubilees* 23, is directed toward the faithful and designed to encourage them to persevere in spite of opposition and persecution (Mk 13:5, 9-13, 19-23, 33-37). Second, the Olivet Discourse rapidly surveys the course of the present age, characterized generally as one of wickedness and evil (Mk 13:7-8). Third, the present age climaxes with a time of unprecedented tribulation (Mk 13:14-23). This is a decisive turning point when God intervenes to bring about the consummation of human history (Mk 13:24-26). Fourth, the righteous play a key role in proclaiming the truth (characterized as either "the covenant," "the laws," "the commandments" or "the path of righteousness" in *Jubilees*, the "good news of the kingdom" in the Synoptic Gospels) during these turbulent end times (Mk 13:9-13). This proclamation results in fierce opposition and persecution. Fifth, the righteous are

---

[40]For fascinating examples from an evangelical author who denies the validity of midrashic exegesis (!), see Robert Gundry, *Matthew,* p. 631.
[41]See Charles, *APOT* 2:8-10.

gathered into the presence of the Lord and rewarded for their faithfulness (Mk 13:27-37). In light of the fact that *Jubilees* was written over 150 years before the Synoptic Gospels, this much similarity is not a mere accident. Clearly the Olivet Discourse is at home in a Jewish milieu and preserves some common expectations that many Jews, including the earliest Christians, would have embraced concerning the end times.

There are, to be sure, significant differences between *Jubilees* 23 and the Olivet Discourse, not least of which is the christological orientation of the latter. *Jubilees* 23 contains no reference to a messianic figure at all, and, even though the author of *Jubilees* probably believed in a messiah from Judah (cf. *Jub.* 31:18-20 and above discussion), salvation was not accomplished by his atoning death and resurrection.

Jubilees confirms our earlier conclusion that the earliest Christians did not devise a new eschatological schema. They adhered to the same one they inherited as Jews, albeit with a radically new focal point: God had acted in Jesus Christ to achieve the fulfillment of the promises of final redemption for Israel and the nations. This was the "good news."

We have already drawn attention to parallels in regard to angelology and demonology between the NT and Tobit, *1 Enoch* 72—82 and the Additions to Daniel. Similar parallels exist between *Jubilees* and the NT.[42] One should note especially the three NT passages that mention angels at Mount Sinai mediating the giving of the law (Acts 7:38; Gal 3:19; Heb 2:2). This, of course, is repeatedly referred to in *Jubilees*. Although R. H. Charles held that Paul, Luke, James, Hebrews and 2 Peter were aware of and influenced by *Jubilees*, this probably overstates the case.[43] Rather, we see instances where the common Jewish milieu of *Jubilees* and the NT shines through.

In conclusion, *Jubilees* represents an important stage in the development of Second Temple Judaism. A crucial aspect of this development centered on the interpretation of the inherited traditions. This was the wellspring from which courage and hope could be summoned to face the uncertainties of the future and the cruel persecution of foes. The biblical texts were contemporized and brought to bear in the midst of a crisis of the human spirit. Here was found hope for hard times.

With the demise of the prophetic office, a new agent arose to provide the needed guidance and encouragement: the learned scribe and interpreter of

---

[42]For further discussion of this point, see ibid., p. 10; and Wintermute, *OTP* 2:47.

[43]For his evidence and argumentation, see his *The Book of Jubilees or the Little Genesis* (London: Adam & Charles Black, 1902), pp. lxxxiii-lxxxv. VanderKam, however, is probably more accurate when he observes: "There is no clear evidence that NT writers were aware of the book of *Jubilees*, but some passages could be illumined from the information contained in it" ("Jubilees," p. 602).

Scripture. From these humble beginnings a long succession of biblical interpreters arose. Interpretation of the sacred Scriptures has occupied countless
hours of devoted study by Jewish and, later, Christian scholars down through
the ages—with no prospect of a moratorium in sight! If this process was
already in evidence by the time of the Chronicler c. 400 B.C., then *Jubilees*
brings us closer to NT times by some 250 years. At the very least, an acquaintance with the approach displayed in *Jubilees* throws light on the NT use of
the OT and the Jesus traditions. In chapter seven we will further discuss this
process of retelling and reinterpreting sacred Scripture when we examine the
famous writings from Qumran.

1 Enoch 83—90

Introduction

We return once again to the Enoch literature, this time taking up Book Four,
the so-called Book of Dream Visions (*1 En.* 83—90). Since we have already
discussed the overall structure of the present text of *1 Enoch,* we proceed
immediately to the section.

This text provides another example of the apocalyptic genre. One can easily discern the similarities in concepts and phraseology between *1 Enoch* 83—
90 and *Jubilees* 23, and Daniel 10—12. As we shall see shortly, it also has clear
affinities to the *Testament of Moses.*

Structure of the Section

Two "dream visions" make up *1 Enoch* 83—90. The first vision covers chapters
83—84. Enoch's grandfather Malalel arouses him from his troubled sleep
because the terrifying nature of the vision causes Enoch to cry out. Enoch
then recounts the content of his dream to his grandfather and then to his son
Methuselah. Essentially the vision concerns the coming destruction of the
world by the great flood of Noah (cf. Gen 6—8). The cause of this worldwide
judgment is attributed to heaven being cast down upon the earth (*1 En.* 83:3),
that is, the fall of the angels (cf. *1 En.* 84:4). This is in harmony with *1 Enoch*
6—11, as we have already seen.

A second, more extensive vision follows, which surveys the history of the
world up to the final consummation. Once again Enoch conveys his vision to
Methuselah. What is noteworthy is that the vision is in the form of an allegory; that is, the leading figures are portrayed as various kinds of animals.
Nonetheless, if one knows biblical and postbiblical history up to the time of
the Maccabees, the allegory is fairly transparent.

Analysis of Content

1. The vision begins with the story of Adam and Eve, under the figure of a

white bull and a heifer. From them come two bulls: a black one, Cain, and a red one, Abel. The story of Cain's murder of Abel and the subsequent birth of Seth is allegorically depicted (*1 En.* 85).

2. The fall of the angels (Gen 6) unfolds in *1 Enoch* 86, drawing attention to the violence that ensued.

3. Enoch's translation to heaven (cf. Gen 5:24) by the seven archangels (cf. *1 En.* 9:1; 20:1-8) is narrated in *1 Enoch* 87. From this vantage point he witnesses the events that will subsequently unfold.

4. In *1 Enoch* 88 one of the archangels imprisons the ringleader of the fallen angels, along with his co-conspirators, in a dreadful abyss (cf. *1 En.* 6—11; 2 Pet 2:4; Jude 6).

5. A disproportionally long section, *1 Enoch* 89, reviews biblical history from Noah through the postexilic period by means of allegorical representation. Most of the figures are easily identified. The narration of Moses and Aaron receives the most extended treatment, as one would suspect. In addition, a fair amount of stress is placed upon Solomon's temple and its fate. The last identifiable figures of the biblical period are Zerubbabel, Joshua the high priest and Ezra the scribe (*1 En.* 89:72-73).

6. With *1 Enoch* 90 we come to the Antiochian persecution and the Maccabean revolt. The thirty-seven shepherds mentioned in this section are probably to be identified with the succession of high priests during the postexilic era up to the time of the revolt. Another group of seventy shepherds appears to refer to angelic beings that are assigned as guardians for the seventy nations, a traditional number of the total of all Gentile nations based upon Genesis 10. Almost certainly *1 Enoch* 90:9 refers to Judas Maccabeus, the first military leader of the revolt and about whom we shall read much more in our next chapter, while *1 Enoch* 90:16 summarizes the protracted warfare during the Hasmonean revolt and the subsequent wars against surrounding neighbors.

Suddenly the text describes the eschatological consummation (*1 En.* 90:18-39). The Lord himself intervenes in the struggle. The sheep (the righteous remnant of Israel) are divinely enabled to destroy their enemies in battle, an idea also found at Qumran in the *War Scroll* (see chapter seven below). The archangels play a leading role in these eschatological events (*1 En.* 90:21). The Lord takes up his seat on the throne of judgment and the books are opened, which is reminiscent of Daniel 7:9-10. Punishment is meted out first to the rebellious angels who have been incarcerated in the abyss all this time, second to the seventy shepherds who failed to lead Israel in the right paths, and third to all apostate and disobedient Israelites (*1 En.* 90:24-26).

This eschatological section builds to a climax with appearance of a new and glorious temple, no doubt inspired by the prophecies of Ezekiel (cf. Ezek

40−48). The Lord takes up his residence in its midst. Furthermore, and quite in contrast to the end-time scenario of *Jubilees*, the remaining Gentile nations are converted to Israel's faith and join with Israel in worship in the new temple. This happy scene concludes with a transformation of all the faithful, both Jews and Gentiles, into the image of a white bull. Just before this happens, there is mention of a white bull whose horns "were big, and all the wild animals and all the birds of heaven were afraid of it and entreated it continually" (*1 En.* 90:37). This is probably a symbol of the Messiah.

Significance for the New Testament

We have already made several references to passages reminding us of certain NT texts. Overall the most obvious parallel in the NT is the Apocalypse, with it bizarre images and symbols. Once one has worked through texts such as *1 Enoch* 83−90 and *Jubilees* 23, however, the decoding of a text like the Apocalypse becomes less mysterious. To be sure, John's Apocalypse is primarily indebted to the OT for its imagery. But understanding how the images and symbols function in *1 Enoch* 83−90 assists us in several instances. For example, the reference to stars falling to the earth—fallen angels or demons—has more in common with *1 Enoch* 83−90 than with any OT passage. Where the OT makes reference to stars (e.g., Is 13:10; 34:4), the referent is nearly always celestial, not angelic (three, possibly four, exceptions are Num 24:17; Job 38:7; Is 14:12-13; and Judg 5:20), as is the case in Revelation and *1 Enoch* 83−90. Note as well that Enoch is caught up to heaven and describes what happens upon the earth. This same supernal viewpoint is reflected in Revelation, where John is raptured to heaven (cf. Rev 4:1).

One is on much surer ground when Revelation's figures and symbols are interpreted against their OT and Second Temple Jewish background rather than from the latest newspaper or television broadcast! Revelation was written for an audience familiar with apocalyptic traditions and conventions. Our task as modern interpreters is to recover *first* the meaning the text had for its original audience *and then* to inquire into its significance for today. This is a much saner (though admittedly less spectacular) approach than trying to connect the latest super computer or world figure with the various images and symbols.[44]

One also recalls the portrayal of Jesus as a Lamb in John's Apocalypse (cf. Rev 5:1-14; 6:1; 8:1; 13:8; 14:1-5; 15:3; 19:9; 21:9; 21:22−22:1). This is a leading motif in the Apocalypse and links it to the Gospel of John (cf. Jn 1:29). Of course, the archenemy of the church is the fiery red dragon, clearly decoded as Satan, while the dragon's master counterfeit, the beast emerging from the

---

[44]For further help on this, see Joel B. Green, *How to Read Prophecy* (Downers Grove, Ill.: InterVarsity Press, 1984).

abyss, is the great nemesis of the church (cf. Rev 13).

Several features of *1 Enoch* with regard to the eschatological consumma-tion find their Christian counterpart in Revelation. In the first place, both works anticipate a New Jerusalem at the end. There is, of course, an impor-tant difference in Revelation in that there is no temple in the New Jerusalem, since God himself and the Lamb dwell with the redeemed. Second, in *1 Enoch* the new age, like Revelation 21–22, is a reversion back to the primordial par-adise of Genesis 2. Third, we suggested above that *1 Enoch* 90 portrays the ultimate end of the redeemed in terms of a transformation into the image of the Messiah. If this is so, we have evidence that already in Judaism such an expectation existed. The parallel to Christian eschatological thought with regard to the glorification of the believer is quite surprising (cf. Rom 8:18, 21, 23, 29-30; 2 Cor 3:18; 5:1-5; Phil 3:20-21; Col 3:3-4; Heb 2:10; 1 Jn 3:2; Jude 23). Finally, the Book of Dreams, so typical of apocalyptic writing, ends with a statement affirming the certainty of all that has been predicted: "everything will come to pass and be fulfilled" (*1 En.* 90:41). One is reminded of the book of Revelation with its concluding affirmations: "These words are trustworthy and true" (Rev 22:6; cf. 21:5).

Several more parallels in phraseology and concept merit mention. Only Paul among the NT writers, and that only one time (1 Cor 2:8), refers to Jesus Christ as "the Lord of glory." Compare this to *1 Enoch* 83:8, where God is so designated. I am also struck by the description of the consummation, when "all the wild animals and the birds of heaven gather together in that house . . . and all the sheep were enclosed in that house" (*1 En.* 90:33-34). This is remi-niscent of Jesus' words: "I have other sheep that do not belong to this fold. I must bring them also, and they will listen to my voice. So there will be one flock, one shepherd" (Jn 10:16). Both texts envision the ingathering of Gentiles into the final kingdom. In short, we clearly have a common background in the eschatological thought of the NT and a work such as *1 Enoch* 83–90.

Testament of Moses (Assumption of Moses)

Introduction

The *Testament of Moses*, like *Jubilees,* retells a familiar biblical narrative, in this case Deuteronomy 31–34. Included in this section of Deuteronomy are the last words of Moses. This is the inspiration for the present work. Our unknown author composes his work by enduing it with the aura of a testa-mentary document—stemming from no less than the great lawgiver of Israel himself. Thus the authority of Moses has been appropriated to validate these "last words."

There is a problem of identification, however. Gelasius of Cyzicus (A.D. 787) quotes from *Testament of Moses* 1:14 and attributes it to a work called the

Assumption of Moses. But other lists of ancient works mention both an "assumption" and a "testament" of Moses. Clearly our work resembles a testament and does not even refer to Moses' assumption. Is this work the *Assumption of Moses,* the *Testament of Moses* or a combination of the foregoing? Scholars have defended all three alternatives, with a majority today following Charles, who argued for the third view.[45] We hold this issue open, but for our present discussion we use the designation *Assumption of Moses (As. Mos.)* as found in Sparks's edition of the Pseudepigrapha.[46]

As was the case in *Jubilees* 23 and *1 Enoch* 85—90, the *Assumption of Moses* predicts the future of Israel up to the consummation of history. *Assumption* is also like the other two works in that no use is made of an angelic guide. This absence distinguishes these three works from other apocalyptic writings in which angelic mediation is a prominent feature.

Purpose

Assumption of Moses 1:16-18 brings us to the heart of what the author wished to convey. In this passage, Moses instructs Joshua to study carefully the writing, consisting of secret prophecies that are to be hidden in clay jars until the time of the end. In reality these "prophecies" are intended for the readers who are the "in-group." By means of this unveiling of the future, the faithful are encouraged to endure to the end. The righteous will be rewarded and the wicked punished at the eschatological consummation. It is evident that the author believed the end was quite near, thus the urgency of persevering. As we will shortly argue, the Antiochian persecutions provided the pattern for this time of final tribulation.

Date and Composition

As in the case of identifying the document itself, considerable problems arise in attempting to place it in its proper historical setting. The reason for this is that two great persecutions are narrated. The first seems clearly to describe the oppression of Herod the Great and the bloody intervention of Varus, the Roman governor of Syria, in 4 B.C. (*As. Mos.* 6:1-8).[47] The second, however, almost certainly describes the even earlier persecution of Antiochus Epiph-

---

[45]*APOT* 2:407-9.

[46]For a discussion of the issues, see R. H. Charles, *The Assumption of Moses* (London: Adam & Charles Black, 1897), pp. xlv-li; Charles, *APOT* 2:407-9; J. P. M. Sweet, *AOT,* pp. 601-2; J. Priest, "Testament of Moses," *OTP* 1:924-25; John J. Collins, "Testaments," in *Jewish Writings of the Second Temple Period,* pp. 344-45; Johannes Tromp, *The Assumption of Moses: A Critical Edition with Commentary,* SVTP 10 (Leiden: E. J. Brill, 1993), pp. 115-16; and D. A. deSilva, "Testament of Moses," *DNTB,* pp. 1192-93.

[47]See Sweet, *AOT,* pp. 602-3.

anes (*As. Mos.* 7:1—10:10). It is in connection with this latter persecution, however, that the end comes. The problem, of course, is the reversal of events in history. Herod actually lived over one hundred years after Antiochus Epiphanes! Scholars have variously accounted for this inversion.

Some take the approach that the last-mentioned event provides the surest guide to the time of writing. On this reckoning, *Assumption* was composed sometime after Herod the Great's death (*As. Mos.* 6:7) and before the revolt against Rome in A.D. 66, since the latter is not mentioned and the temple is still standing (cf. *As. Mos.* 8:5). The section dealing with Antiochus Epiphanes is either a later interpolation, or the author deliberately reversed Herod and Antiochus, applying the traditional descriptions of the latter to the eschatological persecutor of the end times.

Others take the opposite tack and argue that the portion describing Herod and his successors is a later interpolation and updating of a work written during the Antiochian persecution.[48] The evidence does not allow for a definitive answer. We incline to the view that the work originated in the first century sometime between A.D. 6 and 30. We include it here at this point in our survey, however, because it utilizes the persecution of Antiochus Epiphanes in its scenario of the end times. We think the author deliberately and knowingly used the figure of Antiochus as an eschatological persecutor. But more of that below.

Outline of Contents
The contents of *Assumption of Moses* can be outlined as follows:
I.   Charge to Joshua to preserve the secret revelation (1:1-18)
II.   From the conquest to the end of the Hebrew kingdoms (2:1-9)
III. Nebuchadnezzar and the captivity of Judah and Benjamin (3:1-14)
IV.   From Daniel to the return under Nehemiah (4:1-9)
V.   The rise of the hellenizers in Judah (5:1-6)
VI.   The Hasmonean dynasty and Herod the Great (6:1-8)
VII. The end-time persecutions (patterned after Antiochus Epiphanies) (7:1—8:5)
VIII. Taxo and his seven sons (9:1-7)
IX.   Hymn celebrating God's righteous intervention (10:1-15)
X.   Joshua's grief and Moses' reassurance (11:1—12:13)

Analysis
Since *Assumption* covers much the same ground as the other apocalyptic portions we have read, we limit our remarks to a few observations. In the first place, much fascination has centered upon the figure of Taxo and his seven

---

[48]So Nickelsburg, *Jewish Literature,* p. 80; Collins, "Testaments," pp. 347-48.

sons. In our next chapter, we shall read in 1 Maccabees 2:29-38 and 2 Maccabees 2:19-28 passages that may have provided the background for Taxo. The first passage recounts the deeds of pious Jews who chose death over desecrating the sabbath by defending themselves. The second passage features Mattathias and his five sons, who lead an armed struggle against the hellenizers. To this, one should add 2 Maccabees 7, which narrates in gruesome detail the martyrdom of a mother and her seven sons. They refused to violate the strictures in the Mosaic law about eating the flesh of swine. Most likely our author has drawn elements from both 1 and 2 Maccabees for his portrait of Taxo and his sons.

But can we actually identify Taxo with a known historical figure? The number of scholarly suggestions as to the identity of Taxo is at least thirty![49] We will not add another. More important than identifying Taxo is trying to account for his function in the storyline. His death seems to prompt the intervention of God and thus the culmination of human history. Are we then to view Taxo's death as somehow atoning? More likely, his death simply triggers the end times. But even so, this is highly significant. The suffering of the righteous will eventually prompt the Lord to intervene and avenge his holy ones. The operative watchword, then, is faithful endurance. Passive resistance is the divinely ordained method for combating the evil of forced violation of the Mosaic law or required assimilation to a Hellenistic life style. "Sanctification of the Name" is meritorious from our author's point of view.[50]

If we are correct in our assessment, this document is making a rather bold counterstatement. It is saying that the approach of the Hasmoneans, to use whatever force is necessary, is wrong, that militarism in the service of faith is wrong. Given the considerable popularity of the Hasmonean dynasty and their legacy in the first century, our document must be seen as emanating from a minority group that strongly dissented from the majority. It is tempting to identify our author with the Essenes, about whom we shall read in the next two chapters, since there was, among that group, a definite pacifistic stance. Furthermore, *Assumption* contains some stiff criticism of the worship practices in the temple (cf. *As. Mos.* 5:1-6), as does the Essene sectarian writings. Still, there are some significant differences in outlook, so one is better advised to exercise caution. What we can more safely assert is that our writ-

---

[49]For a thorough discussion of the various proposals, see Tromp, *Assumption of Moses,* pp. 124-28.

[50]We are here using terminology from later Jewish history to refer to the practice of preferring martyrdom to any violation or denial of the Jewish religion. It was invoked, tragically, many times during the medieval period when Jews were persecuted by their "Christian" neighbors and has most recently been applied to the extermination of Jews during the Holocaust. See Haim Hillel Ben-Sasson, "Kiddush Ha-Shem and Hillul Ha-Shem," *EncJud* 10:977-86.

ing comes from a pietistic group who believed that the Mosaic law should be observed at all costs and that being faithful unto death is preferable to violent defense of one's faith.[51]

Significance for the New Testament

The most obvious relationship of this work to the NT surfaces in the two little epistles of Jude and 2 Peter. Jude 9 refers to a Jewish tradition involving a dispute between Satan and Michael over Moses' body and contains this quote: "The Lord rebuke you!" Many scholars assume that this episode originally belonged to *Assumption* but is now lost. Note that *Assumption* as we now have it does break off in mid-sentence. If Jude is quoting *Assumption,* this is the second instance in which Jude quotes a pseudepigraphical work (cf. Jude 1:14 with *1 En.* 1:9; see chapter three above). Furthermore, the description of false teachers in both 2 Peter and Jude shares several verbal and conceptual parallels with *Assumption of Moses* 7:1-9 (cf. 2 Pet 2:10b-22; Jude 12-13, 16).[52]

Beyond the allusions or quotations, however, is an even more significant and fascinating relationship. This concerns the description of the end times and the employment of Antiochus Epiphanes as a type of the antichrist in early Christian literature.

In Jesus' Olivet Discourse (cf. Mt 24:15-24; Mk 13:14-23), one finds a reuse of material drawn from Daniel 7:8, 19-25; 8:9-14, 23-25; 11:28-45, passages that in their original setting describe the heinous actions of Antiochus Epiphanes in the second century B.C. But in Jesus' eschatological discourse, the referent is now a figure *yet to appear at the end of the age,* traditionally called the antichrist. Thus the things that the antichrist will do during the end times were already foreshadowed by Antiochus Epiphanes. Paul styles the eschatological

---

[51]John J. Collins has a very balanced assessment: "We can say, then, that TM was produced by a sectarian group around the turn of the era. This group was marked by antagonism to Herod and the Hasmoneans and the rejection of the contemporary temple cult. It called for a complete return to the Mosaic Law. Its model of complete observance involved the sharp rejection of militant nationalism, whether in the Hasmonean or Zealot traditions. It shows certain parallels with the Qumran writings. These parallels suggest that the book may have been written by a group of Essenes, or a group close to the ideology of the Essenes. However, in view of the lack of any indication of an organized community, and above all the absence of the document from the finds of Qumran, it is unlikely that TM was written or preserved in the Qumran community" ("The Date and Provenance of the Testament of Moses," in *Studies on the Testament of Moses,* ed. G. W. E. Nickelsburg, SBLSCS 4 [Cambridge, Mass.: Society of Biblical Literature, 1973], p. 32).

[52]This close verbal similarity, however, should be qualified in that one may find rather stereotypical descriptions of opponents in pagan and Jewish sources. Thus the similarity between Jude and 2 Peter on this point may owe more to a common milieu than to literary borrowing. See A. J. Malherbe, *Moral Exhortation: A Greco-Roman Sourcebook,* LEC 4 (Philadelphia: Fortress, 1986), p. 138.

persecutor of God's elect as "the lawless one" (2 Thess 2:1-12). In the Apocalypse, John portrays him as a beast coming up out of the sea (Rev 13). But there can be little doubt that all three passages refer to the selfsame antichrist. To put it another way, Jesus, Paul and John describe the eschatological antichrist in language that had earlier been employed to describe the depredations of Antiochus Epiphanes against the Palestinian Jews of Judea and Jerusalem.

What is intriguing, however, is the possibility that our unknown Jewish author of the *Assumption of Moses* has already made this appropriation. It may be that shortly before the ministry of Jesus there was *already* a projection into the future of an eschatological figure like Antiochus Epiphanes. Antiochus served as a type of the final persecutor of God's people in some circles of first-century Judaism. This expectation was taken up by Jesus and his apostles and became an important fixture of early Christian eschatology. Such a typological-eschatological reading of the Hebrew Scriptures is but another example of the indebtedness of early Christianity to its Jewish roots.

We also draw attention to the issue of violent versus nonviolent resistance to evil and oppression. Does the NT sanction resistance to the "powers that be" when they demand more than a Christian can morally give? If so, what kind of resistance? This has been a point of disagreement in Christian church history, and a full discussion is beyond our scope. What we can point out, however, is that in the one NT document that speaks most explicitly to this issue and that most clearly has apocalyptic characteristics—the Apocalypse of John—we seem to have a stance similar to that of *Assumption of Moses*. The message of Revelation includes a clarion call for an acceptance of martyrdom rather than violent resistance (cf. Rev 13:9-10).

Conclusion

We conclude this chapter with some comments on Charles's observation that apocalyptic thought lies at the heart of Christianity. Whereas only Revelation and a few isolated passages actually incorporate the formal elements of apocalyptic literature, at the level of the "deep structure" of NT thought we have an apocalyptic worldview. In fact, many NT theologians argue that grasping the apocalyptic nature of NT Christianity is the key that unlocks the NT. I agree.

Jesus, Paul and John, to select three leading witnesses, all share a common perspective on the world, a perspective that is best described as apocalyptic. Thus if one returns to our brief survey of the chief features of apocalyptic thought at the beginning of the chapter, several ideas soon emerge as essential for grasping NT thought:

1. This present world is under Satan's influence (cf. Lk 4:1-13; 2 Cor 4:4; Eph 2:2; 1 Jn 5:19).

2. This present world is soon to pass away (Rom 13:11-12; 1 Cor 7:29-31; 1 Jn 2:17).

3. The powers of darkness (hostile angelic or demonic beings) are arrayed against the church (Mt 16:18; Eph 6:12; Rev 12:17; 13:7).

4. There is a lively expectation that the Lord will soon return to destroy the antichrist and his forces and to reward the righteous with everlasting glory (2 Thess 1:1-10; 2:8; Rev 19:11-21).

The world of NT thought unfolds between two great "moments": the irruption of the new age, inaugurated by the incarnation, ministry, death and resurrection of Jesus; and the consummation of the new age at Jesus' return. Scholars speak of this as the "now but not yet" tension of the NT. Such a notion breathes the very atmosphere of apocalyptic. We could list many more aspects to this apocalyptic worldview but suffice by simply referring the reader to reliable guides into this important area.[53]

Finally, several NT documents should be read against the same backdrop that generated the three Jewish works we have read. Believers (whether Jewish or Christian) must be forewarned of the arduous life of discipleship. Christians must realize that the powers of darkness will not relinquish their grip upon this age without a struggle. The great dragon contests every inch of turf (1 Pet 5:8). Indeed, only the intervention of the church's Lord will bring about ultimate victory and vindication. The church engages the powers of darkness and fights the good fight (2 Tim 4:7) with spiritual armor (Eph 6:10-18), not with worldly motives or means (2 Cor 10:3-6). We think that Paul may have viewed himself somewhat like Taxo. That is, in his ministry to the Gentiles, Paul absorbed a disproportionate amount of suffering, which he likened to the birth pangs that must precede the triumphant coming of the Messiah (Col 1:24). Be that as it may, the church is not called to retaliate in kind. Rather, it is called to resist evil, which calls for patient endurance (Rev 13:9-10). No wonder that the Christian canon concludes with the most overtly apocalyptic work it possesses. The intention to instill faithfulness, courage and hope is the same as that writ large on the pages of the three works we have just read:

Do not be afraid. I am the first and the last, and the living one. I was dead, and see, I am alive for ever and ever; and I have the keys of Death and of Hades. (Rev 1:17b-18)
Be faithful until death, and I will give you the crown of life. (Rev 2:10c)
If you are to be taken captive, into captivity you go; if you kill with the sword,

[53]See George E. Ladd, *A Theology of the New Testament,* rev. ed., ed. Donald Hagner (Grand Rapids, Mich.: Eerdmans, 1993), pp. 54-78; Marvin Pate, *The End of the Age Has Come* (Chicago: Moody Press, 1995).

with the sword you must be killed. Here is a call for the endurance and faith of the saints. (Rev 13:10)

Here is a call for the endurance of the saints, those who keep the commandments of God and hold fast to the faith of Jesus. (Rev 14:12)

Blessed and holy are those who share in the first resurrection. Over these the second death has no power, but they will be priests of God and of Christ, and they will reign with him a thousand years. (Rev 20:6)

For Further Discussion

1. How does the book of Revelation conform to and deviate from the conventions of apocalyptic literature?

2. What features of Jesus' message make it apocalyptic?

3. Why does the author of *Jubilees* expand upon and refashion biblical narratives?

4. Does the NT anywhere utilize a midrashic approach to the OT or the Jesus tradition?

5. What are the implications if one acknowledges that NT authors expanded or embellished OT narratives?

6. Compare and contrast *1 Enoch* 83—90 with the book of Revelation.

7. Compare and contrast the portrayal of Taxo and his sons with that of Jesus in the NT.

8. How does Christian eschatology draw upon its Jewish predecessors?

For Further Reading

D. E. Aune, "Apocalypticism," *DPL*, pp. 25-30.

D. E. Aune, T. J. Geddert and C. A. Evans, "Apocalypticism," *DNTB*, pp. 45-58.

R. H. Charles, "The Assumption of Moses," in *The Apocrypha and Pseudepigrapha of the Old Testament,* ed. R. H. Charles, 2 vols. (Oxford: Clarendon Press, 1913), 2:407-24.

————, "1 Enoch," in *The Apocrypha and Pseudepigrapha of the Old Testament,* ed. R. H. Charles, 2 vols. (Oxford: Clarendon Press, 1913), 2:163-281.

————, "Jubilees," in *The Apocrypha and Pseudepigrapha of the Old Testament,* ed. R. H. Charles, 2 vols. (Oxford: Clarendon Press, 1913), 2:1-82.

J. J. Collins, "Enoch, Books of," *DNTB*, p. 315.

D. A. deSilva, "Testament of Moses," *DNTB*, pp. 1192-99.

E. Isaac, "1 (Ethiopic Apocalypse of) Enoch," in *The Old Testament Pseudepigrapha,* ed. J. H. Charlesworth, 2 vols. (Garden City, N.Y.: Doubleday, 1983), 1:3-12, 61-72.

M. A. Knibb, "1 Enoch," in *The Apocryphal Old Testament,* ed. H. F. D. Sparks (Oxford: Clarendon Press, 1985), pp. 169-83, 274-91.

L. J. Kreitzer, "Apocalyptic, Apocalypticism," *DLNTD*, pp. 55-68.

George W. E. Nickelsburg, "The Bible Rewritten and Expanded," in *Jewish Writings of the Second Temple Period: Apocrypha, Pseudepigrapha, Qumran Sectarian Writings, Philo, Josephus,* ed. Michael E. Stone, CRINT 2 (Assen: Van Gorcum; Philadelphia: Fortress, 1984), pp. 94, 97-104 (*1 En.* 83–84; *Jubilees*).

————, "The Book of Jubilees," "The Testament of Moses," and "1 Enoch 83—90," in *Jewish Literature Between the Bible and the Mishnah: A Historical and Literary Introduction* (Philadelphia: Fortress, 1981), pp. 73-83, 90-95.

J. Priest, "Testament of Moses," in *The Old Testament Pseudepigrapha,* ed. J. H. Charlesworth, 2 vols. (Garden City, N.Y.: Doubleday, 1983), 1:919-35.

C. Rabin, "Jubilees," in *The Apocryphal Old Testament,* ed. H. F. D. Sparks (Oxford: Clarendon Press, 1985), pp. 1-139.

Michael E. Stone, "Apocalyptic Literature," in *Jewish Writings of the Second Temple Period: Apocrypha, Pseudepigrapha, Qumran Sectarian Writings, Philo, Josephus,* ed. Michael E. Stone, CRINT 2 (Assen: Van Gorcum; Philadelphia: Fortress, 1984), pp. 419-20 (*Assumption of Moses*).

J. P. M. Sweet, "The Assumption of Moses," in *The Apocryphal Old Testament,* ed. H. F. D. Sparks (Oxford: Clarendon Press, 1985), pp. 601-16.

James C. VanderKam, "The Book of Jubilees," in *Outside the Old Testament,* ed. M. De Jonge, CCWJCW (New York: Cambridge University Press, 1985).

————, *The Book of Jubilees,* Guides to Apocrypha and Pseudepigrapha (Sheffield: Sheffield Academic Press, 2001).

————, *An Introduction to Early Judaism* (Grand Rapids, Mich.: Eerdmans, 2001), pp. 97-100.

————, "Jubilees," *DNTB,* pp. 600-603.

————, "Jubilees, Book of," *ABD* 3:1030-32.

O. Wintermute, "Jubilees," in *The Old Testament Pseudepigrapha,* ed. J. H. Charlesworth, 2 vols. (Garden City, N.Y.: Doubleday, 1983), 2:35-142.

Five

Resistance Literature

*F*or the English text of 1 and 2 Maccabees, Judith and Baruch, see The New
Oxford Annotated Bible: New Revised Standard Version, *ed. Bruce M. Metzger
and Roland E. Murphy (New York: Oxford University Press, 1991), AP 186-258,
20-40, and 161-68, respectively. One may also consult* The Catholic Study Bible,
*ed. Donald Senior (New York: Oxford University Press, 1990), pp. 550-610, 520-36,
1025-33; and* The Oxford Study Bible: Revised English Bible with the Apocrypha, *ed. M. Jack Suggs, Katharine Doob Sakenfeld, and James R. Mueller (New
York: Oxford University Press, 1992), pp. 1197-1257, 1071-1186, 1177-83. One may
also use the third edition of* New Oxford Annotated Bible, *pp. 32-52, 201-78, 176-
83 Apocrypha; or the* HarperCollins Study Bible: New Revised Standard Version, with the Apocryphal/Deuterocanonical Books, *ed. Wayne A. Meeks et
al. (New York: HarperCollins, 1993), pp. 1459-80, 1645-1722, 1617-26.*

Introduction

Four works engage our interest in this chapter. Each shares a common conviction: Jews must resist all efforts to abandon their ancestral faith or assimilate to a Hellenistic lifestyle. Better by far a martyr's death than deny "the
Name." This strikes the same note we heard in the previous chapter dealing
with apocalyptic literature. The only difference is the literary genre through
which the message is conveyed. Three of our works adopt the more familiar

narrative format, two being ostensibly historical (1 and 2 Maccabees) and a third, fictive (Judith). Baruch, odd man out, embodies a liturgical and confessional style to make the same point.

This chapter involves some of the most interesting and spine-tingling literature we will read. For example, 1 Maccabees, long valued as an essential historical source for the background of the NT, exudes a spirit of nationalistic pride and fervor. It narrates the story of a successful national liberation movement. If you enjoy war stories, 1 Maccabees will not disappoint.

On the other hand, 2 Maccabees breathes an entirely different atmosphere from that of 1 Maccabees. Appealing to the emotions and invoking the miraculous, this work is famous for its gory recounting of the martyrdom of a Jewish mother and her seven sons. It marks the emergence of martyrology as a distinctive literary genre, a genre that would become a long-standing favorite in Christendom. Even now it makes periodic comebacks in the Christian community, underscoring the fact that suffering for one's faith is, unfortunately, never obsolete.

The story of Judith is a literary masterpiece. But beyond its literary merits, this tale of feminine treachery on behalf of religious commitment continues to raise troubling ethical issues. What, after all, is justifiable in defending the faith?

Baruch shares with the foregoing works a steadfast commitment to the Torah. If you enjoy poetry and appreciate word pictures that express the deep yearnings of the heart, Baruch will afford a rewarding experience.

This chapter provides the earliest documentary evidence for the fragmenting of Judaism into the various sects that later vied for prominence and power during the NT era. We begin to see the lineaments of the "three philosophies" Josephus (first century A.D.) described: the Pharisees, the Sadducees and the Essenes. In order for the NT to come into sharper focus, it must be seen through the lens of the literature that we are about to read.

1 Maccabees

Introduction

One finds in 1 Maccabees a historical account of a very turbulent era in the history of the Jewish people.[1] The narrative begins with a brief reprise of the conquests and death of Alexander the Great, then moves quickly to the accession of Antiochus Epiphanes in 175 B.C. and continues down to the death of Simon, the last of the five sons of Mattathias in 134 B.C. This family

---

[1]"No harsher trial ever tested the monotheistic faith of the Jews" (Jonathan A. Goldenstein, *1 Maccabees*, AB 41 [Garden City, N.Y.: Doubleday, 1976], p. 3).

became known as the Maccabees. The term *Maccabee* may have meant something like "the hammer" or "mallet head," a descriptive epithet for the violent blows of this family against the Seleucid dynasty. They were also known as the Hasmoneans.[2] Under the leadership of this family, the Jewish people achieved a period of national independence that lasted until 63 B.C. The narration of these stirring events is straightforward and generally quite trustworthy.[3]

Purpose

One purpose of this historical narrative becomes evident in 1 Maccabees 2. Here we are introduced to the family that will determine the destiny of the Jewish people in this hour of crisis. With a zeal like Phinehas of old, Mattathias stands up to defend the law of Moses (cf. 1 Macc 2:24-26 with Num 25:6-13). Clearly the author of this work is a great admirer of the Hasmonean family and holds almost messianic hopes for its future. This same spirit is conveyed in 1 Maccabees 13:33-53, with its impressively marshaled evidence for the benefactions of Simon's reign. Throughout the narrative of 1 Maccabees one notes the reuse of OT themes such as the holy war of the era of the conquest and the judges. Thus the Maccabee brothers display the charismatic leadership of those venerated heroes of old. The messianic dimensions of Simon's reign shine forth in 1 Maccabees 14:4-15, a hymnic section resonating with the fulfillment of biblical prophecies of the messianic era. By the time we reach 1 Maccabees 16:23-24, our author has made the following points: royal decree, popular acclaim, divine attestation and an alliance with Rome, the emerging superpower of the Mediterranean, all legitimated the Hasmonean dynasty. We should, then, label 1 Maccabees as a tendentious writing, that is, a work written to promote a cause. In short, 1 Maccabees seeks to defend the legitimacy of the Hasmonean high-priestly dynasty.

Going beyond this, however, the author portrays the Jewish people as God's elect, holy congregation. Over against this understanding of the Jewish people stand the hellenizers—both within and without the nation. They are wicked foes whose designs must be resisted with all forces available. Thus the overarching purpose of 1 Maccabees is to remind Jews of their divine destiny: to be a separate and holy people who observe the laws of Moses. As *The New*

---

[2]For a discussion of the various etymological explanations for the meaning of *Maccabee,* see Robert H. Pfeiffer, *History of New Testament Times with an Introduction to the Apocrypha* (New York: Harper, 1949), pp. 461-62.

[3]See the introductory comments in *The New Oxford Annotated Bible: New Revised Standard Version,* ed. Bruce M. Metzger and Roland E. Murphy (New York: Oxford University Press, 1991), AP 186.

Oxford Annotated Bible states in its introduction to 1 Maccabees: "The complex problem of cultural assimilation pervades the book."[4]

Date and Composition

As indicated above, the work itself ends with a covenant of friendship between the Jewish nation and Rome. There is no hint that this relationship would turn sour. Therefore, the composition is almost certainly earlier than 63 B.C., when Pompey entered Jerusalem and effectively ended nearly eighty years of Jewish independence. Since the last named Hasmonean monarch, John Hyrcanus I, reigned from 134 to 104 B.C., we have our range of possible dates: 104-63 B.C.

Based upon the internal evidence of the work itself, it seems that we can make the following judgments about our anonymous, Palestinian author. First, he probably wrote sometime during the reign of Alexander Janneus (103-76 B.C.) with a view to answering critics of the Hasmonean dynasty, namely Pharisees and Essenes. Second, he composed his work in Hebrew and displays a good local knowledge of Palestine. Third, he had a high regard for the Mosaic law and the temple cult. Fourth, the author advocated that extenuating circumstances require a relaxing of sabbath observance and that violent resistance in the name of religious freedom may be necessary. In this regard, our author strikes a quite different stance from that we saw in *Assumption of Moses*. Because our author scrupulously avoids using the divine name, some writers have suggested that he was a Pharisee.[5] On the other hand, since there is no mention of angels or a hope in bodily resurrection, some suggest that he was a Sadducee.[6] Other scholars are more cautious and hold their options open. Metzger's conclusion is the safest course: "It may well be, however, that the author of I Maccabees was neither a Pharisee or a Sadducee."[7]

---

[4]*New Oxford Annotated Bible*, AP 186. J. Julius Scott Jr. has a helpful section on this problem: "At the heart of the anti-Hellenistic reaction were strong views of Israel's election by God and her consequent relation to him and other peoples. Many exponents of the traditional Semitic-Hebraic culture adopted an outlook we may call particularism. In this setting 'particularism' means the belief not only that the Jews alone were God's chosen people, but also that this status necessarily required a specific way of life. Any deviation from it was viewed as dangerous to Israel's relationship with God and to the nation and race as a whole. Deviation could lower barriers and lead to a syncretistic amalgamation of Judaism into an amorphous mass which would leave it indistinguishable from other religions" (*Customs and Controversies: Intertestamental Jewish Backgrounds of the New Testament* [Grand Rapids, Mich.: Baker, 1995], p. 118).

[5]Bruce M. Metzger, *An Introduction to the Apocrypha* (New York: Oxford University Press, 1957), p. 131.

[6]Ibid.

[7]Ibid.

Structure

The entire work, which we will take as a unity, falls generally into three main divisions.[8] These divisions are in chronological order, in keeping with the intention of the original author.

I. Introduction to the crisis (1:1-64)

    A. Alexander the Great and his successors (1:1-9; 331-175 B.C.)

    B. Accession and anti-Judaic activities of Antiochus Epiphanes (1:10-64; 175-167 B.C.)

II. Introduction to the hero and his family (2:1-70; 167 B.C.)

    A. Mattathias and his five sons mourn over the situation (2:1-14)

    B. Mattathias violently resists the Seleucid decree (2:15-28)

    C. Mattathias and his sons attract followers and adopt guerilla warfare (2:29-48)

    D. Mattathias dies and passes on the mantle of leadership to Judas and Simon (2:49-70)

III. Exploits and achievements of the Hasmonean dynasty (3:1—18:24; 166-104 B.C.)

    A. Judas: struggle for religious freedom. Judas leads the revolt, liberates the temple, but eventually loses his life in battle against the forces of Demetrius I, who was seeking to install Alcimus, one of the hellenizers, as high priest (3:1—9:22; 166-160 B.C.)

    B. Jonathan: struggle for political freedom. Jonathan continues the armed struggle, drives the Syrians from the country, becomes high priest, takes various sides in the politics of the empire and finally perishes as a captive (9:23—12:53; 160-142 B.C.)

    C. Simon: independence recognized by the Syrians and the high priesthood conferred upon the Hasmonean dynasty in perpetuity. Simon proclaimed both ethnarch and high priest by acclamation of the Jewish people but falls prey to an assassin's sword (13:1—16:17; 142-135 B.C.)

    D. John Hyrcanus: epilogue (16:18—18:24; 134-104 B.C.)

Three observations should be made about the above outline. (1) The introduction of the family that eventually wrought national deliverance (1 Maccabees 2) is of utmost important and functions as the turning point of the narrative—much like the appearance of Taxo and his sons in *Assumption of Moses*. (2) Nearly 40 percent of the actual narrative is devoted to the brief career of Judas, the son who succeeded Mattathias. Clearly, the author

---

[8]Most scholars conclude that 1 Maccabees is a unity. See Harold W. Attridge, "Jewish Historiography," in *Early Judaism and Its Modern Interpreters,* ed. Robert A. Kraft and George W. E. Nickelsburg (Philadelphia: Fortress; Atlanta: Scholars Press, 1986), p. 317. For the view that the last two chapters were added later in ca. A.D. 70, see Solomon Zeitlin, *The First Book of Maccabees,* JAL (New York: Harper, 1950), pp. 27-33.

accords to Judas a leading role in the revolt. (3) The author frames the exploits of Judas and Simon with two poems that celebrate their heroic achievements (1 Macc 3:3-9; 14:4-15).

Content and Characteristics

What immediately strikes the reader of 1 Maccabees is the focus upon military exploits. The book is filled with vivid descriptions of violent engagements between the greatly outnumbered Maccabean forces and the larger, better-equipped Syrian (Seleucid) armies and their mercenaries. One also senses the brutality of this protracted war. Judas and his men assassinated even Jews who sympathized with the hellenizers; no middle ground was tolerated in the struggle. Initially and out of necessity, Judas and his forces adopted hit-and-run tactics. The Maccabee brothers possessed excellent leadership qualities and military savvy. Employing tactics such as surprise attacks, night marches, feints and, above all, wise selection of the battlefield, they inflicted heavy loses on the numerically superior Seleucid forces.[9] The Jewish nationalists did not, however, escape without severe setbacks (cf. 1 Macc 9:17). In succession, Eleazar, Judas, Jonathan and Simon either fell in battle or were treacherously murdered. The narrative concludes with John Hyrcanus, Simon's son, as king and high priest—the only one to die peacefully! Could Jesus have had the Maccabees in mind when he told Peter, "Put your sword back into its place; for all who take the sword will perish by the sword" (Mt 26:52; cf. Jn 18:11)?

From 167 to 142 B.C., with only intermittent lulls, the struggle of the Jewish freedom fighters continued. Finally the Syrians, exhausted from the struggle and preoccupied elsewhere, recognized the political independence of a Jewish state under Simon the Maccabee. This momentous event receives considerable attention in 1 Maccabees as a grateful nation conferred both the political and spiritual leadership upon Simon. He was acclaimed and accorded the high priesthood with the privilege of hereditary succession. This is clearly the climax to which the book had been aiming, and it underscores the purpose of the author indicated above. There were other military engagements after this, but essentially the Jews had realized their dreams of an independent Jewish state. Initially, most Jews viewed the state as a guardian and champion of the ancestral faith. Political autonomy would last until the fateful intervention of Rome in 63 B.C.

---

[9]See Yohanan Aharoni and Michael Avi-Yonah, *The Macmillan Bible Atlas*, 3d ed. (New York: Macmillan, 1993), pp. 142-55. Lester Grabbe, on the other hand, holds that too much has been made of the David-and-Goliath character of the conflict. He says, "this is part of the myth created by the book" ("1 and 2 Maccabees," *DNTB*, p. 658).

The replacement of the Zadokite priesthood by the Hasmonean princes, however, became a bone of contention for years afterward, as we shall see in the next two chapters of our study. In fact, the Pharisaic, Sadducean and Essene movements, which generated years of bitter, sectarian strife among the Jewish people during the Second Temple period, probably go back to this fateful decision. At any rate, all three movements ultimately traced their beginnings to the stouthearted Hasideans who rallied around Judas Maccabeus.

What should not be lost in all this is the significance of Antiochus Epiphanes' religious persecution, the first of its kind, so far as we know from ancient history. Unfortunately, it would not be the last for the Jewish people, nor have they alone experienced such travail. History is replete with the sad recounting of religious persecution. As we enter the turn of a new millennium, ethnic-religious strife is a continuing scourge. Thus, 1 Maccabees raises in an acute form an important question for Christians and other religions: Is violent resistance an option? We will take this up further on in our study.

Importance for the New Testament
In terms of genre, one NT book approximates 1 Maccabees, namely, the book of Acts. Both works are ostensibly historical in nature and reflect a decided bias. Luke, a companion and great admirer of the apostle Paul, wrote Acts.[10] Scholars have long noted the apologetic purposes of Luke in portraying Paul as an apostle of no less standing than the original Twelve, even if not belonging to this select circle (cf. Acts 1:15-26).[11]

This also explains why, in the last panel or segment of the book (Acts 19:21—28:31), Luke narrates three separate trials and three other occasions when Paul defends his behavior and gospel (Acts 22:1-22; 22:30—23:10; 24:1-22; 25:1-12; 25:23—26:32; 28:17-28). In no instance was Paul guilty of any real crimes or offenses against the Jewish people, their law or their temple (Acts 23:9, 29; 24:12-14, 20; 25:8, 10; 28:17-18). Jewish hostility centered over conflicting views about the function of the Mosaic law and the definition of the true Israel. For Paul, "the law was our disciplinarian until Christ came, so that we might be justified by faith. But now that faith has come, we are no longer subject to a disciplinarian, for in Christ Jesus you are all children of God through faith" (Gal 3:24-26), "the Israel of God" (Gal 6:16). For Paul the "you are all" included Gentiles who had not converted to Judaism and did not observe at least minimal requirements of the Torah (Gal 5:2-6). A corollary to this was that the temple cult no longer held the place it had in most forms of

---

[10]For discussion, see F. F. Bruce, "Acts of the Apostles," *ISBE* 1:35.
[11]For discussion of this point, see Glenn W. Barker, William L. Lane and J. Ramsey Michaels, *The New Testament Speaks* (New York: Harper & Row, 1964), pp. 304-5.

Judaism. For Paul, believers in Christ Jesus were being built "into a holy temple in the Lord" and were the new "dwelling place of God in the Spirit" (Eph 2:21-22, pers. trans.). No doubt Paul shared with other Christian leaders such as Peter and the authors of Hebrews and Revelation the idea that the church is a holy priesthood that offers spiritual sacrifices (cf. Rom 12:1; 15:16; Phil 2:17; 4:18; Heb 13:15; 1 Pet 2:4-9; Rev 1:6; 5:10; 20:6). Such views inevitably sparked confrontation and controversy with Pharisaic and Sadducean Judaism.[12]

Most emphatically, Paul was innocent of any crime against Rome or Roman law (Acts 23:29; 25:18-20, 25; 26:31-32). Clearly, Luke wished to allay any misgivings Roman readers such as Theophilus might have entertained about either the man or his message. Paul's imprisonments and sufferings were a consequence of his being an apostle to the Gentiles, not because he was a subversive or revolutionary. Thus both 1 Maccabees and Acts share an apologetic thrust and manifest a concern to answer criticisms of the principal figures in the narrative. Just as the Hasmonean dynasty was held up for adulation, so Luke unabashedly touts the accomplishments of Paul, the great "apostle to the Gentiles."

The author of 1 Maccabees obviously made use of official documents in compiling his stirring narrative. Several excerpts are sprinkled throughout.[13] The same is true of Acts (cf. Acts 15:23-29; 23:25-30). In addition, 1 Maccabees is punctuated by impassioned speeches by both heroes and villains. One wonders whether these were freely invented by the author or are reliable summaries. Scholarship is divided on the issue. We think a good case can be made that the author, while indulging in some rhetorical flourish and imagination, conveyed what was essentially said on the occasions in question. In this connection, the book of Acts provides a comparable parallel in the NT.[14]

The fervent nationalism so evident in 1 Maccabees must be assumed as part of the background for Jesus' ministry as recorded in the Gospels. We recall our earlier discussion of Tobit along these lines (see chapter two above). One of Jesus' disciples, Simon, is identified as a Zealot (Lk 6:15). The Zealots were a political movement advocating violent overthrow of Roman

---

[12]The Essenes would have been vehemently opposed to Paul's gospel as well, but because they were a separatist sect (as we will see in the next two chapters), they had little or no contact with the early Christian movement.

[13]For an extensive discussion of the hypothetical sources, see Jonathan A. Goldstein, *1 Maccabees,* AB 41 (Garden City, N.Y.: Doubleday, 1976), pp. 37-54, 90-103; for an evaluation of Goldstein's views, see Attridge, "Jewish Historiography," pp. 317-18.

[14]On the question of the historicity of the speeches in Acts, see Joel B. Green, "Acts of the Apostles," *DLNTD,* pp. 10-12; Conrad Gempf, "Public Speaking and Published Accounts," in *The Book of Acts in Its Ancient Literary Setting,* ed. Bruce W. Winter, BAFCS (Grand Rapids, Mich.: Eerdmans, 1993), pp. 259-303; Bruce W. Winter, "Official Proceedings and the Forensic Speeches in Acts 24—26," in *Book of Acts in Its Ancient Literary Setting,* pp. 305-36.

occupation of the Holy Land. The nationalist sentiments of this party found fertile soil especially among the Galileans. The exploits of the Maccabees continued to fire the nationalistic aspirations of many Jews during Jesus' ministry. This helps us appreciate how radically different Jesus' agenda was and how difficult it must have been for some of Jesus' followers to grasp the nature of the kingdom of God that he taught.[15]

Along these same lines, Jesus' teaching struck a quite different note with regard to the manner in which Jews should view non-Jews. As is well known, Jews and Samaritans had a strained and, at times, violent relationship. Yet remarkably, Jesus is recorded as having ministered to Samaritans, even offering them a portion in the kingdom of God (Lk 17:11-19; Jn 4:39-42). Who can forget the memorable parable in which the hero turned out to be a despised Samaritan (Lk 10:29-37)? Furthermore, the Gospels intimate that the kingdom of God is intended for believing Gentiles as well (cf. Mt 13:38; 25:32; 28:19; Lk 2:32; Jn 10:16).

By contrast, 1 Maccabees reflects a process of entrenchment in which Jews tended to insulate themselves from the Gentile world. The author presents Jews as righteous and pure in their motives and intentions; Gentiles are the source of Jewish problems and afflictions.[16] The apostle Paul does not harbor such a one-sided view in Romans: "Therefore you have no excuse, whoever you are, when you judge others; for in passing judgment on another you condemn yourself, because you, the judge, are doing the very same things. . . . For, as it is written, 'The name of God is blasphemed among the Gentiles because of you [i.e., Jews]' " (Rom 2:1, 24). In the final analysis, says Paul, one must realize "that all, both Jews and Greeks, are under the power of sin" and that "all have sinned and fall short of the glory of God" (Rom 3:9, 23). This leaves no room for religious one-upmanship.

We call attention to several conceptual parallels between 1 Maccabees and other NT literature. In 1 Maccabees 2:52 the author inserts into Mattathias's last words to his sons the following rhetorical question: "Was not Abraham found faithful when tested, and it was reckoned to him as righteousness?" This is precisely the point made in James:

> Do you want to be shown, you senseless person, that faith apart from works is barren? Was not our ancestor Abraham justified by works when he offered his son Isaac on the altar? You see that faith was active along with his works, and faith was brought to completion by the works. Thus the scripture was fulfilled that says, "Abraham believed God, and it was reckoned to him as righteousness," and he was called the friend of God. (Jas 2:20-23)

---

[15]See W. H. Brownlee, "Maccabees, Books of," *IDB* 3:206.
[16]Pfeiffer, *History of New Testament Times,* p. 495.

The book of James displays a strong Jewish Christian coloring and may have been responding to an antinomian distortion of Paul's stance with regard to the issue of faith and works (cf. Rom 3:8; 4:1-25; 6:1-2, 15).

Jonathan's letter to the king of the Spartans includes a sentiment that the apostle Paul shared with regard to the sacred Scriptures of Israel: "Therefore, though we have no need of these things [alliances and treaties], since we have as encouragement the holy books that are in our hands, we have undertaken to send to renew our family ties" (1 Macc 12:9-10). Paul likewise reminds his Christian readers in Rome: "For whatever was written in former days was written for our instruction, so that by steadfastness and by the encouragement of the scriptures we might have hope" (Rom 15:4).

An interesting episode is narrated concerning the renegade priest Alcimus. He set about to break down the balustrade that separated Gentiles from the sacred precincts of the Jerusalem temple (1 Macc 9:54). Of course, his motive was to encourage assimilation to a Greek way of life and to break down the barriers that prevented full social intercourse. In this endeavor he was unsuccessful, and our author obviously viewed his death as divine punishment for his insolent disobedience. In Ephesians 2:14 Paul also argues for the abolition of the barrier separating Jew from Gentile. Paul is doubtless referring to the many ritual requirements of the Mosaic law that separated Jews from Gentiles (dietary laws, ritual purity, festivals, circumcision, etc.), but he also is probably alluding to the most tangible outward sign of this separation, namely, the balustrade at the Jerusalem temple. His motive was not, like that of Alcimus, to encourage assimilation to Gentile behavior (cf. Eph 2:1-3; 4:17-24) but rather to exhort his readers to live in accord with an entirely new religious reality: a new creation in Christ in which Jew and Gentile equally share as fellow members.

We also call attention to the eulogy on behalf of Judas Maccabeus. Adopting the style of 1 Kings, our author makes reference to many other deeds that could have been commented upon but were not: "Now the rest of the acts of Judas, and his wars and the brave deeds that he did, and his greatness, have not been recorded, but they were very many" (1 Macc 9:22). Note the similar way in which John's Gospel concludes its account of Jesus' ministry: "Now Jesus did many other signs in the presence of his disciples, which are not written in this book. . . . But there are also many other things that Jesus did; if every one of them were written down, I suppose that the world itself could not contain the books that would be written" (Jn 20:30; 21:25).

Finally, one of the highlights of 1 Maccabees is the rededication of the temple after Judas had won a resounding victory over the army of Lysias (1 Macc 4:26-61). The dedication service reads as follows:

Early in the morning on the twenty-fifth day of the ninth month, which is the month of Chislev, in the one hundred forty-eighth year, they rose and offered sacrifice, as the law directs, on the new altar of burnt offering that they had built. At the very season and on the very day that the Gentiles had profaned it, it was dedicated with songs and harps and lutes and cymbals. All the people fell on their faces and worshiped and blessed Heaven, who had prospered them. So they celebrated the dedication of the altar for eight days, and joyfully offered burnt offerings; they offered a sacrifice of well-being and a thanksgiving offering. They decorated the front of the temple with golden crowns and small shields; they restored the gates and the chambers for the priests, and fitted them with doors. There was very great joy among the people, and the disgrace brought by the Gentiles was removed.

Then Judas and his brothers and all the assembly of Israel determined that every year at that season the days of dedication of the altar should be observed with joy and gladness for eight days, beginning with the twenty-fifth day of the month of Chislev. (1 Macc 4:52-59)

The Gospel of John records a visit to Jerusalem by Jesus during this festival called Hanukkah (Jn 10:22-23). A special feature included the lighting of a special nine-branched candelabrum. The tradition continues to this day. Jewish families light a candle on each successive day of the festival, until all eight shine brightly (the ninth or middle branch is used to light the other eight). According to a legend in the Babylonian Talmud:

When the Temple was rededicated it was discovered that all the oil for the lamp in the Sanctuary had been desecrated by the invaders. After a diligent search, however, a single cruse of undefiled oil sealed by the High Priest was found. In it was oil enough for the lamp to burn but a single day. Then a miracle was wrought for the Maccabees; the oil was multiplied so that it proved to be sufficient to burn for eight days. (*b. Šabb.* 23b)

This festival stirred patriotic feelings among the Jewish people then, and it continues to do so today. The exploits of the Maccabees were rehearsed and hopes for the coming Messiah renewed. It is no surprise that in John's Gospel, on the occasion of Hanukkah (Jn 10:22), the religious authorities huddled around Jesus asked him a very apropos question. "How long will you keep us in suspense? If you are the Messiah, tell us plainly" (Jn 10:24). His answer, according to John's Gospel, was unequivocal (Jn 10:25), but they did not believe him (Jn 10:31). He simply did not fit the expectations created by the Maccabean legacy.

2 Maccabees

Introduction

Contrary to what one might at first surmise, 2 Maccabees is not a sequel to

1 Maccabees, as is the case with canonical 1 and 2 Samuel, 1 and 2 Kings, and 1 and 2 Chronicles. Though 2 Maccabees covers some of the same ground as 1 Maccabees, on closer inspection one discovers that its scope is considerably more restricted. In fact, it begins about five years earlier (c. 180 B.C.) but covers only approximately twenty years down to 160 B.C. Thus, while paralleling the content of 1 Maccabees 1–7, 2 Maccabees is not a reprise; on the contrary, it displays a quite different perspective on those stirring events.

Many readers may well prefer 2 Maccabees. Why? The narrator can weave a good story. Most scholars describe 2 Maccabees as "pathetic" history. By this they mean that the author deliberately crafts the narrative to affect the reader emotionally. Our anonymous author seeks to arouse pity and sympathy for the courageous Hasideans who rose up against the program of hellenization and remained steadfast in the face of the most barbarous torture (the Greek word *pathos* means "passion, suffering"). One could justifiably label this work a romantic melodrama.[17] To this end the author resorts to a number of rhetorical techniques. On the one hand, he milks the last drop of horror and compassion out of the story of the martyrdom of a mother and her seven sons; on the other, he narrates the demise of Antiochus Epiphanes, the archenemy, with a slapstick humor worthy of the Three Stooges.

Outline

One can outline 2 Maccabees in several ways, as indicated below.

I. Two letters from Jews in Jerusalem to the Egyptian Jewish community concerning the new festival of Hanukkah (1:1–2:18)

II. The preface to the epitome (2:19-32)

III. The epitome, or summary, of Jason's history (3:1–15:36)

  A. A threat to the temple during the high priesthood of Onias III is thwarted by a supernatural manifestation (3:1–4:6)

  B. The Hellenistic "reforms" (4:7-50)

  C. The desecration of the temple by Antiochus IV Epiphanes, here pictured as a response to a revolt against the Hellenistic reforms rather than, as in 1 Maccabees, an effort to impose a state religion on the Jews (5:1-27)

  D. Tales of martyrdom (6:1–7:42; cf. 4 Macc 6–12; *As. Mos.* 9; Wis 2:12–5:23)

  E. Judas defeats Nicanor's first invasion (8:1-36)

  F. Antiochus is struck down by God and repents upon his deathbed, leading to purification and rededication of the temple by Judas (9:1–10:9)

---

[17]This is Nickelsburg's descriptive title in *Jewish Literature,* p. 118.

    G. Judas defeats Timothy and Lysias under Antiochus V Eupator (10:10–11:38)
    H. Judas defends Jews in Palestine (12:1-45)
    I. Judas rebuffs an effort by Antiochus V to reinstall Menelaus, high priest during the Hellenistic reforms (13:1-26)
    J. Judas defeats and kills Nicanor (who has undertaken a second campaign) following a vision of the martyred Onias III, the pious high priest, in which Judas receives a sword to defeat his adversaries (14:1–15:36)
IV. The epitomist's conclusion (15:37-39)[18]

We append the following outline, adapted from Nickelsburg, because it reflects his opinion that the book is patterned after the Deuteronomistic view of sacred history as seen in *Jubilees* and *Assumption of Moses.*[19]

I.   Two prefixed letters (1:1-9; 1:10–2:18)
II.   The epitomizer's prologue 2:19-32)
III. The history (3:1–15:36)
    A. Blessing: Jerusalem during the priesthood of Onias (3:1-40)
    B. Sin: hellenization of Jerusalem under Jason and Menelaus (4:1–5:10)
    C. Punishment: Antiochus's reprisals (5:11–6:17)
    D. Turning point: deaths of martyrs and prayers of the people (6:18–8:4)
    E. Judgment and salvation: the victories of Judas (8:5–15:36)
IV. The epitomizer's epilogue (15:37-39)

Content
The author of this work does not claim to be an original historian, candidly admitting that he has abridged the work of one Jason of Cyrene, who wrote no less than a five-volume tome covering this era.[20] Our author does, however, justify his digest in a well-known passage with which students of history can readily identify:

> For considering the flood of statistics involved and the difficulty there is for those who wish to enter upon the narratives of history because of the mass of material, we have aimed to please those who wish to read, to make it easy for those who are inclined to memorize, and to profit all readers. For us who have undertaken the toil of abbreviating, it is no light matter but calls for sweat and

---

[18]This outline is adapted from David W. Suter, "Maccabees, the Second Book of the," *HBD*, p. 637.
[19]*Jewish Literature*, p. 118.
[20]Some scholars think that 2 Macc 3:40; 7:42; 10:9; 13:26; 15:27 are excerpts from the conclusions to each of Jason's five volumes (see Metzger, *Introduction to the Apocrypha*, p. 139).

loss of sleep, just as it is not easy for one who prepares a banquet and seeks the benefit of others. Nevertheless, to secure the gratitude of many we will gladly endure the uncomfortable toil, leaving the responsibility for exact details to the compiler, while devoting our effort to arriving at the outlines of the condensation. For as the master builder of a new house must be concerned with the whole construction, while the one who undertakes its painting and decoration has to consider only what is suitable for its adornment, such in my judgment is the case with us. It is the duty of the original historian to occupy the ground, to discuss matters from every side, and to take trouble with details, but the one who recasts the narrative should be allowed to strive for brevity of expression and to forego exhaustive treatment. (2 Macc 2:24-31)

Scholarly opinion on the reliability of the abridger varies. Most hold that 1 Maccabees is, on the whole, much more accurate and reliable. All agree, however, that 2 Maccabees provides a valuable supplement to the former and, in a few instances, even corrects a too one-sided perspective in 1 Maccabees. Furthermore, all can agree that in terms of entertainment, our digester has scored a hit.[21]

Several features of 2 Maccabees set it apart from 1 Maccabees. Notably, we have a concentration upon the miraculous and supernatural. The author believes in divine intervention in the affairs of the nation, so that 1 Maccabees sounds almost secular by comparison. Apparitions and angels (2 Macc 2:21; 3:24-29; 10:29; 11:8; 12:22; 15:11) punctuate the storyline of 2 Maccabees.

There is a pronounced moralizing throughout. The all-powerful God of Israel rewards the righteous and punishes the wicked in accordance with their evil deeds. The notion of *lex talionis* (the punishment should fit the crime) is assumed as self-evident in the accounts of Andronicus, Jason, Antiochus, Menelaus and Nicanor (cf. 2 Macc 4:38; 5:9-10; 9:5-29; 15:32-33). Especially prominent is the Deuteronomistic theology whereby obedience to Torah leads to blessing but disobedience to punishment for the people of God. This keynote is struck in a clear editorial insertion into Jason's chronicles:

Now I urge those who read this book not to be depressed by such calamities, but

---

[21]Pfeiffer's assessment of our author is worth citing: "He manifestly took considerable liberties, rearranging the order of events wrongly, stressing the religious teaching, exaggerating horrors and miracles, and generally showing less respect for historical reality (cf. 15:37) than Jason, who himself cannot be accused of excessive accuracy. Thus he aggravated the defects of Jason, without making any important contributions. However, we owe the Epitomist a debt for preserving, even though in curtailed and fragmentary form, something of Jason's history; and we should judge him leniently, because he intended to write a popular book—not a scholarly history—for the entertainment and instruction of the general reader among the Alexandrian Jews. If his intentions were better than his achievement, he should be excused, for from all appearances he is right in saying (15:38) that this is the best he could achieve" (*History of New Testament Times,* pp. 521-22).

to recognize that these punishments were designed not to destroy but to discipline our people. In fact, it is a sign of great kindness not to let the impious alone for long, but to punish them immediately. For in the case of the other nations the Lord waits patiently to punish them until they have reached the full measure of their sins; but he does not deal in this way with us, in order that he may not take vengeance on us afterward when our sins have reached their height. Therefore he never withdraws his mercy from us. Although he disciplines us with calamities, he does not forsake his own people. Let what we have said serve as a reminder; we must go on briefly with the story. (2 Macc 6:12-17)

Aim and Purpose

Determining the purpose of this "history with a flair" is complicated somewhat by the two letters that introduce the work. Leaving this aside for the moment and focusing upon the main body of the narrative itself, we can make the following observations. First, the writer was an ardent admirer of Judas the Maccabee. What is especially noteworthy in this regard is the virtual absence of the other Maccabee brothers. They play at best a subsidiary role in the events that transpire. Judas is canonized as the leader of the Hasideans (cf. 2 Macc 14:6). He is portrayed, in contrast to 1 Maccabees, as observant of all ritual requirements of the Torah—even sabbath observance in spite of life-threatening circumstances. He is a model of piety as well as bravery and courage. This leads one to suspect that our author is not enamored with the Hasmonean successors to Judas. They were not Torah-observant, as was Judas. Though one must be careful of reading into the narrative more than is there, it is quite tempting to see here a strong anti-Hasmonean polemic.[22]

A second prominent feature of 2 Maccabees is the great reverence and concern for the temple and its sanctity. The crowning achievement of the resistance movement is not, as in 1 Maccabees, the gaining of political independence but rather the cleansing and rededication of the temple. Several stories narrated in 1 Maccabees that deal with the temple are here elaborated. On the one hand, God intervenes to protect its sanctity (2 Macc 3:4-40); on the other, God may permit its desecration because of the sins of his people (2 Macc 5:17-20).[23] Clearly our author desires to honor this national shrine. The events of Hanukkah are more fully detailed in 2 Maccabees than in the earlier composition. Manifestations of God's power and glory center on this structure.

---

[22]See Attridge, "Historiography," in *Jewish Writings of the Second Temple Period: Apocrypha, Pseudepigrapha, Qumran Sectarian Writings, Philo, Josephus,* ed. Michael E. Stone, CRINT 2 (Assen: Van Gorcum; Philadelphia: Fortress, 1984), p. 177.

[23]Goldstein argues that in fact one of the aims of the abridger was to warn Jews that the temple had not been authenticated as the "holy place" (Jonathan A. Goldstein, *2 Maccabees,* AB 41A [Garden City, N.Y.: Doubleday, 1983], pp. 13-17). We are not entirely convinced by his hypothetical reconstruction of the "situation."

When we read the work as we now have it, however, we must take into account the effect of the two introductory epistles upon the question of the author's purpose. Considerable scholarly debate focuses upon whether the letters are taken from Jason's work, are inserted by our author or are the work of a later editor. We will not enter into this technical discussion here.[24] We will assume that the letters stem from our author and relate to his purpose. If this is correct, then we can add another important reason for this writing. The two letters urge the Jewish community in Egypt to celebrate the new Festival of Hanukkah (2 Macc 1:9; 2:16). Some scholars have hypothesized that in fact the letters also implicitly reject the legitimacy of a Jewish temple at Leontopolis, Egypt.[25] We know that Onias IV, a descendent of the deposed Onias III, presided at a Jewish temple at that location. Our author would then be arguing for the sole legitimacy of the Jerusalem temple and hoping to dissuade Diaspora Jews in Egypt (and perhaps elsewhere) from founding alternative sites for observing the ancestral faith.

Author and Date

Like the other works we have considered, 2 Maccabees is anonymous. We do not even know who Jason of Cyrene was, although there are two men bearing this name mentioned in 1 Maccabees. Most likely our author was an Alexandrian Jew—the two epistles prefixed to the work are directed to Jews in Egypt. He writes in an accomplished Greek hand and imitates the practices and flourishes of Hellenistic historians. As we will argue, the epitomist (the term used to describe the author, since he sought to abridge or epitomize the much longer work of Jason), displays convictions in line with what we know of Pharisaism. *The New Oxford Annotated Bible* follows the majority view in assigning the date of composition to between 104 and 63 B.C.[26]

Importance for the New Testament

For the student of the NT, 2 Maccabees is of considerable importance. Valuable historical light is shed on the background of first-century Judaism, out of which Christianity emerged.[27] Many researchers have remarked on the

---

[24]See Pfeiffer, *History of New Testament Times,* pp. 506-9; Goldstein, *1 Maccabees,* pp. 551-57; Goldstein, *2 Maccabees,* pp. 24-27; Attridge, "Historiography," pp. 177-78; Attridge, "Jewish Historiography," pp. 320-21.

[25]See Nickelsburg, *Jewish Literature,* p. 121.

[26]*New Oxford Annotated Bible,* AP 228. Goldstein has the most complete discussion of the dating in *2 Maccabees,* pp. 71-83.

[27]R. A. Stewart's evaluation of both 1 and 2 Maccabees is worth quoting. "Outside the Protestant canon of Scripture, few documents are of greater importance for the history and theology of the faith" ("Maccabees, Books of," *ISBE* 3:200).

decidedly Pharisaic positions assumed in this work.[28] The intense hostility between the Pharisees and Sadducees, as depicted in the NT, may be better understood after reading 2 Maccabees. Our author seems to be correcting the distortions of 1 Maccabees. We do not have in 2 Maccabees uncritical adulation of the Hasmonean dynasty as the saviors of the nation raised up by God's providence. What we have is a portrait of a pious man, Judas Maccabeus, who was divinely assisted and visited in order to secure religious freedom. Judas was an observant Jew whose views, as they may be determined from the storyline, correspond rather closely to those of the later Pharisees. We hear nothing about the perpetual endowment of priesthood to the Hasmonean dynasty. Contours of the debates among the Pharisees, Sadducees and Essenes over a number of issues dealing with the temple cult, the legitimate priesthood and halakic requirements may already be faintly detected.

The doctrine of bodily resurrection is a cardinal belief for our author. Quite in contrast to 1 Maccabees, this doctrine provides hope and endurance for the faithful martyrs. Judas appeals to this hope as his forces engage the enemy. The student of the NT knows that Pharisees are distinguished from Sadducees on precisely this issue. In Paul's trial before the Sanhedrin, Luke explains for his Gentile readers (probably Romans): "The Sadducees say that there is no resurrection, or angel, or spirit; but the Pharisees acknowledge all three" (Acts 23:8). Earlier Jesus had challenged the Sadducees on their denial of bodily resurrection (cf. Mt 22:23; Mk 12:18; Lk 20:27-40). For the apostle Paul, the doctrine of Jesus' resurrection and the bodily resurrection of believers at the parousia (return of Jesus) is at the very core of Christian tradition (cf. 1 Cor 15:1-8). Paul discloses that at the parousia deceased loved ones who believe in Jesus will return and be reunited with those who survive to the end (1 Thess 4:13-17). The notion of the resurrection being a reunion with one's family is already expressed in 2 Maccabees 7:29.

Martyrology is central to the book, and 2 Maccabees 6 and 7 have exercised immense influence upon both Jews and Christians through the succeeding ages.[29] The church especially cherished the description of the faithful mother and her seven sons. Several church fathers appealed to the story in homilies and writings as an example of steadfastness in the face of torture and death.[30] But even earlier canonical Scripture refers to the persecution of the Hasideans.

---

[28]See Metzger, *Introduction to the Apocrypha*, p. 146.

[29]Metzger nicely summarizes this: "it is probably true to say that in importance for the Christian Church no part of the Apocrypha has been so widely and deeply felt as the narrative of the sufferings of the martyrs recounted in this book" (*Introduction to the Apocrypha*, p. 148). See also Daniel J. Harrington, *Invitation to the Apocrypha* (Grand Rapids, Mich.: Eerdmans, 1999), p. 150.

[30]For references, see Metzger, *Introduction to the Apocrypha*, pp. 148-49.

In the famous "hall of faith" in Hebrews 11, selected heroes and heroines are listed who "won strength out of weakness, became mighty in war, put foreign armies to flight. Women received their dead by resurrection. Others were tortured, refusing to accept release, in order to obtain a better resurrection. Others suffered mocking and flogging, and even chains and imprisonment" (Heb 11:34-36). Not surprisingly, a Jewish Christian author probably wrote Hebrews to a Jewish Christian audience.[31] In the same vein, one notes a passage in Revelation 21:8 that seems to evoke the language of 2 Maccabees 8:13. We place them alongside each other in order to illustrate the parallel:

2 Maccabees 8:13	Revelation 21:8
"Those who were *cowardly* and *distrustful* of God's justice ran off and got away"	"But as for the *cowardly*, the *faithless*, . . . their place will be in the lake that burns"

The parallel is even closer than might at first appear when one consults the Greek lying beneath the English translations: the underlined words are *deilandrountes* and *apistountes* (2 Macc 8:13); and *deilois* and *apistois* (Rev 21:8).[32]

Another interesting parallel with Hebrews occurs in 2 Maccabees 7:28. Here the mother encourages her youngest son (who has witnessed the cruel deaths of his older brothers) to be steadfast in his commitment. "I beg you, my child, to look at the heaven and the earth and see everything that is in them, and recognize that God did not make them out of things that existed." This is foundational to the hope of bodily resurrection: the same God who originally created all things out of nothing can just as easily raise up new bodies. This declaration of *creatio ex nihilo* (creation out of nothing)[33] also finds expression in Hebrews 11:3: "By faith we understand that the worlds were prepared by the word of God, so that what is seen was made from things that are not visible."

There is, finally, the rather famous passage in which Judas offers up prayers for his fallen comrades "that the sin that had been committed might be wholly blotted out" (2 Macc 12:42).[34] We do not cite this as a NT parallel but rather as a text that has been highly controversial within Christendom. In contrast to Protestant Christianity, the Roman Catholic and Greek Orthodox Churches developed a notion of purgatory from these verses. The Reformers

---

[31]See William L. Lane, *Hebrews 9—13*, WBC 47B (Dallas: Word, 1991), pp. 387-89.

[32]See H. Wolf, "Maccabees, Books of," *ZPEB* 4:16-17.

[33]Harrington, however, says, "it is doubtful that the author intended to attribute philosophical significance to her statement" (*Invitation to the Apocrypha*, pp. 150-51).

[34]As *New Oxford Annotated Bible* notes, "this is the first known statement of the doctrine that a *sin offering* and prayer make *atonement* for the sins of *the dead* . . ." (AP 253, note on 2 Macc 12:39-45).

rejected this interpretation as having no basis in canonical Scripture. Of course, the Roman Catholic response was articulated in the Council of Trent (1545-1563), where 2 Maccabees along with most of the other books Protestants designate Apocrypha were declared deuterocanonical, that is, having full authority for faith and practice.[35] Thus Catholics appeal to 2 Maccabees 7:28 as a proof text for the doctrine of purgatory. Rabbinic Judaism appears to have been divided over the question of purgatory.[36]

We think there is sound judgment behind the admonition not to base any doctrine upon an obscure or solitary passage. Furthermore, the meaning of Judas's prayers is far from clear. The doctrine of purgatory goes well beyond what might legitimately be inferred from this one text. Goldstein provides persuasive evidence that Jason the historian misunderstood his source and misconstrued what was really an instance of corporate sin (cf. Lev 4:13).[37]

Judith

Introduction

The book of Judith is a "good read." The art of early Jewish storytelling is raised to a new level with this literary gem.[38] The first assignment is simply to read it through in one sitting, if possible, and to allow the storyline to transport you into its narrative world. Though ostensibly a historical account, on closer inspection, obvious historical errors force us to conclude that these inaccuracies are deliberate—it is fictional work.[39] It is hard to imagine

---

[35]For a review of this history, see Metzger, *Introduction to the Apocrypha,* pp. 175-204.

[36]The view of Orthodox Judaism has been stated as follows: "When a man dies his soul leaves his body, but for the first twelve months it retains a temporary relationship to it, coming and going until the body has disintegrated. Thus the prophet Samuel was able to be raised from the dead within the first year of his demise. This year remains a purgatorial period for the soul, or according to another view only for the wicked soul, after which the righteous go to paradise, *Gan Eden,* and the wicked to hell, *Gehinnom* (Gehinnom; Shab. 152b-153a; Tanh. Va-Yikra, 8)" (Editorial Staff, "Afterlife," *EncJud on CD-ROM* [Judaica Multimedia, version 1.0, 1997]). Reform Judaism has dropped such notions along with a belief in bodily resurrection and focuses instead upon some form of spiritual survival after death (ibid.).

[37]Goldstein, *2 Maccabees,* pp. 449-50. We would add the OT parallel of the sin of Achan as throwing more light on this episode (Josh 7). The sin of one man and his family brought guilt upon the entire community (cf. *HarperCollins Study Bible: New Revised Standard Version, with the Apocryphal/Deuterocanonical Books,* ed. Wayne A. Meeks et al. [New York: HarperCollins, 1993], p. 1716, note on 2 Macc 12:43).

[38]Portions of this section are adapted from my article, "Judith," *DNTB,* pp. 624-27.

[39]See *New Oxford Annotated Bible,* AP 20, for the view that it is a folktale. Pfeiffer has a full discussion of the question of historicity in *History of New Testament Times,* pp. 291-92; cf. also Metzger, *Introduction to the Apocrypha,* pp. 50-51; and George W. E. Nickelsburg, "Stories of Biblical and Post-Biblical Times," in *Jewish Writings of the Second Temple Period,* p. 48.

that any Jew who would offer such a narrative for public consumption could possibly be so misinformed about his own historical heritage! The narrative world, however, is certainly credible, especially after having read 1 and 2 Maccabees. An invasion threatening annihilation thinly veils a "real time" of extreme danger for religiously observant Jews. Nebuchadnezzar functions as a lens through which we see the menacing figure of Antiochus IV Epiphanes; Holofernes conjures up reminiscences of Nicanor, Antiochus's general beheaded by Judas (cf. 2 Macc 15:30-35). The narrative breathes a similar atmosphere as the stirring accounts of the Maccabee brothers. Only in this story, a Jewess is the heroine! Standing in a line of ancient worthies such as Deborah, Jael and Queen Esther, Judith confronts the forces of darkness. By her combination of piety, beauty, cunning and courage, she achieves national deliverance. The moral and ethical problems will engage our attention later.

Author, Date and Purpose

Once again we are confronted with an anonymous work. Internal evidence suggests that our author was a Palestinian Jew. The time of composition comports well with the aftermath of the Maccabean revolt.[40] A widely accepted date is around 150 B.C.[41] On the other hand, some aspects of the story fit nicely into the Persian period. This would include such features as the names Holofernes and Bogoas, the recent return of the Jews to their land (Jdt 4:3), a possible reflex of the Persian title "satrap" (Jdt 2:14), and the symbolism of earth and water for submission (Jdt 2:7). A compromise position suggests that an earlier Persian period tale has been reused and updated in the aftermath of the Maccabean revolt.[42] At any rate, we can be fairly sure that the work in its final form dates to the Maccabean era.

The aim of the author is quite transparent: to call Jews to resist hellenizing pressures and to observe the Torah with minute and steadfast obedience. Thus the theme of the composition is fairly straightforward: God will inter-

---

[40]See *New Oxford Annotated Bible,* AP 20.

[41]See R. A. Stewart, "Judith, Book of," *ISBE* 2:1165. C. C. Torrey makes an interesting case for some time after 120 B.C. following John Hyrcanus's destruction of the Samaritan temple on Mount Gerizim. He also is convinced that Bethulia is Shechem and Betomasthem is Samaria. He believes the author is ridiculing the Samaritans in the story (*The Apocryphal Literature: A Brief Introduction* [New Haven, Conn.: Yale University Press, 1945], pp. 91-92). On the other hand, Edgar J. Goodspeed thinks that the book could not have been written after about 147 B.C., since Jonathan destroyed the city then and the story assumes that the city is still inhabited (*The Story of the Apocrypha* [Chicago: University of Chicago Press, 1939], p. 48).

[42]See James C. VanderKam, *An Introduction to Early Judaism* (Grand Rapids, Mich.: Eerdmans, 2001), p. 72.

vene and defend his people if they but faithfully observe his law. This divine intervention incorporates individuals whose piety is impeccable.

Outline

I. Holofernes' invasion (1:1—7:32)
    A. The western nations, including the Jews, refuse to help Nebuchadnezzar, king of the "Assyrians," in defeating Arphaxad, king of the Medes (1:1-16)
    B. Nebuchadnezzar commissions Holofernes to invade the western nations (2:1-28)
    C. Except for the Jews, all sue for peace and are accepted as vassals (3:1-10)
    D. The Jews are alarmed and cry out to God (4:1-15)
    E. Holofernes prepares to invade Judea; Achior the Ammonite is turned over to the Jews; he is not to see Holofernes' face again until the general has dealt with them (5:1—6:21)
    F. Holofernes besieges Bethulia, and its terrified leaders prepare to surrender (7:1-32)
II. The story of Judith (8:1—16:25)
    A. Judith is introduced as a beautiful, virtuous and pious widow with a plan to deliver her people; she asks the leaders to postpone surrender, noting that, in addition to their town, the sanctuary in Jerusalem is in danger (8:1-36)
    B. Judith's prayer (9:1-14)
    C. She arrays herself in beautiful clothes, provisions herself with kosher foods and, with her maidservant, seeks asylum in Holofernes' camp; he is captivated by her great beauty (10:1—11:23)
    D. For three nights, Judith goes out to pray and bathe in a spring; on the fourth evening, Holofernes throws a banquet at which he plans to seduce her (12:1-20)
    E. Alone in the chambers with the general, Judith decapitates him and, pretending to go out again to bathe, carries his head away to Bethulia in her food bag (13:1-20)
    F. Achior looks upon Holofernes' face and becomes a proselyte, as the Assyrians discover his body (14:1-19)
    G. The Assyrians flee while Judith is honored by the high priest (15:1-14)
    H. The song of Judith (16:1-17)
    I. The spoil is dedicated to the temple and Judith returns home (16:18-25)

As the above outline[43] demonstrates, the book falls into two parts: the first

---

[43]Suter, "Judith, Book of," *HBD*, p. 518.

seven chapters narrate the invasion of the Assyrians; the last nine recount Judith's deliverance. Most readers agree with Goodspeed's observation that the story is a bit slow until Judith makes her appearance.[44] In this regard, one is reminded of *Assumption of Moses* 9:1 and 2 Maccabees 5:27, where the introduction of Taxo and Judas, respectively, is the turning point in the narrative. From the moment that Judith is introduced, however, the storyteller masterfully spins his tale with escalating suspense right up to the spine-tingling climax of the decapitation scene in the tent of Holofernes.

The entire story smacks of irony.[45] That the mighty army of Nebuchadnezzar, which had reduced mighty kingdoms to rubble, could be utterly routed by a small Jewish town in Samaria highlights the most obvious in a series of ironies. Of course, the supreme irony lies in the thematic verse: "But the Lord Almighty has foiled them by the hand of a woman" (Jdt 16:5).[46] This woman, a pious widow of whom no one spoke any ill, lives a celibate life till the day she dies (at the ripe old age of 105!).[47] Yet she possesses such seductive charm that she "turns on" every male who lays eyes on her—not least of whom is the archenemy himself! Several lines offer good examples of double entendre, that is, words or phrases that have a double meaning. For example, several of Judith's utterances to Holofernes have a quite different meaning from what he understands (cf. 11:6 ["my lord/Lord"], 11:16 ["to accomplish with you things that will astonish the whole world"], 11:19 ["I will lead you through Judea"], 12:14 ["it will be a joy to me until the day of my death"], 12:18 ["today is the greatest day in my whole life"]). After reading the entire story, these become clearer and add a touch of humor to the story. One might capture the delightful irony of Judith by observing that Holofernes lost his head before he lost his head![48]

Relevance for the New Testament

Historical background. One may wonder how this novel or folktale throws light upon the NT.[49] We readily admit that it is not of the same importance as other works we have read in this chapter. The book of Judith confronts the reader with a sense of urgency and crisis. The author, whoever he or she might be, has employed a story designed to stir deeply the religious feelings

---

[44] Goodspeed, *Story of the Apocrypha*, p. 50.

[45] "No other biblical book, in either its parts or its totality, is as quintessentially ironic as Judith" (*New Oxford Annotated Bible*, AP 20).

[46] Carey A. Moore has a wonderful discussion on the role of irony in Judith (*Judith*, AB 40 [Garden City, N.Y.: Doubleday, 1985], pp. 78-85).

[47] Cravens points out that the Maccabean era lasted exactly 105 years: 168-63 B.C. (*Harper-Collins Study Bible* [New York: HarperCollins, 1993], p. 1480, note on Jdt 16:23).

[48] With credit to Paul Winter, who first formulated this idea ("Judith, Book of," *IDB* 2:1024).

[49] Metzger calls it a "quasi-historical novel" (*Introduction to the Apocrypha*, p. 51). Carey A. Moore prefers the designation "folktale" ("Judith, Book of," *ABD* 3:1121).

of Jewish readers. Though no NT document can compare with Judith in terms of genre, several convey a similar intensity and urgency, especially Hebrews and the Apocalypse.

While we cannot accept at face value the historicity of the story, this does not mean it has no value for historical purposes. Judith was not a historical figure but a personification (her name means "Jewess"), and as such, she embodies the religious ideals of the author and the community of which he (or she?) was a part. It is precisely in this understanding of our story that a genuine contribution emerges. We are probably overhearing the concerns and theology of a group that will later be identified as the Pharisees.

What characteristics may be discerned in the story that help us understand better the Pharisaic ethos? One of the difficult issues in historical research of early Judaism and Christianity has been an accurate reconstruction of Pharisaism.[50] Judith is valuable in this connection because it seems to portray an earlier phase of Pharisaism than we see in the NT and later rabbinic sources. We may be justified in speaking of pre-Pharisaism in Judith.[51] Following are some features arising from the story:

1. Judith's practice of rigorous fasting goes well beyond what was enjoined in the OT (the only required fast in the OT was on the Day of Atonement) and is in conformity with the injunctions of the Pharisees (Jdt 8:6).[52] In contrast, Jesus' approach to fasting was innovative and distinctive.[53] He rigorously fasted only once, according to the Gospels, and this was in preparation for his ministry (Mt 4:2 and par.). During his ministry there is no mention of regular fasting like that undertaken by the disciples of John the Baptist and the Pharisees (twice a week, on Mondays and Thursdays). He did not forbid his disciples to do so; indeed, he assumed that they would fast as a religious exercise (Mt 6:16-18). On the other hand, when Jesus' disciples were criticized by some for not fasting, he pointed to the incongruous nature of fasting during wedding festivities (Mk 2:19 and par.). This metaphor reflects Jesus' conviction that already the messianic age with its marriage banquet had broken into history. But he was also aware that he, the bridegroom, would be violently taken away from his disciples before the kingdom of God came in all its fullness (Mk 2:20). Thus, fasting still has a place in the spirituality of Jesus' disciples "between the times." Nonetheless, it takes on a quite different character from that of the Pharisees.[54]

---

[50]As pointed out by Jacob Neusner, *From Politics to Piety: The Emergence of Pharisaic Judaism* (Englewood Cliffs, N.J.: Prentice-Hall, 1973), pp. 1-12.

[51]J. M. Grintz, cited by Nickelsburg, "Stories of Biblical and Post-Biblical Times," p. 48.

[52]See the note on Jdt 8:6 in *New Oxford Annotated Bible,* AP 28-29.

[53]See J. Behm, "νῆστις," *TDNT* 4:931.

[54]See ibid.

2. Especially important to the plot of the story is Judith's absolute adherence to ritual purity laws. She carries her own kosher food into Holofernes' camp (cf. Jdt 12:2-4). Pharisees were noted for strict rules governing table fellowship. Paul's confrontation with Peter at Antioch reflects this practice (Gal 2:11-14; cf. Mk 7:3-4).[55] Judith also performs her ritual bathing in running water before prayer, as required by later Pharisaic halakah (Jdt 12:6-9). This, of course, is part of her "game plan" for murdering Holofernes and escaping camp without attracting attention.

3. She also observes set times of prayer when incense was being burned at the Jerusalem temple (Jdt 9:1; cf. Acts 3:1). An important piece of information is Judith's revelation to Holofernes that the elders of Bethulia were about to commit a great sin by eating food that had been tithed to God. This refers indirectly to perhaps the most distinctive feature of Pharisaism as portrayed in the NT, namely, their meticulous tithing of all produce grown in the Holy Land (cf. Mt 23:23).

4. There is also what Nickelsburg considers the most striking evidence for dating the book well after the time of Ezra. This concerns the conversion of Achior the Ammonite (Jdt 14:10).[56] Clearly Ezra disallowed mixed marriages, especially with Moabites and Ammonites (Ezra 9—10). Our document, on the other hand, assumes that an Ammonite could convert—even though Deuteronomy 23:3 forbade the entrance of such into the congregation of Israel unto the tenth generation. Judith reflects a Judaism that is more open and even committed to proselytizing, a stance reflected in the NT (cf. Mt 23:15).

The question of morality. "All is fair in love and war." Or is it? Our author apparently thought so. But for most commentators in the Christian tradition, and for many modern readers, regardless of religious commitments, Judith's deceitful deed is reprehensible. We could offer a legion of quotes to illustrate this perspective.[57] Are there circumstances in which the end justifies the means? Is it wrong for females to use their sexuality in order to defend themselves against evildoers and, even more to the point, others?

The story of Judith has two OT precedents. Jael invited the Canaanite general Sisera, who was fleeing from the battle scene, to seek shelter within her tent (Judg 4:18). There is no explicit indication in the text, however, that sexuality played any significant role in the episode, other than the assumption that pursuing soldiers would not think to check the "women's quarter" of a tent. At any rate,

---

[55]It should be noted, however, that Pharisees were not forbidden generally to eat with Gentiles, and Judith does have dinner with Holofernes. The Pharisees were just forbidden to eat prohibited foods or foods prepared in a non-kashrut manner (i.e., unacceptable or unfit).

[56]Nickelsburg, "Stories of Biblical and Post-Biblical Times," p. 49.

[57]Moore conveniently brings together some highly negative reactions of readers through the centuries—all males, I might add (*Judith*, pp. 64-65).

when the exhausted Sisera was fast asleep, she pounded a tent peg through his skull, a dramatic example of "hitting the nail on the head" (Judg 4:21)! The parallel with Judith lies in the murder by Jael's own hand. The second example is Queen Esther, who, like Judith, enlisted her unusual beauty as an ally in gaining an audience with the king and interceding for her people (Esther 5:1). She did not, however, murder the wicked Haman "by her own hand" (the key phrase in Judith; cf. Jdt 16:5); rather, she "set him up" so that he not only fell from grace but also hung from his own gallows. Judith's sexual enticement in the service of murder appears to be unique in all of Jewish literature.[58]

Where does the NT come down on this issue? The general tenor of NT paraenesis regarding Christian women seems to be against such an activist response (cf. 2 Thess 1:5-12; Heb 11:35; 1 Pet 2:13—3:6), but it must be confessed that this issue is never directly addressed. One must work out an answer on the basis of Jesus' moral and ethical teachings and apostolic teaching as these may be distilled from highly circumstantial writings. Because of the paucity of direct NT teaching on this issue, Christian ethicists must search for underlying principles and appeal to philosophical arguments. Some, for example, subscribe to a hierarchical view of moral principles: higher principles take precedence over lesser ones *when there is a conflict*. Thus it is argued that lying, fornication and adultery might be permissible if the preservation of life were at stake, because this is a higher good. Hierarchialists believe that their system can be supported, inferentially, from Jesus' teachings in the Gospels, where he assigns more worth and value to mercy and justice than tithing, sabbath laws and ritual purity (cf. Mt 23:23). From this one may work out a scale of moral and ethical values and determine which ones take priority when there is a conflict.[59]

Within evangelicalism this is not a question of mere academic interest. There are a few self-professed evangelicals who advocate the killing of abortion-clinic personnel. Their defense is simple: one must defend the defenseless. The example of Dietrich Bonhoeffer, who participated, unsuccessfully, in a plot to assassinate Adolf Hitler, is often brought into this discussion. We can all admire Judith for her courage and commitment; whether we can go further and condone her act of cold-blooded murder is a moot point. Unfortunately, space limitations preclude in-depth discussion.[60]

---

[58]In contemporary film, however, the topic has been quite popular!

[59]For further reading in this area, see James Rachels, *The Elements of Moral Philosophy*, 3rd ed. (New York: McGraw-Hill, 1999); Louis P. Pojman, *Ethics: Discovering Right and Wrong*, 2nd ed. (Belmont, Calif.: Wadsworth, 1995); and, from a Christian perspective, Scott B. Rae, *Moral Choices: An Introduction to Ethics*, 2nd ed. (Grand Rapids, Mich.: Zondervan, 2000).

[60]See further Richard B. Hays, *The Moral Vision of the New Testament: A Contemporary Introduction to New Testament Ethics* (San Francisco: HarperCollins, 1996).

We do, however, urge readers to consider carefully the moral and ethical issues this story raises. A small but growing group of Christians apparently sanctions military action as a legitimate means of preserving "biblical values" in the United States. It would not be hard to imagine a scenario in which a deed comparable to Judith's might be undertaken in defense of personal beliefs.

Jewish feminism before its time. Here is a work that turns on its head feminine stereotypes such as portrayed in Susanna, Tobit and Ben Sira. In the book of Judith, spiritually dwarfed men, roundly rebuked for their lack of faith (cf. Jdt 8:11-27), serve as foils for the stalwart heroine. She is an activist who takes matters into her own hands with the steely determination worthy of Deborah (cf. Judg 4): "Listen to me. I am about to do something that will go down through all generations of our descendants" (Jdt 8:32). Given the culture, the plot is quite radical. One suspects, however, that Judith will get more respect in our own day of female warriors than has been the case in the past!

The one NT writer who is most sensitive to the feminine point of view is Luke. No other NT author devotes as much attention to and favorable comment about women as does Luke.[61] But one should also mention that Hebrews and the Apocalypse employ feminine figures and images in their rhetorical strategy of exhorting the faithful. Note in this regard the worthy women in the "hall of faith" (Heb 11), the positive image of the woman in Revelation 12 and the striking figure of the church as the bride of Christ, who is destined to dwell in the heavenly Jerusalem (Rev 19—22). Comparing the plot of Judith to the storyline underlying the Apocalypse—especially the juxtaposition of Revelation 13 and 14—we suggest an appropriate title for both works might well be "Beauty and the Beast!"[62]

Baruch

Introduction

Baruch does not possess the passion of a Judith; it does, however, reflect the fire of the prophets.[63] The first of several books to be named after the faithful scribe of Jeremiah, Baruch is the only book in the Apocrypha that employs

---

[61]One thinks here especially of the birth narratives in his Gospel (Elizabeth, Mary and Anna in Lk 1—2) but also the "sinful" woman in Lk 7:36-50 and the crippled woman in Lk 13:10-17. In Acts we have several vignettes of early Christian women, most of whom are portrayed positively and sensitively (Dorcas, Acts 9:36-42; Lydia, 16:13-15; Priscilla, 18:2, 26).
[62]With due credit to Moore, *Judith*, p. 56. Note, however, that I have inverted the titles he used to connect more directly with my audience, who may pick up on the Disney movie by the same title. I think the author of Judith would have approved the change!
[63]With credit to Metzger, *Introduction to the Apocrypha*, p. 89, for the phrasing.

the model of an OT prophet.[64] It also shares with Tobit and Wisdom of Solomon a Diaspora perspective. Baruch and Tobit live outside the Promised Land, yet God blesses them. Wisdom is written for those who would discover God's will in a foreign land.

However, Jerusalem is still close to the heart of Baruch. Hope for its restoration provides an anchor in the storms of life. Baruch speaks to a people who are aliens in a foreign land and long for a return. In the meantime, however, they must get on with life. Life still has meaning. "In our homelessness Baruch seeks to impart a sense of prayer—whatever be the situation, we can turn to God."[65] As Stuhlmueller nicely summarizes it, Baruch is a book that teaches "a spirituality for displaced people."[66]

Composition and Date

There is a consensus among modern scholars that Baruch is a composite work. The introduction to *The New Oxford Annotated Bible* suggests that there may have been "as many as four different authors . . . and a final redactor."[67] Nickelsburg, however, sees no reason for denying that an author has taken originally independent compositions and melded them in more or less the existing form.[68] At any rate, the book divides into a prose section, consisting of two parts (Bar 1:1—3:8), and a poetry section, also consisting of two parts (Bar 3:9—5:9).

It is highly unlikely that Jeremiah's devoted scribe wrote any part of the work. There are good reasons for not accepting the introductory historical narrative as factual.[69] This section abounds in a number of anachronisms, and, as we observed with regard to the book of Judith, it is inconceivable that one could be so misinformed. Stuhlmueller is probably correct that the "details about the exile provide a setting in which people can identify who are displaced within their own estrangement, physical or emotional. The details are not chosen at random, but carefully for their message."[70]

The dating of Baruch is not precise; *The New Oxford Annotated Bible* places it

---

[64]Ibid.

[65]Carroll Stuhlmueller, "Baruch," in *The Catholic Study Bible,* ed. Donald Senior et al. (New York: Oxford University Press, 1990), p. 323.

[66]Ibid.

[67]*New Oxford Annotated Bible,* AP 161.

[68]Nickelsburg, *Jewish Literature,* p. 109; Nickelsburg, "The Bible Rewritten and Expanded," in *Jewish Writings of the Second Temple Period,* p. 145; cf. Carol Newsom, in *HarperCollins Study Bible,* p. 1617.

[69]For discussion, see Pfeiffer, *History of New Testament Times,* pp. 413-15.

[70]"Baruch," p. 324.

within the span of 200-60 B.C.[71] Neither internal nor external evidence provides anything secure.[72] Nickelsburg suggests that the fictional date in Baruch 1:2 may provide a clue. Ostensibly, Baruch read out the words of the book five years after the temple had been destroyed by Nebuchadnezzar (582 B.C.). If this really refers to the desecration of the Second Temple by Antiochus IV Epiphanes (i.e., similar to the book of Judith), we are brought to 164 B.C., the time of the Maccabean revolt. Though not without problems, this setting comports reasonably well with the contents, so we will adopt this provisional dating.

Outline and Summary of Contents

Nickelsburg outlines the book in four sections.[73]

Narrative introduction (1:1-14). The introduction places the story in Babylon after the exile. Baruch urges that a collection be taken up and sent to the high priest Jehoiakim in Jerusalem. Baruch also returns the temple vessels that Nebuchadnezzar had removed. Burnt offerings and sin offerings must be presented on the altar. Prayers are also to be lifted up for the king and his son and for the people of the Lord God. On festivals and appointed seasons they are to make confession and read Baruch's scroll.

Prayer (1:15—3:8). The prayer is penitential and reflects the view of Deuteronomy 28—32. The Lord's people have suffered in accordance with their sins (Bar 1:15—3:5). In spite of their sin, the Lord has been faithful and has not abandoned his people (Bar 2:27). The prayer cries out for forgiveness and restoration. This restoration is based upon the Lord's promise to the patriarchs (Bar 2:34-35), not human merit or achievement (Bar 2:19).

Wisdom poem (3:9—4:4). This section switches to poetry. Here we have a personification of Wisdom, identified as the Torah, as we have seen already in Sirach 24.

Zion poem (4:5—5:9). The book concludes with a lovely poem in which the faithful are encouraged by a vision of Zion's future restoration and blessing.[74] Baruch 4:5-29 is a lament over Zion, somewhat in the same vein as Lamenta-

---

[71]*New Oxford Annotated Bible,* AP 161, as does Harrington, *Invitation to the Apocrypha,* p. 94.

[72]In several major Greek MSS of the OT, Baruch is attached to Jeremiah. Emmanuel Tov argues that the translator of the second half of Jeremiah also translated the Hebrew of Baruch 1:1—3:8 into Greek. This suggests that at one time Baruch was attached to the Hebrew scroll of Jeremiah. Since we know that by 132 B.C. (Prologue of Ben Sira) the OT prophetic books were already translated into Greek, Hebrew Baruch must have been written well before this date. Tov feels confident that a *terminus ante quem* would be 116 B.C. (*The Septuagint Translation of Jeremiah and Baruch: A Discussion of an Early Revision of the LXX of Jeremiah 29—52 and Baruch 1:1—3:8* (Missoula, Mont.: Society of Biblical Literature, 1976), pp. 111-33, 165, 169.

[73]"The Bible Rewritten and Expanded," p. 140.

[74]Metzger observes that "the second half of the book is written with deep feeling and no little skill" (*Introduction to the Apocrypha,* p. 91).

tions. Echoing the phraseology of Isaiah 40—66, however, Baruch 4:30—5:9 serves as prophetic paraenesis by sketching God's new acts of mercy: "Look toward the east, O Jerusalem, and see the joy that is coming to you from God" (Bar 4:36); "For God will give you evermore the name, 'Righteous Peace, Godly Glory' " (Bar 5:4).[75]

Features

A striking feature of this work is the passage in which Wisdom is identified as the Torah: "He found the whole way to knowledge, and gave her to his servant Jacob and to Israel, whom he loved. Afterward she appeared on earth and lived with humankind. She is the book of the commandments of God, the law that endures forever" (Bar 3:36—4:1a).[76] We have delved into this theme in our treatment of Sirach 24. This passage takes its place in a developing trajectory that runs from Proverbs 8 and Job 28 through Sirach and Baruch. We will encounter an even more advanced development in Wisdom of Solomon (see chapter eight). The similarity of Baruch to Ben Sira on this point is another inferential piece of evidence for dating Baruch to the same general time period as Ben Sira.

Nickelsburg makes the point, however, that there is a distinction between Ben Sira's treatment of Wisdom and Baruch's. In the former we have a discourse delivered *by* Wisdom herself; in the latter we have a discourse *about* Wisdom.[77] Whether one can infer which is earlier or "more developed," however, is doubtful. More significant is how the book of Baruch utilizes the identification of Wisdom and Torah for its rhetorical purposes. The thrust of this passage is pastoral. One must embrace Wisdom, that is, Torah, or die. If we are correct in our placement of the book in its historical setting of the Maccabean revolt, or its aftermath, this admonition takes on pointed emphasis. "Turn, O Jacob, and take her; walk toward the shining of her light. Do not give your glory to another, or your advantages to an alien people" (Bar 4:2-3). This seems to be aimed at the hellenizers and the Seleucids. Forgiveness and restoration lie in faithful adherence to the law of Moses, God's Wisdom, rather than in assimilation or hellenization.

Especially noteworthy is the fervent hope of national restoration.[78] Since

---

[75]We have used the divine names in the same manner as the author/editor of Baruch. That is, in the first two sections we have Lord (probably Yahweh), and in the second, God (*ʾĕlōhîm*).

[76]See Metzger's discussion of the patristic view that this was a witness to the doctrine of the incarnation of Christ (*Introduction to the Apocrypha*, p. 94).

[77]*Jewish Literature*, p. 112.

[78]Pfeiffer draws attention to the fact that "The future hope is terrestrial, it is the restoration of the nation to its land as it was before the Exile; in this book (as in the Second Isaiah [Is 40—55]) apocalypse and eschatology do not disclose distant chimeric vistas and alluring mirages to a prostrate nation imploring salvation from its God, but merely another chance in the homeland" (*History of New Testament Times*, p. 425).

we have discussed this at length earlier, we simply call attention to this persistent feature of Second Temple literature. Baruch does not envisage any messianic figure, whether divine or human. What it does stress is the need for wholehearted repentance and adherence to Torah.

Importance for the New Testament

Baruch's use of Isaiah 40–66 finds a counterpart in the NT. There are approximately 138 allusions or verbal parallels between Isaiah 40–66 and NT passages (of which approximately thirty-seven are from Paul's letters).[79] Especially noteworthy in this regard would be Romans 9–11.[80] Paul views the majority of Jews—those not believing in Jesus as the promised Messiah—as living in a sort of spiritual Diaspora. For Paul, Israel's problem is not merely failure to obey Torah (as per Baruch); it is the failure to realize that only by faith in Christ can one succeed in fulfilling Torah. In Paul's words: "but Israel, who did strive for the righteousness that is based on the law, did not succeed in fulfilling that law. Why not? Because they did not strive for it on the basis of faith, but as if it were based on works. They have stumbled over the stumbling stone" (Rom 9:31-32). Nonetheless, Paul, like Baruch, maintains an ultimate optimism about the restoration of Israel: "And so all Israel will be saved; as it is written, 'Out of Zion will come the Deliverer; he will banish ungodliness from Jacob' " (Rom 11:26; cf. Is 59:20).

Summary

This chapter has focused on four pieces of literature that we have styled "resistance literature." The crisis surrounding the Maccabean revolt has been our presumed life setting for these works. Each has, in its own way, sought to protect the ancestral faith from the assaults of Hellenism. Fidelity to the Torah is the bottom line. The central pillars of monotheism, election and covenant are the girders that underlie the superstructure.

This crisis exerted a lasting influence on succeeding generations of Jews. Later threats to Judaism resulted in a reuse and reshaping of the images of the Maccabean revolt. Indeed, it appears likely that even Christianity incorporated the imagery, themes and emotive power of this period in defending itself against similar threats and inroads (cf. Heb 11). We have suggested that some NT writers were acquainted with these works and, in a few instances, reflected ideas found in them. What is certain is that martyrology became an important feature of early Christianity. No wonder, then, that among many of the early church fathers these works were regarded as sacred Scripture or at

---

[79]UBS[4], pp. 897-98.
[80]UBS[4] lists six quotations in this section (p. 889).

least conveyed spiritual truths and lessons that Christians could appropriate.

For Further Discussion

1. How are the works of ancient historians different from those of modern historians? How does this affect one's view of the Gospels and Acts?

2. How do the sources read in this chapter throw light on the Pharisees as they appear in the NT?

3. Give your own evaluation of the morality of Judith's actions. Be sure to state clearly the guiding moral principles behind your conclusion.

4. Contrast the view of the Torah in Baruch with that of the apostle Paul.

5. What are some key ideas and concepts in 1 Maccabees that are reflected in the NT?

6. According to 2 Maccabees, how should the Jewish people view persecution and suffering? Is this different from the NT?

For Further Reading

H. W. Attridge, "Historiography," in *Jewish Writings of the Second Temple Period: Apocrypha, Pseudepigrapha, Qumran Sectarian Writings, Philo, Josephus,* ed. Michael E. Stone, CRINT 2 (Assen: Van Gorcum; Philadelphia: Fortress, 1984), pp. 171-84.

————, "Jewish Historiography," in *Early Judaism and Its Modern Interpreters,* ed. Robert A. Kraft and George W. E. Nickelsburg (Philadelphia: Fortress; Atlanta: Scholars Press, 1986), pp. 316-23.

R. Doran, "Narrative Literature," in *Early Judaism and Its Modern Interpreters,* ed. Robert A. Kraft and George W. E. Nickelsburg (Philadelphia: Fortress; Atlanta: Scholars Press, 1986), pp. 302-4.

Jonathan A. Goldstein, *1 Maccabees,* AB 41 (Garden City, N.Y.: Doubleday, 1976).

————, *2 Maccabees,* AB 41A (Garden City, N.Y.: Doubleday, 1983).

L. L. Grabbe, "1 and 2 Maccabees," *DNTB,* pp. 657-61.

Daniel J. Harrington, *Invitation to the Apocrypha* (Grand Rapids, Mich.: Eerdmans, 1999), pp. 27-43, 92-102, 122-51.

Larry R. Helyer, "Judith," *DNTB,* pp. 624-27.

Bruce M. Metzger, *An Introduction to the Apocrypha* (New York: Oxford University Press, 1957), pp. 43-53, 89-94, 129-50.

Carey A. Moore, *Daniel, Esther and Jeremiah: The Additions,* AB 44 (Garden City, N.Y.: Doubleday, 1987), pp. 255-316.

————, *Judith,* AB 40 (Garden City, N.Y.: Doubleday, 1985).

George W. E. Nickelsburg, "The Bible Rewritten and Expanded," in *Jewish Writings of the Second Temple Period: Apocrypha, Pseudepigrapha, Qumran Sectarian Writings, Philo, Josephus,* ed. Michael E. Stone, CRINT 2 (Assen: Van Gorcum; Philadelphia: Fortress, 1984), pp. 46-52.

————, *Jewish Literature Between the Bible and the Mishnah: A Historical and Lit-*

erary Introduction (Philadelphia: Fortress, 1981), pp. 105-21.

——————, "Stories of Biblical and Early Post-Biblical Times," in *Jewish Writings of the Second Temple Period: Apocrypha, Pseudepigrapha, Qumran Sectarian Writings, Philo, Josephus,* ed. Michael E. Stone, CRINT 2 (Assen: Van Gorcum; Philadelphia: Fortress, 1984), pp. 46-52.

Robert H. Pfeiffer, *History of New Testament Times with an Introduction to the Apocrypha* (New York: Harper, 1949), pp. 285-303, 409-25, 461-524.

R. A. Stewart, "Maccabees, Books of," *ISBE* 3:200-205.

James C. VanderKam, *An Introduction to Early Judaism* (Grand Rapids, Mich.: Eerdmans, 2001), pp. 62-69, 72-75, 121-24.

H. Wolf, "Maccabees, Books of," *ZPEB* 4:8-17.

J. E. Wright, "Baruch," *DNTB*, pp. 148-49.

Six

The Dead Sea Scrolls

The New-Covenant Community

*O*ur *basic text for these writings will be the translation by Michael Wise, Martin Abegg Jr. and Edward Cook,* The Dead Sea Scrolls: A New Translation *(New York: HarperCollins, 1999 [1996]). Other easily accessible translations are Geza Vermes,* The Complete Dead Sea Scrolls in English, *5th ed. (London: Penguin, 1998); and Florentino García Martínez,* The Dead Sea Scrolls Translated: The Qumran Texts in English, *trans. W. G. E. Watson (Leiden: E. J. Brill, 1994). We have chosen Wise et al. because of completeness, accuracy and readability. Older English translations are incomplete and do not reflect improved readings for the texts. For those who want the Hebrew text with facing English translation, see J. H. Charlesworth et al., eds.,* The Dead Sea Scrolls: Hebrew, Aramaic and Greek Texts with English Translations, *4 vols. (Tübingen: Mohr Siebeck, 1994-); and Florentino García Martínez and Eibert J. C. Tigchelaar,* The Dead Sea Scrolls Study Edition, *2 vols. (Leiden: E. J. Brill; Grand Rapids: Eerdmans, 2000). The former is still incomplete but is generally more reliable than the García Martínez edition.*

Introduction

This chapter involves us in some of the most fascinating and intriguing literature of the Second Temple period: the writings of the Qumran community. Our brief survey of this rather substantial library will enable us to peer into the fragmented world of Judaism in the first two centuries B.C. and the first century A.D., an era frequently designated as Early Judaism.

Definition and Importance
The Dead Sea Scrolls (hereafter DSS) are the literary remains of a Jewish sect, generally identified as Essenes, who, during the period of about 150 B.C. to A.D. 68, occupied a site along the northwestern shore of the Dead Sea. The importance of this material for an informed view of Christian origins cannot be emphasized enough. These writings have, simply put, revolutionized our understanding of this formative period. The scrolls and the fragments found with them represent the single most important find of manuscripts bearing on the Hebrew Bible, early Judaism and the beginnings of Christianity. It has been called the greatest archaeological discovery of the twentieth century and, in the words of Frank Moore Cross of Harvard University, "set off a series of manuscript finds which are without precedent in the history of modern archaeology."[1]

The Qumran library has generated intense, at times acrimonious, debates over the interpretation of the contents, raised in an acute way the question of proprietorship and rights of publication, and spawned conspiracy theories galore. In short, there is no lack of human interest in the amazing story of its discovery and decipherment, a story whose highlights can only be touched upon in our survey of the literature.[2]

---

[1]*The Ancient Library of Qumran,* 3rd ed. (Minneapolis: Fortress, 1995), p. 19. Similarly, Craig Evans says, "The Dead Sea Scrolls probably constitute the single most important biblically related literary discovery of the twentieth century" (*Noncanonical Writings and New Testament Interpretation* [Peabody, Mass.: Hendrickson, 1992], p. 49).

[2]The story has been told "in many and various ways"! I think the best account is narrated by Yigael Yadin, the son of E. L. Sukenik. The latter was a linguist at Hebrew University and the first scholar to set eyes on the precious documents. Yadin himself was instrumental in acquiring some of the scrolls for the State of Israel (*The Message of the Scrolls* [New York: Simon & Schuster, 1957]). There are many sensationalist approaches to the DSS. Let the reader beware! Here are some books that I think are misguided or just plain foolish: John Allegro, *The Sacred Mushroom and the Cross* (Garden City, N.Y.: Doubleday, 1970); Allegro, *The Dead Sea Scrolls and the Christian Myth* (Buffalo, N.Y.: Prometheus, 1984); Michael Baigent and Richard Leigh, *The Dead Sea Scrolls Deception* (New York: Summit, 1991); Robert Eisenman, *The Dead Sea Scrolls and the First Christians* (Rockport, Mass.: Element, 1996); Eisenman, *James the Brother of Jesus: The Key to Unlocking the Secrets of Early Christianity and the Dead Sea Scrolls* (New York: Penguin: 1996); Norman Golb, *Who Wrote the Dead Sea Scrolls? The Search for the Secret of Qumran* (New York: Macmillan, 1996); Barbara Thiering, *Jesus and the Riddle of the Dead Sea Scrolls: Unlocking the Secrets of His Life Story* (New York: HarperCollins, 1991).

For a well-balanced, readable survey of the DSS, I highly recommend Joseph A. Fitzmyer, *Responses to 101 Questions on the Dead Sea Scrolls* (New York: Paulist, 1992); James VanderKam, *The Dead Sea Scrolls Today* (Grand Rapids, Mich.: Eerdmans, 1994);

The Discoveries of the Manuscripts

As with many other important archaeological finds, the DSS were not discovered initially as the result of a planned excavation.[3] Rather, they were found accidentally by nonarchaeologists.[4] The exact date and circumstances are still disputed, but it appears that sometime between November 1946 and February 1947, three Bedouin named Jum'a Muhammad, Khalil Musa and Muhammad Ahmed el-Hamed, from the Ta'amireh tribe, were herding their sheep and goats along the cliffs of the west shore of the Dead Sea. One of them tossed a rock through a cave opening and heard a shattering sound.

Two days later, however, Muhammad Ahmed el-Hamed (nicknamed edh-Dhib, "the wolf") returned to the cave with at least one other companion. Edh-Dhib slipped into the cave and discovered at least ten clay jars, about 25.5 to 29.5 inches high and almost 10 inches wide. To his initial disappointment—he had hoped they might contain gold or precious stones—all but one of the jars were empty or full of dirt. Inside one of the jars, however, wrapped in linen cloth, were three leather scrolls. Later, the cousins removed four more scrolls from the cave. These nearly complete scrolls were the first seven DSS, and the cave in which they were found is now labeled Cave 1. Eventually, fragments of over eight hundred documents would come to light in a total of eleven caves.

At first, the scrolls from Cave 1 simply hung on a corner tent pole for some months as a trophy for members of the Ta'amireh tribe to admire.[5] Some months later, the Bedouin brought the scrolls to Bethlehem, their trading town, and showed four of them to an antiquities dealer, Khalil Iskandar Shahin, who went by the colorful nickname "Kando." Kando agreed to find a private buyer. As it turned out, he would later play a key role as middleman in the sale of the huge cache of fragments discovered in Cave 4. He took the scrolls to the metropolitan (equivalent to an archbishop) of the Jacobite Syrian Church and the spiritual leader of St. Mark's Monastery in Jerusalem, Mar Athanasius Yeshue Samuel. Eventually, Metropolitan Samuel bought the four scrolls for 24 pounds (equivalent to about

---

Michael Wise, Martin Abegg Jr. and Edward Cook, *The Dead Sea Scrolls: A New Translation* (New York: HarperCollins, 1999 [1996]), pp. 3-45; and Geza Vermes, *An Introduction to the Complete Dead Sea Scrolls* (Minneapolis: Fortress, 1999).

[3]For a careful article rehearsing the details of discovery, see Weston W. Fields, "Discovery and Purchase," *EDSS* 1:208-12.

[4]A delightfully written article by Kenneth Atkinson, "Two Dogs, a Goat and a Partridge: An Archaeologist's Best Friends," retells some accounts of accidental discoveries of great importance (*BRev* 22, no. 1 [1996]: 42-43).

[5]One report says that children playing with one of the scrolls destroyed it, in which case one wonders if there were originally four scrolls instead of three (see Fields, "Discovery and Purchase," 1:208).

$100)—surely one of the best bargains of all time!

The other three scrolls, however, were taken to another antiquities dealer in Bethlehem, Faidi Salahi, and were eventually purchased by Eleazar Lipa Sukenik for the State of Israel. Sukenik was a Jewish archaeologist and philologist at the Hebrew University in Jerusalem and the first scholar to set eyes on these priceless documents. How he acquired them has enough drama and suspense to be worthy of a made-for-television "whodunit"!

Through an intermediary, a fragment of the scrolls was shown to Sukenik. His first glimpse was actually through a barbed-wire barrier separating Arab and Jewish Jerusalem. Tensions ran high during this period, and the British Mandatory Government had divided the city into military zones. Even under these conditions, he realized that the fragment was not a forgery and probably dated to the period of the Second Temple on the basis of its paleography (literally "old writing," referring to the study of ancient writing as a means for deciphering and dating texts). On November 29, 1947, the very day it was expected that the United Nations would vote on partitioning Palestine into Jewish and Arab states, he made a dangerous trip to Bethlehem—the only Jew on an Arab bus—in order to purchase the scrolls. He returned that evening to Jerusalem with the scrolls under his arm wrapped in paper. When he got home and was excitedly reading the scrolls, one of his sons informed him that the United Nations had passed the resolution: there was to be a Jewish state. The occurrence of these two momentous events on the same day profoundly affected Sukenik.

Sukenik learned about the existence of the other four scrolls at St. Mark's Monastery and even gained permission to borrow and examine them. He tried to secure these as well for the State of Israel. In the meantime, however, the metropolitan had solicited an opinion as to their contents and value from scholars at the American Schools of Oriental Research in Jerusalem (now named the W. F. Albright Institute of Archaeological Research). In fact, John C. Trever and William Brownlee had photographed three of the four scrolls (one could not be opened because of its brittleness). Metropolitan Samuel figured that the scrolls would fetch the highest price in the United States, and thus Sukenik's offer was declined. Sukenik did not at the time know why his offer was rejected, and he was heartbroken. In his journal he wrote: "Thus the Jewish people have lost a precious heritage." He died in 1953 thinking that the scrolls were irretrievably lost to the State of Israel. But that did not turn out to be the case.

So how did Israel acquire the other four scrolls from Cave 1? This part of the story also has elements of high drama and the bizarre. Metropolitan Samuel transferred the scrolls to Syria during the fighting that broke out between the neighboring Arab states and Israel in 1948. They were then taken to Lebanon, where, in 1949, Samuel spirited them out of the country and placed them in a safe deposit vault of a New York City bank. Here they remained until 1954. Yigael Yadin, son of Sukenik, was then in New York City lecturing on—the DSS! An ad in the *Wall Street Journal* was brought to his attention, which read as follows:

> "The Four Dead Sea Scrolls" Biblical Manuscripts dating back to a least 200 BC, are for sale. This would be an ideal gift to an educational or religious institution by an individual or group. Box F 206, The Wall Street Journal.

Yadin could scarcely contain himself! By means of an intermediary and Byzantine negotiations, he was able to purchase these scrolls for $250,000. They were then transferred, one by one, under secret code names, back to Jerusalem. Yadin, who gained an international reputation as one of Israel's foremost archaeologists became one of the leading experts in the world on the scrolls and published a splendid edition of the *Temple Scroll,* a document apparently discovered in 1956 in Cave 11.[6]

Thus, all seven scrolls, seven years after they were discovered in Cave 1, were now in the possession of the State of Israel. Today they are housed in a museum built specifically for them in Jerusalem, The Shrine of the Book. The architecture of the building is in the shape of the jar lids found in Cave 1. Inside, in a controlled environment, one may see genuine fragments of the scrolls. Displayed prominently in the center was the magnificent Isaiah scroll, unrolled and mounted on a drum so that one could read all sixty-six chapters. Unfortunately, the scroll developed cracks from being rolled backward, so that today what one sees is a replica.

Cave 1 was not the only cave to yield written material, however. Between February 1951 and January 1956, ten more caves in the general vicinity of Khirbet Qumran (*Khirbeh* is the Arabic word for "a stone ruin") were discovered, and each one had at least some literary remains. Indeed, in the case of Cave 4, over fifteen thousand fragments were recovered! It should also be noted that of the ten caves only two of them (3, 5) were actually discovered by professional archaeologists. Workmen on the site found four (7-10), and the indefatigable Taʿamireh Bedouin uncovered four more (2, 4, 6, 11).[7]

---

[6] I say "apparently" because, in fact, *Temple Scroll*[a] remained in the possession of Kando until after the Six-Day War in 1967. Yadin had learned of its location and was able to enlist the help of the Israeli Army in confiscating it. Kando was later paid more than $100,000 for the document by the Israel Department of Antiquities and Museums (Fields, "Discovery and Purchase," 1:211). Its provenance from Cave 11 and date of discovery in 1956 are presumably based on Kando's testimony. See Florentino García Martínez, "Temple Scroll," *EDSS* 2:927; and VanderKam, *Dead Sea Scrolls Today,* pp. 58-59.
[7] For a map of the Khirbet Qumran area, see VanderKam, *Dead Sea Scrolls Today,* end pages.

Actually, some 225 caves were located in the general area of Qumran, of which thirty-nine had some evidence of human habitation. Only the eleven mentioned above, however, contained any written material. Dr. Eshel Hanan has recently excavated six caves that had been overlooked in previous surveys. Surprisingly, these are very close to the ruins of Khirbet Qumran and the visitor center. The roofs of the caves had collapsed and thus had not been accessible to potential plunderers. So far there is no evidence of written material, although plenty of pottery and coins linking the caves with the Qumran community have surfaced. We eagerly await further updates.[8]

Description of the Scrolls and Fragments from Qumran

The original seven scrolls. The seven original scrolls were promptly published (by 1956 all seven had been published with photographs and transcriptions), and numerous editions and translations are now available in English and many other languages. The amount of secondary literature dealing with the DSS would fill a modern library numbering into the tens of thousands of items!

1. The St. Mark's Monastery Isaiah Scroll (1QIsa[a]).[9] This is a complete copy of Isaiah, the best-preserved scroll from Cave 1, in fact, the only biblical manuscript among the DSS that survived intact. This splendid scroll consists of seventeen sheets of leather sewn together with linen thread and extends to some 23.5 feet long with the width varying from 9.5 to 10.5 inches. The text comes to fifty-four columns beautifully written in Aramaic script, essentially the same script used in modern printed Hebrew Bibles. The sheets were

---

[8]For a brief report on the finds so far, see "Barlines," *BAR* 22, no. 2 (1996): 10, 12.

[9]The explanation for the sigla used for the DSS scrolls is as follows. The caves are numbered in Arabic numerals 1-11. The numbers are occasionally preceded by an abbreviation to indicate the material on which the writing occurs (i.e., pap = papyrus, cu = copper). The abbreviation Q designates Qumran in order to distinguish the finds in the vicinity of Khirbet Qumran from other caves further south such as Khirbet Mird, Wadi Murabbaʿat, Naḥal Ḥever, Naḥal Ṣeʾelim, Naḥal Mishmar, Masada and other locations such as Wadi ed-Daliyeh to the north of Qumran. Then follows an abbreviation for the document itself. If it is an identifiable biblical work, it is so designated (e.g., Isa = Isaiah; Hab = Habakkuk). The sectarian works are given names appropriate to the contents: e.g., S = *Serek Hayaḥad (Rule of the Community)*, CD = Cairo Genizah copy of the *Damascus Document*. The full list of sigla may be found in the official series Discoveries in the Judaean Desert (DJD), 27 vols. to date (Oxford: Clarendon Press, 1955-); Patrick H. Alexander et al., eds., *The SBL Handbook of Style: For Ancient Near Eastern, Biblical, and Early Christian Studies* (Peabody, Mass.: Hendrickson, 1999), pp. 176-233; and *EDSS* 2:1013-49. In DJD each document is assigned a boldface number rather than an abbreviated title. A raised letter following the abbreviation for the work indicates a separate manuscript copy. Thus 1QIsa[a] and 1QIsa[b] distinguish between two different Isaiah scrolls found in Cave 1. For further discussion, see Fitzmyer, *Responses,* pp. xvii-xviii.

scribed horizontally with the writing hanging from the lines.

One of the remarkable characteristics of this scroll is its closeness to the wording of the Masoretic Text, the received Hebrew text that forms the basis of our modern printed editions of the Hebrew Bible. Considering that this copy of Isaiah dates to about 125-100 B.C., one must pay tribute to the care with which the Jewish scribes have transmitted their sacred Scriptures down through the centuries. There are only thirteen substantive differences between the Masoretic Text and 1QIsa[a]! On the other hand, in a public lecture, Martin Abegg conceded that "to be honest, I have to indicate that this scroll does in fact represent a slightly variant tradition as touching on Hebrew dialect and spelling" (pers. comm., August, 1998).

2. The Hebrew University Isaiah Scroll (1QIsa[b]). This scroll is poorly preserved and contains only portions of Isaiah 7—8, 10, 12—13, 15—16, 19—20, 22—23, 24—25, 29—30, 35, 37—41, and 43—51. It dates to about the end of the first century B.C. or the beginning of the first century A.D., that is, about one hundred years later than the St. Mark's copy. Its text conforms even more closely to the Masoretic Text.

3. *Genesis Apocryphon* (1QapGen). Initially this scroll could not be unrolled because of its advanced state of deterioration. Written in Aramaic, a sister language to Hebrew and widely spoken in Palestine at the beginning of the Christian era, it retells the story of the birth of Noah and the story of Abraham and Sarah, following Genesis 12—15. This retelling, however, incorporates many rather fantastic additions to the biblical account. Geza Vermes observes that "this lively and delightful narrative, largely devoid of sectarian bias, throws valuable light on inter-Testamental Bible interpretation. It is a mixture of Targum, Midrash, rewritten Bible and autobiography."[10] Only one copy of this document turned up at Qumran.

4. The Habakkuk Commentary (1QpHab). This scroll contains the text of Habakkuk 1—2 with interspersed interpretations or commentary. This kind of commentary is called a "pesher" (*pesher* means "interpretation"). Composed of two pieces of leather sewn end to end, the scroll extended originally some 5 feet (some of the beginning is missing) and was 7.25 inches wide. The two sheets are ruled both horizontally and vertically. Because it contains historical allusions to contemporary events, the Habakkuk commentary has importance well beyond its length. We will investigate it in more depth later on as we attempt to place the Qumran community in its historical context.

5. *Rule of the Community* (1QS). The *Rule of the Community*, also called the *Manual of Discipline,* is one of the most important of all the discoveries.[11] The

---

[10]Geza Vermes, *The Dead Sea Scrolls in English,* 4th ed. (New York: Penguin, 1995), p. 292.
[11]For details, see Michael A. Knibb, "Rule of the Community," *EDSS* 2:793-97.

scroll is about 6.5 feet long and 10 inches wide, formed by sewing together five pieces of leather. The writing shows many corrections, erasures and additions, indicating that it had much use. Fragments of ten other copies of *Rule of the Community* turned up in Cave 4 (4Q255-264), as well as two tiny fragments in Cave 5 (5Q11) and a quotation from *Rule* in another sectarian text from Cave 5 (5Q13). This testifies to the importance the document possessed for the Qumran community. 1QS also contains two appendices: *Rule of the Congregation* (1Q28a) and *Rule of the Blessings* (1Q28b). Primarily from this document come the raw materials from which we may reconstruct the beliefs and practices of the sect. Since it is so crucial for our understanding, we shall read and analyze this text in some detail.

6. *Thanksgiving Hymns*[a] (1QH[a]). Consisting of hymns much in the style of canonical Psalms, this scroll also provides insight into the ethos and mindset of the Qumran community. At one point the scroll quotes directly Psalm 26:12 (1QH[a] 10:30), but there are many allusions to passages in Psalms, especially sections referring to an innocent sufferer. One also hears echoes of Scripture drawn from Isaiah 40—55 (particularly the "Servant Songs"), Jeremiah, Ezekiel, Job and Proverbs. One estimate places the number of implicit citations and allusions to the OT at around 673.[12] The original scroll was at least 10 feet long and about 12 inches wide. Two scribes can be distinguished by their handwriting. The hymns reveal rich insights into the religious and spiritual life of the community. We will also look at these in more depth.

7. *War Scroll* (1QM). The full title of this scroll is the *War of the Sons of Light and the Sons of Darkness*. It consists of five sheets of leather, nearly 10 feet in length and 6 inches wide, containing twenty columns of text. The columns are ruled both horizontally and vertically, and the handwriting is elegant. The contents are important for at least two reasons: their portrayal of Jewish military strategy and operations, and their portrayal of the eschatological battle at the end of human history.

A survey of the other Dead Sea Scrolls. We can only briefly survey this very considerable body of writings. We will do so by indicating the various categories of texts—biblical texts, Apocrypha and Pseudepigrapha, biblically related writings, and other texts—with a few remarks about noteworthy documents.[13]

The number of biblical texts recovered from the caves of Qumran comes to about 215 (about another 12 come from other sites), constituting about

---

[12]Fitzmyer, *Responses*, p. 32. Abegg adds, "Old Testament vocabulary and phraseology so abound in the *Thanksgiving Psalms* that readers feel they have entered a virtual mosaic of biblical quotations" (in Wise, Abegg and Cook, *Dead Sea Scrolls*, p. 85).

[13]We are greatly indebted to VanderKam, *Dead Sea Scrolls Today.*

one-quarter of the total cache—nearly 900 manuscripts in all.[14] This number demonstrates the importance of the Hebrew Bible for the Qumran sectarians. Of the biblical books represented, the following are listed in order of the number of manuscripts found: Psalms (37), Deuteronomy (30), Isaiah (21), Exodus (17), Genesis (20) and Leviticus (14). The only canonical books not yet identified among the DSS are 1 Chronicles, Nehemiah and Esther. Nehemiah and 1 Chronicles, however, may be represented if, as was the case later, 1-2 Chronicles and Ezra-Nehemiah were reckoned as one book, since a few small fragments of 2 Chronicles and Ezra 4—5 have been found.[15] Fitzmyer thinks the absence of Esther should be attributed to sheer chance,[16] but this is not likely. In the first place, the Festival of Purim, not mentioned in the Pentateuch, is missing from Qumran's sacred calendar. This is hard to explain if Esther were viewed as authoritative. Second, Esther married a Gentile, quite in opposition to the ritual purity standards of Qumran. Third, the book makes no mention of God. Fourth, Esther advocates violent resistance, which is contrary to the pacifism of Qumran. Clearly the theology of Esther and and that of Qumran are not compatible.[17] García Martínez thinks six fragments of an Aramaic work should be called "Proto-Esther,"[18] but most researchers disagree, since nothing in the existing fragments definitely ties it to the story of Esther.[19]

At this point, it is worth noting that if one culls the various OT quotations found in the NT, a similar distribution pattern emerges as in the DSS. That is to say, Psalms (81), Isaiah (66), Deuteronomy (50), Exodus (44), Genesis (34) and Leviticus (17) are the most frequently quoted books in the NT.[20] We will say more of this later.

Two other types of biblical text exist in the Qumran library. First are Targums, translations of biblical books. The language of the Targums is Aramaic, a sister language to Hebrew. In the postexilic period, Aramaic gradually replaced Hebrew as the mother tongue of most Jews, hence the need for a

---

[14]The numbers cited in this section are those of Martin Abegg Jr., Peter Flint and Eugene Ulrich (*The Dead Sea Scrolls Bible: The Oldest Known Bible Translated for the First Time into English* [New York: HarperCollins, 1999], p. xvii).

[15]See the list in Florentino García Martínez, *The Dead Sea Scrolls Translated*, 2d ed. (Grand Rapids, Mich.: Eerdmans, 1996), p. 482. VanderKam prefers not to list Nehemiah, since one cannot prove that Ezra-Nehemiah constituted one book at that time and it is safer to leave it out unless there is actual fragmentary evidence (*Dead Sea Scrolls Today*, p. 31).

[16]*Responses*, p. 14.

[17]See Abegg, Flint and Ulrich, *Dead Sea Scrolls Bible*, pp. 630-31.

[18]See *Dead Sea Scrolls Translated*, pp. 291-92.

[19]See Edward Cook's comments on these fragments in Wise, Abegg and Cook, *Dead Sea Scrolls*, pp. 437-39.

[20]Following UBS[4], pp. 887-88.

translation of the Hebrew Bible. The evidence from Qumran demonstrates that the writing of Aramaic Targums was already well established by the first century B.C. A nice example is the *Targum of Job* (11QtgJob). Second, we can also include in the category of biblical writings the large number of phylacteries (*t*ᵉ*pillîn* in Aramaic, commonly spelled *tephillin*) found at Qumran, since these are small parchments containing passages from Exodus and Deuteronomy (including Ex 12:43—13:16; Deut 5:1—6:9; 10:12—11:21). These parchments were placed in small boxes and strapped to the head and upper left arm during weekday morning prayers. Twenty-one *tephillin* were found in Cave 4 alone. In addition to *tephillin,* eight mezuzot turned up in Qumran excavations. These are boxes containing the above Scripture quotations that are attached to the doorjamb of Jewish homes. Phylacteries and mezuzot are still a vital part of Jewish piety in modern times.

In addition to biblical texts, another important group of writings comes from the Apocrypha and Pseudepigrapha, some of which we have already read in our study. Four works from the Apocrypha have been identified from the Qumran library: Tobit, Ecclesiasticus (Sirach), Letter of Jeremiah and Psalm 151. Three texts belong to the pseudepigraphal writings: *1 Enoch, Jubilees* and fragments of a composite work entitled *Testaments of the Twelve Patriarchs.* In addition, fragments of previously unknown writings surfaced that appear to be pseudepigraphal in nature.

We should also mention a wide assortment of texts that comment upon the biblical text or consist of thematic extracts from biblical passages. An instructive example is *Florilegium* (4QFlor/4Q174). This document brings together in a catena (a closely linked series) a number of scriptural texts connected with the promise of an eternal dynasty for David and comments briefly upon each text. We return to a discussion of this text in chapter seven.

We conclude with a catchall category that includes such diverse genres as halakic texts, calendrical and liturgical compositions, hymnic and poetical works, and astronomical texts. We will sample at least one of each of these works in our survey of this literature.[21] Three scrolls in this category—what can be designated "rules"—require special mention in our brief introductory survey. They legislate both belief and behavior for the community and provide the best entry into the worldview of the community that produced them.

1. Cairo Genizah copy of the *Damascus Document* (CD) and other copies of the *Damascus Document.* Before fragments of this very important document, which is similar to *Rule of the Community* (1QS), were found at Qumran, two copies were discovered by Solomon Schechter in 1897 in a synagogue genizah

---

[21]See García Martínez, *Dead Sea Scrolls Translated,* pp. vi-xvii, for his classification of this material.

(place where worn-out sacred scrolls were stored rather than being burned) in Cairo, Egypt. The copies were in codex form and dated from the tenth and eleventh centuries A.D. Based upon the content, Schechter surmised that they probably derived from the Pharisees. R. H. Charles saw the document as springing from a reform movement within the priesthood, although closely related to the Pharisees.[22] Several scholars suggested that it might be connected in some way with the Essenes. The connection with the Qumran community, however, was not definitely established until fragments of the work turned up in Caves 4 and 6. We will compare it in some of its features to *Rule of the Community* later in order to draw some inferences about the community that valued it. The name *Damascus Document* was given to it because there is mention of a withdrawal of the members to Damascus (the C in the sigla designates the Cairo copies, whereas the Qumran manuscripts are signified by 4QD and 6QD). Schechter had originally bestowed the name *Zadokite Fragments* upon the work because the sect referred to themselves as "the sons of Zadok." This title is no longer used.

2. *Temple Scroll*[a] (11QTemple[a]). The *Temple Scroll*, the longest of the scrolls (ca. 26 feet), is a rewriting of the canonical books of Exodus (the latter part) through Deuteronomy. Another fragmentary copy exists (11Q20), along with three other possible copies (4Q524, 4Q365a, 11Q21).[23] Dominating the document is a grandiose description of the Jerusalem temple, an idealized temple in the same fashion as described in the book of Ezekiel. The plans for this perfect temple, however, do not coincide with those in Ezekiel or, for that matter, the First and Second Temples (cf. 1 Kings 6–7; 2 Chron 3–4; Josephus, *Ant.* 5 and *J. W.* 5; *m. Mid.; m. Tamid*). The copy discovered at Qumran is dated to about 150 B.C., but some scholars think it may go back to an original as early as the sixth century B.C. The *Temple Scroll* frequently quotes from biblical regulations and, in some cases, recasts them in stricter form. Frequently regulations are presented in the first-person singular, as if spoken by God himself. The work thus seems to function as a "new Deuteronomy" for the covenant community.

3. *Copper Scroll* (3Q15). In 1952 the joint expedition team made a startling discovery of a copper scroll found in two pieces on a natural rock ledge inside Cave 3. The problem was trying to unroll it. After consultations, the only technique that proved successful involved sawing with a razor-thin blade, normally used for splitting pen nibs. Carefully sawing between the Hebrew characters, professor H. Wright Baker of the College of Technology at

[22]R. H. Charles, ed., *The Apocrypha and Pseudepigrapha of the Old Testament*, 2 vols. (Oxford: Clarendon Press, 1913), 2:785-94.
[23]See details in Florentino García Martínez, "Temple Scroll," *EDSS* 2:927-33.

Manchester, England, was able to separate the scroll into twenty-three strips of text. The separate pieces were then mounted for display. Even more intriguing were the contents. The text enumerates the hiding places of an immense treasure. It is not certain that this text should even be reckoned as one of the Qumran scrolls. We will discuss later the various scholarly theories as to the nature of this text and its treasure trove. Alas, despite numerous attempts to find the treasure, none has been discovered!

Dating of the Scrolls and Khirbet Qumran

We conclude our introduction with a few words on dating. After all, how do we know for sure that these scrolls and the ruins of Qumran are connected? And do the scrolls really date from the second century B.C. down to the first century A.D.?

Methods of dating the scrolls. There are three primary and independent techniques for dating these manuscripts.

1. The first method is by paleography. Paleography is the study of ancient scripts, paying special attention to the shapes of letters and style of handwriting. Over time these features undergo change and development. For example, one may compare documents in English from different periods and detect considerable changes in orthography, spelling and the shapes of letters. By comparing examples of ancient writings whose dates are already known with an unknown ancient document, trained specialists can assign it on the basis of paleography to its general time period.[24]

How precise can this method be? Frank Moore Cross of Harvard University believes that a trained paleographer can date a manuscript to within twenty-five or fifty years of when it was copied. And what were the results of paleographical analysis? The manuscripts at Qumran fell into three periods: the archaic (250-150 B.C.), the Hasmonean (150-30 B.C.) and the Herodian (30 B.C.-A.D. 70).

2. But for those who distrust the judgments of paleographers, there are more empirical methods available, the most important being radioactive dating techniques. Accelerator Mass Spectrometry (AMS) measures the amount of carbon-14 still found in something organic. All living things on earth have carbon-12 and carbon-13 in their systems. Because of cosmic rays constantly bombarding earth, some of this carbon is changed into a radioactive isotope, carbon-14. Inasmuch as carbon-14 is unstable and decays at a constant rate back into nitrogen, and thus has a known "half-life," one can, by measuring the ratios of carbon-12, -13 and -14, extrapolate backwards and estimate how

---

[24]For specifics on the shape and form of the Hebrew letters at different time periods, see Frank Moore Cross, "Paleography," *EDSS* 2:629-34.

long ago the organic material was alive. Since the material for most of the Qumran documents was vellum or goatskin, this provides an important avenue for determining at least when the animal was alive, and thus an estimate for the earliest possible date for the material to have been prepared for writing. The results correlate nicely with the paleographic dating.[25]

3. A third approach is simply based upon internal evidence. Are there any references to known individuals or events in the manuscripts that would enable us to locate the approximate time of writing? Here the method is admittedly more difficult and subjective. Still, there are specific individuals mentioned in the Qumran literature, such as Demetrius III, Shelamzion Alexandra, either John Hyrcanus I or II and Marcus Aemilius Scaurus (the Roman governor of Syria in 65-62 B.C.). There are also probable allusions to Jonathan, the younger brother of Judah the Maccabee, and to Alexander Janneus, a later Hasmonean king.[26] When all the allusions and references to people, places and events are factored in, the evidence clearly supports the first two mentioned dating methods.

Methods for dating the ruins at Qumran. Besides carbon-14 dating, as mentioned above, there are two other methods that assist us in determining the date of the settlement at Qumran. The first of these is pottery, the archaeologist's best friend. Styles and shapes of pottery, like writing, undergo change and development. The pottery found at Khirbet Qumran, in several of the caves in which documents were found, as well as in caves where no documents were found, all comes from the same time periods as indicated above. Furthermore, the pottery in the caves was apparently even "thrown" at Qumran. This is important because a few scholars have denied that a connection should be made between the scrolls found in the caves and the community that lived at Qumran. A more convincing connection could scarcely be desired.[27]

But the clincher is coins. Hundreds of coins were found in the ruins of the Qumran settlement. Coins regularly have dates stamped on them, so they are crucial for dating purposes. In this regard, the coins themselves date from the Hasmonean era right down to the Jewish revolt against Rome in A.D. 66-70. *In fact, none of the coins are dated later than A.D. 68.* This is extremely important to the issue because that was the year the settlement was destroyed by the Roman legionnaires. The dating and connection of Qumran and the scrolls is beyond serious dispute. "A threefold cord is not quickly broken" (Eccl 4:12).

---

[25]For further details, see VanderKam, *Dead Sea Scrolls Today,* pp. 17-18; and Gregory L. Doudna, "Carbon-14 Dating," *EDSS* 1:120-21.

[26]See Fitzmyer, *Responses,* pp. 19-20. For further discussion of the debate over whether Jonathan ben Mattathias was the "wicked priest," see Hanan Eshel, "Jonathan (Hasmonean)," *EDSS* 1:422-23.

[27]See Jodi Magness, "Pottery," *EDSS* 2:681-86.

Finally, we mention a recent discovery that bears on the discussion. Dr. James Strange, professor of archaeology at South Florida University, in a small dig seeking to discover possible cavities near Khirbet Qumran suggested by seismic scans, accidentally (!) found two ostraca. On one of these ostraca were fifteen crudely incised lines of Hebrew. According to Frank Moore Cross and Esther Eshel, the epigraphers assigned to the ostracon by the dig director, the text records the transfer of the estate of a man named Ḥōni to the "community" (i.e., the community at Qumran). The first line has a date formula: "In year two of the [ ]." Since the handwriting is similar to Late Herodian, and the site at Qumran was destroyed in A.D. 68, Cross and Eshel date the inscription to A.D. 67, though they mention other possibilities. They prefer A.D. 67 because this correlates with year two "of the freedom of Zion," a phrase found on Jewish coins of the First Jewish Revolt (year one being A.D. 66, the beginning of the revolt). In their opinion, this ostracon from the site of Qumran supplies the missing link between the Dead Sea Scrolls and the Qumran community because the inscription records a deed of gift to the "community" (*yahad* in Hebrew), an important self-designation for the Qumran community in their sectarian writings. They read line eight of the inscription as: "when he fulfills (his oath) to the Community." If this reading stands, there can be little doubt that the scrolls should be associated with the Qumran community.[28]

The Life Setting for the Qumran Literature

We set out briefly the background and history of the sect that produced this literature.[29]

---

[28] As is often the case, however, this claim has not gone uncontested. Ada Yardeni translates the crucial line eight as: "and every oth[er(?)] tree [. . .]."Let us just say that the scholarly debate continues and that we may well have many more surprises in store for us from Khirbet Qumran. See Frank Moore Cross and Esther Eshel, "Ostraca from Khirbet Qumrân," *IEJ* 47 (1997): 17-28; Cross and Eshel, "The Missing Link," *BAR* 24, no. 2 (1998): 48-53, 69; Ada Yardeni, "A Draft of a Deed of an Ostracon from Khirbet Qumran," *IEJ* 47 (1997): 233-37; Yardeni, "Breaking the Missing Link," *BAR* 24, no. 3 (1998): 44-47.

[29] I am aware that there are competing views concerning the *Sitz im Leben* for this material. In my opinion, however, the majority view, which I set out in what follows, has the most to commend it. For a concise summary of the critical consensus among authorities on the DSS, see James H. Charlesworth, *Jesus and the Dead Sea Scrolls* (New York: Doubleday, 1992), pp. xxxii-xxv; and George W. E. Nickelsburg, *Jewish Literature Between the Bible and the Mishnah: A Historical and Literary Introduction* (Philadelphia: Fortress, 1981), pp. 122-23. Charlesworth gives a listing of the various scholars, their nationality, religious affiliation (if any) and institutions or organizations. As he points out, the lay reader may not realize the large degree of unanimity that exists because of the sensationalist views in the popular media. Some of these suggest conspiracies, usually to prevent traditional religious views from being undermined. This is poppycock. The reader may sample such notions by reading Baigent and Leigh, *Dead Sea Scrolls Deception*.

Identity

We assume as highly probable that the Qumran sect is the group described by Philo Judaeus (*Good Person* 12 §§75-91), Flavius Josephus (*J.W.* 2.8.2-11 §§119-158 and *Ant.* 18.1.5 §§18-22) and Pliny the Elder (*Nat.* 5.17.4).[30] Pliny stated that the Essenes were located on the west shore of the Dead Sea, north of Engedi and Masada. This of course correlates nicely with Khirbet Qumran. Philo and Josephus both described a celibate, communal sect that pursued a very strict life devoted to personal and corporate purity and holiness. Josephus was aware that there were two groups of Essenes, one celibate and the other not. Those who married lived in cities and villages. He also estimated the total number of Essenes to be about four thousand. Since the maximum number of occupants at Khirbet Qumran has been estimated to be about three hundred, the Qumran community constituted a small minority of the total number of Essenes.[31] Also, the Essene doctrines mentioned by Philo and Josephus correspond closely to the teachings endorsed by the sectarian literature from Qumran. All in all, the parallels are so close that most scholars accept the equation that the Qumran covenanters were the strict order of Essenes mentioned by the above writers of the first century A.D.[32]

History

Correlating the archaeological remains of Qumran with the DSS, we assume that the Essenes occupied Qumran from about 150 B.C. to A.D. 68.[33] More difficult is the question of when the movement itself began. The Cairo Genizah copy of the *Damascus Document* (CD), with which we begin our reading, seems to rather straightforwardly set out a chronological bench-

---

[30]For a discussion of the issues and the consensus view, see Devorah Dimant, "Qumran Sectarian Literature," in *Jewish Writings of the Second Temple Period: Apocrypha, Pseudepigrapha, Qumran Sectarian Writings, Philo, Josephus,* ed. Michael E. Stone, CRINT 2 (Assen: Van Gorcum; Philadelphia: Fortress, 1984), pp. 483-87; Fitzmyer, *Responses,* pp.100-102; VanderKam, *Dead Sea Scrolls Today,* pp. 71-98; Geza Vermes, *The Complete Dead Sea Scrolls in English,* 5th ed. (London: Penguin, 1998), pp. 1-22; Frank Moore Cross, *The Ancient Library of Qumran* (Minneapolis: Fortress, 1995), pp. 54-87; Todd S. Beall, "Essenes," *EDSS* 1:262-69 and secondary sources referred to.

[31]The number of inhabitants at Qumran is based upon Roland de Vaux's lectures published in *Archaeology and the Dead Sea Scrolls* (London: Oxford University Press, 1973).

[32]See VanderKam's discussion of Todd Beall's comparative study of Josephus and the DSS and his own analysis of the wider similarities (*Dead Sea Scrolls Today,* pp. 71-98). Beall's work is *Josephus' Description of the Essenes Illustrated by the Dead Sea Scrolls,* SNTSMS 58 (Cambridge: Cambridge University Press, 1988).

[33]Roland de Vaux had dated the first phase of settlement to the middle of the second century B.C. This is now challenged by later investigation. Some prefer a date of about 100 B.C. See Magen Broshi, "Qumran: Archaeology," *EDSS* 2:737.

mark. We quote the following excerpt:[34]

> A 1 So listen, all you who recognize righteousness, and consider the deeds of God. When He has a dispute with any mortal, He passes judgment on those who spurn him.
>
> For when Israel abandoned Him by being faithless, He turned away from them and from His sanctuary and gave them up to the sword. But when He called to mind the covenant He made with their forefathers, He left a remnant for Israel and did not allow them to be exterminated. In the era of wrath—three hundred and ninety years at the time He handed them over to the power of Nebuchadnezzar king of Babylon—He took care of them and caused to grow from Israel and from Aaron and root of planting to inherit His land and to grow fat on the good produce of His soil. They considered their iniquity and they know that they were guilty men, and had been like the blind and like those groping for the way twenty years. But God considered their deeds, that they had sought Him with a whole heart. So He raised up for them a teacher of righteousness to guide them in the way of His heart. He taught to later generations what God did to the generation deserving wrath, a company of traitors. They are the ones who depart from the proper way. That is the time of which it was written, "Like a rebellious cow, so rebelled Israel" (Hos. 4:16).
>
> When the Man of Mockery appeared, who sprayed on Israel lying waters, he led them to wander in the trackless wasteland. He brought down the lofty heights of old, turned aside from paths of righteousness, and shifted the boundary marks that the forefathers had set up to mark their inheritance, so that the courses of His covenant took hold on them. Because of this they were handed over to the sword that avenges the breach of His covenant.
>
> For they had sought flattery, choosing travesties of true religion; they looked for ways to break the law; they favored the fine neck. They called the guilty innocent, and the innocent guilty. They overstepped covenant, violated law, and they conspired together to kill the innocent, for all those who lived pure lives they loathed from the bottom of their heart. So they persecuted them violently, and were happy to see the people quarrel. Because of this God became very angry with their company. He annihilated the lot of them, because all their deeds were uncleanness to Him.[35]

Should these numbers be taken literally? If so, when should we begin reckoning the 390 years? If we start with the destruction of the First Temple, we have 586-390 = 196 B.C. as the time of formation. Another twenty years means that the Teacher of Righteousness arrived at about 176 B.C. This comports reasonably well with the crisis generated by the hellenizing program instituted by the Seleucids and the archaeological evidence that Qumran was

---

[34]We leave out of the citation the section headings that Wise, Abegg and Cook insert in order to help the reader follow the subject matter.
[35]Edward Cook in Wise, Abegg and Cook, *Dead Sea Scrolls*, pp. 51-52 (A 1:1—2:1).

founded as a religious settlement around 150 B.C.[36] But there are other ways of interpreting this text, and, not surprisingly, some scholars reconstruct the sect's origins in quite different ways.[37]

Jerome Murphy-O'Connor argues for a Babylonian origin during the exile. He views the 390 years as symbolic and patterned after Ezekiel's symbolic action of lying on his side for 390 days for the sin of Israel, a period representing 390 years (cf. Ezek 4:4-6). Devorah Dimant disagrees with a Babylonian origin but, like Murphy-O'Connor, pushes the founding date back to the sixth century. For her the book of Daniel is the exegetical key. The CD years are prophetic years in the manner of Daniel 9:24-27. Furthermore, she takes the *terminus a quo* of the CD quotation as the first deportation of Judeans by Nebuchadnezzar in 605 B.C., as narrated in the book of Daniel (Dan 1:1). This yields the date 605-390 = 215 B.C. and places the sect's formation during the turbulent time of the wars of the Diadochi, the Seleucid and Ptolemaic successors to Alexander the Great, and their struggle to control Palestine.[38]

The present writer follows a well-trodden view in holding that the Qumran community began in the wake of the Hellenistic crisis precipitated by Antiochus IV Epiphanes (175-163 B.C.). It seems that the Qumran community itself resulted from an earlier split within a larger movement, which is probably that designated as Essene by Philo, Josephus and Pliny the Elder. Thus the actual beginnings of the Essene movement may well antedate by some years the settlement of the group at Qumran around 150 B.C. Jerome Murphy-O'Connor's thesis that the Essenes derived from Babylonia in the exilic era has little support, and most researchers agree that the Essenes and the Qumran covenanters had Palestinian roots.[39] We also assume that the celibate version of the Essenes is the group who established a communal center at Khirbet Qumran. More details will be added as we read the literature itself.[40]

---

[36]Though it does not fit as well with the newer proposal of about 100 B.C. for the founding of Qumran.

[37]For a survey of the scholarly views up to the mid-1980s, see Phillip R. Callaway, *The History of the Qumran Community*, JSPSup 3 (Sheffield: Sheffield Academic Press, 1988), pp. 11-27. For more recent scholarship, one may profitably consult Lawrence H. Schiffman, *Reclaiming the Dead Sea Scrolls: The History of Judaism, the Background of Christianity, the Lost Library of Qumran*, ABRL (New York: Doubleday, 1994), pp. 83-95.

[38]See her argumentation in "Qumran Sectarian Literature," pp. 542-47.

[39]For Murphy-O'Connor's arguments, see "The Essenes and Their History," *RB* 81 (1974): 215-44; and Murphy-O'Connor, "The Essenes in Palestine," *BA* 40 (1977): 100-124. For a convenient summary of the position adopted in this book, see Charlesworth, *Jesus and the Dead Sea Scrolls*, pp. 31-35; and VanderKam, *Dead Sea Scrolls Today*, pp. 99-108.

[40]For a lucid treatment of this position, see VanderKam, *Dead Sea Scrolls Today*, pp. 99-108; Todd S. Beall, "Essenes," 1:267-69; and Beall, "Essenes," *DNTB*, pp. 342-48.

Damascus Document

We begin our reading with the *Damascus Document* or, as it is often referred to currently, the *Damascus Covenant* (CD). As indicated above, a medieval copy of this document had already been discovered in a Cairo genizah by Solomon Schechter in 1896 and published in 1910. The discovery in 1952 of a copy dating from the first century B.C. eliminated the notion that this was a medieval composition. Schechter originally thought that the work originated in Pharisaic circles, but most scholars today ascribe the work to the Essenes mentioned by Philo, Josephus and Pliny.[41] R. H. Charles had suggested in his monumental work that it derived from a reformist group of Sadducees.[42] Interestingly, Lawrence Schiffman has recently revived a version of Charles's theory, and others have followed him.[43] We will follow the majority view that the document is Essene.

Date and Composition

The Qumran manuscripts are generally dated on the basis of paleographic analysis to the period between the first half of the first century B.C. and the early first century A.D.[44] Does the document, however, have a prehistory, and is it a composite or unified text? A consensus holds that the text is composite, which introduces a complicating factor into the dating. It may well be that an earlier version of the text goes back to the mid-second century, the time of the formation of the sect.[45] We will leave this issue to the side and focus upon the text as we now have it.

Analysis

The *Damascus Document* falls naturally into two main divisions in terms of content. The first part is a historical retrospect with an admonitory function. That is, the history of the sect is narrated with a view to encouraging the adherents to keep alive the mission and calling of the group. The second section reviews the regulations that define the behavioral, ritual and liturgical standards and expectations of the group.[46] This section affords an opportunity to observe the sect's unique interpretation of Torah.

---

[41]Solomon Schechter, *Fragments of a Zadokite Work: Documents of Jewish Sectaries 1* (New York: Ktav, 1970 [1910]).

[42]Charles, *Apocrypha and Pseudepigrapha of the Old Testament,* 2:785-97.

[43]*Reclaiming the Dead Sea Scrolls,* pp. 65-81.

[44]See Joseph M. Baumgarten, "Damascus Document," *EDSS* 1:166-67.

[45]See, e.g., Jerome Murphy-O'Connor, "A Literary Analysis of Damascus Document VI 2-VIII, 3," *RB* 78 (1971): 210-32.

[46]Vermes neatly divides the work into "an Exhortation and a list of Statutes" (*Complete Dead Sea Scrolls in English,* p. 95).

The admonitions. In terms of genre, this section has biblical prototypes. The book of Deuteronomy provides perhaps the best model for CD. Similar to Deuteronomy 27—33 and Joshua 24, we have a covenant renewal as the occasion of the writing. A good case can be made that the Qumran covenanters celebrated an annual covenant-renewal festival at Pentecost and that the reading of this document played an important role in that ceremony. Just as Moses, the man of God, rehearsed Israel's history for the new generation, so the Teacher of Righteousness (or the community guardians) did the same for the Qumran covenanters. Note also how the admonitions begin by striking a prophetic note reminiscent of the Hebrew prophets. "So listen, all you who recognize righteousness, and consider the deeds of God. When He has a dispute with any mortal, He passes judgment on those who spurn him" (CD 1:1-2). Isaiah's opening indictment of Judah and Jerusalem quickly comes to mind (cf. Is 1:2-9), as do those of Hosea (Hos 4:1-14) and Amos (Amos 3:1-2).

We may outline the section in the following manner: [47]

I.   Recollection of the past (1:1—2:1)

II.   Remembrance of God's foreordination (2:2-13)

III.   The remnant and the last days (2:14—6:2a)

IV.   The role of the Teacher of Righteousness (6:2b-11a)

V.   The rulings of the Teacher of Righteousness: standards of purity and behavior; reward and retribution (6:11b—7:9a)

VI.   The inevitability of judgment upon lawbreakers (7:9b—8:1a)

VII. Alternate version of above (Geniza B 19:7-13)

VIII. Railings against the ruling priestly aristocracy (8:1b-13)

IX.   Reminder to be faithful until Messiah comes (8:14-21, Geniza B 19:33-20:34)

Several items of great importance for understanding the Essene sect's history, theology and self-understanding appear in this document.

Apparently schism and strife rocked the early years of the sect. The revered Teacher of Righteousness was not considered divinely inspired by all the earliest members of this reform movement. Dissenters were designated as "the ones who depart from the proper way" (CD 1:13). CD also castigates the views of the dissenters and charges the advocates of this heretical teaching (from the standpoint of the sect) with physical violence against the community. We will comment on this later.

The primary fault of the dissenters was that they failed to uphold with sufficient rigor and correct interpretation various pentateuchal laws, primarily those concerning ritual purity and the sacred calendar. The Essenes clearly viewed themselves as a community of priests and as *required to maintain a*

---

[47]For another way of outlining the section, see also Nickelsburg, *Jewish Literature,* pp. 124-26.

level of ritual purity that had been reserved for the priest in the OT. This is an important insight into the self-perception of this sect and goes a long way toward helping us understand the nature of the conflict with their opponents.

We also notice in the admonitions a strong note of predestination. In fact, a form of "double predestination" marks the thought of this community. Thus the elect were eternally chosen and the wicked eternally rejected—all before the creation of the world. Nonetheless, God will hold the wicked accountable for their deeds. This view clearly distinguishes the "sons of Zadok" from the Sadducean party as described by Josephus ("The Sadducees . . . deny Fate altogether and . . . say that men are free to choose between good and evil, and each individual must decide which he will follow" [*J. W.* 2.8.14]). It also seems more extreme than the Pharisaic position, which held God's foreordination and human freedom in tension (cf. Josephus, *J. W.* 2.8.14; Acts 5:38-39).

A striking feature of this document, which we shall see reflected in other sectarian writings from Qumran, is the conviction that *the last days have begun and the final intervention of God and his messiah(s) is imminent*. There is a pronounced apocalyptic worldview and perspective operative in the sect's mentality. They are eagerly awaiting the eschatological battle, something described in great detail in the *War Scroll* (1QM). The appearance of the Teacher of Righteousness signaled the beginning of the end times (CD 1:11b-12; 4:4, 10b-13; 6:10-11; 7:10—8.3; 12:23, esp. 20:13b-20). Repentance and rigid obedience to the Teacher's interpretation of Torah was motivated by the immanent appearance of final judgment for the wicked and glory for the righteous, the latter being only those who belonged to the sons of Zadok, the members of the sect.

The commandments. Here are the specifics of living as a "son of Zadok." This section is a halakic commentary on the pentateuchal legislation of the Bible. The word *hālākâ,* meaning "rule or tradition," is a rabbinic term used for the interpretation of the written law. While the term itself is not found in the DSS, the material in this section has clear affinities with what the later sages would call halakah. It is difficult to outline such a diverse collection of legal and ritual requirements. We simply list the main areas of discussion: (1) rules concerning vows; (2) rules concerning admission to the movement and conditions rendering membership impossible; (3) standards of conduct and procedure for discipline; (4) guidelines for trials and hearings; (5) purity laws; (6) sabbath laws; and (7) organization and procedure for communal life.[48]

---

[48]For a sequential outline of the section, see J. M. Baumgarten and D. R. Schwartz, "Damascus Document (CD)," in *The Dead Sea Scrolls: Hebrew, Aramaic and Greek Texts with English Translations, 2: Damascus Document, War Scroll and Related Documents* (Tübingen: Mohr Siebeck; Louisville: Westminster John Knox, 1995), p. 5.

When one compares the halakah of Qumran to that of the Pharisaism depicted in the NT and later in the Mishnah, it is generally more strict and extends the application of the various rulings.[49] They have been aptly called "gap fillers" rather than "fence builders."[50] There are also differences with mainstream Sadducees, as a comparison with 4QMMT[a] seems to imply.[51] In addition to the earlier passage quoted from CD, we cite the following:

> Also they have corrupted their holy spirit, and with blasphemous language they have reviled the statutes of God's covenant, saying, "They are not well-founded." (CD 5:11b-12)
> But the "Shoddy-Wall-Builders" and "White-washers" understood none of these things, for one who deals in mere wind, a spewer of lies, had spewed on them (B reads slightly differently: one who walks in wind, and who deals in storms, one who preaches lies to men), one on whose entire company God's anger had burned hot. (CD 8:12b-13).[52]

Thus for the Qumranites, only the halakah given by the Teacher of Righteousness was correct, and observing it with utter exactness constituted one a member of the true Israel, "sons of light," "sons of righteousness," "a house of holiness," "a sure house," "the community" *(hayyahad)*, "the poor ones," "the many" *(hārabbîm)*, and other titles. These are some of the self-designations used by the Essenes.[53] What is essential for grasping the ethos of this movement is to realize that the elect consisted only of their number. The definition of Israel had been severely delimited. Even Jews who were not a part of the

---

[49]Jacob Milgrom argues that there was both a minimizing and a maximizing hermeneutic at Qumran; that is, high-priestly holiness was required of all Israel—in this case that was only the sectaries of Qumran—but that standard applied within a minimalist space, namely, the temple city of Jerusalem. He speaks of a homogenizing hermeneutic employed by the sectaries as opposed to the rabbis' harmonizing approach. See his "The Scriptural Foundations and Deviations in the Laws of Purity of the *Temple Scroll*," in *Archaeology and History in the Dead Sea Scrolls: The New York University Conference in Memory of Yigael Yadin*, ed. Lawrence H. Schiffman, JSPSup 8, JSOT/ASOR Monographs 2 (Sheffield: JSOT Press, 1990), p. 89. See also the entire article, pp. 82-97.

[50]This phrase comes from a personal note by Martin Abegg (1998).

[51]The hotly debated issues surrounding the interpretation of this fragment will be taken up below.

[52]Edward Cook in Wise, Abegg and Cook, *Dead Sea Scrolls*, pp. 55, 59.

[53]The exact meaning of "Essene" is disputed. VanderKam suggests that it derives from the Hebrew word for "doers" (*'ōśîm; Dead Sea Scrolls Today*, p. 92). But see Cross, *Ancient Library of Qumran*, p. 54 n. 1, for another view and discussion of alternatives. For a full listing of the various self-designations for this group, see William Sanford LaSor, *The Dead Sea Scrolls and the New Testament* (Grand Rapids, Mich.: Eerdmans, 1972), pp. 47-51.

sons of Zadok were sons of darkness and could expect only God's terrible wrath at the day of visitation. For each Jewish movement or sect that we study, this will be a key question: Who is the true Israel? The answer given has been fundamental for the various manifestations of Judaism that have existed, including Christianity.[54]

Relationship to the New Testament

Since we are dealing with such a diverse selection of documents from Qumran, we shall deviate from our usual procedure in earlier chapters and proceed at this point to draw some parallels and observations vis-à-vis NT literature.

Manner of reading Old Testament Scripture. As we look over the shoulders of the sectaries and observe how they read the OT Scriptures, fascinating features appear, one of which is contemporizing OT passages. That is, the community, presumably following the Teacher's exegetical guidance, read OT passages as being fulfilled in the events of the sect's history and current existence. There was a lively sense of fulfilled prophecy. Moses and the prophets spoke of the end times; the end times had begun with the arrival of the Teacher of Righteousness; the events of that day were unfolding according to a predetermined divine plan for the end of the ages. These appear to be the fundamental presuppositions of the community's hermeneutical approach to the Hebrew Scriptures.[55]

Precisely these presuppositions operated within the context of the Christian community.[56] All that is needed is the substitution of Jesus of Nazareth for the Teacher of Righteousness and we have the exegetical keys for discerning early Christian exegesis. Clearly Jesus taught his disciples to read the OT as pointing to him as its ultimate fulfillment. We cite several passages:

> Then beginning with Moses and all the prophets, he interpreted to them the things about himself in all the scriptures. (Lk 24:27)
>
> "These are my words that I spoke to you while I was still with you—that everything written about me in the law of Moses, the prophets, and the psalms must be fulfilled." Then he opened their minds to understand the scriptures, and he said to them, "Thus it is written, that the Messiah is to suffer and to rise from the dead on the third day." (Lk 24:44-46)
>
> Do not think that I have come to abolish the law or the prophets; I have come not to abolish but to fulfill. (Mt 5:17)

---

[54]Or, as Jacob Neusner insists, for the *Judaisms* that have existed. See his discussion in *Self-Fulfilling Prophecy: Exile and Return in the History of Judaism* (Boston: Beacon, 1987), pp. 5-11.

[55]For further discussion, see Cross, *Ancient Library of Qumran*, pp. 90-91.

[56]See also James H. Charlesworth, *Jesus Within Judaism: New Light from Exciting Archaeological Discoveries* (New York: Doubleday, 1988), p. 59.

You search the scriptures, because you think that in them you have eternal life; and it is they that testify on my behalf. (Jn 5:39)[57]

An instructive example occurs in Acts 4:25-28. Here Luke records a sermon by Peter in a post-Pentecost setting in the Jerusalem temple precincts. Peter quotes from Psalm 2:1-2: "Why did the Gentiles rage, and the peoples imagine vain things? The kings of the earth took their stand, and the rulers have gathered together against the Lord and against his Messiah." Notice how Peter comments on this verse: "For in this city, in fact, both Herod and Pontius Pilate, with the Gentiles and the peoples of Israel, gathered together against your holy servant Jesus, whom you anointed, to do whatever your hand and your plan had predestined to take place" (Acts 4:27-28).

Peter identifies the recent events of Jesus' crucifixion as the fulfillment of Psalm 2:1-2. The biblical text is read as a direct prophecy about Jesus and those responsible for his execution. Furthermore, these events unfolded in accordance with a divinely intended plan.

In an earlier sermon, on the Day of Pentecost, Peter quoted from Joel 2:28-32, a passage that begins with the words "In the last days it will be . . ." The outpouring of the Holy Spirit, as prophesied by the prophet Joel, had been fulfilled, according to Peter, at that very moment—the last days had begun!

Once again we point out how important it is to grasp this fundamental presupposition of the earliest Christians: the last days began in the ministry,

---

[57]We could multiply quotations, but our essential point is established. For evangelical Christians this may be a bit disconcerting. If we allow a similarity of approach, do we not call into question the unique, divine authority and inspiration of the NT writings? In short, no. What we acknowledge is that the truth of the gospel has come to us in a thoroughly Jewish mode. This does not undermine the truthfulness of the message of Christ but rather roots it in a tradition that God was pleased to use in redemptive history. Remember Jesus' comment to the Samaritan woman: "Salvation is from the Jews" (Jn 4:22).

As Christians, we do not agree that the interpretations of the Teacher of Righteousness were divinely inspired or that he was God's messenger who prepared a people for the coming of the Messiah(s). Jesus was and is the Messiah of Israel, and John the Baptist was his forerunner. These affirmations are established by faith, the Holy Spirit witnessing with our spirit that these things are true (cf. 1 Jn 2:27; 4:6, 13-16; 5:6-12). Historical research, however, can be helpful in validating competing claims, and the evidences for the truthfulness of Christianity are impressive (cf. Jn 20:30-31; 21:24-25). See further on this Craig Blomberg, "Gospels (Historical Reliability)," *DJG*, pp. 291-97.

In all of this we should remember this fact: the Teacher of Righteousness never claimed, nor did his followers ever claim on his behalf, that his death atoned for the sins of the world or that he would rise from the dead. Jesus of Nazareth, on the other hand, claimed that he came to give his life a ransom for many (Mk 10:45) and that he would rise again on the third day (Mk 8:31). The entire edifice of Christianity rests on the fact that he did as he claimed (cf. 1 Cor 15:3-19). As Charlesworth notes, the Jesus movement, which became the Christian church, was distinguishable from Judaism "essentially in one life and one person" (*Jesus Within Judaism*, p. 58).

death and resurrection of Jesus of Nazareth (cf. 1 Cor 10:11; 1 Jn 2:18). In theological terms, we describe this as "realized eschatology." These last days would, of course, be climaxed by the return of Jesus as rightful heir to the throne of David. His reign over all the earth is the eager expectation of the NT authors (cf. Mt 19:28 and par.; 1 Cor 15:24-25; 2 Tim 2:12; Rev 2:26-27; 3:21; 11:15; 19:11-16; 20:4-6). Thus there exists in Christian thought, as reflected in the NT, the fundamental tension between realized and futuristic eschatology or, in other words, the tension between the "now and not yet" dimension of eschatology (see chapter three). The preaching mission of earliest Christianity operates within this basic orientation.[58]

Morality and ethics. Both communities, Qumran and the earliest Christians, insisted upon a high standard of morality and behavior; indeed, members were disciplined should they fail in this regard: "But all of the members of the covenant who breached the restrictions of the Law, when the glory of God appears to Israel they shall be excluded from the midst of the camp, and with them all who did evil in Judah when it was undergoing trial" (CD B 20:25-27).[59] Paul's pastoral directive with regard to a case of incest at Corinth sounds strikingly similar: "Drive out the wicked person from among you" (1 Cor 5:13b; cf. Gal 6:1-5, 7-8; 2 Thess 3:6, 14-15: 2 Tim 2:12b).

One should also compare the views of the Essenes to Jesus and Paul on the issue of divorce and remarriage. CD 4:15—5:5 identifies one of Belial's traps as taking a second wife while the first is alive. This text refers primarily to polygamy, which, of course, is also prohibited in Christian teaching. [60] More controversial is the question of remarriage following divorce. *Temple Scroll* (11Q19 lvii 17-19) states: "He is not to take another wife in addition to her: no, she alone

---

[58]This, of course, raises the theological question whether we can discern within NT literature a weakening of eschatological fervor. Is there a crisis that develops because of the delay of the return of Christ, and can we detect early Christian responses and adjustments to this problem? For our part, we are not convinced that this ever was a problem or that one can discern theological accommodations to the nonfulfillment of eschatological hopes in the NT era (cf. 2 Pet 3:1-10). For further discussion on this, see Ben Witherington III, *Jesus, Paul and the End of the World* (Downers Grove, Ill.: InterVarsity Press, 1992), pp. 9-44, 232-42.
[59]Edward Cook in Wise, Abegg and Cook, *Dead Sea Scrolls*, p. 60.
[60]Michael A. Knibb comments on 4:21: "The possessive pronoun in 'during their lifetime' is masculine, and the phrase is most naturally taken as referring to the husbands, not the wives; from this it appears that what is attacked here is the whole idea of a man having a second wife during his lifetime, whether through polygamy, or through a second marriage after the divorce or death of a first wife. But from what follows (the quotation of Deut. 17:17 and the reference to David) it seems clear that polygamy is primarily in mind" (*The Qumran Community*, CCWJCW 2 [Cambridge: Cambridge University Press, 1987], p. 43). For further discussion of the Essene view on divorce and remarriage, see Joseph M. Baumgarten, "The Qumran-Essene Restraints on Marriage," in *Archaeology and History in the Dead Sea Scrolls*, pp. 1-24.

shall be with him as long as she lives. If she dies, then he may take himself another wife from his father's house, that is, his family."[61] Even though the text is referring to the king, many have assumed that this prohibition would also apply to the commoner.[62] If this is correct, we have a remarkable parallel to the NT. Mark, Luke and Paul all contain absolute prohibitions against divorce and remarriage regardless of the cause (Mk 10:11-12; Lk 16:18; 1 Cor 7:10-11).[63] The exception clause ("except on the ground of unchastity"), found only in Matthew 5:31-32 and 19:9 may also receive illumination from the *Temple Scroll*. The Greek word is *porneia,* which finds its equivalent in the Hebrew *z^enût*. According to 11Q19 lvii 17-19, one of the two forms of *z^enût* is an illicit marital union, that is, within a forbidden degree of kinship (an aunt/uncle, sister/brother, mother/father, etc.; cf. Lev 18). The Essenes also disallowed union with a niece or nephew (CD 5:7-11). Thus, given the mixed Jewish and Gentile community of Matthew's Gospel, one may infer that Gentile Christians who were married to someone within the prohibited degrees of kinship would be expected to divorce their spouses. But this was the only exception. The upshot of this is that the NT stands in close agreement with the Essenes on the matter of marriage and divorce over against the position of the Pharisees. Matthew 19:3-9 is framed in the context of an inner-Pharisaic dispute between the stricter Shammaites (only *z^enût* was a ground for divorce) and the more liberal Hillelites (nearly anything that grieved the husband was a potential ground for divorce). In all likelihood, the Sadducees were even more lax with regard to divorce.

Explanation for unbelief. Both communities had a similar explanation for the rejection of their message by outsiders. A lack of commitment to the truth was attributed to a lack of understanding. The Essenes appear to have held, however, that this lack of understanding was foreknown, and thus God made his eternal election on the basis of this prior knowledge (cf. CD 2:7-8). With this notion compare 1 Peter 1:b-2a: "who are chosen according to the foreknowledge of God the Father" (NASB). Paul also relates election to foreknowledge (cf. Rom 8:29: "For those whom he foreknew he also predestined"; cf. 11:2).[64] According to the Markan tradition, Jesus likewise traced his gener-

---

[61]Michael Wise in Wise, Abegg and Cook, *Dead Sea Scrolls,* p. 485.

[62]See further Joseph A. Fitzmyer, "Marriage and Divorce," *EDSS* 1:512-13.

[63]On this whole question, see William A. Heth and Gordon J. Wenham, *Jesus and Divorce* (Nashville: Nelson, 1984). For a differing view, refer to Craig Keener, *And Divorces Another: Divorce and Remarriage in the Teaching of the New Testament* (Peabody, Mass.: Hendrickson, 1991). See also Andrew Warren, "Did Moses Permit Divorce? Modal *wĕqātal* as Key to New Testament Readings of Deuteronomy 24:1-4," *TynB* 49 (1998): 39-56.

[64]But see the translation of 1 Pet 1:2 in the NRSV. This gets us into one of the long-standing debates of Christian theology, i.e., the doctrine of unconditional versus conditional election. One may read helpful discussions on the background of the notion of foreknowledge in *NIDNTT* 1:692-97 and *TDNT* 1:689-719.

ation's rejection to a lack of spiritual understanding (Mk 4:10-12), though one may also detect the idea that Satan deceives the unbelieving (Mk 4:15). Luke adds a saying that seems very close to the Qumran idea of prior choice as the prerequisite for understanding (Lk 10:21-23). The Johannine tradition simply states that "they do not know" (Jn 15:21; 16:3; 17:25; 1 Jn 3:1). Certainly Paul can be quoted to the effect that Satan blinds the eyes of unbelievers or that they believe a lie rather than the truth (2 Cor 4:3-4; 2 Thess 2:10-12), similar to the Qumran notion of the "three traps of Belial" (CD 4:13-15).

The new covenant. A striking parallel between Qumran and the NT lies in the conviction of both communities that the new covenant prophesied by Jeremiah (cf. Jer 31:31-34; cf. Ezek 16:60-62) had been established between God and a repentant remnant. A recurring phrase in CD refers to members as those "who enter the covenant" (cf. CD 2:2; 6:11; 8:1). As already mentioned above, a likely life setting for CD, as we now have it, lies in an annual covenant-renewal ceremony. Fragments of CD found in Cave 4 at Qumran seem to specify the time during which this ceremony took place, namely, the Feast of Weeks on the fifteenth day of the third month.[65]

> The Levites and those who live in camps shall convene on the third month and curse those who stray from the Law to the right [or to the left].
>
> This is the exposition of the regulations that they shall follow during the era of wickedness [. . . so that they can] stand firm during all the times of wrath and the stages of the journey made by those [who live in camps and all their cities.
>
> All of] this is on the basis of the most recent interpretation of the Law. (4Q266 18 v 16b-20).[66]

Of course the NT places considerable emphasis upon the new covenant. The Gospel traditions all found the establishment of this covenant with the "little flock" (Lk 12:32) on the authority of Jesus himself (Mt 26:26-29; Mk

---

[65]So Vermes, *Complete Dead Sea Scrolls in English,* pp. 96-97.

[66]Edward Cook in Wise, Abegg and Cook, *Dead Sea Scrolls,* p. 74. The phrase *mdrš h'hrwn* ("the most recent interpretation") is more literally rendered by Florentino García Martínez and Eibert J. C. Tigchelaar as "the last interpretation" (*The Dead Sea Scrolls Study Edition,* 2 vols. [Grand Rapids, Mich.: Eerdmans, 1997-1998], 1:616-17) and by Vermes as "the ultimate interpretation of the Law" (*Complete Dead Sea Scrolls in English,* p. 118).

A word of explanation may be helpful for deciphering DSS citations at this point. In larger collections such as CD, reference is made to column:line (e.g., column 3, line 5 would be cited 3:5). In smaller portions of manuscripts, the student will often encounter, as with 4Q266 18 v 16b-20, reference to a fragment, column and lines. The first arabic numeral (18) identifies the fragment, the roman numeral (v) the column, and the second arabic numeral(s) (16b-20) the lines. One will also often see simply a roman numeral followed by an arabic numeral (e.g., CD B ii 7-8). In this case reference is being made simply to a column and line(s), since the manuscript in question is not made up of various fragments.

14:22-25; Lk 22:15-20). In the setting of a paschal supper, Jesus symbolized the inauguration of the new covenant by means of bread and wine. He interpreted the bread as his body and the wine as the blood of the new covenant. The next day he died on the cross and thereby became the sacrifice of the covenant-making ceremony.[67]

Two NT epistolary documents (2 Cor 3:4-18; Heb 8:6-13) argue for the obsolescence of the old (Mosaic or Sinaitic) covenant and stress the superiority of the new covenant established on the basis of Christ's death and resurrection. In the new covenant the ritual purity laws are no longer binding—having been fulfilled in the work of Christ (cf. Col 2:16-17)—contrary to the convictions of the Qumran community. But the point of similarity lies in the claim of both movements to be the fulfillment of Jeremiah's (and Ezekiel's) prophecies about the establishment of a new covenant between God and a faithful remnant of Israel.

Assorted parallels and similarities. Table 6.1 summarizes some passages from CD that recall similar phraseology, expressions or ideas that point to a common matrix for these two movements within the larger domain of Judaism.

Rule of the Community (Manual of Discipline)

If CD is important for understanding the ethos of this movement, then *Rule of the Community* (1QS) is even more so.[68] Here we have a more developed and elaborated exposition of the faith and praxis of the Essene community. We have already briefly described the physical features of the manuscript found in Cave 1. Fragments of no fewer than ten copies have been recovered from Cave 4, with two tiny fragments coming from Cave 5, showing the importance that it possessed for the community.[69] We proceed to a discussion of the contents.

Unity and Date

Scholars are increasingly convinced that 1QS represents a composite work that has a very complicated textual history. We will not burden the student here with the technical discussion of this point.[70] It is generally dated to about 100-75 B.C.

---

[67]For further discussion of the OT background of covenant making, see Larry R. Helyer, *Yesterday, Today and Forever: The Continuing Relevance of the Old Testament* (Salem, Wis.: Sheffield Publishing, 1996), pp. 13, 103-4, 149-60.

[68]Earlier researchers used the designation *Manual of Discipline*. More recent scholars have generally adopted the name *Rule of the Community*.

[69]For details, see Knibb, "Rule of the Community," 2:793.

[70]See A. R. C. Leaney, *The Rule of Qumran and Its Meaning: Introduction, Translation and Commentary* (Philadelphia: Westminster Press, 1966), pp. 113-16; Nickelsburg, *Jewish Literature*, pp. 132, 156 n. 115; Dimant, "Qumran Sectarian Literature," p. 501, and Knibb, *Qumran Community*, p. 77.

Table 6.1. Parallels between the Damascus Document and the New Testament

CD	NT	Comments
CD 3:1—8:21	Acts 7:2-53; 13:16-41; Heb 3:1—4:11	In sermonic or epistolary exhortation, the NT, like CD, often incorporates a recital of sacred history and sees this as culminating in the life of the movement.
CD 4:21	1 Tim 3:2; cf. Mt 19:1-12	The NRSV renders 1 Tim 3:2: "Married only once." See the discussion above.
CD 3:15b-16a	Gal 3:12	Both quote Lev 18:5. Paul's argument assumes that the Judaizers believed one must follow the law to be saved. CD (and other texts we will read) shows that Essene theology was marked by legalism, i.e., belief in salvation by works. E. P. Sanders argues that Paul does not really accuse his opponents of legalism in Galatians and Romans (*Paul and Palestinian Judaism* [London: SCM Press; Philadelphia: Trinity Press International, 1977]). His thesis overlooks too much evidence to the contrary. For a critique of Sanders's view, see Donald A. Hagner, "Paul and Judaism—The Jewish Matrix of Early Christianity: Issues in the Current Debate," *BBR* 3 (1993): 111-30.
CD 5:18: "raised up Jannes and his brother"	2 Tim 3:8: "As Jannes and Jambres opposed Moses . . ."	Here is the earliest evidence for the Jewish tradition about the names of the Egyptian magicians who remain anonymous in Exodus. Clearly Paul (and Timothy) knew and accepted this tradition.
CD 6:14-21	Mk 7:10-11; 12:40; Lk 20:47; cf. Mt 23	Jesus agrees with some of the Essene criticisms of their opponents, opponents who look to be Pharisees. Note esp. the indictment of "making widows' wealth their booty."
CD 7:4: "not befouling each his holy spirit, just as God has told them so to do."	1 Cor 3:16-17: "Do you not know that you are God's temple and that God's Spirit dwells in you?" (cf. 1 Cor 6:19)	Both communities recognize an indwelling of the Holy Spirit as an essential part of what it means to be the elect people of God. The Jerusalem temple is replaced by the notion of a spiritual temple (cf. Mt 12:6; Mk 14:58; Jn 2:19-21; Eph 2:13-22; 1 Pet 2:4-5; Rev 21:22).

Table 6.1.—*Continued*

CD 15:1-4	Mt 5:33-37; Jas 5:12	Both communities eschew the taking of oaths in God's name. Note that in CD God's name is not even spelled out in the prohibition against it! Jesus enjoins truthfulness and integrity without the need for oaths to bind one to commitment.
CD 15:17: "none of these shall enter the congregation, for the holy angels are in your midst."	1 Cor 11:10: "For this reason a woman ought to have a symbol of authority on her head, because of the angels."	In both communities there appears to have been a conviction that the worship services reflected the heavenly angelic worship. Certain actions or the presence of certain individuals would be an affront to the angelic hosts, conceived of as observing the proceedings (see Morna Hooker, "Authority on Her Head: An Examination of I Cor. xi,10," *NTS* 10 [1963/ 1964]: 412-13).
CD 9:2—10.3; B 20:7-8; cf. 4QD[b] [4Q267] 18 v 1-20	Mt 18:15-17; 1 Cor 5; Gal 6:1-5; 2 Thess 3:14-15	Both communities followed certain procedures in case of erring members. There was a duty to inform the elders of sinning members when it occurred. But safeguards were built in so that one might not simply inform on others with the intent of damaging their reputation. There had to be multiple witnesses or multiple occurrences witnessed by a brother before the accused could be convicted. For further discussion of discipline in the Pauline churches, see T. E. Schmidt, "Discipline," *DPL*, pp. 214-18.
CD 10:21: "One may not travel outside his city more than a thousand cubits."	Acts 1:12: "Olivet, which is near Jerusalem, a sabbath day's journey away."	The Essenes, like the rabbis later, based this distance upon the extent of pastureland allowed outside the Levitical cities (cf. Num 35:4-5). The earliest Christians in Jerusalem accepted the same stricture, as seen in the Acts passage.
CD 11:13-14	Lk 14:5	Jesus agreed with the Pharisaic opinion that one may assist an animal that falls into a well (or pit) on the sabbath. The Essenes forbade such assistance on the sabbath.
CD 13:7-12	1 Cor 4:15; 2 Cor 6:13; 1 Thess 2:7-8, 11; 1 Pet 5:2-4	The apostles described their ministry in terms of a father-son or shepherd-sheep relationship, similar to the "Overseer of a camp" in CD.

Table 6.1.—*Continued*

CD 14:12-17	Acts 2:44-45; 1 Tim 5:3	The earliest Christians held property in common. Later this practice dropped out as a universal rule, but care for those in need is a continuing obligation throughout NT literature.
CD B 20:13-22	2 Thess 2:8-11	For the Essenes, the last times span the period from the death of the Teacher until the coming of the Messiah, a period of forty years. In this connection, it is fascinating to observe that the Thessalonians were expecting an imminent return of Jesus. Paul himself, during his early missionary journeys, may well have believed that Jesus would be returning within a relatively short period of time. He does not, however, nor do any other NT writers, set an exact date for the return of Christ (on Paul's views about Jesus' return, see Witherington, *Jesus, Paul and the End of the World*, pp. 21-35, 152-69).

Outline of Contents

I.   Prologue: mission statement of the community (1:1-15)
II.   Admission procedures of the community (1:16—3:12)
III.   Doctrinal foundation of the community (3:13—4:26)
IV.   Various rules and regulations of the community (5:1—6:23)
V.   Penal code of the community (6:24—7:25)
VI.   Ideals of the community (8:1—9:11)
VII.   Instructions and guidelines of the community (9:12-26)
VIII. Hymns summarizing the mission of the community (10:1—11:22)[71]

A Program for the Community

The nucleus of this work may stem from the Teacher of Righteousness himself,[72] though the document itself is anonymous and contains no direct evidence as to the identity of the author(s). Essentially this work is a programmatic document setting out the purpose, aims and behavior of a par-

---

[71]For other ways of outlining the contents, see Leaney, *Rule of Qumran*, pp. 112-13; and the section headings in Knibb, *Qumran Community*, pp. 78-144; Vermes, *Complete Dead Sea Scrolls in English*, p. 70; J. H. Charlesworth et al., eds., *The Dead Sea Scrolls: Hebrew, Aramaic and Greek Texts with English Translations*, 4 vols. (Tübingen: Mohr Siebeck, 1994-), 1:1; and the helpful sectional summaries in the translation we are using (Wise, Abegg and Cook, *Dead Sea Scrolls*, pp. 126-43).
[72]Cautiously suggested by Leaney, *Rule of Qumran*, pp. 115-16.

ticular community that views itself as the true Israel.

Comparison and contrast with CD. Having read CD, one encounters familiar terrain in 1QS. Despite differences, which we will enumerate shortly, there are common threads. First, we notice in both works an exclusive claim to being the true Israel; the circle of the elect extends no further than the bounds of the new-covenant community. Perhaps the most obvious procedural similarity lies in the process of admission into the community and the yearly review of all members as to their performance and conduct. Common to both documents is the fundamental belief that the community partakes in a new covenant made with the God of Israel, a fulfillment of Jeremiah's new-covenant prophecy. Finally, we note the great importance of following the correct calendar and thus observing the feasts and rituals at their divinely ordained times.

A majority of scholars conclude from this that we are dealing with the same movement in both documents. This view is not, however, without its problems. At least eight points of disagreement or variance may be noted:

1. CD regulated life for a community living in towns and villages and, most importantly, living as families—that is, they married. In contrast, the community of 1QS appears to have been composed of male celibates, somewhat isolated in their desert outpost. Recent study of the Qumran cemetery has indicated that the female skeletons are not to be identified with the Qumran community but are rather dated to the Islamic period.[73]

2. The CD community participated in the Jerusalem temple, though not without rigorous observance of ritual cleanness. On the contrary, 1QS had nothing to do with the Jerusalem temple; indeed, it would appear that they offered up sacrifices independently of the Jerusalem priesthood.

3. At Qumran the *mᵉbaqqēr* (Examiner) acted in concert with a council; in the towns and villages (CD), the *mᵉbaqqēr* presided without associates.

4. The respective penal codes are different, especially with regard to the penalties assessed. At Qumran grievous offenses resulted in expulsion from

---

[73]See Joseph E. Zias, "The Cemeteries of Qumran and Celibacy: Confusion Laid to Rest?" *DSD* 7 (2000): 220-53, for compelling evidence that the female skeletons are probably Bedouin (esp. the glass beads strung together with what looks like a modern button). This is seconded by a majority of researchers, such as James H. Charlesworth, "Jesus and the Dead Sea Scrolls" (public lecture presented at the Forum for Christian-Jewish Relations, Christian Theological Seminary, Indianapolis, Ind., April 8, 2001). On the other hand, not all have conceded. See Jürgen Zangenberg, "Bones of Contention: 'New' Bones from Qumran Help Settle Old Questions (and Raise New Ones)—Remarks on Two Recent Conferences," *QC* 9 (2000): 51-76. For an earlier discussion of the issue and scholarly interaction, see Zdzislaw Jan Kapera, "Some Remarks on the Qumran Cemetery," in *Methods of Investigation of the Dead Sea Scrolls and the Khirbet Qumran Site: Present Realities and Future Prospects,* ed. Michael O. Wise et al., Annals of the New York Academy of Sciences 722 (New York: New York Academy of Sciences, 1994), pp. 97-113.

the community, either temporary or permanent; in the towns offenders were incarcerated or sentenced to death (though most scholars doubt that the Essenes were permitted to carry out capital punishment at this time).

5. The common table and its requisite purity played a leading role at Qumran; this ritual meal is not mentioned as part of the common life in the towns.

6. The source of new members differed in the two communities. 1QS legislated requirements for outsiders who requested entry into the covenant; in CD there were new converts, but provision was also made for sons of members to be admitted as well.

7. The two- to three-year admission process at Qumran (see below) with its instruction about the "two spirits" does not show up in CD.

8. At Qumran there was communal sharing of property and possessions; in the towns and villages there was a common fund to assist those in need but no common ownership of goods and resources.

A majority of scholars have reconciled the above differences between the two groups by assuming that Josephus was correct in his assertion that there were two kinds of Essenes: those who were celibate and those who married (cf. *J.W.* 2.8.13). The former, in all likelihood, were the Qumran sectaries. It may well be that Essenes who lived in towns and villages could opt to join the Qumran community if they wished "to be joined to God's society and walk faultless before Him" (1QS 1:8; cf. 8:1-25). Thus the sanctity and rigor of the Qumranites was greater than their brethren who lived in "camps." Vermes speaks for many scholars in the following summary:

> Yet despite these many dissimilarities, at the basic level of doctrine, aims and principles, a perceptible bond links the brethren of the desert with those of the towns. . . . There can be only one logical conclusion: this was a single religious movement with two branches.[74]

Organization and leadership. Presiding over the community was a council consisting of twelve laymen—representing the biblical ideal of twelve tribes of Israel—and three priests.[75] The group clearly disapproved of the cultic ritual at the Jerusalem temple and viewed itself as the true priesthood (1QS 9:3-5). As a "holy house for Aaron" they awaited the coming of "the Prophet and the Messiahs of Aaron and Israel" (1QS 9:11).

The "sons of Zadok" were the undisputed authorities for the sectarians. We think that Schiffman is probably correct that the original impetus for the sect was a group of priests who resisted the ouster of the Zadokite priestly family

[74]*Complete Dead Sea Scrolls in English,* pp. 16-17.
[75]Some scholars suggest that this council actually went out to Qumran as a pioneer community and lived there two years before incorporating other Jews who shared their vision. See Knibb, *Qumran Community,* p. 129; and Leaney, *Rule of Qumran,* pp. 210-28.

from the Jerusalem high priesthood. These priests became and continued to be the undisputed leaders of the new-covenant community.[76] After some time (CD says twenty years, 1:10-11), the Teacher of Righteousness arose to lead the movement. He was himself a priest, in all likelihood a Zadokite, as indicated by a pesher on Psalm 37:23-24 (4QpPs[a]): "This refers to the priest, the Teacher of R[ighteousness, whom] God [ch]ose to be His servant [and] ordained him to form Him a company [. . .]."[77] The interpretations of the Teacher were considered infallible inasmuch as God directly revealed hidden truth to him. Furthermore, "the teachings of the sect's preeminent leader were still considered authoritative and determined the sect's pattern of behavior long after his death."[78] Interestingly, the Teacher is never mentioned in 1QS. The present form of the text must have been redacted after his death. Its basic teachings, however, are indebted to him. It is very likely that other compositions were either written by him or at least were in harmony with his ideas and teachings.

After the death of the Teacher of Righteousness, an official called the "Overseer" *(m^ebaqqēr)* carried on his role.[79] This leader is mentioned in both CD and 1QS. His duties are outlined most extensively in CD 13:7-19. In 1QS 6:12, 20 he is mentioned as determining who may speak at communal meetings and as the one responsible for oversight of all possessions entrusted to the community. We may summarize his duties as follows: (1) he functioned as the authoritative teacher of the sect; (2) he examined and approved all new members; (3) he supervised all business transactions by members; (4) he approved of marriages and divorces; and (5) he organized the members in accordance with their rank. Comparing CD with 1QS, we conclude that in the towns and villages, each group of Essenes had an Examiner over them but that the Examiner at Qumran held supreme leadership over all the "camps."[80]

1QS 6:12 has an official called the "Overseer of the general membership" or "Inspector of the many"[81] *(hmbqr ʿl hrbm)*, also called "the man appointed as leader of the general membership" (1QS 6:14). Another official mentioned in 1QS 3:13 and 9:12, 16, 21 is styled "the Instructor" (or "the Master" in the translation of Vermes and Charlesworth). The Hebrew term is *maśkîl* and means "one who enlightens." As the name suggests, his primary role was to

---

[76]Schiffman develops this thesis in several works, but his argument is readily accessible in *Reclaiming the Dead Sea Scrolls,* chaps. 5-6.
[77]Edward Cook in Wise, Abegg and Cook, *Dead Sea Scrolls,* p. 222 (4Q171 1-2 iii 15-16).
[78]Schiffman, *Reclaiming the Dead Sea Scrolls,* p. 121.
[79]This title is translated as "Examiner" by Vermes, *Dead Sea Scrolls in English.*
[80]Ibid., p. 122.
[81]The latter is the translation in García Martínez and Tigchelaar, *Dead Sea Scrolls Study Edition,* 1:85.

instruct the members in the proper understanding of Torah, the sectarian interpretation of halakah. Given the similarity in job descriptions, we think this official should probably be equated with the Overseer.[82] The appropriation of the title *maśkil* by the Qumran sect derives from Daniel, a popular book at Qumran, where we find this statement: "None of the wicked shall understand, but those who are wise [*hammaśkilim*] shall understand" (Dan 12:10b). This text occurs in an eschatological passage describing the end times. As noted already, the sect believed it was living in the end times, hence the appropriateness of the title for an official who instructed the members in faith and practice.

According to 1QS, the *maśkil* exercised another role, namely, the recitation of blessings over the holy camp. The content of these blessings probably shows up in a work called *Rule of the Blessings* (1Q28b [1QSb]). Schiffman holds that these blessings were to be recited at the time of the eschatological battle, when all Israel was mustered for battle,[83] but more likely they constituted a covenant-renewal ceremony for restored Israel.[84]

Admission procedures. The heart of the document contains detailed prescriptions for the admission of new members. The process of admission seems to have taken about three years, with several stages:

1. An entrance examination by the Overseer ascertained the suitability of the candidate. He took a solemn oath and thus "entered the covenant" (1QS 5:7-11).[85]

2. Indoctrination into the rules of the community, for an unspecified period of time (1QS 6:14b-15), prepared the candidate for an examination before the congregation to determine his progress. If approved, he was admitted into the council of the community and placed on probation for a period of one year. During this time he was admitted to the purificatory baths but not permitted to eat of the pure meal or touch any of the utensils or plates of the members. His property was turned over to the bursar but not made available to the community at large (1QS 6:17).

3. Following this year, another community evaluation determined his per-

---

[82]Michael A. Knibb holds that the two offices were distinct but related ("Community Organization," *EDSS* 1:135, 137). Schiffman holds that the various terms for leadership "did not coexist at the same time, but rather represent different stages in the organizational history of the sectarian community" (*Reclaiming the Dead Sea Scrolls,* p. 121).

[83]Schiffman, *Reclaiming the Dead Sea Scrolls,* p. 125.

[84]See further Martin Abegg Jr. in Wise, Abegg and Cook, *Dead Sea Scrolls,* p. 147; and Johann Maier, "Rule of Blessings," *EDSS* 2:791.

[85]A question concerns whether the candidate took an oath at the beginning or end of the admission process. See VanderKam, *Dead Sea Scrolls Today,* p. 89. J. Julius Scott Jr. understands it to have been at the end of the process (*Customs and Controversies: Intertestamental Jewish Backgrounds of the New Testament* [Grand Rapids, Mich.: Baker, 1995], p. 223).

formance. If satisfactory to the majority of the community, he was placed on a second probationary year, though he could now share the common meal. He could not, however, share the drink of the community (1QS 6:20-21). This latter circumstance was based upon the ruling that liquids were most prone to the transmission of ritual impurity.

4. After this second year and a successful, final inquiry by the community, the novitiate was enrolled "at the appropriate rank among his brothers" as a full member of the holy community. He was now allowed full access to the pure food and drink, and his possessions became that of the community (1QS 6:21b-23).

Such rigorous admission procedures are not unique to the various forms of Second Temple Judaism. Assuming that the Mishnah and Talmud preserve historical practices from this period, we note that the Pharisees likewise had a multiple-stage admission process to their membership called *ḥªbûrôt* ("fellowships").[86] None of these other movements, however, were as difficult and demanding to join as the Qumran fellowship. Not surprisingly, the degree of commitment displayed by this movement was extraordinary, as testified to by Josephus in his gruesome account of their torture by the Roman soldiers in the revolt against Rome:

> Their spirit was tested to the utmost by the war with the Romans, who racked and twisted, burnt and broke them, subjecting them to every torture yet invented in order to make them blaspheme the Lawgiver or eat some forbidden food, but could not make them do either, or ever once fawn on their tormentors or shed a tear. Smiling in their agony and gently mocking those who tortured them, they resigned their souls in the joyous certainty that they would receive them back. (*J.W.* 2.8.10)

Penal code. The penal code for the sect legislated in both moral and ritual matters. Virtues such as respect, honesty, humility and love for fellow covenanters were enjoined, while retaliation, anger and slander against one's fellow members were conversely proscribed. But separation from and hatred for outsiders were also insisted upon, though it should be noted that the Qumranites were not to act in an unkind way toward outsiders, *unless directed to do so by the community.* Above all, rebellion against the authority of the religious teachings of the sect was simply not tolerated (1QS 5:7; 7:18-19). To apostatize was tantamount to everlasting annihilation—no repentance was possible (1QS 5:13). Of course, ritual purity took on major importance, as we saw in CD as well. The purity standards of 1QS were even more stringent than in CD.

Schiffman gives a helpful chart summarizing the various offenses and their

---

[86]Schiffman, *Reclaiming the Dead Sea Scrolls,* p. 104 and references on p. 424.

Table 6.2. Schiffman's summary of offenses and punishments at Qumran

Offense	Punishment
Misuse of the divine name	Permanent expulsion
Informing against the sect	Expulsion
Rebelling against the teachings of the sect	Separation from pure solid food for one year Reduction of food ration by one-fourth for two years Separation from pure drink for two years [Note that the perpetrator was treated virtually as a novice again.]
Speaking angrily against the priests Intentionally insulting another Knowingly lying about money Gossiping against one's fellow	Separation from pure food and reduction of food ration by one-fourth for one year
Replying stubbornly to a superior sect member	Reduction of food ration by one-fourth for one year
Accidentally speaking angrily against the priests Speaking deceptively to one's fellow Bearing a grudge against one's fellow Walking about unclothed Complaining about one's fellow unjustifiably	Reduction of food ration by one-fourth for six months
Speaking obscenely	Reduction of food ration by one-fourth for three months
Dealing deceitfully with the property of the community	Restitution with penalty or reduction of food ration by one-fourth for sixty days
Falling asleep during the assembly Missing a vote Spitting in the assembly Exposing one's genitals Laughing loudly and foolishly	Reduction of food ration by one-fourth for thirty days
Interrupting one's fellow Absence without reason from the assembly for three days in a session Gesticulating with one's left hand during conversation [the left hand was used to take care of bodily functions, and thus it was considered highly offensive to wave it about publicly]	Reduction of food ration by one-fourth for ten days

corresponding punishments at Qumran (see table 6.2).[87] Some of these seem
rather trivial to us today, for example, falling asleep during assemblies and
spitting. However, this probably says more about our own lack of moral and
spiritual earnestness than about their fastidiousness. One needs to be
reminded that our Pilgrim and Puritan forebears had ushers who patrolled
the aisles in New England congregations with long poles, designed to make
sure the saints were not in the land of Nod during services! When my church
in Hartford City, Indiana, celebrated its sesquicentennial anniversary, the
members chuckled over a rule in the church bylaws, dating to the 1840s,
sternly warning against spitting on the floors!

Doctrinal beliefs. Of central importance to the entire document is the section expounding upon the doctrine of "the two spirits." Vermes calls attention
to the significance of this section by noting that it may be "the only doctrinal
treatise among ancient Hebrew writings."[88] We called attention in our reading
of CD to the predestinarian cast of some passages. 1QS elaborates on this. In
1QS 3:13-24 we have the underlying theological confession that is essential
for understanding the ethos of this sect. In short, God preordained who the
righteous and wicked are:

> All that is now and ever shall be originates with the God of knowledge. Before
> things come to be, He has ordered all their designs, so that when they do come
> to exist—at their appointed times as ordained by His glorious plan—they fulfill
> their destiny, a destiny impossible to change. He controls the laws governing all
> things, and He provides for all their pursuits. (1QS 3:15b-17a)[89]

The doctrine of the two spirits, at first glance, seems to reflect a dualistic
worldview. The dualism, however, is not cosmological—two fundamental and
eternal forces, good and evil, in opposition to one another—but rather ethical.
The Creator places two spirits, the Prince of Light and the Angel of Darkness,
in every human being. But the proportionate influence of these two spirits
varies, a factor predetermined by God (thus not really a dualism, but a
monism).[90] On the face of it, an individual has no choice in the matter ("The
character and fate of all humankind reside with these spirits" [1QS 4:15]). If
the Prince of Light has more power over a person than the Angel of Darkness, then there will be divine assistance and a response to the truth as prop-
agated by the Qumran community. The evil spirit is not removed from the
righteous; indeed, their wrong deeds are directly attributed to the Angel of
Darkness (1QS 11:9-15). On the other hand, the wicked are doomed to walk in

---

[87]Ibid., p. 109.
[88]*Complete Dead Sea Scrolls in English,* p. 41.
[89]Michael Wise in Wise, Abegg and Cook, *Dead Sea Scrolls,* p. 129.
[90]For further discussion of this distinction, see LaSor, *Dead Sea Scrolls,* pp. 75-84.

the way of darkness and ultimately to experience eternal destruction. We cite a text from the *War Scroll* that makes this quite explicit:

> And you, [O God], created us for Yourself as an eternal people, and into the lot of light You cast us in accordance with Your truth. You appointed the Prince of Light from of old to assist us, for in [His] l[ot are all sons of righteous]ness and all spirits of truth are in his dominion. You yourself made Belial for the pit, an angel of malevolence, his [dominio]n is in darkne[ss] and his counsel is to condemn and convict. All the spirits of his lot—the angels of destruction—walk in accord with the rule of darkness, for it is their only [des]ire. But we, in the lot of Your truth, rejoice in Your mighty hand. We rejoice in Your salvation, and revel in [Your] hel[p and] Your [p]eace. (1QM 13:9b-13a)[91]

This extreme determinism distinguishes Essenism from other forms of Second Temple Judaism, as we already noted above in our discussion of CD. There is, however, a certain tension in the thought of the scrolls, since human responsibility does figure prominently and there is great stress upon performance of right deeds. We give one of many such passages:

> Each one who thus enters the Covenant by oath is to separate himself from all of the perverse men, those who walk in the wicked way, for such are not reckoned a part of His Covenant. They "have not sought Him nor inquired of His statutes" (Zeph. 1:6) so as to discover the hidden laws in which they err to their shame. Even the revealed laws they knowingly transgress, thus stirring God's judgmental wrath and full vengeance: the curses of the Mosaic Covenant. (1QS 5:10b-12a)[92]

Perhaps we can say that the Essenes, like many systems of Christian theology, did not have a consistent answer for this vexing theological question![93]

Finally, as we compare 1QS with CD, we note an important difference in the messianic views of the two documents. In 1QS we read about *two* messiahs, one from Aaron and another from Israel: "They shall govern themselves using the original precepts by which the men of the *Yahad* began to be instructed, doing so until there come the Prophet and the Messiahs of Aaron and Israel" (1QS 9:10b-11). Note the plural "messiahs." William Sanford LaSor pointed out that a fragment of CD (4QD[b] = 4Q267) has the singular (messiah), not the plural, and thus emendation of CD should not be allowed.[94] In LaSor's opinion, there never was a belief in two messiahs, priestly and

---

[91]Martin Abegg Jr. in Wise, Abegg and Cook, *Dead Sea Scrolls,* p. 129.
[92]Michael Wise in Wise, Abegg and Cook, *Dead Sea Scrolls,* p. 132.
[93]VanderKam notes that "the Qumran manuscripts apparently contain no extended attempt to deal with the logical perplexities that arise from a system of this kind" (*Dead Sea Scrolls Today,* p. 109).
[94]LaSor, *Dead Sea Scrolls,* p. 102.

Davidic, at Qumran. His position has not, however, been accepted by most scholars, especially now in light of the full availability of all the texts. The *Rule of the Congregation* (1QSa) describes an eschatological meal in which two individuals are present, a priestly leader and a Davidic messiah (1QSa 2:11-22). Not only this, but the pattern of two messianic figures is repeated in a number of Qumran texts and thus tends to confirm the two messiahs view.[95] At some point in the history of the sect, the messianic expectations of the group either underwent a development or the singular form of *messiah* in CD B 20:1 is a scribal error.[96] It is impossible to say at this point which alternative is to be preferred. What is clear, however, is that this belief in two messiahs distinguished Essenes from the Pharisees and the emerging Jesus movement.

Comparison with the New Testament

In terms of genre, we do not have anything in the NT exactly matching the Qumran *Rule of the Community* and the *Damascus Document,* when viewed in whole cloth. However, Paul's Epistles contain a good bit of teaching and paraenetic material that address issues similar to those found at Qumran (see below for specifics). Also, the Pastoral Epistles contain material that resembles a manual of discipline for the church.[97] Here we find emphasis upon certain truths and teachings that serve as the cornerstone of the church. These are frequently introduced by formulaic phrases such as, "the saying is sure and worthy of full acceptance" (1 Tim 1:15; 3:1; 4:9-10; 2 Tim 2:11; Tit 3:8), "now we know" (1 Tim 1:8), "you must understand this" (2 Tim 3:1), "if you put these instructions before the brothers and sisters" (1 Tim 4:6), "these are the things you must insist on and teach" (1 Tim 4:11), "remind them of this, and warn them before God" (2 Tim 2:14) and "but as for you, teach what is consistent with sound doctrine" (Tit 2:1). The ethos of these passages is not far removed from that of Qumran. Thus, in terms both of content and phraseology, we have a number of significant parallels between the manuals of Qumran and Paul's epistolary reminders to Timothy and Titus regarding their oversight of the various house churches in the Aegean and Asia Minor.

Ethical dualism characterizes NT thought. In this the NT, like the Qumran

---

[95]See VanderKam, *Dead Sea Scrolls Today,* pp. 117-18; Scott, *Customs and Controversies,* pp. 308-11; Craig A. Evans, "Messianism," *DNTB,* pp. 701-3; Evans, "Messiahs," *EDSS* 1:537-42.

[96]But Martin Abegg Jr. has argued otherwise in "The Messiah at Qumran: Are We Still Seeing Double?" *DSD* 2 (1995): 125-44, and in "The Hebrew of the Dead Sea Scrolls," in *The Dead Sea Scrolls After Fifty Years: A Comprehensive Assessment,* ed. Peter W. Flint and James C. VanderKam, 2 vols. (Leiden: E. J. Brill, 1998-1999), 2:334-35.

[97]See further, E. E. Ellis, "Pastoral Letters," *DPL,* pp. 663-64; and Ellis, "The Pastorals and Paul," *ExpTim* 104 (1992-1993): 45-47.

sectarian writings, is more indebted to the Hebrew Scriptures and its teaching on "the two ways" (e.g., Ps 1:1; Prov 1—3; Jer 17:5-8) than to anything else.[98] In other words, both literatures share a common heritage. As a reflection of this dualism, one finds the juxtaposition of light and darkness and of categories such as "sons of light" and "sons of darkness," especially in the Pauline literature (cf. Rom 13:12; 2 Cor 11:14; Eph 5:6-14; Col 1:12-13; 1 Thess 5:1-10). Even more pronounced is the dualism of the Johannine writings (cf. Jn 1:4-9; 3:19-21; 5:35; 8:12; 12:36; 1 Jn 1:5-7; 2:8-10). As in CD, an ethical dualism also manifests itself in the angelology of 1QS. (We have already discussed the angelology and demonology of earlier Jewish literature in chapters two and three.) The NT shares the same perspective on the invisible realm of angels and demons.

Of course, both Qumran and the NT share a fervent messianic hope, a hope involving both priestly and kingly functions. Given the Zadokite origins of the movement, it is not surprising that the Qumran community gave priority to the priestly messiah vis-à-vis the Davidic messiah. Nonetheless, in both corpora, the Davidic covenant is a mainstay in the messianic ideology; namely, a descendant of David will rule over Israel and defeat all her enemies. This promise, originally delivered through Nathan the prophet (2 Sam 7:14-17), was reiterated in prophetic and hymnic literature (cf. Ps 89:19-37; Is 9:6-7; 11:1-12; Jer 23:5-6; 30:9; Ezek 34:23-24; Zech 9:9-10). We will examine more closely the Qumranic exegesis of these passages in the next chapter.

In contrast to 1QS, however, the NT *combines* the functions of both the high priest and the Davidic king in the person of Jesus (cf. Mt 1:1; 21:9; 27:11; Lk 23:8; Jn 1:49; Rom 1:3; Heb 1:3; 2:17; 4:14—5:10; 6:19—8:6; 9:11—10:18; Rev 5:5; 22:16). Furthermore, in spite of recent attempts to prove the contrary, there is no clear evidence that links the authoritative Teacher of Righteousness with either the eschatological Priest or the Davidic Messiah.[99] At Qumran there was also a belief in an eschatological prophet who preceded the coming of the two messiahs (1QS 9:11). The NT indicates that this expectation concerning an eschatological prophet was not confined to Qumran but was apparently a rather widely held view. The NT, however, implies that this prophet was John the Baptist (cf. Mt 11:14; 17:10-12; 27:47-49; Jn 1:21-25; 6:14; 7:40).[100]

The process of entry into the Jesus movement differs rather markedly from the procedure at Qumran. We are surprised, in fact, at the immediacy of

[98]Attempts to connect this dualism to Zoroastrianism seem wide of the mark. See LaSor, *Dead Sea Scrolls*, pp. 77-78.
[99]Ibid., pp. 117-30; Fitzmyer, *Responses*, p. 57; Cross, *Ancient Library of Qumran*, pp. 156-65; and Evans, "Messianism," p. 703.
[100]For further discussion, see Scott, *Customs and Controversies*, pp. 308-23.

admission into the fellowship of the earliest church in the book of Acts. Thus on Pentecost Luke informs us that "those who welcomed his [Peter's] message were baptized, and that day about three thousand persons were added" (Acts 2:41). Instruction in the faith then followed ("They devoted themselves to the apostles' teaching and fellowship, to the breaking of bread and the prayers" [Acts 2:42]). The conversion experience was followed immediately by being incorporated into the believing community ("And day by day the Lord added to their number those who were being saved" [Acts 2:47]). This pattern is replicated throughout NT literature. Only later in postapostolic times does one find a period of catechism before the candidate is baptized and formally brought into the church (cf. *Did.* 7.1).

Both groups shared a communal meal and baptism by immersion, although other movements of Second Temple Judaism, such as the Pharisees, also practiced these. For Christians, however, there were distinct differences in the significance of both practices. The meal ("the Lord's Supper") focused on the meaning of Jesus' death for the salvation of the elect. But a strong eschatological note anticipated the messianic banquet at the end of history. In this regard, there is a close parallel between the Qumran community and the Jesus movement (cf. 1QSa 2:11-22 and Mk 14:25 par.; 1 Cor 11:26; Rev 19:9). At Qumran, like the NT, repentance was a precondition for admittance into the community (1QS 2:25b—3:12; Acts 2:37-42). On the other hand, for Christians baptism was an initiatory rite of transfer and symbolized the forgiveness of sins through the atoning work of Jesus. At Qumran, as generally for Second Temple Judaism, regular lustrations were a feature of maintaining ritual purity, though it is possible that there was an initiatory baptism signifying entrance into the *Yahad* (1QS 2:25b—3:12). No doubt the earliest Jesus movement in Jerusalem and its environs continued to observe repeated immersion as a feature of their ongoing life as Jews. But these immersions were not connected to the forgiveness of sins in the name of Jesus. That was a once-for-all event in keeping with its theological significance (cf. Rom 6:1-4).[101] As the church became increasingly Gentile, ritual purity was redefined and immersion in water in order to maintain such purity no longer characterized most Christians (1 Cor 1:13-17; 12:12-13; Gal 3:27-29; Eph 5:26-27; Col 2:11-13).[102]

Another instructive difference between the two communities has to do with attitudes toward those who deliberately broke the standards of belief and behavior. Deliberate sin or rejection of authority at Qumran led to permanent

---

[101] How we are to understand the expression "instruction about baptisms" in Heb 6:2 remains debated. G. W. Bromiley suggests that the plural form refers to the baptism of John, water baptism and baptism by the Spirit ("Baptism," *ISBE* 1:414).

[102] See further Hermann Lichtenberger, "Baths and Baptism," *EDSS* 1:85-88, where he documents certain Jewish-Christian groups who practiced double forms of baptism.

expulsion (1QS 8:21-24; 9:1). There is very little room left for confession and repentance at Qumran. Only if the sin were inadvertent can one be restored, and even then the restoration involved a virtual repeat of the process of novitiate admission.[103] The NT, by contrast, has a more redemptive approach. The moral and ethical standards are as high or higher than at Qumran, but there is a more realistic and compassionate stance with regard to the sin nature and moral failure (cf. 2 Cor 1:23—2:11; Gal 6:1-5).

A major difference, of course, relates to the purity laws. Following the lead of Jesus, the earliest Christians increasingly "sat loose" to external purity regulations (cf. Mt 15:1-20; 23:25-28; Mk 7:1-23). The real turning point for the nascent church was the explosive issue of the conditions for Gentile admittance into the fellowship (cf. Acts 10:1—11:18; 15:1-35; Galatians). Whereas the men of Qumran clearly recognized that the purity rituals were symbolic of sin and holiness, they also insisted upon their complete and uncompromising observance.[104] According to the book of Acts, the majority view of the Jerusalem Church was that these external observances were not binding *on Gentiles* (Acts 15). In the Pauline churches, this was taken even further: the ritual law was fulfilled in the redemptive work of Jesus the Messiah (Rom 14:14, 20; Col 2:16-17, 20-23; cf. Heb 8—10). As already indicated above, many Jewish Christians, however, still continued to observe the ritual law as meaningful expressions of their faith in Jesus the Messiah and, no doubt, as an expression of solidarity with the larger Jewish community (cf., e.g., Acts 18:18-19; 21:20-26; Rom 3:1-2; 9:1—11:36; 14:5-6).

Religion and Authority

What was the purpose of 1QS? Apparently this document served as a basic handbook for the entire community. One gathers from its tone and content that it was designed, at least in part, to silence dissent and to command unwavering allegiance to its teachings and teachers. We may assume that there had in fact been disagreement and schism earlier in the sect's history. In other words, the sectarians had to deal with a common problem found in religious movements, namely, the degree to which dissent is permitted. The Qumran covenanters that we see reflected in 1QS made no allowance for any significant dissent whatsoever. The basis for this extreme position lay in the kind of leadership exercised. The Teacher of Righteousness (or perhaps better, the Right Teacher) was the recipient of direct revelation from God. He

---

[103]This raises the vexed question of the meaning of Heb 6:4-6 and 10:26-31, which on the face of it, do seem to teach that deliberate apostasy could not be forgiven. However, in the context of Hebrews, these warning passages assume that the readers were *not yet* in this state.

[104]See Schiffman, *Reclaiming the Dead Sea Scrolls,* p. 103.

possessed the Holy Spirit in overflowing measure, and his interpretations of Scripture were not merely suggested ways of reading—they were true interpretations. It follows from this that they were a very tightly organized group in which dissenting opinions simply had no place. The faithful were taught what to believe and were to preserve this without deviation. These things were "revealed" to the elect but "hidden" from outsiders. Furthermore, contact with outsiders was greatly restricted for those living in "camps" and almost nonexistent for those at Qumran. The elect would come to the light quite apart from the efforts of the community.

How does this compare to the early church and to later Christian church history? On the one hand, the NT canon does witness to a message that is exclusive. Thus there is no salvation found outside the bounds of the believing community: "There is salvation in no one else, for there is no other name under heaven given among mortals by which we must be saved" (Acts 4:12; cf. 10:42-43; Jn 14:6; 1 Tim 2:5-6). The believing community, however, is "open" to all peoples. The circle of the elect is much larger for the apostolic church than for the Essenes: "[God] desires everyone to be saved" (1 Tim 2:4), and Christians actively engage in witnessing to their faith with a view to winning converts (cf. Mt 28:19-20; Jn 4:35-38; 15:27; Rom 1:14; 2 Cor 5:14, 18-20; Eph 3:9). By contrast, the Qumran community was warned not to share their teachings with outsiders. Whereas their "mysteries" were to be kept secret, the NT speaks of "open mysteries." Paul says his aim is "to make everyone see what is the plan of the mystery hidden for ages in God who created all things; so that through the church the wisdom of God in its rich variety might now be made known" (Eph 3:9-10).

How much dissent was tolerated in the NT community? There were cardinal doctrines to be affirmed and clear behavioral standards to be practiced or one was excluded from the fellowship. Just precisely what constituted this core commitment is more difficult to say.[105] We have several passages that seem to reflect doctrinal confessions (cf. Rom 1:3-5, 15-17; 3:21-26; 10:9-13; 1 Cor 8:6; 12:3; 15:3-6; Eph 4:4-6; Phil 2:6-11; Col 1:15-20; 1 Tim 3:16; 2 Tim 2:11-13; Heb 1:2-3). These center on the person and work of Jesus Christ, involving, at a minimum, a confession of his divine nature, his atoning death on behalf of sinners and, most importantly, his bodily resurrection and exaltation to God's right hand. Certain standards of behavior were also clearly required of members. Disciplinary procedures have already been noted in our previous discussions.

Furthermore, the early church insisted upon apostolic authority. In Paul's

---

[105]This issue of orthodoxy and heresy has been a recurring bone of contention in the church, especially between theologically conservative and liberal Christians. The latter wing of the church tends to downplay or "sit loose" to notions of doctrinal orthodoxy.

letters we read guidelines or boundaries with regard to certain issues: head coverings for women, women speaking in the assemblies, the exercise of spiritual gifts, idleness, sexual promiscuity, sins of the tongue, marriage and divorce, and others (cf. 1 Cor 6:9-10; 7:10; 11:1—14:40; Eph 4:25-32; 1 Thess 4:3-8; 2 Thess 3:6). The basis for apostolic authority, as at Qumran, was rooted in the notion of divine revelation. In several of Paul's letters, where his authority does seem to be challenged, we read of his call experience and his commissioning by the risen Lord (cf. 1 Cor 1:1; 9:1-2; 15:1-11; 2 Cor 3:1-6; 10:1—13:10; Gal 1:1). Rejection of apostolic directives brought one under the threat of excommunication (2 Thess 3:14). Thus to a considerable extent, one would have to acknowledge that a high degree of uniformity of belief and behavior was likewise required in the early church.

Still, we sense that the range of issues regulated by early Christians was considerably smaller than that at Qumran and in the larger Essene movement. Paul discusses issues that he calls "opinions" (Rom 14:1). In matters of food, drink and sabbath observance, room for differences of opinion was allowed. Of course, the Jewish ritual law was not obligatory for either Jewish or Gentile Christians, a feature distinguishing the church from the Essene movement.

What is especially noteworthy in the matter of authority, however, is the reluctance of Paul to assert it among his Gentile churches. When driven to it, Paul does exercise his apostolic authority over recalcitrant congregations, but he much prefers persuasion. He typically appeals to their consciences, the common experience of sharing together in Christ and the guidance of the Holy Spirit over an outright demand for compliance.[106] In general, we sense greater latitude for dissent among the early Christians in all but the most essential beliefs and behaviors. One thinks of Paul's reference to those who preached Christ from envy and rivalry (Phil 1:15). His response, "What does it matter?" (Phil 1:18), is inconceivable in a movement such as we see at Qumran. There conformity was extremely high and a requirement for continuance in the covenantal community.

A good case can be made for a more democratic structure in the Pauline house churches than in the Essene movement. In this regard, early Christianity has more in common with the Pharisaic *ḥᵃbûrôt* than with the Qumran community. Certainly, we do not detect, in the NT documents, the rigid hierarchical structure of the Qumran community, whereby each member is assigned his place or lot.[107] There are, in fact, clear warnings against this kind

---

[106]For a good discussion of this, see Linda Belleville, "Authority," *DPL*, 54-59.

[107]It should be noted here, however, that some researchers are of the opinion that the original, authoritarian and hierarchical leadership gradually gave way to a more democratic structure. See Schiffman, *Reclaiming the Dead Sea Scrolls*, pp. 113-26.

of ranking and elitism (Rom 12:3-8; 1 Cor 3:5-15; 4:1-7; 7:17-24; Gal 6:1-6; Eph 2:11-22; Phil 2:1-4; 1 Pet 5:1-5). According to Acts and the Pauline Epistles, Paul appointed elders and deacons in the churches and entrusted to them the care and oversight of the congregations. There is little evidence that Jerusalem functioned as the "Mother Church" in the Pauline mission. To be sure, Paul initially conferred with the Jerusalem leadership (Gal 1:18-20; 2:1-10) and placed great importance upon his primarily Gentile churches assisting the poor in Jerusalem (Rom 15:25-29; 1 Cor 16:1-4; 2 Cor 8:1—9:15; Gal 2:10). He also urged Gentile Christians to recognize the Jewish roots of their faith (Rom 11:13-36). But in terms of governance, the Pauline churches appear to have been autonomous.[108] In short, we see a more decentralized authority in the early church than at Qumran.

For Further Reading

Edward Cook, *Solving the Mysteries of the Dead Sea Scrolls* (Grand Rapids, Mich.: Zondervan, 1993). Very readable, with the best account of happenings prior to 1992 in the research community.

Frank Moore Cross, *The Ancient Library of Qumran*, 3d ed. (Minneapolis: Fortress, 1995). Written by an expert paleographer and epigrapher of Semitic languages, this volume is very helpful on the history of the discovery and scholarship by a participant from the earliest days of scroll research.

Devorah Dimant, "Qumran Sectarian Literature," in *Jewish Writings of the Second Temple Period: Apocrypha, Pseudepigrapha, Qumran Sectarian Writings, Philo, Josephus,* ed. Michael E. Stone, CRINT 2 (Assen: Van Gorcum; Philadelphia: Fortress, 1984), pp. 483-502. A technical discussion by a leading Jewish scholar of the DSS.

Craig A. Evans and Stanley E. Porter, eds., *Dictionary of New Testament Background* (Downers Grove, Ill.: InterVarsity Press, 2000). The essays in this volume dealing with various aspects of the DSS and Qumran are current and competent.

Joseph A. Fitzmyer, *Responses to 101 Questions on the Dead Sea Scrolls* (New York: Paulist, 1992). Written for the lay reader, this work dispels many of the sensationalist claims made for these writings.

William S. LaSor, *The Dead Sea Scrolls and the New Testament* (Grand Rapids, Mich.: Eerdmans, 1972). Written by a leading evangelical scholar, the work is a bit dated in a few areas now but still useful. It is marked by caution and sound judgment.

George W. E. Nickelsburg, *Jewish Literature Between the Bible and the Mishnah: A Historical and Literary Introduction* (Philadelphia: Fortress, 1981), pp. 122-26,

---

[108]This statement, of course, will not go unchallenged by many who are convinced that the NT displays more of a hierarchical structure than I have allowed. I own up to my Baptistic presuppositions on this point!

132-37. This is a standard survey text by a recognized authority.

Lawrence H. Schiffman, *Reclaiming the Dead Sea Scrolls: Their True Meaning for Judaism and Christianity,* ABRL (New York: Doubleday, 1994), pp. 1-158. This work is written from the perspective of a leading Jewish scholar who wants to place the scrolls in their proper Jewish setting over against a perceived imbalance by Christian scholarship.

Lawrence H. Schiffman and James C. VanderKam, eds., *Encyclopedia of the Dead Sea Scrolls,* 2 vols. (Oxford: Oxford University Press, 2000). A treasure trove of information, this is the most comprehensive collection of information about the scrolls available written by the world's leading authorities on the subject.

James C. VanderKam, *The Dead Sea Scrolls Today* (Grand Rapids, Mich.: Eerdmans, 1994), pp. 1-117. This is probably the best overall introduction to and survey of the topic available for the beginning student.

Geza Vermes, *An Introduction to the Complete Dead Sea Scrolls* (Minneapolis: Fortress, 1999). This is a good survey by a leading authority on the subject.

Yigael Yadin, *The Message of the Scrolls* (New York: Simon and Schuster, 1957). This work is written with flair by a leading Israeli archaeologist and epigrapher.

For a good CD-ROM resource on the DSS, see *The Dead Sea Scrolls Revealed* (Pixel Multimedia and Aaron Witkin Associates, 1994; distributed by Logos Research Systems).

Several popularly written and beautifully illustrated articles in *Biblical Archaeology Review* are also very useful:

Martin G. Abegg Jr., "Paul, Works of the Law, and the MMT," *BAR* 20, no. 6 (1994): 52-55, 82.

Edward E. Cook, "A Ritual Purification Center," *BAR* 22, no. 6 (1996): 39, 48-51, 73.

Alan D. Crown and Lea A. Cansdale, "Qumran—Was it an Essene Settlement?" *BAR* 20, no. 5 (1994): 24-35, 73-78.

Stephen Goranson, "Qumran a Hub of Scribal Activity?" *BAR* 20, no. 5 (1994): 37-39.

————, "Qumran: The Evidence of the Inkwells," *BAR* 19, no. 6 (1993): 67.

Jodi Magness, "Not a Country Villa," *BAR* 22, no. 6 (1996): 37-38, 40-47, 72-73.

Hershel Shanks, "The Qumran Settlement—Monastery, Villa or Fortress?" *BAR* 19, no. 3 (1993): 62-65.

Seven

The Dead Sea Scrolls

Scripture & the End Times

*I*n this chapter we examine some texts from the Qumran library shedding light
on their approach to interpreting Scripture. This exercise will be especially
enlightening as we compare our findings with the NT documents. We already
made mention of this in our discussion of CD in the previous chapter. We take this
up in more depth here.

Presuppositions of Qumran Exegesis

Let us set out more fully the presuppositions that emerge from a careful reading of the biblical commentaries found at Qumran. Four fundamental principles constitute the hermeneutical (i.e., the interpretive or explanatory)
system by which the sectaries read the Hebrew Bible:

1. The prophetic Scriptures of the Hebrew Bible deal primarily with the
end times.

2. The end times have begun. 4QMMT states unequivocally, "this is the
End of Days." This phrase (*ʾaḥᵃrît hayyāmîm*) occurs more than thirty times
in the DDS and is derived from the OT Prophets, where it refers to the decisive events leading up to the Day of the Lord. *The Rule of the Congregation*
(1Q28a 1:1) begins with this pronouncement: "This is the rule for all the
congregation of Israel in the Last Days, when they are mobilized [to join the

Yahad]."[1] The arrival of the Teacher of Righteousness was a key event heralding these perilous days. We think it likely, in fact, that he, more than any other individual, was responsible for the system of interpretation employed by the Qumran community.[2]

3. Embedded in the prophetic texts of the Hebrew Bible are cryptic references to contemporary events (contemporary to the Qumran community). These references were referred to as "mysteries."

4. The Teacher of Righteousness possessed the God-given ability to ferret out these "mysteries." His interpretation of Scripture was guided by the Spirit and thus infallible.[3]

Even though the Teacher of Righteousness was the interpreter par excellence at Qumran, he was not the innovator of an entirely new method of exegesis. The basic approach appears even earlier than the Qumran sectarian literature. Thus in works such as *Jubilees, 1 Enoch* 85—90 and the *Testament of Moses* one finds examples of texts from the Hebrew Prophets applied to events contemporary with the author and readers.[4] This illustrates the basic presupposition that the prophets spoke primarily of the end times, a period now beginning to unfold.

Pesher Interpretation

We turn next to an analysis of a distinctive method of exegesis employed at Qumran, namely, pesher (Heb *pešer*), the basic meaning of which is "solution" or "interpretation." The pesharim are generally classified into two cate-

---

[1] Translation by Michael Wise in Michael Wise, Martin Abegg Jr. and Edward Cook, *The Dead Sea Scrolls: A New Translation* (New York: HarperCollins, 1999 [1996]), p. 144.

[2] See further John J. Collins, "Eschatology," *EDSS* 1:256-61.

[3] See the in-depth treatment of Maurya P. Horgan, *Pesharim: Qumran Interpretations of Biblical Books,* CBQMS 8 (Washington, D.C.: Catholic Biblical Association of America, 1979), pp. 229-59.

[4] With regard to *Testament of Moses,* there is a question of dating. We think that a good case can be made for the second century B.C. This is argued by George W. E. Nickelsburg, *Jewish Literature Between the Bible and the Mishnah: A Historical and Literary Introduction* (Philadelphia: Fortress, 1981), pp. 212-14. For a defense of the first century A.D. date, see J. Priest, "Testament of Moses," *OTP* 1:920-21; and J. J. Collins, "Testaments," in *Jewish Writings of the Second Temple Period: Apocrypha, Pseudepigrapha, Qumran Sectarian Writings, Philo, Josephus,* ed. Michael E. Stone, CRINT 2 (Assen: Van Gorcum; Philadelphia: Fortress, 1984), pp. 347-48. We are of the opinion that the parallels between *Jubilees, 1 Enoch* and the *Testament of Moses* suggest a close relationship between the Qumran community and the group(s) responsible for the above-mentioned works. The relationship was probably a genetic one; that is, the Essenes of Qumran were a splinter group who broke off from a larger movement whose views are reflected in works such as *Jubilees, 1 Enoch* and possibly the *Testament of Moses.* This, however, is not capable of proof, given the present nature of the evidence, and must be held as a theory only.

gories: continuous and thematic. In the former, the commentary typically singles out sections of text and comments verse by verse. In the latter, we find selected portions of Scripture with interpretive comments organized around a central theme or idea.

Continuous Pesher

We will examine first examples of the continuous commentaries on portions of Habakkuk, Psalms, Nahum and Isaiah. As noted, the commentator typically quotes a verse or verses and then follows this with a formal introductory phrase: "its interpretation concerns" *(pišrô ʿal)* or "the interpretation of the passage is" *(pešer haddābār)*. The meaning of the verse under scrutiny is explained in terms of the fulfillment of prophecy, a prophecy actualized in the life of the Qumran community. Thus the distinctive feature about pesher is that it denotes an interpretation of Scripture whereby the words of the prophet actually referred to the experiences of the sect. These experiences covered the historical roots of the movement, the coming of the Teacher of Righteousness and significant events up to the era of Roman domination over Judea. Thus under the tutelage of the spirit-guided Teacher of Righteousness, the Qumran community read Scripture with a lively sense of their own participation in the events leading up to the culmination of God's redemptive plan.

The Habakkuk commentary (1QpHab). We begin with a pesher on one of the shortest of the OT books, Habakkuk. Its length, however, belies its importance for both the Qumran community and the NT. This particular Qumran commentary happens to be the best preserved of the whole lot. In addition, we have comments on the entirety of Habakkuk 1 and 2, thus providing us with an extensive example of Qumran exegesis at work. Furthermore, within the commentary itself are explicit statements that articulate some of the principles of Qumran hermeneutics (the art of interpretation). No wonder the pesher on Habakkuk holds such importance in the world of Qumran scholarship.

The Habakkuk commentary, for one thing, offers us tantalizing glimpses into the history of the sect. For example, 1QpHab 1:11-15 interprets Habakkuk 1:4c as referring to two individuals; they are none other than the central figure of the Qumran sect, namely, the Teacher of Righteousness, and his arch rival, "the Wicked Priest." Unfortunately, neither protagonist can be identified with certainty in 1QpHab, nor anywhere else in the extant sectarian writings or, for that matter, in any other writing of the Second Temple period! We postpone momentarily a discussion of this intriguing riddle.

Column 2 brings into the mix a third character, another bitter opponent: "the Man of the Lie." This individual apparently once belonged to the movement but disagreed with the views of the Teacher of Righteousness and drew away a number of followers. This latter group is castigated as traitors. It would seem that at one point in the pesher they are referred to as "the family of Absalom" (1QpHab 5:9-10).[5] From the standpoint of the writer of the commentary, the Teacher of Righteousness is the undisputed leader because God raised him up "to explain all the words of His servants the prophets, through [whom] God has foretold everything that is to come upon His people and [His land]" (1QpHab 2:8-10). In 1QpHab 7:4-5 the Teacher of Righteousness is further described as one "to whom God made known all the mysterious revelations of his servants the prophets." Here we see evidence for some of the hermeneutical presuppositions mentioned above.

The nature of the dispute between the Man of the Lie and the Teacher of Righteousness no doubt revolved around halakic issues, questions of ritual purity and calendrical observance. 1QpHab 1:4-5 implies that the followers of the Teacher of Righteousness suffered persecution and betrayal because of their particular views on these matters. In this connection, the document called *A Sectarian Manifesto* (4QMMT)[6] may supply crucial information bearing on the rift.[7] This letter discusses some twenty-four halakic differences between the Qumran community and another group in Jerusalem, presumably a priestly group. Although the tone of the letter is cordial, one may suppose that the issues in question became highly charged and divisive, leading eventually to mutual excommunication by the contending factions. In the Habakkuk commentary the invective leaves no doubt about the intense hostility that developed.

As for the Wicked Priest, 1QpHab 8:8b-13a (commenting on Hab 2:5-6) contains several charges against him for which he is vilified by the Qumran brethren. We cite the passage in full:

> This refers to the Wicked Priest who had a reputation for reliability at the beginning of his term of service; but when he became ruler over Israel, he became proud and forsook God and betrayed the commandments for the sake of riches. He amassed by force the riches of the lawless who had rebelled against God, seizing the riches of the peoples, thus adding to the guilt of his crimes, and he committed abhorrent deeds in every defiling impurity.

---

[5] All subsequent quotations taken from Edward Cook in Wise, Abegg and Cook, *Dead Sea Scrolls*, pp. 115-22.

[6] It is often referred to in other works as the "Halakhic Letter" (cf. Florentino García Martínez and Eibert J. C. Tigchelaar, *The Dead Sea Scrolls Study Edition,* 2 vols. [Grand Rapids: Eerdmans, 1997-1998], 2:790).

[7] For a brief discussion and a translation of one portion, see Geza Vermes, *The Complete Dead Sea Scrolls in English,* 5th ed. (London: Penguin, 1998), pp. 181-82. For a translation of all fragments and a composite text, see Florentino García Martínez, *The Dead Sea Scrolls Translated: The Qumran Texts in English,* trans. W. G. E. Watson (Leiden: E. J. Brill, 1994), pp. 77-85.

This description has led many scholars to suggest that the Wicked Priest must have been either Jonathan or Simon, the Maccabee brothers.[8] In our review of 1 Maccabees we had occasion to read about some of the events surrounding these two brothers during the Hasmonean revolt. A close reading of 1 Maccabees 9–10 and 14 is especially important in this regard. We think the case for Jonathan is slightly more compelling than for Simon. First, he was the first to be proclaimed high priest as well as military and political leader (cf. 1 Macc 9:28-31; 10:18-21). Second, the details of his demise correspond more closely with the Habakkuk commentary's description. The commentary on Habakkuk 2:8b says of the Wicked Priest:

> This refers to the Wicked Priest. Because of the crime he committed against the Teacher of Righteousness and the members of his party, God handed him over to his enemies, humiliating him with a consuming affliction with despair, because he had done wrong to His chosen. (1QpHab 9:9-11)

A comparison with the account of Jonathan's death in 1 Maccabees fits tolerably well (1 Macc 12:46, 48):

> Jonathan trusted him [Trypho] and did as he said; he sent away the troops, and they returned to the land of Judah. . . . But when Jonathan entered Ptolemais, the people of Ptolemais closed the gates and seized him, and they killed with the sword all who had entered with him.

In short, the situation seems to be one in which the high priesthood was taken over by a non-Zadokite family, namely, the Hasmoneans. By assuming the power and prerogatives of both the political and spiritual leadership of the Jewish people, the Hasmonean princes incurred the wrath of at least some of the Zadokite priests. Furthermore, the Teacher of Righteousness, who was probably a Zadokite priest, *may* have been the acting high priest replaced by the Hasmoneans. In any case, we have the dynamics for a bitter conflict that resulted in an exile in the desert of Judea at Qumran for the Teacher and his followers. Precisely when the dispute with the Man of the Lie occurred relative to the break with the Hasmoneans is difficult to say.[9]

A fourth party playing a leading role in the events alluded to in the commentary are the "Kittim." Whereas in some Jewish literature this term referred to the Greeks (cf. 1 Macc 1:1; 8:5), the consensus view of modern scholarship

---

[8]A few scholars have suggested that the title "Wicked Priest" refers to the entirety of the Hasmonean priest-kings. See W. H. Brownlee, "The Wicked Priest, the Man of Lies, and the Righteous Teacher—The Problem of Identity," *JQR* 73 (1982): 1-37. He is followed in this by Craig A. Evans, *Noncanonical Writings and New Testament Interpretation* (Peabody, Mass.: Hendrickson, 1992), p. 51. Timothy H. Lim puts the number of identifications of the Wicked Priest at over twenty! See his discussion in "Wicked Priest," *EDSS* 2:973-76.
[9]See further Michael A. Knibb, "Teacher of Righteousness," *EDSS* 2:918-21.

identifies the Kittim in 1QpHab with the Romans (cf. Dan 11:30 MT and LXX). This being the case, the commentary was written at least after Pompey's conquest of Jerusalem in 63 B.C. This provides a *terminus a quo* (earliest possible date) for the document and comports well with the paleographical evidence, which dates the Qumran copy to the latter half of the first century B.C. The description of the power and success of the Kittim fits nicely the expansion of Rome into the eastern Mediterranean during the first century B.C. Furthermore, the observation that "they sacrifice to their standards, and . . . their weapons are what they worship" (1QpHab 6:3b-5a) accords with Josephus's description of Roman practices in the Jewish war against Rome (cf. *J.W.* 6.2 §331). What is notably absent in the commentary is any indication of the terribly inept administration by the Roman procurators during the era of A.D. 44-66 and the destruction of Jerusalem in A.D. 70 by the Romans.

All of this, together with the relevant material from CD and 1QS, provides a possible reconstruction of the history of the sect at Qumran. With its roots in the Hasidim of the Maccabee uprising (167 B.C.), there was a traumatic break with the Hasmoneans upon the acceptance by Jonathan (151 B.C.) or Simon (142 B.C.) of the high priesthood. The dispossessed Zadokites retreated to their desert outpost at Qumran and sought to reconstitute the true Israel. After some time, perhaps twenty years (cf. CD 1:8-11), the Teacher of Righteousness joined them and provided authoritative guidance as an inspired interpreter of the prophetic Scriptures and of the halakah. At some point a bitter schism occurred in which the authority of the Teacher was challenged and rejected. Perhaps a majority, pejoratively referred to as "the family of Absalom," followed the "Liar." A minority, "the Elect" or "the Poor," remained at Qumran under the leadership of the Teacher and his successors.

We cannot prove this scenario because of the paucity of sources and the inherent difficulties and uncertainties in the interpretation of those sources that we do possess. While this remains one of several possible reconstructions, we think it has the most to commend it.[10]

---

[10]For further discussion on the question of the history of the sect, see Todd S. Beall, "Essenes," *EDSS* 1:267-68; Frank Moore Cross, *The Ancient Library of Qumran*, 3rd ed. (Minneapolis: Fortress, 1995), pp. 88-120 (he argues that Simon was the Wicked Priest); Devorah Dimant, "Qumran Sectarian Literature," in *Jewish Writings of the Second Temple Period: Apocrypha, Pseudepigrapha, Qumran Sectarian Writings, Philo, Josephus*, ed. Michael E. Stone, CRINT 2 (Assen: Van Gorcum; Philadelphia: Fortress, 1984), pp. 508-10; Lawrence H. Schiffman, *Reclaiming the Dead Sea Scrolls: The History of Judaism, the Background of Christianity, the Lost Library of Qumran*, ABRL (New York: Doubleday, 1994), pp. 83-95; James VanderKam, *The Dead Sea Scrolls Today* (Grand Rapids, Mich.: Eerdmans, 1994), pp. 99-108; Vermes, *Complete Dead Sea Scrolls in English*, pp. 23-40 (he argues for Jonathan as the Wicked Priest); and Vermes, *An Introduction to the Complete Dead Sea Scrolls* (Minneapolis: Fortress, 1999), pp. 127-44.

We call attention to an extraordinary event referred to in the commentary. The Wicked Priest suddenly showed up at Qumran and harassed the Teacher of Righteousness and his followers. He may even have put him to death. The relevant passage reads as follows:

> This [Hab 2:15] refers to the Wicked Priest, who pursued the Teacher of Right-eousness to destroy him in the heat of his anger at his place of exile. At the time set aside for the repose of the Day of Atonement he appeared to them to destroy them and to bring them to ruin on the fast day, the Sabbath intended for their repose. (1QpHab 11:4-9a)

The fact that a high priest from Jerusalem would persecute the Teacher on a high, holy day is explicable only on the understanding that the calendars differed between the two groups—it was *not* the Day of Atonement according to the Wicked Priest. We will examine other pesharim for evidence of this dramatic confrontation between the Wicked Priest and the Teacher of Righteousness.

We have sampled enough of this pesher to gain a feel for Qumran hermeneutics. The plain meaning of the text, the setting in the sixth century of Habakkuk's day, was bypassed and instead a contemporary event was read out of the text. This was justified by making explicit the underlying assumption, namely, that Habakkuk was really speaking of the end times, times that were currently unfolding in the life of the Qumran community (1QpHab 1:1-2; 7:1-5). The only instance where the plain meaning *(peshat)* is adopted is where the Gentiles are condemned for idolatry. Even here, however, the commentator assumes that the passage speaks of an eschatological judgment and not one of the sixth century B.C. (1QpHab 13:1-4).

There is one more point to be made about this commentary. The Qumran community's understanding of Habakkuk 2:4 and the apostle Paul's are quite different. Both cite this short text; in fact Paul cites it in two of his letters (Rom 10:5; Gal 3:11). But in Paul's case, the text is cited to buttress his contention that one is not put right with God by performing "works of the law." At Qumran, exactly the opposite point is made: one gains God's grace and favor by a punctilious observance of all the law, in this case, of course, the halakic interpretation advocated by the Teacher of Righteousness.[11] This pesher on Habakkuk is evidence that Paul's polemic against salvation by works is not a

---

[11]On this same point in connection with 4QMMT, Robert H. Eisenman and Michael Wise comment: "Both the Qumran letters and Paul's are operating in similar ideological frameworks, the only difference being that the Qumran ones are completely 'works' and *Torah*-oriented; Paul's, the opposite" (*The Dead Sea Scrolls Uncovered* [New York: Penguin, 1992], p. 184 [italics theirs]). We are not, however, convinced by Eisenman and Wise's historical reconstruction of the setting of 4QMMT (see ibid., pp. 182-96).

fabrication on his part.[12] We can be quite sure that legalism was a real danger, not only at Qumran but also among the Pharisees. This needs to be stated in opposition to the "new perspective on Paul" movement, which insists that such a reading of Paul stems more from the Reformation than from the real life setting of Paul's letters.

Commentary on Psalms (4Q171 or 4QpPs^a).[13] This commentary deals with Psalm 37. Four columns of a pesher on Psalm 45 also exist, but we will concentrate on Psalm 37. The script is Herodian and thus dates to the end of the first century B.C.

We single out some comments that add more information to the key actors and episodes sketched out in the pesher on Habakkuk. Note first of all the titles given to the Qumran community. They are variously styled as "the company of the poor" (4Q171 2:9; 3:10), "the society of the *Yahad* ["the Council of the Community" in Vermes's translation]" (4Q171 2:15), "the ones who return from the wilderness" (4Q171 3:1), "all who return to the Law" (4Q171 2:2-3) and "the company of His chosen" or "God's chosen people" (4Q171 2:5; 3:4-5; 4:14).

We also meet again the archenemy, "the Man of the Lie who led many people astray with deceitful statements, because they had chosen trivial matters but did not listen to the spokesmen for true knowledge" (4Q171 1:26-27). The latter is obviously the Teacher of Righteousness. The Liar is said to have acted "impertinently with an arrogant hand" (following García Martínez's translation of 4Q171 4:15). His followers "will perish and be exterminated from the company of the *Yahad*" (4Q171 4:18-19). The "cruel Israelites in the house of Judah who plot to destroy those who obey the Law" (4Q171 2:13-14) probably refers to these schismatics.

The Wicked Priest and his henchmen also appear in the commentary. The "wicked of 'Ephraim and Manasseh' " (4Q171 2:17) probably refers to the Pharisees and Sadducees, as we will see shortly in our study of the pesher on Nahum. At any rate, in this commentary, they are condemned to future judgment for their attempt to "do away with the Priest and the members of his party" (4Q171 2:17b-18a). It would seem, then, that the Teacher of Righteousness, here clearly designated a priest, had run-ins with virtually all the known groups in Second Temple Judaism! This should not be surprising considering the nature of the claims the Teacher made for himself. Self-styled religious authorities claiming infallible interpretations, both then and now, invariably generate controversy and conflict.

Of special interest in the pesher are the promises to the elect, provided

---

[12]See Martin Abegg, "Paul, 'Works of the Law' and MMT," *BRev* 20, no. 6 (1994): 52-55, 82.

[13]The two sigla represent the two different ways the document is designated in Vermes's and García Martínez's translations.

they remain faithful to the law as interpreted by the Teacher. They "will inherit the earth" (4Q171 2:4 applies Ps 37:9b to the "company of His chosen"), "are delivered from all the snares of Belial" and "will enjoy all the [. . .] of the earth and grow fat on every human [luxury]" (4Q171 2:9-11). The land in question is no doubt the promised land of the Hebrew Bible, the land promised to the patriarchs in Genesis. In 4Q171 3:1-2 the reward of the faithful is to live for a thousand generations—probably a metaphor for everlasting life—and to receive the inheritance of Adam and his descendants. There appear to be honors for those who are especially devoted to the Lord in that they will be given positions of leadership in the future days (4Q171 3:5-6). In 4Q171 3:10 the inheritance of the saints includes the whole earth, though the centerpiece of this great kingdom is still Jerusalem—the "lofty mount of Is[rael and] . . . His holy mount" (4Q171 3:11).

The destiny of the wicked and the just stand in sharp contrast: annihilation versus everlasting life (4Q171 4:1-3, citing Ps 37:28). As for the Wicked Priest, he will experience the vengeance of "the cruel Gentiles" (4Q171 4:9-10). This seems to correlate with the fate of Jonathan the Maccabee, as suggested above. As for the Liar, he "will perish and be exterminated from the company of the *Yahad*" (4Q171 4:18-19). Ephraim and Manasseh, like the Wicked Priest, undergo judgment at the hands of "the wicked Gentiles" (4Q171 2:20). In short, all but the Qumran sectaries will be utterly destroyed.

Sectarianism of any kind tends to display the same sort of mentality toward those who are on the outside, especially those who actively oppose the group. One senses sharp lines of demarcation between "them" and "us." A lack of compassion and understanding for outsiders often accompanies this sort of exclusiveness. Modern evangelicals are likewise not immune to this sort of "demonizing" of nonbelievers. Unfortunately, it becomes especially noticeable during election years![14]

The Jesus tradition in the Synoptic Gospels shares with the pesher on Psalm 37 a common expectation for the righteous. In the Beatitudes Jesus sets out an eschatological blessing in these familiar words: "Blessed are the meek, for they will inherit the earth" (Mt 5:5).[15] Of course, this is almost certainly a quotation from Psalm 37:11, showing a common indebtedness for both the Teacher of Right-

---

[14]Richard Mouw provides sage counsel on how evangelicals can relate to the secular arena in *Uncommon Decency: Christian Civility in an Uncivil World* (Downers Grove, Ill.: InterVarsity Press, 1992).

[15]For an example of five beatitudes grouped together, see 4Q525 (Wise, Abegg and Cook, *Dead Sea Scrolls,* pp. 423-24; García Martínez, *Dead Sea Scrolls Translated,* p. 395). On the literary and tradition-history background of the beatitudes in the Sermon on the Mount, see Robert Guelich, *The Sermon on the Mount* (Grand Rapids, Mich.: Eerdmans, 1982), pp. 62-97, 109-18.

eousness and Jesus. We have argued above that the early Christians, in keeping with their Jewish roots, shared a hope of a renewed earth as an everlasting inheritance. The centerpiece of this earthly kingdom was Jerusalem. Jesus promised his disciples that they would reign with him over the twelve tribes of Israel (Mt 19:28-30; Lk 22:28-30). Furthermore, the apostle Paul reminded his Gentile converts that they too would exercise positions of leadership in the future kingdom, if they proved faithful in the here and now (1 Cor 6:2).[16]

Nahum Commentary (4Q169 or 4QpNah). This fascinating pesher, covering portions of Nahum 1–2 and 3:1-14, continues the story of conflict in the Qumran community even further. The paleography and internal evidence place the copy in the reign of Alexander Janneus (103-76 B.C.).

As noted above, the "Kittim" are the Romans. The group called "the Flattery Seekers" must be the Pharisees. This derogatory nickname derived from the fact that, according to the *Yahad,* the Pharisees' halakah was too lenient and in error. This title probably incorporates a play on words inasmuch as $h^a laq\hat{o}t$ ("easy" or "smooth") sounds similar to $h^a l\bar{a}k\hat{o}t$ ("rules or interpretations").

The "Lion of Wrath" (4Q169 3-4 i 5) must be Alexander Janneus, since it says of him that he "used to hang men alive" (4Q169 3-4 i 7); that is, he crucified them (cf. 4QpHos[b]). Josephus attributes an atrocity to Alexander Janneus in which the latter crucified eight hundred rebel leaders in the middle of the city of Jerusalem (*J. W.* 1.4.6 §97). Furthermore, this incident occurred in the aftermath of a battle with a Greek king named Demetrius. The Nahum commentary explicitly refers to a "[Deme]trius, king of Greece" (4Q169 3-4 i 2). This Demetrius is probably Demetrius III Eukairos (95-88 B.C.). Since in 4Q169 3-4 ii 2, "the city of Ephraim" is equated with "the Flattery-Seekers in the Last Days," we have confirmation that "Ephraim" refers to the Pharisees.

Another group castigated in the commentary is "Manasseh in the Last Days, for his kingdom shall be brought low in Is[rael]" (4Q169 3-4 iv 3). The commentary's identification of "No-Amon" and "the streams" from Nahum 3:8 (NRSV renders these two terms as "Thebes" and "the Nile") as "Manasseh" and "the nobles of Manasseh, the respectable" (4Q169 3-4 iii 9), seems to point to an aristocratic element in Jewish society, suggesting an allusion to the party of the Sadducees. This should be compared with the reference to Ephraim and Manasseh in the Habakkuk commentary, as noted above.

In sum, the Qumran sectarians held that the prophet Nahum foretold the horrible atrocities that would befall both the Pharisees and the Sadducees. Furthermore, the Qumran community viewed these judgments as the just deserts of their erring opponents.

---

[16]See further on Jesus' view of the future in Ben Witherington III, *Jesus, Paul and the End of the World* (Downers Grove, Ill.: InterVarsity Press, 1992), pp. 36-44, 59-72.

Commentaries on Isaiah (4QpIsa^{a-e} [4Q161-165]). The last example of pesher
we consider consists of fragments from five commentaries on the book of Isaiah, one of the most frequently quoted canonical works at Qumran. In these
pesharim we meet the familiar figures we have already seen: the Kittim
(4Q161 frags. 8-10), the Teacher of Righteousness (4Q163 frag. 21 lines 5-6;
4Q165 frags. 1-2 line 3) and, of course, the Qumran community identified as
those who "return from the 'wilderness of the Gen[tiles' " (4Q161 frags. 5-6
lines 15-16), the remnant of Israel (4Q163 6-7 ii 8 [?], 10, 17 [?], "the society of
the *Yahad* . . . the company of His chosen" (4Q164 2-3) and their leaders, the
"Zadokite [priests]" (4Q163 frag. 22 lines 1-3). The "Men of Mockery who are
in Jerusalem" (4Q162 ii 6-7; cf. 4Q163 23 ii 10) may refer to the Pharisees,
since it is said that "He [God] stretched out his hand against them and struck
them so that the mountains shook and the corpses lay like garbage in the
middle of the streets" (4Q162 ii 8-10). This sounds similar to the episode in
which Alexander Janneus crucified eight hundred Pharisees.

There is also reference to a king of the Kittim who "marches inland from
the Plain of Akko to fight against [. . . the leader of the Na]tion" (4Q161 frags.
5-6, lines 25-26). It is tempting to see here an allusion to Pompey in 63 B.C.
Devorah Dimant, however, suggests that it refers to an attempted march on
Jerusalem by Ptolemy Lathyrus during Alexander Janneus's reign (cf. Josephus *Ant.* 13.12.2-13.13.3 §§324-64; *J.W.* 1.4.2 §§86-87). Since the biblical text
narrates the miraculous escape of Jerusalem from the attack of the Assyrian
monarch Sennacherib, she suggests that Cleopatra's restraining of Ptolemy's
intentions was likewise viewed as a miraculous intervention.[17]

Of considerable interest to Christian readers is a pesher on Isaiah 11:1-5, in
which we have a clear reference to a Davidic messiah (4Q161 frags. 8-10). His
role is military and political. He executes all God's enemies and reigns over
all peoples. Even Magog, a symbol of the farthest removed of all peoples on
earth, comes under his sovereignty (cf. Ezek 38–39). Right at the end of the
fragment we read that "[he will be advised by the Zadokite priests,] and as
they instruct him, so shall he rule, and at their command [he shall render
decisions; and always] one of the prominent priests shall go out with him, in
whose hand shall be the garments of [. . .]" (4Q161 frags. 8-10 line 25). Is this
interpretation an allusion to Zechariah 3:1-10? In the latter passage the high
priest Joshua exchanges his filthy clothes for festal apparel. This symbolizes
cleansing in connection with the coming of the Messiah. If so, both Zechariah
and our pesher feature a priestly figure (or figures) and a Branch of David
who is a political figure. Unfortunately, no pesher on Zechariah, which might
throw more light on our question, has been found at Qumran. We do, how-

---

[17]"Qumran Sectarian Literature," in *Jewish Writings of the Second Temple Period,* p. 513.

ever, have a commentary on Genesis, perhaps the blessing on Judah (Gen 49:8-12), which makes reference to the two anointed ones of Zechariah 4:14: "[. . . 'These are] the two anointed sons who [stand by the Lord of the whole earth.' . . .] those who keep the commandments of God [. . .] for the men of the *Yahad* [. . .]" (4Q254 frag. 4). To this we should add 4Q285, where we have a commentary on Isaiah 10:34—11:1:

> This is the] Branch of David. Then [all forces of Belial] shall be judged, [and the king of the Kittim shall stand for judgment] and the leader of the nation—the Bra[nch of David]—will have him put to death. [Then all Israel shall come out with timbrel]s and dancers, and the [High] Priest shall order [them to cleanse their bodies from the guilty blood of the c]orpse[s of] the Kittim. (4Q285 frag. 5 lines 3-6)[18]

Taken together, 4Q161, 4Q254 and 4Q285 strengthen the claim that the Qumran community held to both a Davidic and a priestly messiah. Furthermore, one senses that the priestly messiah took precedence over the Davidic scion.[19]

Finally, we should observe another allusion to the Pharisees: "This passage is for the Last Days and refers to the company of Flattery-Seekers who are in Jerusalem" (4Q163 23 ii 10-11). García Martínez renders the Hebrew *dwršy hhlqwt* as "those l[ooking] for easy interpretations."[20] Nickelsburg renders it as "Facile Interpreters" and claims that it is "almost certain" that the expression comes from Isaiah 30:10b: "speak to us smooth things, prophesy illusions."[21] Here was a scriptural designation that served to characterize all that was wrong about Pharisaic interpretation! As Nickelsburg points out, this passage in Isaiah must have been especially meaningful to the Qumran community, because just a few verses down in Isaiah 30 we read the following: "Though the Lord may give you the bread of adversity and the water of affliction, yet your Teacher will not hide himself any more, but your eyes shall see your Teacher" (Is 30:20).[22] This text was no doubt explicitly connected with the Teacher of Righteousness in pesharim that have not survived the ravages of time.

Relevance for New Testament Interpretation

Pesher in the New Testament. An issue bearing on the interpretation of the NT confronts us in these brief examples of pesharim from Qumran. In short, the

---

[18]See Abegg's discussion on the initial excitement and controversy surrounding this text (Wise, Abegg and Cook, *Dead Sea Scrolls*, pp. 291-92).

[19]See further on this, John J. Collins, *The Scepter and the Star: The Messiahs of the Dead Sea Scrolls and Other Ancient Literature*, ABRL 10 (New York: Doubleday, 1995), pp. 74-95; and Craig A. Evans, "Messiahs," *EDSS* 1:537-42.

[20]García Martínez and Tigchelaar, *Dead Sea Scrolls Study Edition*, 1:324-45.

[21]*Jewish Literature*, pp. 131-32.

[22]Ibid.

question is whether NT authors also employed the pesher technique in their interpretation of the OT prophetic writings (which includes some Psalms). This is a controversial subject, and we can but mention some contours of the issue.[23]

As a point of entry, we reexamine an extraordinary event: the day of Pentecost (Acts 2). According to Luke's account, Peter stood up to speak to the bewildered crowd of onlookers and launched into a proclamation of the kerygma (the basic content of the gospel, from the Greek word meaning "preaching"). His message was essentially an interpretation of an eschatological prophecy describing the messianic age (Joel 2:28-32). Peter introduced the quotation with the phrase "this is what was spoken through the prophet Joel" (Acts 2:16). In short, Peter proceeded to inform his listeners that the ancient prophecy of Joel about the messianic age was now being fulfilled in their very presence and actualized in the lives of Jesus' "witnesses" (Acts 2:32). The listeners were urged to respond to the promise and experience eschatological salvation (Acts 2:38-40). The last days had begun!

What is striking is the similarity to the Qumran pesharim. Although Acts 2 does not have the exact, linguistic equivalent for the typical introductory formula used in the Qumran pesharim ("This refers to" [*pišrô ʿal, pišrŏ ʾašer, pišrô hûʾ* or *pešer haddābār*]), it does have a phrase close to one occasionally employed at Qumran ("for this is as it is said" or "for this is what it says" [Heb *kî hûʾ ʾašer ʾāmar*]).[24] In any case, Acts 2 demonstrates essentially the same exegetical method as at Qumran, namely, a contemporizing of the prophecy in the new-covenant community. Defined broadly, this falls within the orbit of pesher.[25]

---

[23]As a point of departure one may profitably consult E. E. Ellis, *Paul's Use of the Old Testament* (Edinburgh: Oliver & Boyd, 1957); F. F. Bruce, *Biblical Exegesis in the Qumran Texts* (Grand Rapids, Mich.: Eerdmans, 1959); Richard Longenecker, *Biblical Exegesis in the Apostolic Period* (Grand Rapids, Mich.: Eerdmans, 1975); Craig A. Evans, "Old Testament in the Gospels," *DJG*, pp. 579-90; M. Silva, "Old Testament in Paul," *DPL*, pp. 630-42; G. J. Brooke, "Pesharim," *DNTB*, pp. 778-82; C. Marvin Pate, *Communities of the Last Days: The Dead Sea Scrolls, the New Testament and the Story of Israel* (Downers Grove, Ill.: InterVarsity Press, 2000), pp. 85-106; and Shani L. Berrin, "Pesharim," *EDSS* 2:644-47.

[24]See Berrin, "Pesharim," 2:645; Bernstein, "Pesher Habakkuk," *EDSS* 2:648.

[25]We are aware that not all would agree with this assessment. G. J. Brooke, e.g., wants to limit pesher to cases "where the NT author engages in the interpretation of unfulfilled or partially fulfilled blessings, curses and other prophecies." He makes the point that most of the scriptural interpretation in the NT "that is usually associated with the Qumran pesharim depicts the Scriptures as having been fulfilled" ("Pesharim," p. 782). We think this is a distinction without a difference. At Qumran both fulfilled and unfulfilled prophecies (from the vantage point of the interpreter) were introduced with formulas signaling pesher comments. Also, to argue from Matthew's Infancy Narrative that Matthew reverses the order of Scripture-event, as at Qumran, to event-Scripture confuses pesher with a genre, not a technique. Of course Matthew proceeds from event to Scripture—after all, a Gospel is essentially a biographical narrative—but ancient prophecies are actualized in the life of Jesus. This in our judgment is what pesher is all about. See further on this in Pate, *Communities of the Last Days*, pp. 85-106.

Did Peter (or Luke) come up with this approach on his own? As we have already shown, the Qumran sectaries were employing the technique long before the Jesus movement began. Just as the Teacher of Righteousness instructed the *Yahad,* so Jesus taught his disciples how to read the OT. A promising avenue of investigation focuses on the possibility of Essene influence upon Jesus' interpretation of Scripture.[26]

Several passages from the Gospels provide examples of a form of exegesis employed by Jesus having considerable similarity to the pesher technique found at Qumran. As a matter of fact, Richard Longenecker maintains that Jesus' "most characteristic employment of Scripture is portrayed as being a pesher type of interpretation. The 'this is that' fulfillment motif, which is distinctive to pesher exegesis, repeatedly comes to the fore in the words of Jesus."[27] Longenecker further says that if all we had were just two passages from the Gospels, we would have grounds for saying that "it was Jesus himself who gave the impetus to the explication of the fulfillment theme and of a pesher approach to Scripture in the early Church."[28]

The first of these two passages is the famous Nazareth sermon recorded in Luke 4:16-21. Placed right at the beginning of Jesus' public ministry by Luke, this sermon is paradigmatic for the message of the entire Gospel. Jesus rose to read the haphtarah (a reading selection from the Prophets, read in the synagogue service on the sabbath following each lesson from the Torah). I think it likely there was already a lectionary in place in the Palestinian synagogues and the reading for that particular Sabbath was from Isaiah 61. Jesus gained the entire congregation's attention by reading Isaiah 61:1-2a and then suddenly breaking off in the middle of a sentence—why hadn't he finished the reading? He next electrified the synagogue with his dramatic announcement: "Today this scripture has been fulfilled in your hearing" (Lk 4:21). Jesus' messianic status and mission could hardly have been made clearer, since this text was almost certainly understood by first-century Jews to refer to the Messiah. Clearly the Qumran sectaries so understood it, as may be seen in 11QMelch 2:4.[29] The messianic age was breaking into history!

The second passage, John 5:39-47, occurs in the setting of the third of

---

[26]Bruce Chilton makes much of the formative influence of John the Baptist upon Jesus. Among other things, according to Chilton, John taught Jesus Merkabah (the throne-chariot of God) mysticism (*Rabbi Jesus: An Intimate Biography* [New York: Doubleday, 2000], chap. 3). This line of argument does not persuade us. A more convincing case could be made for pesher interpretation being mediated by John the Baptist from the Essenes to Jesus, although even this overreaches the available evidence.

[27]*Biblical Exegesis,* p. 70.

[28]Ibid.

[29]See further discussion of this text in Wise, Abegg and Cook, *Dead Sea Scrolls,* pp. 455-56; Evans, *Noncanonical Writings,* pp. 178-79.

Table 7.1. Longenecker's observations of Jesus' pesherlike approach

NT Passage	Introductory Formula	OT Text Quoted (see Gleason L. Archer and Gregory Chirichigno, *Old Testament Quotations in the New Testament* [Chicago: Moody Press, 1983])	Comment
Mk 12:1-12	"Have you not read this scripture" (Mk 12:10).	Ps 118:22-23: "The stone that the builders rejected has become the cornerstone."	The rejection of Jesus by the religious leaders was prophesied (or foreshadowed) in this royal psalm.
Mk 14:26-27	"For it is written" (Mk 14:27).	Zech 13:7: "I will strike the shepherd, and the sheep will be scattered."	Jesus' death and desertion by his disciples was foreseen in this messianic oracle.
Mt 11:7-19	"This is the one about whom it is written" (Mt 11:10).	Mal 3:1: "See, I am sending my messenger ahead of you, who will prepare your way before you."	John the Baptist is identified as the messenger who prepares for the coming of the Lord (now identified as Jesus).
Mt 13:10-16	"With them [Jesus' listeners] indeed is fulfilled the prophecy of Isaiah that says" (Mt 13:14).	Is 6:9-10: "You will indeed listen, but never understand. . . ."	This explains why most Jews rejected Jesus' message.
Mt 15:1-9	"Isaiah prophesied rightly about you when he said" (Mt 15:7).	Is 29:13: "This people honors me with their lips, but their hearts are far from me. . . ."	This explains why the scribes and Pharisees rejected Jesus' teaching.
Lk 22:35-38	"For I tell you, this scripture must be fulfilled in me . . . and indeed what is written about me is being fulfilled" (Lk 22:37).	Is 53:12: "And he was counted among the lawless."	Jesus' condemnation as a criminal was prophesied in this messianic oracle (the fourth of the Servant Songs).
Jn 6:41-51	"It is written in the prophets" (Jn 6:45).	Is 54:13: "And they all shall be taught by God."	Jesus is God's unique teacher, and all God's children respond to him.

Table 7.1.—*Continued*

NT Passage	Introductory Formula	OT Text Quoted	Comment
Jn 13:12-20	"But it is to fulfill the scripture" (Jn 13:18).	Ps 41:9: "The one who ate my bread has lifted his heel against me."	Judas's betrayal was prophesied in this psalm.
Jn 15:18-25	"It was to fulfill the word . . . written in their law" (Jn 15:25).	Ps 35:19: "They hated me without a cause."	This citation explains the hatred directed at Jesus' followers.

seven "signs" Jesus performs in John 1—11 to display his glory. He heals at the Pool of Bethesda a man who has been lame for thirty-eight years. A sharp dispute breaks out with the religious authorities over the perceived breach of sabbath laws. At the conclusion of this argument, which is essentially over the question of religious authority, Jesus says: "You search the scriptures because you think that in them you have eternal life; and it is they that testify on my behalf" (Jn 5:39). He follows up this astounding claim by adding, "If you believed Moses, you would believe me, for he wrote about me" (Jn 5:46). Assuming that this truly reflects Jesus' self-understanding, we should not be surprised that Peter and the apostles saw the events of Pentecost as the fulfillment of end-times prophecy. Their contemporizing of scriptural prophecy—the essence of pesher—was learned at the feet of Rabbi Jesus.

Luke's Gospel makes this point explicit in the memorable story of the two disciples on the way to Emmaus on Easter eve. Jesus rebukes them for their slowness "to believe all that the prophets have declared! . . . Then beginning with Moses and all the prophets, he interpreted to them the things about himself in all the scriptures" (Lk 24:25, 27). Luke's account of a forty-day period of postresurrection instruction during which Jesus taught about the kingdom of God (Acts 1:3) surely included further sessions on Jesus' fulfillment of OT prophecy. There are other instances where Jesus adopted a pesherlike approach to the OT. Longenecker briefly discusses nine such passages (see table 7.1).[30]

Would Paul, trained at Jerusalem under the renowned Pharisee Gamaliel, have been likely to employ pesher interpretation, especially considering the hostility between Essenes and Pharisees? Earle Ellis argued some years ago that about twenty Pauline quotations could be classified as pesher.[31] Though some have challenged his claim,[32] we think his essential point remains valid,

---

[30]*Biblical Exegesis*, pp. 70-73.

[31]*Paul's Use of the Old Testament*, p. 144.

[32]See, e.g., Walter C. Kaiser Jr., *The Uses of the Old Testament in the New* (Chicago: Moody Press, 1985), pp. 226-28.

even if the number of examples should probably be reduced owing to uncertainty about distinguishing between textual variants and ad hoc interpretations.[33]

Before looking at Paul's letters for evidence, consider Luke's narrative of Paul's preaching at Antioch of Pisidia. In this sample sermon given to a Jewish audience, Paul employs a promise-fulfillment scheme that flows out of a traditional rehearsal of salvation history (Acts 13:17-22): "Of this man's [David's] posterity God has brought to Israel a Savior, Jesus, as he promised" (Acts 13:23). But, according to Paul, the Jerusalemites and religious leaders "did not recognize him or understand the words of the prophets that are read every Sabbath . . . [but] fulfilled those words by condemning him," and in so doing, "they had carried out everything that was written about him" (Acts 13:27-29). Then Paul strings together four OT citations: Psalm 2:7; Isaiah 55:3; Psalm 16:10 and Habakkuk 1:5. He introduces the citations with the following quotation formulas: "as also it is written in the second psalm," "he has spoken in this way," "he has also said in another psalm" and "what the prophets said."

The Habakkuk quotation is fascinating because, as we have already noted, this text was also commented upon in 1QpHab. Both 1QpHab and Paul apply the biblical text to *contemporary,* unbelieving Israelites (Jews). We cite a portion of 1QpHab to show this phenomenon:

> They are the cru[el Israel]ites who will not believe when they hear everything that [is to come upon] the latter generation that will be spoken by the Priest in whose [heart] God has put [the ability] to explain all the words of His servants the prophets, through [whom] God has foretold everything that is to come upon His people and [His land]. (1QpHab 2:6-10)

Assuming that Luke gives a reliable précis of Paul's synagogue sermon, we have initial evidence that Paul did employ pesher interpretation in his use of the OT.

Can this be verified, however, from his actual letters? We can give what is to my mind a convincing example. In Romans 10:6-8 Paul paraphrases Deuteronomy 30:12-14. As the reader can quickly confirm, the quotation is not verbatim. Furthermore, it does not conform to either LXX or MT in any of its known forms. Paul has rather freely adapted the Deuteronomy passage and contemporized its meaning in his own proclamation of the kerygma. Possibly he is also indebted to a Targum of the Deuteronomy passage in which reference is made to Moses, who ascended to heaven to get the law, and to Jonah, who descended into the Abyss.[34] At any rate, Paul's pesherlike com-

---

[33]See Longenecker, *Biblical Exegesis,* pp. 129-30.
[34]For the details, see Evans, *Noncanonical Writings,* pp. 185-86.

ments (see table 7.2) are signaled by the formula "that is" *(tout' estin)*.

Table 7.2. Paul's pesherlike comments

OT Citation	Introductory Formula	Paul's Interpretation (Pesher)
"Do not say in your heart, 'Who will ascend into heaven?' " (Deut 30:12)	"that is"	"to bring Christ down"
"or 'Who will descend into the abyss?' " (Deut 30:13)	"that is"	"to bring Christ up from the dead"
"The word is near you, on your lips and in your heart" (Deut 30:14)	"that is"	"the word of faith that we proclaim"

We agree with Moisés Silva that the crucial contrast between Qumran exegesis and that of NT writers lies in the completely different identification of the events and persons that fulfilled biblical prophecy. We think, however, that his drawing a distinction between the verse-by-verse interpretation of the Qumran pesharim and Paul's letters once again confuses genre and methodology.[35] Obviously, it was not Paul's intention to do verse-by-verse exegesis in his letters. In the course of his letters, however, we occasionally discover approaches to Scripture that can best be described as pesherlike.

Another example is 2 Corinthians 6:2, where Paul quotes from Isaiah 49:8: "At an acceptable time I have listened to you, and on a day of salvation I have helped you." This citation is preceded by the formula, "For he [God] says." Paul then adds his pesher: "See, now is the acceptable time; see, now is the day of salvation!" The actualization of the prophecy is unmistakable.

Beyond this we have several passages that are not, strictly speaking, pesher exegesis. Rather, they demonstrate Paul's basic presupposition underlying pesher, namely, that God has revealed the mysteries of his saving plan with Paul himself as a key element in making that known, especially among the Gentiles.

In the ideology of Qumran, the term "mystery" (Aramaic *rāz*) was impor-

---

[35]"Old Testament in Paul," *DPL*, pp. 636-37. Silva does admit, however, that "there is a rough parallel between this approach [pesher] and the conviction of the NT writers, including Paul, that the coming of Jesus Christ was to be understood as the fulfillment of the OT prophecies" (p. 636).

tant.[36] God revealed many mysteries to the Teacher of Righteousness, and he in turn taught his followers what those mysteries were (cf. 1QH 9:21; 12:6-11, 23-28). Many of those mysteries were divinely revealed to the Teacher as he read and meditated upon Scripture. Pesher exegesis is all about elucidating those revealed mysteries that are embedded in Scripture itself.

Likewise for the apostle Paul, the concept of mystery looms large; the term occurs twenty-one times in Pauline literature. For Paul the concept of "mystery" (the Gk translation of Aramaic *rāz* is *mystērion)* was crucial to his self-understanding as an apostle to the Gentiles. Like the Teacher of Righteousness, Paul was the recipient of divine revelation (Gal 1:15-16). Like the Teacher, Paul understood the prophetic Scriptures to contain these divinely revealed truths about God's saving activity.

To be sure, the content of Paul's mysteries differs markedly from that of the Teacher. Furthermore, the Teacher sought to preserve and protect his mysteries for the elect community alone. Paul, on the other hand, committed himself to proclaiming the revealed mysteries of the kingdom of God to both Jew and Gentile (the latter group were beyond the pale of salvation for the Essenes). In Paul's own words:

> I became its servant according to God's commission that was given to me for you, to make the word of God fully known, the mystery that has been hidden throughout the ages and generations but has now been revealed to his saints. To them God chose to make known how great among the Gentiles are the riches of the glory of this mystery, which is Christ in you, the hope of glory. (Col 1:25-27)
>
> For surely you have already heard of the commission of God's grace that was given me for you, and how the mystery was made known to me by revelation. . . . In former generations this mystery was not made known to humankind, as it has now been revealed to his holy apostles and prophets by the Spirit: that is, the Gentiles have become fellow heirs, members of the same body, and sharers in the promise in Christ Jesus through the gospel. (Eph 3:2-6)
>
> Paul, a servant of Jesus Christ, called to be an apostle, set apart for the gospel of God, which he promised beforehand through his prophets in the holy scriptures, the gospel concerning his Son. (Rom 1:1-3)
>
> Now to God who is able to strengthen you according to my gospel and the proclamation of Jesus Christ, according to the revelation of the mystery that was kept secret for long ages but is now disclosed, and through the prophetic writings is made known to all the Gentiles . . . (Rom 16:25-26)

When all is said and done, it is hard to avoid the conclusion that Paul shared with Qumran an approach to the Scripture that we can designate as pesher.

---

[36]The word occurs about twenty-seven times in James H. Charlesworth, ed., *Graphic Concordance to the Dead Sea Scrolls* (Tübingen: Mohr Siebeck; Louisville: Westminster John Knox, 1991), p. 487.

Other NT writers besides the Evangelists and Paul display the pesher technique. Longenecker draws attention to the employment of a pesher type of approach to Scripture in the Petrine epistles and Jude as well.[37]

Polemics in the New Testament. The Qumran commentaries we have examined thus far illuminate the deep divisions and animosities that existed within Second Temple Judaism in the first century B.C. and first century A.D. The harsh denunciations of the Pharisees and Sadducees found in the Qumran writings should be compared with Jesus' condemnation of the selfsame groups.

The language of Jesus' charges, especially in a passage such as Matthew 23, has occasioned some misgivings. After all, did not Jesus himself warn his followers about angry words and passing judgment on others (cf. Mt 5:22, 44; 7:1-5; 12:36-37)? In response to this, some scholars remind us that, when placed in the context of the polemics of Second Temple Judaism, Jesus' criticisms are not exceptional.[38] That is, his accusations employed the conventional language of the era that dissenting groups used with reference to each other. While helpful, this still does not alleviate the perceived problem.

We also need to remind ourselves that Jesus was probably closest theologically to the position of the Pharisees. The common ground shared by Jesus and the Pharisees was considerably greater than that of any other known sect within Second Temple Judaism. Thus the dispute was intramural in nature. Jesus did not totally repudiate the Pharisees. In fact, Matthew records Jesus as saying, "The scribes and the Pharisees sit on Moses' seat; therefore, do whatever they teach you and follow it" (Mt 23:2-3). This is not the case with the Sadducees. Jesus' blunt reply to the hypothetical question concerning resurrection and marriage posed by the Sadducean party demonstrates this: "You are wrong, because you know neither the scriptures nor the power of God" (Mt 22:29). One should also recall here that, according to Luke, the apostle Paul identified himself as a Pharisee in a hearing before the Sanhedrin (Acts 23:6), which is quite remarkable, since by that time he had been a follower of Jesus for over twenty years (cf. Gal 1:14; Phil 3:5). According to Luke, in the late 50s the church in Jerusalem had thousands of believers, all of whom were "zealous for the law" (Acts 21:20). It sounds as though one could be a Christian Pharisee, at least as far as the Christians were concerned. Whether the Pharisees officially accepted this combination is doubtful, especially if we acknowledge the historical reliability of John's Gospel (cf. Jn 9:22; 12:42; 16:2).

---

[37]*Biblical Exegesis*, pp. 200-204.

[38]See Luke T. Johnson, "The New Testament's Anti-Jewish Slander and the Conventions of Ancient Polemic," *JBL* 108 (1989): 419-41.

The nature of Jesus' dispute with the Pharisees concerned the "tradition of the elders" (Mk 7:3-4). This was in all likelihood the oral law that we have spoken about previously (see chapter three). Thus the primary contention with the Pharisaic party centered on the validity of their halakic interpretations of the Mosaic law. Interestingly enough, Jesus sided with the Sadducees on one point, namely, that the written Torah alone possessed binding authority for faith and practice (cf. Mt 5:17-20; 15:2-9; Mk 7:8-13). According to Jesus, the halakah of the Pharisees was not of divine origin, though he did apparently instruct his followers to respect the teaching authority of the Pharisees and to conform, *for the meantime*, to their legislation (Mt 23:1-3).[39] On the other hand, he characterized Pharisaic interpretations as burdensome and hard to bear (Mt 23:4) and criticized its implementation by the Pharisees as hypocritical (Mt 23:1-36). Jesus' primary critique of the Pharisaic system was that it focused on externals and incidentals: "[You] have neglected the weightier matters of the law: justice and mercy and faith. It is these you ought to have practiced without neglecting the others" (Mt 23:23b).

We do not sense in Jesus' accusations anything that could truly be called anti-Judaic or anti-Semitic.[40] He had an undying love for his people and did not separate himself from his opponents, as was the case with the *Yahad*. He maintained a dialogue with the Pharisees and Sadducees right up to the end and taught his disciples to bless and pray for their enemies. Sadly, the church has not always heeded his words or followed in his footsteps. We will say more about this in chapter fourteen.

A number of scholars have suggested that at least several of Jesus' sayings and parables may well have had the Essenes as the intended foil. Perhaps the clearest instance occurs in the Sermon on the Mount. In the section called "the antitheses," Matthew places the following on Jesus' lips: "You have heard that it was said, 'You shall love your neighbor and hate your enemy' " (Mt

---

[39]This surprising concession by Jesus should be seen in light of the larger history of redemption. The mission to Israel had not yet concluded. Jesus did not want his disciples to alienate the most respected and powerful religious body in Israel by ignoring or rejecting their halakah. As the church became increasingly a Gentile-dominated movement, this counsel became irrelevant. For a different approach to this passage, see Richard T. France, "Matthew," in *New Bible Commentary*, ed. D. A. Carson et al., 4th ed. (Downers Grove, Ill.: InterVarsity Press, 1994), p. 934.

[40]Scholars in the liberal tradition often absolve Jesus of any guilt in this matter by asserting that the anti-Judaism of the NT is really the creation of the later church, who put such sayings on the lips of Jesus. Allegedly, this was an unfortunate consequence of the church's struggle with the synagogue. See, e.g., Sidney G. Hall III, *Christian Anti-Semitism and Paul's Theology* (Minneapolis: Fortress, 1993), pp. 26-28. Conservative scholars, who have a higher view of the reliability of the Gospel traditions, cannot entertain such an option. For them, the issue must be faced head on. For a good treatment, see J. A. Weatherly, "Anti-Semitism," *DJG*, pp. 13-17.

5:43). The first part of the citation is, of course, found in the Hebrew Bible (cf. Lev 19:18; Deut 10:19), but nowhere in Jewish sources do we find an exhortation to hate one's enemies, except in the sectarian literature stemming from Qumran (cf. 1QS 1:4, 9-10).[41] He may have been deliberately contrasting his behavioral standard for disciples with that of the Essenes.[42] Certainly the Gospel portrayal of Jesus' ministry distances him considerably from the austere, separatist lifestyle of the Qumran community. Jesus' openness to and engagement with all strata of Jewish society stands in sharp contrast to the exclusive nature of the sectarians.[43]

Parallels in the church today. Are there not parallels to the attitudes of the Qumran covenanters in Christian circles? Not infrequently we encounter bitter intramural disputes among groups that are quite close theologically. The differences, however, assume monumental importance, and the rhetoric employed, like a ratchet, intensifies the disagreement, resulting in a split or schism. Not a few denominations trace their history back to one or several disputes over relatively minor differences that assumed great significance for the contending parties.[44] Whether the dispute concerns the nature of church government, the mode of baptism, the frequency and manner of observing the Lord's Supper, the role and function of women in the church, spiritual gifts (especially tongues) or the details of the second coming, the result is a highly charged atmosphere in which accusations and recriminations fly back and forth. The venom manifested in disputes of this nature often far exceeds that directed toward complete outsiders and antireligious movements! This phenomenon, of course, is not unique to Christianity but occurs in all the major religions of the world. A study of American Judaism, for example, contains fascinating parallels to disputes in various Christian denominations.[45]

One of the benefits of reading the surviving writings of the Qumran sect is that it prompts us to reflect upon our attitudes toward "outsiders" as well as "insiders" with whom we share a great deal but differ with on a few points of doctrine and practice. Where does one draw the line of fellowship? Among

---

[41]See further, James H. Charlesworth, "The Dead Sea Scrolls and the Historical Jesus," in *Jesus and the Dead Sea Scrolls* (New York: Doubleday, 1992), pp. 23-24.

[42]See further Heinz-Wolfgang Kuhn, "Jesus," *EDSS* 1:406.

[43]David Flusser argues that Jesus criticizes the Qumran view of refusing to share goods with nonbelievers ("The Parable of the Unjust Steward: Jesus' Criticism of the Essenes," in Charlesworth, *Jesus and the Dead Sea Scrolls,* pp. 176-97).

[44]For a helpful resource that gives a brief historical sketch of the various denominations in the United States, see Frank S. Mead and Samuel S. Hill, eds., *Handbook of Denominations in the United States,* 9th ed. (Nashville: Abingdon, 1992).

[45]See, e.g., Max Dimont, *The Jews in America: The Roots, History and Destiny of American Jews* (New York: Simon & Schuster, 1978); and more recently, Samuel G. Freedman, *Jew vs. Jew: The Struggle for the Soul of American Jewry* (New York: Simon & Schuster, 2000).

the challenges of the new millennium will certainly be the tension between commitment to the unity of the church, on the one hand, and the truth of the gospel, on the other. Another will be our attitude toward those who are hostile to all expressions of Christianity. One of the primary lessons we can learn from the Qumran community is that intolerance for those who reject our views and withdrawal from society at large are not viable options. It was not the way of Jesus, and it should not be ours either (cf. 1 Pet 2:1, 21-23; 3:15-18; 4:8-9, 12-19).

Thematic Pesharim

We give two examples of the second main type of pesher. Here, instead of the verse-by-verse approach thus far examined, we find a few instances in which the members of Qumran juxtaposed several different scriptural texts, resulting in a kind of intertextual commentary. Interspersed between the scriptural texts are comments making a thematic connection between them.[46]

Midrash on the Last Days (4Q174) (= Florilegium [4QFlor])

This text is in a Herodian hand and dates to the last part of the first century B.C. In terms of composition, there are two parts: a citation of 2 Samuel 7:10-11 with explanatory glosses incorporating other texts from Exodus 15:17-18, Deuteronomy 23:3-4 and Ezekiel 44:9 (the latter two are not explicitly cited but clearly are the source of the comments); and a citation of 2 Samuel 7:12-14, once again followed by interpretations utilizing quotations from Deuteronomy 33; Amos 9:11; Isaiah 8:11; Ezekiel 37:23; Psalm 2:1; Daniel 11:32, 35; 12:10; Psalm 5:2-3; and Isaiah 65:22-23.[47] The guiding assumption is that similar words and phrases occurring in different prophetic texts may be combined in order to provide a synoptic view of some future individual or event. Michael Wise observes: "This approach is essentially the classical technique of Protestant Christianity, 'Scripture interprets scripture.' The type of rabbinic biblical interpretation known as *midrash* operated by similar methods."[48]

4Q174 is of special interest to students of the NT because it describes an eschatological scenario similar to the NT. Thus we read of a time of great trial for the faithful (styled the "House of Judah") brought on by Belial but terminated by God's intervention and destruction of the wicked (4Q174 2:12—4:7). Two figures attend the events of the end, namely, the Shoot of David, also styled the Branch of David, and the Interpreter of the Law (4Q174 3:10-13).

---

[46]For a good explanation of thematic pesharim, see André Dupont-Sommer, *The Essene Writings from Qumran*, trans. G. Vermes (Gloucester, Mass.: Peter Smith, 1973), pp. 310-11.

[47]See ibid, pp. 310-11, for a different analysis into three sections.

[48]In Wise, Abegg and Cook, *Dead Sea Scrolls*, p. 225.

The former is the Davidic Messiah; the latter may be the eschatological Chief Priest who instructs the Davidic Messiah (as in 4Q161) and who presides over the *Yahad* during the eschatological war (cf. 1QM 10:2—14:1; 15:4; 16:13—17:9; 18:5—19:8; 19:11-14).

Surprisingly, the pesher speaks of a future temple in which the elect will offer up "proper sacrifices" (4Q174 3:2-7). This stands in some tension with the community's view of itself as already a living, spiritual temple (cf. 1QS 9:18).[49] In spite of this, they apparently anticipated, at the end of days, a "Temple of Adam" (or "Temple of Humankind") to appear (4Q174 3:6). This difficult phrase *(mqdš 'dm)* is taken by some authorities to refer to the First Temple of Solomon or to a spiritualized concept of the temple. We think a good case can be made for an actual eschatological temple.[50] If we are correct in this, our text may then illustrate another presupposition of the Qumran exegetes, namely, the notion that the end recapitulates the beginning.[51] Thus the final age would see a return to the perfect worship of Adam in the garden.

The NT shares with 1QS the notion of the community of the faithful constituting a temple. In 1 Corinthians 3:16-17 we read: "Do you not know that you are God's temple and that God's Spirit dwells in you? If anyone destroys God's temple, God will destroy that person. For God's temple is holy, and you are that temple." The pronoun "you" in this passage is plural, thus stressing the corporate nature of this metaphor. In 1 Corinthians 6:19-20, Paul again uses the analogy of the temple but individualizes it in terms of each believer's body being a temple of the Holy Spirit. Paul's most impressive use of this imagery is in Ephesians 2:19-22: "In him the whole structure is joined together and grows into a holy temple in the Lord; in whom you also are built together spiritually into a dwelling place for God" (Eph 2:21-22).

Paul is not the only NT writer to liken the church to a spiritual temple. Peter likewise employs the idea in a passage having many points of similarity to the

---

[49]We have already seen evidence of the Qumran rejection of the extant Jerusalem temple and its priesthood in CD and 1QS—both were defiled, in the estimation of Qumran.

[50]For a good treatment of the issue, see Johann Maier, "Temple," *EDSS* 2:921-27. García Martínez's translation differs from that of Wise: "And he commanded to build for himself a temple of man, to offer him in it, before him, the works of thanksgiving" (*Dead Sea Scrolls Translated,* p. 136). Theodore Gaster comments on this passage: "What (in fact) God here declares is that (in the future) there shall be built for Him a sanctuary constituted out of mankind itself—a sanctuary in which performance of the things laid down in the Law shall rank as the equivalent of the (erstwhile) burning of incense in His presence" (*The Dead Sea Scrolls in English Translation* [Garden City, N.Y.: Doubleday, 1956], pp. 446-47). But it is questionable that this eschatological sanctuary was viewed in nonmaterial terms. The context seems to point to an actual structure of some type (see Maier, "Temple," 2:923, 926).

[51]See Michael Wise in Wise, Abegg and Cook, *Dead Sea Scrolls,* p. 226. We have already seen this notion in several apocalyptic works such as *1 Enoch, Testament of Moses* and *Jubilees.*

Qumran self-conception: "Like living stones, let yourselves be built into a spiritual house, to be a holy priesthood, to offer spiritual sacrifices acceptable to God through Jesus Christ" (1 Pet 2:5). Peter cites Isaiah 28:16, Psalm 118:22 and Isaiah 8:14 as proof texts for his simile. As it turns out, in the material preserved from Qumran, there are no known instances where the sectaries cite the above scriptural passages to buttress their contention that they were the true temple of God. It would not be surprising, however, if, in fact, they did so.

On the other hand, Paul may, in one passage, also refer to an eschatological temple. This occurs in an apocalyptic passage in 2 Thessalonians 2, where Paul is detailing the sequence of events that will lead up to Jesus' parousia. According to Paul, the lawless one "takes his seat in the temple of God, declaring himself to be God. Do you not remember that I told you these things when I was still with you?" (2 Thess 2:4b-5). Did Paul think that the lawless one would actually carry out this sacrilege in the Jerusalem temple, which was still standing when he wrote his letter (A.D. 51/52), or was he projecting this episode into a more distant future? Or is his reference to the temple of God merely a figurative expression? Opinions vary.[52] Paul's instruction probably goes back to Jesus' teaching as preserved in the Olivet Discourse, in which a "desolating sacrilege" was to be "set up where it ought not to be" (Mk 13:14). Matthew specifies more narrowly the location as "the holy place" and supports this with an allusion to Daniel (Mt 24:15). The Apocalypse, also drawing heavily from Daniel, makes reference to the Jerusalem temple, trampled down for forty-two months during the end-time events (Rev 11:1-2). Accordingly, we are inclined to think that Paul expected this act of blasphemy to be perpetrated in an actual Jerusalem Temple—especially in light of the importance of Daniel 9:20-27; 11:31; 12:11 for all three witnesses, Jesus, Paul and John. If this is correct, the Qumran community clearly had a much more positive expectation for their "Temple of Adam" than either Paul or John had for their eschatological temple (the third temple?).

There are, of course, several references to God's heavenly temple in the book of Revelation (Rev 7:15; 11:19; 14:15, 17; 15:5-6, 8; 16:1, 17) and in Hebrews (Heb 8:1-5; 9:11-12, 24-28; 10:19-21). This idea is also reflected in the DSS, most notably in the *Songs of the Sabbath Sacrifice* (4Q400-407). However, as we have noted earlier, in striking contrast to the ultimate eschatological expectations of Qumran, the Apocalypse definitely says there will be no temple in the New Jerusalem (Rev 21:22).

---

[52]See, e.g., Thomas L. Constable, "2 Thessalonians," in *The Bible Knowledge Commentary on CD-ROM* (Logos Library System, version 2.0c, 1995, 1996); Pheme Perkins, "2 Thessalonians," in *Bible Knowledge Commentary on CD-ROM;* F. F. Bruce, "1 and 2 Thessalonians," in *WBC on CD-ROM* (Logos Library System, version 2.1, 1998).

We should also note the messianic expectation connected to the Davidic covenant of 2 Samuel 7 in 4Q174. The earliest Christians did not "discover" 2 Samuel 7:12-16 as a messianic proof text; the same connection had already been made by the Qumran sectaries. Indeed, it would appear that this text was widely viewed as messianic by most Jews in the pre-Christian era (cf. Jn 7:42).[53] At any rate, the apostles took up that expectation and identified Jesus of Nazareth as the fulfillment (cf. Acts 2:30; 13:23). In his Gospel, Luke draws a clear connection between the promise to David and its fulfillment in Jesus Christ (Lk 1:32-33). Thus Qumran and the Palestinian Jesus movement shared the basic conviction that the Messiah was the "Son of David" (cf. Mt 1:1; 9:27; 12:23; 21:9, 15; 22:42).

Another foundational OT text for NT Christology is Psalm 2. NT writers make no fewer than fourteen citations or allusions to this psalm, a royal psalm in terms of literary genre. That is, Psalm 2 and several others in the Psalter (e.g., Pss 20; 21; 45; 72; 89; 102; 110; 132) focus on some aspect or function of the Davidic king. There is a difference in application between Qumran and the NT, however. The former interprets the "anointed" as the "chosen of Israel," the Qumran community (4Q174 3:18-19); the latter interprets it as a prophecy about Jesus, the Davidic heir (cf. Mk 1:11; 9:7 and par.; Phil 2:10-11; Heb 1:2; Rev 2:26-27; 12:5).

As an example, in a section extolling the superiority of Jesus over angels, the author of Hebrews cites Psalm 2:7: "For to which of the angels did God ever say, 'You are my Son: today I have begotten you'?" (Heb 1:5a). Note also that the very next quotation in the Hebrews catena (a string of citations) is from 2 Samuel 7:14 (Heb 1:5b). The writer to the Hebrews exhibits the same exegetical technique as 4Q174. In both cases the writers weave together a series of texts, indeed, some of the very same texts, to make a point. Thus we see close parallels in both exegetical techniques and in messianic proof texts between the two religious communities. Both communities made use of collections of *testimonia*, proof texts that exegetically support their claims.[54]

Messianic Anthology or Testimonia (4Q175)

We examine briefly one other example from Qumran of a thematic pesher. In

---

[53]E. P. Sanders downplays the importance and widespread expectation of a Davidic Messiah in our era. See his *Judaism: Practice and Belief 63 BCE-66 CE* (London: SCM Press; Philadelphia: Trinity Press International, 1992), pp. 295-98. In my opinion, a more accurate perspective is provided by Collins, *Scepter and Star,* pp. 1-101; and J. Julius Scott Jr., *Customs and Controversies: Intertestamental Jewish Backgrounds of the New Testament* (Grand Rapids, Mich.: Baker, 1995), 308-10.

[54]For other NT examples, see Rom 9—11; 15:9-12.

this instance we have four texts from the Pentateuch (Deut 5:28-29; 18:18-19; Num 24:15-17; Deut 33:8-11) and one from the Former Prophets (Josh 6:26).[55] Actually, the Joshua passage is more correctly from an apocryphal work, *The Psalms of Joshua* (4Q379).[56] We do not have explanatory glosses, as in 4Q174, but rather an implied theme that arises from an association of the ideas found in the quotations. The pentateuchal citations draw attention to three distinct figures: the prophet like Moses, the Star from Jacob (the Davidic Messiah) and Levi. In all likelihood this catena deliberately focuses on the three eschatological figures expected at Qumran: the Prophet, the Davidic messiah, and the Priestly messiah. We have already discussed above the Christian interpretation of these figures.[57]

The citation of the Joshua passage may describe the nefarious activities of the Wicked Priest. The point of the quotation is to draw attention to the fulfillment of Joshua's curse upon the one who rebuilds Jericho. The Qumran scribe, however, transfers the accursed city from Jericho to Jerusalem.[58] The "cursed man, one belonging to Belial," with his two "instruments of wrongdoing" rebuild the city while committing profanation and great blasphemy (1Q175 1:23, 25). They shed blood like water. Is this interpretation speaking of a father and his two sons who commit outrageous and ungodly acts? The tantalizing challenge is to find a match between this description and what we know of the Hasmonean priest-kings.

Dupont-Sommer argues at length that Alexander Janneus is the cursed man and his two sons are Hyrcanus II, the elder, and Aristobulus II, the younger. In his reconstruction, Hyrcanus II becomes the Wicked Priest who killed the Teacher of Righteousness—and thus committed the most heinous crime in the eyes of the sect. Wise, Abegg and Cook concur.[59] We have already argued above that either Jonathan or Simon better fit the allusions

---

[55]In the Hebrew Bible the books designated as Historical Books in our English Bibles (following the LXX and Vulgate) make up the first of the two sections designated as the Prophets. The prophetic books so called in the English versions are called the Latter Prophets in the Hebrew Bible.

[56]For translation, see Michael Wise in Wise, Abegg and Cook, *Dead Sea Scrolls,* pp. 339-42. This looks like an instance in which a noncanonical book is cited as authoritative scripture, but this is a disputed issue (see ibid., pp. 339-40).

[57]We are not convinced by Dupont-Sommer's contention that the Qumran messianic ideology focused the triple quality of prophet, priest and king upon the Teacher of Righteousness (*Essene Writings,* p. 318). For a critique of Dupont-Sommer's view, see William Sanford LaSor, *The Dead Sea Scrolls and the New Testament* (Grand Rapids, Mich.: Eerdmans, 1972), pp. 117-30. A helpful overview of the question may be found in VanderKam, *Dead Sea Scrolls Today,* pp. 177-80.

[58]Dupont-Sommer notes that this is a rather common feature of the pesharim (*Essene Writings,* p. 355).

[59]Wise, Abegg and Cook, *Dead Sea Scrolls,* pp. 229-30.

in CD and the pesharim. However, Schiffman provides a salutary warning to all researchers by observing:

> In the absence of any firm historical evidence, it is not possible to decide to which Hasmonean ruler—Simon or his son John Hyrcanus—this dually preserved text applies. The text shows us that even after the lifetime of the Wicked Priest, the Qumran sectarians continued to be anti-Hasmoneans, considering the descendants of the Maccabees as transgressors who led their people astray.[60]

The Thanksgiving Hymns (1QH)

Introduction

We conclude our survey of the exegetical traditions of Qumran with a slightly different kind of work. *Thanksgiving Hymns* is not, strictly speaking, an exegetical piece. However, the compositions are so saturated with the language and style of the canonical Psalms that we may consider the collection under this heading. It imitates the book of Psalms, yet it is a free composition, not a paraphrase or commentary. The individual pieces are essentially prayers and meditations. Because of their personal nature, they provide a window into the soul of both an individual, perhaps the Teacher of Righteousness, and the community to which he belonged. There is much in these poems of spiritual benefit for Christian readers.

Date and Composition

Fortunately, *Thanksgiving Hymns* was one of the original finds from Cave 1 that was relatively intact. The paleographic evidence points to a date sometime around the beginning of the Christian era. Fragments of six other manuscripts were recovered from Cave 4. These were older than the manuscript from Cave 1, with the oldest being from shortly after 100 B.C.[61] The twenty-five distinct poems fall into two main categories: individual and communal. The difference is signaled by the use of either the first-person singular pronoun or the first-person plural. They are called *Hodayot*, "thanksgivings," because each composition begins with the Hebrew phrase 'wdk 'dwny ("I give thanks to you, O Lord") or brwk 'th 'dwny ("Blessed are you, O Lord"). A passage from Philo of Alexandria may well provide the setting for these hymns. In a description of a sect in Egypt called the Therapeutae—probably related to the Essenes—Philo provides this enlightening passage:

> When, therefore, the president appears to have spoken at sufficient length, and to have carried out his intentions adequately, so that his explanation has gone on felicitously and fluently through his own acuteness, and the hearing of the others

---

[60]*Reclaiming the Dead Sea Scrolls,* p. 236.
[61]See Émile Puech, "Hodayot," *EDSS* 1:366.

has been profitable, applause arises from them all as of men rejoicing together at
what they have seen and heard; and then some one rising up sings a hymn which
has been made in honour of God, either such as he has composed himself, or
some ancient one of some old poet, for they have left behind them many poems
and songs in trimetre iambics, and in psalms of thanksgiving and in hymns, and
songs at the time of libation, and at the altar, and in regular order, and in choruses,
admirably measured out in various and well diversified strophes.

And after him then others also arise in their ranks, in becoming order, while
every one else listens in decent silence, except when it is proper for them to take
up the burden of the song, and to join in at the end; for then they all, both men
and women, join in the hymn.[62]

Vermes infers from this passage that on the Feast of the Renewal of the Covenant the Guardian and the newly initiated members of the sect may have
recited the hymns.[63] It is certainly a plausible setting for the hymns.

The individual hymns are highly personal in nature and include a number
of biographical details. Reading these hymns in the context of the larger
Qumran corpus, one is tempted to designate the Teacher of Righteousness as
the author. Eleazar Sukenik, the first to read *Thanksgiving Hymns*, already
suggested this connection. Nickelsburg believes that at least seven of the
hymns should be attributed to the Teacher.[64] We will assume that he is the primary creative genius behind all the hymns.[65]

Themes

The sovereignty of God. Perhaps the best way to appreciate these hymns is to
focus on their leading themes. The sovereignty of God is a keynote throughout. The Teacher of Righteousness believed that God was the blessed control-
ler of all things and foreordained all things that transpire in the world.

By Your wisdom [You have establish]ed the successive [generations] and before
You created them You knew [all] their works for ever and ever. [For apart from
You no]thing is done, and without Your will nothing is known. You have formed
every spirit and [You determined their] de[eds] and judgment for all their works.
(1QH 9:7-9)

---

[62]Philo, *Contempl. Life* 79-80 in *The Works of Philo*, trans. C. D. Yonge, new ed. (Peabody, Mass.: Hendrickson, 1993), p. 705.
[63]*Complete Dead Sea Scrolls in English*, pp. 189-90.
[64]*Jewish Literature*, p. 137. See also Dupont-Sommer, *Essene Writings*, pp. 200-210; Dimant, "Qumran Sectarian Literature," p. 523 and notes. More cautious is Vermes, *Complete Dead Sea Scrolls in English*, p. 189.
[65]See Martin Abegg, "4Q491, 4Q427, and the Teacher of Righteousness," in *Studies in the Dead Sea Scrolls and Related Literature*, ed. Martin G. Abegg Jr. and Peter W. Flint, vol. 1: *Eschatology, Messianism, and the Dead Sea Scrolls*, ed. Craig A. Evans and Peter W. Flint (Grand Rapids, Mich.: Eerdmans, 1997), pp. 71-72.

[You determined] all Your works before You created them, together with the host of Your spirits and the assembly of [Your holy ones], Your holy expanse [and all] its hosts, together with the earth and all that springs from it, in the seas and the deeps [according to] all Your designs for the end of time and the eternal visitation. For You have determined them from of old, and also the work of [unrighteousness . . .] in them so that they may tell of Your glory throughout all Your dominion. (1QH 5:13-17)[66]

A clearer statement of God's sovereignty could scarcely be stated.

The innocent sufferer. In this collection of prayers and meditations, one quickly senses that the Teacher and his devoted followers endured unrelenting opposition and persecution from their opponents. Echoes of this hostility resonate in the following passages:

You have appointed me as an object of shame and derision to the faithless, but a foundation of truth and understanding for the upright. And because of the iniquity of the wicked, I have become slander on the lips of the brutal, and scoffers gnash their teeth. I have become a taunt-song for the rebellious, and the assembly of the wicked have stormed against me. They roar like a gale on the seas, when their waves churn, they cast up slime and mud. (1QH 10:9b-13a)

Brutal men seek my soul, while I hold fast to Your Covenant. (1QH 10:21b-22a)

I myself have said, mighty men have camped against me, they have surrounded me with all their weapons of war. Arrows burst forth without ceasing, and the blade of the spear devours trees as fire. (1QH 10:25b-26)

They set [my] soul as a boat in the depths of the sea, and as a fortified city befo[re her enemy]. I am in distress, as a woman about to give birth to her firstborn. (1QH 11:6b-7)

And who are the opponents? Once again we meet familiar imagery that helps to identify who these might be: "I have become a man of contention for the mediators of error, but a purveyor of peace unto all the seers of righteousness. I have become impassioned against those who seek fl at[tery], [so that all] the men of deceit roar against me" (1QH 10:14b-16a; cf. 1QH 10:31b-32a; 1QH 12:7-16). In light of the expression "those who seek flattery," one group of opponents must have been the Pharisees, as we saw above in the pesharim. There are also passages that imply an internal rift, a rejection of the Teacher's authority. This may be a reference to the schism led by the Liar (cf. 1QH 12:22b-28).

The sinfulness of human beings. The Teacher recognized the profound sin-

---

[66]The numbering in Abegg's translation (Wise, Abegg and Cook, *Dead Sea Scrolls,* pp. 87, 91) differs from that of Vermes and García Martínez. He was able to incorporate the latest research of Émile Puech.

fulness of all flesh.[67] As a consequence of this depravity, one must depend totally upon God for salvation. It did not lie within the human grasp to contribute toward one's deliverance from sin. Several passages poignantly make this point:

> These things I know through Your understanding, for You have opened my ears to wonderful mysteries even though I am a vessel of clay and kneaded with water, a foundation of shame and a spring of filth, a melting pot of iniquity and a structure of sin, a spirit of error, perverted without understanding and terrified by righteous judgments. (1QH 9:21-23a)
>
> What is mortal man in comparison with this? And where is the vessel of clay that is able to carry out wondrous deeds? For he is sinful from the womb and in the guilt of unfaithfulness until old age. I know that man has no righteousness, nor does the son of man walk in the perfect way. (1QH 12:29b-31a)

There is no self-congratulatory note in this! Here is a humble, honest recognition of moral failure—in short, the neglected word, sin. This frank acknowledgment of sinfulness, however, needs to be placed in the larger scheme of things. That is, the doctrine of the two spirits actually attributes the evil impulse to God. Though accountable for their sin, the wicked, by virtue of God's eternal plan, have no recourse but to succumb to the evil angel and the resultant misdeeds. This theological problem is never raised or discussed in the Qumran literature; it is simply assumed as a fact.

The necessity for God's grace and mercy. So how does one experience forgiveness and cleansing? The Teacher, like the NT writers, located the source of cleansing in the prevenient grace of God. Several passages make this crystal clear:

> But all the children of Your truth You bring before You in forgiveness, cleansing them from their rebellious acts in the multiplicity of Your goodness, and by the abundance of Your compassion maintaining them before You for ever and ever. (1QH 15:29b-31a)
>
> I know that man has no righteousness, nor does the son of man walk in the perfect way. All the works of righteousness belong to God Most High. (1QH 12:30b-31a)
>
> For [I] rested in Your mercies and the abundance of Your compassion. For You atone for iniquity and purif[y] man from guilt by Your righteousness. But not for man, [but for] Your [glory]. (1QH 12:36b-38; cf. 1QH 8:17b-18)

---

[67]Note here the usage of *flesh*. As with the apostle Paul, the Teacher uses the expression to refer to the evil inclinations that all human beings possess as well as to describe people who are so controlled by this evil influence. There is an opposition set up between flesh and spirit. See further Karl Georg Kuhn, "Temptation, Sin, and Flesh," in *The Scrolls and the New Testament,* ed. Krister Stendahl (New York: Harper, 1957), pp. 101-8.

We will comment below on whether the NT has precisely the same perspective on salvation by grace as the *Hodayot*.

The correct interpreter of the law. As we have already seen in the sectarian writings, the men of Qumran adhered strictly to the interpretations of Scripture rendered by the community leadership. We think that the Teacher of Righteousness was the fountainhead of this interpretive tradition and that his views were zealously maintained in the ongoing life of the community. Several passages allude to or explicitly mention this unique revelatory role of the Teacher:

> These things I know through Your understanding, for You have opened my ears to wonderful mysteries. (1QH 9:21)
>
> I seek You, and as an enduring dawning, as [perfe]ct ligh[t], You have revealed Yourself to me. (1QH 12:6a)
>
> You display Your might through me, and reveal Yourself to me in Your strength as perfect light. You do not cover with shame the faces of all those who are sought by me, who are meeting together (*or* in the *Yahad*) in accordance with Your covenant. (1QH 12:23b-24a)
>
> But by me You have illumined the face of many (*or* the general membership) and have strengthened them uncountable times. For You have given me understanding of the mysteries of your wonder. (1QH 12:27b-28a)
>
> And from my youth You have shined the insight of Your judgment on me. With a sure truth You have supported me, and by Your holy spirit You have delighted me; even until this day. (1QH 17:31b-32; cf. 1QH 18:14-15; 19:16-17a; 20:19; etc.)

Significance for New Testament Interpretation

Do we have anything like the *Hodayot* in NT literature in terms of form and style? The basic forms of NT literature—Gospels, apologetic-historical (Acts), epistles and apocalypse—do not share the same form and function. On the other hand, do we have snippets of hymnic and meditative pieces that are similar to *Hodayot?* Let me suggest some similarities.

We pointed out at the beginning of our discussion of *Hodayot* that each poem characteristically begins with the phrase "I thank you, O God." It is interesting to observe that the translational counterpart in Greek occurs in the NT. For example, the Greek phrase *ho theos, eucharistō soi* ("God, I thank you") is placed in the mouth of a Pharisee at prayer (Lk 18:11).

Not surprisingly, Jesus' prayers employ this expression as well: "Father, *I thank you* for having heard me" (Jn 11:41).[68] The phrase occurs frequently in

---

[68]Of course, the distinctiveness of this prayer lies in the direct address to God as "Father." See further Joachim Jeremias, *New Testament Theology: The Proclamation of Jesus* (New York: Charles Scribner's Sons, 1971), pp. 63-68.

Paul's letters as an unconscious expression of his religious convictions and piety (cf. Rom 1:8; 1 Cor 1:4; 14:18; 2 Cor 8:16; Phil 1:3; Col 1:3; 1 Thess 1:2; 2:13; 3:9; 2 Thess 1:3; 2:13; 1 Tim 1:12; 2 Tim 1:3; Philem 4). In other words, as a Pharisee and as a Christian, Paul regularly and naturally gave thanks for God's providential care and grace in Christ. We are not arguing that Jesus and Paul were indebted to the Teacher of Righteousness for this expression; its usage by all three figures simply reflects a common background in first-century Judaism. As a matter of fact, there are even similarities in the phraseology of prayers originating from Hellenistic religions.[69]

Of more import would be an examination of NT hymns and meditations in order to see if there are stylistic and formal parallels to the *Hodayot*. This is, unfortunately, a neglected area of scholarship, so we can only suggest possible links for further study.[70]

It seems to me that the closest literary parallel occurs in Ephesians 1:3-14, a meditative passage evoking sentiments quite similar to the *Hodayot*. In both we have a focus on God's mysterious plan and purpose realized in the life of the elect. God's glory revealed in his plan for the ages is a keynote in both. Of course, the Christology and implicit trinitarianism clearly demarcates the Ephesians passage as a Christian composition.

Luke's Gospel also provides a point of contact with *Hodayot*. Embedded in Luke's infancy narratives are snatches of paeans and prayers that have a decidedly Jewish cast to them. Indeed, some scholars have argued that such well-beloved sections as the Magnificat, the Benedictus, the Gloria in Excelsis Deo and the Nunc Dimittis reflect a Christian use of essentially Jewish prayers and hymns.[71] The interesting point of comparison between these Lukan hymns and the *Hodayot* is the adaptation of OT Scripture. The Magnificat is based largely on Hannah's prayer in 1 Samuel 2:1-10; the Benedictus is a pastiche of selected Psalms and Malachi; the Nunc Dimittis builds upon Isaiah 52:10; 42:6; 49:6. Add to this the eschatological interpretation placed upon these passages and one has the, by now familiar, common exegetical framework of both Qumran and early Christianity; namely, the end times have begun and the believing community is the fulfillment of OT prophecy.

Like the *Hodayot*, the NT also emphasizes God's sovereignty. One recalls the apostle Paul's ringing affirmation: "We know that all things work together

---

[69]See Ralph P. Martin, "Hymns in the NT," *ISBE* 2:788.

[70]See the comments of James H. Charlesworth, "Jewish Hymns, Odes, and Prayers (ca. 167 B.C.E.-135 C.E.)," in *Early Judaism and Its Modern Interpreters,* ed. Robert A. Kraft and George W. E. Nickelsburg (Philadelphia: Fortress; Atlanta: Scholars Press, 1986), p. 411.

[71]See Charlesworth, "Jewish Hymns," p. 419 and secondary literature cited there. See also Ralph P. Martin, "Hymns, Hymn Fragments, Songs, Spiritual Songs," *DPL,* pp. 419-20.

for good for those who love God, who are called according to his purpose" (Rom 8:28). Paul, like the Teacher, believed that the elect were predestined unto salvation: "In Christ we have also obtained an inheritance, having been destined according to the purpose of him who accomplishes all things according to his counsel and will" (Eph 1:11). Paul does not, however, explicitly state the contrary, namely, that the wicked are predestined to damnation. The closest Paul comes to such a position is his hypothetical statement in Romans 9:22-23:

> What if God, desiring to show his wrath and to make known his power, has endured with much patience the objects of wrath that are made for destruction; and what if he has done so in order to make known the riches of his glory for the objects of mercy, which he has prepared beforehand for glory—including us whom he has called, not from the Jews only but also from the Gentiles?[72]

By a steadfast trust in the sovereign God, the Teacher of Righteousness also found the courage and persistence to carry on in the face of unrelenting opposition.

There are many similarities between the Teacher of Righteousness and Jesus of Nazareth. Both individuals were loyal sons of Israel and held the sacred Scriptures in high regard. Both were esteemed as authoritative, charismatic teachers, with a circle of followers or disciples gathered around them. Both, of course, encountered bitter opposition from the entrenched religious leadership, whether Sadducee or Pharisee, and, apparently, both suffered as martyrs for their beliefs. The Gospel of Mark, for example, presents the story of Jesus as a crisis; indeed, the Gospel seems intended for an audience that would soon face a crisis.[73] Within the Gospel narratives one finds many instances in which the Servant Songs of Isaiah (Is 42:1-4; 49:1-6; 50:4-11; 52:13—53:12; 61:1-3) or the laments of an innocent sufferer from the canonical Psalms are cited as being fulfilled in Jesus of Nazareth.[74]

As one reads the *Hodayot,* one also encounters echoes of passages from Psalms that have been appropriated by the Teacher. The Teacher of Righteousness read off his life story from the cries and laments of the innocent sufferers in sacred Scripture. Jesus did the same and taught his disciples to read the OT Scriptures accordingly (cf. Lk 24:44). In the passion narratives,

---

[72]Not all will agree with our characterization of Paul's statement as hypothetical. What we mean is that *for the sake of argument* Paul assumes the stated position. For further discussion of the debated area of conditional clauses in Greek, see Daniel Wallace, *Greek Grammar Beyond Basics: An Exegetical Syntax of the New Testament* (Grand Rapids, Mich.: Zondervan, 1996), pp. 679-712.

[73]For further development of this point, see William Lane, *The Gospel According to Mark,* NICNT (Grand Rapids, Mich.: Eerdmans, 1974), pp. 12-17.

[74]See index of quotations from Isaiah 42—61 and the Psalms in the NT in UBS[4].

the Evangelists Matthew and Mark depict Jesus as reciting portions of Psalm 22 (a lament of an innocent sufferer) as he was dying on the cross (Mt 27:46; Mk 15:34).[75]

Like *Hodayot*, one finds in the NT exhortations to faithfulness in the face of persecution. Furthermore, in both corpora the exhortations frequently appeal to the glory that awaits the faithful. Consider, for example, this passage: "For You have brought [Your] t[ruth and g]lory to all the men of Your council, in the lot together with the angels of presence" (1QH 14:12b-13). This future glory is sometimes referred to as the "glory of man (*or* Adam)" (cf. 1QH 4:15). Many NT passages could be cited as parallels, such as Paul's well-known line: "I consider that the sufferings of this present time are not worth comparing with the glory about to be revealed to us" (Rom 8:18). Paul's eschatology envisions an investiture of glory greatly exceeding Adam's prefall splendor and glory (cf. Rom 8:28-30; 1 Cor 15:42-53; 2 Cor 4:4-6).

The theme of enduring persecution figures prominently in such books as Hebrews, 1 Peter and Revelation, though it is not absent in most other NT literature as well (cf. 1 Pet 1:3-7, 13, 22-25; 2:21-23; 4:1-7; Rev 4—5). A passage from Hebrews illustrates our point:

> But recall those earlier days when, after you had been enlightened, you endured a hard struggle with sufferings, sometimes being publicly exposed to abuse and persecution, and sometimes being partners with those so treated. For you had compassion for those who were in prison, and you cheerfully accepted the plundering of your possessions, knowing that you yourselves possessed something better and more lasting. Do not, therefore, abandon that confidence of yours; it brings a great reward. For you need endurance, so that when you have done the will of God, you may receive what was promised. (Heb 10:32-36)

In both corpora, the reward of the righteousness is a primary motivation for perseverance.

Modern readers of the *Hodayot* may be put off by what seems to be a morbid preoccupation with sin. Today we try to accent the positive. It may well be that too much preoccupation with our sins and failures can be emotionally crippling and counterproductive. However, our modern culture, so permeated with moral relativism and permissiveness, must not throw the baby out with the bathwater! We desperately need to recover the NT teaching that "all have sinned and fall short of the glory of God" (Rom 3:23). The depravity of human beings is not a Reformed and Puritan invention; it is the consequence of sober exegesis of NT texts. Self-esteem is possible only after the really bad news has been squarely faced: we are sinners in need of forgiveness and cleansing. The

---

[75]See further J. B. Green, "Passion Narrative," *DJG*, pp. 601-4.

Teacher of Righteousness deeply sensed this, and so did NT authors.

Of course, the good news as proclaimed by the Teacher and Jesus was not the same news.[76] We think a patient and fair reading of the NT and the Qumran literature, the *Hodayot* in particular, demonstrates that salvation was viewed differently in the respective communities. Though both stressed the priority of grace, for the Teacher, "works of the law" were essential for obtaining final salvation. For the NT, "works of the law" result in condemnation (Gal 2:16; 3:10-14).[77] Instead, one needs to be liberated from the "works of the law" and united with Jesus Christ in his death, burial and resurrection (Rom 6:1-4, 15-19; 7:1-11). This, paradoxically, results in a true fulfillment of the law (cf. Rom 8:1-8). Union with Christ brings about justification and sanctification (Rom 8:1-17). As a result, the love of God floods the believer's life and issues in a lifestyle exceeding all the law's demands—this is the new "law of Christ" (1 Cor 9:21; Gal 5:13-25). Paul's critique of his nonbelieving fellow Jews captures the soteriological difference between the Teacher of Righteousness and the message of the gospel:

> Israel, who did strive for the righteousness that is based on the law, did not succeed in fulfilling that law. Why not? Because they did not strive for it on the basis of faith, but as if it were *based on works*. They have stumbled over the stumbling stone, as it is written, "See, I am laying in Zion a stone that will make people stumble, a rock that will make them fall, and whoever *believes in him* will not be put to shame." (Rom 9:31-33, italics added)

In the above quotation Paul interprets a prophetic text christologically—an adaptation of the pesher technique—so that in Isaiah 8:14; 28:16, Jesus of Nazareth is now the object of saving faith. This gets to the heart of the difference between Qumran and Christianity. The latter experience salvation by trusting in and becoming joined to the one who took the curse of the law in their place and absorbed their just punishment as lawbreakers. His righteousness is then reckoned to them by faith in him (2 Cor 5:21).

Finally, we must draw attention to that most crucial difference between

---

[76]For some helpful comparisons and contrasts by scholars of various theological persuasions, see Hartmut Stegemann, "Jesus and the Teacher of Righteousness," *BRev* 10, no. 1 (1994): 42-47, 63; James H. Charlesworth, "Jesus as 'Son' and the Righteous Teacher as 'Gardener,' " in *Jesus and the Dead Sea Scrolls*, pp. 140-75; Dupont-Sommer, *Essene Writings*, pp. 368-78; LaSor, *Dead Sea Scrolls*, pp. 106-30, 237-54.

[77]This is a disputed point. For the view that "works of the law" can be understood as a reflection of genuine faith, see Daniel E. Fuller, *The Law and the Gospel: Contrast or Continuum?* (Grand Rapids, Mich.: Eerdmans, 1980), pp. 65-120. We think that Stephen Westerholm lays out the best statement of this controversial issue in *Israel's Law and the Church's Faith* (Grand Rapids, Mich.: Eerdmans, 1988), pp. 105-222. For a slightly different perspective, see Thomas Schreiner, *The Law and Its Fulfillment: A Pauline Theology of Law* (Grand Rapids, Mich.: Baker, 1993).

Table 7.3. Assorted parallels between the Hodayot and the New Testament

Hodayot	NT	Point of Comparison
1QH 11:20: "You have raised me up to an eternal height, so that I might walk about on a limitless plain."	Col 3:1: "So if you have been raised with Christ . . . seated at the right hand of God."	Both passages exhibit realized eschatology (unless 1QH reflects a visionary experience, as in 2 Cor 12:2-5, in which case see the excursus below).
1QH 11:35b-36: "The war of the heroes of heaven shall spread over the world and shall not return until an annihilation that has been determined from eternity is completed. Nothing like this has ever occurred" (cf. 1QM).	Rev 9:13-19; 16:12-16; 17:12-17; 19:11-21; 20:7-10	The NT, like 1QH, anticipates a final battle between good and evil, the time of which is predetermined.
1QH 13:23b-24a: "Ev[en those who sha]re my bread have lifted up their heel against me."	Jn 13:18: "But it is to fulfill the scripture, 'The one who ate my bread has lifted his heel against me.' "	Both the Teacher and Jesus quote this passage from Ps 41:9 and apply it to disloyal followers. In the case of Jesus, it is in reference to only one person, Judas.
1QH 14:12b-13a: "For You have brought [Your] t[ruth and g]lory to all the men of Your council, in the lot together with the angels of presence."	Col 1:12: "who has enabled you to share in the inheritance of the saints in the light" (cf. Mt 18:10; 22:30; Heb 12:22).	In both corpora, the redeemed share in a heavenly existence with the angels.
1QH 14:25b-27a: "For you set a foundation upon the rock, and beams upon a just measuring line, [ins]pecting the tested stones with a true plumb line so as to build a strong [wall] which shall not be shaken. All who enter it shall not totter."	Mt 16:18: "on this rock I will build my church, and the gates of Hades will not prevail against it."	There are some striking similarities in imagery and concepts. In both cases we have a leader promising his followers security and eventual triumph. The common imagery and motifs spring from a common religious heritage.

Table 7.3.—*Continued*

Hodayot	NT	Point of Comparison
1QH 14:29b-30: "Then the sword of God shall hasten to the time of judgment and all the children of His truth shall awaken to put an end to [the children of] wickedness, and all the children of guilt shall be no more. The hero shall draw his bow, and the fortification shall open."	Rev 19:15: "From his mouth comes a sharp sword with which to strike down the nations, and he will rule them with a rod of iron."	The imagery of the final battle and the fate of the wicked in both writings are similar.
1QH 15:12: "For all who attack me You will condemn to judgment, so that in me You might divide between the righteous and the ungodly."	Mt 25:32: "he will separate people one from another" (cf. verses 31-46). Jn 12:48: "The one who rejects me and does not receive my word has a judge; on the last day the word that I have spoken will serve as judge."	In both documents, the Teacher and Jesus play a role in final judgment. There is, however, an important difference in that Jesus himself is the saving agent (cf. Jn 5:25-30).

the Teacher of Righteousness and Jesus of Nazareth. The bones of the former are somewhere in the wilderness of Judea; those of Jesus are not. Therein lies the climax of the Gospels: "Do not be alarmed; you are looking for Jesus of Nazareth, who was crucified. He has been raised; he is not here. Look, there is the place they laid him" (Mk 16:6 and par.). The apostolic message is clear: "This Jesus God raised up, and of that all of us are witnesses. . . . Therefore let the entire house of Israel know with certainty that God has made him both Lord and Messiah" (Acts 2:32, 36; cf. 1 Cor 15:3-20). Once again, several passages have bearing on the interpretation of the NT (see table 7.3).

Excursus: The Relationship of the Angelology of Qumran and the False Teaching at Colossae

In this addendum we wish to reopen a long-debated question with regard to the interpretation of Colossians. This has to do with the nature of the false teaching threatening the congregation. In our opinion the library of Qumran may throw some welcome light on this question.

Already in 1878, the great Cambridge scholar J. B. Lightfoot, on the slender basis of what was known about the Essenes from classical sources (Pliny, Philo and Josephus), posited a connection between the Colossian heresy and the Essenes. The connection that Lightfoot detected is best stated in his own words: "It will appear from the delineations of ancient writers, more especially of Philo and Josephus, that the characteristic feature of Essenism was a particular direction of mystic speculation, involving a rigid asceticism as its practical consequence."[78] Lightfoot argued that there was already current in the mid- to late first century A.D. a tendency that one could identify as Gnostic. This was a theosophical, mystical worldview that sought to reconcile the problem of an absolute, good God with the presence of evil in the universe. The proposed solution was a dualism that separated the transcendent God from the world of created matter. In this scheme, matter is the creative act of an emanation (a derived deity of much less glory and power) far removed from the God of light. This emanation or demigod is basically evil. Thus human beings are entombed in a body that is necessarily evil.[79]

Salvation essentially consists of escaping the clutches of the evil body and world in which one lives by returning to God Most High who dwells in light. Only a select few have a spark of the true light and have a chance to return, however. These elect must be informed of their destiny and learn the secrets of how to ascend back to their true source. Hence the term *gnōsis* ("knowledge") refers to the enlightenment that comes to the elect whereby they achieve deliverance or salvation. Gnostics had to learn how to control the evil urges of their bodies and keep their spirits pure. This involved a complete regimen of discipline and rigorous observances. In some forms of Gnostic thought, however, an opposite tack was taken on the basis of an assumption that the body had no influence or bearing whatever on the spirit, the upshot being that deeds done in the body were irrelevant. Thus we have two possible behavioral consequences: asceticism and libertinism or antinomianism. Libertinism and antinomianism refer to the attitude and practice in which there is moral license to do as one wants. In sum, Gnosticism refers to a dualistic worldview that purports to explain the mystery of evil and provide a way of salvation for the enlightened.

The full-blown system of Gnosticism is a post-Christian development of the second century A.D. Lightfoot posited, however, that it had a pre-Christian origin and that Judaism may well have contributed to that early tendency. This is where the Essenes come in. Gnostic ideas find little or nothing in

---

[78]James Barber Lightfoot, *Saint Paul's Epistles to the Colossians and to Philemon* (London: Macmillan, 1890), p. 83.
[79]The choice of the word *entombed* is deliberate in order to capture a play on words that was current in ancient times. The slogan was *sōma, sēma* ("the body is a tomb") and thus made explicit this dilemma as the Gnostic saw it.

common with the Pharisees or Sadducees, but from what we have already read in the DSS we may, like Lightfoot, discern some interesting echoes or parallels. Now that all fragments of the Qumran library are available to scholars, the time may be ripe for a reappraisal of Lightfoot's thesis.

Let us lay out the essence of the Colossian heresy as nearly as we can reconstruct it from Paul's letter. It would seem that the main feature was a visionary ascent into the heavenly realms in order to observe or participate in angelic worship. *It is not likely that this angelic worship was worship of humans directed toward angels, but rather worship of angels directed toward God.*[80] Our reasoning is that if the error had actually involved veneration and adoration of angels by humans, we can scarcely conceive of Paul's relatively calm response. We have already seen his abhorrence for idolatry in our earlier discussions in chapter two. Paul's response to teachings undermining or denying the gospel are typically vitriolic; one need only recall his vehement response to the Galatian Judaizers in which he anathematized them for believing a different gospel.

Furthermore, in the Colossian letter, Paul singles out as a characteristic of the false teachers that "such a person goes into great detail about *what he has seen,* and his unspiritual mind puffs him up with idle notions" (Col 2:18b NIV, italics added). This seems like a trivial objection to fasten on if actual human worship of angels was occurring. His real quarrel with this aberration is that the mystical experience displaces Christ as the central focus of worship and is really of no value "in checking self-indulgence" (Col 2:23). In short, a mystical experience had assumed an all-absorbing focus and thereby missed the essence of authentic Christian experience, "not holding fast to the head [Christ]" (Col 2:19; cf. 1:15-20; 2:2-4, 8-15). The Jewish rituals, prescribed as a prerequisite for the visionary experience (Col 2:16, 21-22), are dismissed by Paul as "only a shadow of what is to come." On the contrary, says Paul, "the substance belongs to Christ" (Col 2:17).

Are there features of Essenism in the error Paul appears to be attacking in Colossians? We would cautiously suggest the following items.

1. In Colossians there is a decided emphasis upon knowledge *(gnōsis).* Note how Paul makes a point of locating the source of all "treasures of wisdom and knowledge" *(gnōsis)* in Christ (Col 2:2-3) in a passage just prior to his first clear warning about being taken captive "through philosophy and empty deceit" (Col 2:8). We have seen already how often in CD, 1QS and 1QH the text stresses the special knowledge made available to the elect community by

---

[80]In short, the problem is whether to take the phrase "worship of angels" as an objective or subjective genitive. Note that in English we have the same ambiguity as in Greek. Only the context may decide the question of which it is.

means of divine revelation to the Teacher ("For You have given me understanding of the mysteries of Your wonder" [1QH 12:27b-28a]). To this should
be added *Songs of the Sabbath Sacrifice* (4QShirShabb [4Q400-407]), a work that
revels in this mysterious knowledge.[81]

2. In Colossians the focal point of the false teaching centers on visionary
experience, seemingly in the very presence of the angels (Col 2:18, 20; cf.
2:8). What is fascinating is that one can make a plausible case that either the
Teacher of Righteousness believed that he actually ascended to the very
throne room of God, sat on a throne himself and joined in the angelic worship or his later followers made that claim about him.[82] Listen to the fantastic
claim:

> . . . a mighty throne in the congregation of the gods. None of the ancient kings
> shall sit on it, and their nobles [shall] not [. . . There are no]ne comparable [to
> me in] my glory, no one shall be exalted besides me; none shall associate with
> me. For I dwelt in the [. . .] in the heavens, and there is no one [. . .]. I am reck-
> oned with the gods and my abode is in the holy congregation. [My] desi[re] is not
> according to the flesh, and everything precious to me is in the glory [of] the holy
> [habit]ation. [Wh]om have I considered contemptible? Who is comparable to me
> in my glory? Who of those who sail the seas shall return telling [of] my [equal]?
> Who shall [experience] troubles like me? And who is like me [in bearing] evil? I
> have not been taught, but no teaching compares [with my teaching]. Who then
> shall attack me when [I] ope[n my mouth]? Who can endure the utterance of my
> lips? Who shall arraign me and compare with my judgment [. . . Fo]r I am
> reck[oned] with the gods, [and] my glory with *that of* the sons of the King.
> (4Q491 MS C 11 i 12-18)[83]

To this should be compared another of the *Hodayot:*

> For as for me, [my] office is among the gods, [and glory and majes]ty is not as
> gold [. . .] for me. Neither pure gold or precious metal [. . . for me . . .] shall [not]
> be reckoned to me. Sing praise, O beloved ones, sing to the King [of glory, rejoice
> in the congre]gation of God. Sing for joy in the tents of salvation, praise in the
> [holy] habitation. [E]xalt together with the eternal hosts, ascribe greatness to our
> God and glory to our King. [Sanct]ify His name with mighty speech, and with
> eminent oration lift up your voice together. [At a]ll times proclaim, speak it out,
> exult with eternal joy. There shall be no [ce]asing to bow down together in
> assembly. Bless the One who performs majestic wonders. (4Q427 7 i 11-18)[84]

We think this would qualify for Paul's censure, "puffed up without cause by

---

[81] See Wise in Wise, Abegg and Cook, *Dead Sea Scrolls,* pp. 365-77; García Martínez, *Dead Sea
Scrolls Translated,* pp. 419-31.
[82] Abegg, "4Q491, 4Q427, and the Teacher of Righteousness," pp. 70-73.
[83] Abegg in Wise, Abegg and Cook, *Dead Sea Scrolls,* p. 171.
[84] Ibid., p. 113.

a human way of thinking"! Especially interesting in this regard is Paul's counter argument in Colossians. He says that the Colossian believers (most of them Gentiles) were *already* "seated at the right hand of God," "where Christ is" (Col 3:1). This is a nice piece of realized eschatology. What is noteworthy by its absence is any reference to Paul's own visionary experience as recorded in 2 Corinthians 12:1-10. That might play into the hands of the opponents. Apparently he felt that the best way to counter the Colossian error was not by denying the reality of visionary ascent per se but by minimizing its significance and importance for a full and meaningful Christian life (Col 2:19, 23). Union with Christ *now* amounts to an ascent to the heavenly throne (Col 3: 3) and will certainly eventuate in the glories of the throne room at the parousia (Col 3:4).

3. An obvious point of contact between Colossians and the DSS is the angelology. With the publication of all the texts of Cave 4, we are now in possession of some new material that highlights this aspect of Qumran belief. It is precisely in *Songs of the Sabbath Sacrifice* (hereafter *Songs*) that we have a fascinating conjunction of esoteric knowledge (see above) and elaborate descriptions of angels and the heavenly sanctuary. We can only briefly mention some similarities. *Songs* celebrates the kingdom of God with all his holy ones (4Q400 frag. 2 lines 3-4). Paul celebrates the transfer of believers "into the kingdom of his [God's] beloved son" (Col 1:13). *Songs* mentions the "war of the godlike beings" that transpires in the heavens and "[weap]ons of war[f]ar[e]" (4Q402 frags. 3-4 lines 7-8). Paul extols Christ, who "disarmed the rulers and authorities and made a public example of them, triumphing over them in it [the cross]" (Col 2:15). *Songs* praises God, who created the "godlike beings of utter holiness" (4Q400 1 i 2). These beings came into existence as "part of His glorious creation, and were [part] of His [plan] before ever they came to be" (4Q402 frags. 3-4 line 15). Paul's matchless confession of the person of Christ attributes to him the creation of all things, including the invisible realm of "thrones or dominions or rulers or powers" (Col 1:16), these latter being categories of angelic beings (see chapter two above). The extensive descriptions of the heavenly sanctuary with its rituals and attendants in *Songs* may provide the substance of the vaunted visions of the Colossian errorists (Col 2:18), who may have been perpetuating the visionary experiences of the Teacher of Righteousness.

We should also recall that the book of Revelation is addressed to the seven churches of Asia, of which one, Laodicea, was right next door to Colossae and Hierapolis in the Lycus Valley. *Songs* makes reference to the "exalted angels" who are seven in number and offer "seven words of wondrous glorification" (4Q403 1 i 1-29), reminding us of the seven spirits (archangels?) who surround the throne in Revelation. The mention of times of silence in heaven, the throne room, the throne-chariot and the increasing volume of heavenly songs, among other features, adds to the Jewish setting. This fascination with the angelic worship may be the problem Paul faces in Colossians.[85]

This leads us to a crucial phrase in Paul's letter to the Colossians, namely, "the elemental spirits of the universe" (Col 2:20). Much ink has been spilled in the explication of this intriguing expression. One surmises there is a problem, since the NRSV provides a textual note giving an alternate translation: "the rudiments of the world."[86] A survey of major commentaries on Colossians and special monographs devoted to the topic will turn up several vying alternatives.[87] These options range from the notions of basic elements of the universe to astral spirits inhabiting the stellar regions! The expression occurs one other time, in Paul's letter to the Galatians, where it is applied to the kind of religious system sponsored by the Judaizers. This is a factor in a few scholars' equation of the two erring systems at Galatia and Colossae.[88]

A passage from 4Q405 provides a fascinating parallel:

> At their wondrous stations are spirits, clothed with embroidery, a sort of woven handiwork, engraved with splendid figures. In the midst of what looks like glorious scarlet and colors of utterly holy spiritual light, the spirits take up their holy stand in the presence of the [K]ing—[splendidly] colored spirits surrounded by the appearance of whiteness. . . . These spirits are the leaders of those who are wondrously clothed for service, the leaders of each and every holy kingdom belonging to the holy King, who serve in all the exalted temples of His glorious realm.
>
> The leaders of the exaltation possess tongues of knowledge [so as] to bless the God of knowledge for all His glorious works. (4Q405 23 ii 7b-12a)

Unquestionably there was a fascination with the astral beings at Qumran. They played a much larger role in the cosmos than one would have thought possible on the basis of contemporary Jewish sources outside Qumran. There are veiled references to the "two powers in heaven" in later rabbinic sources, but nothing like the angelology we discover at Qumran in sources clearly

---

[85] This is a very complicated issue, and the secondary literature is sizable. As an entry into this question, see P. T. O'Brien, "Colossians, Letter to the," *DPL*, 148-50 and the accompanying bibliography. Yigael Yadin argued that the book of Hebrews should also be read against the backdrop of a Christian Essenism. See his "The Scrolls and the Epistle to the Hebrews," in *Aspects of the Dead Sea Scrolls,* ed. Chaim Rabin and Y. Yadin, ScrHier 4 (Jerusalem: Magnes, 1958), pp. 36-55.

[86] See also the NIV and NASB translations.

[87] For recent surveys or attempts to reconstruct the false teaching, see Markus Barth and Helmut Blanke, *Colossians,* trans. Astrid B. Beck, AB (New York: Doubleday, 1994), pp. 10-41; Clinton E. Arnold, *The Colossian Syncretism: The Interface Between Christianity and Folk Belief at Colossae* (Grand Rapids, Mich.: Baker, 1996).

[88] See, e.g., N. T. Wright, *The Epistles of Paul to Colossians and to Philemon* (Grand Rapids, Mich.: Eerdmans, 1986), pp. 21-30.

belonging to the first two centuries B.C. into the first century A.D. Consequently, we are inclined to think that one need not go outside a Jewish orbit in order to explain the *stoicheia tou kosmou* ("the elemental spirits of the universe"). We are not opposed in principle to a derivation from the world of Hellenistic religions; it is purely a historical question. We know that syncretism was operative in this era and that Judaism was not immune to it. Indeed, the Qumran system may have been influenced to some degree by Iranian thought. But the Gnostic flavor that seems to be present in the false teaching at Colossae could just as easily be accounted for by its Essene roots rather than as a borrowing from Hellenistic mysticism and angelology.

4. The ritual observances mentioned by Paul almost certainly are Jewish: "food and drink . . . festivals, new moons, or sabbaths" (Col 2:16). The regulations of the false teaching that Paul quotes, "Do not handle, Do not taste, Do not touch" (Col 2:21) certainly have an Essene ring to them. We have already observed the incredible discipline and self-denial practiced by the Qumran community. Rigorous asceticism seems to feature prominently in the false teaching at Colossae. To be sure, Paul's passing references provide little to go on. For that matter, one could adduce parallels in this regard from a wide variety of Hellenistic religions as well. For Gentile Christians, mysticism was not something unknown from their pagan past. There were mystery religions aplenty throughout Asia. It might have seemed rather natural to observe a regimen like that prescribed by the false teachers. But the Jewish cast of the false teaching is unmistakable, and we think Essenism is a plausible source.[89]

We suggest that the Lycus Valley may have been home to an Essene community. We know from Josephus that Jews were already settled in the region by Antiochus III in the second century B.C. (*Ant.* 12.3.4 §§147-153). Clearly Philo describes a group that seems to be very much like the Essenes in Egypt (cf. *Contempl. Life* §§11-90). If such a community existed at some considerable distance from Judea and Qumran, there is no serious objection to positing other Essene settlements in the Diaspora. The weakness of my suggestion, of course, is lack of documentary evidence for any other Diaspora community of Essenes other than the one in Egypt. Unfortunately, no major excavation has yet been carried out at Colossae, so there is no immediate prospect that inscriptional data of any kind will be forthcoming.

However we reconstruct the false teaching at Colossae, Epaphras was uncertain how to confront this aberration and sought the counsel of his mentor, Paul. The result is a magnificent exposition of the lordship of Jesus Christ.

---

[89]For a well-argued case that the Colossian heresy should be identified with a local pagan cult emphasizing visionary ascent and angelic veneration, see Arnold, *Colossian Syncretism*.

Concluding Remarks on the Dead Sea Scrolls

The DSS provide an opportunity to reflect upon a pressing issue in the modern church, namely, the degree of separation required of faithful Christians from the larger society. Clearly the Qumran covenanters withdrew and consigned all those outside to the category of the wicked, to be annihilated at the end of days. Christendom has struggled with the same problem. Just how much separation is required? One thinks of the monastic movement that began in the late third and early fourth centuries and continues within the Eastern Orthodox and Roman Catholic traditions. This ascetic expression of Christianity in effect "encourages the idea of a double standard, with a spiritual elite set above the general level of Christians . . . [and] the additional step of withdrawing from society and seeking solitude."[90] In this we certainly hear echoes of the men of Qumran.

Within theologically conservative, Protestant circles, this continues to be a contentious issue. Some, often labeled fundamentalists, insist upon separatism.[91] Adherence to a carefully spelled out confessional statement is required. Besides an affirmation of the doctrines of historic Christianity, these statements also typically include issues that, for the most part, are matters of indifference to mainline churches (i.e., denominations that participate in the ecumenical movement and are generally identified as more theologically liberal: American Baptist, Church of Christ, Episcopalian, Lutheran, Methodist, Presbyterian, etc.). Examples include the young-earth view of creation (as opposed to evolution),[92] the inerrancy of Scripture, independent church governance and premillennial eschatology, to name a few of the most prominent. In regard to eschatology, probably no doctrine defines fundamentalism, as it exists today, more reliably than the pretribulational second coming of Christ. This is a touchstone of orthodoxy for most fundamentalists. Because of their eschatology, most, but not all, support Zionism. They are also alarmed by the feminist movement and reaffirm male headship in the home, church and society as a biblical doctrine.

Behavioral standards such as total abstinence from alcoholic beverages, drugs, premarital sex and tobacco are stoutly maintained. A generation ago fun-

---

[90]Michael A. Smith, "Christian Ascetics and Monks," in *Eerdmans' Handbook to the History of Christianity,* ed. Tim Dowley et al. (Grand Rapids, Mich.: Eerdmans, 1977), p. 204.

[91]For a definition and overview, see G. M. Marsden, "Fundamentalism," in *New Dictionary of Theology,* ed. Sinclair B. Ferguson, David F. Wright and J. I. Packer (Downers Grove, Ill.: InterVarsity Press, 1988), pp. 266-68.

[92]This involves a completely literal interpretation of Gen 1 in which the earth was created only some thousands of years ago in six solar days. For a discussion of this issue, see Larry R. Helyer, *Yesterday, Today and Forever: The Continuing Relevance of the Old Testament* (Salem, Wis.: Sheffield Publishing, 1996), pp. 24-38.

damentalists also proscribed dancing, movies, gambling and, in some circles, mixed swimming; however, these "vices" have quietly disappeared from the "list," with certain qualifications, for many, if not most, fundamentalists today.[93]

Furthermore, a clear majority of fundamentalists subscribe to a conservative Republican political agenda. In contrast to Essenism, and in contrast to a former generation of fundamentalists, many contemporary fundamentalists actively participate in the political process. They are especially distressed by the perception that the government and secular humanists are steadily undermining the Christian foundations and values of the United States of America. Fundamentalists are virtually unanimous in their opposition to abortion, are in favor of prayer in public schools and typically refuse to cooperate with mainline churches in any kind of endeavor, whether evangelistic or social service. On the fringes of this movement are those who advocate violence directed toward abortion clinics and who participate in various paramilitary groups. The overwhelming majority of fundamentalists, however, reject this kind of violence as unbiblical and morally wrong.

While fundamentalists do not consign all those outside the movement to eternal destruction, a circle of fellowship is nearly always drawn, and it is assumed that only this circle truly conforms to biblical standards. They regularly define evangelicals who do not subscribe to their narrow doctrinal basis as "liberals," neo-orthodox," or "neo-evangelicals." Fundamentalists may even distinguish among themselves, whether they are "militant" or "compromising" fundamentalists. The former do not cooperate with those who deviate even slightly from their position and publicly attack those who do.[94]

Our intent here is simply to point out the similar (by no means identical) kinds of religious debates that occur within the larger Judeo-Christian traditions. It is quite revealing to study the disputes and disagreements that arise among Orthodox Jewish groups and to compare these to the controversies among conservative, evangelical or fundamentalist Christians.[95] In so many

---

[93]For an interesting discussion of the changing mores of evangelicals and Protestant fundamentalists, see Richard Quebedeaux, *The Worldly Evangelicals* (San Francisco: Harper & Row, 1978).

[94]Those who surf the Internet may already have discovered home pages of Protestant fundamentalists who excoriate "neo-evangelicals" for their failures to be doctrinally and behaviorally "biblical." Note in this regard the interesting parallel with the Qumran community's disparaging labels for various opponents. An important distinction between the controversies of the men of Qumran and militant fundamentalists is that the former were concerned about ritual purity whereas the latter are concerned primarily about doctrinal purity.

[95]For concrete examples in the American Jewish community, see Samuel G. Freedman, *Jew Versus Jew: The Struggle for the Soul of American Jewry* (New York: Simon & Schuster, 2000).

respects, we truly are mirror images of one another! The DSS enable us to observe how one group of committed Jews approached this matter of separation and conformity. Since we have no emotional investment in the issues that elicited such a vehement response from them, we can more objectively evaluate their stance. Perhaps we can extrapolate from the core issues that fueled the acrimonious debate between the Essenes and their opponents in order to draw some lessons for our own times. Just how separate from the larger culture should we be as modern Christians? How much uniformity and authoritarianism should we expect and allow today? What doctrines and standards of behavior form the irreducible core of Christian faith and life? These are important and still debated issues in the church. And perhaps—just perhaps—after languishing nearly two thousand years in their dark grottoes, the scrolls and fragments from Qumran may illuminate our own controversies!

Excursus: The Dynamics of Sects and Cults

A recurring feature of Christian church history is the formation of splinter groups and sects. Typically these are founded or led by an authoritarian leader who has a "direct line to God." The teachings of this leader are viewed as the very word of God, and extremely high uniformity is demanded of disciples.

The problems of psychological and physical abuse in these sects are well known. One of the more publicized examples is a cult known as Children of God founded by David Berg in 1968 as a spin-off from the Jesus movement of the 1960s. In the early 1980s they renamed the group Family of Love. This cult practices a form of charismatic Christianity and lives communally. They attracted public attention because of the practice of free sex among the group members and sexual solicitation as a means of evangelism (some of the female members called themselves "hookers for Jesus"). In October of 1995 a British court awarded five thousand pounds to a former member who had been sexually abused by the sect from the age of three years old. David Berg, who has since died, styled himself as Moses and communicated with the various communes across the United States, Europe, India and Australasia by means of letters called "Mo Letters." Despite their lax sexual practices, Berg insisted upon harsh, restrictive living conditions for group members. His directives were viewed as the very word of God.

Sometimes disastrous consequences ensue when people commit themselves to such authoritarian sects. In 1978 a cult led by the Reverend Jim Jones, called the Peoples Temple, committed mass suicide by drinking cyanide-laced Kool-Aid—at his insistence—in Jonestown, Guyana, South America, where Jones had fled to avoid prosecution in the United States. In all, 913 people died, including women and children. The Reverend Jim Jones, an ordained clergyman belonging to the Church of God (he pastored a church in Indianapolis, Indiana, during the 1950s and 1960s), increasingly became an autocrat, illegally diverting and extorting millions of dollars of his members' money. His manipulation of followers included blackmail, threats, beatings and, in all likelihood, death. His delusions of grandeur finally led to the claim that he was God himself.

Similarly, on February 28, 1993, in Waco, Texas, officers of the department of Alcohol, Tobacco and Firearms assaulted an armed cult called the Branch Davidians holed up in their compound under the direction of David Koresh. In the ensuing inferno, eighty-two members perished.[96] This cult, originally an offshoot of the Seventh-day Adventist Church, held to an imminent return of Jesus Christ. Koresh, who was thrown out of the SDA in 1979 for being a troublemaker, wrested leadership of the Branch Davidians away from the former leader George Roden. Once in power, he exercised absolute control over his disciples and, like David Berg, engaged in illicit sex with female members, including minors. Only he was allowed such liberties, however, and discipline was severe under his leadership. After a pilgrimage to Jerusalem in 1985, he declared himself "the sinful Messiah." He indoctrinated his followers with his idiosyncratic views about the coming of Christ and the end of the world based upon certain prophetic and apocalyptic passages of Scripture, especially in the book of Revelation.

On March 28, 1997, thirty-nine members of a cult called Heaven's Gate committed suicide in Rancho La Mesa, an exclusive suburb twenty miles north of San Diego. They were under the spell of Marshall Applewhite, son of a Presbyterian minister. He had come to the bizarre notion that the group had to escape the earth before its imminent destruction by rendezvousing with a spaceship hovering just behind the then-prominent Hale-Bopp comet. This cult, a strange mixture of recycled Gnosticism tweaked with Star Trek imagery, exhibited a highly ascetic lifestyle, shunning all manifestations of sexuality, even to the point of voluntary castration for some members. As is typical of such cult leaders, Applewhite claimed to have a "hot line" to heaven and manipulated the lives of his followers.

Reading the DSS forces us to rethink the nature of religious authority and the constant danger of abusing power. Each of the above-mentioned cults, *though differing from the Qumran community in many respects,* does have some features in common. Authoritarianism (requiring absolute obedience to authority) is one such common thread. Evangelicalism, while believing in God's revelation in authoritative Scripture, must always be vigilant against the pitfall of authoritarianism. The Reformation principle of the freedom of each believer's conscience must be safeguarded. The right of private judgment and the accountability of leaders to the church must balance faithfulness to the apostolic teachings. Both

---

[96]For an account of this tragedy, see James D. Tabor, "Apocalypse at Waco: Could the Tragedy Have Been Averted?" *BRev* 9, no. 5 (1993): 24-33.

Testaments of Scripture contain warnings against false prophets and tests for discerning those who are (Deut 13:1-5; 18:14-22; Jer 23:1-40; 28:1-17; Ezek 13:1-23; Mt 7:15-20; 1 Cor 14:29; 1 Tim 4:1-5; 2 Tim 3:1-9; 2 Pet 2:1-22; 1 Jn 2:18-23; 4:1-3; 2 Jn 7-11; Jude 3-23; Rev 2—3).[97] The NT also gives qualifications and guidelines for exercising leadership in the church (cf. 1 Tim 3:1-13; 4:11—5:2, 17-22; 6:3-16, 20; 2 Tim 2: 1-7: 2:14—4:5). These must be diligently upheld lest some fall prey to false teachers such as David Berg, Jim Jones, David Koresh, Marshall Applewhite and a disconcertingly large number of others.

For Further Discussion

1. What is the relationship of Qumran to the DSS?
2. How do the DSS illuminate the world of Early Judaism?
3. Who were the Essenes, and what were they all about?
4. What are some basic theological convictions reflected in the DSS?
5. What do the DSS contribute to our understanding of apocalyptic literature?
6. How do the DSS illuminate the world of the NT?
7. How is the NT use of the OT similar to that of Qumran? How is it different? What difference does it make?
8. What is the essence of pesher interpretation?
9. Does acceptance of pesher interpretation by NT writers undermine the truthfulness of the NT message?
10. What light do the pesharim throw on the NT's claim that Jesus fulfilled messianic prophecies in the OT?
11. What are some parallels between the DSS and the NT in terms of organization and behavioral issues?
12. Compare and contrast the scrolls and the NT on the degree of separation "from the world" demanded of the faithful.
13. What dangers are inherent in tightly structured, rigid faith communities?

For Further Reading

Moshe J. Bernstein, "Interpretation of Scripture," *EDSS* 1:376-83.
————, "Pesher Habakkuk," *EDSS* 2:647-50.
————, "Pesher Isaiah," *EDSS* 2:651-53.
————, "Pesher Psalms," *EDSS* 2:655-56.
Shani L. Berrin, "Pesharim," *EDSS* 2:644-47.
————, "Pesher Nahum," *EDSS* 2:653-55.
George J. Brooke, "Florilegium," *EDSS* 1:297-98.
————, "Pesharim," *DNTB,* pp. 778-82.
F. F. Bruce, *Biblical Exegesis in the Qumran Texts* (Grand Rapids: Eerdmans, 1959).

---

[97]For a discussion of these, see Helyer, *Yesterday,* pp. 292-98.

James H. Charlesworth, ed., *Jesus and the Dead Sea Scrolls,* ABRL (New York: Doubleday, 1992), esp. pp. 1-74, 140-75.

————, *John and the Dead Sea Scrolls* (New York: Crossroad, 1991).

Devorah Dimant, "Qumran Sectarian Literature," in *Jewish Writings of the Second Temple Period: Apocrypha, Pseudepigrapha, Qumran Sectarian Writings, Philo, Josephus,* ed. Michael E. Stone, CRINT 2 (Assen: Van Gorcum; Philadelphia: Fortress, 1984), pp. 503-31.

André Dupont-Sommer, *The Essene Writings from Qumran,* trans. G. Vermes (Gloucester, Mass.: Peter Smith, 1973), pp. 164-278, 310-19.

Joseph A. Fitzmyer, *Essays on the Semitic Background of the New Testament,* SBLSBS 5 (Missoula, Mont.: Scholars Press, 1974), pp. 3-58.

————, " '4QTestimonia' and the New Testament," *TS* 18 (1957): 513-37.

————, "The Qumran Scrolls and the New Testament After Forty Years," *RevQ* 13 (1988): 609-20.

————, "The Use of Explicit Old Testament Quotations in Qumran Literature and in the New Testament," *NTS* 7 (1960-1961): 297-333.

Michael A. Knibb, *The Qumran Community,* CCWJCW 2 (Cambridge: Cambridge University Press, 1987), pp. 157-82, 207-66.

T. H. Lim, *Holy Scripture in the Qumran Commentaries and Pauline Letters* (Oxford: Oxford University Press, 1997).

Richard Longenecker, *Biblical Exegesis in the Apostolic Period* (Grand Rapids, Mich.: Eerdmans, 1975). An important work by an evangelical scholar in which NT appropriation of the OT is compared to that of Qumran.

George W. E. Nickelsburg, *Jewish Literature Between the Bible and the Mishnah: A Historical and Literary Introduction* (Philadelphia: Fortress, 1981), pp. 126-41.

C. Marvin Pate, *Communities of the Last Days: The Dead Sea Scrolls, the New Testament and the Story of Israel* (Downers Grove, Ill.: InterVarsity Press, 2000). A helpful discussion by an evangelical scholar of the hermeneutics and theological positions of the Qumran community.

Cecil Roth, "The Subject Matter of Qumran Exegesis," *VT* 10 (1960): 51-68.

Lawrence H. Schiffman, *Reclaiming the Dead Sea Scrolls: The History of Judaism, the Background of Christianity, the Lost Library of Qumran,* ABRL (New York: Doubleday, 1995), pp. 223-41, 257-71, 317-39, 351-66.

James VanderKam, *The Dead Sea Scrolls Today* (Grand Rapids, Mich.: Eerdmans, 1994), pp. 43-55.

Geza Vermes, *An Introduction to the Complete Dead Sea Scrolls* (Minneapolis: Fortress, 1999), pp. 182-91.

Michael Wise, Martin Abegg Jr. and Edward Cook, *The Dead Sea Scrolls: A New Translation* (New York: HarperCollins, 1999 [1996]). The introductions and section headings of this translation are quite helpful.

Eight

"Down in Egypt Land"

Unfortunately, Aristeas to Philocrates *is not included in Sparks's edition, so we must resort to the more compendious collection of James H. Charlesworth, ed.,* The Old Testament Pseudepigrapha, *2 vols. (New York: Doubleday, 1983), 2:7-34. It is also found in R. H. Charles, ed.,* The Apocrypha and Pseudepigrapha of the Old Testament, *2 vols. (Oxford: Oxford University Press, 1913), 2:83-122. Both* 3 Maccabees *and* Wisdom of Solomon *are found in* The New Oxford Annotated Bible: New Revised Standard Version, *ed. Bruce M. Metzger and Roland E. Murphy (New York: Oxford University Press, 1991), AP 285-99 and 57-85, respectively, though* 3 Maccabees *may also be consulted in Charlesworth, ed.,* Old Testament Pseudepigrapha, *2:531-64, and* Wisdom of Solomon *in the New American Bible translation in* The Catholic Study Bible, *ed. Donald Senior (New York: Oxford University Press, 1990), pp. 799-821; and* The Oxford Study Bible: Revised English Bible with the Apocrypha, *ed. M. Jack Suggs, Katharine Doob Sakenfeld and James R. Mueller (New York: Oxford University Press, 1992), 1099-1115.*

Overview

During the first century B.C. and the first Christian century, a very large Jewish community lived in Egypt, especially in the great city of Alexandria. In fact, there had been a substantial settlement of Jews in Egypt since the Babylonian invasion by Nebuchadnezzar in the sixth century B.C. (cf.

2 Kings 25:26; Jer 43:7; and chapter one above). This community generated a number of significant Jewish writings. Owing to space limitations, we will have to make a selection out of the larger extant corpus.[1] We will examine four texts that date from approximately 140 B.C. to about A.D. 50. Each of these is preoccupied with the problems of life in Diaspora. The burning question is, How should Jews relate to Gentiles? The *modus vivendi* (way of living) suggested by these writings contrasts markedly from *Jubilees,* the resistance literature we read in chapter five, and the writings from Qumran in chapters six and seven.

We begin with an examination of a work purporting to inform us how the Septuagint (LXX) was translated, *Aristeas to Philocrates* (often called the *Epistle of Aristeas).* Remember that this Greek version of the Hebrew Bible became *the* Bible of the early church. Only toward the end of the first century A.D. did the NT documents begin to take their place alongside the LXX as sacred Scripture (cf. 2 Pet 3:16). The LXX was, for example, the Bible that Paul the apostle typically used in his mission to the Gentiles.

As a classic example of how a cultured Jew could synthesize Hellenism and the Hebrew traditions, we turn to the Wisdom of Solomon. This masterpiece of Diaspora Judaism has considerable significance for the interpretation of the NT. We also glimpse, in 3 Maccabees, the ever-recurring curse of anti-Semitism. Alexandria was for centuries a hotbed for such sentiment, and one reads in this work some of the slanders and stereotypes leveled against Jews that continue their baleful influence to this very day.

The premier author, however, who has bequeathed us the fruit of his labors while in Alexandria is Philo Judaeus. We can only sample his voluminous works, but enough will be read to appreciate the intellectual achievement of this Diaspora Jew. Because of Philo's large output, we devote an entire chapter to his work (chapter nine). According to Philo, Moses actually anticipated the philosophical thought of Plato, the Pythagoreans and the Stoics. The allegorical method, which Philo employed in order to achieve his synthesis of Greek philosophy and the Hebrew traditions, has had an enormous impact on the Christian tradition.

---

[1]We will not cover the Elephantine correspondence (fifth century B.C.), the Story of Ahikar and the large corpus of papyri stretching from Ptolemaic down to Byzantine times that were recovered from Oxyrhynchus. Neither will we read Book 3 of the *Sybilline Oracles.* This is part of a larger collection (twelve books) of predictions attributed to women who spoke oracles under divine impulse, usually in a state of ecstasy. These oracular utterances were originally pagan in background but were taken up by later generations of pagans, Jews and Christians and adapted to their particular viewpoints. Book 3 is generally dated to ca. 150 B.C. and attributed to a Jewish author living in Egypt. In its own way, this work reveals some indications of the situation of Jews in Egypt under the Ptolemies. For the text and introduction, see John J. Collins, "The Sybilline Oracles," *OTP* 1:317-26, 362-80.

Aristeas to Philocrates

Introduction

As George W. E. Nickelsburg observes, "In the whole of our literature this writing presents the most positive estimate of the Greeks and Greek culture and of the possibility for peaceful and productive coexistence between Jews and Greeks."[2] That Diaspora Jews displayed more willingness to coexist amicably with their Gentile neighbors than Palestinian Jews is not surprising. Certainly it was in their self-interest to do so. As we will discover, anti-Semitism was a very real danger for Diaspora communities, and their continued existence depended upon their ability to maintain the goodwill of their more numerous Gentile neighbors.

So what is the *Epistle of Aristeas* all about? It purports to be a letter by one Aristeas, an influential Gentile courtier of Ptolemy II Philadelphus (283-247 B.C.), to his brother Philocrates, a distinguished intellectual. The "letter" (it is really a first-person narrative) explains how it came about that a Greek translation of the Hebrew Scriptures was executed by a group of Palestinian Jewish scholars in a mere seventy-two days at the bequest of the Egyptian monarch himself.

Structure

The letter does not lend itself to a neat outline, but the flow of the document can be seen in twelve main sections as follows:

Prologue: Explanation of letter to Philocrates (lines 1-8)

I.   Ptolemy II orders his librarian Demetrius to collect all the books in the world for the library of Alexandria (lines 9-11)

II.   First digression: Aristeas details his successful petition on behalf of Jews who had been deported to and enslaved in Egypt (lines 12-27)

III.   Letter of Demetrius to high priest requesting the translation and its acceptance (lines 28-82)

IV.   Description of Palestine, the temple, the high priest's vestments and the qualifications and virtues of the translators (lines 83-127)

V.   Second digression: the law in Judaism (lines 128-172)

VI.   Arrival of translators and a royal banquet prepared (lines 173-186)

VII.   Questions of the king and replies of the translators during the seven-day banquet (lines 187-294; the bulk of the letter)

VIII. Third digression: apology for the length of the foregoing section (lines 295-300)

IX.   Work begins on the translation in the specially prepared quarters and is

---

[2]*Jewish Literature Between the Bible and the Mishnah: A Historical and Literary Introduction* (Philadelphia: Fortress, 1981), p. 165.

completed in exactly seventy-two days (lines 301-307)

X. The version is read aloud to the Jewish community with a great ovation and is designated as the authorized Greek translation (lines 308-311)

XI. The king rejoices in the completed project, and special instructions are given Demetrius concerning the care of these books (lines 312-317)

XII. Translators depart for home after further compliments and gifts (lines 318-321)

Epilogue: Philocrates' special interest in such projects recalled (line 322)

Occasion and Purpose

The ostensible occasion cannot be accepted at face value. There are compelling arguments that the work is not contemporary with the narrated events, nor is it historically accurate in all that it narrates.[3] What does stand out in terms of the content is the strong apologetic tone in defense of Judaism and especially its two central symbols and institutions, the law and the temple.[4] This makes sense if we place the document in the period of the Hellenistic crisis surrounding Antiochus Epiphanes. No doubt the repercussions of Antiochus's Hellenistic reforms were felt in the very large Diaspora community at Alexandria. There could be no question of any kind of armed resistance or takeover there. In order to survive, the Jewish community needed to elicit the goodwill and respect of their Gentile overlords. Without capitulating to Hellenism entirely and abandoning the ancestral faith, the Jewish residents of Alexandria and other Egyptian cities sought to extol the virtues of their faith. Significantly, in this work, Ptolemaic figures (the king himself!) go out of their way to praise and admire the Jewish law and ritual.

The letter is not intended for internal consumption alone; it is intended to impress pagans with the excellencies of Judaism.[5] Such a system of belief would not only be beneficial to have in one's midst but would be an attractive option for one's own life—so the implied argument of the letter. We thus have a document that aggressively promotes the superiority of Judaism vis-à-vis

---

[3]For specific evidence, see Sidney Jellicoe, *The Septuagint and Modern Study* (Oxford: Clarendon Press, 1968), pp. 47, 52-58; Nickelsburg, *Jewish Literature*, p. 77; M. Hadas, ed., *Aristeas to Philocrates*, JAL (New York: Harper, 1951), pp. 6-9; Herbert T. Andrews, "The Letter of Aristeas," *APOT* 2:83-84; and C. C. Caragounis, "Aristeas, Epistle of," *DNTB*, pp. 115-16.

[4]See Jellicoe's concise discussion in *Septuagint*, p. 47.

[5]Caragounis, however, criticizes the notion that it was also intended for Gentile readers: "its simplistic narrative and historical blunders could not but alienate them and thus defeat its purpose. It was written for Jewish consumption outside Palestine, in particular Alexandria" ("Aristeas," p. 117). But would this not also have been a problem for many Jewish readers? It is very difficult to assess the psychological impact of writings upon people who lived a long time ago. Our author apparently was not concerned about this.

paganism.[6] Few scholars have questioned the essential unity of the work as we have it.

Date, Author and Provenance

The dating of this work is notoriously difficult.[7] But if our reconstruction of the occasion is approximately correct, the composition falls somewhere between 170 and 130 B.C.[8] Although the author identifies himself as one Aristeas, a Greek pagan serving as an official in the court of Ptolemy Philadelphus, he is obviously a Hellenistic Jew. The extravagant praise of the Jewish law and temple along with many indications of Jewish bias and interest, something entirely out of character for a pagan, render this judgment almost certain.[9] The affinities of the work with other Jewish Alexandrine writings, such as Wisdom of Solomon, 3 Maccabees and Philo, strongly point to Alexandria as the home of our pseudonymous author.

Features

As we have seen in our discussion of the purpose of *Aristeas*, the document is not primarily a narrative about how the LXX was translated—one sentence is all this receives in the entire work! Rather, the aim was to argue for "rapprochement without assimilation."[10] The author is clearly at home in the Greek language and possesses a fair amount of traditional Hellenistic learning and culture. He is familiar with figures well known from the Hellenistic era. Our author displays his literary craft by means of a number of Hellenistic genres, such as the *prooemium* (preface; lines 1-8), a utopian travelogue (lines 107-120), an *ekphrasis* (a listing of gifts bestowed; lines 51-82), a symposium (discussions accompanying a banquet or social gathering; lines 172-300) and an epilogue (line 322). The work as a whole resembles the *chreia*, a homily or written speech, for that is the best way to describe *Aristeas*, with its thoroughly Greek vocabulary and style after the manner of the Cynics and Stoics.[11]

---

[6]Robert H. Pfeiffer summarizes the purpose accordingly: "This fanciful story of the origin of the Septuagint is merely a pretext for defending Judaism against its heathen denigrators, for extolling its nobility and reasonableness, and for striving to convert Greek-speaking Gentiles to it" (*History of New Testament Times with an Introduction to the Apocrypha* [New York: Harper, 1949], p. 225).

[7]See G. E. Ladd, "Pseudepigrapha," *ISBE* 3:1041; cf. Jellicoe, *Septuagint*, pp. 48-52; Caragounis, "Aristeas," pp. 116-17.

[8]Hadas sifts through all the arguments and decides that 130 B.C. is "least liable to objection" (*Aristeas to Philocrates*, pp. 9-54, with summary statement on p. 54).

[9]In Hadas's words: "His knowledge of and devotion to the traditions of Judaism are incredible in a pagan" (ibid., p. 5).

[10]Nickelsburg, *Jewish Literature*, p. 79.

[11]Ibid., p. 78.

Of special interest is the section that describes Jerusalem, the temple and the sacrificial ritual. Although one must take with a grain of salt some of the descriptions—clearly extravagant embellishments—we are still indebted to the writer for some valuable details of pre-Herodian Jerusalem and the Temple Mount. The description of the temple as being on the top of a hill and towering over the city corresponds to the topography of the area. Aristeas also says, correctly, that the temple was oriented toward the east. Of special interest is Aristeas's account of the veil:

> The configuration of the veil was in respects very similar to the door furnishing, and most of all in view of continuous movement caused to the material by the undercurrent of the air. It was continuous because the undercurrent started from the bottom and the billowing extended to the rippling at the top—the phenomenon making a pleasant and unforgettable spectacle. (*Aristeas* 86)[12]

Most likely, this veil separated the vestibule from the nave, or holy place, and was not the one that separated the holy place from the holy of holies. Josephus agrees with Aristeas that there was a curtain in front of the door admitting one to the holy place (*J.W.* 5.5.4 §212), but the Mishnah does not mention such a curtain.[13] At any rate, Aristeas's comment seems to have been based upon actual observation.[14]

Aristeas also was impressed by the elaborate and extensive underground system of reservoirs. These provided the necessarily large water supply for cleansing the area of the "many thousands" of sacrifices offered during the festivals. Modern surveys of the Haram es-Sharif ("The Venerable Sanctuary," the Arabic name for the area surrounding the Dome of the Rock and the El Aqsa Mosque) have confirmed the presence, beneath the existing platform, of numerous cisterns.[15] Note that according to Aristeas the temple was sur-

---

[12]All translations of *Aristeas* are by R. J. H. Shutt, "Letter of Aristeas," in *The Old Testament Pseudepigrapha,* ed. James H. Charlesworth (New York: Doubleday, 1983), 2:12-34.

[13]H. G. Stigers suggests that "the curtain of which Josephus wrote may have been added at a later time when fears of defilement of the Temple by even a look by a foreigner were felt" ("Temple, Jerusalem," *ZPEB* 5:646).

[14]Hadas, however, mentions that the literary *ekphrasis* involved the technique of including descriptions that seemed to be eyewitness accounts (*Aristeas to Philocrates,* p. 133, note on paragraph 86).

[15]See, e.g., the diagram in Leibel Reznick, *The Holy Temple Revisited* (Northvale, N.J.: Jason Aaronson, 1993), p. 35. Stigers is probably wrong in asserting that "Aristeas described the presence of an inexhaustible spring within the Temple precincts" ("Temple, Jerusalem," 5:644). He follows the translation of Andrews for paragraph 89: "And there is an inexhaustible supply of water, because an abundant natural spring gushes up from within the temple area" ("Letter of Aristeas," 2:103). Hadas's translation is very close to that of Andrews (Hadas, *Aristeas to Philocrates,* p. 135). Shutt, on the other hand, renders the pas-

rounded by three enclosing walls (*Aristeas* 84). This is confirmed by 1 Maccabees 4:38; 9:54, which mention or imply that the sanctuary was surrounded by more than one courtyard.

Aristeas's most effusive praise, however, centers upon the work of the priesthood. In his words: "The ministering of the priests was absolutely unsurpassable in its vigor and the arrangement of its well-ordered silence" (*Aristeas* 92). His description of the strength and speed displayed by the priests, as they literally "rip" the bones apart, seems overdone, to say the least. He says that more than seven hundred priests were on duty—he must be referring to festival days (cf. *Aristeas* 88-89)—and that these were aided by a "large number" of assistants, no doubt Levites. But beyond all the sights witnessed by Aristeas, none could match that of the high priest Eleazar. "I emphatically assert that every man who comes near the spectacle of what I have described will experience astonishment and amazement beyond words, his very being transformed by the hallowed arrangement on every single detail" (*Aristeas* 99). Included in Aristeas's account of the accoutrements of Eleazar are his "garment" of precious stones (cf. Ex 39:2-26), the golden bells on the hem (Ex 39:25-26) and the tiara with its miter and the ineffable name of God (Yahweh) inscribed upon it.

Aristeas also mentions a fortress for the protection of the temple that overlooks the entire area. This fortress seems to be the same one known in 1 Maccabees as "the citadel" or "Akra" (1 Macc 4:41; 13:49-50). The tight security measures by which the guards operated drew special comment from Aristeas (*Aristeas* 100-104). Most scholars hold that Herod the Great later enlarged and strengthened this citadel, the foundations of which are situated on the north side of the Temple Mount, and renamed it "Antonia" after his friend Mark Antony. Some prefer to locate the citadel of Aristeas and the Maccabean era to the south of the Temple Mount, near the present El Aqsa Mosque, agreeing that Herod later relocated it.

This grandiose description of the temple, with its ministry and priesthood, and of the city and its environs argues persuasively for the unsurpassed excellence of the Jewish religion. Of course, even more prominent is the very long digression—for which the author feels compelled to apologize—narrating the seven-day banquet and the questions put by the king himself to these philosopher-translators. Couched in the language of Hellenistic political theory and practice, the answers are nonetheless undergirded by Jewish mono-

---

sage: "There is an uninterrupted supply not only of water, *just as if* there were a plentiful-spring rising naturally from within, but also of indescribably wonderful underground reservoirs" ("Letter of Aristeas," *OTP*, 2:18, italics added). This seems more accurate to me, since the Greek has the subjunctive particle.

theism and the ideals of the law. Our author was writing to bolster commitment by his co-religionists and to invite conversion by his pagan neighbors.

Another feature that jars modern readers concerns the view of women that surfaces in one of the banquet questions: " 'How can one reach agreement with a woman?' 'By recognizing,' he replied, 'that the female sex is bold, positively active for something which it desires, easily liable to change its mind because of poor reasoning powers, and of naturally weak constitution'" (*Aristeas* 250). This uncomplimentary assessment aligns itself with Ben Sira and the Qumran literature but stands in contrast to Judith. One needs to be aware, however, of the generally suspicious and patronizing view of women widespread in Greek literature "from Semonides of Amorgos onwards."[16] The school of the Peripatetics (literally "those who walk about," i. e., followers and imitators of Aristotle, who, when he taught at the Lyceum at Athens, strolled about the premises) held as a doctrine that females were inferior to males. Given the popularity of the Peripatetics at Alexandria, we should not be surprised that a negative view of women appears in *Aristeas*.

Relevance for the New Testament

As already mentioned, the LXX played a vital part in the life of the earliest church. Although the members of the first community of believers in Jerusalem were all Jews (or proselytes to Judaism; cf. Acts 6:5) and spoke Aramaic or Hebrew, many also spoke Greek and were familiar with the LXX. As the church moved out of its Jewish enclave in Jerusalem and then made the huge breakout into the Gentile world, primarily under the impetus of the Pauline mission, the LXX became the basic Bible of these house churches.[17] When one examines Paul's letters and studies his use of the OT in them, it quickly becomes apparent that this was the version he cited.[18] Consequently, even though we cannot accept prima facie the particulars of Aristeas's tale, it nonetheless supports the probable existence, by the third century B.C., of a Greek translation of the Hebrew Pentateuch. Sound evidence also exists supporting the claim that by the second century B.C. the entire Hebrew Bible existed in a Greek translation.[19]

Aristeas is an apologetic tract. The objective of the apology was to demon-

---

[16]Hadas, *Aristeas to Philocrates*, p. 198, note on paragraph 250. For a general discussion of the role of women in Greco-Roman culture, see Helen King, "Women," *OCD*, pp. 1623-24.

[17]For further evidence of its importance to the early church, see Jellicoe, *Septuagint*, pp. 74-99.

[18]David Winston, *The Wisdom of Solomon*, AB 43 (New York: Doubleday, 1979), p. 182. On Paul's use of the LXX, see M. Silva, "Old Testament in Paul," *DPL*, pp. 630-42.

[19]For the background of the different recensions of the LXX, see Melvin K. H. Peters, "Septuagint," *ABD* 5:1093-1104.

strate the superiority of Judaism to paganism. The closest analogy in the NT is the book of Hebrews. Granted that the specific life settings and occasions were different,[20] there is still this common ground: both argue for the superiority of a religious system over against a rival. For Hebrews, the rival to "the new and living way" (Heb 10:20) was Diaspora Judaism. As is well known, Hebrews is punctuated by the repeated use of the terms "better" (cf. Heb 6:9; 7:19, 22; 8:6; 9:23: 10:34; 11:4, 16, 40; 12:24) and "superior" (Heb 1:4; 8:6). The argument of the homily consists of a series of well-developed "proofs" in which faith in Jesus is demonstrated as far superior to the ancestral faith.[21] Angels, Moses, Joshua, the temple and the Aaronic priesthood all pale in comparison to the excellence and majesty of Jesus and his new priesthood after the order of Melchizedek. There is a significant difference from *Aristeas* in this regard, however. Hebrews does not resort to blatant ridicule. It is respectful, even appreciative, of the ancestral faith. Arguing from the perspective of salvation history and realized eschatology, Hebrews sees continuity between the "long ago" of "our ancestors" and the "better," the "perfect" and the "final" that has now come through the Son (Heb 1:1-2). One cannot, however, miss the sustained argument of Hebrews, in which the ineffectiveness and obsolescence of the old covenant is repeatedly asserted (cf. Heb 7:18; 8:6-13; 9:1—10:18). Glory, perfection and rest, says the homilist (one who preaches a sermon), lies in the finished work of the great high priest after the order of Melchizedek, not in the shadows of the old covenant with its regulations and rituals. Furthermore, to remain in or return to the old covenant is to fall into a "consuming fire" (Heb 12:29). "Sitting on the fence" is not an option.

To draw another parallel, *Aristeas* is a narrative written for a distinguished individual having interest in the matters to be related, which leads one to think of the two volumes in the NT dedicated to Theophilus. The introduction to the Gospel of Luke is reminiscent of *Aristeas:* "I too decided, after investigating everything carefully from the very first, to write an orderly account for you, most excellent Theophilus, so that you may know the truth concerning the things about which you have been instructed" (Lk 1:3-4; cf. *Aristeas* 1-2, 5-8, 120, 322). Theophilus appears to have been a Gentile convert to Christianity and may have been the patron who underwrote the expenses of publication. The major difference between the two works in this regard lies in Luke's avoidance of an overly fawning attitude toward his recip-

---

[20]Although in this regard we do have a point of similarity, namely, that Hebrews was also written to a faith community that was in great danger from its pagan and unbelieving neighbors. For the life setting of Hebrews, see William Lane, *Hebrews,* WBC 47A (Waco, Tex.: Word, 1991), pp. li-lxiii.

[21]On Hebrews as a homily, see ibid., p. lxxi.

ients or patron. Both writers do, however, insist on the accuracy and care with which they have undertaken their researches and writing (Lk 1:1-4; *Aristeas* 295-300). One should also note that among the Synoptic Gospels, only Luke tells us that there was a preaching and healing mission involving seventy or seventy-two disciples sent out in pairs (Lk 10:1, 17). Given Luke's fondness for the LXX, this detail may be indebted to Aristeas's account of the translation of the Hebrew Scriptures into Greek.[22]

Incorporated into *Aristeas* are excerpts of letters written by the king of Egypt, the high priest Eleazar, the librarian Demetrius, and other officials. The standardized form of Hellenistic letters followed the pattern of opening ("A to B, greetings"), prayer or wish for good health, the body of the letter and a closing ("farewell"). Precisely this pattern appears in the NT, a nice example being 3 John. Luke, like *Aristeas,* cited letters in the book of Acts, and these duplicate the same pattern as above (cf. Acts 15:23-29; 23:26-30). Paul adapted this basic form as an aspect of his pastoral work among his churches.[23] The essential pattern, however, remained the same. Thus early Christians continued and adapted the letter format for pastoral purposes.

We also mention the reference to "the woman as the weaker sex" in 1 Peter 3:7. This is close to the phrase "of naturally weak constitution" in *Aristeas* 250. Whether Peter's comment refers only to physical strength or carries other negative connotations is difficult to say. At any rate, 1 Peter does not accuse women of dubious motives and faulty reasoning. Furthermore, Peter notes immediately after his comment about the weaker sex that "they too are also heirs of the gracious gift of life."

In this regard, the Pastoral Epistles may provide the closest NT parallel to Aristeas's denigration of women. The well-known prohibition against women teaching men ("I permit no woman to teach or to have authority over a man; she is to keep silent. For Adam was formed first, then Eve; and Adam was not deceived, but the woman was deceived and became a transgressor" [1 Tim 2:12-14]), the refusal to put younger widows on the list for church support ("for when their sensual desires alienate them from Christ, they want to marry. . . . Besides that, they learn to be idle, gadding about from house to house; and they are not merely idle, but also gossips and busybodies, saying what they should not say" [1 Tim 5:11, 13]) and the vulnerability of some women to false teachers ("For among them are those who make their way into households and captivate silly women, overwhelmed by their sins and

---

[22]This is argued more fully in Jellicoe, *Septuagint*, p. 45. See also Jellicoe's "St. Luke and the Seventy(-Two)," *NTS* 6 (1959-1960): 319-21; Jellicoe, "St. Luke and the Letter of Aristeas," *JBL* 80 (1961): 149-55.
[23]See P. T. O'Brien, "Letters, Letter Forms," *DPL*, pp. 550-53.

swayed by all kinds of desires, who are always being instructed and can
never arrive at a knowledge of the truth" [2 Tim 3:6-7]) all seem to reflect a
less-than-desirable view of women.[24]

These descriptions and directives, however, need to be read in the context
of the letters as a whole in which false teachers (male) were exploiting uned-
ucated women as a means of gaining new adherents for their sect. Furthermore, as Craig Keener notes, Paul gives both short-term and long-term
directives to deal with the situation: women should, for the present, be prohibited from teaching in the house churches but encouraged to learn from
their husbands at home so that they could contribute later.[25] In light of that,
we are hesitant to understand the negative descriptions of women in the Pastorals and the prohibition against their teaching in the church as normative
for the modern church, certainly the modern North American church.[26]

Finally, Aristeas's description of the veil in the vestibule of the temple,
with its undulations, calls for comment. Several NT writers display fascination with the temple veil, though their interest lay with the veil before the
holy of holies. The Synoptic Gospels recount the extraordinary circumstance that, when Jesus died, the veil rent in two from top to bottom (Mt
27:51; Mk 15:38; Lk 23:45). The book of Acts says that a number of priests
came to faith in Jesus in those first few years after Jesus' death (Acts 6:7).
One wonders if the impact of this event was instrumental in their joining
this new movement within Judaism. It is, however, the author of Hebrews,
perhaps also an Alexandrian Jew, who explicitly draws out the theological
significance of this moment. He urges his readers to enter into the most
holy place "behind the curtain, where Jesus, a forerunner on our behalf,
has entered" (Heb 6:19b-20a). Later on, he typologically identifies the curtain as Jesus' flesh (Heb 10:20), probably an allusion to the Synoptic Gospels' reference to the rending of the curtain when Jesus died. The point is
that Jesus, like the Aaronic priests, brought blood into the holy of holies as
an atoning sacrifice, but, unlike them, after the order of the new and better
Melchizedekian priesthood, offered his own blood as a once-for-all sacrifice

---

[24]On male attitudes toward women in Greco-Roman culture, see King, "Women," pp. 1623-
24; Emily Kearns, "Women in Cult," *OCD*, pp. 1624-25; and Craig S. Keener, "Man and
Woman," *DPL*, pp. 583-92.

[25]For a defense of this position, see Keener, "Man and Woman," pp. 590-91.

[26]For a carefully argued hermeneutic in dealing with the role of women in the church, see
William J. Webb, *Slaves, Women and Homosexuals: Exploring the Hermeneutics of Cultural
Analysis* (Downers Grove, Ill.: InterVarsity Press, 2001), esp. the appendices in pp. 257-
78. In fairness, one should also see the arguments for the traditional view that the prohibition against teaching still obtains. See Andreas J. Köstenberger, Thomas R. Schreiner
and H. Scott Baldwin, eds., *Women in the Church: A Fresh Analysis of 1 Timothy 2:9-15*
(Grand Rapids, Mich.: Baker, 1995).

(Heb 9:24-27; 10:10-20). A new and living way into the holy of holies was now available.[27]

Wisdom of Solomon

The Wisdom of Solomon, that "most beautiful of all late Jewish writings,"[28] is a work of considerable importance in its own right and has more than a little significance for the NT, especially the Pauline Epistles. In terms of genre, Wisdom falls into the category of sapiential (Latin, "wisdom") literature. It takes its place in the trajectory of wisdom literature that we have previously mentioned in connection with Ben Sira and Baruch. Indeed, one may justifiably place Wisdom at the apex of this fascinating development.[29] It is distinguishable from canonical Proverbs, which consists of short, pithy aphorisms and observations, and from Ecclesiastes, which features a monologue type of discourse. Metzger characterizes Wisdom as a theological treatise.[30] Nickelsburg, following David Winston, more narrowly specifies it by the term "protreptic," meaning a treatise that makes "an appeal to follow a meaningful philosophy as a way of life."[31] This designation is followed by the introduction in *The New Oxford Annotated Bible*.[32]

---

[27]For further discussion, see F. B. Huey Jr., "Veil," *ZPEB* 5:862-63. Leen Ritmeyer has recently drawn attention to the apparent discrepancy in the description of the veil found in Josephus and in the Mishnah. Josephus seems to speak of but one veil separating the holy place from the most holy place (*J.W.* 5.5. §219). In the latter there are *two* veils, which the high priest had to pass by going laterally between the two barriers (*m. Yoma* 5:1; *b. Yoma* 52b). It should be noted, however, that the Mishnah cited also contains a dissenting opinion by Rabbi Yose that there was only one veil. Ritmeyer suggests that the Mishnaic description is correct for the period *after* the crucifixion of Jesus. In other words, that event momentarily exposed the holy of holies to the gaze of priests other than the high priest. In order to prevent a similar occurrence, a second veil was added for the period A.D. 30-70 ("Rediscovering Herod's Temple," paper presented at the annual meeting of the Evangelical Theological Society, Nashville, Tenn., November, 2000).

[28]The description of R. Reitzenstein, *Zwei religionsgeschichtliche Fragen* (Strassburg, 1901), p. 109, cited by Pfeiffer, *History of New Testament Times*, p. 334.

[29]See Hagner, "Wisdom of Solomon," *ZPEB* 5:945.

[30]*An Introduction to the Apocrypha* (New York: Oxford University Press, 1957), p. 66.

[31]*Jewish Literature*, p. 175, quoting James M. Reese, *Hellenistic Influence on the Book of Wisdom and Its Consequences*, AnBib 41 (Rome: Biblical Institute, 1970), pp. 117-21. Winston qualifies the genre of Wisdom with this distinction: "Although it is clear that the author of Wisd has shaped his work in the form of a protreptic discourse it is equally clear that his argumentation . . . is largely rhetorical rather than demonstrative." He goes on to describe it as "a highly charged appeal designed to persuade a large audience to succumb to the charms of the philosophical life" (*Wisdom of Solomon*, p. 20). Daniel J. Harrington simply says: "It is an exhortation to seek wisdom and live by it" (*Invitation to the Apocrypha* [Grand Rapids, Mich.: Eerdmans, 1999], p. 55).

[32]Ed. Bruce M. Metzger and Roland E. Murphy (New York: Oxford University Press, 1991), AP 57.

M. Gilbert, however, persuasively argues that Wisdom best conforms to a genre called "encomium" (Latin, "tribute, eulogy"). This type of discourse was aimed at convincing a reader or listener to admire someone, to practice a particular virtue or to develop a desired quality.[33] Regardless of Wisdom's literary genre,[34] there is widespread agreement that Wisdom of Solomon attempts to combine conventional, orthodox Jewish piety with the Greek intellectual tradition.

Outline and Structure

In broadest terms, Wisdom of Solomon falls into three main sections. Section one (chaps. 1—5) is basically an exhortation and warning to Jews: seek justice and righteousness, since God will judge evildoers. The second section (chaps. 6—9) is an essay on the origin and benefits of wisdom. Solomon is the assumed speaker throughout. Section three (chaps. 10—19) consists, for the most part, of a retelling of the biblical story from creation to the exodus and conquest.[35] Here the intended audience is primarily Gentile (esp. in chaps. 13—15). The focus is upon God's acts of judgment in history, with special attention given to the account of the plagues on Egypt. Throughout this section there are several digressions and constant moralizing. But there is more of a highly crafted organizational structure than the above summary suggests.

The following outline is based upon a close literary analysis disclosing the tightly symmetrical and proportional plan by which the author of Wisdom shaped his composition. Particularly noteworthy are *inclusio* (a poetic device in which the opening word or theme reappears at the end) and a variety of symmetrical patterns, such as concentric, parallel and quantitative (i.e., the author has even counted his verses so that they are proportional in the sections).[36]

I.   The praises of wisdom (1:1—11:1)

    A. Immortality is the reward of wisdom (1:1—6:21)

       1. Exhortation to justice (1:1-15)

---

[33]For a detailed analysis of Wisdom and its conformity to the Aristotelian aspects that should characterize encomium, see M. Gilbert, "Wisdom Literature," in *Jewish Writings of the Second Temple Period: Apocrypha, Pseudepigrapha, Qumran Sectarian Writings, Philo, Josephus,* ed. Michael E. Stone, CRINT 2 (Assen: Van Gorcum; Philadelphia: Fortress, 1984), pp. 307-8. For a detailed analysis of literary features, see also Pfeiffer, *History of New Testament Times,* pp. 319-34.

[34]Lester L. Grabbe suggests that one may make a good case for a variety of genres in the book (*Wisdom of Solomon* [Sheffield: Sheffield Academic Press, 1997], pp. 25-28).

[35]Grabbe (ibid., p. 18) has a slightly different organization: 1—5: Book of Eschatology; 6—9: Book of Wisdom; 10—19: Book of History.

[36]See A. G. Wright, "The Structure of the Book of Wisdom," *Bib* 48 (1967) 165-84; Wright, "Wisdom," in *JBC on CD-ROM* (Logos Library System, version 2.0c, 1995, 1996); and Winston, *Wisdom of Solomon,* pp. 9-12.

2. The wicked invite death (speech of the wicked) (1:16—2:24)
3. The hidden counsels of God (3:1—4:19)
    a. Suffering (3:1-12)
    b. Childlessness (3:13—4:6)
    c. Early death (4:7-19)
2'. The final judgment (speech of the wicked) (4:20—5:23)
1'. Exhortation to seek Wisdom (6:1-21)[37]
B. The nature of wisdom and Solomon's quest for her (6:22—11:1)
    1. Introduction (6:22-25)
    2. Solomon's speech (7:1—8:21)
        a. Solomon is like other men (7:1-6)
        b. Solomon prayed, and wisdom and riches came to him (7:7-12)
        c. Solomon prays for help to speak of wisdom (7:13-22a)
        d. The nature of wisdom (7:22b—8:1)
        c'. Solomon sought wisdom, the source of knowledge (8:2-8)
        b'. Solomon sought wisdom as his counselor and comfort (8:9-16)
        a'. Solomon realizes the wisdom is a gift of God (8:17-21)
    3. Solomon's prayer for wisdom (9:1-18)
    4. Transitional section: wisdom saves her own (10:1—11:1)
II. God's fidelity to his people in the exodus (11:2—19:22)
    A. Introductory narrative (11:2-4)
    B. Theme: Israel is benefited by the very things that punish Egypt (11:5)
    C. Illustration of the theme in five antithetical diptychs (11:6—19:22)
        1. First diptych: water from the rock instead of the plague of the Nile (11:6-14)
        2. Second diptych: quail instead of the plague of little animals (11:15—16:15)
            a. 11:15-16 plus digression on God's power and mercy (11:17—12:22)
            b. 12:23-27 plus digression on false worship (13:1—15:17)
            c. 15:18—16:4 plus digression on the serpents in the desert (16:5-15)
        3. Third diptych: a rain of manna instead of the plague of storms (16:16-29)
        4. Fourth diptych: the pillar of fire instead of the plague of darkness (17:1—18:4)
        5. Fifth diptych: the tenth plague and the exodus by which God pun-

---

[37]The observant reader will note that this outline is slightly different from our general survey of the contents. As Harrington observes, "The parts are linked together so that it is possible to take chapter 6 as the end of Part 1 or the beginning of Part 2, and chapter 10 as the end of Part 2 and the beginning of Part 3" (*Invitation to the Apocrypha*, p. 56).

ished the Egyptians and glorified Israel (18:5—19:22)
  a. 18:5-19 plus digression on the plague in the desert (18:20-25)
  b. 19:1-5 plus digression on creation (19:6-21)
  c. Conclusion (19:22)

Date and Author

Though Solomon is the implied author, clearly the work is much later than the tenth century B.C. Like canonical Ecclesiastes, Wisdom conveniently employs Solomon as the speaker because of his reputation as the sage par excellence. As *The New Oxford Annotated Bible* points out, Solomon's prayer for wisdom seems deliberately modeled after the biblical exemplars in 1 Kings 3:6-9 and 2 Chronicles 1:8-10.[38] The consensus of scholars today is that Wisdom is a unified composition.[39] Suggestions as to authorship are closely bound up with one's assessment of the date and include possibilities such as Philo Judaeus or even the Apollos who is mentioned in the NT (Acts 18:24-28). Neither of these suggestions is very likely. Note, however, that both candidates are Alexandrian Jews. Most scholars generally accept the Alexandrian provenance of the work. Once again we must be content with a pseudonymous author.

But is the work from the first century A.D.? The argument in favor stems from the story of the persecuted righteous one and the oppression of Israel by the Egyptians. Some have inferred from these two episodes that we have a setting in the time of Caligula (A.D. 37-41), a period in which the Jewish community suffered greatly. On the other hand, times of oppression for Jews in Alexandria were not confined to the reign of Caligula, and, furthermore, our author shows no awareness of Philo's writings (first century A.D.). Since our author quotes from the LXX version of the prophets and seems to know Ben Sira in its Greek translation, we may set a *terminus a quo* (earliest date) at about 100 B.C. Coming at it from a different angle, Gilbert infers from a supposed reference to the *pax Romana* (the period of Roman peace) in Wisdom 14:22 that the date of composition could not be earlier that 30 B.C., when Augustus ushered in this era. Admittedly, the foregoing discussion does not offer very firm ground for dating. Accordingly, we must be content with the broad range of 100 B.C. to A.D. 40.[40]

Purpose

Our author seems to be waging an intellectual and spiritual battle on two

---

[38] AP 57.

[39] Winston, *Wisdom of Solomon*, pp. 12-14.

[40] See Metzger, *Introduction to the Apocrypha*, p. 67; Hagner, "Wisdom of Solomon," 5:947; Nickelsburg, *Jewish Literature*, p. 184; David Winton, "Solomon, Wisdom of," *ABD* 6:120-27; and D. A. deSilva, "Wisdom of Solomon," *DNTB*, p. 1269.

fronts, much like the author of *Letter of Aristeas*. On the one hand, he speaks to disaffected Jews who have either apostatized or were in danger of doing so. As Goodspeed puts it: "The writer's purpose was to protect the Jews in Egypt from the danger of falling into skepticism, materialism, and idolatry, and of yielding to the pressure of persecution to which they had evidently been exposed."[41] In this connection, one recalls the earlier wisdom tradition of Israel and the more contemporaneous work of Ben Sira. These works were aimed primarily at Jewish young men; so too, it would seem, is Wisdom of Solomon. On the other hand, this work is not for internal consumption alone. There are too many indicators of a polemic against the evils of the Gentile world, especially idolatry. This author, like *Aristeas*, appeals to rational arguments in order to persuade and convince pagans of the truth found in the Jewish tradition. They also can discover God's wisdom and order their lives aright. Indeed, the ancestral faith is recast in the language of Hellenistic thought.[42] It is precisely this delicate balancing act of adaptation and opposition that characterizes these works of Alexandrian origin. Thus Metzger nicely summarizes the purpose of Wisdom in three statements: (1) to rekindle zeal for God's Law in the heart of apostates (chaps. 1—5); (2) to encourage and fortify Jews who were wavering and disheartened (chaps. 10—12, 16—19); and (3) to convert Gentiles (chaps. 6—9, 13—15).[43] Some earlier scholars saw another purpose, namely, a refutation of the canonical book of Ecclesiastes or, as it is known in the Hebrew canon, Qoheleth.[44] This position has not, however, garnered much support in more recent research.

Features

Several distinctive teachings emerge clearly in Wisdom. Whereas the taproot of our author's thought grows out of the OT, there can be little doubt that he has incorporated ideas from Greek philosophy, especially Stoicism. We digress here briefly to summarize Stoic thought.

This school, founded by Zeno (335-263 B.C.), was named after the Stoa or porch in Athens where he taught his students. Well-known disciples of Zeno included Cleanthes of Assos (331-232 B.C.) and later, in Rome, Cicero (106-43

---

[41] Edgar J. Goodspeed, *The Story of the Old Testament Apocrypha* (Chicago: University of Chicago Press, 1939), p. 90.

[42] "He seems obviously to be formulating the faith of his fathers in the thought categories of the educated man of his day. . . . He is saying that the Jewish religion is no less satisfying than Gr. philosophy, and that the concepts of the latter can be most helpful in revealing the true depth of the former" (Hagner, "Wisdom of Solomon," 5:948).

[43] *Introduction to the Apocrypha*, p. 68. See also deSilva, "Wisdom of Solomon," p. 1271.

[44] See W. O. E. Oesterley, *An Introduction to the Books of the Apocrypha* (New York: Macmillan, 1935), pp. 214-17.

B.C.). The aim of Stoicism was to acquire wisdom in order to discover the greatest happiness possible in life. Discovering what can be changed and accepting with dignified resignation what cannot constituted the agenda of Stoicism.

The Stoic theory of knowledge was as follows: at birth one possesses a blank page, as it were. This was what John Locke would later call the *tabula rasa* (Latin, "erased tablet"). The mind, however, has the innate capability of processing new bits of information and organizing it into coherent patterns and systems. Thus there is a developmental process in the acquisition of knowledge and wisdom. Harnessing this increasing store of ideas and concepts is what leads to greater happiness.

The Stoics held that matter is the basic "stuff" of reality. Everything in the universe is some form of matter. Matter itself may be either inert or active. The latter expresses itself in an elemental force or power operative in the universe. This fundamental force is fire and moves in everything like an air current. Fire provides vitality to all of life. There is a hierarchy of beings in the universe, with rationality as the highest form. This leads to the essential point of Stoicism, namely, that rationality, identified as God, permeates everything. All of nature is filled with the principle of reason. It follows necessarily from this that all things are under the control of the Logos (Gk, "reason" or "rationality"). This Logos could also be styled as the Pneuma (Gk, "spirit").

Since God is conceived of as a sort of "world-soul," each human being is a part of God (cf. today's New Age teachings). The soul is corporeal (having bodily form) and is transmitted by human generation. For the Stoics, the soul centered in the heart and permeated the entire body by means of the bloodstream. Because a human being is a part of God, rationality is possible because God is ultimate rationality. Furthermore, the ability to exercise rational thought leads to an awareness of God as well as to an awareness of the order and operation of the universe. This is an inadequate summary of Stoic philosophy, but perhaps enough has been said to at least show how the author of Wisdom has borrowed and adapted some of its ideas.[45]

Our author employs phraseology and terminology reminiscent of Stoicism in his description of wisdom (Wis 7:22-24). Note, for example, passages such as the following: "all-powerful, overseeing all, and penetrating through all spirits that are intelligent, pure, and altogether subtle. For wisdom is more mobile than any motion; because of her pureness she pervades and penetrates all things" (Wis 7:23b-24). To be sure, one may find the ideas of omnipotence, omnipresence, sovereignty and so forth in the OT (cf. Ps 139; Is 40).

---

[45]See further, Julia Annas, "Stoicism," *OCD*, p. 1446; J. C. Thom, "Stoicism," *DNTB*, pp. 1139-42.

But the terminology employed in Wisdom of Solomon is quite different from that of the OT. It is, on the other hand, very much like that of Stoicism. The notion of a "world-soul" seems to have been taken over by our author from the Stoics (cf. Wis 1:7; 7:24; 8:1). The idea that the world has been arranged "by measure and number and weight" (Wis 11:20) is also typical of Stoicism and finds no counterpart in the OT.

We should also note that Wisdom manifests marked similarities to the Cynic-Stoic diatribe style, a public discourse intended to argue the merits of a position over against opposing viewpoints.[46] Very often rather harsh and abusive language was employed, and a key feature was anticipating objections by an imaginary opponent and answering them before a reply could be offered. Note how the author of Wisdom puts speeches into the mouths of the "wicked" and then responds with withering criticism (cf. Wis 2:2-20 to 2:21—4:20). Also to be mentioned in regard to literary style is the fact that Wisdom, like the Greek rhetorical tradition, displays nice examples of alliteration, assonance, chiasmus (arrangement of a literary unit in the form of an a-b-b-a pattern), sorites (a chain pattern in which the predicate of each link is the subject of the next), syncrisis (a comparison) and catalogues.[47]

Other features of Wisdom show an acquaintance with concepts in Greek philosophy. A rather clear instance is in Wisdom 8:7, a listing of virtues: "for she [wisdom] teaches self-control and prudence, justice and courage." Plato and the Stoics considered these the four cardinal virtues. The reference to creation as arising out of formless matter (Wis 11:17) seems borrowed from Plato, although the Stoics too may have accepted this. The reference to "a perishable body [that] weighs down the soul" (Wis 9:15) sounds very much like Plato. The latter two ideas, by the way, stand in sharp antithesis to the biblical doctrine of creation. In Wisdom 8:19-20 the author seems to accept the Platonic idea of the preexistence of souls: "a good soul fell to my lot; or rather, being good, I entered an undefiled body." But the last part of that quotation asserts the Hebraic insistence upon the essential goodness of God's material creation.[48] A rather obvious instance of borrowing from Plato is Wisdom's insistence upon the immortality of the soul: "But the righteous live forever" (Wis 5:15; cf. 2:23; 3:1-9). It would seem that the unrighteous also continue to exist after death, though in torment (cf. Wis 3:10-19; 4:18-20; 17:21).

We conclude, therefore, that our author explicated the earlier ideas of wisdom found in Job 28, Proverbs 8:22-31 and Sirach 24 by borrowing the Stoic

---

[46]For further discussion, see S. E. Porter, "Diatribe," *DNTB*, pp. 296-98.

[47]Pfeiffer gives a detailed listing of examples in *History of New Testament Times*, pp. 329-34.

[48]See note on Wis 8:19-20 in *The New Oxford Annotated Bible: New Revised Standard Version*, ed. Bruce M. Metzger and Roland E. Murphy (New York: Oxford University Press, 1991), AP 68.

idea of the Logos. In so doing he has given the Hebrew wisdom traditions a metaphysical twist.[49] In this regard we have an example of the highest degree of assimilation of Greek thought in any of the literature we have read thus far. Only Philo will take this further. It is worth noting that, in contrast to Ben Sira and Baruch, Wisdom of Solomon does *not* identify wisdom with the Torah. This makes aligning our author with a particular sect of Judaism quite problematic. It simply points out again the considerable diversity that existed at this point in Jewish history.

There is a significant addition to Wisdom of Solomon that sets it apart from its predecessors. Included in Wisdom 10:1—11:4 is an appeal to salvation history as a part of the author's argument. Wisdom actively involved herself in the unfolding of the lives and events of the patriarchs. The lack of explicit appeal to Israel's salvation history has been a long-debated aspect of OT wisdom literature. What interface was there between the prophetic and wisdom traditions of ancient Israel? How do we account for the near absence of salvation history in the OT wisdom books? To be sure, Ben Sira includes a long encomium praising the fathers of Israel (Sir 44:1—50:21), but it does not function as a vital part of his argument, as it does in Wisdom of Solomon.

Why this should be so and what factors facilitated it are probably beyond our ability to recover. One of the hallmarks of Judaism during the Hellenistic age was its ability to synthesize Hellenism and the ancestral faith of Sinai. That synthesis involved new ways of understanding the old traditions. For our author, both sage and prophet must be heard. In other words, the timeless world of ideas (Hellenism) has not swallowed up history (Judaism). In fact, God's progressive, unfolding, saving plan provides *the* definitive framework from which one perceives reality. This insight may be the single most important contribution our author makes and is, at the very least, the prime example of his originality.

Importance for the New Testament
Donald A. Hagner asserts that "the influence of the book on the Early Christian Church appears to have been remarkable, and far surpasses all other OT

---

[49]So Metzger, *Introduction to the Apocrypha,* p. 73. So also Nickelsburg, *Jewish Literature,* p. 181; Winston, *Wisdom of Solomon,* p. 182. But Gilbert's assessment should be carefully considered: "Finally, the originality of Wisdom may be seen from the way it assimilates Hellenistic culture. Not only does the author write in Greek, use a Greek literary genre and take over, with due modifications, the Stoic doctrine of *pneuma,* but closely akin to the bible though he is, he adopts the imagery, vocabulary and theories of contemporary Stoicism, a component of Middle Platonism. But he shows no mastery of these philosophies. His knowledge, indirect, seems to derive only from his general education" ("Wisdom Literature," p. 312).

Apoc. [Apocrypha] in importance." [50] We concur. The evidence is as follows.

Pride of place belongs to the contribution that our work makes to NT Christology. We can offer only a brief discussion of a huge topic. [51] The key passage is Wisdom 7:22—8:1, which Hagner calls "the climax of all Jewish writing on wisdom." [52] What is impressive is the degree to which our author personifies wisdom. It is very close to what we call hypostatization, that is, the ascription of material existence to an abstraction; in this case, wisdom is hypostatized as a distinct person alongside God. [53]

Note the characteristics our author ascribes to wisdom. These phrases immediately bring to mind the manner in which Christians describe Jesus Christ in the NT. Three NT writers in particular are worthy of close comparison: Paul, John and the anonymous writer to the Hebrews. Each of these authors composes passages celebrating the person and work of Christ in language similar to Wisdom. Table 8.1 illustrates this more fully.

Table 8.1. Parallels between Wisdom of Solomon and the NT

"Because the spirit of the Lord has filled the world, and that which holds all things together *[kai to synechon ta panta]* knows what is said" (Wis 1:7).	". . . the fullness of him who fills all in all" (Eph 1:23). "He himself is before all things, and in him all things hold together *[kai ta panta en autō synestēken]*" (Col 1:17). "He sustains all things *[pherōn te ta panta]*" (Heb 1:3b).
"For she is a reflection of eternal light *[apaugasma gar esti phōtos aidiou]*, a spotless mirror of the working of God, and an image *[eikōn]* of his goodness" (Wis 7:26).	"He is the reflection *[apaugasma]* of God's glory and the exact imprint of God's very being" (Heb 1:3a). "The life was the light *[phōs]* of all people . . . the true light" (Jn 1:4b, 9a). "He is the image *[eikōn]* of the invisible God" (Col 1:15a).
". . . who have made all things by your word, and by your wisdom have formed humankind" (Wis 9:1b-2a).	"All things came into being through him, and without him not one thing came into being" (Jn 1:3).

---

[50]"Wisdom of Solomon," 5:948.

[51]The beginning student will find I. H. Marshall's little volume *The Origin of New Testament Christology* (Downers Grove, Ill.: InterVarsity Press, 1976) a helpful point of departure.

[52]"Wisdom of Solomon," 5:946.

[53]This despite Pfeiffer's strong protest: "The horrible word 'hypostasis' should be avoided entirely in this connection, since it is only a bone of contention among ancient Christians, and the only problem raised by our book is whether the author thought of wisdom as a person (or thing) distinct from God. Wisdom is strongly personified: is that mere

The contribution of Wisdom of Solomon can be more specifically set out as follows. One of the challenging tasks of NT theology is reconstructing the process whereby the earliest followers of Jesus ascribed to him a cosmic role in creation and redemption. In Rudolf Bultmann's famous dictum: "How did the proclaimer become the Proclaimed?"[54] That is, in the Synoptic Gospels Jesus' teaching focuses upon the kingdom of God and the God of the kingdom. Nowhere does he explicitly indicate his role in the original creation, nor do we have any clear indication that he would bring about a radically new creation on a cosmic scale.[55] But if not, was it the early church that gradually came to ascribe such functions to him? Is it true that a "high Christology" is the creation of individuals such as Paul, John and the later church fathers rather than being something that Jesus himself would have endorsed and believed?[56] This question is of crucial importance for Christians who still adhere to the ancient creeds of Christendom.

We summarize our reflections on this issue. First, within the ministry of Jesus there were several instances of "nature miracles." These included changing water to wine, multiplying loaves of bread and, especially, calming the storm and walking upon the Sea of Galilee. These miracles demonstrated

---

rhetoric or a real conviction of the author? Let better men decide" (*History of New Testament Times,* pp. 350-51). We claim not to be a "better man," simply unconvinced that ancient controversy is sufficient to side-step a legitimate question of both historical and theological importance. D. A. deSilva has no such qualms about the notion of hypostasis: "The figure of Wisdom . . . is developed to new heights of personification, even hypostatization" ("Wisdom of Solomon," p. 1271).

"He who formerly had been the *bearer* of the message was drawn into it and became its essential *content. The proclaimer became the proclaimed*—but the central question is: In what sense?" (*Theology of the New Testament,* trans. Kendrick Grobel [New York: Scribners, 1951, 1955], p. 33, emphasis original).

[55]One might wonder why this is the case. But if one thinks about it, Jesus' silence on this point becomes comprehensible. Being a master teacher, he followed the dictum: one must start with where the learners are and take them step by step to where you want them to go. Imagine Jesus informing his disciples that he had actually created the sun, moon, stars, earth and all that is in it—the reaction would have been incredulity; they would have thought him mad! Thus, there was a progressive unfolding of his true identity. The climactic revelation was, of course, the resurrection and ascension. Aiding in digesting this almost overwhelming reality—even today!—was the assistance of the Comforter, the Holy Spirit, who brought to remembrance what had been taught and led them into a fuller apprehension of the Truth.

[56]In this connection, James Dunn doubts that Paul himself actually taught a cosmic Christology in the ontological sense, i.e., that the preexistent Son of God, now known to us as Jesus Christ, was in fact the Creator of the universe. Dunn thinks this notion did not enter the church until the very end of the first century A.D. in the writings attributed to John. We have responded to this assertion in Larry R. Helyer, "Cosmic Christology and Col 1:15-20," *JETS* 37 (1994): 235-46. Cf. also the incisive remarks of G. B. Caird, *New Testament Theology* (Oxford: Clarendon Press, 1994), pp. 281-85.

that Jesus had authority over even the fundamental forces of nature. The Essenes of Qumran, by the way, already seemed to expect this capability of the Messiah. In a text called the *Messianic Apocalypse* (4Q521), we read: "[. . . For the hea]vens and the earth shall listen to his Messiah [and all w]hich is in them shall not turn away from the commandments of the holy ones."[57] Second, in his teaching Jesus assumed the prerogatives of God, such as forgiveness of sins (Mk 2:6-12). He spoke directly as an authoritative messenger of God himself. He could amend or even abrogate certain aspects of the sacrosanct Torah because, as the promised Messiah, he brought out its true and intended meaning (Mt 5:17-48).[58] He was thus Lord of the law and Lord of the sabbath (Mk 2:23-28). Third, he indicated that he would be present at the final assize—Daniel's "one like a son of man" (Dan 7:9-14; cf. Mt 16:27; 26:64). Thus he possessed an eschatological role that was truly cosmic in scope. Fourth, and of tremendous significance, was Jesus' resurrection. This event radically altered the disciples' conception of Jesus. Before this event, there were several occasions in which they inquired with bewilderment: "Who is this person?" After the resurrection they knew—he is Lord. Once this fundamental affirmation was made—and it appears to have been right after Jesus' resurrection—an immediate resource lay at hand. Following the lead of Jesus, who taught his disciples to read the OT christologically, they linked OT Scriptures to the saving deeds of Jesus by means of the promise-fulfillment pattern (cf. Lk 24:25-27, 44-49). Among those OT passages were ones in which the Lord (Yahweh) was portrayed as the mighty Creator. Some of these were then applied to Jesus the Lord. This can be seen in the series of OT quotations in Hebrews 1:5-13.[59]

But there is another piece to the puzzle of NT Christology. An important catalyst that made cosmic Christology possible derived from the wisdom tradition. Beginning already in Proverbs 8:22-31 there was a biblical precedent for the role of God's wisdom as preexistent before and instrumental in creation and providence. Second Temple Judaism carried this notion even further. Wisdom of Solomon represents the most advanced development, thus

---

[57]Translation of 4Q521 frags. 2 + 4 ii 1-2 by Martin Abegg Jr. in Michael Wise, Martin Abegg Jr. and Edward Cook, *The Dead Sea Scrolls: A New Translation* (New York: HarperCollins, 1999 [1996]), p. 421.

[58]For a defense of this understanding of what Jesus meant by "fulfilling the Law," see Donald A. Hagner, "Matthew," in *WBC on CD-ROM* (Logos Library System, version 2.0c, 1995, 1996).

[59]For a helpful discussion of the background and development of NT Christology, see G. B. Caird, *New Testament Theology* (Oxford: Clarendon Press, 1994), pp. 279-344. Also useful is C. F. D. Moule, *The Origin of Christology* (Cambridge: Cambridge University Press, 1977). For the catena in Heb 1:5-13, see Larry R. Helyer, "The Prototokos Title in the New Testament," *Studia Biblica et Theologica* 6 (1976): 3-28.

far, of this trajectory. As we argued above, we have something approaching, if not attaining, a hypostatization of Wisdom. The keen mind of the apostle Paul was already programmed with this background. It seems inconceivable that he could have studied at Jerusalem and not have known a work such as Wisdom of Solomon. Some might object that since Wisdom did not make it into the Hebrew canon, Pharisees would not have studied it. This assumes an insularity of Pharisaic thought that is unjustified. But beyond this, the similarity of thought between several Pauline passages and Wisdom of Solomon strongly suggests his awareness of it.

We draw attention to some striking parallels between the letters of Paul and Wisdom of Solomon. In the first place, Paul argues in Romans 1:19-25 that God's power and wisdom are clearly seen in creation itself:

> For what can be known about God is plain to them, because God has shown it to them. Ever since the creation of the world his eternal power and divine nature, invisible though they are, have been understood and seen through the things he has made. So they are without excuse; for though they knew God, they did not honor him as God or give thanks to him, but they became futile in their thinking, and their senseless minds were darkened. (Rom 1:19-21)

Listen to Wisdom make the similar point: "For all people who were ignorant of God were foolish by nature; and they were unable from the good things that are seen to know the one who exists, nor did they recognize the artisan while paying heed to his works" (Wis 13:1). Paul's description of the effects of idolatry upon pagan society echoes the same point pursued with some relish by Wisdom 11—14. Paul's discussion of God's sovereignty in Romans 9:19-23 resonates with language quite similar to Wisdom, as may be seen more clearly when we place the respective passages side by side, as in table 8.2.

Other parallels may be found listed in reference works and commentaries dealing with Wisdom. Though one may not justifiably say that Paul directly quotes Wisdom, we have marshaled enough evidence to conclude that Paul was influenced by certain ideas and phraseology found in the Wisdom of Solomon.[60] It should also be obvious from the above comparisons that Paul, like Wisdom, employed the diatribe style in his writing of Romans. Numerous passages, especially in Romans 2—6, 9, 11 and 14, feature the diatribe.[61]

Paul is not, however, the only NT writer to employ the category and terminology of preexistent Wisdom in framing a doctrine of the mediatorship of Christ in both the old and new creations, what we call "cosmic Christology."

---

[60]See further deSilva, "Wisdom of Solomon," p. 1274.
[61]See further D. F. Watson, "Diatribe," *DPL,* pp. 213-14; Porter, "Diatribe," pp. 296-98.

Table 8.2. God's sovereignty in Wisdom of Solomon and Romans

Wisdom of Solomon	Romans
"For who will say, 'What have you done?' Or will resist your judgment? Who will accuse you for the destruction of nations that you made? Or who will come before you to plead as an advocate for the unrighteous?" (Wis 12:12).	"You will say to me then, 'Why then does he still find fault? For who can resist his will?' " (Rom 9:19).
"A potter kneads the soft earth and laboriously molds each vessel for our service, fashioning out of the same clay both the vessels that serve clean uses and those for contrary uses, making all alike; but which shall be the use of each of them the worker in clay decides" (Wis 15:7).	"But who indeed are you, a human being, to argue with God? Will what is molded say to the one who molds, it, 'Why have you made me like this?' Has the potter no right over the clay, to make out of the same lump one object for special use and another for ordinary use?" (Rom 9:20-21).

The prologues of John's Gospel and the book of Hebrews also reflect indebtedness to the wisdom tradition. To be sure, they go well beyond the received wisdom traditions in that they *incarnate* Wisdom in the person of Jesus Christ. In this regard their thought represents "one great leap for mankind."[62] Here we have an unquestioned instance of hypostasis. The early church fathers and ecumenical creeds simply elaborated upon what was already present *in nuce* in the NT.[63] But in all this, let us not forget that Ben Sira, the author of Baruch and especially Wisdom of Solomon, in a real sense contributed toward the formulation of NT Christology. They provided a crucial category that Christians adapted and incorporated in order to express the almost inexpressible: "the knowledge of the glory of God in the face of Jesus Christ" (2 Cor 4:6). "He is the image of the invisible God" (Col 1:15), "the reflection of God's glory and the exact imprint of God's very being" (Heb 1:3), and the Word of God who was with God in the beginning and was God (Jn 1:1). Furthermore, he is the one in whom, through whom and for whom all things were created, indeed, the one who holds all things together (cf. Jn 1:3; 1 Cor 8:6; Col 1:15-17; Heb 1:2-3).

---

[62]With due credit to Neil Armstrong's famous statement as he stepped off the Apollo lander to the surface of the moon in July 1969.

[63]Donald A. Hagner observes in this connection: "It may certainly be said, however, that the early Christian formulations of the doctrine of the Trinity in language and concept, often bear a great resemblance to our author's discussion of wisdom and her relationship to God, and that the latter not only anticipated, but to some extent prepared the way for those formulations" ("Wisdom of Solomon," 5:948).

We noted above that a unique contribution of Wisdom lay in its insistence that salvation history provides the interpretive framework for understanding reality. There is one NT work in particular that shares this perspective, namely, Hebrews. Interestingly, this work may also have Alexandrian roots, especially if we connect its authorship with Apollos (Acts 18:24). However that may be, there can be little doubt that the author of Hebrews operated within the framework of an eschatological dualism (i.e., a contrast between the present age and the age to come). At first glance, Hebrews seems to reflect a vertical or cosmological dualism (a contrast between the heavenly, eternal ideas and their earthly, temporal shadows), after the fashion of Plato and Philo. But this is not really determinative for Hebrews.[64] Like Wisdom, Hebrews refuses to let go of salvation history in favor of a retreat into the ahistorical world of Greek "ideas." Unfortunately, this is precisely what the Gnosticism of the second and third centuries A.D. did.[65]

Finally, we note three passages in Wisdom that were misinterpreted by some early Christian fathers and fancifully applied to Jesus. The first is in Wisdom 14:7: "For blessed is the wood by which righteousness comes." Though often interpreted as a reference to the cross, the context makes clear that it refers to Noah's ark. The second has more plausibility. Wisdom 2:12-20 bears some resemblance to the Synoptic Gospels' description of the scoffing and derision of the religious leaders at Jesus' crucifixion (cf. Mt 27:43). But as Metzger points out, the author of Wisdom may just as well have been indebted to the stories in the books of Maccabees or Glaucon's description in Plato's *Republic* of a just man's martyrdom.[66] Finally, an eloquent passage in Wisdom 18:15-16a was taken by many church fathers as a reference to the incarnation: "Your all-powerful word leaped from heaven, from the royal throne, into the midst of the land that was doomed, a stern warrior carrying the sharp sword of your authentic command." As one can see, the context does not support such a fanciful interpretation, since the passage is speaking of the events surrounding the exodus from Egypt.[67]

3 Maccabees

Introduction

Despite its name, this work has nothing to do with 1 and 2 Maccabees but is rather a fictional story about a dire threat of extermination for the entire Jew-

---

[64]In fact, some modern scholars suggest more plausibly that the background of Hebrews lies in apocalyptic Judaism rather than in Philonic adaptations of Plato. See Lane, *Hebrews*, pp. ciii-cx.

[65]See further on this E. M. Yamauchi, "Gnosticism," *DNTB*, pp. 414-18.

[66]*Introduction to the Apocrypha*, p. 76.

[67]Ibid.

ish community of Egypt. As such, it clearly recalls the book of Esther set in the Persian Empire. The underlying concern of *Aristeas* and Wisdom of Solomon about the possible rejection of Jews and Judaism by pagan neighbors is not merely a theoretical issue in 3 Maccabees, but a grim reality. The story has a historical core, since there were periodic pogroms (organized and often officially encouraged massacres or persecutions of a minority group) that erupted in Egypt and Alexandria in particular. The precarious nature of Jewish life in Diaspora confronts us dramatically in this historical novel or romance. Whereas all turns out well in this story, the historical reality is that many such incidents did not. We need to read this story with that in mind.

Author and Date

As we now have it, 3 Maccabees begins abruptly with an account of a military campaign and the contribution of a certain apostate Jew by the name of Dositheus. Scholars are agreed that the beginning of the story is lost. Another reference in the work to an episode assumed as already known by the reader (3 Macc 2:25) confirms that something is missing. Thus we are bereft of any clues that a prologue may have provided. Since we do not have even the literary device of an assumed name, as in *Aristeas,* we are once again dealing with an anonymous author. Given the fact that the major concern of the book centers on the Jewish people, our author is almost certainly Jewish. Parallels to the previously discussed works above lead to the inference that our author was likewise an Alexandrian Jew.[68]

The outside dates for the composition are the Battle of Raphia in 217 B.C. (since that is narrated in 3 Macc 1:1) and the fall of Jerusalem to the Romans in A.D. 70 (since temple services are viewed as still continuing in 3 Macc 1:9). If weight be given to the literary affinities of our work to 2 Maccabees and *Letter of Aristeas,* its composition would fall into the latter part of the second century or the first part of the first century B.C.[69]

Outline and Synopsis

The outline in *The New Oxford Annotated Bible* helpfully draws attention to the careful construction of this piece. We reproduce the outline as follows:[70]

A Ptolemy's threat to desecrate the temple (1:1-29)

B Simon's prayer of intercession (divine intercession) (2:1-24)

---

[68]For a full discussion of sources that may have been utilized by or influenced this work, see Moses Hadas, *The Third and Fourth Book of Maccabees,* JAL (New York: Harper, 1953), pp. 6-16.
[69]H. Wolf ("Maccabees, Books of," *ZPEB* 4:18) summarizes the arguments for a first-century B.C. dating and is followed by D. A. deSilva, "3 and 4 Maccabees," *DNTB,* p. 662.
[70]AP 285.

C Ptolemy's cruel treatment of the Jews (2:25—4:13)
D Thwarting the registration (divine intervention) (4:14-21)
C' Ptolemy's cruel treatment of the Jews (5:1-51)
B' Eleazar's prayer of intercession (divine intervention) (6:1-29)
A' Ptolemy's deliverance and defense of the Jews (6:30—7:23)

As indicated in the outline, the arrangement of the work is in concentric circles, with the hinge being the episode whereby the registration is thwarted in 3 Maccabees 4:14-21. The story itself is about a Ptolemaic king, Philopator, who acts arrogantly and with murderous intent against the Jewish people, just as Antiochus Epiphanes had done earlier. Recalling motifs from Esther, the story narrates how Philopator became incensed when he was not permitted to enter the most holy place in the Jerusalem temple. This snub festered into a plan to exterminate all Jews in Egypt, just as the wicked Haman had deigned to do in the book of Esther. The whole point of the story is the deliverance. Against all odds, the entire Jewish community of Egypt, having been transported to a great stadium for a public spectacle of mass execution, was spared by a series of divine interventions. The author narrates the story in the style of "pathetic history" after the pattern of 2 Maccabees. Appeal to emotion is uppermost. The story itself is beyond credibility and is clearly designed to entertain as well as persuade. The stays of execution give evidence of a "dark humor" that characterizes so much of later Jewish literature and entertainment. Here too we see a parallel with 2 Maccabees and its description of Antiochus's death throes (2 Macc 9:5-29).

Purpose

As in *Aristeas* and Wisdom of Solomon, 3 Maccabees is primarily an exhortation to the Jewish community and, by application, to the Jewish Diaspora to remain faithful to the ancestral tradition even in the face of threats to their very existence. Shining forth from the pages of this story is a firm belief in the "invincible providence of him who was aiding the Jews from heaven" (3 Macc 4:21; cf. 7:6). Besides encouraging wavering Jews, the storyline also conveys a stiff warning: more than three hundred Jews who had apostatized under duress were put to death (3 Macc 7:10-15).

On the other hand, 3 Maccabees has a slightly different tack to the problem of Jews living in Diaspora from either *Aristeas* or Wisdom. The latter two works seem much more open and accepting of Hellenistic culture, without, of course, abandoning the basic commitment to the ancestral faith. In contrast, 3 Maccabees is not as sanguine about or open to acculturation. Furthermore, 3 Maccabees seems to correct the view implied in Esther. The degree of assimilation in Esther is considerably more than that found in our Alexandrian Jewish literature.[71] Thus 3 Maccabees tries to find a middle ground in this delicate and often dangerous task of living among the Gentiles.[72]

Features

This work depicts anti-Semitism as a deadly reality for Jews already in the pre-Christian era.[73] Of special note are the various accusations and calumnies hurled at them. They are listed in the order in which they appear within the story:

1. "they hindered others from the observance of their customs" (3:2).
2. "they kept their separateness with respect to foods" (3:4).
3. "they appeared hateful to some" (3:4; cf. 4:1: "inveterate enmity").
4. "loyal neither to the king nor to his authorities, but were hostile and greatly opposed to his government" (3:7).
5. "those wicked people who never cease from their folly" (3:16).
6. "they were carried away by their traditional arrogance. . . . They become the only people among all nations who hold their heads high in defiance of kings and their own benefactors, and are unwilling to regard any action as sincere" (3:18-19).
7. "in their innate malice . . . they incline constantly to evil" (3:22).

What is startling in this list is how contemporary it sounds. Modern anti-Semitism basically continues this litany of imagined but unfounded Jewish stereotypes. About all that is lacking from 3 Maccabees is some notion of financial wizardry and manipulation of the media! There is even implied in 3 Maccabees 3:26 a very common theme among modern anti-Semites, namely, a conspiracy to control the government: "We are sure that for the remaining time the government will be established for ourselves in good order and in the best state."

The mysterious phenomenon of anti-Semitism has a core of recurring stereotypes that are constantly recycled from one generation to another.[74] Among these are the following: (1) the avaricious Jew; (2) the disloyal Jew;

---

[71]We are here speaking of the Hebrew Esther. The LXX additions to Esther clearly modify the viewpoint of the earlier Hebrew version by providing a religious dimension and "explaining" the problem of Esther's intermarriage with a Gentile. See Nickelsburg, *Jewish Literature*, pp. 172-75.

[72]See further Hadas, *Third and Fourth Book of Maccabees*, p. 24.

[73]There is a semantic problem here in using the term "anti-Semitism," which was not even coined until the end of the nineteenth century, for the phenomenon that would more accurately for our period be called anti-Judaism. Nonetheless, we do not think the reader will be misled since it conveys what was originally intended and is an expression widely used and recognized.

[74]For a thorough survey of anti-Semitism, see Anthony Lerman, Julia Schopflin and Howard Spier, "Anti-Semitism," in *EncJud on CD-ROM* (Judaica Multimedia, version 1.0, 1997).

(3) the egocentric and exclusive Jew; (4) the immoral Jew; and (5) the intellectual and successful Jew.[75] Unfortunately, even some very conservative Christians perpetuate these stereotypes.[76] This shameful state of affairs is a betrayal of the heritage to which we are indebted and stands at odds with the basic thrust of NT teaching. It behooves us to be vigilant in our efforts to prevent such a "root of bitterness" (Heb 12:15) from springing up in our society.[77]

Let us note the actual steps that are mentioned in the spiral of persecution devised by Philopator. First he openly slandered the Jews among his high-ranking officials (3 Macc 2:26). This did not go unheeded. As always, those who would climb to the top in politics "trim their sails to the winds." It was evident to them that the king "proposed to inflict public disgrace on the Jewish community" (3 Macc 2:27). This created a climate in which "Jew-bashing" would be acceptable. Second, the king took away the civil rights of Jews in his kingdom. They were subjected to a poll tax and reduced in status to slaves (3 Macc 2:28). Any Jews who objected were immediately executed (3 Macc 2:28). This decree was publicly promulgated so that all citizens knew of this new status for Jews (3 Macc 2:27). Third, all Jews were required to wear an identifying badge, a tattoo in the form of an ivy-leaf, a symbol of the Greek god Dionysus. There was an "out" for Jews, however. If they became devotees of Dionysus, as evidenced by their initiation into the mysteries (secret rites and ceremonies), they could possess Alexandrian citizenship. Thus, their only escape hatch lay in conversion to paganism.

When but a small minority took advantage of this option and the majority sought by bribes to avoid implementation of the decree, Philopator was enraged and resorted to more draconian measures. He put in motion his "final solution,"[78] a plan to exterminate all Jews throughout Egypt. In order to secure public support for such a horrific undertaking, he circulated rumors about the danger of Jews to the public welfare. They were por-

---

[75]See the study of anti-Semitism among various Christian groups by Charles Y. Glock and Rodney Stark, *Christian Beliefs and Anti-Semitism* (New York: Harper, 1966).

[76]As a sad example of this, see Theodore Winston Pike, *Israel Our Duty . . . Our Dilemma* (Oregon City, Ore.: Big Sky, 1984). For earlier examples such as Gerald Winrod, see David A. Rausch, *Fundamentalist Evangelicals and Anti-Semitism* (Valley Forge, Penn.: Trinity Press International, 1993).

[77]For helpful direction in becoming aware of anti-Semitism and taking steps to combat it, see David A. Rausch, *A Legacy of Hatred: Why Christians Must Not Forget the Holocaust* (Chicago: Moody Press, 1984); Rausch, *Building Bridges* (Chicago: Moody Press, 1988); Marvin R. Wilson, *Our Father Abraham: Jewish Roots of the Christian Faith* (Grand Rapids, Mich.: Eerdmans; Dayton: Center for Judaic-Christian Studies, 1989).

[78]An anachronistic use of the Nazi plan, implemented in 1942, to exterminate Jews in the death camps by using Zyklon B gas.

trayed as despicable and worthy of death. Official letters, sent to leading military figures throughout the country, castigated the Jews as state enemies, disloyal to the crown and just waiting for the opportunity to overthrow the government (3 Macc 3:12-24). The leaders were ordered to round up all Jews—men, women and children—bind them with iron fetters, inflict them with "insulting and harsh treatment" and send them to a place to be determined for mass execution (3 Macc 3:25). If anyone should disobey the edict, the same fate was to befall that person. In addition, the king offered as reward any information concerning Jews who might be hiding. The homes of those sheltering Jews would be burned to the ground (3 Macc 3:28-29).

The shocking thing about the decree was its jubilant acceptance by the general public. Our author simply notes that "the inveterate enmity that had long ago been in their minds was now made evident and outspoken" (3 Macc 4:1). He further graphically describes the rounding-up process and deportation: "In bonds and in public view they were violently dragged along as far as the place of embarkation. . . . They were brought on board like wild animals. . . . They were confined under a solid deck, so that, with their eyes in total darkness, they would undergo treatment befitting traitors during the whole voyage" (3 Macc 4:7, 9-10). Once at the hippodrome, the Jews were locked in and isolated from all outside contact.

To be sure, the author narrates this section with "purple prose" for rhetorical effect,[79] but anyone who has read about the Holocaust or seen movies dealing with the Nazi death camps—such as *Schindler's List*—can hardly read this without a sense of *déjà vu*. This whole episode, narrated no later than the first century A.D., has an unnerving similarity to Hitler's "war against the Jews" in World War II. It is almost as if the Nazis incorporated these very pages for the implementation of Hitler's "final solution."[80] Of course, the "final solution" of Philopator was carried out not with the bureaucratic efficiency of the isolated Nazi death camps but with a circus and carnival atmosphere. The hippodrome (an oval-shaped stadium for horse and chariot racing) of Alexandria was selected as the site of execution. The means of death devised by Philopator was by five hundred enraged elephants (drugged by frankincense and wine), which were supposed to trample some hundreds of thousands of Jews for the entertainment of the crowds. This, of course, stretches credulity to the breaking point. Many scholars suggest that our author has incorporated a legend at

---

[79]See Hadas, *Third and Fourth Book of Maccabees*, pp. 5-6, 15, 22.
[80]There are many good resources for pursuing this further. For a useful overview, see Rausch, *Legacy of Hatred*, pp. 53-146.

this point.[81] We should not, however, let this obscure the main point, namely, that murderous anti-Semitic attitudes existed already in major cities of the Diaspora. The book of Esther depicts a similar situation in the Persian era; the situation was little different in Ptolemaic Egypt.

Before leaving this topic, however, we draw attention to one bright spot. The author mentions that "some of their neighbors and friends and business associates had taken some of them aside privately and were pledging to protect them and to exert more earnest efforts for their assistance" (3 Macc 3:10). Thankfully, there were then, as there were during the Nazi regime, a few "righteous Gentiles" who stood against anti-Semitism.

Relevance for the New Testament

The book of 3 Maccabees is an important reminder that anti-Semitism was "in the air" when Christianity sprang up from its Jewish roots. In time, tragically, Christians would contribute to the persistence and virulence of anti-Semitism. We will say more about that in chapter fourteen. For now, however, we bring to the reader's attention evidences from NT literature of anti-Semitism on the part of pagans. In fact, early Christians had to contend with this phenomenon themselves, because for several decades Christianity was considered a sect of Judaism. Some of the onus of anti-Judaic sentiment was transferred by association to this new movement.

Our best source for this is the book of Acts. Several incidents reflect anti-Judaic attitudes and actions. For example, when Paul and Silas were in Philippi, an incident occurred that manifested the hostility Gentiles had toward Jews generally. After exorcising a demon from a slave girl who provided a good income for her owners by divination, Paul was hauled before the magistrates. The slave girl's owners charged, "These men are disturbing our city; they are Jews and are advocating customs that are not lawful for us as Romans to adopt or observe" (Acts 16:20b-21). Rather than settling this in court, however, the crowd "joined in attacking them, and the magistrates had them stripped of their clothing and ordered them to be beaten with rods" (Acts 16:22). In time this precipitous punishment without due process occasioned much embarrassment and concern when the officials learned that Paul was a Roman citizen. Yet the point is that in response to Jews, a crowd and authorities reacted with considerable venom.

This is not an isolated event, as may be seen in several other instances

---

[81] Hadas observes: "The number would strike an ancient reader as so fantastic (the 73 elephants Philopator had at Raphia were impressive) that he would likely adjust his reception, as the author doubtless intended he should, to the key of romance rather than history" (*Third and Fourth Book of Maccabees*, p. 60, note on v. 2). See also H. Anderson, "3 Maccabees: A New Translation and Introduction," *OTP* 2:511.

related in Acts. In Acts 18 the Jewish community sought to halt Paul's successful ministry in Corinth by taking him before the proconsul Gallio. Their strategy appears to have been to charge Paul with propagating a cult not recognized by the Roman imperial government (cf. Acts 17:7). The technical term for this was *religio illicita* (an unsanctioned religion). If Gallio had indeed upheld such a charge, it would have been a serious setback for Paul's missionary effort. What happened was quite contrary to the Jewish community's expectations. Gallio dismissed the case without a hearing (Acts 18:14-16). Apparently he considered Christianity a sect of Judaism, a *religio licita* (a sanctioned religion). It is what happens next, however, that is relevant for our discussion: "Then all of them seized Sosthenes, the official of the synagogue, and beat him in front of the tribunal. But Gallio paid no attention to any of these things" (Acts 18:17). While there is some ambiguity as to the identity of "all of them," we think the most likely interpretation is that they were lictors, the equivalent of our police. The fact that they could "rough up" the Jewish litigants in the tribunal without Gallio paying the least attention speaks volumes about latent anti-Semitic attitudes at the highest level of government as well as among the masses.[82]

A third instance narrated by Luke occurred when Paul was in Ephesus, the Roman provincial capital of Asia, in modern western Turkey. Once again Paul's success in evangelizing Gentiles led to trouble. The silversmiths, led by a certain Demetrius, sought to curb his influence, inasmuch as the demand for the silver figurines of the goddess Artemis had greatly declined, owing to large numbers of converts to Christianity. A massive demonstration was staged at the large theater of Ephesus, capable of holding some twenty thousand spectators. Luke notes that most of the participants did not even know why they were there (Acts 19:32)!

Because the disturbance was over the goddess Artemis, some of the Jewish citizens of Ephesus put forward one of their own, no doubt an official of some standing in the city, to "make a defense before the people" (Acts 19:33). Why did they do this? Almost certainly because the Jews did not want to be

---

[82]Conrad Gempf, however, offers a different view. He notes that "groundless prosecution was a serious problem in the Roman world at this time, and during Paul's lifetime laws were being passed to discourage the practice of accusing enemies in order to have them locked up for a time when one had no real case against them" ("Acts," in *New Bible Commentary: 21st Century Edition*, ed. G. J. Wenham, J. A. Motyer, D. A. Carson and R. T. France [Downers Grove, Ill.: InterVarsity Press, 1994], p. 1095). Even so, a public beating is not the same as a lockup. We doubt that Greek citizens would have been so treated. We think Craig S. Keener is closer to the mark when he observes that this episode "betrays more than a tinge of Roman impatience for Jewish religious disputes. Many upper class Romans viewed Jews as uncultured troublemakers" (*The IVP Bible Background Commentary: New Testament* [Downers Grove, Ill.: InterVarsity Press, 1993], p. 376).

considered the cause of the turmoil about Artemis. The strong rejection of idolatry by Jews was well known. The Ephesian Jewish community did not want to bear the brunt of any retaliation for perceived insults against paganism.[83] Perhaps the Jews even thought they had an opportunity to direct the wrath of the masses against Paul and the Christians. The response of the mob toward Alexander's attempt to silence them, however, speaks volumes: "But when they recognized that he was a Jew, for about two hours all of them shouted in unison, 'Great is Artemis of the Ephesians!' " (Acts 19:34). Hostility toward Jews is unmistakable in this incident.

Because of the origin of the church in Judaism and the continuation of some of Judaism's central beliefs, it is no surprise that pagans also reacted strongly against early Christianity. Whereas "boundary markers" such as circumcision, dietary laws and sacred seasons were no longer binding on Gentile converts—and thus less likely to engender hostility from pagans—Christians, like Jews, affirmed ethical monotheism and forbade involvement in idolatry (cf. 1 Cor 8—10, esp. 8:6; 1 Jn 5:21; Rev 2:14-16, 20-22). Likewise, 1 Peter 4:4 speaks of a situation that was no doubt widespread: "They [pagans] are surprised that you no longer join them in the same excesses of dissipation, and so they blaspheme." There were also "cultured despisers" as well, like the Areopagus crowd, who balked at Christianity's insistence upon the resurrection of Christ as the lynchpin of the gospel (Acts 17:32; cf. 1 Cor 15).

Very early on Christianity was accused of being atheistic, hostile toward non-Christians and disloyal to the empire. Most of these accusations grew out of misperceptions because Christians no longer supported the imperial cults by burning incense to Caesar or to the patron deities so important to the ideology of the Roman imperial state. Thus, in the first two centuries of the church's existence, there was a residual hostility transferred from Jews to Christians. This is not to say that Jews no longer experienced hostility and persecution but rather that Christians *also* came under fire for some of the same reasons.

Finally, we draw attention to a term used in 3 Maccabees that throws light on NT usage. It is the term *epiphaneia* ("manifestation"). Several times the author employs the word to magnify God's mighty acts and mercy in the course of history (cf. 3 Macc 2:9, 19; 5:8, 35, 51; 6:18). Six times this term is used in the NT, each time in connection with the anticipated return of Jesus Christ on the last day (2 Thess 2:8; 1 Tim 6:14; 2 Tim 1:10; 4:1, 8; Tit 2:13). "NT use of ἐπιφάνεια signifies that in the Christ-event God has appeared in the world and believers are summoned before the appearance of the judge of

---

[83]Keener, *IVP Bible Background Commentary,* p. 381.

the world in decision, confession, and responsive action."[84] We are not suggesting literary dependence but simply the taking over of a Hellenistic concept and filling it with a distinctly Christian content.

For Further Discussion

1. Compare and contrast the view of women in the *Letter of Aristeas* and the NT.

2. How did the LXX affect Judaism and Christianity?

3. Compare the stance toward pagan Gentiles in the *Letter of Aristeas,* the Wisdom of Solomon and the NT.

4. Why is Wisdom of Solomon important for NT Christology?

5. What similarities are there between the anti-Judaism seen in 3 Maccabees and modern manifestations of anti-Semitism?

6. What features of Judaism adopted by Christians caused a strong negative reaction from pagans?

For Further Reading

Aristeas

H. Andrews, "The Letter of Aristeas," in *The Apocrypha and Pseudepigrapha of the Old Testament,* ed. R. H. Charles, 2 vols. (Oxford: Oxford University Press, 1913), 2:83-122.

C. C. Caragounis, "Aristeas, Epistle of," *DNTB,* pp. 114-18.

M. Hadas, *Aristeas to Philocrates,* JAL (New York: Harper, 1951).

Burton L. Mack and Roland E. Murphy, "Wisdom Literature," in *Early Judaism and Its Modern Interpreters,* ed. Robert A. Kraft and George W. E. Nickelsburg (Philadelphia: Fortress; Atlanta: Scholars Press, 1986), pp. 378-79.

G. W. E. Nickelsburg, *Jewish Literature Between the Bible and the Mishnah: A Historical and Literary Introduction* (Philadelphia: Fortress, 1981), pp. 165-69.

————, "Stories of Biblical and Early Post-Biblical Times," in *Jewish Writings of the Second Temple Period: Apocrypha, Pseudepigrapha, Qumran Sectarian Writings, Philo, Josephus,* ed. Michael E. Stone, CRINT 2 (Assen: Van Gorcum; Philadelphia: Fortress, 1984), pp. 75-80.

R. J. H. Shutt, "Letter of Aristeas," in *The Old Testament Pseudepigrapha,* ed. James H. Charlesworth, 2 vols. (New York: Doubleday, 1983), 2:7-34.

James C. VanderKam, *An Introduction to Early Judaism* (Grand Rapids, Mich.: Eerdmans, 2001), pp. 81-85.

3 Maccabees

H. Anderson, "3 Maccabees," in *The Old Testament Pseudepigrapha,* ed. James H.

---

[84]P.-G. Müller, "ἐπιφάνεια," *EDNT,* 2:44.

Charlesworth, 2 vols. (New York: Doubleday, 1983), 2:509-16.

John J. Collins, "3 Maccabees: Introduction," in *The HarperCollins Study Bible: New Revised Standard Version* (New York: HarperCollins, 1993), pp. 1752-54.

D. A. deSilva, "3 and 4 Maccabees," *DNTB,* pp. 661-63.

M. Hadas, *The Third and Fourth Books of Maccabees,* JAL (New York: Harper, 1953).

Daniel J. Harrington, *Invitation to the Apocrypha* (Grand Rapids, Mich.: Eerdmans, 1999), pp. 173-84.

George W. E. Nickelsburg, *Jewish Literature Between the Bible and the Mishnah: A Historical and Literary Introduction* (Philadelphia: Fortress, 1981), pp. 169-72.

————, "Stories of Biblical and Early Post-Biblical Times," in *Jewish Writings of the Second Temple Period: Apocrypha, Pseudepigrapha, Qumran Sectarian Writings, Philo, Josephus,* ed. Michael E. Stone, CRINT 2 (Assen: Van Gorcum; Philadelphia: Fortress, 1984), pp. 80-84.

James C. VanderKam, *An Introduction to Early Judaism* (Grand Rapids, Mich.: Eerdmans, 2001), pp. 78-81.

Wisdom of Solomon

D. A. deSilva, "Wisdom of Solomon," *DNTB,* pp. 1268-76.

Donald A. Hagner, "Wisdom of Solomon," *ZPEB* 5:945-49.

Daniel J. Harrington, *Invitation to the Apocrypha* (Grand Rapids, Mich.: Eerdmans, 1999), pp. 55-77.

M. Gilbert, "Wisdom Literature," in *Jewish Writings of the Second Temple Period: Apocrypha, Pseudepigrapha, Qumran Sectarian Writings, Philo, Josephus,* ed. Michael E. Stone, CRINT 2 (Assen: Van Gorcum; Philadelphia: Fortress, 1984), pp. 301-13.

Lester L. Grabbe, *Wisdom of Solomon* (Sheffield: Sheffield Academic Press, 1997).

Burton L. Mack and Roland E. Murphy, "Wisdom Literature," in *Early Judaism and Its Modern Interpreters,* ed. Robert A. Kraft and George W. E. Nickelsburg (Philadelphia: Fortress; Atlanta: Scholars Press, 1986), pp. 380-87.

Bruce M. Metzger, *An Introduction to the Apocrypha* (New York: Oxford University Press, 1957), pp. 65-76.

George W. E. Nickelsburg, *Jewish Literature Between the Bible and the Mishnah: A Historical and Literary Introduction* (Philadelphia: Fortress, 1981), pp. 175-85.

James C. VanderKam, *An Introduction to Early Judaism* (Grand Rapids, Mich.: Eerdmans, 2001), pp. 138-42.

David Winston, *The Wisdom of Solomon,* AB 43 (New York: Doubleday, 1979).

Nine

Philo Judaeus

*F*or Philo we make use of The Works of Philo: Complete and Unabridged, *new ed., trans. C. D. Yonge (Peabody, Mass.; Hendrickson, 1993). For those who would like to have the critical edition of the Greek text with a facing English translation, see F. H. Colson, G. H. Whitaker and R. Markus, eds. Philo, 10 vols. and 2 supplementary vols., LCL (Cambridge, Mass.: Harvard University Press, 1927-1962).*

Introduction

For a good grasp of the Western intellectual tradition, familiarity with Philo of Alexandria is a necessity. Given the fact that, after Aristotle, he is the only writer whose philosophical writings exist beyond mere fragments and that he alone among Diaspora Jews has left behind any extensive corpus, one may readily appreciate his importance. He remains a prime example of the degree to which Hellenism influenced Judaism. For this reason he is essential for understanding Diaspora Judaism as well as the NT.

First, however, we summarize what may be known about his life.[1] He was a contemporary of both Jesus of Nazareth (c. 6/5 B.C.-A.D. 30-33) and the apostle Paul (c. A.D. 1-c. 64-68). Philo is generally reckoned to have been born around 20 B.C., to have lived to at least A.D. 40, when he represented

---

[1]For a good summary of Philo's life and background, see Peder Borgen, "Philo of Alexandria," in *Jewish Writings of the Second Temple Period: Apocrypha, Pseudepigrapha, Qumran Sectarian Writings, Philo, Josephus,* ed. Michael E. Stone, CRINT 2 (Assen: Van Gorcum; Philadelphia: Fortress, 1984), pp. 252-59; and G. E. Sterling, "Philo," *DNTB,* pp. 789-90.

the Alexandrian Jewish community before the Roman emperor Caligula, and probably to have died around A.D. 45-50. As already indicated, Philo lived his entire life in Alexandria, Egypt. He must have been held in high regard by the Jewish community of Alexandria, since he was selected to head up the Jewish delegation arguing their case before Caligula in the aftermath of a pogrom in A.D. 38. Unfortunately, we know few details about his personal life. He never mentions a wife or children. He had a brother named Alexander, who served in the Roman administration of Egypt and contributed his own money to plate the gates of the Jerusalem temple. This indicates that Philo's family was quite wealthy and also explains why he had the leisure to be a man of letters. He also had a nephew, Tiberius Alexander, who served in various capacities for Rome, including stints as procurator of Palestine and prefect of Egypt. Tiberius, in contrast to Philo, became thoroughly assimilated to Greco-Roman society and was not an observant Jew, a source of deep concern for Philo.[2]

Philo undoubtedly received a typical Jewish training as a youth, but his first language was Greek, not Hebrew. He was educated in the standard Greek curriculum, as evidenced from his writings. He was also familiar with Greek history, literature and philosophy. By temperament and inclination, Philo was drawn to philosophy and contemplation. Though forced by necessity and a sense of duty to fulfill throughout his adult life civic responsibilities to the Jewish community as well as the larger Gentile community of Alexandria, his real love was the pursuit of integrating faith and learning.[3]

His Writings

The best word to describe the extent of Philo's writings is voluminous. They occupy twelve volumes in the standard Loeb edition, and this is only what has been preserved! Many works have not survived or exist only in a fragmentary state. Can we somehow classify this mass of material into identifiable divisions? At the risk of oversimplification, we may say that generally Philo's writings fall into three major divisions: (1) apologetic works addressed to Gentiles; (2) exegetical and expositional works designed to illustrate how

---

[2]R. M. Wilson observes: "Living as they did in a predominantly gentile environment, exposed daily to the attractions of Hellenistic culture, the Jews of Alexandria were constantly tempted to abandon their ancestral faith and conform to the customs of their neighbors. The case of Tiberius Alexander is significant, since he could not have held the offices he did without relaxing his observance of the Jewish faith. There were presumably others who, whether for the material advantage to be gained or because of the attractions of an apparently superior culture and philosophy, turned away from Judaism and became completely assimilated to their gentile neighbors" ("Philo Judaeus," *ISBE*, 3:847).

[3]For a nice summary of Philo's nature, see J. N. Birdsall, "Philo," *NBD*, p. 923.

the biblical and Greek sources are really complementary (sometimes called the *Exposition of the Law*); and (3) a consecutive series of treatises (often called the *Allegory of the Jewish Law*), devoted primarily to passages found in Genesis.[4] The latter is considered to be Philo's major and most developed work.[5] We will select portions from each of these three major divisions. The first two divisions seem directed to Gentiles or to Jews who had thoroughly assimilated to Hellenistic culture. The third division assumes an audience that already understands Philo's hermeneutical method. Two of Philo's surviving works are historical essays *(Against Flaccus* and *On the Embassy to Gaius)* designed to respond to the unrest that erupted between Gentiles and Jews during the reign of Caligula (A.D. 12-41).

The Historical Essays

Against Flaccus. We begin with this work in order to illustrate the ongoing tension between Jews and Gentiles and the increased virulence of anti-Semitism in the Roman imperial age, especially in the large city of Alexandria, Egypt. Philo tells us that no fewer than a million Jews lived in Alexandria and the rest of Egypt (*Flacc.* 43).

Basically this is an account of a Roman governor of Egypt who, after exercising his sovereignty with admirable skill and justice for some five years, inexplicably turned venomous in his hatred of the Jews and sought by several degrading and barbaric measures to destroy them. His murderous designs, however, were at last overturned by the providence of God, who keeps watch over his people Israel and delivers them from such tyrants.

This account has similarities to 3 Maccabees, also set in Alexandria, with its graphic account of an Egyptian pogrom. The narrative of Flaccus's downfall, including arrest, accusations by former underlings, public humiliation, banishment and gruesome execution, is written in a style that reminds us of the demise of Antiochus Epiphanes in 2 Maccabees 9:5-29. In the end, Philo places in Flaccus's mouth this acknowledgment:

> O King of gods and men! you are not, then, indifferent to the Jewish nation, nor are the assertions which they relate with respect to your providence false; but those men who say that that people has not you for their champion and defender, are far from a correct opinion. And I am an evident proof of this; for all the frantic designs, which I conceived against the Jews, I now suffer myself. (*Flacc.* 170)[6]

---

[4]For a fivefold division, see Sterling, "Philo," pp. 790-91.
[5]See E. R. Goodenough, "Philo Judeus," *IDB* 3:796-97.
[6]This and subsequent translations are those of C. D. Yonge, *The Works of Philo: Complete and Unabridged,* new ed. (Peabody, Mass.; Hendrickson, 1993).

Philo's account does not explicitly quote Scripture, but throughout there are several scriptural themes that appear, especially the notion of *lex talionis,* that is, the punishment should fit the crime (cf. Ex 21:23-25).

On the Embassy to Gaius. This floridly written account of a Jewish delegation from Alexandria, headed by Philo, affords a graphic example of how intensely anti-Jewish sentiment might be held by certain individuals and groups within the empire. The cause célèbre was Gaius Caesar Germanicus's ("Caligula") demand that a statue of himself be placed in the holy of holies of the Jerusalem temple and that he be worshiped as a god by the Jews. This is an appalling narrative demonstrating how bad dictatorships can be when the person at the top is hardly sane! One gathers, however, that Caligula's hatred of Jews went well beyond their refusal to accord him divine status. One reads of large numbers of people throughout the narrative who slander and ridicule Jews for a wide range of perceived errors, misdemeanors and felonies.

One is disappointed at the end of the account to read that a recantation by Caligula is to follow immediately *(Embassy* 373), only to learn that such a work is not extant. Presumably, Philo wrote it somewhat in the vein of *Against Flaccus,* in which the arch villain confessed the error of his ways and acknowledged the one true God of Israel. We do know from other accounts that members of the Praetorian Guard in the palace assassinated Gaius on January 22 or 24, A.D. 41, thus ending a potential conflict between Rome and Judea with huge casualties on both sides. Claudius, the successor to Gaius, reverted to the precedent of Augustus and Tiberius, who had exempted Jews from some civic duties, such as participation in the imperial cult.

Relevance for the New Testament. Several passages in these two works, while not necessarily being parallels, nonetheless throw light on or afford interesting comparisons to NT texts. In Philo's opening section of *Against Flaccus,* he adopts the diatribe style (a dispute or debate with an imaginary opponent), much like Paul in Romans 1—7. Even closer to home, at one point Philo raises an imaginary opponent's question: "Are you not doting and mad? I am not mad, my friend, nor am I a downright fool so as to be unable to see the consequences of connexion of things" *(Flacc.* 6). This reminds us of Luke's account of Paul's trial before the Roman governor Festus and Herod Agrippa II (the son of Herod Agrippa I who wrote the letter of entreaty to Caligula to desist from placing a statue of himself in the Jerusalem temple; cf. *Embassy* 261-329): "While he was making his defense, Festus exclaimed, 'You are out of your mind, Paul! Too much learning is driving you insane!' But Paul said, 'I am not out of my mind, most excellent Festus, but I am speaking the sober truth' " (Acts 26:24-25).

The attitude of Flaccus toward Jewish delegates before his tribunal, while much more calloused and insensitive, reminds us of Gallio's cool reception and deliberate disregard of unruly behavior toward the Jewish litigants at his court in Corinth (cf. *Flacc.* 24; Acts 18:12-17; and the discussion in chapter eight on 3 Maccabees).

Philo places in the mouths of anti-Semites in Alexandria accusations against Herod Agrippa I concerning his arrogant, overbearing demeanor (*Flacc.* 30). Apparently there was some truth to their slanders, since both Luke and the first-century A.D. Jewish historian Josephus narrate an episode in the life of Agrippa that portrays him as pretentious and extravagant:

> On an appointed day Herod put on his royal robes, took his seat on the platform, and delivered a public address to them. The people kept shouting, "The voice of a god, and not of a mortal!" And immediately, because he had not given the glory to God, an angel of the Lord struck him down, and he was eaten by worms and died. (Acts 12:21-23)

> On the second day of which shows he put on a garment made wholly of silver, and of a contexture truly wonderful, and came into the theatre early in the morning; at which time the silver of his garment being illuminated by the fresh reflection of the sun's rays upon it, shone out after a surprising manner, and was so resplendent as to spread a horror over those that looked intently upon him; and presently his flatterers cried out . . . that he was a god. . . . Upon this the king did neither rebuke them, nor reject their impious flattery. But, as he presently afterwards looked up, he saw an owl sitting on a certain rope over his head, and immediately understood that this bird was the messenger of ill things, as it had once been the messenger of good tidings to him; and fell into the deepest sorrow. A severe pain also arose in his belly, and began in a most violent manner. . . . And when he had been quite worn out by the pain in his belly for five days, he departed this life, being in the fifty-fourth year of his age, and in the seventh year of his reign. (Josephus, *Ant.* 19.8.2 §§344-50, Whiston)

Philo's account of the oppressed Jews of Alexandria mentions that after Flaccus had been arrested, the Jewish community "poured out through the gates at the earliest dawn, and hastened to the nearest point of the shore, for they had been deprived of their usual places for prayer" (*Flacc.* 122). The reason, of course, for no "usual places for prayer" was that Flaccus had allowed the mobs to burn, desecrate and pillage all the synagogues in Alexandria. In the book of Acts, Luke narrates: "On the sabbath day we went outside the gate by the river, where we supposed there was a place of prayer" (Acts 16:13). We infer from this that there was no synagogue at Philippi, probably because the Jewish community was quite small. Later Jewish sources specify a minimum of ten adult Jewish males (a *minyān*) in order to conduct a regular synagogue service (*b. Ber.* 21b; *b. Meg.* 23b). However, when no synagogue was available, because of the ritual purity laws, places near running water or the sea were preferred for saying the traditional prayers.

There are also two phrases from Flaccus's speech of contrition and confession that are similar to Pauline expressions. First, Flaccus pessimistically observes: "and I am thoroughly assured that even this is not the limit of my misfortunes, but that others are still in store for me, to fill up the measures as a requital for all the evils which I have done" (*Flacc.* 174). Compare this with Paul's bitter outburst against his Jewish opponents: "Thus they have constantly been filling up the measure of their sins; but God's wrath has overtaken them at last" (1 Thess 2:16).[7] The second follows close thereafter when Flaccus says: "I may say, every hour, I die before my time, enduring many deaths instead of one, the last of all" (*Flacc.* 175). In its context, this refers to Flaccus's dread that Gaius will not be content with his banishment but will devise some cruel way to do away with him. In this he was not wrong, as Philo rather expansively narrates. Paul, in his great chapter on the resurrection written to the Corinthians, cries out, "And why are we putting ourselves in danger every hour? I die every day!" (1 Cor 15:30-31a). Paul's point is not so much his dread of such an occurrence but the very real prospect of being murdered by his opponents every day he stayed in Corinth.

The Exposition of the Laws of Moses

This division was a comprehensive whole and consisted of the following sections: (1) *On the Creation;* (2) *On Abraham;* (3) *On Isaac;* (4) *On Jacob;* (5) *On Joseph;* (6) *On the Decalogue;* (7) *On the Special Laws;* (8) *On the Virtues;* (9) *On Rewards and Punishments;* and (10) *On the Life of Moses 1* and *2.* Of these *On Isaac* and *On Jacob* are no longer extant. As Borgen points out, Philo seems to provide an outline of his exposition at the beginning of *Rewards* 1.1: "We find, then that in the sacred oracles delivered by the prophet Moses, there are three separate characters; for a portion of them relates to the creation of the world, a portion is historical, and the third portion is legislative."[8] This corresponds nicely, then, to the narrative framework of the Pentateuch. In this regard we recall a similar paraphrase of the Pentateuch in *Jubilees* as well as the *Genesis Apocryphon* from the Dead Sea Scrolls.[9]

On the Life of Moses 1 and 2. This work covers most of the story of Moses as recorded in the Pentateuch, the most notable omission being the narrative of Moses on Mount Sinai. This is probably because Philo dealt with this important moment in more detail in *On the Decalogue.* The overall scheme of books

---

[7]Precisely what this "wrath" refers to has been subject to considerable debate. Some see it as a historical manifestation such as a pogrom. Others connect it to God's eschatological judgment upon unbelievers. See G. L. Borchert, "Wrath, Destruction," *DPL,* 991-93.

[8]Cf. Borgen, "Philo of Alexandria," in *Jewish Writings of the Second Temple Period,* p. 234.

[9]"Philo covers the biblical story from creation to Joshua's succession to Moses; *Jubilees* narrates the story from creation to the giving of the Law on mount Sinai" (ibid., p. 234 n. 7).

1 and 2 portrays Moses as embodying the four offices of king, priest, prophet and lawgiver. In this endeavor Philo sought to extol Moses as without peer among the ancient heroes and, of course, to place the law of Moses above all other philosophies and traditions. Book 1, with its historical or biographical approach, focuses on Moses' kingly office, whereas book 2 develops the other three offices. The major part of book 2 consists of a selective examination of individual teachings in the Pentateuch, demonstrating in each case what to Philo was self-evident, namely, the vast superiority of the Mosaic legislation to anything Egyptian, Greek or otherwise non-Hebrew. *On the Life of Moses* has a strong apologetic thrust and reflects the tension between Jews and Gentiles in Alexandria. Peder Borgen identifies Philo's purpose as a justification for Jews pursuing and being admitted to the larger arena of political and social life at Alexandria.[10]

Philo was constrained to argue for the superiority of the law of Moses over against the Greek and pagan traditions; to this end his argument proceeded along several lines. First, he argued for the unparalleled character of the lawgiver, Moses:

> The man who desires to be an excellent and perfect lawgiver ought to exercise all the virtues in their complete integrity and perfection. . . . Therefore, it is a very great thing if it has fallen to the lot of any one to arrive at any one of the qualities before mentioned, and it is a marvellous thing, as it should seem, for any one man to have been able to grasp them all, which in fact Moses appears to have been the only person who has ever done, having given a very clear description of the aforesaid virtues in the commandments which he established. (*Moses* 2.8, 10; cf. 1.1)

Second, Philo drew attention to the unchanging nature of the Mosaic law ("not even the smallest and most unimportant of all his commandments was changed" [*Moses* 3.15]) and its nearly universal recognition and influence ("in short, the whole habitable world from one extremity to the other" [*Moses* 2.20; cf. 1.2: "for the glory of the laws which he left behind him has reached over the whole world, and has penetrated to the very furthest limits of the universe"]). Third, he gave an account of the translation of the Hebrew Scriptures (Philo uses the term "Chaldean" for Hebrew) into Greek, quite exceeding that of the *Epistle of Aristeas* in fabulous embellishment, with the obvious intent of demonstrating its divine nature. We quote a section that crosses the line of credibility:

> They [the translators], like men inspired, prophesied, not one saying one thing and another, but every one of them employed the self-same nouns and verbs, as

---

[10]Ibid., p. 235.

if some unseen prompter had suggested all their language to them. And yet who is there who does not know that every language, and the Greek language above all others, is rich in a variety of words, and that it is possible to vary a sentence and to paraphrase the same idea, so as to set it forth in a great variety of manners, adapting many different forms of expression to it at different times.

But this, they say, did not happen at all in the case of this translation of the law, but that, in every case, exactly corresponding Greek words were employed to translate literally the appropriate Chaldaic words, being adapted with exceeding propriety to the matters which were to be explained. (*Moses* 2.37-38)

Compare this with *Epistle of Aristeas,* in which the process was described in a much more realistic manner: "They set to completing their several tasks, reaching agreement among themselves on each by comparing versions" (*Aristeas* 302). Clearly Philo indulged in a little rhetorical overkill to make his case for the superiority of the Mosaic laws. His fervent wish was cast in the form of an expectation for the future:

I think that in that case every nation, abandoning all their own individual customs, and utterly disregarding their national laws, would change and come over to the honour of such a people only: for their laws shining in connection with, and simultaneously with, the prosperity of the nation, will obscure all others, just as the rising sun obscures the stars. (*Moses* 2.44)[11]

Book 1 of *On the Life of Moses* essentially traces the life of Moses based upon the pentateuchal narratives. There are, however, fascinating expansions, concerning whose origins we can only speculate. Were these already part of Jewish oral traditions, or did Philo create some of these expansions ad hoc? We give only one example to illustrate. In the account of Moses' rescue by Pharaoh's daughter, Philo informs us:

Now the king of the country had an only daughter, whom he tenderly loved, and they say that she, although she had been married a long time, had never had any children, and therefore, as was natural, was very desirous of children, and especially male offspring, which should succeed to the noble inheritance of her father's prosperity and imperial authority, which was otherwise in danger of being lost, since the king had no other grandsons.

And as she was always desponding and lamenting, so especially on that particular day was she overcome by the weight of her anxiety, that, though it was her ordinary custom to stay in doors and never to pass over the threshold of her house, yet now she went forth with her handmaidens down to the river, where the infant was lying. (*Moses* 1.12)

We do not know who the "they" of "they say" might be, but it must be

---

[11] Borgen views this as an eschatological expectation on the part of Philo (ibid.). This may be so, but the context is not explicit in this regard.

admitted that the addition makes the story more interesting.[12] There are numerous such expansions, each one of which is interesting for the light it sheds on how the Hebrew Scriptures were read and expanded by a highly cultured Diaspora Jew seeking to provide credibility for his ancestral traditions.

On the Creation. This work, which is the first part of Philo's "Exposition," deals with Genesis 1–3. *On the Creation* enables us to perceive both Philo's indebtedness to and his opposition against various ideas originating in Greek philosophy. We also gain an appreciation for his exegetical approach to the scriptural text whereby he was able to harmonize Greek philosophy with his own Jewish traditions, at least to his own satisfaction. The means whereby he sought to achieve this synthesis was in the deployment of a literal-allegorical method of interpretation. When it suited his purpose, or in order to resolve questions and to reply to ridicule arising from a strictly literal interpretation, he resorted to a hidden or deeper meaning, a meaning that coheres with or derives from Greek philosophical thought. Of course, for Philo, Moses already held such views. Philo did not, however, abandon literal interpretation, as may be seen throughout his writings, and, for the most part, his allegorical meanings bear some relationship to the literal meaning.

The outline of this work is straightforward: after an introduction (1-12), Philo comments on each of the six days of creation (13-88); expands on the significance of the seventh day, the sabbath (89-128); comments on the second creation account in Genesis 2, which he takes, with indebtedness to Plato, to be the external and perceptible creation as opposed to the incorporeal and imperceptible ideas that preceded them in Genesis 1 (129-50); discusses the fall of Adam, for which he lays the blame squarely at the feet of Eve (151-69); and, last of all, adduces five lessons that Moses wished to convey (170-72).

Philo praises Moses' account of creation effusively: "His exordium [introduction] . . . is most admirable. . . . Accordingly, no one, whether poet or historian, could ever give expression in an adequate manner to the beauty of his ideas respecting the creation of the world; for they surpass all the power of language, and amaze our hearing, being too great and venerable to be adapted to the sense of any created being" (*Creation* 3-4).

In this introduction, Philo took pains to refute the Aristotelian view that the universe had no beginning. In Philo's view, "Moses, who had early reached the very summits of philosophy, and who had learnt from the oracles of God the most numerous and important of the principles of nature was well aware that it is indispensable that in all existing things there must be an

---

[12]For suggested Jewish sources other than the Bible, see Peder Borgen, "Philo," *ABD* 5:333-42.

active cause, and a passive subject; and that the active cause is the intellect of the universe" (*Creation* 8).

On the other hand, Philo employed Neo-Pythagorean philosophy to argue for the necessity of six days for the creation. It was not, Philo averred, because God needed that amount of time; it was, rather, because "the things created required arrangement; and number is akin to arrangement; and, of all numbers, six is, by the laws of nature, the most productive . . . [and] the first perfect one. . . . It was fitting therefore, that the world, being the most perfect of created things, should be made according to the perfect number" (*Creation* 13-14).

Central to Philo's understanding of the creation account in Genesis 1 was the notion of an archetype. Genesis 1 is really an account of the model or plan that originated in the mind of God and can only be perceived by the intellect. Here Philo shows his indebtedness to Plato (esp. in *Timaeus*) and the Stoics. Thus it was self-evident to Philo that "the archetypal seal, which we call that world which is perceptible only to the intellect, must itself be the archetypal model, the idea of ideas, the Reason of God" (*Creation* 25).

Several Philonic views are worth mentioning since they are still relevant for modern cosmological theories and debates. Philo, in contrast to Plato, upheld an absolute creation by God, who is the Creator of the Ideas (*Creation* 17-19). It is also evident from reading *On the Creation* that Philo employed forms of what philosophers would call the cosmological and teleological arguments for the existence of God. Meaning, purpose and design are all manifestations of a supreme all-knowing Mind, an architect who for Philo is the God of the Hebrew Scriptures. Philo held that time was created "either simultaneously with it [the world], or after it . . . [since] to assert that it is older than the world is absolutely inconsistent with philosophy" (*Creation* 26). He also understood the first sentence of Genesis 1 to mean that the heavens were the first thing created rather than the sentence being an introduction or title for the whole section in Genesis 1:2—2:4 (*Creation* 27-28).[13] Philo articulated a view that today is labeled mature creationism; that is, God made the various kinds of living things fully mature: "God produced the whole race of trees out of the earth in full perfection, having their fruit not incomplete but in a state of entire ripeness, to be ready for the immediate and undelayed use and enjoyment" (*Creation* 42). This concept is an

---

[13]Contrast this to OT scholar Bruce Waltke, who holds that Gen 1:1 is really the title to the entire creation account and describes a precreation chaos concerning which we are left in the dark, with the actual creation account beginning in v. 2 (*Creation and Chaos* [Portland, Ore.: Western Conservative Baptist Seminary, 1974]). Many evangelical commentators follow Philo's approach.

important plank in the argument of biblical creationists or young-earth advocates today.[14]

Philo expounded at length upon the significance of the fourth day for two reasons: (1) it prevents us from falling into the nearly universal error of ascribing divinity to the heavenly bodies; and (2) the number four is "the origin and source of the all-perfect decade" (*Creation* 47), "comprehends the principles of the harmonious concords in music" (*Creation* 48), is the "number that first displayed the nature of the solid cube" (*Creation* 49) and "is the first number which is a square" (*Creation* 51). Lest the significance of this escape the reader, Philo summarized why the fourth day carries such weight:

> It was the foundation of the creation of the whole heaven and the whole world. For the four elements, out of which this universe was made, flowed from the number four as from a fountain. And in addition to the four elements the seasons of the year are also four, which are the causes of the generation of animals and plants, the year being divided into the quadruple division of winter, and spring, and summer, and autumn. (*Creation* 52)

Once again we discern the influence of the Neo-Pythagorean philosophers, who devoted so much study to the importance of numbers for perceiving the true nature of things (*Creation* 45-52). This is even more evident in Philo's long digression on the seventh day and the significance of the number seven, concerning which we shall not digress!

Philo, of course, recognized and emphasized the place of human beings in the created order. For Philo, the original man "was really good and perfect . . . the most beautiful of all beings" (*Creation* 136, 138). Furthermore, Philo did not subscribe to any notion of common descent, as in modern evolutionary theory, since "God does not seem to have availed himself of any other animal existing in creation as his model in the formation of man; but to have been guided . . . by his own reason alone" (*Creation* 139). The primary distinction between animals and humans is explained in terms of the degree to which they partake of soul. Thus fish are lowest on the scale, since they partake least in soul; birds and terrestrial animals have a higher degree, but pride of place belongs to man "to whom he [God] gave that admirable endowment of mind—the soul, if I may so call it, of the soul, as being like the pupil to the eye" (*Creation* 66). The mind, according to Philo is that aspect of man in which the image of God consists. Here Philo reasserted the Jewish view of the incorporeality of God:

---

[14]For further discussion and bibliography, see Larry R. Helyer, *Yesterday, Today and Forever: The Continuing Relevance of the Old Testament* (Salem, Wis.: Sheffield Publishing, 1996), pp. 25-29, 65-66.

And let no one think that he is able to judge of this likeness from the characters
of the body; for neither is God a being with the form of a man, or is the human
body like the form of God; but the resemblance is spoken of with reference to
the most important part of the soul, namely, the mind: for the mind which
exists in each individual has been created after the likeness of that one mind
which is in the universe as its primitive model. (*Creation* 69)

We must say something about Philo's understanding of the fall (the first
sin of Adam and Eve). He seems to have offered two different, even conflicting, explanations for the first transgression. First Philo attributed it to the
very nature of things: "But since nothing in creation lasts for ever, but all
mortal things are liable to inevitable changes and alterations, it was unavoid-
able that the first man should also undergo some disaster" (*Creation* 151). But
this seemingly naturalistic explanation quickly gives way to another, namely,
that the original sin was sexual pleasure, "which is the beginning of iniquities
and transgressions, and it is owing to this that men have exchanged their previously immortal and happy existence for one which is mortal and full of mis-
fortune" (*Creation* 151; cf. 161). Apparently, Philo reconciled these two
positions by implying, if not actually asserting, that the woman was not as
fully in the image of God as the man. Thus she was capable of subverting the
pure state in which the man existed while he was single (*Creation* 151)
because she was the source of great pleasure, which can easily become unbri-
dled passion. To this one may ask how Philo avoided imputing the origin of
evil to God, since God created the woman? Philo's answer appears to be as follows: God the Father ("the one who is") created all things that are good and all
things that are neutral, but those things that contain vice or evil are attributed to his assistants (*Creation* 72-76). Philo did not discuss who these are
here, but elsewhere he spoke of two other powers, called "God" and "Lord,"
who act upon the world (*Abraham* 119-23). This, of course, raises other problems, but Philo either did not sense them or simply ignored them. At any
rate, Philo stated that women are to be identified with sensations and men
with mind or reason.[15] The challenge for men now was to make sure that reason keeps control of sensations and passions (*Creation* 165). Here we detect
the influence of the Stoic school of philosophy. Philo's view of women is certainly more in accord with those of Ben Sira, *Aristeas,* the Dead Sea Scrolls
and some latter rabbis than that of the author of Judith.[16] Furthermore, his

[15]On this see further, Judith Romney Wegner, "Philo's Portrayal of Women—Hebraic or
Hellenic?" in *Diaspora Jews and Judaism: Essays in Honor of, and in Dialogue with, A. Thomas Kraabel,* ed. J. Andrew Overman and Robert S. MacLennan, South Florida Studies in
the History of Judaism 41 (Atlanta: Scholars Press, 1992), pp. 41-66, esp. p. 64.
[16]See further on this Dorothy Sly, *Philo's Perception of Women,* BJS 209 (Atlanta: Scholars
Press, 1990).

view of the origin of evil reflects the tensions and contradictions that we have already witnessed in Jewish literature such as the Enoch traditions, *Jubilees* and the Dead Sea Scrolls.

In his section on the fall we see Philo's allegorical method at work. In commenting on the tree of the knowledge of good and evil and the tree of life, Philo admits that

> no trees of life or of knowledge have ever at any previous time appeared upon the earth, nor is it likely that any will appear hereafter. But I rather conceive that Moses was speaking in an allegorical spirit, intending by his paradise to intimate the dominant character of the soul, which is full of innumerable opinions as this figurative paradise was of trees. And by the tree of life he was shadowing out the greatest of the virtues—namely, piety toward the gods . . . and by the tree which had the knowledge of good and evil, he was intimating that wisdom and moderation. (*Creation* 154)

The serpent, too, is treated allegorically as "the symbol of pleasure" (*Creation* 157), in support of which Philo offers a long list of reasons. In this regard, one need not agree with the specific allegorical interpretations that Philo proffers without, at the same time, being willing to acknowledge that Genesis 2—3 do in fact contain elements of symbolism.[17]

The weakness in Philo's allegorical method is that he did not let the biblical account provide its own clues as to the presence of the symbolic but rather read wholesale into the scriptural text various features of Greek philosophy in a highly eclectic manner, whether Platonic, Stoic, Neo-Pythagorean or whatever. In this case his literary instincts about the text were correct, but his execution was flawed. To compound the problem, however, as we read in his discussion of the creation account in Genesis 1 and in other historical narratives in the Pentateuch, Philo found symbolism everywhere, even when there is no literary justification for it whatsoever (i.e., there is no indication that the author intended the narrative to be read symbolically or allegorically).

Selected Passages and Their Relevance for the New Testament

In this section we simply select out of Philo's vast writings a few passages that may have some bearing on the interpretation of the NT.

Creation and the Origin of Evil

Like Philo, NT writers affirm the Jewish doctrine of absolute creation by one self-existent, all-powerful, all-knowing, good God (cf. Rom 11:36; 1 Cor 8:6;

---

[17]See Helyer, *Yesterday*, pp. 72-73.

2 Pet 3:5). Whereas Philo speaks of the Father's "assistants," NT writers place Jesus the Son of God alongside the Father and affirm his essential equality with the Father (Jn 1:1; Phil 2:6; Col 1:15, 19; 2:9). The Son, however, voluntarily subordinates himself to the Father in the economy of redemption (1 Cor 15:27-28; Phil 2:7-8). The NT ascribes to the Lord Jesus Christ an active role in the creation (Jn 1:1-3; Col 1:15-17; Heb 1:2-3). We shall say more about Philo's doctrine of the Logos shortly. Paul explicitly denies that anything God created is evil (1 Tim 4:4). Furthermore, Hebrews 11:3 likewise affirms creation without pre-existing matter.

With regard to the origin of sin, one passage is superficially similar to Philo. In 1 Timothy 2:11-15, Paul enjoins women to be silent in the church meetings. He has two arguments for this injunction: Adam was formed first, the argument apparently being that priority of creation entails authority over women; and it was Eve who was deceived, apparently implying that she was more susceptible to enticement than Adam. It is the latter argument that bears some similarity to Philo's rather disparaging description of Eve: "she, without any inquiry, prompted by an unstable and rash mind, acquiesced in his advice" (*Creation* 156). But one should be cautious here, because Paul does not actually say that Eve was especially susceptible to temptation, only that it was in fact she who first transgressed. Also, in Romans 5:12-21 Paul lays full blame in the lap of Adam without so much as a reference to Eve. Nowhere in Paul, or in the rest of the NT for that matter, do we have an argument to the effect that the fall was something inevitable for created beings and that with passing generations there would have been a diminution of the perfections of the first man (cf. *Creation* 140-41).

The Problem of Circumcision
In *On the Special Laws* Philo responded to ridicule of the Jews for their practice of circumcision, which was especially abhorrent to Greeks and Romans. Philo's argument first proceeds, for the most part, along the lines of good hygiene. Circumcision prevents a painful disease he calls carbuncle, prevents bodily uncleanliness and, in fact, leads to more offspring. Philo also includes a strange argument about the similarity between the part circumcised and the heart, an argument we can simply attribute to the shortcomings of medical knowledge in Philo's day (*Laws* 1.1-7).

Philo then advances what to him is the real heart of the matter. Circumcision should be seen as a symbolic ritual speaking to important issues of life. The action of circumcision symbolizes the cutting off of pleasures that delude the mind. In Philo's words:

Since of all the delights which pleasure can afford, the association of man with woman is the most exquisite, it seemed good to the lawgivers to mutilate the organ which ministers to such connections; by which rite they signified figuratively the excision of all superfluous and excessive pleasure, not, indeed, of one only, but of all others whatever, though that one which is the most imperious of all. (*Laws* 1.9)

Philo also sees in circumcision an act that reminds man of his creaturely status and prevents that vain opinion whereby a man thinks himself a god. Given Philo's experience with Gaius Caesar, we can at least understand why this was part of Philo's defense of circumcision.

What has this to do with the NT? The ritual of circumcision looms large in a major controversy of the early church. What requirements should Gentiles meet in order to join the Palestinian Jesus movement? The book of Acts witnesses to the difficulty this posed. Many Jewish Christians could not imagine that God's commandment to Abraham (Gen 17) could ever be abolished or ignored. The Jerusalem Council met to resolve this thorny question (Acts 15). The decision, probably rejected by considerable numbers of Jewish Christians, was that Gentiles were not to be required to be circumcised in order to become full-fledged members of the messianic community. A prime exponent of Gentile liberty in this matter was the apostle Paul, and several of his letters, especially Galatians, refer to this issue (Gal 5:6; 6:15).

But what especially interests us in this connection is the fact that Paul also, in at least two passages, views circumcision as a symbol of something deeper. It occurs in Romans 2, where he debates an imaginary Jewish objector to his gospel: "For a person is not a Jew who is one outwardly, nor is true circumcision something external and physical. Rather, a person is a Jew who is one inwardly, and real circumcision is a matter of the heart—it is spiritual and not literal. Such a person receives praise not from others but from God" (Rom 2:28-29). We think Paul is making essentially the same point in Colossians 2:11-12, which presents baptism as an outward sign of a spiritual resurrection and identifies this moment as a "spiritual circumcision" (Col 2:11). Paul describes this spiritual circumcision as a "putting off the body of the flesh." While for Paul the term "flesh" has wider connotations than Philo's "pleasure," the essential point of both is rather close.[18] Paul is not nearly as ascetic as Philo, but he does recognize the power of sexual passion and always warns his converts about keeping it in check (cf. Rom 13:13; 1 Cor 5:9; 6:9, 12-20; 7:2, 5, 9, 36; Eph 2:3; 4:19; 5:3). One should also compare Paul's comments in Philippians 3:3 and Ephesians 2:11, where he clearly spiritualizes circumcision.

---

[18]See further on this R. J. Erickson, "Flesh," *DPL,* pp. 303-6.

The Logos

Students of the NT have long been aware of the remarkable discussions in Philo about the Logos or Word of God, an aspect of God's being that seemingly takes on a distinct personality. Since the notion of a world-soul or mind occurs in Stoic and Pythagorean thought, many have supposed that Philo simply incorporated this into his own Jewish tradition. This may be so, but one should not forget the OT and the later Jewish wisdom tradition in Sirach, Baruch, and Wisdom of Solomon, in which much importance is laid on the notion of creation by the Word (Logos [Gk *logos*]) of God. Attention should also be given to the influence of the Targumim (Aramaic paraphrases of the Hebrew Bible used in the synagogues), whereby Wisdom and the Word of God are said to have created "in the beginning." [19]

In his work *On the Confusion of Tongues* Philo is at pains to deny a strictly literal meaning of the phrase "The LORD came down to see the city and the tower" (Gen 11:5) because this would localize God, who cannot be confined to any one point:

> All places are filled at once by God, who surrounds them all and is not surrounded by any of them, to whom alone it is possible to be everywhere and also nowhere. . . . But the power of this being which made and arranged everything is with perfect truth called God, and it contains everything in its bosom, and pervades every portion of the universe. (*Confusion* 136-37)

Philo argues that one must recognize such language as anthropomorphic (*Confusion* 135) and that there is a deeper, hidden meaning beneath the literal. In his words: "But we must not suppose that such a plain and unquestionable fact as that ['which mortals had built,' Gen 11:5b] is what is intended to be conveyed by the mention of it in the holy scriptures, but rather there is some hidden meaning concealed under these apparently plain words which we must trace out" (*Confusion* 143). This illustrates again Philo's allegorical method.

But in the course of his explanation of the "deeper" meaning of the expression, Philo exhorts his readers to

> labour earnestly to be adorned according to his first-born word, the eldest of his angels, as the great archangel of many names; for he is called, the authority, and the name of God, and the Word, and man according to God's image, and he who sees Israel. . . . For even if we are not yet suitable to be called the sons of God, still we may deserve to be called the children of his eternal image, of his most sacred word; for the image of God is his most ancient word. (*Confusion* 146-47)

---

[19]See Craig A. Evans, *Noncanonical Writings and New Testament Interpretation* (Peabody, Mass.: Hendrickson, 1992), p. 84.

It would seem that this Word is to be identified with the "archetypal model, the idea of ideas, the Reason of God" spoken of in *On the Creation* 25. This is confirmed by a passage in *On Flight and Finding* where Philo, in commenting on the cities of refuge, once again resorts to an allegorical interpretation. He identifies these cities as powers of God, the chief of which is the divine word. This divine word

> does not come into any visible appearance, inasmuch as it is not like to any of the things that come under the external senses, but is itself an image of God, the most ancient of all the objects of intellect in the whole world, and that which is placed in the closest proximity to the only truly existing God, without any partition or distance being interposed between them. (*Flight* 101)

Again, commenting on Genesis 9:6, Philo describes the Logos further:

> For no mortal thing could have been formed on the similitude of the supreme Father of the universe, but only after the patter[n] of the second deity, who is the Word of the supreme Being; since it is fitting that the rational soul of man should bear it the type of the divine Word; since in his first Word God is superior to the most rational possible nature. But he who is superior to the Word holds his rank in a better and most singular pre-eminence, and how could the creature possibly exhibit a likeness of him in himself? (*QG* 2.62)

We have read enough from Philo's discourses on the Logos to realize that there are some similarities in his description of the Logos and the way Jesus Christ is described by Paul, John and the author of Hebrews. Inasmuch as we have already discussed the wisdom tradition and its influence upon NT writers, we keep our comments short. The striking thing about Philo's Logos is his assertion that (1) he is so close to God the Father as to be almost indistinguishable and (2) he was the primary agent in the actual creation of the visible world. Both of these concepts are quite close to Pauline and Johannine Christology as well as that of Hebrews (cf. Jn 1:1-3; 1 Cor 8:6; 2 Cor 4:4; Phil 2:6; Col 1:15-17; 2:9; Heb 1:1-3).

We should not, however, go as far as some of the early church fathers in thinking that Philo actually anticipated or held to trinitarian thought. After all, Philo was, in the end, speaking not about a real hypostasis but about aspects or powers of the one true God the Father.[20] Besides, his allegorical method lent itself to misunderstanding, and he was not innocent of contradictions and imprecise language here and there. What we can say is that before Paul, John and the author of Hebrews framed their understanding of Jesus Christ, we have a Hellenistic, Diaspora Jew who could speak of a plurality of powers emanating from the one true God. It is not a great distance

---

[20]G. H. Clark, "Philo Judaeus," *ZPEB* 4:775-76.

from this to the NT understanding of the Word of God who was "with God" and "was God" (Jn 1:1). On the other hand, it is a giant step away from the NT proclamation that the "Word became flesh and lived among us" (Jn 1:14). Nonetheless, Philo remains an eloquent witness for the claim that NT Christology is deeply rooted in a Jewish substratum.

Adam Christology

Closely related to Philo's teaching about the Logos is the notion of a perfect man. Remember that Philo, in *On the Creation,* held that the first man created in Genesis 1 was created in the image of God. Furthermore, this man was an invisible, incorporeal archetype who continues to maintain that exalted status. On the other hand, the second man, Adam, who was created in Genesis 2, while being in the image of God so far as his mind was concerned, was also created a sensual being. Alas, this man succumbed to the enticements of sexual pleasure and fell from his initial state of creaturely perfection and innocence. Philo elaborates on this in *On the Confusion of Tongues* 62-63, *Questions and Answers on Genesis* 2.4 and *On the Virtues* 205.

This notion of two Adams has some similarity to a central idea in the thought of the apostle Paul. In 1 Corinthians 15:21-28, 45-49 and Romans 5:12-21, Paul develops what we can label an "Adam Christology." For Paul two Adams are determinative for all human existence: one is either in the first Adam, that is, fallen and unredeemed, or in the second, last Adam, Jesus Christ, and thus reconciled and redeemed. Aside from Philo's obvious indebtedness to the Platonic notion of "ideas," something not detected in Paul, we should also note Paul's explicit reversal in the order of the first and second Adams. It is the second Adam who is "from heaven," the "life-giving spirit," the Lord Jesus Christ (1 Cor 15:45-47). In this latter passage Paul is speaking in terms of salvation history and not metaphysics. It is possible that he did conceive of Jesus Christ as the preexistent model or archetype after which the first or earthly Adam was created, but the evidence is not clear from Paul's writings and can only be inferred. The most that can be said is that "Paul's typology may be assuming a distinction between the two Adams of the two creation accounts that approximates Philo's exegesis."[21]

Substance and Shadow

Students of the NT book of Hebrews have long been fascinated by features that might be labeled as Philonic. Both works display a highly refined, elegant Greek; rhetorical devices and flourishes typical of the Greek gymna-

---

[21] Evans, *Noncanonical Writings,* p. 85. See further on this Larry Kreitzer, "Adam and Christ," *DPL,* pp. 9-15.

sium; and reliance upon the LXX as the scriptural text. But the foregoing does not necessarily make Hebrews Philonic. Much more impressive is the pronounced dualism of Hebrews, which is expressed in vocabulary similar to that used by Philo. Here is a passage from Philo's *On the Migration of Abraham:*

> For it is absurd for a shadow *[skia]* to be looked upon as of more importance than the bodies *[sōmata]* themselves, or for an imitation to carry off the palm from the model. Now the interpretation resembles a shadow and an imitation, but the nature of things signified under these expressions, thus interpreted, resemble the bodies and original models which the man who aims at being such and such rather than at appearing so must cling, removing to a distance from the other things. (*Migration* 12)

To this we compare a passage from Hebrews:

> Thus it was necessary for the sketches of the heavenly things to be purified with these rites, but the heavenly things themselves need better sacrifices than these. For Christ did not enter a sanctuary made by human hands, a mere copy of the true one, but he entered into heaven itself. . . . the law has only a shadow *[skian]* of the good things to come and not the true form *[eikona]* of these realities. (Heb 9:23-24; 10:1)

To be sure, Philo is borrowing Neoplatonic notions and is speaking onto-logically, whereas the author of Hebrews, while employing a vertical dualism in his argument for the superiority of Christ, never abandons an essentially eschatological dualism. The author of Hebrews is not really enamored with or indebted to the Platonic concept of ideas. The vertical dualism is sub-sumed under the controlling notion of salvation history, which is a horizontal dualism between the present age and the age to come (cf. Heb 2:5; 6:5; 9:26-28; 11:10; 12:22-28; 13:14).[22] The tension between the "now but not yet" is pri-mary in Hebrews. Still, the author of Hebrews may have found the Philonic contrast between substance and shadow a most useful one for his own, quite different, polemical purpose.[23]

It is tempting to suggest Apollos as the anonymous author of Hebrews, since no other NT writing has as much in common with Philo. The link is that Luke describes Apollos as "a native of Alexandria" and "an eloquent man, well-versed in the scriptures" (Acts 18:24). Apparently some at Corinth com-pared Paul unfavorably to the gifted orator Apollos (cf. 1 Cor 1:12; 2:4-7; 3:4-15, 22; 4:6-7; 2 Cor 10:11). Could it be that Apollos knew of the writings of his

---

[22]See further D. M. Martin, "Philo," *DLNTD*, pp. 932-33.
[23]On the purpose of Hebrews, see William L. Lane, "Hebrews," *DLNTD*, pp. 447-54; and his more full treatment in *Hebrews*, WBC 47A (Waco, Tex.: Word, 1991), pp. xcviii-ci.

fellow Alexandrian and even attended the same synagogue for awhile? Certainly the time frame would permit such a connection (Apollos was in Corinth shortly after A.D. 51, by which time Philo may have just recently died), but it must be admitted that this is purely conjecture.[24]

Before we leave this topic of Philo's contrast between substance and shadow, it is worth noting that Paul's letter to the Colossians has an even closer verbal parallel to Philo than Hebrews. We have discussed earlier the nature of the false teaching at Colossae (see chap. seven). Paul dismisses the ritual observances of the false teaching by commenting: "These are only a shadow *[skia]* of what is to come, but the substance *[sōma]* belongs to Christ" (Col 2:17). The point made is different from Philo's, but the terminology is the same.

Mysticism

Philo was a mystic, not in the sense of an absorption mysticism, whereby the initiate loses all personal identity by merging with the "wholly Other," but rather in the sense of a rational mysticism, that is, a mysticism consisting of an unmediated experience of God through contemplation of the world of invisible ideas—the real. Paul, too, was a mystic, but of a different kind. Though a good case can be made that Saul the Pharisee practiced Merkabah mysticism before his conversion, there can be no doubt that as a Christian he had remarkable experiences with the risen Christ, experiences that can rightly be described as mystical.[25] As to the former experiences, Paul puts little stock, even disparaging the pursuit of such, without actually denying their reality, in Colossians 2:18 and his so-called "fool's speech" in 2 Corinthians 12:1-13. But central Pauline themes, such as "dying and rising with Christ," living together with other believers "in Christ" and "sharing the sufferings of Christ," to say nothing of Paul's visionary experiences, including an ascent to the third heaven (2 Cor 12:1-7), all point to a decidedly mystical dimension to his faith and theology.[26]

At several places in Philo's writings, he seems to describe an ascent of the soul into the realm of the heavenly ideas, indeed, the very presence of God

---

[24]Donald A. Hagner sums up his discussion of the authorship of Hebrews as follows: "The only drawback to the suggestion that Apollos was the author of Hebrews is the lack of any ancient testimony supporting it. Because we know so little, Apollos can only be a guess. But it is a very good guess, and perhaps the best that can be offered" (*Hebrews* [San Francisco: Harper & Row, 1983], p. xxi; cf. R. M. Wilson, "Philo Judaeus," 3:849).

[25]See further W. R. Stegner, "Jew, Paul the," *DPL*, pp. 508-9; and P. T. O'Brien, "Mysticism," *DPL*, pp. 623-25.

[26]For a helpful discussion of Christian mysticism, see Winfried Corduan, *Mysticism: An Evangelical Option?* (Grand Rapids, Mich.: Zondervan, 1991).

himself. Moses is said to have experienced this when he was on Mount Sinai (*Moses* 1.158), and Philo himself gives the impression that he experienced something similar (*Migration* 34-36; cf. *Creation* 70-71; *Flight* 137-41).[27] In this connection it is worth noting again that Paul countered the Colossian heresy by insisting that believers in Jesus are already joined in fellowship with God in the heavenly realms by virtue of their union with Christ (Col 3:1-4; see the earlier discussion in chap. seven). This is one of the most dramatic instances of realized eschatology in the entire Pauline corpus, yet it still preserves the tension of the unfulfilled "not yet" ("When Christ who is your life is revealed" [Col 3:4]). Ephesians also is marked by an emphasis on a mystical union with Christ in the heavenly realms, something already capable of being experienced (Eph 1:3, 17-23; 2:6; 3:12, 17-19; 6:12).

But there is a fundamental difference between Philo and Paul that should be grasped. If we ask what the unifying idea of each was, I think we can make a good case for the following: Philo saw the Jewish people, the chosen people, as the integrating point of the cosmos and the Jerusalem temple as the crown jewel of this bridge between the divine, heavenly realm and the earthly. In Peder Borgen's words:

> Looking for a dominant feature in Philo's thought, some scholars have pointed to the tendency to bridge the gap between the transcendent God and man by intermediaries, such as Logos, the powers, etc. This is not enough. To Philo, it is specifically the Jewish people which intermediates between God and man. The notion of the cosmic and universal significance of Israel dominates in this thought.
>
> The center of Jewish existence is Jerusalem and its Temple. All Jews see Jerusalem as mother city, their metropolis. Its earthly buildings are not its totality, but essentially represent God's cosmos. Surprisingly, the Logos is equally characterized as a "metropolis," and Philo regards Jerusalem as a manifestation of the divine Logos spoken by God when he created the world. Indeed the chief, surest, and best mother city—which is more than just a city—is the Divine Logos, and to take refuge in it is supremely advantageous. Furthermore, Philo seems to expect that all Jews of the Diaspora would be brought back to Jerusalem and the Holy Land in the eschatological age.

---

[27]This would strengthen the theory that Jewish mysticism was in fact the problem at Colossae in that something similar can be documented for a Diaspora, Hellenistic Jew who was at the same time halakically observant. However, we must concede that Philo says little about angels and nowhere designates them with individual names such as Michael, Gabriel and so forth. He subsumes them under the category of the powers *(dynameis)* of God. Still, he has great admiration for the Essenes, who did make much of angels and who manifested mystical tendencies in their rituals and theology, and he greatly praises the Therapeutae, a similar Jewish sect, who engaged in mystic contemplation (cf. *Contempl. Life* II [11-12]).

Equally, the Temple in Jerusalem is an earthly counterpart of the cosmic heavenly Temple.[28]

For Paul the great unifying principle in the cosmos is the last Adam and the new humanity created through his death and resurrection (Rom 5:12-21; 6:1-11; 1 Cor 15:21-22; 2 Cor 5:17). There is a new people of God, and they are now made up of Jew and Gentile, slave and free, male and female, joined together in one new humanity, one new temple, one new body. We string together several Pauline passages in order to illustrate this new perspective:

> There is no longer Jew or Greek, there is no longer slave or free, there is no longer male and female; for all of you are one in Christ Jesus. And if you belong to Christ, then you are Abraham's offspring, heirs according to the promise. (Gal 3:28-29)
>
> With all wisdom and insight he has made known to us the mystery of his will . . . as a plan for the fullness of time, to gather up all things in him [Christ], things in heaven and things on earth. (Eph 1:8b-10)
>
> For he [Christ] is our peace; in his flesh he has made both groups [Jew and Gentile] into one and has broken down the dividing wall, that is, the hostility between us . . . that he might create in himself one new humanity. . . . for through him both of us have access in one Spirit to the Father. So then you are no longer strangers and aliens, but you are citizens with the saints and also members of the household of God, built upon the foundation of the apostles and prophets, with Christ Jesus himself as the cornerstone. In him the whole structure is joined together and grows into a holy temple in the Lord. (Eph 2:14, 18-21)
>
> To them God chose to make known how great among the Gentiles are the riches of the glory of this mystery, which is Christ in you, the hope of glory. (Col 1:27)
>
> [You] have clothed yourselves with the new self, which is being renewed in knowledge according to the image of its creator. In that renewal there is no longer Greek and Jew, circumcised and uncircumcised, barbarian, Scythian, slave and free; but Christ is all and in all! (Col 3:10-11)

Allegorical Interpretation
We conclude our discussion of Philo's relevance for the NT by asking if any NT writer ever adopts the allegorical method. There are two instances, in my opinion, where Paul allegorizes an OT passage: the allegory of the

---

[28]Peder Borgen, "Philo," *ABD* 5:333-42. Philo comments as follows: "We ought to look upon the universal world as the highest and truest temple of God, having for its most holy place that most sacred part of the essence of all existing things, namely, the heaven. . . . But the other temple is made with hands: for it was desirable not to cut short the impulses of men who were eager to bring in contributions for the objects of piety" (*Special Laws* XII [66-67]). The similarity of this to a major argument in Heb 8–10 is obvious.

unmuzzled ox in 1 Corinthians 9:8-10 (cf. 1 Tim 5:17-18) and the famous allegory on Sarah and Hagar in Galatians 4:21-31.[29] What is fascinating is to compare Philo's allegorizing of this latter passage with Paul's. In *Questions and Answers on Genesis* 3, Philo comments on selected verses that cover the story of Sarah and Hagar in Genesis 16—17. Hagar, symbolically perceived, represents an immature level of instruction and knowledge. Unfortunately, this tractate breaks off at Genesis 17, and we do not have Philo's comments on the section where Hagar is sent away by Abraham in Genesis 21. We know what Philo would have said, however, because in *On the Cherubim* he does refer to that episode and there identifies Hagar as "the middle kind of encyclical instruction," "those elementary branches of instruction which bear the name of Agar" (*Cherubim* 6, 8). Philo reads the story literally to mean that Ishmael was illegitimate; but allegorically or symbolically Ishmael is castigated as belonging to the sophists (*On Drunkenness* 8-9), and both mother and child, symbolically understood, "shall undergo eternal banishment, God himself confirming their expulsion" (*Cherubim* 9).

Paul, of course, is arguing a different point in Galatians. But he does want the Galatians to drive out the Judaizers, whom he firmly believes are illegitimate and whose system leads to bondage. Paul labels this section an allegory. (He actually uses the present participle of the verb *allēgoreō* as a substantive.) In Paul's allegory Hagar and Sarah represent two contrasting covenants. Hagar comes from Mount Sinai and represents "the present Jerusalem," that is, any form of Judaism still trusting in the Mosaic covenant for salvation; Sarah is "the Jerusalem above," the new-covenant, messianic community who trust in Jesus as Savior and Lord. What Paul wants is for his Galatian converts to expel the Judaizing interlopers just as Abraham expelled Hagar and her son Ishmael. And make no mistake about it, just like Philo, Paul sees no middle ground in this debate: "But even if we or an angel from heaven should proclaim to you a gospel contrary to what we proclaimed to you, let that one be accursed!" (Gal 1:8). There is no reason to think that Paul was directly indebted to Philo for the polemical use of the Hagar story, but it is remarkable how only this one time Paul resorts to a typically Philonic approach to Scripture.[30]

---

[29]See further on this Richard N. Longenecker, *Biblical Exegesis in the Apostolic Period* (Grand Rapids, Mich.: Eerdmans, 1975), pp. 126-29.

[30]Borgen suggests that "the similarities between Paul and Philo in this respect are probably due to expository traditions which each develops in his own way" ("Hebrew and Pagan Features in Philo's and Paul's Interpretation of Hagar and Ishmael," in *The New Testament and Hellenistic Judaism*, ed. Peder Borgen and Søren Giversen [Peabody, Mass.: Hendrickson, 1995], p. 161).

Impact of Philo on Later Christian Tradition

Philo's allegorical method cast a long shadow in the history of biblical exegesis, especially for the Christian church. Allegorical interpretation became the regnant method from the time of Clement and Origen, both Alexandrians, until the end of the Middles Ages; it was not seriously challenged until the Reformation and Enlightenment. Indeed, under new guises it still continues today. Surely Christian scholars such as Clement and Origen were not oblivious to the prodigious labors of Philo the Jew, nor did they devise the allegorical method on their own initiative. Rather, they appropriated Philo's hermeneutical approach, enabling them to grapple with a similar problem, namely, how to reconcile two bodies of seemingly diverse literature. For Christian scholars, that meant explaining the relationship of the Hebrew Scriptures (eventually called the Old Testament) to the Greek writings deemed apostolic that would bear the name New Testament. Just as Philo discovered Greek philosophy beneath the letter of Moses, so Christian theologians discovered Christian doctrine hidden throughout the OT by essentially the same method.[31] The OT was thus seen to be essentially a Christian book. The Reformation and the Enlightenment adopted different approaches to answering this fundamental question of the Christian church.[32]

For Further Discussion

1. Based on the works *Against Flaccus* and *On the Embassy to Gaius,* how would you characterize Gentile attitudes toward Jews during the time of Jesus? What contribution does the NT make in this regard?

2. How did Philo respond to Hellenistic ideas that he perceived as threatening to Judaism?

3. Philo advocated a relatively young earth. Why did he do so, and what was at stake?

4. How did Philo explain the origin of evil?

5. Philo's allegorical interpretation of Scripture has had an immense influence on Christian interpretation of the OT. In your opinion, is this a valid approach for interpretation today? Why or why not?

6. Compare Philo's understanding of circumcision with that of the apostle Paul.

---

[31] Borgen summarizes the impact of Philo on Christian exegetical tradition as follows: "Philo remained almost unknown in Jewish tradition until the 16th century. It was the Christian Church which preserved and adopted Philo; Byzantine anthologies even cite excerpts of Philo under the heading 'of Philo the Bishop.' Clement of Alexandria, Origen, and Ambrose were influenced by Philo in their allegorical exegesis and their use of such concepts as wisdom, Logos, and faith" ("Philo," *ABD* 5:341).

[32] See further D. P. Fuller, "Interpretation, History of," *ISBE* 2:863-74.

7. Summarize Philo's characterization of the Logos. Compare this to the NT presentation of Jesus Christ as the Wisdom and Word of God.

8. Philo was a mystic. Was Paul a mystic, and is there such a thing as Christian mysticism?

For Further Reading

Standard Critical Text

L. Cohn et al., eds., *Philonis Alexandrini opera quae supersunt,* 7 vols. (Berlin: G. Reimer, 1896-1930; 2d ed., 1962).

English Translations

F. H. Colson, G. H. Whitaker and R. Markus, eds., *Philo,* 10 vols. and 2 supplementary vols., LCL (Cambridge, Mass.: Harvard University Press, 1927-1962).

The Works of Philo, trans. C. D. Yonge, with an introduction by David M. Scholer (Peabody, Mass.: Hendrickson, 1993).

Selections with Brief Introductions and Comments

C. K. Barrett, *The New Testament Background: Selected Documents,* rev. ed. (San Francisco: Harper & Row, 1987), pp. 252-68.

Lawrence H. Schiffman, *Texts and Traditions: A Source Reader for the Study of Second Temple and Rabbinic Judaism* (Hoboken, N.J.: Ktav, 1998), pp. 203-6, 220-30.

Secondary Literature

Peder Borgen, "Philo of Alexandria," in *Jewish Writings of the Second Temple Period: Apocrypha, Pseudepigrapha, Qumran Sectarian Writings, Philo, Josephus,* ed. Michael E. Stone, CRINT 2 (Assen: Van Gorcum; Philadelphia: Fortress, 1984), pp. 233-82.

—————, *Philo of Alexandria—An Exegete for His Time* (Leiden: E. J. Brill, 1997).

G. H. Clark, "Philo Judaeus," *ZPEB* 4:773-76.

Craig A. Evans, *Noncanonical Writings and New Testament Interpretation* (Peabody, Mass.: Hendrickson, 1992), pp. 80-86.

Erwin R. Goodenough, *An Introduction to Philo Judaeus,* 2d ed. (Oxford: Basil Blackwell, 1962).

Burton L. Mack and Roland E. Murphy, "Wisdom Literature," in *Early Judaism and Its Modern Interpreters,* ed. Robert A. Kraft and George W. E. Nickelsburg (Philadelphia: Fortress; Atlanta: Scholars Press, 1986), pp. 387-95.

Samuel Sandmel, *Philo of Alexandria* (Oxford: Oxford University Press, 1979).

G. E. Sterling, "Philo," *DNTB,* pp. 789-93.

—————, "Philo Judaeus," *EDSS* 2:663-69.

Ronald Williamson, *Jews in the Hellenistic World: Philo,* CCWJCW (Cambridge: Cambridge University Press, 1989).

R. M. Wilson, "Philo Judaeus," *ISBE* 3:847-50.

Ten

Flavius Josephus

The House That Herod Built

*F*or Josephus we draw upon the convenient translation of William Whiston, updated and republished by Hendrickson (The Works of Josephus: Complete and Unabridged *[Peabody, Mass: Hendrickson, 1987]). For those who can read Greek, the standard critical edition is B. Niese, ed.,* Flavi Iosephi Opera, 7 vols. *(Berlin: Weidman, 1885-1895). A convenient and scholarly edition that has both the Greek text and a facing English translation is H. St. J. Thackeray, R. Marcus and L. H. Feldman, eds.,* Josephus, 9 vols., LCL *(Cambridge, Mass.: Harvard University Press, 1926-1965). There are two other English editions for the Jewish War: G. A. Williamson and E. Mary Smallwood,* Josephus: The Jewish War, *rev. ed. (New York: Penguin Books, 1981); and G. Cornfeld et al., eds.,* Josephus: The Jewish War *(Jerusalem: Masada; Grand Rapids, Mich.: Zondervan, 1982), the latter complete with splendid photographs.*

Introduction

The Jewish historian Josephus is essential reading for understanding the Second Temple period, especially the last half of the first century B.C. and the first half of the first century A.D. Since the latter is also the era during which Jesus lived and the church began, Josephus is of utmost importance for understanding early Christianity.

By this time, the relationship between the Jewish commonwealth and Rome, which began on such a promising note in the days of the Hasmonean princes, had begun to sour. The Romans had, in fact, administered the *coup de grâce* to Hasmonean hegemony in 63 B.C., when Pompey stormed Jerusalem, effectively annexing Palestine to the empire. Under Herod, a client king of Rome (40-4 B.C.), the land of Israel experienced sweeping changes. It was a time of turmoil, deep divisions, oppression, violence and, paradoxically, splendor and luxury. Momentous decisions had to be made about radically differing visions of what Judaism should be and the agendas to achieve those aims.

The Life of Flavius Josephus

Joseph ben Mattathias, better known by his adopted Roman name, Flavius Josephus, was born around A.D. 37/38 and died about A.D. 100. His career as a writer, both as a historian and an apologist for Judaism, was preceded by a stint in the military (A.D. 66-67), during which time he served as a general of the Jewish forces in Galilee during the ill-fated revolt against Rome. For the latter service he has not earned endearment and honor from the Jewish people, inasmuch as he surrendered to the Romans and turned traitor by assisting the Romans for the duration of the war. At its bloody and devastating conclusion, he retired to Rome and lived as a pensioner under the good graces of the emperors Vespasian, Titus and Domitian. For obvious reasons, his works were not cherished in Jewish circles and, were it not for Christians, might well have disappeared. Modern historians, whether religious or not, agree that we are fortunate to possess his writings, since they are an unparalleled source of information for this period.

Josephus informs us that he was born of a priestly family, being descended on his mother's side from the royal Hasmonean family. His parents provided him with a religious education, and he informs his readers that he was possessed of an extraordinary mind (*Life* 2 §9). At the age of sixteen, he engaged in an intense period of investigation in order to determine which "philosophy" of Judaism he should join.[1] He studied the three major sects, Pharisees, Sadducees and Essenes. As to the latter, Josephus says he studied for three years in the wilderness of Judea with a certain hermit named Bannus. At the age of nineteen, Josephus became a Pharisee (*Life* 2 §12). Despite this, in his collected writings he expresses great admiration for the Essenes and appears critical of the Pharisees at several points. Perhaps this is typical of many of us who rarely find a group with which we can totally agree.[2]

---

[1]Josephus uses the word *philosophy* to refer to a sect, or as we would say in the Protestant tradition, a denomination. He chooses the word *philosophy* in order to appeal to his cultured readers at Rome.

[2]According to Steve Mason, however, Josephus really "writes from the inner circle of the ancient priestly aristocracy" ("Josephus: Value for New Testament Study," *DNTB*, p. 599).

At any rate, in his twenty-ninth year (A.D. 64) he made a trip to Rome, a trip that inspired awe and respect for the power of Rome. His mission at that time was as part of a delegation to plead on behalf of some priests who had been sent to Rome by Felix, the procurator of Judea, to stand trial before Nero for various charges. This is the very same procurator before whom Paul stood trial earlier at Caesarea, sometime between A.D. 56 and 59 (Acts 23:24; 24:1-27). One is reminded in this regard of Philo and his earlier delegation to Rome in the days of Caligula (A.D. 39-40; cf. Josephus, *Ant.* 18.8.1 §§259-260). As it turns out, Josephus was successful in freeing the accused priests, largely through his contacts with Poppea, Nero's wife. Precisely how he pulled this off is not clear, but he met her through a mutual friend, a Jewish actor in Rome (*Life* 3 §§13-16).

When Josephus returned to Palestine, the whole country was in turmoil; rebellion hung in the air. According to his version of matters in *Life,* Josephus tried vainly to dissuade the Jewish leadership against the folly of revolt (*Life* 4-5 §§17-23). In *Jewish War* (his first work), Josephus makes no mention of attempts to dissuade the revolt; on the contrary, he energetically set about the defense of Galilee, after being appointed as general of all Galilee by the Jerusalem leadership. In *Life,* Josephus defends his actions against accusations by another Jewish historian, Justus, whose portrayal of Josephus was highly uncomplimentary, to say the least. Josephus thus proceeds to provide a somewhat different version of what happened from what he had earlier reported in *Jewish War.* Not surprisingly, he accuses Justus of having base motives and of being a liar (*Life* 9 §§36-40). On the other hand, Josephus's changed story does not build confidence in his objectivity.[3]

According to *Jewish War,* Josephus made his services available and was assigned a commission in Galilee, the northern part of the country and the most vulnerable to Roman attack. Apparently his loyalties were under suspicion, and those passed over for the commission (Josephus had no prior military experience) deeply resented him, since Josephus informs us of numerous accusations and plots against his life by enemies. His most bitter enemy was a certain John of Gischala, who accused Josephus of treachery. Josephus scarcely survived the stratagems of John (*Life* 13-25 §§70-125; *J.W.* 2.21.1-7 §§585-631). When he was not trying to outmaneuver his opponents, Josephus made preparations for the inevitable invasion by the imperial forces of Rome (*Life* 25-73 §§122-404). Nero entrusted this operation to a well-decorated soldier, Titus Flavius Vespasianus, who dispatched three legions to

---

[3]For a good discussion of the issues, see Steve Mason, *Josephus and the New Testament* (Peabody, Mass.: Hendrickson, 1992), pp. 73-76; Mason, "Josephus: Value for New Testament Study," pp. 596-600.

Judea to supplement the forces already in the region. Josephus had barely six months to prepare for the onslaught.

Vespasian met with little resistance from the Jewish forces of Galilee and quickly subdued the major centers of the rebellion, bottling up Josephus and his demoralized troops in Jotapata in the spring of A.D. 67. After a siege of forty-seven days the town fell (*J.W.* 3.7.3-36 §§141-339). In the melee that ensued, Josephus and two others hid in a cave inside the town. At this point, over the objections of Josephus, they elected to commit suicide rather than be captured by the Romans. They cast lots to determine the order in which they should kill each other, with the last person killing himself. Josephus (fortuitously?) drew the second-to-last lot. When only the two of them were left, Josephus was able to talk the other survivor into surrendering themselves to the Romans (*J.W.* 3.8.6-7 §§383-391). When Josephus was led into Vespasian's presence, he dramatically prophesied that Vespasian would become the next emperor (*J.W.* 3.3.9 §§399-401).

For whatever reason, whether owing to idle curiosity or possibly a bribe, Vespasian kept Josephus alive (*J.W.* 3.3.9. §408). As it turned out, Vespasian's troops acclaimed him emperor in A.D. 69 after Nero's suicide (in A.D. 68), and he freed Josephus before returning to Rome to be formally inaugurated as emperor in A.D. 70. Vespasian entrusted the remaining campaign into the hands of his very capable son, Titus. Josephus accompanied the latter to the siege of Jerusalem, where he served as an interpreter and mediator—the latter duty with singular lack of success.

After the destruction of Jerusalem and the burning to the ground of its crown jewel, the Second Temple, Josephus departed with Titus to Rome, where he settled into an imperial apartment. Here he entered upon his career as a writer and lived out his days. His domestic life seems to have been nearly as turbulent and unsuccessful as his military career, since he married four times. He had three sons by his third wife and two more sons by his fourth wife.

Jewish War

Composition and Outline

Four works by Josephus survive. The earliest is *Jewish War*, dated in its Greek edition to sometime between A.D. 75, the last dated event in the book, and A.D. 79, the death of Vespasian, Josephus's great benefactor. Josephus says this was in fact preceded by an Aramaic version intended for a Jewish audience in the region of Parthia and Babylonia (*J.W.* preface 1 §3; 2 §6). Most modern scholars agree, however, that the Greek version we possess is not a mere translation from the Aramaic (which we do not possess) but an edition displaying a sophistication and refinement quite worthy of an accomplished author of literary Greek. This means that we have an account of the war written by a participant and spectator just a few short years after the events it narrates.

The work falls into seven books: (1) book 1: Antiochus Epiphanes' sack of Jerusalem to the death of Herod the Great (ca. 168-4 B.C.); (2) book 2: the death of Herod the Great to the outbreak of the Jewish revolt (ca. 4 B.C.-A.D. 66); (3) book 3: Vespasian's Galilean campaign (ca. 1 year); (4) book 4: the fall of Gamala to the beginning of the siege of Jerusalem (ca. 1 year); (5) book 5: the Siege of Jerusalem (ca. 6 months); (6) book 6: the fall of Jerusalem (A.D. 70); and (7) book 7: aftermath of the fall of Jerusalem (ca. 3 years). One can readily see that Josephus focuses considerable attention upon the climactic events of the destruction of Jerusalem and the fall of Masada, events that signaled the collapse of Jewish resistance in Palestine.

Purpose

After a brief introduction to the work as a whole, Josephus sets out his reason for writing. It is, in short, to set forth the facts of the matter in opposition to misrepresentations and distortions by individuals whom he says "have the confidence to call their accounts histories . . . [but] fail of their purpose" (*J. W.* preface 3 §7). The blame for the war he lays squarely at the feet of certain Jewish leaders whom he labels as "party chiefs and bandits." These misguided zealots brought catastrophe upon the heads of their own people.

Though earlier scholarship tended to view *Jewish War* as a piece of imperial propaganda designed to forestall any further attempts at rebellion against the Roman Empire, there is sufficient evidence to doubt this assessment.[4] In his prologue, which was for books in antiquity the place where an author tried to make clear what the writing was designed to accomplish, Josephus indicates his displeasure with false and misdirected accounts of the war. He objects to writers who

> have a mind to demonstrate the greatness of the Romans, while they still diminish and lessen the actions of the Jews, as not discerning how it cannot be that those must appear to be great who have only conquered those that were little; nor are they ashamed to overlook the length of the war, the multitude of the Roman forces who so greatly suffered in it, or the might of the commanders,—whose great labors about Jerusalem will be deemed inglorious, if what they achieved be reckoned by a small matter. (*J. W.* preface 3 §§7-8, Whiston)

It can hardly be said that this is simply imperial propaganda. The portrayal of the Jewish resistance is narrated with scarcely disguised pride in the

---

[4]I am indebted to Mason, *Josephus and the New Testament,* pp. 58-64, for the following discussion.

pluck of the Jewish forces. As Mason clearly shows, "Josephus was confronted with potentially conflicting loyalties." [5] The way he handled this delicate problem was

> by developing an interpretation of the Jewish war that allows him both to remain loyal to his patrons and to speak as a committed Jew. His essential thesis (*J.W.* 1.9-12) is that the revolt was caused by only a few troublemakers among the Jews—power-hungry tyrants and marauders who drove the people to rebel against their will. The vast majority of Jews, he contends, have always been peace-loving, devoted to the Roman virtues of order and harmony. Those who fomented revolt were aberrations from true Judaism.[6]

To be sure, Josephus wrote from a pro-Roman perspective and would have us believe that Rome was a reluctant destroyer of both Jewish statehood and shrine. Still, Josephus did not write as one obsessed with hatred of his own Jewishness, nor did he repudiate Judaism as he understood it. One cannot read this without sensing considerable pride in his heritage. Furthermore, in spite of being misguided by zealot bandits, the Jewish resistance movement was finally crushed only because God so willed it. The Romans had conquered no inconsequential people.

There seems to have been, then, both an overt and a covert message to *Jewish War.* On the one hand, it was a piece of political propaganda aimed at dissuading rebellious provinces and regions from attempting a similar liberation movement. Mighty Rome was equal to any and every challenge. Not surprisingly, the work was published under the auspices of the Flavian dynasty. On the other hand, the work served to rehabilitate the reputation of Jews in the empire. Quite evidently, some writers made use of the humiliating defeat to draw unwarranted conclusions about Jews generally. Josephus was waging a war on two fronts. He was seeking to deflect criticism and blame from himself as a traitor to the cause by explaining, from his point of view, that the cause itself was misguided and not in the best interests of the Jewish people. But he was also responding to anti-Semites for whom the war against Rome had provided new grist for the mill. We sense that Josephus found himself in a somewhat similar situation as Philo earlier faced in Alexandria, Egypt. It has been, alas, the recurring burden of many Jewish intellectuals.

Sources

A close reading of Josephus reveals several sources for his narrative. On the one hand, there is abundant evidence that he was in fact a participant and observer. The amount and accuracy of details justify us in attributing the

---

[5]Ibid., p. 60.
[6]Ibid., pp. 60-61.

work to an eyewitness. This is not to say that Josephus can be taken at face value for everything he narrates, but it is to acknowledge that enough independent verification has been made possible through archaeological excavations and a careful comparison with other written sources, both biblical and nonbiblical, to accord to Josephus essential reliability as a historian. In addition to his own observations, Josephus apparently had access to official records and diaries of the Romans. Finally, he acknowledged his indebtedness to Nicolaus of Damascus for events before his own time. Regrettably, we know next to nothing of this Nicolaus, and his work lives on only in fragments incorporated by Josephus. Not to be overlooked, of course, is the Hebrew Bible in Greek translation, which Josephus drew upon for earlier material and for allusions.

Features

Josephus says at the conclusion of his preface that he has "written . . . for the sake of those that love truth, but not for those that please themselves" (*J.W.* preface 12 §30). But most will agree, after reading his work, that Josephus could also spin a good tale. Numerous passages are recounted in the best tradition of a suspense thriller. Josephus regales the reader with treacherous deeds and appalling actions, as well as noble and heroic undertakings. Though tame by modern standards, he even weaves romance into the fabric of this masterpiece.

Josephus's account of the war begins, significantly, with the depredations of Antiochus IV Epiphanes. Antiochus functions as an archetype who prefigures the dire fate of Jerusalem and the Jewish nation. Of course, we have a parallel and more fulsome account of this protracted struggle in 1 and 2 Maccabees. By contrast, Josephus quickly summarizes the Maccabean liberation movement, an important milestone of which was the alliance Judas forged with Rome in the early years of the struggle. The struggle culminated in the climactic moment when Simon "was made high priest, and also freed the Jews from the dominion of the Macedonians, after a hundred and seventy years of the empire" (*J.W.* 1.2.2 §53). But immediately thereafter, "Simon had also a plot laid against him, and was slain" (*J.W.* 1.2.3 §54).

This tragedy was paradigmatic from Josephus's point of view. Just at the point of seemingly their greatest achievement, internal fratricide plunged the nation into more suffering. Like a musical motif, this unfortunate, political dynamism returns again and again in Josephus's narrative. For example, in the days of John Hyrcanus a similar episode unfolded. In a glowing tribute to Hyrcanus's achievements, Josephus informs us that "He it was who alone had three of the most desirable things in the world—the government of his nation, and the high priesthood, and the gift of prophecy" (*J.W.* 1.2.8 §68). But in the next breath Josephus says that John Hyrcanus "foresaw and foretold that his two eldest sons would not continue masters of the government; and it will highly deserve our narrations to describe their catastrophe, and how far inferior these men were to their father in felicity" (*J. W.* 1.2.8 §68).

The catastrophe to which Josephus adverted involved the Romans. It was Pompey who, in 63 B.C., intervened in the power struggle between the two sons of Queen Alexandra (Hyrcanus II and Aristobulus II) and effectively swept the Jewish nation into Rome's orbit. The account of their folly is virtually a type scene for the even greater catastrophe of the great war against Rome about a century later. What is evident in all this is that Josephus had a keen eye for recurring patterns. Of course, as a faithful son of Israel, Josephus placed all of this in the ultimate context of God's inscrutable providence and just government of the world.

The Antiquities of the Jews

Purpose and Date

In a second and much longer work, *Jewish Antiquities,* Josephus offered a general history of the Jewish people with a clearly apologetic purpose designed to counter vicious slanders against the Jews. Once again we are reminded of earlier works such as *Aristeas,* 3 Maccabees and the writings of Philo Judaeus. Indeed, the familiar canards found in those works resurface in Josephus's apology for the Jewish people. This work, which retells in its first eleven books the biblical history and continues in the next nine to narrate Jewish history right up to the eve of the Jewish war—thus overlapping here with his first piece—was published about twenty years later, in about A.D. 93/94.

Outline of Contents

The twenty books of *Jewish Antiquities* fall into five major divisions: (1) books 1-10: from the primeval period to the captivity (essentially a retelling of the biblical history); (2) book 11: the age of Cyrus the Great; (3) books 12-14: from Alexander the Great to the accession of Herod the Great; (4) books 15-17: the reign of Herod the Great; and (5) books 18-20: from the death of Herod the Great to the outbreak of the revolt against Rome.

Features and Sources

An intriguing feature of *Jewish Antiquities* lies in Josephus's retelling of the stories in the Hebrew Bible. It is surprising how freely Josephus revised, adapted or even completely recast the biblical narratives. This is all the more surprising since in his opening statement he had said: "I shall accurately describe what is contained in our records, in the order of time that belongs to them; for I have already promised so to do throughout this undertaking, and this without adding anything to what is therein contained, or taking away anything therefrom" (*Ant.* preface 3 §17). In this regard, we recall a similar characteristic of the sectarian and biblical writings found at Qumran. *Jewish Antiquities* reinforces the modern scholarly view that the biblical text was still somewhat fluid in the first century A.D. Josephus really gives us an expanded paraphrase of biblical history.

The biblical text Josephus used, most scholars agree, was a version of the Septuagint (LXX).[7] Whereas some modern scholars have doubted that Josephus could even read biblical Hebrew, this has no basis and stands opposed to what he narrates about his early life (*Life* 1-2 §§1-9). Rather, Josephus's use of the LXX was in keeping with his Greek-speaking audience, not his inability to read Hebrew.[8]

Josephus's additions and omissions provide insight into his agenda, namely, a defense of Judaism. Because Roman society valued law and order, Josephus's portrait of Judaism highlights this very aspect. Moses was supremely the great lawgiver (the biblical portrait stresses his status as the great prophet) and Judaism itself was a well-ordered "philosophy," bearing striking resemblance to Stoicism—though, of course, Moses was much earlier than, and thus more venerable than, the school of the Stoics.

Anti-Semitic slurs are met head on by Josephus's retelling of the biblical history. For instance, several Roman intellectuals slandered Moses as a leper. Against this, Josephus embellishes the birth narratives in Exodus such that none other than an Egyptian scribe prophesied Moses' great destiny (*Ant.* 2.9.2 §205), and Pharaoh's daughter was captivated by Moses' "largeness and beauty" (*Ant.* 2.9.5 §224). Furthermore, Josephus says that Moses banished all lepers from the Jewish community (*Ant.* 3.11.4 §§265-268). Significantly, Josephus does not narrate the account of Moses' murder of an Egyptian but substitutes an otherwise unknown story about Moses' military exploits against the Ethiopians (*Ant.* 2.10.1-2 §§238-253). Josephus's omission of the golden calf incident and Moses' sending his wife back to Egypt on a donkey is almost certainly owing to vicious slanders that Antiochus Epiphanes had discovered a golden donkey's head in the most holy place in the Jerusalem temple (*Ag. Ap.* 2.7 §§79-88). Many other examples could be listed, but these will suffice. Mason has not overstated the case when he observes that "Josephus' *Antiquities* is an all-out campaign to dispel the ridicule and misinformation that characterized literate Roman portrayals of the Jews. It is a massive effort at legitimation, seeking to dem-

---

[7] E. C. Ulrich shows that Josephus used a proto-Lucianic version (*The Qumran Text of Samuel and Josephus,* HSM 19 [Missoula, Mont.: Scholars Press, 1978]).

[8] See Abraham Schalit, "Josephus Flavius," *EncJud* 10:251-66.

onstrate the great antiquity and nobility of Jewish traditions."[9]

Not all embellishments, however, should be credited to Josephus's invention. We cannot rule out the influence of traditional Jewish readings. For example, some of Josephus's embellishments resemble the later midrashim (Jewish commentaries on the Hebrew Bible written after A.D. 400 but incorporating much earlier traditions). It is likely that Josephus employed some of these haggadic midrashim in his retelling of the stories. Furthermore, book four describes some halakot that are otherwise unknown. For example, proceeds from the sale of female dog skins were forbidden as sacrifice (*Ant.* 4.8.9-10 §§206-207); there were seven judges in each town instead of twenty-three (*Ant.* 4.8.14 §214; the Mishnah specifies the number of judges for particular cases, and never are there seven—there may be three, five or twenty-three [cf. *m. Sanh.* 1:1-6]); women were not admitted as witnesses (*Ant.* 4.8.15 §219); and aristocracy was the preferred form of government (*Ant.* 4.8.17 §223). In all likelihood, these were authentic rather than an error on Josephus's part, since the halakah evolved over the centuries.

Josephus's approach is best placed in a larger literary context, namely, that of a Hellenistic writer.[10] Accordingly, the biblical stories are constantly shaped to suit the audience. This is illustrated, for example, in the account of Joseph and Potiphar's wife (*Ant.* 2.4.1-5 §§39-59). According to Josephus, Potiphar "taught him [Joseph] the learning that became a free man"(*Ant.* 2.4.1 §39). This strikes a common chord with one of the ideals of Hellenism. The entire episode is cast in terms of the familiar Stoic emphasis upon reason guiding the passions (*Ant.* 2.4.1-5 §§40, 43-44, 53) and the importance of listening to one's conscience (*Ant.* 2.4.4 §52). In fact, Josephus does not even mention the biblical emphasis upon sin being essentially an affront to God.

In the course of his writing, Josephus quotes from a number of Hellenistic writers. Among them are Agatharchides of Cnidus (ca. 215-145 B.C.; see, e.g., *Ant.* 12.1.1 §§5-7; cf. *Ag. Ap.* 1.23 §§205-212), Cleodemus called Malchus (*Ant.* 1.15 §240), Berossus (fl. 290 B.C.; cf., e.g., *Ant.* 1.3.6 §93; 1.3.9 §107), Manetho (fl. 280 B.C.; *Ant.* 1.3.9 §107; numerous citations in *Ag. Ap.*), Menander of Ephesus (*Ant.* 8.5.3 §144; 8.13.2 §324) and Polybius (ca. 200-118 B.C.; *Ant.* 12.3.3 §§135-137; 12.9.1 §§358-359). It is also likely that Josephus had access to a general history such as that of Alexander Polyhistor (b. ca. 105 B.C.; cf. *Ant.* 1.15 §240). Polyhistor compiled geographical material and wonder stories of various lands and peoples, among which were the Romans, Delphi,

---

[9]Mason, *Josephus and New Testament,* p. 71.

[10]See further Harold W. Attridge, "Jewish Historiography," in *Early Judaism and Its Modern Interpreters,* ed. Robert A. Kraft and George W. E. Nickelsburg (Philadelphia: Fortress, 1986), p. 326 and references.

Egypt, the Chaldeans and the Jews).[11] Book eleven contains a quote from an unnamed source describing a murder in the Jerusalem temple during the Persian period. This source may have had a Samaritan provenance.[12]

Josephus did not have much in the way of sources for the Ptolemaic period, and this weakness is evident in his wrong placement of events and in his superficial treatment of the period. He does, however, quote from three important documents issued by Antiochus III: his proclamation rewarding the Jews for their assistance (*Ant.* 12.3.3 §§137-144), a decree upholding the ritual prohibitions regarding the temple (*Ant.* 12.3.3 §§145-146) and a decree that Jewish settlers be transferred from Babylonia to Lydia and Phrygia in order to help pacify the region (*Ant.* 12.3.3 §§147-53). The genuineness of all three is not in doubt.[13]

For the Maccabean era, Josephus obviously employed 1 Maccabees and more than likely had other histories of that time period at hand. A major source was the work of Nicolaus of Damascus (already mentioned in connection with *Jewish War*), whom Josephus quoted and acknowledged several times (see, e.g., *Ant* 12.3.2 §126; 13.12.6 §347; and the index in Whiston). In addition, Josephus clearly was aware of information about Diaspora communities, citing several proclamations by Roman emperors and governors with regard to the rights of Jews in various cities and provinces (cf., e.g., *Ant.* 19.5.2 §279-285).

For the Herodian period, Josephus had available his earlier *Jewish War*, and he relied upon his own recollections—though now somewhat modified in light of criticisms directed at him by members of the Jewish community, such as Justus of Tiberias, and by anti-Semites such as Apion. In addition, Josephus may have copied the work of his rival Justus for the reign of Agrippa I (*Ant.* 19.6-8 §§292-353). He was obviously indebted to Strabo (b. c. 64 B.C.), particularly for the Augustan age, whom he quoted numerous times in both *Jewish War* and *Jewish Antiquities* (cf. *Ant.* 13.10.4 §§286-287; 13.11.3 §319). Furthermore, book eighteen tells the story of two Babylonian Jews, the brothers Anilaeus and Asinaeus, and the hatred for Jews that existed in Mesopotamia (*Ant.* 18.9.1-8 §§310-379), while book twenty narrates the conversion of the royal house of Adiabene (*Ant.* 20.2-4 §§17-96). Josephus may well have incorporated these stories as well. Book twenty, for the most part, may be attributed to his participation in the events narrated.[14]

---

[11]See further, J. Strugnell, "Introduction: General Introduction, with a Note on Alexander Polyhistor," *OTP* 2:777-79, 790-93.

[12]Ibid.

[13]Ibid.

[14]See ibid. for further discussion.

Life and Against Apion

Two further works exist, both of which are somewhat like sequels to the preceding writings. Josephus's *Life* appears in all known manuscripts as an appendix to *Jewish Antiquities*. This work, the earliest known example of an autobiography, focuses primarily upon that period of time during which Josephus was commander of the Galilean forces. Obviously he was responding to personal attacks and slanders upon his integrity. This work should be dated to several years after *Jewish Antiquities*.

The last work of which we have knowledge is Josephus's *Against Apion*, also appearing as an appendix to *Jewish Antiquities*. It is another impassioned defense of Jewish history and religion against the attacks of anti-Semites. One of these attacks was by an Egyptian scholar named Apion, whose name has been supplied as the title for the entire work, even though he is only mentioned as an opponent in the first half of the second volume. Since it appears that this work was responding to a negative review of *Jewish Antiquities*, we must allow for a few years' lapse, thus suggesting a time around A.D. 97-100 for its publication. This, then, is the Josephan corpus as we have received it. As with the voluminous works of Philo, we can only sample Josephus's literary output.

The War Against Rome

The Events That Led to the Great War Against Rome
"The war of the Jews against the Romans was the greatest of our time: greater too, perhaps, than any recorded struggle whether between cities or nations" (*J.W.* preface 1 §1]).[15] So begins Josephus's account of this epic struggle against Rome. Josephus's writings are invaluable for tracing the incidents that finally precipitated the Jewish revolt. Like so many wars, the actual outbreak of hostilities came after a long series of grievances and offenses.[16] Josephus indicates that a leading factor was simply mismanagement by a series of incompetent, Roman-appointed governors. After the death of Herod Agrippa I in A.D. 44 (cf. Acts 12:19-23; *Ant.* 19.8.2 §§343-52), the Roman Senate decided that his son Agrippa II was too young to assume leadership of all his father's realm and reverted to a governor holding the rank of procurator. We list these procurators and the incidents during their tenure that fueled the flames of revolt.

---

[15]The translation is by G. A. Williamson and E. Mary Smallwood, *Josephus: The Jewish War*, rev. ed. (New York: Penguin, 1981), p. 27. Unless otherwise noted, subsequent translations are from Whiston.

[16]For a discussion of various scholarly opinions on the causes of the war and its uniqueness, see Doron Mendels, *The Rise and Fall of Jewish Nationalism: Jewish and Christian Ethnicity in Ancient Palestine,* 2d ed. (Grand Rapids: Eerdmans, 1997), pp. 355-58 and the notes included there.

Cuspius Fadus (c. A.D. 44-46) sought to confiscate the high-priestly vestments, which previously had been under the custody of Herod Agrippa I. This prompted a massive outcry, and Fadus relented. When a self-proclaimed prophet, Theudas, gathered a large following at the Jordan River to witness his parting of the river (like a new Joshua), Fadus descended upon them with force and killed many. Theudas, whose vain exploits are referred to in passing in Acts 5:36, was beheaded (*Ant.* 20.5.1 §§97-99).

Tiberius Julius Alexander (c. 46-48), a nephew of Philo and an apostate from Judaism, stirred the pot when he crucified the two sons of a certain Judas the Galilean, who had earlier led an uprising in A.D. 6 (*Ant.* 20.5.1 §§100-102; cf. Acts 5:37).

Ventidius Cumanus (48-52) ratcheted the tension to new levels during his procuratorship. During the Feast of Unleavened Bread (in the spring), when pilgrims thronged the temple courtyards, a Roman soldier standing guard on the roof of the colonnaded porticoes "mooned" the pilgrims below, complete with sounds effects and commentary (*J.W.* 2.12.1 §§223-224)! The reaction was predictable: the crowds demanded punishment for this obscene gesture in a holy shrine. Young Jews took matters into their own hands and starting throwing rocks at the soldiers. Cumanus called in more troops, with the result that the multitudes of pilgrims fled in panic and crushed each other in the narrow streets. In *Jewish War* Josephus says that ten thousand people died on that one occasion alone (*J.W.* 2.12.1 §§225-227), a number that he increases to twenty thousand in his later account in *Jewish Antiquities* (*Ant.* 20.5.3 §§105-112). Even if he exaggerated the numbers, one can easily accept that there would have been many deaths under such circumstances.[17] The resentment toward the Roman occupation was seething.

This was followed by another incident during Cumanus's tenure. This time robbers made off with some furniture belonging to a servant of Caesar's. Cumanus dispatched troops out into the surrounding villages looking for the perpetrators. During this search, a Roman soldier proceeded to tear up and burn a copy of the sacred Torah. Again there was a public outcry and protest to Cumanus about this desecration. Eventually, Cumanus executed the soldier and allayed the outrage of the Jewish community (*J.W.* 2.12.1 §§228-231; *Ant.* 20.5.4 §§113-117).

But this was not the end of it. An even more serious incident arose in the autumn Festival of Tabernacles (in September-October). Samaritans murdered a Jewish pilgrim from Galilee as he was going up to Jerusalem.

---

[17]One may recall that in recent years there have been several episodes in which dozens of Islamic pilgrims lost their lives by being crushed in the courtyard surrounding the Kaaba at Mecca in Saudi Arabia during the annual Haj.

Galilean Jews did not wait for Roman justice; they proceeded to organize a punitive raid on the Samaritans. When Cumanus failed to act promptly on this threat, other Jews from Jerusalem left the feast and joined in the attack on several Samaritan villages. At this point Cumanus did act and with great severity, killing many of the Jewish attackers and imprisoning others. When the Samaritans appealed to Quadratus, governor of the province of Syria and immediate supervisor of Cumanus, he likewise stalled in examining and adjudicating the dispute. When he finally did go to Caesarea, he crucified the prisoners Cumanus had taken. He then sent leading delegates of both the Jewish and Samaritan communities to plead their respective cases before Caesar. Cumanus was also ordered to appear and answer for his actions, with the result that he was removed from office and replaced by Felix (*J.W.* 2.12.1 §§232-246; *Ant.* 20.6.1-3 §§118-136).

Felix (c. 52-60) was not qualified to govern a peaceful province, much less one so volatile as Galilee, Samaria and Judea. He secured the job through his brother Pallas, an influential courtier at Rome (*J.W.* 2.12.1 §247). Suffice it to say, during Felix's tenure conditions rapidly deteriorated with numerous groups of terrorists operating in the cities and countryside. An especially dangerous group was the *sicarii,* named after the daggers they carried concealed under their robes. These used with deadly efficiency in political assassinations (*Ant.* 20.8.5 §§164-165). Anyone collaborating with the Romans was a possible target, but the most prominent victim was none other than the high priest Jonathan. Members of the priestly aristocracy feared for their lives (*J.W.* 2.13.3 §§254-257). Felix responded by crucifying as many of the terrorists as he could lay hands on and punishing all sympathizers.

In one noteworthy incident, an Egyptian self-proclaimed prophet rallied a large number of followers (Josephus says thirty thousand) to attack Jerusalem and drive the Romans out. Felix, with the assistance of most of the citizens of Jerusalem, fell upon this ragtag army and killed many of them, imprisoning the survivors (*J.W.* 2.13.5 §§258-263). For all this, at the end of Felix's administration the countryside was infested with robbers and private armies of terrorists. Furthermore, a violent clash between Syrians and Jews at Caesarea led to armed intervention by Felix's troops and the deaths of many more Jews (*Ant.* 20.8.7 §§173-178).

Porcius Festus succeeded Felix (c. 60-62). Though Festus was a decent man (cf. Acts 25:1—26:32), the situation was so precarious that he could do little to alleviate matters. Josephus says that, although he was able to capture and execute many of the marauders (*J.W.* 14.1 §271), he died in office and was replaced by Albinus.

Albinus (62-64) opened the floodgates further. The *sicarii* began kidnapping servants belonging to the high priest Ananus and demanding the release of their imprisoned colleagues in exchange. This continued with such regularity that before long the *sicarii* were nearly back at full strength (*Ant.* 20.9.3 §§208-210). Besides accepting bribes and embezzling funds, Albinus cooperated with the *sicarii* and, at the end of his administration, freed all the imprisoned terrorists (*J.W.* 2.14.1 §§271-276; *Ant.* 20.9.2-6 §§204-218).

Under the procuratorship of Gessius Florus (64-66), we pass the point of no return. The man was totally venal; Josephus waxes eloquent depicting his depravity:

> He omitted no sort of rapine, or of vexation; where the case was really pitiable, he was most barbarous; and in things of the greatest turpitude, he was most impudent; nor could anyone outdo him in disguising the truth; nor could anyone contrive more subtle ways of deceit than he did. He indeed thought it but a petty offense to get money out of single persons; so he spoiled whole cities, and ruined entire bodies of men at once, and did almost publicly proclaim it all the country over, that they had liberty given them to turn robbers, upon this condition, that he might go shares with them in the spoils. (*J.W.* 2.14.2 §§277-278; cf. *Ant.* 20.11.1 §§252-258)

It was as if he had set himself up as the boss of a mob controlling the entire province. Corruption hit an all-time high.

The spark that ignited the explosion began at Caesarea in a property dispute between Greeks and Jews. A synagogue was located right next to a Greek workshop. Following a series of disputes, a pagan deliberately sacrificed birds right outside the synagogue entrance. This led to verbal abuse followed by physical violence among the young people of both parties. When Jewish leaders went to the procurator Florus to protest, he charged them with illegally removing their sacred books from the synagogue (which they had done in protest) and proceeded to imprison them (*J.W.* 2.14.4-5 §§284-292). According to Josephus, what happened next was deliberately intended by Florus to provoke war. He capped off his misdeeds by robbing the temple treasury, claiming that Caesar had need of the funds.

In spite of this, the Jerusalem leadership made one last attempt to pacify Florus and prevent war. Florus, however, refused all offers of apology and ordered his soldiers to plunder the Upper Market and kill all they should encounter. Citizens who were not even involved were rounded up, and some were crucified. When the bloodbath was over, 3,600 men, women and children had perished. Public opinion began to swing to the Zealots, who for years had been agitating for armed revolt; the war was all but inevitable.

Still, even at this stage, according to Josephus, Agrippa II nearly averted war. He and his sister Bernice pleaded with the multitudes to refrain from the folly of rebelling against the invincible Romans. Josephus includes Agrippa's lengthy oration, but its content strikes precisely the same themes that Jose-

phus makes throughout his narrative, leading one to suspect that the sentiments were primarily Josephus's literary creation (*J.W.* 2.16.4-5 §§345-404).
Especially noteworthy is the argument that God would not assist the Jews in
this rebellion because he had ordained Roman domination and his laws
would be transgressed in the prosecution of the war. That is, the Romans
would wage war on the sabbath, and the Jews would be forced to do the same,
thus breaking God's law and bringing his certain judgment.

Agrippa's plea went unheeded primarily because of the innovators, says
Josephus. Indeed, their hostility forced Agrippa and his sister to withdraw
from the city. Then two events happened that plunged the nation into open
war with Rome. First, some Zealots took Masada by treachery and massacred
the Roman garrison. Second, and even more decisively, the temple sacrifice
for Caesar was cancelled by none other than the governor of the temple precincts, one Eleazar, son of Ananias the high priest (*J.W.* 2.17.2 §408).

The high priests and Pharisaic leaders still sought to head off war, but the
Zealots prevailed with the multitudes, especially after the archives were
raided and all bonds of indebtedness were burned. The revolt now became as
much a struggle of the lower classes and disenfranchised against the wealthy
as it did a struggle for independence from Rome. The mobs captured and
burned the Tower of Antonia, killing all the Roman soldiers stationed there.
The high priest Ananias was discovered in the underground aqueducts,
where he had fled, and was put to death. The city itself was divided into factions headed up by self-proclaimed leaders and warlords who battled each
other for control of the city (*J.W.* 2.17.3-9 §§411-440).

The cities in the surrounding regions erupted into violence, with Gentiles
massacring Jews and Jews retaliating and massacring Gentiles. Cestius Gallus, the governor of Syria, mobilized the Twelfth Legion (nicknamed *Fulmi-
nata,* "the Thundering One") with a number of supporting troops and
auxiliaries coming to well over twenty thousand in all, and advanced along
the Palestinian coast and up to Jerusalem (*J.W.* 2.18.1-11 §§457-512).

As Josephus narrates it, Cestius would surely have taken the city of Jerusalem and brought the revolt to a speedy end, if he had persevered. Not knowing how close he was to success, and with winter setting in, Cestius lost his
nerve and decided to withdraw back to Caesarea. The insurgents took heart
from this unexpected turn of events and harassed the Roman retreat with
great success, killing some 5,680 soldiers and capturing a great quantity of
supplies and military equipment. Josephus saw in this an instance of God's
providence whereby the war would be prolonged and the calamity and suffering of the Jewish people greatly augmented by this seeming victory by the
rebels (*J.W.* 2.19.4-9 §§527-555). Rome must and would respond; the Second
Commonwealth was doomed.

For his part, Nero appointed Titus Flavius Vespasianus, the most experienced and decorated soldier available. Vespasian set out overland to Syria, organizing forces while his son Titus went to Alexandria, Egypt, to mobilize the Fifth and Tenth legions (*J.W.* 3.1.1-3 §§1-8).

Highlights of the Roman Subjugation of Galilee and Judea

As was typical of Roman campaigns, Vespasian went about quelling the revolt methodically and unrelentingly. The Fifth, Tenth and Fifteenth legions reinforced the bloodied Twelfth, to which were added auxiliary troops from the region, bringing the total to some eighty thousand troops. Ptolemais became the base camp for the first phase of the war.

Galilean campaign of A.D. *67.* Vespasian first concentrated on the rebellious cities in Galilee. One by one these pockets of rebellion were overwhelmed and reduced to rubble. The loss of life was enormous. One sea battle is worth mentioning, since we probably have mute evidence of this conflict in a museum at Nof Ginosaur today. Several years ago, when the Sea of Galilee was at a record low level, several members from Kibbutz Nof Ginosaur saw something protruding from the shoreline. On further examination it turned out to be a boat. Archaeologists were brought in, and the boat was recovered intact. After being submersed in a special solution for several years to prevent it from drying out and virtually disintegrating, it has been placed on display at a museum on the Kibbutz. Although dubbed the "Jesus boat," it almost certainly was one that was destroyed in the sea battle narrated at some length by Josephus (*J.W.* 3.10.1-9 §§462-542).

During this phase, Josephus was bottled up in Jotapata and besieged for forty-seven days. Of course, this part of the story is told at some length, and we have already discussed the rather suspicious circumstances under which Josephus managed to surrender himself and gain the confidence of Vespasian (*J.W.* 3.7.1-8 §§132-408).

The siege of Gamala, overlooking the Sea of Galilee, is also worth mentioning, especially if one has had the opportunity to visit the site as a tourist. Josephus narrates with vivid detail the difficulties and setbacks endured by the Romans and the tragedy that befell the inhabitants. Reading Josephus's account when visiting Gamala, one gains appreciation for his essentially accurate depiction of the terrain.[18] Josephus even takes credit for making the

---

[18] I say "essentially accurate" because, throughout his work, Josephus tends to describe heights as if they were dizzying and enormous. The consistent exaggeration in this regard has led some scholars to suspect that Josephus was rather near-sighted so that the heights *did* seem more pronounced to him than they actually were (Anson Rainey, pers. comm., 1969). Be that as it may, his accounts are still quite reliable and may generally be taken at face value.

fortifications of Gamala more formidable. Agrippa had previously tried unsuccessfully to take Gamala with the forces available to him for seven months, but Roman persistence and valor eventually triumphed (*J.W.* 4.1.1-10 §§1-83).

The campaign of A.D. *68.* During the spring of 68, Vespasian renewed the war by completely isolating Judea. Thus the district of Perea (on the east side of the Jordan River and today primarily located in modern Jordan) was subdued with the only fortress yet standing at Macherus overlooking the Dead Sea. Vespasian next attacked the coastal plain and regions to the southwest of Jerusalem. The Fifth Legion was stationed at Emmaus to the west of Jerusalem. Next, the entire Jordan Valley was secured, cutting off all access from the east, and the Tenth Legion was posted at Jericho. Hapless Jerusalem lay astride the Judean hills completely hemmed in by Roman forces.

In the spring of 68, revolts against Nero broke out in various parts of the empire. Nero himself committed suicide on June 9. During the next year, three emperors ruled briefly, none of them dying peacefully. Vespasian waited on the sidelines during this time of uncertainty and turmoil, and the Jewish insurgents received an unexpected reprieve. Then in July 69, Vespasian was proclaimed emperor by his troops, and in the spring of 70 he ascended the throne. His son Titus was entrusted with the final campaign against Jerusalem.

The siege of Jerusalem. In the spring of 70, Titus approached Jerusalem with two legions, the Twelfth and Fifteenth, and was met by the Tenth Legion coming up from Jericho to the east and the Fifth Legion advancing from Emmaus on the west. To these were added a large number of auxiliaries, bringing the total to some 80,000 troops. The insurgents could muster at most about 25,000. Two Zealot factions, led by Simon bar Giora and John of Gischala, now defended the city. They finally ceased their internecine strife and assigned respective sections of the wall to defend. Simon's forces guarded the northeastern corner all the way to the southwestern corner at the Pool of Siloam, and John's manned the eastern wall.

The following is a brief chronology of this horrific siege. In April of 70 Titus completed the investment of Jerusalem. This procedure cut off all aid and prevented escape for all except those who were willing to pay large bribes to the Romans and could escape detection by the partisans inside the city.

By May 25, the Third Wall was breached. Herod Agrippa II had begun construction on this wall but had never finished it. After the revolt, the insurgents hastily threw up stoneworks along its projected course to provide another line of defense on the vulnerable north side of Jerusalem. Though scholarly debate still continues, a majority of archaeologists believe that the remnants of a wall in the vicinity of the American Schools of Oriental Research are part of this Third Wall.[19] Once inside, Titus moved his camp within the northern part of the city, at the so-called Assyrian Camp (cf. 2 Kings 19:35), opposite the Second Wall. The Third Wall was razed, as was much of this quarter of the city (*J. W.* 5.7.2-3 §§296-303).[20]

On May 30 the Second Wall was breached (though not without difficulties and setbacks) just to the east of the present-day Damascus Gate. Titus transferred his main camps inside the city, with the Fifth and Twelfth Legions positioned to the north of the well-fortified Fortress Antonia and the Tenth and Fifteenth in the vicinity of what is today Jaffa Gate. The Second Wall was demolished (*J. W.* 5.8.1-2 §§331-347).

On June 16 Titus ordered an all-out assault on the three towers guarding Herod's Palace (Phasael, Hippicus, Mariamne) and the Fortress Antonia guarding the north end of the temple. The Jewish defenders repelled this massive assault (*J. W.* 5.11.4-6 §§466-490), so Titus ordered a siege dike to be thrown up around the remaining city, which effectively prevented any food from being smuggled in (*J. W.* 5.12.2 §§502-511). The renewal of partisan strife among the defenders only intensified the desperate condition of the insurgents. Josephus narrates a particularly gruesome account of a woman eating her own infant son (*J. W.* 6.3.3-5 §§193-219).

Since the Zealots refused all offers to surrender, Titus was left no choice but to proceed with a bloody assault. This began on July 20; by July 24 the chief obstacle in the temple area, the Fortress Antonia, fell. Josephus records in vivid and gory detail the desperate fighting that raged during this time and narrates deeds of bravery and courage on both sides (*J. W.* 6.1.1-8 §§1-92). One is reminded here of the classic work by Homer, *The Iliad,* in which the battle scenes are punctuated by accounts of individual bravery and single-handed combat between two opponents. On August 6 the sacrifices ceased in the Jerusalem temple (*J. W.* 6.2.1 §§93-94). They have never been reinstituted to this day.

On August 27 the temple gates were burned, and on the August 28 the temple itself was completely burned. This date, called the Ninth of Ab (or Av) in the Jewish calendar, is fraught with deep sadness in Jewish history, since it was the same calendar day on which the First Temple was destroyed by Nebuchadnezzar in 586 B.C.—an irony not missed by Josephus (*J. W.* 6.4.5 §§249-251). Both destructions are recalled in synagogue services today. Ironi-

---

[19]For further discussion, see S. Ben-Arieh, "The 'Third Wall' of Jerusalem," in *Jerusalem Revealed: Archaeology in the Holy City 1967-1974,* ed. Y. Yadin (Jerusalem: Israel Exploration Society, 1975), pp. 60-62.
[20]Note the typographical error in the Hendrickson Whiston edition. There are two number 2s on page 712.

cally, a number of tragic events have also occurred on this same calendar day in Jewish history.[21]

By August 30 the Romans had captured the Lower City and set fire to it (*J.W.* 6.7.2 §363). John of Gischala made his escape to the Upper City, where his forces held out until September 26, which is the ninth of Elul in the Jewish calendar (*J.W.* 6.8.4-5 §§392-408). The entire city of Jerusalem including the temple area was ordered leveled and the pitiful survivors sent into captivity. Only the three massive towers of Phasael, Hippicus, and Mariamne were left standing as a testament to the valor and might of imperial Rome (*J.W.* 6.9.1-3 §409). Over the desolate remains Titus posted the Tenth Legion; they remained there some two hundred years in the area known today as the Armenian Garden. In this area a water pipe and personal seals have been found bearing the name of the Tenth Legion. Not far from Jaffa Gate, next to the New Imperial Hotel, one may see a dedicatory column erected about A.D. 200 in honor of Marcus Iunius Maximus, a Legate of the Tenth Legion and governor of Judea.[22]

In the summer of 71 a joint triumph (a victory parade) celebrated Vespasian and Titus's victory over the Jews. Today one may admire the impressive triumphal arch of Titus at the site of the ancient Forum, standing as a silent sentinel to this epic struggle. Roman soldiers are sculpted on an inside panel of the arch, shown carrying off the menorah from the temple. Roman coins were minted all over the empire commemorating the victorious legions. Thousands of gold, silver and bronze coins of various denominations depict a mourning female figure beneath a palm tree. Her identity is no mystery, as an inscription tersely announces: *Judaea Capta.* No other Roman victory received such widespread notice as this one, a testament to the difficulty of subduing the Jewish insurgents. At this same triumph the two ringleaders, Simon bar Giora and John of Gischala, were punished: Simon was publicly executed and John imprisoned in the salt mines.

Right at the top of "must see" sites in Rome today is the massive Colosseum—originally 165 feet high, with five tiers, eighty entrances, and a capacity reported as 87,000. This amphitheater was built over a period of years beginning with Vespasian (69-79), continued by Titus (79-81) and completed by Domitian (81-96). Nerva (96-98) and Trajan (98-117) made further additions to this architectural marvel, and in the middle of the second century Antoninus Pius authorized restoration of the entire edifice.

The name *Colosseum* apparently derives from a colossal statue of Nero (54-

---

[21] See "Av, The Ninth of," *EncJud* 3:936-40.

[22] See Jerome Murphy-O'Connor, *The Holy Land: An Archaeological Guide from Earliest Times to 1700,* 3d ed. (Oxford: Oxford University Press, 1992), p. 64.

68) that once stood nearby. Remember that it was during his reign that the ill-fated First Jewish Revolt began (66). Since the building was not formally dedicated until the year 80, Jewish prisoners did not, in all likelihood, meet their fate in this arena. So why do I mention it? The connection is this. We know that the economic and financial condition of the empire when Vespasian became emperor was critical. So how was the Roman government able to finance such an enormous undertaking? The answer is almost certainly this: plunder from Judea and especially from the Jerusalem temple. This conclusion is inferred from a "ghost" inscription next to one of the entryways to the Colosseum. That is to say, an inscription with metal letters fastened to a stone slab (the "ghost" inscription) was removed, smoothed over and over-written by a later inscription carved into the stone. Through careful analysis of the hole placements and comparison with other dedicatory inscriptions of the period, Professor Géza Alföldy was able to decipher the original inscription. He translates it as follows: "The emperor Titus Caesar Vespasian Augustus ordered the new amphitheater to be made from the (proceeds from the sale of the) booty."[23] Added to this is the testimony of Josephus that in the triumphal procession in Rome "there was here to be seen a mighty quantity of silver and gold and ivory . . . running along like a river" (*J.W.* 7.5 §134). The amount of booty taken from defeated Judea could easily have been the equivalent of hundreds of millions of dollars. No doubt it was from this influx of revenue that Rome erected this monumental public building as a showplace to proclaim its powers and glory. This was the final irony in this tragic story of the relationship between Jews and Romans that began so auspiciously in the days of the Hasmoneans.[24]

Remarkably, there still remained a few pockets of resistance in Judea. Titus returned to Rome with Josephus and entrusted the mopping-up operations to Lucius Bassus, governor of Judea, and to Silva, a top general. Bassus took the fortresses of Herodium and Macherus, and Silva finally captured Masada in the spring of 73 or 74. Those who have visited the site will resonate with Jerome Murphy-O'Connor's statement that "Masada is the most spectacular site in the country and the scene of one of the most dramatic epi-

---

[23]Cited by Louis H. Feldman, "Financing the Colosseum," *BAR* 27, no. 4 (2001): 20-31, 60. The translation in German may be consulted in Géza Alföldy, "Eine Bauinschrift aus dem Colosseum," *Zeitschrift für Papyrologie und Epigraphik* 109 (1995): 195-226. Feldman's article is a fascinating account of the Colosseum and its connection to the First Jewish Revolt and contains splendid pictures and a reconstruction of the inscription.

[24]Unfortunately, this would not be the last time Jews underwrote, against their will, the grand designs of empires. For example, Christopher Columbus's epic voyage to the New World was financed, at least in part, by wealth confiscated from the Jews by King Ferdinand and Queen Isabella of Spain after their edict of expulsion in 1492.

sodes in its history."[25] This last siege has fired the imaginations of many and still figures in the national psyche of the modern State of Israel.[26]

Josephus's description displays his storytelling ability at its best; it has also sparked considerable scholarly controversy. Can one take Josephus's account of the mass suicide of the 960 Jewish defenders at face value, or has he indulged his national pride and invented a heroic, albeit tragic, finale? We leave the question to the scholars.[27] But every student of Josephus should at least read the stirring oration attributed to the Zealot leader Eleazar (*J. W.* 7.8.6-7 §§320-388). According to Josephus, only two women and five children survived to tell about the details of the suicide, which ironically occurred on the fifteenth of Nisan, the first day of Passover commemorating the liberation and exodus from Egypt.

We break off our story here, since for all practical purposes the last center of Jewish resistance had been crushed. Only a few isolated incidents of Jewish rebellion occurred in Egypt and North Africa after the fall of Masada.

Importance of Josephus for the NT

Literary Features

The closest parallel in the NT to the works of Josephus are the Gospel of Luke and the book of Acts—both traditionally ascribed to Luke, Paul's travelling companion. Luke is the one NT author who self-consciously sets out to give a historical account of the Jesus movement and of the earliest church. It may come as a surprise to the reader of the NT to realize that Mark, generally thought to be the earliest of the Gospels, does not give one date with which to locate Jesus' ministry. Only the mention of Pilate as the governor before whom Jesus stood trial (Mk 15:1-15) helps us know the approximate time of Jesus' death (Pilate was governor from A.D. 26-36). Matthew, thought by most scholars to have used Mark in the composition of his Gospel, also provides no dates, though he does place Jesus' birth in the time of Herod the Great, thus giving us an approximate date for Jesus' birth (Herod died in 4 B.C.). It is Luke, however, who provides the chronological pegs that locate Jesus' minis-

---

[25]*Holy Land,* p. 343.

[26]Thus various units of the Israeli military have a swearing-in ceremony on top of Masada with the vow "Masada shall not fall again!"

[27]For a good popular discussion of the issue with excellent photographs and diagrams, see Hershel Shanks, "Questioning Masada," *BAR* 24, no. 6 (1998): 30-31, as well as the accompanying articles in the same issue: Nachman Ben-Yehuda, "Where Masada's Defenders Fell," pp. 32-39; Joseph Zias, "Whose Bones?" pp. 40-45, 54-66; and Ze'ev Meshel, "Governments-in-Exile," pp. 46-53, 68. For a scholarly discussion, see M. Stern, "The Suicide of Eleazar ben Jair and His Men at Masada and the 'Fourth Philosophy,'" in his *Studies in Jewish History* (Jerusalem: Magnes, 1991), pp. 313-43.

try within a year or two. In Luke, the Palestinian Jesus movement unfolds within the larger context of Roman history. See especially Luke 3:1-2, where we have a full listing of the various provincial governors and regional rulers in Tiberius Caesar's fifteenth year (either A.D. 26 or 27), which signaled the beginning of John the Baptist's ministry.

In addition, Luke displays a style and flourish imitative of the Greek and Roman historians.[28] To illustrate this point, we quote from several prominent Greek and Roman historians as they introduce their respective works to their readers and compare this to both Josephus and Luke:

> In this book, the result of my inquiries into history, I hope to do two things: to preserve the memory of the past by putting on record the astonishing achievements both of our own and of the Asiatic peoples; secondly, and more particularly, to show how the two races came into conflict. (Herodotus, *History* 1.1 [fifth century B.C.])
>
> Thucydides, an Athenian, wrote the history of the war between the Peloponnesians and the Athenians, beginning at the moment that it broke out, and believing that it would be a great war, and more worthy of relations than any that had preceded it. . . . Indeed this was the greatest movement yet known in history, not only of the Hellenes, but of a large part of the barbarian world—I have almost said of mankind. For though the events of remote antiquity, and even those that more immediately precede the war, could not from lapse of time be clearly ascertained, yet the evidences which an inquiry carried as far back as was practicable leads me to trust, all point to the conclusion that there was nothing on a great scale, either in war or in other matters. (Thucydides, *Peloponnesian War* 1.1 [fifth century B.C.])
>
> Famous writers have recorded Rome's early glories and disasters. The Augustan Age, too, had its distinguished historians. But then the rising tide of flattery had a deterrent effect. The reigns of Tiberius, Gaius, Claudius, and Nero were described during their lifetimes in fictitious terms, for fear of the consequences; whereas the accounts written after their deaths were influenced by still raging animosities. So I have decided to say a little about Augustus, with special attention to his last period, and then go on to the reign of Tiberius and what followed. I shall write without indignation or partisanship: in my case the customary incentives to these are lacking. (Tacitus, *Annals of Imperial Rome* 1.1 [first century A.D.])

For comparison we excerpt sections of Josephus's introduction to his *Jewish War* and *Antiquities*.

> Whereas the war which the Jews made with the Romans hath been the greatest of all those, not only that have been in our times, but, in a manner, of those that ever were heard of; both of those wherein cities have fought against cities, or

---

[28]See further Attridge, "Jewish Historiography," p. 327 and references.

nations against nations; while some men who were not concerned in the affairs themselves, have gotten together vain and contradictory stories by hearsay, and have written them down after a sophistical manner; and while those that were there present have given false accounts of things, and this either out of a humor of flattery to the Romans, or of hatred towards the Jews; and while their writings contain sometimes accusations, and sometimes encomiums, but nowhere, the accurate truth of the facts, I have proposed to myself, for the sake of such as live under the government of the Romans, to translate those books into the Greek tongue, which I formerly composed in the language of our country, and sent to the Upper Barbarians; I Joseph, the son of Matthias, by birth an Hebrew, a priest also, and one who at first fought against the Romans myself, and was forced to be present at what was done afterwards, [am author of this work]. (*J.W.* preface 1 §1)

Those who undertake to write histories do not, I perceive, take that trouble on one and the same account, but for many reasons, and those such as are very different one from another; for some of them apply themselves to this part of learning to show their skill in composition, and that they may then acquire a reputation for speaking finely; others of them there are who write histories, in order to gratify those that happened to be concerned in them, and on that account have spared no pains, but rather go beyond their own abilities in the performance; but others there are, who, of necessity and by force, are driven to write history, because they are concerned in the facts, and so cannot excuse themselves from committing them to writing, for the advantage of posterity; nay, there are not a few who are induced to draw their historical facts out of darkness into light, and to produce them for the benefit of the public on account of the great importance of the facts themselves with which they have been concerned. Now of these several reasons for writing history, I must profess the two last were my own reasons also; for since I was myself interested in that war which we Jews had with the Romans, and knew myself its particular actions, and what conclusion it had, I was forced to give the history of it, because I saw that others perverted the truth of those actions in their writings.

Now I have undertaken the present work, as thinking it will appear to all the Greeks worthy of their study; for it will contain all our antiquities, and the constitution of our government, as interpreted out of the Hebrew Scriptures; and indeed I did formerly intend, when I wrote of the war, to explain who the Jews originally were,—what fortunes they had been subjected to,—and by what legislator they had been instructed in piety, and the exercise of other—what wars also they had made in remote ages, till they were unwillingly engaged in this last with the Romans; but because this work would take up a great compass, I separated it into a set treatise by itself, with a beginning of its own, and its own conclusion; but in process of time, as usually happens to such as undertake great things, I grew weary, and went on slowly, it being a large subject, and a difficult thing to translate our history into a foreign, and to us unaccustomed, language. However, some persons there were who desired to know our history, and so exhorted me to go on with it; and, above all the rest, Epaphroditus, a man who is a lover of all kind of learning, but is principally delighted with the knowledge of history; and this on account of his having been himself concerned in great affairs, and many turns of fortune, and having shown a wonderful vigor of an excellent nature, and an immovable virtuous resolution in them all. I yielded to this man's persuasions, who always excites such as have abilities in what is useful and acceptable, to join their endeavors with his. I was also ashamed myself to permit any laziness of disposition to have a greater influence upon me than the delight of taking pains in such studies as were very useful: I thereupon stirred up myself, and went on with my work more cheerfully. Besides the foregoing motives, I had others which I greatly reflected on; and these were, that our forefathers were willing to communicate such things to others; and that some of the Greeks took considerable pains to know the affairs of our nation. (*Ant.* preface 1 §§1-2)

These lengthy introductions by Josephus clearly imitate the Hellenistic and Roman historians. We now cite Luke's introduction to his Gospel and Acts:

Since many have undertaken to set down an orderly account of the events that have been fulfilled among us, just as they were handed on to us by those who from the beginning were eyewitnesses and servants of the word, I too decided, after investigating everything carefully from the very first, to write an orderly account for you, most excellent Theophilus, so that you may know the truth concerning the things about which you have been instructed. (Lk 1:1-4)

In the first book, Theophilus, I wrote about all that Jesus did and taught from the beginning until the day when he was taken up to heaven, after giving instructions through the Holy Spirit to the apostles whom he had chosen. (Acts 1:1-2)

What stands out in this comparison of prefaces is the concern of the historians to indicate to the reader (1) the aim and scope of the work; (2) the importance of the subject matter; (3) the credentials and accuracy of the historian; and (4) the inadequacies of previous efforts. Thus both Josephus and Luke consciously set about their respective tasks with a shared tradition of how historiography ought to be done.[29]

Luke, like Josephus, also wrote a sequel to his first work and, in the opening preface, draws the readers' attention to that fact (Acts 1:1). The opening line of Acts also assists the reader in knowing that this is volume two, not volume one. Recall that books were produced as scrolls and not in codex form, as became customary in the second century A.D. and later.[30] Hence the necessity of indicating right at the beginning of a scroll if it is a sequel to another. There is also a dedication to a patron: in the case of Josephus it was to a certain Epaphroditus; for Luke it was to Theophilus. These were at least inter-

---

[29]See further Mason, *Josephus and the New Testament,* pp. 186-88.
[30]See Bruce Metzger, *The Text of the New Testament,* 3rd ed. (Oxford: Oxford University Press, 1992), pp. 5-6.

ested readers and may have underwritten the costs of publication (Lk 1:3; Acts 1:1).

Both Josephus and Luke wrote their histories from an apologetic stance. We have already seen how Josephus clearly pursued his apologetic interests in both *Jewish War* and *Jewish Antiquities*. Luke's apologetic purpose has been widely recognized by NT scholars as being a defense of the Jesus movement and one of its most prominent missionaries, Paul, against the charge of being subversive and revolutionary.[31] The trial scenes of Jesus and Paul (three of them in Acts) make a clear point: nothing in this new movement should be seen as a threat to Rome's political control.

Another literary feature shared by Josephus and Luke is the insertion of speeches reportedly uttered by various individuals on certain occasions. A close examination of these speeches in both writers points to their programmatic function within the composition as a whole. In other words, the themes of the speeches tend to echo the sentiments of the historian himself. This, of course, raises the knotty problem of the genuineness of the speeches, especially in the case of Luke. Since close study demonstrates that both writers display a degree of looseness and invention in their speeches, we need to recognize this as a part of the literary conventions of that time. It is a mistake to judge ancient historians by the standards of modern ones! On the other hand, neither Luke nor Josephus resorted to wholesale fabrication. The essence of the speeches corresponded to the convictions of the individuals making them, *in the view of our first-century historians.*[32]

A rather important issue concerns the question of literary dependence between Josephus and Luke-Acts. Scholars have weighed in on both sides of the issue. The fact is that in addition to the features mentioned above, both authors recorded a rather large number of common incidents. For example, the following events occur in both sets of writings: the census under Quirinius (Lk 2:1-3; cf. *J.W.* 2.8.1 §§117-118; *Ant.* 18.1.1 §§1-5); the insurrections of Judas the Galilean, Theudas and the Egyptian prophet (Acts 5:36-37; 21:38; cf. *J.W.* 2.13.4-5 §§259, 261-263; *Ant.* 20.5-8 §§97, 102, 171); an account of King Agrippa I's death; the governor Felix and his Jewish mistress Drusilla; Agrippa II and his sister Bernice; mention of Lysanias as tetrarch of Abilene; the famine under Claudius; and perhaps Pilate's attack on some Galilean pilgrims to Jerusalem.

These shared incidents do not automatically indicate literary dependence; it is entirely possible that both had access to common traditions. Beyond this,

---

[31]See, e.g., E. M. Blaiklock, "Acts of the Apostles," *ZPEB* 1:45-47; F. F. Bruce, "Acts of the Apostles," *ISBE* 1:44-46; and J. B. Green, "Acts of the Apostles," *DLNTD,* pp. 16-23.

[32]See further, Green, "Acts of the Apostles," pp. 10-12.

however, are the shared themes and vocabulary. These might suggest more than merely shared traditions.[33] On the other hand, the issue of dating enters the picture. In order for Luke to have used Josephus, one would have to date Luke-Acts to the 90s, since *Jewish Antiquities* was published around A.D. 93. Conservative scholarship has usually not dated Luke-Acts this late.[34] If one dates Luke-Acts early, that is, in the 60s, then Josephus *may* have had access to Luke-Acts, though it hardly seems likely that he would have consulted a Christian work.[35] Most scholars today deny any dependence one way or the other, and we think this judgment is correct.[36]

Key Figures

Josephus's works illuminate several key players on the stage of NT history. The first is Herod the Great. We are extremely grateful to Josephus for a lively, at times riveting, account of the rise of this man to power and his extraordinary achievements. As magnificent as his accomplishments were, these almost fade by comparison to his incredible personal tragedies. Herod the Great is like a combination of Judas Maccabeus and Antiochus Epiphanes; he elicits both admiration and abhorrence.

Scholars have noted that Josephus's portrayal of Herod varies in his earlier *Jewish War* and his later *Jewish Antiquities*.[37] Herod is more sinister and self-seeking in the latter. Perhaps the best single depiction of Herod by Josephus comes in a well-known passage from *Jewish Antiquities* 16.4 §§150-159. Here Josephus reduced the seeming contradictions in Herod's life to one fatal flaw: "a man ambitious of honor, and quite overcome by that passion" (*Ant.* 16.4 §150).

For Herod's contemporaries, assessment of the man depended upon where one stood in the complex political spectrum of the day. That Herod had supporters is clear. Even the NT indicates that he had a party of backers (the "Herodians"; cf. Mk 3:6; 12:13). That he had opponents goes without saying. It is safe to say that a majority of Jews detested him. This fact shaped to a considerable extent the course of Jewish history for nearly half a century.

Unanimously appointed client-king over Judea by the Roman Senate in 40

---

[33]See the specific points in Mason, *Josephus and the New Testament*, pp. 214-25.
[34]See, e.g., Blaiklock, "Acts of the Apostles," 1:43-44.
[35]William Whiston's view that Josephus became a Christian (see Dissertation 6 in *The Works of Josephus: Complete and Unabridged* [Peabody, Mass: Hendrickson, 1987]) is uniformly denied by modern scholars.
[36]Mason states: "I find it easier to believe that Luke knew something of Josephus' work than that he independently arrived at these points of agreement. Nevertheless, we await a thorough study of the matter" (*Josephus and the New Testament*, p. 225). In "Josephus: Value for New Testament Study," however, he is content to note that "most scholars think that he [Luke] did not [know Josephus]" (p. 599).
[37]For particulars, see Mason, *Josephus and the New Testament*, pp. 90-96.

B.C. (*Ant.* 14.3-5 §§377-389), Herod fought until 38/37 B.C. before he actually gained control over Antigonas, a Hasmonean rival (*Ant.* 15.1-14 §§394-467). Herod eliminated the last Hasmonean claimant to the throne after a bloody siege of Jerusalem, which ironically, Josephus informs us, occurred on the same calendar day twenty-seven years after Pompey had sacked Jerusalem in 63 B.C. (*Ant.* 16.1-4 §§468-491). Eventually Herod's domain included Perea, Samaria, Galilee, Iturea and Traconitis (the latter two regions being in the modern Golan Heights and Jordan).

Herod's reign can be divided into three distinct periods: an early phase, in which he had to consolidate his kingdom and fight off rivals and predators (40-30 B.C.); a prosperous middle phase marked by great building projects, of which the temple was the crown jewel (30-10 B.C.); and a final turbulent and troubled phase in which Herod battled internal squabbles and international crises to remain in power and secure dynastic succession (10-4 B.C.). He finally succumbed to a painful and revolting illness (*Ant.* 17.6.1-5 §§146-171; *J.W.* 1.33.5-9 §§565-673)—one thinks here of the account of Antiochus Epiphanes' demise in 2 Maccabees 9:5-29.[38]

The only explicit mention of Herod the Great in the NT occurs in Matthew's infancy narrative (Mt 2:1-19; cf. Lk 1:5). The slaughter of the innocents in the region of Bethlehem highlights the paranoid and cruel side of this man during the last phase of his life. Josephus's depiction of Herod's mental state provides the larger context for such an atrocity. The fact that it was but one of many such atrocities probably accounts for its omission by Josephus.

Though he is not mentioned again by name in the Gospels, Herod the Great left a lasting legacy as a builder, and some of his architectural and engineering accomplishments are mentioned or alluded to in the NT. An extremely valuable passage in *Antiquities* describes the magnificent temple that Herod enlarged and beautified (*Ant.* 15.11.17 §§380-425). This temple is the setting for many Gospel narratives: (1) Jesus' dedication as an infant (Lk 2:22-38); (2) his brief stay in the temple area during his twelfth year (Lk 2:41-50); (3) his temptation by Satan on the "pinnacle of the temple" (Mt 4:5-7; cf. Lk 4:9-12);[39] (4) his cleansing of the temple (Mk 11:15-19; cf. Mt 21:12-17; Lk 19:45-48); (5) his frequent teaching in the cloisters or porticoes of the temple when he visited Jerusalem (Mk 11:15; 12:35; 14:49; cf. Lk 19:47; Jn 7:14, 28;

---

[38]See further, Nikos Kokkinos, "Herod's Horrid Death," *BAR* 28, no. 2 (2002): 28-35, 62, and "What Killed Herod?" *BAR* 28, no. 2 (2002): 16.

[39]Precisely where this was is not certain. Generally scholars place it on the southeast corner. This seems to be the place from which, according to Josephus, one's "sight could not reach to such an immense depth" (*Ant* 15.11.5 §412). But see our earlier comment on Josephus's poor eyesight (n. 20). Many would understand the account to be visionary in nature and not literal.

8:20: 10:23; 11:56); (6) his observation of a poor widow putting in her two small copper coins in the offering boxes of the treasury, surrounding the Court of the Women (Mk 12:41-44; Lk 21:1-4); and (7) the remarkable phenomenon whereby the curtain shielding the holy of holies tore from top to bottom at the moment of Jesus' death (Mk 15:38; cf. Mt 27:51; Lk 23:45).

An important reference to the temple also occurs in John's Gospel when, in a retort to Jesus' claim to be able to raise up the temple in three days, the religious leaders incredulously reminded Jesus that the temple had already been under construction forty-six years and was not yet completed (Jn 2:13-22). This time frame correlates nicely with Luke's notation that Jesus was baptized in the fifteenth year of Tiberius (ca. A.D. 25/26). Since Herod began work in 20 B.C., forty-six years brings us quite close to the first year of Jesus' ministry (ca. A.D. 27). According to Josephus, the entire temple complex was not finished until A.D. 64, just before the outbreak of the revolt in 66. The Synoptic Gospels all record the reaction of Jesus' disciples to the outward beauty and splendor of the buildings (Mt 24:1; Mk 13:1; Lk 21:5). Josephus likewise took some pride in the splendor of this complex and obviously enjoyed describing its construction and appointments. His sadness at its destruction is palpable (*J.W.* 6.4.8 §§267-270). The disciples, for their part, were deeply shocked to hear Jesus' prediction that "not one stone will be left upon another" (Lk 21:6).[40]

According to the book of Acts, the porticoes surrounding the temple were a regular place of worship and witnessing (Acts 2:46; 3:1—4:1; 5:12, 21, 42). Paul's arrest on his last visit to Jerusalem took place in the temple precincts, and he spent a short while in the Fortress Antonia, described by Josephus as guarding the temple complex, before being transferred to Caesarea (Acts 21:27—23:31). Peter also may have been incarcerated in Antonia and miraculously delivered by an angel (Acts 12:3-11).

Though not mentioned in the NT, Herod's reign was characterized by building on a grand scale all over the country, indeed, even in other Roman provinces (*Ant.* 16.5.2 §§142-149). Samaria, renamed Sebaste in honor of Augustus Caesar, was rebuilt as a Greco-Roman city of the first order. It became the site for games like the Olympics held every five years (*Ant.* 16.5.1 §§136-141). Herod transformed Caesarea by the sea, formerly known as Strato's Tower,

---

[40]The present writer attended a public lecture by E. P. Sanders in which he made the point that Jesus' prediction did not literally come to pass, as anyone who visits the Western Wall (called the "Wailing Wall" before the Israelis captured the Old City in 1967) may see ("Jesus, Paul and Other Jews," lecture presented at the Thirteenth Forum on Jewish/ Christian Relations, Christian Theological Seminary, Indianapolis, Ind., March 21, 1994). During a question-and-answer session, I asked Dr. Sanders if the retaining wall really qualified as part of the temple buildings (*hieron* in Gk). His reply was that my "question was very shrewd"!

into the major seaport and center of government (*Ant.* 15.9.6 §§331-341). The artificial harbor with breakwater and tower, the warehouses, theaters, amphitheater, hippodrome, baths and forum are coming to light in modern excavations.[41] Paul spent several years under detention at Caesarea (Acts 23:33–26:32). Jericho, an important commercial center, also became a winter resort for Herod and his family. It was the hometown of the wealthy tax farmer Zacchaeus and the blind Bartimaeus (Mk 10:46; Lk 19:1-10). Many other cities were founded or rebuilt throughout the region (*Ant.* 16.5.2 §§142-149).

In addition, Herod built a series of fortresses to protect his kingdom from invaders such as the Parthians and Nabateans and from poachers such as Cleopatra of Egypt, who had designs upon certain of Herod's holdings, especially Jericho with its balsam groves (*Ant.* 15.4.1-2 §§88-98). Josephus's description of Cleopatra and her antics is worthy of any soap opera! Although she turned her seductive charms on Herod, he resisted, not because of moral scruples, but out of purely pragmatic considerations (*Ant.* 15.2.2 §§97-103). Herod's fortresses, however, also served as safe havens from his own subjects. Later, during the First Jewish Revolt, fortresses such as Alexandrium, Macherus, Masada and Herodium were seized by the insurgents, and only after immense effort and huge loss of life on both sides were the Roman legions able to subdue them. In addition to being fortresses, Macherus and Hyrcania were dreaded state prisons. Few if any ever returned from stints in these locations. John the Baptist was beheaded at the eastern fortress of Macherus in what is today Jordan (*Ant.* 18.5.2 §119; cf. Mt 14:1-12; Mk 6:14-29; Lk 3:20). Masada and Herodium are spectacular tourist sites, and one can only marvel at the engineering skill, architectural splendor and artistic grace that went into their construction. Herodium was the site of Herod's burial (*Ant.* 17.8.3 §§196-199).[42]

Just before his death, Herod the Great designated Archelaus (4 B.C.-A.D. 6) as ethnarch ("national ruler"). Archelaus ruled over Judea, Samaria and the coastal plain until he was removed from office for incompetence by Caesar Augustus. He is mentioned but once in the NT, in Matthew's infancy narrative (Mt 2:22). Some scholars think that Jesus' parable about a nobleman who went "to a distant country to get royal power for himself and then return" (Lk 19:12) reflects the circumstances of Archelaus's struggle for succession to his father's kingdom (*J.W.* 2.1-2 §§1-37).

Antipas (4 B.C.-A.D. 34), another of Herod's sons, was appointed by Herod

[41]See the articles with excellent photographs by Robert J. Bull, "Caesarea Maritima—The Search for Herod's City," *BAR* 8, no. 3 (1982): 24; and Robert L. Hohlfelder, "Caesarea Beneath the Sea," p. 42.

[42]See Ehud Netzer, "Searching for Herod's Tomb," *BAR* 9, no. 3 (1983): 30. The search for Herod's sepulchre has thus far been unsuccessful. See also Eric Wargo, "Where Is Herod Buried?" BAR 28, no. 2 (2002): 33, 63.

and confirmed by Caesar as tetrarch ("ruler of a quarter") of Galilee and Perea. He had actually been named king in a second version of Herod's will but was finally demoted to tetrarch in the turbulent days surrounding Herod's death (*J.W.* 1.33.7 §646; *Ant.* 17.8.1 §188). Not without good cause Jesus called him a "fox" (Lk 13:32)—he fell in love with his niece Herodias, wife of his brother Herod Philip.[43] He promised Herodias he would divorce his first wife, daughter of the Arabian king Aretas (Lk 3:19). This action, among other things, led to armed conflict with Aretas, a battle in which Antipas lost most of his army and survived only because the Romans intervened and threatened Aretas with military action (*Ant.* 18.5.1 §§109-115).

One of his more infamous acts was ordering John the Baptist beheaded. Josephus says it was Antipas's concern over the popular support given the Baptist (*Ant.* 18.5.2 §§116-119), whereas the Gospel of Mark focuses on the personal enmity of Herodias (Mk 6:14-29).[44] Eventually, Herodias's envy of her brother Agrippa's good fortune was her undoing; Antipas was accused of plotting rebellion, and she and Antipas were exiled to Lyons in Gaul (*Ant.* 18.7.1-2 §§240-256).

Luke had two informants who were "insiders" in the court of Antipas: Joanna and Manaen (Lk 8:3; Acts 13:1). The former was the wife of Chuza, Herod Antipas's steward, and the latter was a close friend of Antipas and later became a leading teacher in the church at Antioch on the Orontes. Probably they supplied further details involving Antipas, such as his perplexity about who Jesus was, his desire to see Jesus perform a sign and his shameful and abusive treatment of Jesus during the trial (Lk 9:7-9; 23:6-12).

King Agrippa I and his son Agrippa II both appear briefly in Acts. The former figures in two episodes in Acts 12. First Agrippa I imprisoned Peter, intending to put him to death in order to please the religious leaders, but eventually his overweening pride led to his death at the hands of an angel of the Lord. Josephus's depiction of Agrippa I fits reasonably well with both of these episodes in Acts, though it recounts only the latter. The imprisonment of Peter in order to curry the favor of the Jewish leadership certainly accords well with Agrippa's general modus operandi as sketched by Josephus (cf. *Ant.* 19.6.1-2 §§292-298; 19.7.3 §§328-331). More closely, both Acts and Josephus indicate that Agrippa I died because he accepted worship due only to God (*Ant.* 19.8.2 §§343-350; Acts 12:20-23). The details of Agrippa's death differ, however, in the two sources; Luke attributes the death to an angel of the Lord, whereas Josephus mentions only an omen and Agrippa's realization of divine retribution. Furthermore, Luke says Agrippa died immediately of worms, whereas Josephus says it was a bowel disorder that lasted five days.

---

[43]Not to be confused with the tetrarch Philip Herod II mentioned in Lk 3:1.

[44]Josephus actually names Herod Philip's wife Salome. See below for further discussion.

These differences are, however, more a matter of perspective than substance.

Agrippa II appears in the NT only in Acts, when he interviews Paul at Caesarea following the latter's appeal to be tried before Caesar (Acts 25:13—26:32). Josephus's description of Agrippa II and some of his behavior illuminate the context of this encounter. We learn from Josephus that Agrippa II had been carrying on an affair with his sister Bernice (*Ant.* 20.7.3 §§145-146). This scandalous relationship is not mentioned in Acts, but once it is assumed Paul's words take on an ironic tone: "you [King Agrippa] are especially familiar with all the customs and controversies of the Jews" (Acts 26:3).

No doubt one of the most infamous NT characters is the procurator Pontius Pilate (A.D. 26-36), about whom Josephus provides additional information.[45] A key issue has been the differing assessment of Pilate's role in the trial and death of Jesus as found in Josephus and the Gospels. The Gospels present Pilate as unwilling to sentence Jesus to death and as even trying to negotiate an exchange for a certain Jesus Barabbas, probably a Zealot terrorist. On the one hand, we see an increasingly negative portrayal of the Jewish religious leaders in Mark, Matthew, Luke and John, and, on the other, a steadily more positive and sympathetic depiction of Pilate (Mk 15:6-15; Mt 27:1, 11-26; Lk 23:1-25; Jn 18:28—19:16).[46] Pilate is most sympathetic to Jesus in John, where we are told that the religious leaders pressured Pilate to sentence Jesus to death by threatening to complain to Caesar that Pilate was "no friend of the emperor" by releasing a revolutionary (Jn 19:12). In Matthew, Luke and John, Pilate seeks to absolve himself of any involvement in and guilt for Jesus' death. Matthew's Gospel has "the people as a whole" take an oath in which they affirm: "His blood be on us and on our children!" (Mt 27:25).

Josephus helps us understand better the complexity of the situation. We learn that Pilate precipitated a number of crises and run-ins with the Jews of Judea and Galilee and with the Samaritans during his tenure. Jesus' comment about the blood mingled by Pilate in the offerings of the Galileans, though not recorded by Josephus, is at least consistent with the picture that emerges from *Jewish War* and *Jewish Antiquities* (Lk 13:1-3; cf. *Ant.* 18.4.1 §§85-89; *J.W.* 2.9.2-4 §§169-177). Tiberius eventually removed Pilate from office for incompetence.

---

[45]The title for the earlier Roman-appointed governors was "prefect," as an inscription discovered in 1961 at Caesarea Maritima mentioning Pilate confirms. For a transcription, translation and discussion, see Craig A. Evans, "Pilate Inscription," *DNTB*, pp. 803-4. Thus Josephus's use of the term "procurator" *(epitropos)* for Pilate is anachronistic. The NT Gospels use a generic term "governor" *(hēgemōn)*, as does Josephus occasionally.

[46]We are assuming Markan priority, whereby Mark is the earliest of the canonical Gospels, Matthew and Luke used Mark, and John was last (near the end of the first Christian century) and represents an independent account though aware of the others.

The rising tension between synagogue and church from the middle of the first century and the necessity of the early Christian movement to answer charges of disloyalty and sedition help explain why there are differing perspectives on Pilate in Josephus and the Gospels.[47] Luke most insistently draws attention to Pilate's expostulations to the religious leaders and the crowd to the effect that Jesus was innocent of the charges (Lk 23:4, 13-16, 22). Luke continues to stress that Christianity is not a dangerous, subversive sect in his volume two, the book of Acts (Acts 18:14-16; 19:23-41; 24:12-13; 25:10-12; 26:30-32).

Josephus had a quite different agenda from that of the Gospel writers. He wished to show that provocations of the Roman governors and the ill-advised "innovations" of a Jewish minority led to the disastrous war. It seems to me that both depictions are compatible; in fact, each throws light on the other. As always, in reading ancient sources, one must try to discover the intentions and tendencies of the authors. An author's selectivity and shaping of the information available is a key factor in interpretation.

Figures in Early Christianity

John the Baptist. We mentioned John the Baptist already in connection with Herod Antipas. In that same section (*Ant.* 18.5.2 §§116-119), Josephus also provides a sketch of John's ministry. Josephus's portrait of John resembles that of a persecuted philosopher, a well-known figure in Greco-Roman society (e.g., Socrates). Furthermore, John's preaching is cast in the terminology of popular Roman morality; that is, it strikes the keynotes of virtue and piety, qualities Josephus wished to make synonymous with Judaism.[48] Nonetheless, Josephus and the NT agree that John required repentance followed by immersion in water as an outward sign of commitment to righteous behavior (cf. Mt 3:7-10; Lk 3:7-9).

Josephus does not seem aware of any connection between John the Baptist and Jesus, but one must remember that John had died years before Josephus was even born. Nowhere in his writings does Josephus give any indication of any firsthand knowledge of Christianity,[49] and he was likely dependent upon Jewish sources for this brief sketch.

James the brother of Jesus. Josephus narrates James's martyrdom just after Festus died and Albinus his successor was en route (*Ant.* 20.9.1 §200). Josephus refers to James as "the brother of Jesus," reminding us of Paul's reference to James as "the Lord's brother" (Gal 1:19). According to Josephus's

---

[47]See further Mason, *Josephus and the New Testament,* p. 117.
[48]Ibid., pp. 152-54.
[49]Note, however, Whiston's "Dissertation 1" (*Works of Josephus,* p. 819) and "Dissertation 6" (pp. 872-79) for the view that Josephus did become a Christian.

account, James was hailed before the Sanhedrin and executed by stoning on the charge of being a "breaker of the law." This is a bit perplexing, since the NT represents James in Acts and Paul's letters as being an advocate of Torah observance, at least for Jewish Christians (cf. Acts 21:18-25; Gal 2:12; Jas 1:25; 2:8-12; 4:11). Perhaps James's death was brought about by the fact that some Jewish Christians did not observe the ritual purity laws or, at least, the Pharisaic interpretation of the pentateuchal laws (the "tradition of the elders"). James, as leader of the Jerusalem church (cf. Acts 12:17; 15:13-21; Gal 2:9), was held liable for the views of all who confessed being followers of Jesus.

Jesus of Nazareth. Finally, we draw attention to what is probably the main reason Josephus has been valued by Christian scholarship down through the ages. This concerns his comments about Jesus of Nazareth, the so-called *testimonium flavianum* (*Ant.* 18.3.3 §§63-64), that appear in connection with Pilate's governorship. The authenticity of this passage has generated considerable debate. The positions range from denial that any of it is genuine to a complete acceptance of the entire paragraph.[50] The truth probably lies somewhere in between. Since Josephus later states that Ananus, the high priest, "assembled the Sanhedrin of judges, and brought before them the brother of Jesus, who was called Christ, whose name was James" (*Ant.* 20.10.1 §200), this presupposes an earlier reference to Jesus. Historian John Meier reconstructs what he believes to be the most likely original reading as follows:

> At this time there appeared Jesus, a wise man. For he was a doer of startling deeds, a teacher of people who receive the truth with pleasure. And he gained a following both among many Jews and among many of Greek origin. And when Pilate, because of an accusation made by the leading men among us, condemned him to the cross, those who loved him previously did not cease to do so. And up until this very day the tribe of Christians, named after him, has not died out.[51]

The passage thus stands as an independent witness to the historicity of Jesus and the bare essentials of his ministry and death under Pilate. The continuing influence of Jesus upon his followers at the end of the first century is also worth noting. Beyond that we probably cannot go without additional textual evidence.

Historical Background
High priesthood. Josephus provides welcome light on the institution of the

---

[50]For a defense of its authenticity, see Whiston, "Dissertation 1," *Works of Josephus,* pp. 815-22. We think Mason has a balanced view of the question (*Josephus and the New Testament,* pp. 163-75).
[51]John P. Meier, "The Testimonium: Evidence for Jesus Outside the Bible," *BRev* 7, no. 3 (1991): 23.

Jewish high priesthood. For example, he helps us resolve what appears to be an inconsistency in the Gospels concerning the identity of the high priest who condemned Jesus to death. Mark omits his name, whereas Matthew says it was Caiaphas (Mt 26:55-58; Mk 14:48-54). Luke, however, mentions Annas *and* Caiaphas (Lk 3:2). The Gospel of John agrees that Caiaphas was a high priest but qualifies this by saying "who was high priest that year" (Jn 11:49). According to John's Gospel, Annas was the father-in-law of the high priest (Jn 18:13), but later Annas is referred to as the high priest (Jn 18:15, 19, 22). However, when Jesus is sent to Caiaphas, the latter is called "the high priest" (Jn 18:24). A careful reading of Josephus suggests an answer to this seeming confusion. Apparently, the high priest held the office for life and could be referred to as such even when not serving actively in office (*J. W.* 2.17.9 §441; *Ant.* 20.9.2 §205; *Life* 38 §193). We know from Josephus that, in addition to his son-in-law Caiaphas, Annas had five sons who served as high priests at various times (*Ant.* 20.9.1 §198). We also know that the Roman government frequently replaced the high priest during this era. Not all the problems are resolved on this issue, but when read in light of each other, there is significant agreement between Josephus and the Gospels.[52]

The repeated mention in the Gospels of a Jewish council called the Sanhedrin, presided over by the high priest, is confirmed by Josephus (Mk 11:27; 14:1, 53; Acts 5:21-39; 22:30–23:10; *J.W.* 2.17.3 §411; *Life* 38-39 §§193-197). In all likelihood, for Jews living in the Holy Land during the time of the NT, matters of personal status (marriage, divorce, inheritance, transfer of property, ritual questions, small claims, etc.) as well as limited civic and political control were vested in the Sanhedrin.[53] This council included Pharisees and leading citizens, but the Sadducees, headed up by the high priests, had the final say, an arrangement sanctioned by the Roman government. Thus, even though there was bitter hostility between Pharisees and Sadducees—a fact that both the NT and Josephus clearly agree on—we can understand how political necessity forced them to cooperate with each other under Roman hegemony. It also demonstrates that they could occasionally act in concert against a common foe or perceived threat, as in the case of Jesus (Mt 16:1; 21:45-46; 26:3-5; Mk 14:1-2, 43, 53; 15:1).

Jewish sects. Perhaps the single most important contribution Josephus makes toward illuminating the background of the NT is in his descriptions of

---

[52]On the problems see Mason, *Josephus and the New Testament,* pp. 125-31; and Bruce Chilton, "Annas," in *ABD on CD-ROM* (Logos Library System, version 2.0c, 1995, 1996).

[53]For further discussion of a much-debated issue, see Anthony J. Saldarini, "Sanhedrin," in *ABD on CD-ROM* (Logos Library System, version 2.0c, 1995,1996). For a different opinion, see E. P. Sanders, *Judaism: Practice and Belief 63 BCE-66 CE* (London: SCM Press; Philadelphia: Trinity Press International, 1992), pp. 458-90.

the major Jewish sects. Outside of Josephus and the NT, we have no other contemporary description of these groups. Five passages in Josephus's works devote some space to these "philosophies" (*J.W.* 2.8.1-14 §§117-166; *Ant.* 13.5.9 §§171-173; 13.10.5-6 §§288-298; 18.1.2-6 §§11-25; *Life* 2 §§10-12). He uses the term *philosophy* because this carries more esteem with his Roman audience than the less respectable sobriquet of *sect*.[54] According to Josephus, there were four philosophies: the Pharisees, the Sadducees, the Essenes and the Zealots. Actually, in only one passage are the Zealots included as a "philosophy," and it is clear that they differed little from Pharisees except that they were committed to a military response to Roman occupation (*Ant.* 18.1.6 §§23-25). Josephus castigates the Zealots for their ill-advised "innovations" in *Jewish War* but expresses admiration for their willingness to suffer and die for their cause in *Jewish Antiquities*.

According to Josephus the following features characterized the Pharisees:

1. The hallmark of Pharisaism was belief in the twofold Torah: the Written Torah of Moses and the oral interpretations of the law handed down by the elders—also said to have been vouchsafed to Moses on Mount Sinai. Championing the twofold Torah set the Pharisees in opposition to the Sadducees, who held that only the pentateuchal laws were authoritative and binding.

2. They were esteemed by the majority of Jews as the most accurate interpreters of the laws and thus were the leading sect of the first century, even though they numbered only about six thousand (*Ant.* 17.2.4 §42) out of a total population of some two million.[55] According to Josephus, the majority of Jews living in towns followed their interpretations of the proper prayers and divine rituals. This latter observation is important in that it shows that the real strength of Pharisaism lay with the middle class: small businessmen, merchants and property owners. According to Josephus, even Sadducees serving in the priestly office had to accommodate themselves to Pharisaic opinion on "the way things were to be done" in order not to engender hostility by the masses.[56]

3. They held to both providence and free will.

4. They believed in the immortality of the soul and the bodily resurrection of the righteous. Josephus tends to downplay the concept of bodily resurrec-

---

[54]On the problems of using the term *sect* for English speakers, see J. Julius Scott Jr., *Customs and Controversies: Intertestamental Jewish Backgrounds of the New Testament* (Grand Rapids, Mich.: Baker, 1995), p. 200. He suggests the term *denomination*.

[55]Actually, Josephus says that at a Feast of Unleavened Bread an assemblage of Jews numbering three million protested against Florus (*J.W.* 2.14.3 §280). One can scarcely take this at face value, however.

[56]But see Sanders, *Judaism*, pp. 388-412, 458-90, for a spirited denial that Pharisees actually wielded that much influence.

tion for his Roman readership. He speaks of the righteous as receiving the "power to revive and live again." His description tends to make the Pharisees sound more Greek than they really were (e.g., the wicked suffer eternal punishment under the earth).

5. They practiced a civil and polite manner of interaction with themselves and others and lived as simply as possible.

This portrait in Josephus comports reasonably well with the NT documents.[57] The NT confirms that a hallmark of the Pharisees was their commitment to the "tradition of the elders" (Mt 15:2; Mk 7:3-4) or the "traditions of the ancestors" (Gal 1:14). This was the Oral Torah discussed earlier, the ongoing, living tradition specifying how the pentateuchal laws were to be applied to daily life. In Matthew, Jesus acknowledges the dominant place that Pharisaic scribes held in terms of religious and ritual matters—they occupied "Moses' seat" (Mt 23:1-12)—but the Synoptic portrayal of Jesus also has him consistently at odds with the Pharisees over "their tradition" (cf. Mt 15:1-20; Mk 7:5-23).

The NT also confirms, albeit indirectly, Josephus's declaration that Pharisees adhered to both the sovereignty of God and freedom of the will.[58] One only has to follow Paul's argument in Romans 9–11 to see that, as a Christian, Paul still held both of these concepts in tension (cf. Rom 9:11-16 with 10:9-17). Beyond that, Gamaliel's speech in Acts 5:34-39 is a perfect exemplar of this theological position as well as a model of how Pharisees sought to accommodate dissenting views.

What the NT adds to Josephus's portrait of the Pharisees is their preoccupation with tithing and ritual purity laws (cf. Mt 23:23-28; Lk 11:37-42). Josephus omits this in his histories, no doubt because it was not likely to be of interest to his Roman readers and may even have occasioned some hostility. We know that in some Roman writers (Horace, Martial, Chaeremon, Cicero, Juvenal, Tacitus), Jewish fastidiousness over such matters was a recurring criticism and butt of jokes and satire.[59]

The NT also attributes to Pharisees a belief in angels and demons (Acts 23:8). Even though Josephus does not list this as a specific item in his discussion of the various "philosophies," he himself does make reference to, and apparently put credence in, the reality of such beings (cf. *Ant.* 1.3.1 §§72-73).

---

[57]On the problems of harmonizing Josephus and the NT on this point, see Scott, *Customs and Controversies,* pp. 202-6; and Mason, *Josephus and the New Testament,* pp. 131-48.

[58]Mason discusses why this theme received prominence in Josephus (*Josephus and the New Testament,* p. 146).

[59]See further Joseph Heinemann and Joshua Gutmann, "Anti-Semitism, In Antiquity," *EncJud* 3:87-96. See also Lawrence H. Schiffman, *Texts and Traditions: A Source Reader for the Study of Second Temple and Rabbinic Judaism* (Hoboken, N.J.: Ktav, 1998), pp. 199-218.

In *Jewish War*, we read of an angelic apparition seen just before the fall of Jerusalem (*J. W.* 6.5.3 §§297-300). As previously discussed, the NT assumes the reality of angelic and demonic beings, and numerous passages in Paul reflect continuing Pharisaic belief incorporated into a Christian worldview. In Acts the Pharisaic position on bodily resurrection figures directly in Paul's trial before the Sanhedrin and the Roman governors. With a sly sense of humor Luke depicts courtroom chaos when Paul pits the Pharisaic doctrine of bodily resurrection against the Sadducean denial of the same (Acts 23:6-10).

The matter of a simple lifestyle mentioned by Josephus seemingly stands contradicted in one particular by Luke's Gospel. In Luke 16:14 the Pharisees are accused of being "lovers of money." This may be accounted for by standard polemical rhetoric on the part of Luke (i.e., accusations of being lovers of money were widespread amongst opposing groups in the first century, as they are today).[60] Luke's indictment, however, does not stand alone. Jesus also attacked the scribes—most likely the legal experts of the Pharisaic party—for preying on the estates of widows (Mk 12:40; Lk 20:47). On the other hand, there may be no real contradiction at all—loving money, even hoarding it, and living a simple, frugal lifestyle are not necessarily mutually exclusive, as the lives of not a few miserly millionaires demonstrate!

According to Josephus the Sadducees were characterized by the following:

1. They held that only the pentateuchal laws were binding. They thus rejected the Pharisaic idea of the "tradition of the elders," the Oral Torah.

2. They rejected fate (really predestination) and affirmed free will.

3. They rejected the notion of posttemporal rewards or punishments. The soul ceased to exist at death, and thus they rejected the idea of bodily resurrection.

4. They were relatively few in number and constituted a wealthy aristocracy.

5. Their focal point of interest was the temple, its supervision and ritual.

6. They behaved rudely toward each other and to outsiders.

Once again, the NT generally agrees with Josephus's portrait of the Sadducees. Interestingly, Jesus' own theological position was closer to that of the Pharisees. Indeed, Matthew and Mark attribute to Jesus this blunt response to the Sadducean denial of bodily resurrection: "You are wrong, because you know neither the scriptures nor the power of God" (Mt 22:29; cf. Mk 12:24). As mentioned earlier, however, on the question of the oral tradition, Jesus' own position seems to have been closer to that of the Sadducees.

The passion narratives agree that the high priests and Sadducees took the initiative in seeking to destroy Jesus. Jesus' cleansing of the temple seems to have been the decisive event that precipitated his crucifixion (Mt 21:12-17;

---

[60]See further Mason, *Josephus and the New Testament*, p. 147.

Mk 11:15-19; Lk 19:45-48). Jesus' action directly challenged those who controlled the temple (Jesus styled the temple "a den of robbers" [Mt 21:13; Mk 11:17; Lk 19:46]) and threatened to remove a most lucrative income from their coffers (cf. Jn 11:48). Visual evidence of the opulent lifestyle of Sadducees has come to light in excavations conducted by Nachman Avigad in the Jewish Quarter of Jerusalem since the Six-Day War.[61] Not surprisingly, the Sadducean party united with the Pharisees to silence this dangerous critic.

In addition, the portraits of the high priests sketched in the Gospels and Acts are not very complimentary and conform to Josephus's description in the *Jewish War:* "The behavior of the Sadducees one towards another is in some degree wild; and their conversation with those that are of their own party is as barbarous as if they were strangers to them" (*J.W.* 2.8.14 §166). For example, in John we have this outburst by Caiaphas directed at his colleagues: "You know nothing at all! You do not understand that it is better for you to have one man die for the people than to have a whole nation destroyed" (Jn 11:49b-50). Later, Ananias's treatment of Paul before the Sanhedrin does not speak well of his general deportment or justice (Acts 23:1-5). Incidentally, Josephus tells us that not too long after this, Ananias was sent off to Rome in chains to defend Jewish actions in the incident with the Samaritans leading up to the revolt of A.D. 66 (*Ant.* 20.6.2 §131). Ananias was eventually slain by the Zealots during the revolt (*J.W.* 2.17.9 §441).

Paramount, however, are the trial scenes and crucifixion of Jesus. The Gospels present the chief priests (cf. Acts 5:17; cf. 4:1) as prime movers in arresting and convicting Jesus on charges of blasphemy and sedition before the tribunal of the Roman governor (Mt 26:3-5, 57-68; 27:20, 62-64; Mk 14:53-65; 15:10-15; Lk 22:63-70; 23:1-5, 13-25). For many readers of the NT, the lingering impression of the chief priests and Sadducees consists of their sneering, calloused demeanor at Jesus' crucifixion (Mt 27:41-43; Mk 15:31-32; Lk 23:35) and their bribery of the guards after the resurrection (Mt 28:11-15). Great care must be taken to read such passages historically and not to transfer this depiction to Jews generally, as has repeatedly happened throughout history. These passages must be read and interpreted with keen sensitivity to anti-Semitism and the specter of the Holocaust. Tragically, Jews have had to live (and die) under the onus of "Christ-killers." [62] That was not what the NT authors intended, nor should it be an unconscious consequence of committing oneself to the authority of Scripture.

---

[61] See further Nachman Avigad, "Excavations in the Jewish Quarter of the Old City of Jerusalem, 1970," *IEJ* 20 (1970); and Avigad, "How the Wealthy Lived in Herodian Jerusalem," *BAR* 2, no. 4 (1976): 1.

[62] See further David A. Rausch, *A Legacy of Hatred: Why Christians Must Not Forget the Holocaust* (Chicago: Moody Press, 1984), pp. 21-30.

Of the three main "philosophies," Josephus gives more attention to the Essenes. Curiously, the NT does not explicitly mention them. Since we have already devoted two chapters to this sect and the question of whether Josephus's Essenes should be identified with the sect that wrote the Dead Sea Scrolls, we will not discuss further their distinctive tenets.

Josephus's discussions about the "Jewish philosophies" is a salutary reminder that first-century Judaism was by no means monolithic. As is the case with religions today, diversity and divisiveness characterized first-century Judaism. Thus Philo, Josephus and the NT are independent witnesses to the fractured nature of Judaism during this era. There is general agreement among modern scholars that other groups existed as well.[63] Thus, in addition to the Samaritans, for example, the NT mentions "Herodians" (Mt 22:16; Mk 3:6; 12:13), and Philo mentions "Therapeutae" (*Contempl. Life* §§11-90), who are similar to but apparently not identical to Essenes. The Dead Sea Scrolls may also witness to other apocalyptic groups whose names have not been preserved (i.e., the community from whom *Jubilees* came).

As we leave Josephus, we do so with profound appreciation for his contribution. It is to be lamented that so few Christian readers these days have any knowledge of Josephus's writings. In the light of his works, much that is obscure in the NT comes into focus. Though one may fault Josephus for obvious failings as a historian, without his work we would be looking at the equivalent of a "black hole" in terms of Jewish history during this period. Evangelical Christians should also be grateful for his stout defense of the integrity and superiority of revealed religion.[64] God's revelation to Moses is foundational to Christianity as well as to Judaism.

For Further Discussion

1. Should Josephus be viewed as a traitor or as a patriot?

2. What were Josephus's purposes for writing his four undisputed works?

3. How are we to assess Josephus as a credible historian? Should ancient historians be judged by the standards of modern historiography? Why or why not?

---

[63]See Schiffman, *Texts and Traditions*, pp. 231-34; Scott, *Customs and Controversies*, pp. 21, 120, 144-46, 195-232 and notes included there.

[64]Thus many Christian apologists have had occasion to research and cite the works of Josephus in their defense of Christianity. H. Schreckenberg notes that "already in the Middle Ages he was often seen almost as a church father, and in more recent times his work has sometimes been regarded—half jestingly—as a 'Fifth Gospel' or 'Small Bible.' . . . As late as the 19th cent., especially in the English-speaking world, the reading of Josephus in many private homes was second only to the reading of the Bible" ("Josephus, Flavius," *ISBE* 2:1133).

4. In what ways is Josephus helpful for a better understanding of Luke-Acts?

5. How does Josephus characterize the relationship between Jews and Romans from 63 B.C. up to the time of his writing?

6. Give a brief description of Josephus's four "philosophies" among the Jewish people. Have any of these influenced Christianity? If so, how?

For Further Reading

Critical Text

Benedictus Niese, ed., *Flavii Iosephi Opera,* 7 vols. (Berlin: Weidmann, 1887-1895).

Text and Translation

H. St. J. Thackeray et al., trans., *Josephus,* 10 vols., LCL (Cambridge, Mass.: Harvard University Press, 1926-1965).

William Whiston, trans., *The Works of Josephus: Complete and Unabridged* (Peabody, Mass.: Hendrickson, 1987).

Secondary Sources

Harold W. Attridge, "Jewish Historiography," in *Early Judaism and Its Modern Interpreters,* ed. Robert A. Kraft and George W. E. Nickelsburg (Philadelphia: Fortress; Atlanta: Scholars Press, 1986), pp. 324-29.

————, "Josephus and His Works," in *Jewish Writings of the Second Temple Period: Apocrypha, Pseudepigrapha, Qumran Sectarian Writings, Philo, Josephus,* ed. Michael E. Stone, CRINT 2 (Assen: Van Gorcum; Philadelphia: Fortress, 1984), pp. 185-232. This is a fine overview by a recognized expert on Josephus.

Craig A. Evans, *Noncanonical Writings and New Testament Interpretation* (Peabody, Mass.: Hendrickson, 1992), pp. 86-96. Although brief, this is a useful overview of Josephus and the NT, with bibliography.

L. H. Feldman, "Josephus," *ABD* 3:981-98.

————, "Josephus," *EDSS* 1:427-31.

————, "Josephus: Interpretive Methods and Tendencies," *DNTB,* pp. 590-96. This article is a useful survey of main issues by a specialist on Josephus, with bibliography.

Steve Mason, *Josephus and the New Testament* (Peabody, Mass.: Hendrickson, 1992). This book offers a good introduction to the writings of Josephus and their importance for the study of the NT.

————, "Josephus: Value for New Testament Study," *DNTB,* pp. 596-600. This is a convenient summary of Mason's views on Josephus, with helpful bibliography.

Tessa Rajak, *Josephus: The Historian and His Society* (London: Duckworth; Philadelphia: Fortress, 1983).

Abraham Schalit, "Josephus Flavius," *Encyclopedia Judaica on CD-ROM* (Judaica

Multimedia, version 1.0, 1997).

Lawrence H. Schiffman, *From Text to Tradition: A History of Second Temple and Rabbinic Judaism* (Jerusalem: Ktav, 1991).

E. Mary Smallwood, introduction to *Josephus: The Jewish War,* trans., G. A. Williamson (New York: Penguin, 1981). This is a concise overview of Josephus and his work.

Henry St. J. Thackeray, *Josephus: The Man and the Historian* (New York: Ktav, 1967 [1929]). Though dated, this is perhaps the best general introduction available.

Eleven

Coping with Calamity

*F*or The Psalms of Solomon, *the Similitudes (1 Enoch 37—71) and* 2 Enoch, *we use H. F. D. Sparks, ed.,* The Apocryphal Old Testament *(Oxford: Clarendon Press, 1985), pp. 649-82, 221-56, 321-62, respectively. These works are also available in J. H. Charlesworth, ed.,* The Old Testament Pseudepigrapha, *2 vols. (Garden City, N.Y.: Doubleday, 1983), 2:639-70, 1:29-50, 91-222, respectively; and in the older work of R. H. Charles, ed.,* The Apocrypha and Pseudepigrapha of the Old Testament, *2 vols. (Oxford: Clarendon Press, 1913), 2:625-52, 208-37, 425-69, respectively. For 4 Ezra/2 Esdras 3—14 and 4 Maccabees we draw upon the text in* The New Oxford Annotated Bible: New Revised Standard Version, *ed. Bruce M. Metzger and Roland E. Murphy (New York: Oxford University Press, 1991) AP 300-40, 341-61, respectively. One may also consult 2 Esdras 3—14 in* The Oxford Study Bible: Revised English Bible with the Apocrypha, *ed. M. Jack Suggs, Katharine Doob Sakenfeld, and James R. Mueller (New York: Oxford University Press, 1992), 1026-57; and in Charlesworth,* Old Testament Pseudepigrapha, *1:517-60 (called* 4 Ezra *in this edition). Finally, 4 Maccabees is also in Charlesworth,* Old Testament Pseudepigrapha, *2:531-64; and Charles,* Apocrypha and Pseudepigrapha of the Old Testament, 2:653-85.

Introduction

The Jewish literature sampled in this chapter includes the *Psalms of Solomon*, noteworthy for its fervent prayers for a Davidic Messiah; the much-debated

Similitudes (*1 Enoch* 37—71), in which we read of a transcendent Son of Man figure; *2 Enoch*, a further elaboration of the earlier Enoch traditions; 4 Maccabees with its panegyric for Jewish martyrs; and *4 Ezra* (2 Esdras 3—14), an apocalyptic work trying to come to grips with the disaster of A.D. 70. As we have seen in the previous chapter, this was a turbulent period of Jewish history. Not surprisingly, many found refuge and hope in apocalypticism and fervent messianism. Some resorted to extreme sectarianism, as seen in *2 Enoch*. But a shared commitment emerges in all the pieces, most graphically in 4 Maccabees: steadfast commitment to the Torah.

We think the above works fit generally into the following chronological framework. The *Psalms of Solomon* was written fairly soon after the Roman takeover of Palestine (63 B.C.) and the consequent end of the Hasmonean dynasty. The Similitudes, *2 Enoch* and 4 Maccabees probably derive from the first century A.D., the era of the Herodian dynasty, Roman procurators and rise of early Christianity. It is almost certain that *4 Ezra* was written after the First Jewish Revolt of A.D. 66-73. In all three eras, political realities forced religious Jews to reassess their commitments. Their varied responses provide a point of contact with the NT.

2 Enoch (Slavonic Book of Enoch, The Book of the Secrets of Enoch)

Genre and Structure

In *2 Enoch* we revisit the esoteric world of apocalyptic as reflected in the Enoch traditions. However, *2 Enoch* is not a pure example of an apocalypse. In fact, its underlying literary structure is more in the nature of a midrash, a creative retelling of the biblical story of Enoch's life up to the flood. The apocalyptic elements and motifs are embedded in this midrash and, at times, all but efface the story line. Furthermore, the writing consists of apocalyptic materials reworked and reformulated in a testamentary setting. That is, the work as we now have it purports to be the visions of Enoch passed along to his posterity. Coupled to this are passages that recall the wisdom tradition of Israel, particularly Ben Sira, with its earnest appeals to moral and ethical behavior. Clearly, we have before us a work displaying a mix of genres.

The book falls into three major sections (with corresponding portions of *1 Enoch* placed alongside where similar or related themes appear): (1) Enoch's ascent (1—11; cf. *1 En.* 12—36); (2) Enoch's return and instruction (13—22; cf. *1 En.* 81, 91—105); and (3) Melchizedek's miraculous birth (23; cf. *1 En.* 106—7).[1]

---

[1]Note that the chapters do not correspond in the Sparks edition *(AOT)* and the Charlesworth edition *(OTP)*. See *AOT*, pp. 321-23, and *OTP* 2:91-94 for an explanation. I follow the *AOT* numeration.

Date and Provenance

The date and provenance of *2 Enoch* are problematic. Scholars have championed widely differing views. At one end of the spectrum, R. H. Charles dated it to the first century B.C. in Alexandria, Egypt;[2] at the other end, A. S. D. Maunder concluded that it was a Bogomil (Bulgarian) work dating to some time between the twelfth and fifteenth centuries A.D.[3] Not quite so late was the estimate of J. T. Milik, one of the original Qumran scholars, who dated it to the ninth century A.D. in eastern Europe.[4]

Michael Stone and George Nickelsburg, while acknowledging the complexities and enigmas of *2 Enoch,* nonetheless hold that there are no compelling arguments for rejecting a date as early as the first century A.D. Andersen and Stone prefer a Palestinian provenance, whereas Nickelsburg and Collins opt for a Diaspora setting, most likely Egypt.[5] There is no consensus, but a majority holds that the original was in Greek and was later translated into Slavonic. One cannot, however, rule out completely the possibility that there was a Semitic original. Francis Andersen sums it up by saying, "The origins of *2 Enoch* are unknown. Research has not reached any consensus about the time, place, or contents of its first published form."[6]

The most obvious source to which *2 Enoch* is indebted is *1 Enoch.* One may well suppose that the author(s) of *2 Enoch* reworked and adapted earlier Enoch traditions. Even the casual reader detects the similarities, and specialized studies point out the specific parallels. Still, there are significant differences between the two works, and a direct relationship is not likely. Unlike *1 Enoch,* to date no fragments of *2 Enoch* have turned up at Qumran.

Some scholars have detected ancient Mesopotamian motifs, but as Andersen points out, "these could be floating folk motifs that could surface anywhere at any time."[7] Of course the basic story line is from Genesis 5:18-31, but it is worth noting that there are fewer allusions to the Hebrew Bible than one

---

[2]See his comments in *APOT* 2:429.

[3]See the discussion in A. Pennington, "2 Enoch," *AOT,* p. 323.

[4]J. T. Milik and Matthew Black, *The Books of Enoch: Aramaic Fragments of Qumran Cave 4* (Oxford: Clarendon Press, 1976), pp. 109-10.

[5]See George W. E. Nickelsburg, *Jewish Literature Between the Bible and the Mishnah: A Historical and Literary Introduction* (Philadelphia: Fortress, 1981), p. 188; Michael E. Stone, "Apocalyptic Literature," in *Jewish Writings of the Second Temple Period: Apocrypha, Pseudepigrapha, Qumran Sectarian Writings, Philo, Josephus,* ed. Michael E. Stone, CRINT 2 (Assen: Van Gorcum; Philadelphia: Fortress, 1984), p. 406; F. I. Andersen, "2 (Slavonic Apocalypse of) Enoch," *OTP* 1:94-97; and J. J. Collins, "Enoch, Books of," *DNTB,* p. 316.

[6]"Enoch, Second Book of," *ABD* 2:520; cf. his "2 (Slavonic Apocalypse of) Enoch," *OTP* 1:94-97. He notes regarding the historical importance of *2 Enoch,* "In every respect 2 Enoch remains an enigma" ("2 [Slavonic Apocalypse of] Enoch," 1:97).

[7]Andersen, "Enoch, Second Book of," 2:519.

might expect for a piece of Jewish literature of the Second Temple period. Charles was convinced that *2 Enoch* was Egyptian in origin, but none of the features he adduced are really determinative for the question of origin.[8]

One might even suggest an Essene origin. The story of Melchizedek's miraculous birth in *2 Enoch* 23 and the Essene fascination with Melchizedek (see chapter seven above) tempt us to establish a connection, especially in light of the shared insistence upon the solar calendar and the importance of the sun in its heavenly movements. Still, one must somehow account for the fact that distinctive Essene thought is simply not present in *2 Enoch*. Note carefully that not once is the law of Moses referred to; rather, one is to do the "will of God" as this has been vouchsafed to Enoch. This is quite at odds, in fact, with the known movements of the Pharisees, Sadducees and Essenes. Andersen notes that some features of *2 Enoch* remind one of Philo's Thera-peutae, but the latter, in contrast to *2 Enoch*, revered Moses and the law (cf. Philo, *Contempl. Life* 75-78).[9]

Most likely, the community represented by *2 Enoch* was an unknown Jewish sectarian group, which offers once again evidence of pluralism within first-century A.D. Judaism. Several teachings have no counterpart in known Jewish thought. For example, the notion that humans were created in the likeness of God's own face (*2 En.* 13:42) and that one should never kill an animal without first binding it cannot be paralleled in any other known forms of Judaism (*2 En.* 15:9; 21:9; 22:23).[10] We may rule out the possibility that the work is Christian, since it is hard to imagine a Christian author not making some clear allusion or direct reference to Jesus Christ.[11]

Purpose

The testamentary nature of this work points to its purpose. The information that Enoch receives, as he passes upward through the multiple heavens, is passed on to his descendants and to the faithful at his return. The basic content of the revealed truths has to do with creation and eschatology. Enoch's ascent climaxes in the seventh heaven, where God's throne is located. Enoch listens to a long discourse on how God created the world. This material, Enoch is informed, was previously unknown, even by angels. Of particular importance

---

[8]For details, see Charles, *APOT* 2:426; and Andersen, "Enoch, Second Book of," 2:519.

[9]Andersen, "2 (Slavonic Apocalypse of) Enoch," 1:96.

[10]The Babylonian Talmud refers to heretics *(mînîm)* who tie sacrificial animals (*b. Tamid* 31b). This strengthens the argument that *2 Enoch* has at least portions that are Jewish and predate the medieval era.

[11]Andersen notes, "There is not a distinctively Christian idea in the book. Alleged use of it in the New Testament . . . is in passing phrases of a very general kind" ("2 [Slavonic Apocalypse of] Enoch," 1:95).

are the descriptions of paradise and hell (*2 En.* 5). Thus it is fundamentally important that the readership of this work grasp the true nature of the created order and understand the doctrine of eschatological reward and punishment.

In the course of this revelation, Enoch enjoins strict standards of behavior. This brings us to the heart of what *2 Enoch* is all about. Obedience to the things written down by Enoch in 360 books is essential in order to enjoy the fruits of paradise. Failure to do righteousness, as so defined, leads to the miseries and torments of hell. What we have, then, is an appeal, couched in visionary trappings, to uphold the moral and ritual purity laws of a Jewish sectarian movement.

If the work does date to the first century A.D., we may very provisionally offer a life setting. The longer recension of *2 Enoch* assumes that the temple is still standing.[12] If so, we may be close to the era of the First Jewish Revolt (A.D. 66-74). These were tumultuous times. Thus, *2 Enoch*, ostensibly the last will and testament of Enoch, garbed in the trappings of apocalyptic and wisdom, is essentially an exhortation to hold on until the "flood," that is, the day of judgment when God will reward the righteous and punish the wicked.

Comparison with the New Testament
In light of the uncertainty of *2 Enoch*'s date and provenance, we simply point out some similarities of thought and expression, without suggesting any dependence one way or the other. We may rather consider that *2 Enoch* and the NT share a broad cultural milieu.

The vision of the various heavens (*2 En.* 3—9), especially the seventh (*2 En.* 9), with its archangels, sea of glass and throne of God, has a number of similarities to the throne-room scene in Revelation 4, with its different categories of angelic beings arrayed around God's throne. Angelic functions are similar in *2 Enoch* and the Apocalypse (i.e., certain angelic beings control or exercise power over different aspects of the created order [Rev 8—9; 16]). More striking than this, however, is the description of the third heaven, said to be in the midst of Paradise (*2 En.* 5). One is immediately reminded of the apostle Paul's description of one of his visions in which he "was caught up to the third heaven . . . up into Paradise" (2 Cor 12:2, 4). This is another indication of the importance of apocalyptic thought for the theology of Paul.[13]

In *2 Enoch* 5:16-17 some of the behaviors that characterize the inhabitants of hell are listed. Among them is the charge that they "left the man who is

---

[12]The student should know that the Sparks edition of *2 Enoch* translates the "shorter" Slavonic text. For particulars, see the introduction to *2 Enoch* in *AOT* and especially the discussion by Andersen in "Enoch, Second Book of." The reference to the temple is in the "longer" recension.

[13]See D. E. Aune, "Apocalypticism," *DPL,* pp. 25-35.

hungry to die of starvation when they could have satisfied him, and have stripped the naked when they could have clothed them" (cf. *2 En.* 15:21-22). This reminds one of Jesus' parable of the sheep and goats on the day of judgment in which one's actions speak louder than words (Mt 25:41-44).[14]

In addition, *2 Enoch* 11:2 gives voice to the notion that God created all things out of nothing (cf. 2 Macc 7:28), "from what is invisible into what is seen." This is reminiscent of Hebrews 11:3, which states that "By faith we understand that the worlds were prepared by the word of God, so that what is seen was made from things that are not visible." Enoch is also informed that even the angels do not know how they themselves were formed. Likewise, Paul affirms that Christ created the invisible things as well as the visible (cf. Col 1:16; 3:10).

In *2 Enoch* 11:37-38 we find sentiments that resemble John's Gospel. Enoch is promised: "For a place is prepared for you, and you shall live in my presence for ever." One recalls Jesus' promise to his followers: "If it were not so, would I have told you that I go to prepare a place for you? And if I go and prepare a place for you, I will come again and will take you to myself, so that where I am, there you may be also" (Jn 14:2b-3). In the book of Acts the apostles are said to be witnesses of the resurrection (Acts 1:8; 2:32; 3:15). Enoch was designated to serve as a witness for God at the day of judgment (*2 En.* 11:37).

In *2 Enoch* 13:12 Enoch views the lowest levels of hell, called Tartarus, a term borrowed from Greek mythology and religion to refer to the deepest region of the underworld. Likewise, 2 Peter 2:4 (cf. Jude 6), also referring to this place, uses the Greek verb *tartaroō* ("to cast into Tartarus"; translated in NRSV as "cast them into hell").

An interesting similarity occurs in *2 Enoch* 13:64-71, where we have seven beatitudes forming part of a larger section containing ethical, moral and ritual instruction. The beatitude form, of course, immediately recalls the Sermon on the Mount, where we have eight beatitudes—the eighth being elaborated and expanded (Mt 5:3-12). Only two of the Enoch beatitudes actually correspond in content to the Matthean examples, the blessedness of the peacemaker (*2 En.* 13:69-70). The climactic Enoch beatitude has to do with peacemaking, whereas Jesus' beatitudes build up to being persecuted for righteousness' sake, a key issue in the Sermon on the Mount.[15]

The most striking similarity in *2 Enoch* to NT thought is the section deal-

[14]In fact, Andersen notes that "2 En comes closer in language and ideas to Mt than to any other part of the NT" ("2 [Slavonic Apocalypse of] Enoch," 1:95 n. 13).
[15]On this see further, S. McKnight, "Justice, Righteousness," *DJG*, pp. 413-15.

ing with Melchizedek (2 *En.* 22—23). Though 2 *Enoch's* view is quite independent of the development of Melchizedek in the book of Hebrews (Heb 6:20—
8:13), both writings stress the everlasting nature of his priesthood. Unique to
2 *Enoch* is the miraculous birth story, which has only the most tenuous connection to the birth stories of Jesus.[16] Melchizedek's preservation during the
flood by being kept in Paradise is also quite without parallel in extant sources,
whether Jewish or Christian. Not to be lost in this discussion is an interesting
observation, namely, that the author of 2 *Enoch* believes that because
Melchizedek has an everlasting priesthood someday the tabernacle will be
restored. Note how this resonates with earlier Jewish literature on the notion
of restoration (i.e., Tobit and Qumran sectarian writings such as *Temple Scroll*
[11Q19-20] and *New Jerusalem* [1Q32, 2Q24, 4Q554-555, 5Q15, 11Q18]). The
author of 2 *Enoch* still held on to a basic hope in a future blessedness centered on a "pure" worship led by Melchizedek, perhaps performed in the original tabernacle but transferred to the heavenly realm.[17] The NT goes in an
entirely different direction by affirming that Jesus Christ has *already* passed
through the heavens (Heb 4:14) into the heavenly sanctuary, not made with
human hands (Heb 9:11-12), and that his high-priestly ministry *replaced* the
old tabernacle and old Levitical priesthood (Heb 8:1-7; 9:11-14).

Perhaps 2 *Enoch* is most relevant for NT literature at the level of paraenesis (moral exhortation and admonition): both exhort believers to hold on in
the present afflictions and persecutions and to ride out the "flood" (functioning typologically for the final judgment). Jesus Christ will return and reward
the righteous and punish the wicked (Rom 13:11-14; Col 3:6; 2 Thess 1:5-12;
1 Pet 4:12-13; 2 Pet 3:1-10; Rev 11:15-18; 16:1-21; 19:1-8).

Similitudes (or Parables) of Enoch (1 Enoch 37—71)

Content and Structure

The Book of Similitudes is composed of three "parables," each describing
Enoch's visions as he ascended to the throne room of God. Accompanying
angels answer Enoch's questions, providing dialogue for the narrative. Each
parable underscores the conviction that righteousness shall at last triumph
over wickedness. The section is capped by a double epilogue. Similitudes
divides as follows:

---

[16]See D. C. Allison Jr., "Melchizedek," *DLNTD*, p. 730.

[17]If the longer text is used, there is a very interesting parallel to the notion of a millennium
found in Rev 20:1-5. According to the longer version, the earth will last six thousand
years, one thousand years for each day of creation (Gen 1). Augustine and others adopted
the Hexaemeron, creation of the world in six days, as the key to earth history. Then there
will be a one-thousand-year interim kingdom after which time shall cease and an eternal
state will ensue.

I.   Introduction: Identity of visionary and summary of experience (37)
II.   First parable: revelation of eschatological rewards and punishments (38—44); the Chosen One appears and cosmic secrets are divulged to Enoch
III. Second parable: revelation of the Son of Man, the Chosen One (45—57); war against the wicked; judgment of wicked; transformation of heaven and earth by the Son of Man
IV.   Third parable: revelation of the flood (58—69); cosmic eschatological judgment executed by the Chosen One
V.   Epilogue (70—71)

The focus of Similitudes is upon the great throne room where a transcendent figure styled "the Chosen One," "the Righteous One," "the Son of Man" and "God's Anointed One" stands ready to exercise judgment upon all humanity and to vindicate the righteous.

Composition

We recall that *1 Enoch* is really a compilation of five different works (see chapter three above). The particular section we now examine poses a problem: we are not certain if Similitudes dates to a time prior to the writing of the NT. This uncertainty remains because thus far no fragments of *1 Enoch* 37—71 have turned up at Qumran. This has confirmed for many scholars the suspicion, based on internal evidence, that it was added to the larger Enoch corpus at a later date. It will come as no surprise to learn that the debate on this question is long and involved. We will only give a bare summary of the status of the question.

Though Milik, one of the original Dead Sea Scrolls inner circle, dated Similitudes to the third century A.D., most researches place it somewhere between the last quarter of the first century B.C. and the first century A.D.[18] Perhaps a majority would locate it in the first century A.D. If so, this makes it contemporaneous with NT literature. The earlier (B.C.) dating takes the reference in *1 Enoch* 56:5 to the "Parthians and Medes" as alluding to the Parthian invasion of 40 B.C. (cf. Josephus, *Ant.* 14.13.3 §330) and reads *1 Enoch* 67:8-13 as a veiled allusion to Herod the Great and his recourse to the mineral waters of Calirrhoe (cf. *Ant.* 17.6.5 §171). The first-century A.D. dating simply aligns Similitudes with similar types of apocalyptic material that flourished in both Jewish and Christian circles during the last half of the first century A.D., thus arguing from analogy.[19]

---

[18]On the shortcomings of Milik's dating, see John J. Collins, "Apocalyptic Literature," in *Early Judaism and Its Modern Interpreters,* ed. Robert A. Kraft and George W. E. Nickelsburg (Philadelphia: Fortress; Atlanta: Scholars Press, 1986), p. 358; and E. Isaac, "1 (Ethiopic Apocalypse of) Enoch," *OTP* 1:6-7.

[19]See Collins, "Enoch, Books of," p. 316.

Likewise, the question of the circles in which the material originated cannot be definitely established, but a majority of scholars prefer a sectarian movement having affinities, though not necessarily identity, with the Essenes. This seems the best hypothesis at present. That the group or community stands apart from the Pharisees and Sadducees seems evident from a statement such as the following: "Wisdom found no place where she could dwell, and her dwelling was in heaven. Wisdom went out in order to dwell among the sons of men, but did not find a dwelling; wisdom returned to her place and took her seat in the midst of angels" (*1 En.* 42:1-2). This stands in stark contrast to the affirmations of Baruch, Ben Sira and Wisdom of Solomon that wisdom was embodied in the Torah and dwelt among Israel. One senses from this that the author of Similitudes had given up on the leading factions, who claim to be the true Israel, and had essentially confined Wisdom to his own sect.

Relevance for the New Testament

From our previous exposure to *1 Enoch* (and *2 Enoch*), we are already familiar with material detailing the cosmic workings of the universe and describing the angelic orders, the throne room, paradise and hell. What is different in Similitudes, however, and the most fascinating feature, is the transcendent figure, "the Righteous One" or "the Chosen One." We note several items about this person. First, he is presented as a preexistent figure; that is, he predates creation (*1 En.* 48:2-7; 62:7). Second, he is enthroned and possesses authority and power normally ascribed only to God (*1 En.* 49:1-4). Third, he is entrusted with the final judgment of all humankind, determining the punishment of the wicked and the blessedness of the righteous (*1 En.* 45:2-6; 46:4-8; 51:1-5; 61:8-9; 62:14-16; 69:26-27). Christian readers immediately detect a remarkable similarity to the NT portrayal of Jesus Christ. No wonder this section has generated so much scholarly interest.

The question, of course, is whether this material predates the NT writings and thus might have been a source for christological reflection or whether this material is in fact Christian.[20] Another alternative would be that the core of the material is Jewish but has been interpolated by Christians at a later date.[21] Similitudes does not, however, identify Jesus as the Son of Man. Conceivably, the work might also be a Jewish apologetic work designed to provide a response to the Christian claim that Jesus of Nazareth is the Son of

---

[20]For the view that the material is Christian, see Milik and Black, *Books of Enoch*, pp. 91-92.
[21]Remember that the pseudepigraphal writings were preserved in Christian, not Jewish, circles.

Man.[22] Surprisingly, in *1 Enoch* 71 Enoch himself is declared (or transformed into) the Son of Man.[23] This identification of Enoch with the Son of Man stands in considerable tension with the earlier presentation of this preexistent figure.[24] In light of this, some conjecture that *1 Enoch* 71 is an appendix added by another sectarian group.[25] We think the arguments favor the view that Similitudes is pre-Christian.[26]

Summarizing an immense discussion,[27] we observe that most researchers are agreed that Daniel 7 is related to the portrait of the Son of Man in Similitudes, the "man from heaven" in *Sibylline Oracle* 5[28] and the "man from the sea" in *4 Ezra* 13 (see below). In addition, most accept the notion that there was a rather fluid depiction of this figure and that he was sometimes identified with either the archangel Michael (Dan 12:1; 1QM 17:6-7) or Melchizedek (11Q13).[29] More important for our purposes is the recognition that in Second Temple Judaism, before the writing of the NT, there was a "hope of salvation mediated by a supernatural, heavenly savior figure, which might be fulfilled in any of a number of ways."[30]

In my view, Daniel 7 is the taproot for speculation about the "Son of Man" in Similitudes.[31] However, it is not quite so simple. Similitudes (cf. *1 En.* 48:4-

---

[22]John J. Collins entertains this view in "The Son of Man Who Has Righteousness," in *Ideal Figures in Ancient Judaism: Profiles and Paradigms,* ed. John J. Collins and George W. E. Nickelsburg, SBLSCS 12 (Missoula, Mont.: Scholars Press, 1980), pp. 111-33; and in "Enoch, Books of," p. 316.

[23]Carsten Colpe notes: "The pt. is simply that En. is instituted into the office and function of the eschatological Son of Man, with perhaps a suggestion that the earthly man En. is transformed into the heavenly being, the Son of Man" ("ὁ υἱὸς τοῦ ἀνθρώπου," *TDNT* 8:427).

[24]C. K. Barrett sagely observes: "This identification cannot be rationally conceived; but rationality is perhaps the last quality we should expect in an apocalypse, and the wisest course may be to suppose that there were circles in Judaism in which this strange belief was held. There are several other pieces of evidence which attest the belief that Enoch was translated to heaven to become a celestial being. If there were, in the first century AD, Jews who believed that it was possible for a man to be exalted to heaven so as to be identified with a supernatural being who was called Son of man and was to come in glory as judge and saviour, their existence and their belief can hardly fail to be relevant to the study of the Gospels" (*The New Testament Background: Selected Documents,* rev. ed. [San Francisco: Harper & Row, 1987], p. 344).

[25]Colpe, "ὁ υἱὸς τοῦ ἀνθρώπου," 8:426-27; Nickelsburg, *Jewish Literature,* p. 221.

[26]For specific arguments, see Nickelsburg, *Jewish Literature,* p. 222.

[27]See ibid., pp. 44-430; and Collins, "Apocalyptic Literature," pp. 352-53 and bibliography.

[28]We will briefly examine this work in the next chapter. Like *1 Enoch,* it is a composite work. The fifth oracle is thought by many scholars to date to sometime after the fall of Jerusalem in A.D. 70.

[29]For translation of 11Q13, see Michael Wise, *The Dead Sea Scrolls: A New Translation* (San Francisco: HarperSanFrancisco, 1996), pp. 455-57.

[30]Collins, "Apocalyptic Literature," p. 353.

[31]This is supported by Stone, "Apocalyptic Literature," p. 402.

5) also recalls passages in Isaiah in which we have a figure called the "Servant of the Lord" (Is 42; 49; 50; 52—53). In the Isaiah passages, this individual is not explicitly called a descendant of David or straightforwardly identified as the one who fulfills the Davidic promise of 2 Samuel 7:12-17. The author of Similitudes, on the other hand, conflates the two figures of Daniel 7 and the Isaianic Servant into one. Additionally (cf. *1 En.* 46:4-6), the author incorporates imagery taken from the traditional expectations of a Davidic Messiah as found in the OT (i.e., from the prophetic [Is 9:6-7; 11:1-9; Jer 23:5-6; 33:14-26; Ezek 34:23-24; Zech 9:9-10] and hymnic literature [Ps 2; 72; 110]).

This is precisely what the NT does with these three seemingly unrelated figures of the Hebrew Scriptures. Jesus of Nazareth, as portrayed by the NT, combines the attributes and functions of all three figures.[32] This is not to argue that Similitudes is a Christian work; after all, it goes in a quite different direction. For example, there is no indication that the Son of Man in Similitudes is a mediator of creation, nor is he the very image of God—affirmations made of Jesus Christ, as we have already discussed in connection with Wisdom (see chapter three above). Furthermore, Similitudes does not betray any notion of a vicarious sacrifice for the sins of the whole world, and, of course, there is no hint of a resurrection.

What seems to be the case, however, is that the earliest Christians, following the lead of their teacher, saw the fulfillment of these three eschatological figures in Jesus of Nazareth. He was the one "like a son of man." The conflation of the three OT figures may not be a Christian innovation—it may even have been assisted by Jewish sectarian exegesis—but identifying this majestic person as Jesus of Nazareth was. In contrast to some Jewish thought, however, there is no evidence that the earliest Christians identified Jesus with any archangel or angel (cf. the polemic of Hebrews), or with Melchizedek, who only serves as a type for the greater priesthood of Jesus (Heb 7:3).[33] On the other hand, later church fathers and Christian theologians up to the present day have identified the preincarnate Christ with the OT angel of the Lord.[34]

Psalms of Solomon

Introduction

This piece falls into the category of hymnic literature and reminds us of the *Thanksgiving Hymns* of Qumran. The work consists of eighteen psalms attrib-

[32]See further Nickelsburg, *Jewish Literature,* p. 223; and Larry R. Helyer, *Yesterday, Today and Forever: The Continuing Relevance of the Old Testament* (Salem, Wis.: Sheffield Publishing, 1996), pp. 316-24.
[33]See further Gerhard Kittel, "ἄγγελος," *TDNT* 1:85.
[34]See G. B. Funderburk, "Angel," *ZPEB* 1:1622-63.

uted to Solomon, though, of course, that is hardly the case, and we must once again simply be content with an anonymous author. *Psalms of Solomon* was originally written in Hebrew, though only a few Greek and Syriac manuscripts survive.[35]

Date and Provenance

Most scholars date *Psalms of Solomon* to the mid-first century B.C., placing it shortly after the intervention of Pompey and the end of Hasmonean hegemony (63 B.C.). This dating is based in large part on several historical allusions to Pompey's depredations (cf. e.g., *Pss. Sol.* 2:1-2, 26-28 [30-31]; 8:15-22 [16-26]; cf. Josephus, *Ant.* 14.4.1-4 §§54-76).[36]

The work probably originated in Palestine, and a majority of researchers are inclined to identity the Pharisees as the group from which its author emanated.[37] This identification is based upon several internal features: (1) a denunciation of the Hasmonean dynasty (*Pss. Sol.* 1:4-8; 2:2-13); (2) an affirmation of the resurrection of the dead (*Pss. Sol.* 3:12 [16]); (3) a fervent messianism (*Pss. Sol.* 17–18); and (4) concern for rigorous piety and observance of the Law (*Pss. Sol.* 14:2-3). The opening section, in which the writer describes himself as one "full of righteousness" (*Pss. Sol.* 1:2), reflects a Pharisaic self-perception (cf. Lk 18:9-14; Phil 3:5-6).

Thus far, the features of the "righteous" eliminate the Sadducees but could include the Essenes. We are not, however, dealing with sectarian Jews in the *Psalms*. Note that our author believes in freedom of choice (*Pss. Sol.* 9:4-5 [7-9]), in sharp opposition to the Essenes, and that none of the distinctive traits or beliefs of Essenism are anywhere apparent. On the other hand, the "wicked" of these compositions accord quite well with the Sadducees, *as seen by Pharisees*. These two groups, then, constitute our protagonists and antagonists in the *Psalms*.

Features

Psalms of Solomon is obviously patterned after the canonical book of Psalms, with which it has many features in common (e.g., lament, praise, doxology, imprecation). The pieces divide into two categories by type: communal (*Pss. Sol.* 1; 2; 7; 8; 11; 17; 18) and individual (*Pss. Sol.* 3; 4; 6; 9; 10; 13–16). In the individual psalms, however, the individual speaks as a member of a community designated as the "righteous" and "the poor and needy." Like canonical

---

[35]On text-critical issues, see M. Lattke, "Psalms of Solomon," *DNTB*, pp. 853-54.
[36]For an overview of dating issues, see ibid., p. 855.
[37]Though this has been recently challenged, with suggestions that the group responsible had points of contact with the Essenes or is otherwise unknown. For discussion and bibliography, see ibid., pp. 855-57.

Psalms 37 and 73, the *Psalms of Solomon* are chiefly didactic; that is, they explain why the nation and the righteous are suffering such calamity.

Especially heinous to the author are sexual sins (*Pss. Sol.* 2:11, 13; 4:4-5). But pride and insolence also rank high in the list of transgressions (*Pss. Sol.* 1:6; 2:1), as do hypocrisy (*Pss. Sol.* 4:6-8), covetousness (*Pss. Sol.* 5:16-17; 8:11) and profanation of the temple (*Pss. Sol.* 1:8; 2:3). The latter is not spelled out in detail, but most likely it involves ritual disputes and lack of personal piety by officiants. We do not hear of any disputes over calendrical matters or over interpretations about what constitutes "uncleanness" and how it is transmitted—with one exception, the issue of menstrual blood [*Pss. Sol.* 8:12]—as we did in the Qumran sectarian scrolls. Once again this points to the opposition being Sadducean.

Since psalms are literary expressions of devotion and worship, it is of some interest to note that the prime function of God that is highlighted in these eighteen compositions is that of judge. The desire for God's vindication and justice are uppermost in the sensibilities of our author(s).

Purpose

The latter observation assists in discerning the purpose of these psalms. These heartfelt cries for God's forgiveness of national sin and for divine intervention reflect a political and religious crisis for the community of the faithful and dispossessed. The work thus had therapeutic value for those who were suffering. According to our author, however, relief would not be forthcoming from the present leadership, the "wicked."

But this is not the literature of mere resignation; there is long-range optimism. The hope of restoration and regathering resounds throughout this work (*Pss. Sol.* 7:8; 8:28; 9:19; 11:1-9; 17:26-31 [28-34]). God's intervention by means of his chosen Davidic king resonates in two of these psalms (*Pss. Sol.* 17—18). The royal scion will overthrow the usurpers (Sadducees), expel the invaders (Romans) and establish the promised and long-awaited kingdom. Thus, by means of the language of prayer and worship we hear the aspirations of a Pharisaic Jew who doubtless wished to encourage his co-religionists not to give up their messianic hopes.

There is one important observation in this connection, however. Our author, unlike apocalyptic groups of the time, does not evidence a sense of the imminent intervention of God. Rather, he anticipated an unspecified time in which God would act ("the time which thou didst foresee" [*Pss. Sol.* 17:21]; "Blessed are they who shall be in those days" [*Pss. Sol.* 18:6]). Nickelsburg nicely captures the distinction: "We miss here the white heat of apocalyptic expectation."[38]

---

[38]Nickelsburg, *Jewish Literature*, p. 209.

Relevance for the New Testament

The importance of *Psalms of Solomon* for the NT lies primarily in its messianic expectations. These are similar in certain respects to that of the NT. We list some correspondences:

1. The Messiah will be a human being who is descended from the royal family of David (*Pss. Sol.* 17:4, 24; cf. Mt 1:1; 9:27; 15:22; Mk 10:47; Lk 1:32; Rom 1:3; 2 Tim 2:8; Heb 7:14; Rev 22:16).

2. The Messiah will fulfill the ancient covenant promise (2 Sam 7:14-16; Ps 89:19-37) to David that a descendant of his would rule over Israel forever (*Pss. Sol.* 17:4, 21-24, 26-31; cf. Mt 1:1-17; 19:28; Lk 22:28-30; Acts 13:23; Heb 1:5b; Rev 1:5, 7; 2:26-28; 3:21; 5:1-5; 11:15-18; 12:5, 10; 19:11-16).

3. The Messiah will manifest divine characteristics. His righteousness, strength and wisdom will exceed greatly that of mere mortals (*Pss. Sol.* 17:22-23, 32; cf. 1 Cor 1:30), and he will be pure from sin (*Pss. Sol.* 17:36; cf. Jn 8:46; 2 Cor 5:21; Heb 4:15; 7:26). Of course, the NT goes far beyond mere attribution of divine superlatives to the risen Jesus; it acclaims him as God in flesh (cf. Jn 1:1-5; Phil 2:6; Col 1:15; 1 Tim 3:16; Heb 1:1-3).

4. The functions of the Messiah will include defeat of enemies, expulsion of sinners (Sadducees, among others), regathering of the tribes, expansion of the homeland, establishment of holiness as the standard for behavior, the shepherding of Israel and the exaltation of Israel over the nations (*Pss. Sol.* 17:21-46). Many of these, with due allowance for a broadening of the notion of the people of God to include Gentiles and a corresponding broadening of the scope of the kingdom to a truly cosmic dimension, are taken up in NT depictions of the role and functions of Jesus Christ (cf. Mk 13:26-27 and par.; Rom 16:20; 1 Cor 6:2-3; 15:24-28; 2 Cor 4:16-18; Phil 3:20-21; Col 3:3-4; 2 Thess 1:5-10; 2:8; 2 Pet 3:10-13). The NT shatters the narrow nationalism of *Psalms of Solomon*. This very significant difference no doubt played a leading role in the partings of the ways between Judaism and Christianity (see chapter fourteen below).

5. The kingdom of Messiah will be an ideal age. The psalmist encourages his readers by assuring them of the blessedness of those days: "Blessed are they who shall be in those days, Seeing the good things of Israel which God shall accomplish in the gathering of the tribes" (*Pss. Sol.* 17:44; cf. 18:6). This benediction echoes a similar expectation of an unknown dinner guest who listened to Jesus' teaching: "Blessed is anyone who will eat bread in the kingdom of God!" (Lk 14:15). Jesus' response may have dampened his enthusiasm somewhat ("For I tell you, none of those who were invited will taste my dinner" [Lk 14:24]), but basically Jesus shared his contemporaries' belief that the culmination of God's kingdom would indeed be a time of blessedness for the truly righteous (cf. Mt 5:3-10; 25:34). The real innovation in his teaching (and that of his apostles) lay in the notion that the kingdom was *already here* in a

hidden form and that kingdom blessing was a *present* experience, though not
the ultimate state of beatitude: "Blessed are the eyes that see what you see!
For I tell you that many prophets and kings desired to see what you see, but
did not see it, and to hear what you hear, but did not hear it" (Lk 10:23b-24).
One is also reminded of the book of Revelation with its concluding beatitude:
"Blessed are those who wash their robes, so that they will have the right to
the tree of life and may enter the city by the gates" (Rev 22:14). This text captures nicely the tension between the "now but not yet" character of salvation.

There is, however, another feature of *Psalms of Solomon* that is relevant for
a study of the NT. As noted earlier, *Psalms of Solomon* places great emphasis
upon the notion of righteousness. A close study of the context of the *dikai-*
word group (the basic Gk stem for words such as upright, just, right, righteous, justification) in the piece demonstrates that for the author/community
of these psalms, righteousness was primarily a forensic idea; that is, it had to
do with a legal declaration by a judge or court. One who was "righteous" was
declared to be "in the right" by a judge or court. In *Psalms of Solomon*, God
himself is declared to be "in the right" by the devout in regard to his actions
and judgments (*Pss. Sol.* 2:15; 3:5; 4:8; 8:7, 26), and it is God who declares who
those "in the right" are (*Pss. Sol.* 8:23; 9:2). Though still intensely debated by
NT scholars, many would acknowledge that Paul, at least in some contexts,
speaks of righteousness in just such terms (Rom 4:3-12, 22-25; Gal 3:6-14).
This is not to deny, however, that Paul's fundamental understanding of the
righteousness of God should probably be conceived of as God's saving deed.[39]

4 Ezra (2 Esdras 3—14)

Composition

Several works feature the stalwart priest and scribe Ezra.[40] This particular
work, another in the apocalyptic genre, challenges the modern reader not
familiar with its "code." The extant work known as 2 Esdras is a composite,
falling into three sections. The earliest of these (2 Esd 3—14; these chapters
are also designated *4 Ezra*) consists ostensibly of seven visions granted to
Ezra in Babylon. One may infer from 2 Esdras 11—12 that it was written
after the fall of Jerusalem, perhaps right around A.D. 100, almost certainly

[39]For an extensive discussion of the modern debate, see K. L. Onesti and M. T. Brauch,
"Righteousness, Righteousness of God," *DPL*, pp. 827-37.
[40]Thus, in addition to canonical Ezra, we have 1 Esdras (a slightly different version of
canonical Ezra; 2 Chron 35:1—36:23; Neh 7:73—8:12), 2 Esdras, and much later works
attributed to him such as the *Greek Apocalypse of Ezra* (second to ninth centuries A.D.),
the *Vision of Ezra* (fourth to ninth centuries A.D.), the *Revelation to Ezra* (before the ninth
century A.D.) and a work heavily dependent upon *4 Ezra*, the *Apocalypse of Sedrach* (second to fifth centuries A.D.).

in Hebrew.[41] It thus provides an important window into the psyche of at least some Jews in the aftermath of this calamity.

Subsequently, the book was translated into Greek—there are quotations from it in Greek authors—though this version has not survived either. Existing manuscripts are in Latin, Syriac, Ethiopic, Arabic, Armenian and Georgian. To this basic work two Christian supplements were added: 2 Esdras 1—2 *(5 Ezra)* and 2 Esdras 15—16 *(6 Ezra)*. The former dates to about the middle of the second century A.D., and the latter probably comes from the middle of the third century A.D.

The Christian orientation of 2 Esdras 1—2 becomes evident in the section that describes a vision of heavenly Mount Zion (2 Esd 2:42-48, recalling Heb 12:22-24; Rev 7:9), when a young man is identified as "the Son of God" (2 Esd 2:47). But 2 Esdras 1:30 also clearly echoes a saying of Jesus in Matthew 23:37, and 2 Esdras 1:28-40 recalls John 20:29. Furthermore, we read in 2 Esdras 1 a lengthy recital of Israel's failings followed by the Lord's rhetorical question: "What shall I do to you, O Jacob?" The answer forthcoming is clearly Christian: "You, Judah, would not obey me. I will turn to other nations and will give them my name, so that they may keep my statutes" (2 Esdr 1:24; cf. Mt 21:43; 22:7-10). Here is already evidence for supersessionism (i.e., the view that the church replaces the Jewish people as the true Israel) within Christianity during the second century A.D. (see further discussion on this in chapter fourteen below). The Christian nature of 2 Esdras 15—16 is not as apparent. However, two historical allusions to events of the third century A.D. (2 Esd 15:11, a terrible famine in Alexandria, Egypt, during the reign of Gallienus [A.D. 260-268]; 2 Esd 15:28-63, the invasion of Syria by King Sapor I of Persia [A.D. 240-273]) make it likely that this too is a Christian addition.

Outline
The central section of 2 Esdras (2 Esd 3—14 = *4 Ezra*), which is our focus in this study, falls naturally into seven parts, corresponding to the seven visionary experiences narrated by the seer.

Introduction: identification of the seer and the circumstances of his vision
      (3:1-3)

I.   Vision one: the main problem raised—how can one justify God's treatment of Israel? (3:4—5:20)

---

[41]Scholars often understand the chronological notation "the thirtieth year after the destruction of the city" (2 Esd 3:1) typologically. Thus, it really refers to the thirtieth year after the fall of Jerusalem to the Romans, i.e., about A.D. 100. On the issues of dating, see Bruce M. Metzger, "The Fourth Book of Ezra," *OTP* 1:520 and bibliography cited there. The three heads are generally identified as Vespasian, Titus and Domitian. See Michael E. Stone, *Faith and Piety in Early Judaism: Texts and Documents* (Philadelphia: Fortress, 1983), p. 166.

II.   Vision two: reiteration of basic complaint, vision of the succession of the
        ages and the end of the age (5:21—6:34)

III.   Vision three: God's work of creation, a vision of the messianic era and
        final judgment and the plight of the mass of humanity (6:35—9:25)

IV.   Vision four: The glory of the Mosaic law, the sad plight of present Jeru-
        salem and a vision of the heavenly Jerusalem (9:26—10:59)

V.   Vision five: vision of eagle (Rome), its sins and judgment (11:1—12:51)

VI.   Vision six: vision of the Son of Man and his deliverance (13:1-58)

VII.   Vision seven: Legend of Ezra and the restoration of the Scriptures (14:1-48)

In the first three visions, Ezra dialogues with his angelic guide and raises
the basic question that haunts our author: Is God just in his dealings with
Israel? Ezra does not receive a direct answer. In this regard, one is reminded
of the book of Job. In the fourth vision, Ezra encounters a woman in deep
mourning, later interpreted as historic Zion, that is, Jerusalem. After Ezra
consoles her, she is transformed into the heavenly Jerusalem. The fifth and
sixth visions portray various aspects of the coming destruction of the Roman
Empire and all the wicked nations. The Messiah plays a leading role in this
judgment. The seventh and final vision depicts how Ezra preserved the Scriptures and was raptured to heaven.

Purpose

The burning question of *4 Ezra* is this: How can God allow Israel to experience humiliation at the hands of a godless enemy? There is little doubt that
the godless enemy is imperial Rome. We are brought to the heart of the issue
in 2 Esdras 6:55-59. The question, of course, was not a new one in the history
of Israel. Already in the canonical Scriptures the prophet Habakkuk struggled
with a similar question when Judah collapsed before the onslaught of the
Neo-Babylonian empire in the sixth century B.C. (cf. Hab 1:13).

The answer forthcoming in *4 Ezra* is this: Ezra must wait until the eschatological consummation for vindication and restoration. In the short run, he
must simply hold fast to the traditional answer to the problem of evil and be
faithful unto the end. The traditional answer is that God has ordained all that
comes to pass without being in any way the author of evil. Human beings are
the source of sin and responsible for it. Thus, in spite of the author's sorrow
and pessimism, his strong faith enables him to ride out the storm and to
encourage his readers to do the same.[42]

---

[42]Bruce M. Metzger nicely captures the tone of this book as follows: "In spite of the essentially pessimistic outlook of II Esdras, the author's strong religious faith often enables
him to rise above the fires of adversity to the very highest spiritual levels. His agonizing
is both honorable and pathetic as he seeks 'to justify the ways of God to man' " (*An Introduction to the Apocrypha* [New York: Oxford University Press, 1957], p. 30).

Features

Placing Ezra in the thirtieth year after the fall of Jerusalem to Babylon is anachronistic, inasmuch as Ezra's ministry was at least a century later (cf. Ezra 7:1-6). As most scholars recognize, one should see this as a code for Rome's destruction of Jerusalem in A.D. 70.

However, the ostensible setting may also function in another way: the author deliberately credits Ezra with a life span exceeding that of Moses. Ezra's role as a "new Moses" seems intentional.[43] In 2 Esdras 14 Ezra assembles the people and gives an exhortation somewhat in the manner of Moses' speeches in Deuteronomy. Ezra then dictates to five assistants ninety-four books (2 Esd 14:37-48), books lost in the destruction of Jerusalem (2 Esd 14:21). Of these, twenty-four were to be made public, the other seventy being reserved only for the "wise." The twenty-four books must surely be the canonical Scriptures as they are reckoned in the Hebrew Bible.[44] The tantalizing seventy secret books likely refers to those books that we today include in the Apocrypha and Pseudepigrapha.[45]

What stands out is the lack of confidence in possessing the law, quite in contrast to other first-century Jewish movements, such as the Pharisees (and the later rabbinic tradition), the Sadducees and the Essenes. Whence this pessimism? We cannot say for sure. The collapse of the Second Commonwealth, however, probably lies at the bottom of it. This calamity prompted profound reflection on the whole issue of law and righteousness and found the prevailing views unacceptable.

A fascinating feature of *4 Ezra* concerns the shift in viewpoint of the assumed author, Ezra. In the first three dialogues, Ezra clearly has a major disagreement with God's justice. In this we recall the plight of Job (cf. Job 9). An angel represents God's interests and seeks to persuade Ezra. Though even the third dialogue by no means convinces Ezra, one can still see a softening of his position. As the book further unfolds, Ezra at last adopts the

---

[43]Michael E. Stone observes: "In the seventh vision at first he is promised esoteric teaching (14:7–8); but only after his special prayer (14:19–22) does God also grant him the revelation of esoteric teaching, the 24 books of the Bible. Only with this does he become equal to Moses. The number of days of the first six visions totals 40, corresponding to the 40 days of the seventh vision (and of course to Moses' time on Mt. Sinai). The seventh vision tells of a revelation that parallels and complements the revelation of the first six visions. Ezra has moved from his doubts to a full prophetic position, indeed to the role of Moses. The transcending of doubts is the transcending of the problems raised by the destruction and the acceptance of divine governance of the world and divine determination of its history" ("2 Esdras," *ABD* 2:611-14).

[44]Josephus divided them into twenty-two books (*Ag. Ap.* 1.8 §§38-40). Rabbinic Judaism followed the count as given in *4 Ezra*.

[45]See J. H. Charlesworth, "Introduction for the General Reader," *OTP* 1:xxi-xxvii.

perspective of his angelic guide. Stone's suggestion that the fourth vision is crucial in that Ezra finally internalizes the position of the angelic guide deserves consideration. This gradual development of Ezra's view in the course of the book is fascinating and invites the fitting title "Odyssey of Ezra's Soul."[46]

Relevance for the New Testament

On the level of literary features, the most obvious comparison to the NT is the Apocalypse. Both works, having been written quite close in time at the end of the first century A.D., display common apocalyptic features: visions and raptures, angelic guides, strange beasts representing historical persons or entities, numbers freighted with symbolism and a pronounced ethical dualism. As noted above, *4 Ezra* is organized around seven basic visions. One can make a good case for Revelation also being constructed around seven basic visions; there can be no doubt about the importance of the "sevens" in this book (e.g., seven seals, seven trumpets, seven angels, seven bowls, etc.). The Apocalypse, like other apocalyptic works, and *4 Ezra* in particular, has a strong sense of the imminence of the end (Rev 1:1, 7; 6:10-11; 16:15; 22:20; cf. 2 Esd 4:26, 49-50).

Noteworthy also is *4 Ezra*'s view of the law. Whereas the apocalyptist revered the law of Moses, he also struggled with a major problem in reference to it. The problem was human inability and thus inevitable condemnation (2 Esd 7:20-24, 45-48; 8:35-36). According to our author, the law made one acutely aware of unfaithfulness to its demands (2 Esd 9:36; cf. 3:20-26) but was utterly incapable of actually assisting one to carry out those demands. This problem sounds remarkably like Paul's argument in opposing Judaizers. As Paul trenchantly points out several times, the law cannot justify; it can only define and condemn sin (Rom 3:19-20; 4:15; 7:7-24; 8:3-4; Gal 2:16-21).

As we discussed earlier in connection with the Dead Sea Scrolls, there is evidence that some Jews of the first century A.D. did indeed hold a legalistic view of the law, and some, like our author, saw this as a problem. The "New Perspective on Paul" movement, inaugurated by E. P. Sanders, rejects the view that first-century Judaism was legalistic.[47] In the prosecution of his case, however, Sanders has overlooked the viewpoint of *4 Ezra* (and, we should add, 4QMMT), since it undercuts his thesis about the nature of first-century

---

[46]See further Michael E. Stone, "The Way of the Most High and the Injustice of God in 4 Ezra," in *Knowledge of God in the Graeco-Roman World,* ed. R. van den Broeck, T. Baarda and J. Mansfeld (Leiden: E. J. Brill, 1988), p. 735; and Stone, "2 Esdras," 2:613.

[47]See his *Paul and Palestinian Judaism: A Comparison of Patterns of Religion* (Philadelphia: Fortress, 1977), pp. 70, 180, passim.

Judaism.[48] Note that Paul adopts the same stance as *4 Ezra* with respect to the problem of the law, namely, the human inability to keep it. Paul, of course, departs radically from *4 Ezra* in that he provides a christological answer to the dilemma. Christ assumed the inevitable curse of the law for believers (Gal 3:10-14), imputes to them his own righteousness (2 Cor 5:21) and, by means of the Holy Spirit, imparts a righteousness that exceeds all the requirements of the law (Rom 8:1-4; Phil 3:8-9).

Connected to the problem of human inability to keep the law is another: the seeming imbalance in God's economy tortured Ezra's soul. Why is the number of the elect so small compared to the masses destined to perdition? No direct answer is forthcoming. The angel simply informs Ezra that God has his own purposes, that all receive what they deserve in the end and that the elect are very precious in God's sight. This same question arises in NT literature, as attested by several sayings of Jesus, which seem to adopt a position similar to that of *4 Ezra:*

> Enter through the narrow gate; for the gate is wide and the road is easy that leads to destruction, and there are many who take it. For the gate is narrow and the road is hard that leads to life, and there are few who find it. (Mt 7:13-14)
>
> Someone asked him, "Lord, will only a few be saved?" He said to them, "Strive to enter through the narrow door; for many, I tell you, will try to enter and will not be able." (Lk 13:23-24)

On the other hand, the NT generally affirms that there will be a multitude of the elect (cf. Col 1:5-6; Rev 7:9). For those who question God's fairness in election, Paul curtly replies: "But who indeed are you, a human being, to argue with God? Will what is molded say to the one who molds it, 'Why have you made me like this?' " (Rom 9:20).

Our apocalyptist, like others of his mindset, goes back to Genesis for an explanation of the origin of sin. Unlike the Enoch traditions, however, the lustful angels are not to blame. Rather, Adam's personal act of disobedience is the source of human sin (2 Esd 3:21). In a poignant outcry our author laments: "O Adam, what have you done? For though it was you who sinned, the fall was not yours alone, but ours also who are your descendants" (2 Esd 7:48 [118]). The connection between Adam's sin and the sin of all his descendants is similar to that found in rabbinic theology, in which Adam's sin serves as a bad example, an example invariably followed by all (2 Esd 3:26; 8:35).

There is more to be said than this, however. According to our author, Adam

---

[48]There is not one reference to *4 Ezra* in all the many references in his book. In his defense, we should note that 4QMMT was not available at the time he wrote his book. For a valuable overview of Sanders's "new perspective" against the backdrop of larger Pauline studies, see Scott J. Hafemann, "Paul and His Interpreters," *DPL,* pp. 666-79.

had a grain of evil implanted from the very beginning of his existence (2 Esd 4:30). This view, on first glance, is similar to the Essene position concerning the "two spirits," as we read in chapter seven. It is difficult, on such a view, to avoid attributing evil to God. However, *4 Ezra* is actually closer to the Pharisaic stance on this issue by insisting that, in spite of the "evil implantation," each individual is fully responsible and capable with God's help of withstanding the evil seed.

> He answered and said, "This is the significance of the contest that all who are born on earth shall wage: if they are defeated they shall suffer what you have said, but if they are victorious they shall receive what I have said. For this is the way of which Moses, while he was alive, spoke to the people, saying, 'Choose life for yourself, so that you may live!' But they did not believe him or the prophets after him, or even myself who have spoken to them. Therefore there shall not be grief at their destruction, so much as joy over those to whom salvation is assured." (2 Esd 7:57 [127]-61 [131]; cf. 8:55-58)

Although several times Paul refers to the transgression of Adam and Eve (Rom 5:12-21; 1 Cor 11:3; 15:21-22; 1 Tim 2:14), nowhere do we detect explicit mention of the idea that Adam possessed an implanted evil seed (i.e., an evil inclination), as depicted in *4 Ezra*.[49] On the other hand, his anthropological views include the notion that unbelievers are dominated by sin (viewed as a force) or the "flesh" (i.e., the lower or sin nature; cf. Rom 6:1—8:11) and that believers continue to struggle between the opposing desires of the "flesh" and the Spirit (cf. Gal 5:16-26) until their glorification (Rom 8:28-30; Phil 3:20-21; Col 3:1-11).[50] This reminds us of the Pharisaic view that human beings were created with two "urges" or impulses within them: the *yēṣer haṭṭôb* (the good impulse) and the *yēṣer hārāʿ* (the evil impulse).

On the whole, however, Paul was much more pessimistic about the human plight than was Pharisaic teaching or even *4 Ezra*. In contrast to *4 Ezra* and rabbinic theology (the later development of Pharisaism), Paul denied that an individual outside Christ was truly free to decide which impulse would dominate. For Paul, all unbelievers suffer under abject servitude to sin (Rom 5:6; 6:6, 17, 20; 7:14-24). Only in Christ can one truly be liberated (Rom 7:25; 8:1-4).

This leads to another issue: Does *4 Ezra* teach or imply the imputation of Adam's sin to all humanity? In other words, did Adam's original sin constitute all humanity liable for his trespass and result in hereditary corruption of nature? There is no indication that *4 Ezra* presupposes such a notion. Even

---

[49]"Paul does not see sin as part of human nature as God created it. God is not responsible for a flawed creation" (Leon Morris, "Sin, Guilt," *DPL,* p. 878).

[50]See further, George E. Ladd, *A Theology of the New Testament,* rev. ed., ed. Donald A. Hagner (Grand Rapids, Mich.: Eerdmans, 1993), pp. 435-47, 509-17.

more assuredly, no such notion can be found in rabbinic literature.[51] What is taught in Jewish sources, whether the Hebrew Bible, Second Temple Judaism or later rabbinic Judaism, is that Adam's sin resulted in death for all.[52] Thus all experience the consequences of Adam's sin, but not the guilt of it. Apparently, each person becomes his or her own Adam or Eve as each gives way to the implanted evil seed.

As for the NT, we enter an area of long theological dispute among Christian theologians, and we can only outline the issues in the barest fashion.[53] Suffice it to say, a large theological edifice has been erected upon Romans 5:12-21 (cf. 2 Cor 5:14-16, 21). Within the Reformed tradition it has been customary to speak of the federal headship of Adam and the forensic (i.e., judicial) imputation of Adam's sin to all his descendants.[54] Thus Adam's trespass, inasmuch as he acted as the representative for all his offspring, resulted in a legal declaration from the Most High Judge to the effect that all his descendants are held accountable for his one act of disobedience. In this view, the imputation of Adam's sin is strictly paralleled by the imputation of the sins of God's people to Jesus Christ and the imputation of Christ's perfect righteousness to all his people (cf. 2 Cor 5:21). Others within this tradition prefer to speak of a seminal or realistic participation of all Adam's descendants in his one act of disobedience (i.e., all Adam's descendants did actually participate in his offense, though not individually and consciously, because Adam *was* the human race at that point).[55]

Those outside the Reformed tradition are more likely to be content to affirm the hereditary transmission of a corrupt nature, which invariably gives rise to personal sin. Or, they teach that all invariably follow the example of Adam and thus commit personal acts of sin, like the view of traditional Judaism.[56] Since Paul delves into this discussion only in Romans 5:21-21 and the passage in question operates within a typological contrast between the first Adam and the second Adam, with a long digression between verses 12 and 18, one faces considerable difficulties trying to say precisely what Paul's views were. What we can say with some confidence, however, is that for Paul, as for *4 Ezra*, the sin of Adam is the taproot of sin in the human race. Given Paul's

---

[51]See Louis Jacobs, "Sin," *EncJud* 14:1587-94.

[52]See George Foot Moore, *Judaism in the First Centuries of the Christian Era: The Age of the Tannaim*, 3 vols. (Cambridge, Mass.: Harvard University Press, 1958 [1927-1930]), 1:475-79.

[53]For a survey, see S. Lewis Johnson, "Romans 5:12-21—An Exercise in Exegesis and Theology," in *New Dimensions of New Testament Study*, ed. Richard N. Longenecker and Merrill C. Tenney (Grand Rapids, Mich.: Zondervan, 1974), pp. 298-316.

[54]See a classic exposition of this view in Charles W. Hodge, "Imputation," *ISBE* 2:812-15.

[55]As argued by William G. T. Shedd, *A Critical and Doctrinal Commentary on the Epistle of St. Paul to the Romans* (Grand Rapids, Mich.: Zondervan, 1967 [1879]), pp. 120-30.

[56]This seems to be the position of Larry J. Kreitzer, "Adam and Christ," *DPL*, pp. 12-13.

recognition of the solidarity of humanity—a view arising out of the OT and continued in Second Temple Judaism—he most likely held that Adam's fall was humanity's fall by virtue of a seminal or realistic participation.

Messianism is a leading theme of *4 Ezra,* as it was in the Similitudes (*1 En.* 37—71). In common with the latter, *4 Ezra* pictures a transcendent figure who is hidden with God until the appointed time for his revelation to the world (2 Esd 12:31; 13:26, 32).[57] So far as we are aware, for the first time in Jewish literature (excluding the NT), we encounter the notion of a dying Messiah (2 Esd 7:28-30; cf. 13:52).[58] Only in the later Tannaitic material of the Talmud (*b. Sukkah* 52a)[59] and in the Targums and midrashim (*Tg. Ps.-J.* on Ex 40:11; *Pesiq. Rab.* on Song 4:5) do we read of a Messiah ben Joseph (or Ephraim) who precedes the Davidic Messiah and fights the enemies of God and Israel.[60] Messiah ben Joseph dies in battle, but his death does not atone for the sins of Israel, much less for Gentiles. In *4 Ezra* the Messiah participates in the final

---

[57]The question of preexistence is not clearly stated but may be implied in 2 Esd 12:32; 13:52; 14:9. See Jacob M. Myers, *I and II Esdras: Introduction, Translation, and Commentary,* AB 42 (Garden City, N.Y.: Doubleday, 1974), p. 127.

[58]Robert Eisenman created a media sensation when he announced that a Qumran text made mention of a "dying Messiah." For background on this, see John J. Collins, *The Scepter and the Star: The Messiahs of the Dead Sea Scrolls and Other Ancient Literature,* ABRL 10 (New York: Doubleday, 1995), pp. 58-60 and nn. 36-46. Eisenman later publicly recanted in the face of scholarly critiques of his view (Collins says that Eisenman and M. O. Wise "still defend their original interpretation as possible" [*Scepter and Star,* p. 70 n. 36]). Sound reasons exist for denying any notion of an executed Messiah in the Dead Sea Scrolls. See Lawrence H. Schiffman, *Reclaiming the Dead Sea Scrolls: Their True Meaning for Judaism and Christianity,* ABRL (New York: Doubleday, 1994), pp. 344-47; and Abegg in Wise, Abegg and Cook, *The Dead Sea Scrolls,* pp. 291-94. For a popular account of the controversy, see James D. Tabor, "A Pierced or Piercing Messiah?—The Verdict Is Still Out," *BAR* 18, no. 6 (1992): 58-59.

[59]We cite the relevant passage: "What is the cause of the mourning [mentioned in the last cited verse]? —R. Dosa and the Rabbis differ on the point. One explained, The cause is the slaying of Messiah the son of Joseph, and the other explained, The cause is the slaying of the Evil Inclination. It is well according to him who explains that the cause is the slaying of Messiah the son of Joseph, since that well agrees with the Scriptural verse, And they shall look upon me because they have thrust him through, and they shall mourn for him as one mourneth for his only son; but according to him who explains the cause to be the slaying of the Evil Inclination, is this [it may be objected] an occasion for mourning? Is it not rather an occasion for rejoicing? Why then should they weep? . . . Our Rabbis taught, The Holy One, blessed be He, will say to the Messiah, the son of David (May he reveal himself speedily in our days!), 'Ask of me anything, and I will give it to thee', as it is said, I will tell of the decree etc. this day have I begotten thee, ask of me and I will give the nations for thy inheritance. But when he will see that the Messiah the son of Joseph is slain, he will say to Him, 'Lord of the Universe, I ask of Thee only the gift of life'. 'As to life', He would answer him, 'Your father David has already prophesied this concerning you', as it is said, He asked life of thee, thou gavest it him, [even length of days for ever and ever]" (*b. Sukkah* 52a, in *The Soncino Talmud on CD-ROM,* The CD-ROM Judaic Classics Library [Davka, 1973, 1990]).

[60]For a full discussion, read Moore, *Judaism in the First Centuries,* 2:323-76.

resurrection but does not inaugurate it (cf. 2 Esd 7:31-32). Some have plausibly suggested that the presence of a dying Messiah in *4 Ezra* represents a Jewish apologetic response to the Christian preaching of the gospel (cf. Rom 1:3-6; 1 Tim 1:15; 2 Tim 1:10; 2:8; 1 Jn 2:2; Rev 5:5-10).

When the Messiah is revealed, he reigns on earth with the righteous for a period of four hundred years.[61] After this, all those still living die, including the Messiah, and there is primeval silence for seven days. Then follows the renewal of all things, resurrection and reward for the righteous, and resurrection and eternal punishment for the wicked (2 Esd 7:28-44). The final judgment of the wicked lasts seven years (2 Esd 7:43). One is immediately reminded of the Apocalypse, in which one reads of an earthly, messianic kingdom lasting one thousand years—the millennial reign of Christ—followed by the second resurrection, the Great White Throne judgment and the eternal state (Rev 20—22). Many scholars have argued that Paul's eschatology is also compatible with millennialism (cf. 1 Cor 15:22-26).[62]

Another significant feature of *4 Ezra* is its lengthy description of the "intermediate state," that is, the status of those who die and await their final destiny (2 Esd 7:75-105). The rather full description of the fate of the ungodly in *4 Ezra* contrasts with the NT's reticence on this subject. We do have sayings of Jesus in which he warns of a fiery punishment in Gehenna (Mt 5:22; cf. Mt 5:29-30 par. Mk 9:43-48; Mt 10:28), described as an eternal fire (Mt 18:8-9; 25:41). He also solemnly affirms that evil persons will be thrown into "the furnace of fire, where there will be weeping and gnashing of teeth" (Mt 13:50). But these passages seem to refer to final judgment, not the intermediate state, and are sparse in description.

We have only the parable (if such it is) about the rich man and Lazarus (Lk 16:19-31), affording a brief glimpse into the condition of the wicked before they experience final judgment. This passage, by the way, reflects the common views of Second Temple Judaism in regard to the fate of the wicked. In contrast to Luke 16:10-31, *4 Ezra* seems to teach that the ungodly are shown their mistake for seven days and then must wait in anxiety and dread until the carrying out of their future punishment. The righteous, on the other hand, appear to enjoy something like "soul sleep" in heavenly chambers (2 Esd 7:85, 95; cf. *1 En.* 91:10; 92:3). This notion does not comport well with

---

[61]The versions vary at 2 Esd 7:28. See NRSV notes. Some versions have thirty years and others one thousand years.

[62]On 1 Cor 15:22-26 see Wilber B. Wellis, "The Problem of an Intermediate Kingdom in 1 Corinthians 15:20-28," *JETS* 18/4 (1975): 229-42. For a survey of opinion, see L. Joseph Kreitzer, *Jesus and God in Paul's Eschatology*, JSNTSup 19 (Sheffield: Sheffield Academic Press, 1987), pp. 130-54. For a convenient survey of the various millennial views, see R. J. Bauckham, "Millennium," in *New Dictionary of Theology*, ed. Sinclair B. Ferguson and David F. Wright (Downers Grove, Ill.: InterVarsity Press, 1988), pp. 428-30.

Paul's brief statements in which he anticipates being "with the Lord" or "with Christ" (2 Cor 5:1-10; Phil 1:21-23). He expects to be fully conscious, as is the case with the deceased saints in Revelation 6:9-11 and 7:9-17. To be sure, Revelation 14:13 speaks of deceased saints resting from their labors, but this seems to be metaphorical rather than literal.

We make one final observation: in 4 Ezra the author stresses that God created all things by himself (2 Esd 3:4-5; 6:6; 8:7; 9:18). He was not dependent upon or assisted by anyone else. Special emphasis upon God's singular work in creation leads us to suspect that we may be overhearing a Jewish response to the Christian teaching of Jesus Christ's role in creation (cf. our earlier discussion in connection with the books of Baruch, Ben Sira and Wisdom of Solomon and the works of Philo).[63] Christology was the primary bone of contention that led to the mutual "divorce" of church and synagogue at the end of the first century. Obviously, we hear the Christian side of the argument in the Apocalypse, which affirms Jesus Christ as the mediator of creation (Rev 3:14; cf. Prov 8:22-31; Rev 1:8; 22:12).

4 Maccabees

Content and Genre

Our last selection in this chapter is another bearing the name Maccabees. Its connection to the other works already examined lies in its focus on the martyrdom of Eleazar and a mother and her seven sons narrated in 2 Maccabees 6—7. Indeed, the latter work served as the primary source for our author, who greatly elaborated, embellished and adapted it for his own purposes. In 4 Maccabees each of the martyrs refuses to eat pork and food sacrificed to idols in the presence of the archenemy, Antiochus Epiphanes. Each one chooses to endure torture and death rather than violate the law of Moses. After watching each of her seven sons die horrible deaths, the mother not only encourages each to die nobly and honorably but also actually throws herself into the fire rather than allow the soldiers to touch her body. The work concludes with a stirring encomium and exhortation to emulate these heroes of the faith.

In terms of genre, the work is mixed. It begins like a philosophical discourse on the superiority of reason, but the discourse soon becomes a eulogy in honor of nine Jewish martyrs. At points in the eulogy, however, the writer returns to a philosophical mode to drive home his point. In the end, both

---

[63]Myers suggests rather that this formulation comes "at a time when there was a tendency to associate wisdom or the logos with God in the former [creation] and the messiah in the latter [consummation]" (*I and II Esdras,* pp. 121, 201). This is doubtless so, but early Christians also associated both creation and consummation with Jesus Christ.

genres are vehicles of moral exhortation.[64] Employing standard Greek rhetorical conventions and devices, our author's style at points reminds us of the wisdom genre, especially Wisdom of Solomon. The result is a rather remarkable piece of writing. The style is florid and expansive, appealing to reason, but calculated to appeal to the emotions.

Outline
I   The thesis announced: reason sovereign over emotions (1:1-6)
II. The thesis illustrated from Jewish history (1:7—4:26)
III. Martyrdom of Eleazar (5:1—7:23)
IV. Martyrdom of the seven sons (8:1—14:20)
V.   In praise of the mother and concluding moral exhortation (15:1—18:24)

Purpose
The author announces his theme at the outset: "The subject that I am about to discuss is most philosophical, that is, whether devout reason is sovereign over the emotions" (4 Macc 1:1). His aim is straightforward: "I could prove to you from many and various examples that reason is dominant over the emotions" (4 Macc 1:7). Though it is not mentioned explicitly until 4 Maccabees 1:17, our author assumes that the Torah is the epitome of reason. Thus the basic thesis defended by our author is that total faithfulness to Torah enables one to rule over the emotions and results in blessedness.[65] The main emotion or passion that reason must overcome is fear. The bulk of the work portrays how seven Jewish martyrs did exactly that. Like emotional tracts for the times, this work seeks to involve the reader viscerally, which it does by its gruesome, theatrical recital of torture and death. This work is essentially a funeral oration praising the martyrs' faithfulness unto death. Clearly the eulogy urges Jews likewise to be faithful. We infer that it was written during a time when many Jews faced just such a decision.[66]

---

[64]R. B. Townsend speaks of it as having "the nature of a sermon" ("The Fourth Book of Maccabees," *APOT* 2:654).

[65]According to G. E. Ladd, our author's purpose was "to show that the Jewish belief in the divinely given Law was not incompatible with Greek philosophy but was in fact the way the goals of philosophy could be realized. In fact, only Judaism embodied the true philosophy" ("Pseudepigrapha," *ISBE* 3:1042).

[66]Townsend captures nicely the issue at stake: "Every far-sighted man, such as the author of this book must have been, could not but recognize, even during the more clement days of Augustus and Tiberius, that as soon as ever Jews were required to offer public sacrifice at the imperial altars an impossible test would be imposed. Every true Jew knew that he must refuse, and it was not hard to foresee what would happen then, when once the passions of the vilest mob in the world were let loose. To meet and endure the coming persecution the sons of Israel would need all their courage, and how better could the Jewish-hellenic philosopher steel the hearts of his brethren than by holding up to

Authorship and Date

The author of our work is anonymous. Eusebius (*Hist. eccl.* 3.10.6) and Jerome (*De viris illustribus* 13) both attributed the work to Josephus and entitled it "On the Sovereignty of Reason." Whereas the title is certainly appropriate, modern scholars, with good reason, do not accept the attribution of authorship, even though the work is found in several manuscripts that also contain Josephus's works. The style, method and basic position of 4 Maccabees are very hard to reconcile with Josephus's acknowledged works.[67] Though it is reminiscent of Philo in some passages, neither should the work be attributed to him.[68] Originally written in Greek by one conversant with Greek rhetorical devices and philosophy, the work conforms to what is called the "Asianic" style of writing, as distinct from the classical, Attic style. The most that can safely be assumed is that our author was a Diaspora Jew who possessed a Greek education, though his understanding of Greek philosophy was not extensive. Given the importance of Alexandria, Egypt, and the philosophical works of Philo, who hailed from this city (cf. chapter nine above), one is tempted to locate the work there.[69] On the other hand, early Christian tradition located the tombs of the martyrs in Antioch of Syria.[70] We leave the place of writing an open question.

The date is also uncertain. Some scholars date it to Caligula's insane attempt to erect an image of himself in the Jerusalem temple (ca. A.D. 40).[71] Certainly this was a time calling for unflinching commitment to Torah. We recall Philo's *Embassy to Gaius,* in which this crisis loomed large, and Josephus's account of this near disaster (*J.W.* 2.10.1-5 §§184-203; *Ant.* 18.8.1-9 §§257-309).

Of course, there were many other such crises during the first century A.D., so other scholars prefer to place the writing during the era of Hadrian (A.D. 117-138). The appeal of the latter date is the reference in rabbinic tradition to the martyrdom of a mother and her seven sons when Hadrian was emperor (*b. Giṭ.* 57b).

---

them the self-abnegating virtues of Stoicism and the sublime heroism of the Maccabean martyrs?" ("Fourth Book of Maccabees," 2:654).

[67] For details, see Hugh Anderson, "4 Maccabees (First Century A.D.): A New Translation and Introduction," *OTP* 2:533; and Townsend, "Fourth Book of Maccabees," 2:656-57.

[68] Hugh Anderson speaks of "numerous echoes of the thought and exegetical methods of Philo" ("Maccabees, Books of," *ABD* 4:453).

[69] Townsend thinks this is the best choice for location ("Fourth Book of Maccabees," 2:657). He is followed in this by Herbert Wolf, "Maccabees, Books of," *ZPEB* 4:19; and Ladd, "Pseudepigrapha," 3:1042.

[70] See Moses Hadas, "Introduction," in *The Third and Fourth Books of Maccabees,* JAL (New York: Harper, 1953), 112; and Anderson, "4 Maccabees (First Century A.D.)," 2:534-37.

[71] Townsend fittingly notes that "we might well call [Caligula] the Second Brilliant Madman," the first, of course, being Antiochus IV Epiphanes, whom Jews nicknamed Epimanes, "the madman" ("Fourth Book of Maccabees," 2:653).

What may tip the scales in favor of a mid-first century A.D. date is the mention of Simon's trip to see "Apollonius, governor of Syria, Phoenicia, and Cilicia" (4 Macc 4:2). Only during the years A.D.19-54 did Cilicia and Syria form one administrative province in the Roman Empire.[72] If this clue is decisive for dating, the writing of 4 Maccabees coincides with the career of Philo as well as with the early missionary work of the apostle Paul.

Features

Several features of this work merit discussion. The adoption of Greek philosophical terminology and concepts is noteworthy.[73] As we have seen earlier in our study, Jewish thinkers were not reluctant to incorporate and adapt aspects of Hellenistic thought and culture. Our author has obviously received a basic Hellenistic education and can make his way reasonably well through the curriculum. Most pronounced in the work are the points of contact with Platonic and Stoic thought.

In this regard one notes several references to the four cardinal virtues so highly valued in Platonic and Stoic philosophy (4 Macc 1:2-4, 18; 5:23-24 [note that in the latter passage piety is one of the four virtues, in keeping with Xenophon and Philo]). Reason, says our author, prefers a life of wisdom, and wisdom includes learning "divine matters." Thus, for our author, the law of Moses (divine matters) takes its place as the highest form of learning. But wisdom also includes "human affairs to our advantage," a phrase borrowed from the Stoic definition of wisdom (4 Macc 1:15-19). Likewise, 4 Maccabees 2:23 strikes a familiar Stoic keynote of the wise man being a king who rules over his senses. Like Aristotle, our author divides the passions into pleasure and pain (4 Macc 1:20-23). The description of David's thirst as a "frenzied desire" picks up the notion of the Greek mythological gadfly *(oistros)*, a symbol of sexual desire (4 Macc 3:17). In 4 Maccabees 5:13 one meets the phrase "some power watching over," a Greek philosophical expression. The author pictures the sons "grouped about their mother as though a chorus" (4 Macc 8:4), recalling the conventions of the Greek theatrical productions. In 4 Maccabees 9:7 we have a clear borrowing of the Stoic principle that suffering does not affect the essential nature of the wise ("do not suppose that you can injure us"). The author seems to adopt the Platonic idea of the natural immortality of the soul (4 Macc 9:22). The phrase in 4 Maccabees 15:4 "of mind and of form" is a borrowing from Stoic terminology.

---

[72]See E. J. Bickerman, "The Date of Fourth Maccabees," in *Studies in Jewish and Christian History*, 3 vols., AGJU 9 (Leiden: E. J. Brill, 1976-1986), 1:277.

[73]G. E. Ladd says "This book illustrates better than any other book of the Pseudepigrapha the fusion of Hebrew and Greek culture" ("Pseudepigrapha," 3:1042).

These are but some of the instances of borrowing by our author.[74]

The main feature that characterizes this discourse is the remarkable capacity of the nine martyrs (in particular, the mother) to endure such horrific torture, when all they had to do was accede in what might seem an insignificant violation of Torah. In this regard we note that, in contrast to 2 Maccabees 7:9, 11, 14, 23, our author does not mention the resurrection of the body as the reward of the righteous martyrs. Rather, they enter into a state of immortality (4 Macc 7:19; 9:22; 14:5; 15:3; 16:13; 17:12; 18:23). Most scholars assume that our author did not believe in the resurrection of the body. I question this judgment. An argument from silence is not the strongest that can be mustered. For some time scholars held that the Qumran community likewise rejected resurrection, since no explicit mention of it was made in the central documents such as *Damascus Document* and *Rule of the Community*. Now, however, recently published texts and a rereading of the previously known ones have tipped the scales in the other direction.[75] We suggest one should therefore exercise caution here. As an example from the NT, Paul held to both concepts but does not always mention them together in the Thessalonian and Corinthian correspondence.[76] We can say confidently that the concept of immortality in 4 Maccabees is not like Plato's notion of an inherent quality but is rather a gracious gift of God for obedient faith.[77]

In many ways, the mother is the chief figure in the oration. She is a mother in Israel who takes her place alongside such stalwarts as Sarah, Deborah, Susanna and Judith. Once again we note that despite a tendency to deprecate women in some of the literature we have read, there are pieces that elevate them to the level of national heroines. The role of Jewish mothers in preserving Jewish tradition has a long pedigree, and 4 Maccabees must be seen in this storied tradition.[78] Judaism simply would not have survived the centuries had it not been for the steely determination of Jewish mothers to "sanctify the Name" at whatever cost. The phrase "sanctification of the Name" (*kidduš haššēm*) embodies the resolve of a people who were prepared to die rather than renounce their faith. It has unfortunately been a recurring necessity in Jewish history since the days of 4 Maccabees. One thinks here of the

---

[74]For discussion, see Hadas, "Introduction," pp. 115-18.

[75]For discussion and texts, see James C. VanderKam, *The Dead Sea Scrolls Today* (Grand Rapids, Mich.: Eerdmans, 1994), pp. 78-81.

[76]See Ladd, *Theology of the New Testament*, pp. 597-603; L. J. Kreitzer, "Eschatology," *DPL*, pp. 260-61; and J. J. Scott, "Immortality," *DPL*, pp. 431-33.

[77]Ladd, "Pseudepigrapha," 3:1042.

[78]Townsend rightly points out that our author does, however, get in a rather extraneous point about feminine virtue in 4 Macc 18:6-9. Jewish women were thus exhorted to guard their virtue at all costs ("Fourth Book of Maccabees," 2:655).

"Dark Night" of the Middle Ages when Jews were repeatedly massacred for various alleged offenses.[79] Even in the modern age we have faced the horrors of a Holocaust *(Shoah)* in which Jews were given no choice whether they would voluntarily renounce their faith. In short, the issue that dominates 4 Maccabees is still relevant; it weaves itself through the tapestry of Jewish history and culture.[80]

Relevance for the New Testament

In terms of genre, there is no example of NT literature or, for that matter, contemporary Hebrew literature that corresponds to 4 Maccabees. On the other hand, there is a section of Hebrews that invites comparison. Significantly, Hebrews is a homiletic discourse and thus has at least a point of contact with 4 Maccabees. Though not containing a lengthy, gory description of torture, Hebrews 11 narrates the sufferings and torture of some unnamed "heroes and heroines of faith."

> Others were tortured, refusing to accept release, in order to obtain a better resurrection. Others suffered mocking and flogging, and even chains and imprisonment. They were stoned to death, they were sawn in two, they were killed by the sword; they went about in skins of sheep and goats, destitute, persecuted, tormented—of whom the world was not worthy. They wandered in deserts and mountains, and in caves and holes in the ground. (Heb 11:35b-38)

Like 4 Maccabees, Hebrews urges its readers to endure suffering for a supreme good. In the case of Hebrews, it is the city that is coming (Heb 11:10; 12:22; 13:14), the new heavenly reality. The author challenges readers to let nothing hinder them from this objective, even death (Heb 12:4-12). Of course, the difference between 4 Maccabees and Hebrews lies in the latter's christological basis for perseverance rather than in reason (cf. Heb 2:9—3:6; 4:14—5:4; 7:26—8:7; 9:11—10:39; 12:1-4; 13:12, 20-21). In this regard, it is noteworthy that the NT passion narratives display remarkable restraint in their description of the crucifixion of Christ. This stands in marked contrast, of course, with later Christian depictions and embellishments of the crucifixion. These later traditions, in fact, owe as much to 4 Maccabees as to the NT.[81]

Beyond this we find commonplace similarities in the use of metaphors or images. In 4 Maccabees 17:14-15 one notes the image of a great athletic stadium, notably present in Hebrews 12:1 as well (cf. 1 Cor 9:24-27; Gal 2:2; Phil

---

[79]For background on this, see Haim Hillel Ben-Sasson, "Kiddush Ha-Shem and Hillul Ha-Shem," *EncJud* 10:978-86.

[80]For a survey of Jewish persecution through history, see Graham Keith, *Hated Without A Cause? A Survey of Anti-Semitism* (London: Paternoster, 1997).

[81]On the impact of 4 Maccabees, see ibid., pp. 123-27.

2:16; 2 Tim 4:7). Like the author of Hebrews, 4 Maccabees is fond of nautical imagery (Heb 2:1; 6:19; cf. 4 Macc 7:1-3; 13:6-7; 15:31-32). These simply demonstrate a common cultural heritage in the Greco-Roman world.

A major issue in comparing 4 Maccabees with NT thought centers on four remarkable passages that view the deaths of the martyrs as having atoning significance (4 Macc 1:11; 6:28-29; 17:21-22; 18:4). We cite the third: "they having become, as it were, a ransom for the sin of our nation. And through the blood of those devout ones and their death as an atoning sacrifice, divine Providence preserved Israel that previously had been mistreated" (4 Macc 17:21b-22). This seeming parallel to the substitutionary atonement of Jesus Christ as found in the NT requires comment (cf., e.g., Mt 20:28; Mk 10:45; Rom 3:24-26; 5:6-11; 1 Tim 2:6, Heb 9:12). Is there indebtedness in one direction or the other here? Or are both concepts drawing upon a common Jewish tradition that was already current in first-century Judaism? Few today would argue that the NT is dependent upon 4 Maccabees, and even fewer would argue vice versa.[82] The most likely explanation is that both works drew upon preexisting Jewish tradition, though each developed it in a different direction.

Whereas one may note some similarity in various pagan ideas about atoning for the transgressions of a community or group,[83] the most obvious taproot for vicarious suffering is the OT. The sacrificial ritual of ancient Israel involved the fundamental notion of substitution (cf. Lev 1:4; 4:1—5:19). Deriving from the priestly traditions, we also have the Day of Atonement (Yom Kippur) ritual in which an animal sacrifice (a scapegoat) expiated the sins of the entire nation (Lev 16:7-22). Another interesting instance involves the substitution of the Levites in place of the Israelite firstborn males as servants in the Tabernacle ("But you shall accept the Levites for me—I am the LORD—as substitutes for all the firstborn among the Israelites" [Num 3:41]). Furthermore, in Deuteronomy we read of a procedure for exculpating a community from bloodguilt when a homicide was discovered and the guilty party could not be determined (Deut 21:1-9). The procedure in this case, however, called for a heifer to be killed by having its neck broken, not by shedding its blood. We also have the dramatic episode in which Moses offered to forfeit his place in God's book of the living, if this would atone for the sin of Israel in making the golden calf. His request was rejected: "Whoever has sinned against me I will blot out of my book" (Ex 32:33). Finally, we recall David's census of all Israel and the three choices placed before him in order to atone

[82]H. Rashdall held that it was "highly probable" that Paul borrowed from 4 Maccabees (cited in Hans-Georg Link and Colin Brown, "ἱλάσκομαι," *NIDNTT* 3:164).
[83]For examples, see Sam K. Williams, *Jesus' Death as Saving Event,* HDR 2 (Missoula, Mont.: Scholars Press, 1975), pp. 137-61.

for this sin (2 Sam 24:1-17). David chose to fall into the hands of the Lord, which, in this case, resulted in a plague killing some seventy thousand people. By their deaths the nation as a whole was spared. When Jerusalem itself was threatened, David pleaded with the destroying angel to take out his vengeance on him alone, seeing that he was responsible for the census. As in the case of Moses, this was not done, but it is instructive for its concept of the one who offers to die for the many.

Even more determinative for the idea of vicarious atonement by an individual (or group) is the famous Suffering Servant passage in Isaiah 52:13–53:12. This text, predating considerably both 4 Maccabees and the NT, features an innocent, elect individual who was destined by the Lord to die for the sake and in the place of others. Unlike Moses and David, the Servant *is* accepted in place of the many.

> But he was wounded for our transgressions, crushed for our iniquities; upon him was the punishment that made us whole, and by his bruises we are healed. All we like sheep have gone astray; we have all turned to our own way, and the LORD has laid on him the iniquity of us all. . . . Yet he bore the sin of many, and made intercession for the transgressors. (Is 53:5-6, 12b)

Scholars have called attention to the fact that a belief in vicarious atonement seems to have flourished in apocalyptic circles.[84] Thus we note a similar idea in *Testament of Benjamin* 3:8, a work generally dated to the Maccabean era (mid-second century B.C.):

> Through you will be fulfilled the heavenly prophecy concerning the Lamb of God, the Savior of the world, because the unspotted one will be betrayed by lawless men, and the sinless one will die for impious men by the blood of the covenant for the salvation of the gentiles and of Israel and the destruction of Beliar and his servants.

This passage, however, almost certainly contains a Christian interpolation ("the Lamb of God, the Savior of the world" [Jn 1:29]; perhaps also "by the blood of the covenant" [Mt 26:28]).[85] Still, it does witness to the idea of vicarious redemption accomplished by a messianic figure among apocalyptic groups in intertestamental Judaism.

At Qumran we find the notion that by living a life devoted to the covenant of the community, the covenanters could "atone for all those in Aaron who volunteer for holiness, and for those in Israel who belong to truth, and for Gentile proselytes who join them in community" (1QS 5:6). The mission of

---

[84]So Hadas, *Third and Fourth Books of Maccabees,* p. 122.
[85]The translation is by H. C. Kee, "Testaments of the Twelve Patriarchs," *OTP* 1:826. See the textual variants and discussion there.

the covenanters was to "preserve the faith in the land with self-control and a broken spirit, atoning for sin by working justice and suffering affliction" (1QS 8:3-4a; cf. 8:10; 9:4).[86] Only those, however, who joined the new covenant community actually experienced the benefits of atonement. All others in Israel were excluded (see chapters six and seven above).

The NT strikes a quite different note when it insists that none but Jesus Christ can atone for sins. It hardly needs mentioning that the NT clearly identifies the Suffering Servant of Isaiah as Jesus of Nazareth. According to the NT, he alone possesses the merit and ability to remove sin (Heb 7:23-28; 1 Pet 1:19-21; 2:24). In contrast, then, to some streams of intertestamental and later rabbinic Judaism, in the NT no one can contribute toward or augment this once-for-all sacrifice for sin (Rom 3:21-31; 5:1-21; Heb 2:14-18; 5:1-10; 7:11—8:7; 9:11—10:17).[87]

Furthermore, the nature of the atonement does not seem to be precisely the same in 4 Maccabees and the NT.[88] In the former, the primary benefit of the martyrs' atoning death was the removal of God's wrath and the securing of his favor *for the enjoyment of national life in the ancestral homeland* ("they became the cause of the downfall of tyranny over their nation" [4 Macc 1:11]; "divine Providence preserved Israel that previously had been mistreated" [4 Macc 17:22]; "Because of them the nation gained peace" [4 Macc 18:4]). To be sure, according to 4 Maccabees the martyrs were welcomed into the presence of the patriarchs at their deaths; they thus experienced personal salvation and entered into immortality (4 Macc 7:19; 16:25; 17:12, 18; cf. Lk 16:9, 22). But this was their personal reward for devotion to Torah; their sufferings, on the other hand, worked toward the betterment of Israel's existence on earth.

Perhaps 4 Maccabees 6:28-29 refers to the salvation of individual Israelites at the day of judgment ("Be merciful to your people, and let our punishment suffice for them. Make my blood their purification, and take my life in exchange for theirs" [Eleazar's speech]). Even here, however, the text may have national redemption in view. Note that this is a prayer that God *might* account Eleazar's death as having atoning value; there is no guarantee that it actually *would* atone. At any rate, the personal dimension of the atoning death of the martyrs is not foremost in our author's theology. Actually, the above speech of Eleazar may be rather close in thought to that of Paul in

---

[86]The translations are by Michael Wise in Wise, Abegg and Cook, *Dead Sea Scrolls,* pp. 132, 137.

[87]For a quotation from the Talmud (*b. Sukkah* 45b) by a rabbi who was confident his righteousness could exempt all his contemporary co-religionists from judgment, see Link and Brown, "ἱλάσκομαι," 3:161.

[88]For an insightful discussion of atonement in the OT, see J. Milgrom, "Atonement in the OT," *IDBSup,* pp. 78-82.

Colossians 1:24: "I am now rejoicing in my sufferings for your sake, and in my flesh I am completing what is lacking in Christ's afflictions for the sake of his body, that is, the church." Thus Eleazar and Paul may have shared the notion that one may vicariously absorb *a larger proportion of the destined sufferings* of the people of God before the messianic age arrives in all its fullness (designated as "the birth pangs of the Messiah" in rabbinic literature).[89]

Jesus' atonement in the NT, by contrast, is *cosmic in scope* and *certain in its benefits*. It focuses upon the personal, spiritual and cosmic dimensions of a restored relationship with God (cf. Eph. 1:3-14, 21-22; 2:6, 21-22; 3:10; Col 1:15-20) and thus transcends narrow, nationalistic aspirations. The gospel guarantees the salvation of all who embrace its message by faith (Acts 2:32-29; 4:12; Heb 6:13-20), though, like Qumran, only those who personally do so enjoy its fruits (Mt 7:21-23; Acts 4:12).

There is another interesting point of contact between 4 Maccabees and the NT. Our author depicts Antiochus trying to reason with Eleazar. Simply submitting "out of compulsion" to a royal decree, argues Antiochus, is not a violation of any true philosophy (4 Macc 5:10-13). To this Eleazar replies that there are no gradations of sin: "to transgress the law in matters either small or great is of equal seriousness" (4 Macc 5:20). Thus sin has a uniform character, namely, disobedience to the great Lawgiver. This reminds us of Paul's argument against the Judaizers in Galatians. He assumes that if one tries to be justified by works, one must observe the law in its entirety: "Once again I testify to every man who lets himself be circumcised that he is obliged to obey the entire law" (Gal 5:3; cf. 3:10-14). It also comes to expression in James's statement that "whoever keeps the whole law but fails in one point has become accountable for all of it" (Jas 2:10).

Finally, we note some assorted similarities between 4 Maccabees and the NT. Paul's conviction that the mind *(nous)* or inmost self *(esō anthrōpon)* cannot control the desires of the flesh (Rom 7:14-25) reminds us of a concession made in 4 Maccabees. Although reason *(logismos)* is dominant over the emotions *(pathē)* that hinder the cardinal virtues, it cannot control its own emotions: forgetfulness and ignorance (4 Macc 1:5-6). Paul taught that all those outside of Christ are slaves to sin (Rom 6:17-22). But he also taught that believers in Christ, though set free from bondage to sin, cannot obtain perfection in this life; they are still in need of constant *reminder* and *instruction* about what it means to walk worthy of the Lord (Rom 6:12-14; Gal 5:7-26; 6:1-10; Eph 4:17—5:20; Phil 3:12-16).

---

[89]See further P. T. O'Brien, *Colossians, Philemon*, WBC 44 (Waco, Tex.: Word, 1982), p. 79. Scott J. Hafemann, however, rejects this interpretation of Paul's statement ("Suffering," *DPL*, p. 920).

We also wonder if Paul was thinking of 4 Maccabees when he said that even if he handed over his body but had not love, it gained nothing (1 Cor 13:3).[90]

We have already noted some similarities of Hebrews to 4 Maccabees. The stress in Hebrews upon the cleansing effect of Jesus' blood seems to echo the sentiment in 4 Maccabees that the martyrs' blood purified the land and people (4 Macc 1:11; 6:29: 17:21-22; cf. Heb 1:3; 2:11; 10:10, 14, 29; 13:12). In both writings faith distinguishes those who persevere and lay hold of God's promises (4 Macc 16:22; 17:2; cf. Heb 11:1-2, 6, 8, 13-16, 39). Both employ the metaphor of a great crowd at a stadium watching the competition (4 Macc 17:11-16; Heb 12:1-2). There is also a rare phrase shared by both works in the last-named parallel, namely, *aphoraō eis* ("looking unto"). In 4 Maccabees 17:10 the martyrs look unto God, whereas in Hebrews 12:2 believers are urged to look unto Jesus.

The Johannine writings share with 4 Maccabees a fondness for the word *nikaō*, "to conquer" (cf. 4 Macc 1:11; 6:10; 7:4, 11; 9:6, 30; 16:14 with Jn 16:33; 1 Jn 2:13-14; 5:4-5; Rev 2:7, 11, 17, 26; 3:5, 12, 21). There is also the common feature of the martyrs appearing before the throne of God after their ordeal (4 Macc 17:18; cf. Rev 7:15).

Influence

This book might not seem to be of much moment for Christians. We should remember, however, that it was Christians who preserved and valued it. Among the Eastern and Western Churches, the stories of Eleazar and the mother and her seven sons became a model for Christian martyrdom.[91] Gregory Nazianzen even sees a connection between the mother of the seven and the Mother of Sorrows (i.e., Mary, the mother of Jesus).[92] It still has a haunting quality about it and poses afresh the question of what one is willing to die for.

For Further Discussion

1. What was the purpose of *2 Enoch?*
2. What are some apocalyptic features of *2 Enoch* shared with the NT, and

---

[90]Note the textual variants at 1 Cor 13:3. Some MSS read as NRSV: "if I hand over my body so that I may boast." Other authorities read: "if I hand over my body to be burned." In either case the situation seems to be martyrdom.

[91]For details see Townsend, "Fourth Book of Maccabees," 2:657-662; Hadas, *Third and Fourth Books of Maccabees,* pp. 123-27.

[92]The mother is called "Felicitas" in a Christian work coming from the fourth century. In Jewish tradition she is called "Miriam" in *Lamentations Rabbah* 1:50 and "Hannah" in *Josippon* (Hadas, *Third and Fourth Books of Maccabees,* p. 127).

how do you explain the common material?

3. Summarize the significant similarities between the depiction of the Son of Man in the Similitudes and the NT. How do you account for the close parallels?

4. What is the assumed life setting of the *Psalms of Solomon,* and what was the author trying to accomplish?

5. Compare and contrast the portrait of the Davidic Messiah in *Psalms of Solomon* with that of Jesus as Messiah in the NT.

6. What contribution does *Psalms of Solomon* make to understanding Paul's doctrine of justification by faith?

7. Compare and contrast *4 Ezra*'s view of sin and the law with that of the apostle Paul.

8. What ideas do *4 Ezra* and Revelation share in common? How are they different?

9. Is the NT indebted to 4 Maccabees for its doctrine of the substitutionary atonement of Jesus Christ? Why not?

10. How has 4 Maccabees influenced the church generally?

For Further Reading

Yehoshua Amir (Neumark), "Maccabees, Fourth Book of," *EncJud* 11:662.

F. I. Andersen, "Enoch, Second Book of," *ABD on CD-ROM* (Logos Library System, version 2.0c, 1995, 1996).

——————, "2 (Slavonic Apocalypse of) Enoch," in *The Old Testament Pseudepigrapha,* ed. J. H. Charlesworth, 2 vols. (Garden City, N.Y.: Doubleday, 1983), 1:91-213.

H. Anderson, "4 Maccabees," in *The Old Testament Pseudepigrapha,* ed. J. H. Charlesworth, 2 vols. (Garden City, N.Y.: Doubleday, 1983), 2:531-64.

——————, "Maccabees, Books of," *ABD* 4:452-54.

J. J. Collins, "Enoch, Books of," *DNTB,* pp. 316-17.

M. Gilbert, "Wisdom Literature," in *Jewish Writings of the Second Temple Period: Apocrypha, Pseudepigrapha, Qumran Sectarian Writings, Philo, Josephus,* ed. Michael E. Stone, CRINT 2 (Assen: Van Gorcum; Philadelphia: Fortress, 1984), pp. 316-19 [4 Maccabees].

M. Hadas, *The Third and Fourth Books of Maccabees,* JAL (New York: Harper, 1953).

Daniel J. Harrington, *Invitation to the Apocrypha* (Grand Rapids, Mich.: Eerdmans, 1999), pp. 207-18.

M. Lattke, "Psalms of Solomon," *DNTB,* pp. 853-57.

Burton L. Mack and Roland E. Murphy, "Wisdom Literature," in *Early Judaism and Its Modern Interpreters,* ed. Robert A. Kraft and George W. E. Nickelsburg (Philadelphia: Fortress; Atlanta: Scholars Press, 1986), pp. 396-98.

B. M. Metzger, "The Fourth Book of the Maccabees," in *The New Oxford Annotated Bible: New Revised Standard Version,* ed. Bruce M. Metzger and Roland E. Murphy (New York: Oxford University Press, 1991), pp. 309-29.

George W. E. Nickelsburg, *Jewish Literature Between the Bible and the Mishnah: A Historical and Literary Introduction* (Philadelphia: Fortress, 1981), pp. 185-93, 203-30 [*2 Enoch, Psalms of Solomon, 1 Enoch 37—71*, 4 Maccabees].

George W. E. Nickelsburg and Michael E. Stone, eds., *Faith and Piety in Early Judaism: Texts and Documents* (Philadelphia: Fortress, 1983), pp. 161-68.

Slomo Pines, "Enoch, Slavonic Book of," *EncJud on CD-ROM* (Judaica Multimedia, version 1.0, 1997).

Michael E. Stone, "Apocalyptic Literature," in *Jewish Writings of the Second Temple Period: Apocrypha, Pseudepigrapha, Qumran Sectarian Writings, Philo, Josephus*, ed. Michael E. Stone, CRINT 2 (Assen: Van Gorcum; Philadelphia: Fortress, 1984), pp. 395-407 [*1 Enoch, 2 Enoch*].

Thomas H. Tobin, "4 Maccabees: Introduction," in *The HarperCollins Study Bible: New Revised Standard Version*, ed. Wayne A. Meeks et al. (New York: HarperCollins, 1993), pp. 1814-16.

Joseph L. Trafton, "Solomon, Psalms of," *ABD on CD-ROM* (Logos Library System, version 2.0c, 1995, 1996).

James C. VanderKam, *An Introduction to Early Judaism* (Grand Rapids, Mich.: Eerdmans, 2001), pp. 10-12, 128-31.

R. B. Wright, "Psalms of Solomon," in *The Old Testament Pseudepigrapha*, ed. J. H. Charlesworth, 2 vols. (Garden City, N.Y.: Doubleday, 1983), 2:639-70.

Twelve

The Reconstruction of Judaism

For 2 Baruch *and* 4 Baruch (Paraleipomena of Jeremiah), *we will use H. F. D. Sparks, ed.,* The Apocryphal Old Testament *(Oxford: Clarendon Press, 1985), pp. 835-95 and 813-33, respectively. One may also find both texts in J. H. Charlesworth, ed.,* The Old Testament Pseudepigrapha, *2 vols. (Garden City, N.Y.: Doubleday, 1983), 1:615-52, 2:413-25; and* 2 Baruch *in R. H. Charles, ed.,* The Apocrypha and Pseudepigrapha of the Old Testament, *2 vols. (Oxford: Clarendon Press, 1913), 2:470-526.* Sibylline Oracle 5 *is available in Charlesworth,* Old Testament Pseudepigrapha, *1:390-405; and in Charles,* Apocrypha and Pseudepigrapha of the Old Testament, *2:397-406. Other sources drawn upon in this chapter as extracts are identified in footnotes.*

Introduction

In this chapter we survey the course of Jewish history from the destruction of the Second Temple (A.D. 70) up to the codification of the Mishnah in about A.D. 200. A primary focus will be Jewish responses to the devastating wars against imperial Rome, the First Jewish Revolt of A.D. 66-73 and the Second Jewish or Bar Kokhba revolt of A.D. 132-135. How did this people once again survive as a cohesive, self-identifiable group after the loss of nationhood and temple? The destruction of Herod's temple led to the demise of Second Temple Judaism and to the rise of a new Judaism, one that nonetheless fervently prayed for a third temple.

The literature we examine in this chapter provides insight into the survival of Jews as a distinct religious-ethnic group. Apocalyptic works such as *2 Baruch* and *Sibylline Oracle* 5 as well as the midrash in *4 Baruch* (*Paraleipomena of Jeremiah*) afford a window into the hearts and minds of at least some Jews as they sought to find meaning in these national disasters. Somehow the ways of God had to be justified and reconciled with received traditions.

The Quiet Before the Storm

Unfortunately, we have little documentation for Jewish life in Palestine after the destruction of Jerusalem and prior to the Second Jewish Revolt. Two major changes transpired. Having at last learned from their mistakes of the past, the Roman imperial government installed a higher-ranking official over the province of Judea. This officer was now an imperial senatorial legate holding the rank of praetorian rather than equestrian. As a result, Judea was generally governed by a more capable individual, the lack of which had earlier fostered the First Jewish Revolt. The province itself was upgraded so that the legate of Judea no longer reported to the Syrian legate. This meant that the governor of Judea could make immediate policy decisions.

Furthermore, more military forces were stationed in the vicinity of Jerusalem rather than on the coast at Caesarea. We know from archaeological evidence that the Tenth Legion *(Fratensis)* was bivouacked on the remains of the city, especially around the foundations of the great towers Herod the Great had erected: Phasael, Hippicus and Mariamne. A Roman column bearing the inscription of the Tenth Legion may still be seen in the Muristan area of the Old City of Jerusalem.[1]

A few Jewish cities and towns, such as Sepphoris, remained loyal to Rome in the First Jewish Revolt and thus did not suffer devastation. Furthermore, many Jews who had fled the region during the fighting later returned. Remarkably, the Jewish population in general appears to have remained intact.[2] The empire confiscated some lands formerly owned by Jews, and not a few Jews sold their land to Roman soldiers as a ransom for their lives. An interesting passage in the

---

[1]The Column itself dates to ca. A.D. 200. For discussion of the inscription, see Jerome Murphy-O'Connor, *The Holy Land: An Archaeological Guide from Earliest Times to 1700*, 3d ed. (Oxford: Oxford University Press, 1992), p. 64.
[2]As Isaiah Gafni points out, "no major mass exodus of Jews followed the destruction" ("Historical Background," in *Jewish Writings of the Second Temple Period: Apocrypha, Pseudepigrapha, Qumran Sectarian Writings, Philo, Josephus*, ed. Michael E. Stone, CRINT 2 [Assen: Van Gorcum; Philadelphia: Fortress, 1984], p. 28). L. L. Grabbe observes: "The Jews as a whole seem to have recovered from the A.D. 66-70 war fairly quickly. The destruction of Jerusalem and its surroundings was great, but much of the rest of the country had got off relatively lightly" ("Jewish History: Roman Period," *DNTB*, p. 579).

Mishnah deals with the recovery of land that had been sold to Roman soldiers by Jews. The ruling required the Jewish buyer to pay the original owner the actual value of the property, not what the soldier paid for it (*m. Giṭ.* 5:6).

All Jews in the empire, however, suffered reprisals and humiliations as a result of the First Jewish Revolt. Suetonius informs us of a tax imposed upon Jews, the *Fiscus Judaicus*, which replaced the voluntary contribution Jews made to support the Second Temple:

> Besides other taxes, that on the Jews was levied with the utmost rigor, and those were prosecuted who without publicly acknowledging that faith yet lived as Jews, as well as those who concealed their origin and did not pay the tribute levied upon their people. I recall being present in my youth when the person of a man ninety years old was examined before the procurator and a very crowded court, to see whether he was circumcised. (Suetonius, *Domitian* 12.2)[3]

Renewed Jewish life in Palestine involved major adjustments. With the cultic center of Jewish life in ruins and no immediate prospect of rebuilding, the rabbis under the direction of Yohanan ben Zakkai (c. A.D. 1-80) stressed the role of good deeds as taking the place of the sacrificial ritual. A passage from a minor Talmudic tractate entitled *ʾAbot de Rabbi Nathan* places in the mouth of Rabbi Yohanan ben Zakkai the following declaration: "be not grieved; we have another atonement as effective as this [the temple sacrificial ritual], and what is it? It is acts of loving kindness, as it is said: 'For I desire mercy and not sacrifice' " (Hos. 6:6)."[4] An interesting passage in the Tosefta[5] attributed to Rabbi Joshua (one of the inner circle of Yohanan ben Zakkai's disciples)[6] basically insists that Jews get on with their lives rather than spend an inordinate amount of time mourning the destruction of the temple: "Not to mourn at all is not feasible, for the decree has already been decreed. But further, to mourn excessively (also) is not feasible. Rather, thus the sages have said, 'A man shall plaster his home with plaster and leave over a small bit as a remembrance of Jerusalem' " (*t. Soṭah* 15:12).

As already mentioned, the purity laws of the priesthood were adapted to the home. Yohanan ben Zakkai established an academy at Yavneh (Jamnia)

---

[3]J. C. Rolfe, trans., *Suetonius II,* Loeb Classical Library (Cambridge, Mass.: Harvard University Press, 1979).

[4]*ʾAbot R. Nat.* 4:5. The translation is by Judah Goldin. Judah Goldin notes that although the compilation of *ʾAbot* dates to sometime between the seventh and ninth centuries, the composition goes back to the third century, with parts perhaps dating back to the first century (*The Fathers According to Rabbi Nathan* [New Haven, Conn.: Yale University Press, 1955], p. xxi).

[5]The Tosefta is a supplement to the rulings in the Mishnah. Though appended to the Talmud and possessing less authority than the Mishnah, it nevertheless preceded them by some 150-250 years.

[6]He lived between the end of the first century A.D. and the beginning of the second.

along the Palestinian coast, about ten miles south of modern Tel Aviv, and this reflected the transition to a new religious authority: the teacher-rabbi instead of the priest.[7] The mission of Yohanan ben Zakkai and his academy was essentially to devise a system whereby "Israel could remain holy, even without its holy city and Temple."[8]

The story (or legend) of how Yohanan ben Zakkai escaped from Jerusalem during the siege is worth citing:

> Abba Sikra the head of the biryoni [zealots] in Jerusalem was the son of the sister of Rabban Johanan b. Zakkai. [The latter] sent to him saying, Come to visit me privately. When he came he said to him, How long are you going to carry on in this way and kill all the people with starvation? He replied: What can I do? If I say a word to them, they will kill me. He said: Devise some plan for me to escape. Perhaps I shall be able to save a little. He said to him: Pretend to be ill, and let everyone come to inquire about you. Bring something evil smelling and put it by you so that they will say you are dead. Let then your disciples get under your bed, but no others, so that they shall not notice that you are still light, since they know that a living being is lighter than a corpse. He did so, and R. Eliezer went under the bier from one side and R. Joshua from the other. When they reached the door, some men wanted to put a lance through the bier. He said to them: Shall [the Romans] say. They have pierced their Master? They wanted to give it a push. He said to them: Shall they say that they pushed their Master? They opened a town gate for him and he got out.
>
> When he reached the Romans he said, Peace to you, O king, peace to you, O king. He [Vespasian] said: Your life is forfeit on two counts, one because I am not a king and you call me king, and again, if I am a king, why did you not come to me before now? He replied: As for your saying that you are not a king, in truth you are a king, since if you were not a king Jerusalem would not be delivered into your hand, as it is written, And Lebanon shall fall by a mighty one. "Mighty one" [is an epithet] applied only to a king, as it is written, And their mighty one shall be of themselves etc.; and Lebanon refers to the Sanctuary, as it says, This goodly mountain and Lebanon. As for your question, why if you are a king, I did not come to you till now, the answer is that the biryoni among us did not let me. He said to him: If there is a jar of honey round which a serpent is wound, would they not break the jar to get rid of the serpent? He could give no answer. R. Joseph, or as some say R. Akiba, applied to him the verse, [God] turneth wise men backward and maketh their knowledge foolish. He ought to have said to him: We take a pair of tongs and grip the snake and kill it, and leave the jar intact.
>
> At this point a messenger came to him from Rome saying, Up, for the Emperor is dead, and the notables of Rome have decided to make you head [of

---

[7]For further discussion on this, see Gafni, "Historical Background," p. 28.

[8]Jacob Neusner, *Self-Fulfilling Prophecy: Exile and Return in the History of Judaism* (Boston: Beacon, 1987), p. 15.

the state]. He had just finished putting on one boot. When he tried to put on the other he could not. He tried to take off the first but it would not come off. He said: What is the meaning of this? R. Johanan said to him: Do not worry: the good news has done it, as it says, Good tidings make the bone fat. What is the remedy? Let someone whom you dislike come and pass before you, as it is written, A broken spirit drieth up the bones. He did so, and the boot went on. He said to him: Seeing that you are so wise, why did you not come to me till now? He said: Have I not told you?—He retorted: I too have told you.

He said; I am now going, and will send someone to take my place. You can, however, make a request of me and I will grant it. He said to him: Give me Jabneh and its Wise Men, and the family chain of Rabban Gamaliel, and physicians to heal R. Zadok. R. Joseph, or some say R. Akiba, applied to him the verse, "[God] turneth wise men backward and maketh their knowledge foolish". He ought to have said to him; Let them [the Jews] off this time. He, however, thought that so much he would not grant, and so even a little would not be saved. (*b. Giṭ.* 56a)[9]

Despite obvious embellishments and some similarity to Josephus's account of how he was able to get into the good graces of Vespasian (*J.W.* 3.8.1-9 §§340-408), there is probably a historical core to the story. This passage illustrates some characteristic features of rabbinical writings, such as scriptural quotation accompanied by interpretation frequently bypassing the literal meaning and substituting a rather fanciful meaning. The next chapter briefly discusses some of the hermeneutical guidelines employed in rabbinical writings. The above selection also highlights the use of humor and irony in rabbinical literature.

Especially important is the mention of Yavneh and the scholars designated as "Wise Men." This academy, acting in place of the now defunct Sanhedrin, ruled on various matters concerning halakah, festivals and calendars and carried on deliberations about which books were canonical or, in their words, "defiled the hands." Modern scholars have debated whether these discussions actually established the canon or merely formalized already-existing attitudes toward the sacred Scriptures. Gamaliel II, the successor of Zakkai, may also have authorized a new translation of the Hebrew Scriptures into Greek, carried out by a Jew named Aquila. This was probably in response to the wide use of the Septuagint among the growing Christian community.[10] The Yavneh scholars thus

---

[9]S. Berrin, trans., cited in Lawrence H. Schiffman, ed., *Texts and Traditions: A Source Reader for the Study of Second Temple and Rabbinic Judaism* (Hoboken, N.J.: Ktav, 1998), pp. 455-57.
[10]See further Gafni, "Historical Background," pp. 29-30; and S. Jellicoe, *The Septuagint and Modern Study* (Oxford: Oxford University Press, 1968). Suzanne Daniel suggests that the Jewish community was also concerned about the increasing textual corruption and difficulties in the LXX, especially after the Hebrew canon was fixed at Yavneh ("Bible, Translations," *EncJud on CD-ROM* [Judaica Multimedia, version 1.0, 1997).

issued authoritative rulings regarding a whole range of normative belief and ritual practice; in short, they redefined who constituted the true Israel.

Unfortunately, we possess no sources that throw light on Jewish life in Palestine during the reigns of Titus (A.D. 79-81), Domitian (81-96), Nerva (96-98) and Trajan (98-117). At the outbreak of the First Jewish Revolt, Agrippa II reigned over Chalcis, the tetrarchy of Philip (essentially the area today called the Golan Heights), as well as areas around Tiberias (on the western shore of the Sea of Galilee) and Abila (located in ancient Gilead and today the modern state of Jordan). He lived until some time between A.D. 93-100.[11] After the war he was reconfirmed as ruler in his Palestinian holdings, with some new territory added. In A.D. 75 Agrippa II and his sister went to Rome, where she became Titus's mistress. When this caused a scandal, she returned to Palestine, presumably with Agrippa. We may surmise that Jews thrived in Agrippa's territories, as evidenced by coins minted in the mid-80s bearing the initials SC (*Senatus Consultum*, "Resolved by the Roman Senate"). The Talmud may be referring to Agrippa II in passages where Rabbi Eliezer ben Hyrcanus is dialoguing with a certain Agrippa. These passages present Agrippa in a favorable light and may indicate that Agrippa II sought to fill the vacuum left by the destruction of Jerusalem with its temple and priesthood.[12] Beyond this, we know that Agrippa corresponded with Josephus about his *Jewish War,* concerning which Agrippa, not surprisingly, had high praise. When he died, the Herodian dynasty came to an end.[13] The districts formerly under his control reverted to provincial administration.

Revolt Under Trajan

The relative calm among Jewish communities in the empire was shattered in A.D. 115-117.[14] Again Jews rose in revolt against Roman rule, this time the initial focal point being Egypt, where, as we have previously seen, Gentile-Jewish relationships had long been at a flash point. The revolt spread to Jewish communities living in Cyrene (modern Libya), Cyprus and Mesopotamia (modern Syria and Iraq).

The immediate occasion was Trajan's campaigns in Mesopotamia against the Parthians. We may surmise that the underlying reasons were the continued national humiliation in the aftermath of the First Jewish Revolt and

---

[11]For his role in the First Jewish Revolt, see chapter ten.

[12]See Lee I. A. Levine, "Judaism from the Destruction of Jerusalem to the End of the Second Jewish Revolt," in *Christianity and Rabbinic Judaism: A Parallel History of Their Origins and Early Development,* ed. Herschel Shanks (Washington, D.C.: Biblical Archaeology Society, 1992), p. 132 and n. 14, p. 338.

[13]See H. W. Hoehner, "Herod," *ZPEB* 3:144-45.

[14]See Grabbe, "Jewish History: Roman Period," pp. 579-80; and Grabbe, "Jewish Wars with Rome," *DNTB*, pp. 587-88.

harsh conditions for Jewish communities brought about by Gentile domination and reprisals. Added to this were no doubt continuing messianic expectations among many Jews. Eusebius, a fourth-century chronicler of Christian church history, provides a brief comment on this uprising:

> The emperor was now advancing into the eighteenth year of his reign, and another commotion of the Jews being raised, he destroyed a very great number of them. For in Alexandria and the rest of Egypt, and also in Cyrene, as if actuated by some terrible and tempestuous spirit, they rushed upon seditious measures against the Greeks of the same place. Having increased the insurrection to a great extent, they excited no inconsiderable war the following year, when Lupus was governor of all Egypt. And in the first conflict, indeed, it happened that they prevailed over the Greeks; who, retreating into Alexandria, took and destroyed the Jews that were found in the city. But the Jews of Cyrene being deprived of their assistance, after laying waste the country of Egypt, also proceeded to destroy its districts, under their leader Lucuas. Against these the emperor sent Marcius Turbo, with foot and naval forces, besides cavalry. He, however, protracting the war a long time against them in many battles, slew many thousand Jews, not only of Cyrene, but also of Egypt that had joined them, together with their leader Lucuas. But the emperor, suspecting that the Jews in Mesopotamia would also make an attack upon those there, ordered Lucius Quietus to clear the province of them, who also led an army against them, and slew a great multitude of them. Upon which victory, he was appointed governor of Judea by the emperor. These things are recorded by the Greek writers of the day, in nearly the same words. (*De ecclesiastic theologia* 4.2)

Though Eusebius and other historians mention no revolt in Palestine, it is difficult to imagine there was no resistance there.[15] The fact that Lucius Quietus was appointed as Judean legate in A.D. 116 or 117 implies that this too was a trouble spot. Evidence from Roman milestones in Palestine dating to A.D. 120 indicates that the Second Trajana Legion was stationed there in the aftermath of this revolt.[16] From Jewish sources we learn that this uprising was called "Polemus Quietus" after the name of the legate.[17]

---

[15]For a much more cautious approach to the involvement of Judah in the revolt during Trajan's reign, see Lester L. Grabbe, *Judaism from Cyprus to Hadrian,* 2 vols. (Minneapolis: Fortress, 1992), 2:566-69. He writes, "In light of arguments advanced so far, it seems best to allow for the possibility of a Palestinian revolt but to recognize that the evidence is uncertain" (2:569).

[16]See B. Isaac and I. Roll, "Judaea in the Early Years of Hadrian's Reign," *Latomus* 38 (1979): 54-66.

[17]For sources, see Doron Mendels, *The Rise and Fall of Jewish Nationalism,* rev. ed. (Grand Rapids, Mich.: Eerdmans, 1997), p. 392 n. 4.

2 Baruch (Apocalypse of Baruch)

Introduction

We turn aside momentarily to consider an apocalyptic work perhaps written during this period. This work, though generally designated an apocalypse, in fact contains a variety of literary genres and features: lamentations, prayers, didactic passages (questions and answers), homilies and a letter to Diaspora Jews as well as revelations of future events so characteristic of apocalyptic. A notable feature is its alternation between prose and poetic passages. The document in its extant form consists of eighty-seven chapters written in Syriac, a language related to Hebrew. Scholars are fairly certain there was an earlier and slightly longer version in Greek.[18] Behind the Greek text there probably was a Hebrew original, but no textual evidence has yet confirmed this assumption.

The leading figure of the work is Jeremiah's faithful associate and scribe Baruch. Because of Baruch's role in the events surrounding the collapse of Judah in the sixth century B.C., a number of traditions grew up around his name. We have already examined an earlier work entitled Baruch found in the Apocrypha (see chapter five), but in addition to this there are works such as *The Rest of the Words of Baruch, Gnostic Book of Baruch* and the *Greek Apocalypse of Baruch*.[19] Our anonymous author thus employs a well-worn figure to encourage his co-religionists at a very difficult time in Jewish history.[20]

Outline

I.   The destruction of Jerusalem (1:1—8:5)
II.   Seven-day fast and lamentation to God (9:1—12:4)
III.   Seven-day fast followed by questions about God's justice (12:5—20:4)
IV.   Seven-day fast followed by the revelation of God's final plan (20:5—30:5)
V.   Baruch's warning of tribulation before the end (31:1—34:1)
VI.   Baruch's vision in the holy of holies concerning the end (35:1—43:3)
VII.   Baruch's sermon on God's judgment (44:1—46:7)
VIII. Seven-day fast and the question of predestination (47:1—48:50)
IX.   Question about the resurrection body (49:1—52:7)
X.   Vision of a cloud and waters (53:1—74:4)
XI.   Thanksgiving and sermon about the saved (75:1—77:26)

---

[18]There is a fragment from the Oxyrhynchus papyri dating to roughly the fourth or fifth centuries A.D. (A. F. J. Klijn, "2 (Syriac Apocalypse of) Baruch," *OTP* 1:616).

[19]Unfortunately, space limitations prevent us from exploring the first two works further. For the *Greek Apocalypse of Baruch (3 Baruch)*, see pp. 437-43.

[20]See further J. E. Wright, "Baruch, Books of," *DNTB*, pp. 148-51.

XII.   Letter of exhortation to the nine and a half tribes (78:1−87:1)[21]

Date and Provenance

Like so many works written during the Second Temple era, *2 Baruch* is difficult to date with any precision. Several internal clues, however, may assist us
in locating it approximately. We can be fairly sure that the work is post-A.D.
70, since *2 Baruch* 32:2-4 presupposes that there have been two destructions
of the temple. Though ostensibly set in the time of the Babylonian destruction (587/586 B.C.), the author knows that a rebuilt temple "will again be
uprooted." Furthermore, in *2 Baruch* 67:1, the author identifies the eleventh
black waters as "the disaster which has befallen Zion now." This would seem
to be the period after A.D. 70. In *2 Baruch* 68 he refers to the twelfth bright
waters, during which time there is a restoration of the temple. This restoration occurs after a "short time," and it will bring "joy one day." But just prior
to that is a time of such distress for Israel "that they are all together in danger
of perishing." It is tempting to connect these two events with the excitement
caused by Hadrian's plan to rebuild the Jewish temple, but it is difficult to
know if our author then spoke of Bar Kokhba's Revolt and the devastation
that followed or of the eschatological judgment. In *2 Baruch* 70 the author
clearly connects the "last black waters" with a cosmic "great tribulation"
before the Lord returns to rescue Israel and the Holy Land and to punish the
wicked.

Another factor in the dating of *2 Baruch* concerns the many points of contact with *4 Ezra*, which dates to sometime around A.D. 90-100. Furthermore,
Epistle of Barnabas 11:9 quotes *2 Baruch* 61:7. The *Epistle of Barnabas* dates to
sometime between A.D. 117 and 132. Based upon this internal evidence, most
scholars place *2 Baruch* into the time period of A.D. 100-132.

The place of writing was probably Palestine, in keeping with the presumed
Hebrew original and affinities with other Palestinian apocalyptic writings.
Thus, *2 Baruch* testifies to the acute theological crisis for Jews in Palestine
during these turbulent times.

Features

This work wrestles with theodicy. How could God punish his people Israel
whom he had elected and separated from all the nations (*2 Bar.* 42:5; 48:20;
77:2-5)? The answer, in short, was that Israel had sinned and deserved this

---

[21]Some see *2 Baruch* as arranged in "seven distinct sections each separated from its neighbor by a fast" (Michael E. Stone, "Apocalyptic Literature," in *Jewish Writings of the Second
Temple Period,* p. 409). While the seven fasts are important to the structure, the work as
we now have it incorporates these into a larger overarching structure.

punishment (*2 Bar.* 4:1; 6:9; 13:9; 78:3, 5; 79:2). God had not, however, rejected his people (*2 Bar.* 13:9-10; 52:6). They will enjoy a restoration (*2 Bar.* 78:7) and participate in resurrection life on a new earth (*2 Bar.* 30:1-2). Baruch should not be overwrought about the destruction of the temple: "This building, which now stands in your midst, is not the one that is to be revealed, that is with me now, that was prepared beforehand here at the time when I determined to make Paradise" (*2 Bar.* 4:3). Baruch is informed that Adam, Abraham and Moses all glimpsed this glorious temple (*2 Bar.* 4:3-7).

One notes many similarities to *4 Ezra,* yet there are distinct differences. The author of *2 Baruch* does not struggle as much as *4 Ezra;* the answers are more forthcoming, and there is less doubt and ambiguity. Take for example, the role of the law in the respective works. Our author is not pessimistic about human ability to keep the law, as is the author of *4 Ezra.* In this regard, *2 Baruch* strikes a very Pharisaic note.[22] According to *2 Baruch* every person has the freedom and capability of choice (*2 Bar.* 54:15, 19; 85:7). Furthermore, the law itself assists those who are committed to it: "And the law which is with us will help us, And the matchless wisdom which is in our midst will sustain us" (*2 Bar.* 48:24). This stands in opposition to *4 Ezra,* where the law brings certain condemnation (cf. chapter eleven above).

Both works trace sin back to Adam's transgression, which brought about physical death, pain and a general diminishment of the enjoyment of life (*2 Bar.* 17:3; 19:8; 23:4; 48:42-43, 50; cf. 2 Esd 3:7). Neither speculates about the involvement of fallen angels or Satan, as in *1 Enoch* and *2 Enoch.* One passage in *2 Baruch* seems to imply belief in hereditary corruption ("O Adam, What was it that you did to all your posterity? And what should be said to Eve who first listened to the serpent? For all this multitude is going to corruption: innumerable are those whom the fire will devour" [48:42]). This seems echoed in *4 Ezra:* "For the first Adam, burdened with an evil heart, transgressed and was overcome, as were also all who were descended from him. Thus the disease became permanent; the law was in the hearts of the people along with the evil root; but what was good departed, and the evil remained" (2 Esd 3:21-22). In another passage in *2 Baruch,* however, such a connection is disavowed. "For though Adam first sinned and brought untimely death upon all men, yet each one of those who were born from him has either prepared for his own soul its future torment or chosen for himself the glories that are to be. . . . Thus Adam was responsible for himself only, each one of us is his own Adam" (*2 Bar.* 54:15, 19). This more nearly corresponds to the rabbinical view of the evil tendency *(yēṣer hārāʿ)* that appears already in Ben Sira.

The Messiah ("my Anointed One") figures prominently in *2 Baruch.* This is

---

[22]Charles notes that "This book is of a strongly Pharisaic character" (*APOT* 2:478).

seen in the three messianic apocalypses that punctuate the book (*2 Bar.* 27–30; 36–50; 53–76).[23] He will come after a time of intense tribulation that is cosmic in scope. He overcomes the forces of darkness, tries and executes the last wicked ruler, and assumes dominion over all the earth (*2 Bar.* 39:7–40:2). His reign will be characterized by a time of unparalleled abundance (*2 Bar.* 74:1-4). Included in this reign is the notion of a restored temple ("Zion will be rebuilt, and its offerings will be restored again, and the priests will return to their ministry, and the Gentiles also will come and acclaim it" [*2 Bar.* 68:5]). Thus the messianic reign is not restricted to faithful Israelites but will be open to "every nation which has not known Israel and which has not trodden down the seed of Jacob" (*2 Bar.* 72:3-4). We seem to have a clear instance in *2 Baruch* of an intermediate kingdom that precedes the eternal state (*2 Bar.* 29:1–30:5).[24]

As we read *2 Baruch*, we need to remind ourselves that we are listening to a voice not far removed in time from the Academy of Yavneh and the rabbis of the early Tannaitic period. To be sure, Yavneh turned away from the explicit eschatology of *2 Baruch*, but the traditions preserved in rabbinical sources dovetail at several points with that of *2 Baruch*. For example, in *2 Baruch* 10:18, before the destruction of the temple, the priests throw the keys of the sanctuary up to heaven. This is also mentioned in the Babylonian Talmud (*b. Taʿan.* 29a; cf. *Lev. Rab.* 19:6).[25] Baruch enters Paradise alive (*2 Bar.* 13:3-4), an episode mentioned in *Sipre Numbers* 99. The legend about the articles of the temple being swallowed up by the earth (*2 Bar.* 6:7-8; cf. *b. Yoma* 21b; *Num. Rab.* 15:10) and that the patriarchs knew and observed the Torah, even the dietary laws, are common traditions (*b. Yoma* 28b; *b. B. Meṣiʿa* 87a). Further parallels include the notion that the earthly temple is modeled after

---

[23]See further Larry J. Kreitzer, *Jesus and God in Paul's Eschatology*, JSNTSup 19 (Sheffield: JSOT, 1987), pp. 69-74.

[24]*Pace* Klijn, who writes, "He rejected the idea of a messianic kingdom on earth" ("2 [Syriac Apocalypse of] Baruch," 1:619). For arguments in favor of an interim messianic kingdom in *2 Baruch*, see Kreitzer, *Jesus and God*, pp. 74-80.

[25]We cite the text: "Our Rabbis have taught: When the First Temple was about to be destroyed bands upon bands of young priests with the keys of the Temple in their hands assembled and mounted the roof of the Temple and exclaimed, 'Master of the Universe, as we did not have the merit to be faithful treasurers these keys are handed back into Thy keeping'. They then threw the keys up towards heaven. And there emerged the figure of a hand and received the keys from them. Whereupon they jumped and fell into the fire. It is in allusion to them that the prophet Isaiah laments: The burden concerning the Valley of Vision. What aileth thee now, that thou art wholly gone up to the house tops, thou that art full of uproar, a tumultuous city, a joyous town? Thy slain are not slain with the sword, nor dead in battle. Of the Holy One, blessed be He, also it is said, Kir shouting, and crying at the mount" (*b. Taʿan.* 29a, *The Soncino Talmud on CD-ROM*, The CD-ROM Judaica Classics Library [Davka, 1991-1995]).

a heavenly prototype (*2 Bar.* 4:3; cf. *Sipre Deuteronomy* 37), the reference to the temple being seen by Abraham "between the pieces of the sacrifice" (*2 Bar.* 4:4; cf. *Gen. Rab.* 44:21; 56:10), the souls in the treasury (*2 Bar.* 30:2; cf. *b. Yebam.* 62a; *Sipre Numbers* 139; *b. Šabb.* 152b) and the miraculous abundance of the messianic reign (*2 Bar.* 73—74).[26] A. F. J. Klijn summarizes the contribution of *2 Baruch* by observing:

> After the destruction of the Temple, a new period arrived that was characterized by the influence of the rabbis. The author opened a way for studying the Law after a period of apocalyptic expectations. He was an expert on both apocalyptic imagery and rabbinic teaching, and, as such, was one of the Jews who managed to bring Judaism in a new era.[27]

Relevance for the New Testament

Numerous and striking parallels with the NT appear. Literary dependence one way or the other is not likely. The best explanation is shared religious and cultural traditions. The most obvious common feature is messianism and apocalyptic features. Both expect a period of great tribulation followed by the advent of a messianic kingdom (with a messiah figure sometimes explicitly mentioned in *2 Baruch* and sometimes not). A physical resurrection, with glorification for the faithful and torment for the wicked, accompanies this kingdom. Beyond a similar eschatological framework, however, there are a number of specific similarities. It should be noted that the largest number of parallels occurs in NT passages that are apocalyptic in outlook or form.

We conclude with a tribute to the literary skill of our unknown author. No passage demonstrates this more eloquently than his poignant hope that Israel's travail is almost over: "For the youth of the world is past, and the strength of the creation already exhausted: the times have run their course and the end is very near. The pitcher is near the cistern, the ship to port, the traveler to the city, and life to its consummation" (*2 Bar.* 85:10).

The Second Jewish Revolt

Amazingly, the flames of revolt flared up one more time in a desperate struggle to liberate the Holy Land from Roman domination. This bitter war, sometimes called the Bar Kokhba revolt, was precipitated by Hadrian's policy toward the Jews of Palestine and of the empire in general. As to the former, he decided upon a plan to rebuild Jerusalem in the style of a magnificent Roman city and to rename it Aelia Capitolina. Prominent in this new city

---

[26]See further Yehoshua M. Grintz, "Baruch, Apocalypse of, " *EncJud on CD-ROM* (Judaica Multimedia, version 1.0, 1997).

[27]"2 (Syriac Apocalypse of) Baruch," 1:620.

Table 12.1. Parallels between the New Testament and *2 Baruch*

New Testament	2 Baruch	Connection
Mt 3:16-17; Mk 1:10; Lk 3:21-22; Jn 12:28; Rev 4:1	22:1	Heavens opened and visionary experience with heavenly voice; common feature of Jewish apocalyptic literature
Mt 24:3; Mk 13:4; Lk 21:7	3:7-9	Common apocalyptic motif involving questions about signs and events of the end times
Mt 24:23-26, 30; Mk 13:21-23, 26	27:6	Signs of the last days, famines, earthquakes, etc., and especially the "sign" of the Most High (*2 Baruch*) or of the Son of Man (Synoptics)
Gal 4:26; Heb 12:22; 13:14; cf. Jn 14:2-3	4:1-2	Common notion of a heavenly Jerusalem in Jewish apocalyptic
2 Thess 2:6-7	12:4; 51:11	Common notion of a restraining force or agent that will be removed just before the end times
Rom 1:18-21, 32; 2:1-10	15:5-8	Knowledge of God is accessible to all people and thus rejection of him is inexcusable
2 Cor 4:4; Gal 1:4; Eph 1:21; 2:2; 6:12	15:8; 44:15	Common tradition of the "two ages"
Rev 1:1; 10:6, 11	20:6	Common idea of the unveiling of the course of this world and the note of imminence ("no delay")
Heb 11:3	21:5-6	Shared idea of creation out of nothing (cf. 2 Macc 7:28)
Heb 1:7	21:6	Both works draw upon Ps 104:4 in describing angels as flames of fire
1 Cor 15:19	21:13	Common paraenetic tradition whereby the faithful are assured of future blessing in the eschaton (end of the age)
2 Pet 3:15	21:20-21	Explanation for the Lord's delay in coming
Rom 11:28	21:21	The people of Israel are called "a beloved people" by God

Table 12.1.—*Continued*

New Testament	2 Baruch	Connection
Rom 5:12-14; 2 Cor 11:3; 1 Tim 2:13-14	23:4; 48:42-43	Connection of Adam and Eve's sin with death and corruption; a common Second Temple conviction
Rom 13:11	23:7	Common expectation in apocalyptic literature of the nearness of the end
Rev 20:11-15	24:1	Common tradition of a "book of deeds" at last judgment
Rev 13:1-4	29:4	Eschatological beasts connected with end-time events
Rev 20:7-15	30:1-5	Resurrection and judgment at the conclusion of the millennial age
Heb 12:26-28	32:1-4	Eschatological shaking of the earth and the permanence of the New Jerusalem (cf. Hag 2:6)
2 Thess 2:8; cf. 1:7-9; Rev 14:9-11; 16:12-16; 19:19-21; 20:10	40:1-4	Common tradition about the defeat and judgment of the lawless leader of the end times (the beast or man of sin)
Mt 11:29	41:3	The obligations of the law commonly called "the yoke of the law" by the rabbis
1 Cor 15:42-55	42:7-8	Common view of the differing destinies of the wicked and righteous at the resurrection
Rom 11:33-36	44:6	Common acknowledgment of God's unfathomable wisdom
Lk 2:25	44:7	The consolation of Zion/Jerusalem a common expectation in Judaism
1 Cor 15:53-54	44:9-12	Common expectation of a transformation of bodies/cosmos in the age to come
2 Pet 2:4; Jude 6; Rev 20:1, 3; cf. 9:1-2, 11, 11:7; 17:8 (NIV)	44:15 (implied but not directly stated); 56:13-15	Common view of an abyss as punishment for the wicked angels and humans and chains for rebellious angels

Table 12.1.—*Continued*

New Testament	2 Baruch	Connection
Rom 6:12-14; 7:23; 1 Cor 15:35-49	49:2-3	Shared notion of the transformation of the resurrection body and the members of the "old" body as instruments of sin
Mt 22:30; 2 Cor 3:18; Phil 3:20-21	51:1-6, 10	Transformation of the righteous into ever greater degrees of glory at the resurrection and having the appearance of angels
Col 3:1-3	51:8-9	The invisible world of the spirit to be revealed at the resurrection
Mt 16:26; Lk 9:25; 12:15	51:15	Common idea of the folly of saving one's life at the expense of one's soul
Rom 8:18-25; Jas 1:2-4; 1 Pet 2:13-25; 3:8—4:6	52:5-7	The righteous should rejoice in suffering in light of future reward and glory
Rom 1:18-32	55:2	The wicked know that God is real and that they are accountable for their sins
Rev 12:14-16	71:1	The righteous protected by the land itself during the final tribulation
Mt 25:31-46	72:1-6	The Gentiles judged by the Messiah in accordance with their treatment of Israel
Mt 12:36-37; Rom 2:16; 1 Cor 14:25	83:2-3	Secret thoughts and deeds exposed at day of judgment
Col 3:2-4	83:5	The righteous ought not to focus on this world but on the coming one
Rom 13:11-14; 1 Cor 7:29, 31	83:22-23; 85:10	Nearness of the end times
Eph 4:4-6	85:14-15	Stress upon the unity of God and of faith
Col 4:16-17; cf. 2 Thess 3:14	86:1-3	Exhortation to read and obey letters written by religious authorities (apostles or seers)
Gal 6:11; 2 Thess 2:2; 3:17	87:1	Need for authenticating writings and letters against possible forgery

were pagan temples featuring one dedicated to Jupiter on the remains of the Second Temple. This plan was especially galling to Jews because there had been some hopes earlier that Hadrian would authorize the rebuilding of a Jewish temple.[28]

Added to this was a direct assault upon the very heart of Judaism in which Hadrian forbade the practice of circumcision.[29] Suddenly, the grim specter of Antiochus Epiphanes once again overshadowed all of Jewish life. Hadrian's actual motivation for the ban appears not to have been a direct attempt to suppress Judaism but a profound disgust for the physical act. To him, it was barbarous and akin to emasculation.[30] This prohibition ignited a blaze. Long-simmering resentment at Roman retribution and outrage at the thought of a pagan temple on the holy site of the Second Temple were fanned into flame by this direct threat to the ancestral faith.

The Jews had learned from bitter experience that Rome could not be challenged unless there was a unified command and battle plan. Furthermore, it was obvious that a disparity in trained forces and weaponry meant that open engagement must be avoided. Instead, the rebels adopted guerrilla warfare, holing up in well-concealed, stockpiled caves and tunnels rather than in fortresses. Sudden raids followed by retreat and hiding were unleashed upon Roman and sympathizing forces with considerable effect. Today, one still marvels at the ingenuity and industry of the rebels when visiting such sites as the Herodium, where one can actually traverse some of these tunnel systems.[31]

Unfortunately, we lack a chronicler like Josephus. We have only snatches of rabbinic comments on the war in Talmudic sources, a small cache of personal letters written by Jewish rebels and their family members, and a few passages by later historians such as Dio Cassius and Eusebius.

From these we may piece together the following scenario. The revolt began, appropriately, near the site of the Hasmonean family home of Modein (apparently the village of Caphar-harub). The rebels waited until Hadrian departed from the region—he had visited in the autumn of A.D. 129. The

---

[28]See Y. Yadin, "Bar Kochba," *IDBSup*, p. 90.

[29]This cause has been called into question, I think unconvincingly, by several recent studies. See Grabbe, "Jewish Wars with Rome," *DNTB*, p. 587.

[30]See *Historia Augusta*, a fourth-century compilation of material about the Roman emperors. In the section *Hadrian* 14.2 one reads of Hadrian's law. See John H. Hayes and Sarah R. Mandell, *The Jewish People in Classical Antiquity: From Alexander to Bar Kochba* (Louisville: Westminster John Knox, 1998), p. 211.

[31]See the discussion and excellent pictures in Ehud Netzer, "Jewish Rebels Dig Strategic Tunnel System," *BAR* 14, no. 4 (1988): 18-33; Amos Kloner, "Name of Ancient Israel's Last President Discovered on Lead Weight," *BAR* 14, no. 4 (1988): 12-17; Joseph Patrich, "Hideouts in the Judean Wilderness—Jewish Revolutionaries and Christian Ascetics Sought Shelter and Protection in Cliffside Caves," *BAR* 15, no. 5 (1989): 32-42.

revolt began in the fall of 131.[32] Military service for Jews became compulsory. The Roman governor, Tinius Rufus, was so taken by surprise that he had to evacuate the Tenth Legion from Jerusalem and beat a hasty retreat to Caesarea. The rebels took over the city and joyfully proclaimed its liberation. A new calendar heralded "The Year One of the Redemption of Israel," and coins were minted proclaiming the same. A new government with district commanders was put in place.

Bar Kokhba, the rebel leader, about whom we will say more shortly, tried to enlist Galilean Jews in the uprising as well. Though some portions of Palestine outside Judea were taken over, it appears that for the most part he was unsuccessful, which was a severe blow to the rebel cause.[33] For their part, the Roman government exerted every effort to crush the uprising. Hadrian himself returned to the area and recalled his best general from Britain, the proconsul Julius Severus. Severus was entrusted with the overall command of Roman forces in Palestine.

In addition to the Sixth and Tenth Legions, already stationed in Palestine, additional troops were brought in from surrounding regions. All or portions of no less than twelve Roman legions were brought in to quell the revolt (among which were the Tenth *[Fratensis]*, Sixth *[Ferrata]*, Twenty-second *[Diotrajana]*, Third *[Cyrenaica]*, Fourth *[Scythica]*, Second *[Trajana]* and Fifth *[Macedonica]*), a good indication of the severity of the struggle.[34] In the initial fighting, the Twenty-second Legion had been virtually annihilated when they made a rapid advance into the interior of Judea (remember a similar error by Cestius Gallus and the Twelfth Legion at the beginning of the First Jewish Revolt). Severus adopted a cautious, piecemeal approach, methodically attacking each fortified position and village. He waged a war of attrition against the rebels.

The third and fourth years of the war turned in Rome's favor. Assembling a very large force, they began to annihilate whole villages and communities. A major victory fell to the Romans at the site of Emmaus. This town commanded the ascent to Jerusalem from the west. Thereafter, Roman forces strategically deployed to the west (Emmaus, renamed Nicopolis), north (Bethel) and south (Caphar-Laqitiyah) of Jerusalem, virtually sealing the

---

[32]Mendels's date of spring 132 refers to the outbreak of hostilities (*Rise and Fall of Jewish Nationalism*, p. 388).

[33]Yadin claims that Bar Kokhba gained control over "large sections of the rest of the country" ("Bar Kokhba," p. 90). He is followed in this opinion by Hayes and Mandell, *Jewish People in Classical Antiquity*, p. 214. This is disputed by others, such as Grabbe, *Judaism from Cyrus to Hadrian*, 2:578; Lee I. A. Levine, "Judaism from the Destruction of Jerusalem," p. 147; and Mendels, *Rise and Fall of Jewish Nationalism*, pp. 390, 393 n. 17.

[34]Yadin, "Bar Kochba," p. 90.

rebels in a small enclave of some twenty by thirty miles. Finally, the Romans were able to force the rebel forces under the leadership of Bar Kokhba into the fortress of Betar (Beththera), about ten miles southwest of Jerusalem. By the end of the summer (135), the Romans breached the walls, having built a siege dam across the fosse (moat or ditch) on the south of the fortress, and massacred all the surviving defenders, including Bar Kokhba.[35] Ironically, according to Jewish tradition, this was the very same calendar day as the fall of the First and Second Temples, the ninth of Ab. The Romans sought to forestall another Jewish revolt by declaring Jerusalem off-limits to all Jews, the penalty for violation of this decree being death. Adding insult to injury, the Romans changed the official name of the province from "Judea" to "Syria Palaestina."

All that remained after the decisive battle at Betar were pockets of rebels who fled to caves high up in the cliffs above the Dead Sea. The Romans pursued the rebels even to their cave hideouts and either ferreted or starved them out. Archaeologists have discovered several of these caves and given them colorful names such as "Cave of the Pool," "Cave of Letters" and "Cave of Horror." Each one is a mute witness to the tragic end of the Second Jewish Revolt. But perhaps we should not say mute. Artifacts and letters found in the caves still give voice to these Jewish nationalists who, in spite of a war that swirled about them, carried on with the daily routine of life right up to the end.[36]

One such individual was Babatha. She was the daughter of Simon from the village of Maoza in the district of Zoara (in the southern region of the Dead Sea). Interestingly, both her first husband and her son were named Jesus. In A.D. 128, having already been widowed in 124, she became the second wife of Judah ben Elazar Khthousion. He was a relatively well-to-do Jewish landowner at En-Gedi, an oasis town situated along the Dead Sea about thirty miles south of Jericho. When Roman military forces moved toward En-Gedi, Babatha, her family and her neighbors fled to previously prepared caves high up in the cliffs overlooking the Dead Sea at Naḥal Hever, three miles south of En-Gedi.

Amazingly, in the 1960s, when intrepid archaeologists excavated the cave of Babatha, carefully packaged documents from her personal papers were found still intact. These papers included items such as "legal suits over pay-

---

[35]For details, see Yohanan Aharoni and Michael Avi-Yonah, *The Macmillan Bible Atlas,* ed. Anson F. Rainey and Ze'ev Safrai, 3d ed. (New York: Macmillan, 1993), p. 197 map 268.

[36]For details about the documents see Yadin, "Bar Kochba," pp. 91-92. For a spellbinding account of the discovery of the artifacts and letters, see Antony J. Saldarini, "Babatha's Story," *BAR* 24, no. 2 (1998): 28-32, 36-37, 72-73; and David Harris, "I Was There," *BAR* 24, no. 2 (1998): 34-35. Most recently the site has again been excavated with new interpretations of the occupational history and artifacts in Richard A. Freund and Rami Arav, "Return to the Cave of Letters: What Still Lies Buried?" *BAR* 27, no. 1 (2001): 25-39.

ments and property, the guardianship of her minor son, petitions to the court, marriages, summons, leases and deeds."[37] They are invaluable in affording us a small window into the daily lives of Jews at this period of time. In all there were thirty-five documents, of which twenty-six were written in Greek, six in Nabatean (an Aramaic dialect) and three in Aramaic.[38] Besides her documents, Babatha also stashed items such as "a beautiful jewelry box, bowls, and knives, a frying pan, a mirror, clothing, sandals, cloth and jugs."[39] Babatha's cache also included expensive clothes, cosmetics and an assortment of utensils.

One thing made quite clear by Babatha's documents is that Jews interacted with their non-Jewish neighbors and adopted the prevailing legal customs and laws of the Greco-Roman era. This is of great significance for interpretation of this period. As Saldarini notes:

> Interpretations of the Mishnah and Talmud that picture Jewish life in the second century C.E. as separate, independent and self-defining do not accord with what we see here, and the view they imply probably needs revision. The noticeable absence of the rabbinic system from these documents accords well both with the general tendency of Jews in the Roman period to follow the laws of the lands they lived in and with the slow spread of rabbinic influence and power among Jewish communities.[40]

So what happened to Babatha? We do not know. The Cave of Letters had the skeletons of eight women, six children and three men. Was one of them Babatha, or did she surrender and face execution or slavery by the Romans? At least this much is certain: she never returned for her precious documents and personal items that she jammed into a crevice of the cave.

Dio Cassius attests to the fact that the Bar Kokhba revolt was a bloody war with huge casualties on both sides:

> Very few of them in fact survived. Fifty of their most important outposts and 985 of their most famous villages were razed to the ground. 580,000 men were slain in the various raids and battles, and the number of those that perished by famine, disease and fire was past finding out. Thus nearly the whole of Judea was made desolate. . . . Many Romans, moreover, perished in this war. Therefore, Hadrian in writing to the Senate did not employ the opening phrase commonly affected by the emperors, "If you and your children are in health, it is well; I and the legions are in health." (*Roman History* 69.33-45)

---

[37]Saldarini, "Babatha's Story," p. 29.
[38]Ibid., p. 30. For a critical edition of the texts, see Naphtali Lewis, Yigael Yadin and Jonas C. Greenfield, eds., *The Documents from the Bar Kokhba Period in the Cave of Letters,* JDS (Jerusalem: Israel Exploration Society, 1989).
[39]Saldarini, "Babatha's Story," p. 30.
[40]Ibid. p. 72.

Two passages, one from the Jerusalem Talmud and the other from the Babylonian Talmud, also testify to the horrible carnage suffered by the Jewish rebels (*y. Taʿan.* 4:6 §§68d-69a; *b. Giṭ.* 57a). They speak of casualties as high as 800,000 for Betar alone and mention the brains of three hundred children being found on one rock. The blood of Betar was said to have flowed all the way to the Mediterranean and also served as manure for Gentile vineyards for seven years after the conflict! The obvious exaggeration does not belie the enormous loss of life.

Surprisingly, among the letters discovered in the caves above the Dead Sea were some by Bar Kokhba himself. These consisted of correspondence with surrounding leaders and villages. In them we learn that his name was actually Simeon bar Kosiba. Here are some excerpts.[41]

> Simeon Bar Kosiba to Yehonathan and to Masabala, a letter:
> That every man from Tekoa and from Tel Adirin who is with you, you shall send them to me without delay. And if you shall not send them, let it be known to you, that I will exact punishment from you.
> Salisu [son of] Yose wrote it.

> Simeon, son of Kosiba, the ruler over Israel, to Jonathan and Masabal, peace!
> That you should inspect and take the wheat which Han bar Yishaʿel has brought, and send me, after inspection, one hundred. And you should give them with assurance for they have been found to be stolen. And if you do not do this, then retribution will be exacted from you. And send me the man immediately with assurance.
> And every Tekoan man who is with you, the houses in which they dwell will be burned down, and from you I will exact retribution.
> (As for) Joshua, son of the Palmyrene, you shall seize him and send him to me with assurance. Do not hesitate to seize the sword which is upon him. You shall send him.
> Samuel, son of Ammi.

> Letter of Simeon bar Kosiba, peace!
> To Yehonatan son of Baʿaya [my order is] that whatever Elisha tells you do for him and help him [in every] action. Be well.

> From the Administrators of Beth Mashko, from Yeshua and from Eleazar to Yeshua ben Galgoula chief of the camp, peace.
> Let it be known to you that the cow which Yehoseph ben Ariston took from

---

[41]These excerpts are from Lawrence H. Schiffman, *Texts and Traditions: A Source Reader for the Study of Second Temple and Rabbinic Judaism* (Hoboken, N.J.: Ktav, 1998), pp. 489-91. He has made slight additions to or modifications of the translations by J. Fitzmyer and D. J. Harrington (*A Manual of Palestinian Aramaic Texts* [Rome: Biblical Institute Press, 1978]), K. Beyer (*Die Aramäischen Texte vom Toten Meer* [Göttingen: Vandenhoeck & Ruprecht, 1994]) and Y. Yadin (*Bar-Kochba* [New York: Random House, 1971]).

Ya'akov ben Yehudah, who dwells in Beth Mashko, belongs to him [i.e., to Ya'akov] by purchase. Were it not for the Gentiles [i.e., the Romans] who are near us, I would have gone up and satisfied you concerning this, lest you will say that it is out of contempt that I did not go up to you. Be you well and the whole House of Israel.

Yeshua ben Elazar has written it [i.e., dictated it]
Eleazar ben Yehoseph has written it
Ya'akov ben Yehudah, for himself
Sha'ul ben Eliezar, witness
Yehoseph ben Yehoseph, witness
Ya'akov ben Yehoseph, testifies [scribe or notary].

Simeon, son of Kosiba, to Jonathan, son of Ba'yan, and Masabala, son of Simeon:

You are to send to me Eleazar, son of Ḥitta, immediately before the Sabbath. . . . Simeon, son of Judah, wrote it.

Simeon, son of Kosiba, to Jonathan, son of Ba'yan, and Masabala who is in Ḥotah and to Masabala on the frontier, my brother, peace. . . .

. . . the Romans. You are to take Tirsos, son of Tinianos, and let him come with you, because we are in need of him. . . . Be in peace.

Simeon to Yehudah bar Menashe to Qiryath 'Arabya:

I have sent to you two donkeys so that you shall send with them two men to Yehonathan bar Ba'ayan and to Masabala in order that they shall pack and send to the camp, to you, palm branches *[lulavin]* and citrons *[ethrogin]*. And you, from your place, send others who will bring you myrtles *[hadasin]* and willows *['aravin]*. See that they are tithed and send them to the camp. (The request is made) since the army is large. Be well.

From Simeon ben Kosiba to Yeshua ben Galgoula and to the men of the fort, peace!

I take heaven to witness against me that unless you mobilize [destroy?] the Galileans who are with you every man, I will put fetters upon your feet as I did to ben Aphlul.

[Si]meon be[n Kosiba wrote it].

From Simeon bar Kosiba to the people of Ein Gedi, to Masabala and Yonathan bar Ba'ayan, peace.

In comfort you sit, eat and drink from the property of the House of Israel, and care nothing for your brothers. . . .

. . . my house . . . till the end . . . , [send] me grain, for there is no bread [in their] district . . . they have [fl]ed [to] your father . . . to the Fortress of the Hasidim. And my brothers in the sou[th] . . . [Many] of these were lost by the sword . . . these my brothers.

From these extracts we make some observations about Bar Kokhba and his revolt. One senses clearly the dictatorial powers Bar Kokhba wielded. In contrast to the First Jewish Revolt, in which various warlords struggled against each other as well as the Romans, all military and civil authority was entrusted to the hands of one man and his small group of officers and administrators. The upshot was a well-organized and disciplined army.

The official title of Bar Kokhba was "Nasi" ("prince"), already connected with the king in the OT and at Qumran (Ezek 12:10, 12; 34:24). In 1987 at a site called Horvat Alim in the Shephelah (western slopes of Judea), a lead weight was discovered in the cave system dug during the Bar Kokhba revolt. This rectangular lead tablet had an inscription on front and back. The face inscription read: "Simeon ben Kosba president *[nasi]* of Israel and his economic chief Peras." The other side read: "Ben Kosba president of Israel and his economic chief Simeon Dasoi. Peras."[42] Not everyone, however, knuckled under to this "last president of Israel." Clearly there were pockets of rebellion whom Bar Kokhba threatened with ruthless measures and, apparently, punished whenever possible.

We also note the poor food-supply situation. In one passage the Gentiles (Romans) are mentioned as close at hand. This must have been an ever-deepening crisis for the rebel cause. In spite of these difficulties, however, we read of their plans to observe the holiday of Sukkoth with the required branches of four different kinds. The army seems to have been made up, for the most part, of observant Jews. We do read, however, of some non-Jews who joined in the revolt. These were no doubt Gentiles who also suffered exploitation under the Roman imperial system and had grievances for which there was no means of redress short of violent resistance.

The intriguing question concerns the messianic status of Bar Kokhba. Though none of his letters provides direct evidence on this point, we do possess both rabbinical and Christian sources attesting to messianic claims at least made by others on his behalf.[43] In the Jerusalem Talmud we have a passage debating the status of Bar Kokhba:

> Rabbi Simeon bar Yoḥai taught, "Akiva, my master, expounded, 'A star will go forth from Jacob' (Num 28:17), (as) 'Koziba has come forth from Jacob.' " When Rabbi Akiva would see Bar Koziba, he would say, "This is the King Messiah!" Rabbi Yoḥanan ben Torta said to him, "Akiva, grass will grow on your cheeks and still the Son of David will not have come." (*y. Ta'an.* 4:6 §§68d-69a)

---

[42]Kloner, "Name of Ancient Israel's Last President," p. 14.

[43]For a very cautious survey of the evidence and scholarly opinion, see Grabbe, *Judaism from Cyrus to Hadrian,* 2:579-81. He writes, "It seems clear that some, including probably Aqiva, identified Bar Kochba as the messiah" (2:580). More certain that Simon was viewed as the Messiah is Craig Evans, "Simon ben Kosiba," *DNTB,* pp. 1114-15.

The Church historian Eusebius seems to confirm the messianic claims made for Bar Kokhba:

> The leader of the Jews at this time was a man by the name of Bar Cocheba (which signifies a star), who possessed the character of a robber and a murderer, but nevertheless, relying upon his name, boasted to them, as if they were slaves, that he possessed wonderful powers; and he pretended that he was a star that had come down to them out of heaven to bring them light in the midst of their misfortunes. (*Hist. eccl.* 4.6.6-12)

Eusebius also records a statement to the same effect by the postapostolic church father Justin Martyr (died ca. A.D. 165) that is quite likely correct:

> The same writer [Justin Martyr], speaking of the Jewish war which took place at the time, adds the following: "For in the late Jewish war Bar Cocheba, the leader of the Jewish rebellion, commanded that Christians alone should be visited with terrible punishments unless they would deny and blaspheme Jesus Christ." (*Hist. eccl.* 4.8.18-22)

This violent persecution directed at Christians is not surprising, given the apparent messianic status of Bar Kokhba and the desperate nature of the struggle with Rome. Jews who did not join in the war effort were viewed as traitors. The Bar Kokhba revolt marked a watershed in Christian-Jewish relations. Both sides in the dispute over who constitutes the True Israel now hardened their positions, and in effect a final divorce between these two faiths became a *fait accompli*. As it turned out, even the Jewish community eventually denounced Bar Kokhba's messianic claims, as seen in rabbinic literature. Messianism as a political option was stifled by the post–Bar Kokhba rabbis, and Jewish nationalism resurfaced as a viable political option only in modern times.

Reaction to the Failure of Bar Kokhba's Revolt

In chapter fourteen we will pursue further the rift between church and synagogue. For now, however, we briefly investigate two Jewish works, perhaps redacted just after the Bar Kokhba revolt. Once again the issue of theodicy looms large. What are Jews to make of this devastating loss and apparent end of all hope for a renewed national life and a rebuilt temple?

Baruch (The Paraleipomena of Jeremiah)

Introduction

This interesting little work may well be the original Rip Van Winkle story. The two leading figures in the story are Jeremiah and his faithful scribe Baruch; but it is Abimelech's sixty-six-year nap that nabs one's attention. The title of the work, *paraleipomena*, means "the things left out." Thus we have a work purportedly informing us of matters not recorded by canonical

Jeremiah. Other titles for this work, however, are found in the various extant translations. In the Ethiopic manuscript the work is titled *The Rest of the Words of Baruch*. Modern scholars, in trying to distinguish the work from others dealing with Baruch, sometimes assigned the titles *3 Baruch* or *4 Baruch*.[44] The recent preference, however, is to revert back to the oldest title that we have, which is found in the Greek manuscripts.

Synopsis

The story begins on the eve of Nebuchadnezzar's assault of Jerusalem. The Lord warns Jeremiah and Baruch to flee the city because its destruction has been decreed. To show Nebuchadnezzar and his army that the capture of the city was not due to their military prowess, the angels of God actually open the city gates for the invaders (*4 Bar.* 1—2). Before this happens, however, Jeremiah and Baruch hide the temple vessels in the ground. Jeremiah then requests that his friend Abimelech (cf. Ebed-melech in Jer 38:7-13) be spared the sight of the temple's destruction (*4 Bar.* 3). This having been granted, Jeremiah takes the keys to the temple and hurls them to the sun for safekeeping until the day of restoration. Baruch sings a lament over the destruction of Jerusalem that highlights the sin of Israel as the cause of this devastation (*4 Bar.* 4). Abimelech goes as bidden by Jeremiah to Agrippa's vineyard to gather figs. While there he falls into a slumber lasting sixty-six years, thus not seeing the destruction of the city. When he awakes, he goes back to the city but is thoroughly confused, for everything is different. At last an old man informs him of the time lapse and what had happened. Because Abimelech's figs are still fresh, both men believe that a miracle has occurred (*4 Bar.* 5). An angel leads Abimelech to Baruch, who was sitting on a tomb. Baruch confirms that the figs constitute a sign of both personal resurrection and national restoration. He then composes a letter, conveyed by an eagle to Jeremiah in Babylon, in which he urges Jeremiah to bring back a repentant remnant to Jerusalem (*4 Bar.* 6). Jeremiah responds by letter and is aided in convincing the people by a miraculous return to life of a man who was being buried (*4 Bar.* 7). The people journey to the Jordan River, where they are required to leave behind their Babylonian spouses (cf. Ezra and Nehemiah for a similar measure imposed on the postexilic community in Judea). Those who refuse (fully half the group) return to Babylon but are rejected and expelled by the Babylonians. These Jews then trek westward again and finally settle in

---

[44]See, respectively, M. R. James, *Apocrypha Anecdota: Second Series*, Texts and Studies 5, no. 1 (Cambridge: Cambridge University Press, 1897), pp. 53, 71; and R. H. Charles, *APOT* 2:471. We are following the notation *4 Baruch* because this is the title used in *OTP*.

Samaria (*4 Bar.* 8). Meanwhile, Jeremiah, after offering sacrifice continuously for ten days, experiences a vision of celestial glory. He then appears to die. After three days he comes to life and describes his vision. It concerns Jesus Christ "the Light of all the ages, the unquenchable Lamp, the Life of faith," and his coming back in 477 years. Upon this the people stone him for blasphemy, and Baruch and Abimelech erect a stone memorial at his tomb (*4 Bar.* 9). At this point the book abruptly ends.

Composition, Date and Provenance

There are several incongruities in *4 Baruch,* not least of which is the surprise ending with a prophecy about Jesus Christ and Jeremiah's death by stoning. Most scholars are of the opinion that it has undergone at least three different redactions, the last being by a Christian.[45] We think a good case can be made for the essentially Jewish nature of the original work, with a major Christian interpolation being *4 Baruch* 9:10-32. It may be that *4 Baruch* 6:23 is also a Christian interpolation, inasmuch as the baptism at the Jordan River is called "the sign of the great seal" (cf. Jn 6:27; Eph 1:13; 4:30; 2 Tim 2:19; Rev 7:2, 4). But otherwise the ideas expressed move comfortably within a Jewish ambiance.

The original language was probably Hebrew, though conclusive proof is lacking. The transliteration of the Hebrew word *zār* ("foreign") and certain Hebraisms, like the redundant use of personal pronouns following a relative pronoun and intensive verbal constructions, among others, point in this direction.[46] The only manuscripts that we possess are in Greek (at least thirteen), Ethiopian, Armenian, Old Church Slavonic and Romanian.

The date is difficult to specify, but several internal features point us to the first third of the second century A.D. Of particular interest is the reference to Agrippa's vineyard. Since Agrippa II did not control Judea until A.D. 41, we have our earliest possible date. If the destruction of Jerusalem in A.D. 70 is the real focal point of the work and we use Abimelech's long siesta of sixty-six years as a yardstick, we may assign a date of A.D. 136 as the terminal point. This would fit nicely with the anticipation of restoration so prominent in the work, particularly in light of the harsh reality of Hadrian's edict forbidding Jews to enter Jerusalem on pain of death after the last Jewish forces fell in A.D. 135.

The place of composition best fits Palestine and, even more narrowly, Jerusalem. The geographical allusions, such as Agrippa's vineyard and the market of the Gentiles, are the primary evidence for this. A Hebrew original would also argue for a Palestinian setting.

---

[45]See S. E. Robinson, "4 Baruch," *OTP* 2:415.
[46]Ibid., 2:414.

Purpose

The purpose of this writing emerges from the twin foci of the destruction of Jerusalem and its restoration. Under the guise of an untold story about Jeremiah, Baruch and Abimelech, the Jewish author inspires hope that the city and its temple would again be restored. As with other writings we have examined earlier, this one served as a "tract for the times." If we are correct in assuming that its composition should be dated around A.D. 136, it came at a time when many Jews had lost all hope for a brighter tomorrow. Hadrian had forbidden Jews even to set foot in Jerusalem on pain of death. Yet, in spite of the outward circumstances, God's promise of a New Jerusalem and a glorious temple were reaffirmed in this tale about Jeremiah and his friends. As events turned out, there was a modest historical vindication for our unknown author's convictions. In time, the Hadrianic decree was rescinded, and Jews could once again live in Jerusalem and at least pray at the only remains of the Second Temple, the so-called Wailing Wall or, as it is styled today, the Western Wall. A Jewish community did reestablish itself in the city of Jerusalem and carried on its rich traditions, with only a few interruptions, up to our own times.[47] Of course, a third temple did not materialize. Today, some Orthodox Jews, a very small minority, still harbor hopes for a third temple.[48] God alone knows whether this ancient hope will ever be realized in history.[49]

Features

Ostensibly, this story concerns the destruction of Jerusalem by Nebuchadnezzar in 586 B.C. Once again, however, as we have seen in other Second Temple writings (cf. Tobit, Judith, *Assumption of Moses, Jubilees, 1 Enoch*), there is a typology at work. The destruction of the First Temple actually mirrors the tragedy of the Second Temple or, in this case perhaps, the Bar Kokhba revolt.

One of the noteworthy features of this book is Jeremiah and Baruch's interment of the temple vessels in the earth; the earth actually swallows them up.

---

[47] A tragic instance being the First Crusade (A.D. 1099) in which the victorious Crusader army burned alive the Jewish community in one of its synagogues. The story is told that the Crusaders sang the hymn "Fairest Lord Jesus" as this atrocity was being perpetrated. For details on the First Crusade and this particular episode see Steven Runciman, *History of the Crusades*, 2 vols. (Cambridge: Cambridge University Press, 1968).

[48] There is an organization called "the Temple Faithful" who study the biblical and rabbinic sources with an eye to reestablishing the priestly ritual. They demonstrate for and propagate zealously their aspirations for a rebuilt temple. It should be emphasized that they do not represent the official position of the State of Israel in this regard. The state stands committed to the continuation of the so-called "Status Quo." This means that each religious community in Israel maintains control over its respective holy sites.

[49] Considerable debate in evangelical circles continues over the question of whether there will be a divinely authorized third temple or not.

We have noted already in our reading that this idea was widespread in Jewish circles (cf. 2 Macc 2:4-5; *2 Bar.* 6:7-10; *Num. Rab.* 15:10).[50] The exact spot of burial is not specified in *4 Baruch*. In 2 Maccabees, however, we read that it was a cave on Mount Nebo, in what is today modern Jordan, overlooking Jericho.

These references to the stashed temple vessels have spawned a wave of modern "arkeologists." Several years ago a Kansan, Tom Crotser, conned some supporters into funding his quest for the ark of the covenant. Unfortunately, he had neither the proper credentials nor permission to go on his "arkeological" adventure. On October 31, 1981, he illegally entered a cave and passageway on Mount Pisgah (near Mount Nebo) and dug through three existing walls where, he claimed, he did indeed find and photograph the ark of the covenant in a rock-hewn chamber. Several papers in the United States published an article by a UPI reporter in Kansas about this sensational discovery. A professor of archaeology at Andrews University in Michigan, Dr. Seigfrid Horn, very dubious about the alleged discovery, examined Crotser's color photographs of the ark. Dr. Horn was not impressed, since the box in the photograph clearly had a modern-looking nail at one end. Furthermore, the metal sheet surrounding the box looked like it had been machine worked![51] Needless to say, Mr. Crotser has not been invited back to Jordan, and, if he should go, he would probably spend some time behind bars. I have personally known another individual who has devoted much of his adult life in search of the ark, thus far without success.[52] One would do better, in my opin-

---

[50]"And so, when the Temple was destroyed, the candlestick was [divinely] stored away. It was one of the following five things that were so stored away: The ark, the candlestick, the fire, the Holy Spirit, and the cherubim. When the Holy One, blessed be He, in His mercy will again build His Temple and His Holy Place, He will restore them to their position in order to gladden Jerusalem; as it says, The wilderness and the parched land shall be glad; and the desert shall rejoice, and blossom as the rose. It shall blossom abundantly, and rejoice. (Isa. XXXV, 1 f.)" (*Num. Rab.* 15:10, *The Soncino Midrash Rabbah on CD-ROM*, The CD-ROM Judaica Classics Library [Davka, 1992-1995]).

[51]For a summary see "Tom Crotser Has Found the Ark of the Covenant—Or Has He? *BAR* 9, no. 3 (1983): 66.

[52]This man is Vendyl Jones, a one-time fundamentalist prophecy buff who wrote for a publication specializing in biblical prophecy and Jewish evangelism. Later he founded and became director of the Institute for Judaic-Christian Research. He has been involved in a number of "unofficial" digs in Israel, some of which actually turned up some very interesting and valuable finds (see e.g., Patrich, "Hideouts in the Judean Wilderness," pp. 32-42; and "Giving Credit Where Credit Is Due" [letter to the editor] *BAR* 16, no. 1 [1990]: 64-65). Jones claims to have discovered a place where the Jerusalem priests dumped the ashes of the red heifer in the wilderness of Judea. In addition to the ark of the covenant, he has been involved in a quest for the other ark, i.e., Noah's ark. He participated, as an archaeological expert, in a PBS program devoted to alleged sightings of Noah's ark. He also claims that the movie figure "Indiana Jones" (played by Harrison Ford) was actually based upon his own life! At any rate, he has in recent years converted to Judaism and continues his quest for both arks.

ion, watching the movie rather than going on the quest![53]

Scholars have long noted the similarities between *4 Baruch* and *2 Baruch*. One scholar even argued that *4 Baruch* is literarily dependent upon *2 Baruch*.[54] Most scholars, however, conclude that common traditions lie behind both works and that this accounts for the similarities.[55]

Relevance for the New Testament

There is little here of direct relevance for study of the NT. What this work does demonstrate, however, is that Christians found it useful in validating their faith commitments. The Christian redactions probably reflect a continuing witness, as well as an apologetic response, to the Jewish community concerning the messianic status of Jesus. The work may also bear witness to the persistence of Christian belief in an interim messianic kingdom (the millennium) and the restoration of the temple, since the redactor(s) would hardly have taken over without correction such a view if it were unacceptable. This chimes in with the millenarian views of such church fathers as Papias, Justin Martyr, Irenaeus and Tertullian, all of whom lived during the second century A.D.[56] Of course, corporate and individual bodily resurrection receives great emphasis in *4 Baruch,* a major reason such a work was preserved by Christians.

We note several minor parallels. In *4 Baruch* 7:1 we read: "And Baruch stood up and went out of the tomb and found the eagle sitting outside the tomb. And conversing in a human voice, the eagle said to him, 'Hail, Baruch, the steward of the faith!' " The point of comparison is the use of the term "the faith" to designate a body of teaching or doctrine that is normative. In the Pauline epistles widely accepted as authentic by modern scholars, we never find this use of *pistis* (faith). Rather, Paul uses *pistis* to refer to the intellectual and volitional commitment that places one in a right relationship before God. However, we find in the Pastoral Epistles a very similar usage as in *4 Baruch* (cf. 1 Tim 3:9: "hold fast to

---

[53]I am referring to the Hollywood blockbuster *Raiders of the Lost Ark,* starring Harrison Ford. More recently Larry Blaser of Englewood, Colorado, thought that he had discovered the cave in which the ark of the covenant was hidden. His candidate was a cave above En-Gedi along the shores of the Dead Sea. The site was examined, without success, by a professional archaeologist of international reputation, Dr. James F. Strange. For details and pictures, see "The Ark That Wasn't There," *BAR* 9, no. 4 (1983): 58-61.

[54]P. Bogaert, *Apocalypse de Baruch* (Paris, 1969), pp. 186-92, cited in Robinson, "4 Baruch," 2:416.

[55]See George W. E. Nickelsburg, *Jewish Literature Between the Bible and the Mishnah: A Historical and Literary Introduction* (Philadelphia: Fortress, 1981), p. 316; Nickelsburg, "Stories of Biblical and Early Post-Biblical Times," in *Jewish Writings of the Second Temple Period,* p. 75; and Robinson, "4 Baruch," 2:416-17.

[56]As R. J. Bauckham notes, "This belief was . . . a continuation of Jewish apocalyptic expectation of an interim messianic kingdom" (*New Dictionary of Theology,* ed. Sinclair B. Ferguson, David F. Wright and J. I. Packer [Downers Grove, Ill.: InterVarsity Press, 1988], p. 428).

the mystery of the faith"; 4:1: "some will renounce the faith"). In *4 Baruch* 9:4 we have a phrase that recalls the prologue in John's Gospel: "true light that enlightens me until I am taken up to you." Compare this to John 1:9, where we have the affirmation: "The true light, which enlightens everyone, was coming into the world." In *4 Baruch* 9:14 we read the summons: "Glorify God with one voice! All (of you) glorify God, and the Son of God who awakens us, Jesus Christ the light of all the aeons." This reminds us of Paul's benediction in Romans 15:5b-6, where he prays that his readers would live "in accordance with Christ Jesus, so that together you may with one voice glorify the God and Father of our Lord Jesus Christ." There are several other allusions to NT passages (*4 Bar.* 9:20; cf. Jn 1:9; Acts 1:11-12; *4 Bar.* 9:21; cf. Mt 5:6; 14:19-20).

Sybilline Oracle 5

We consult several brief passages from *Sybilline Oracle* 5, dating approximately to the time of the Bar Kokhba Revolt. As one might expect, bitter hostility permeates these passages, given the horrific reprisals the Romans inflicted upon both the Palestinian and Diaspora Jewish communities.

Date and Provenance

The factors determining one's assessment of date are as follows. First, Nero plays a leading role as the great adversary of the end times. Therefore, the work must be later than A.D. 68 when Nero committed suicide (*Sib. Or.* 5:214-238, 361-385). Second, the Second Temple has been destroyed for some time (*Sib. Or.* 5:397-402). Third, there are references to the destruction of pagan temples (*Sib. Or.* 5:52-59, 484-491). This could well refer to the uprising of Jews in the Diaspora, especially Egypt, during the reign of Trajan around A.D. 115. Finally, there is a favorable reference to Hadrian (*Sib. Or.* 5:46-50); thus the work in its final form must be before A.D. 132. Scholars are nearly unanimous in favor of an Egyptian provenance.[57] The work originated in a Jewish environment, and only lines 256-259 reflect any Christian redaction.[58]

> *Oracle against Rome (lines 162-178)*
> You will be among evil mortals, suffering evils,
> but you will remain utterly desolate for all ages yet,
> (it will exist, but it will remain utterly desolate forever),
> despising your soil, because you desired sorcery.
> With you are found adulteries and illicit intercourse with boys.

---

[57] See the evidence and arguments in John J. Collins, "Sibylline Oracles: A New Translation and Introduction," *OTP* 1:390-91.

[58] Collins notes that "even here it is probable that a reference to a Jewish savior figure in the original Jewish oracle has been modified only by an allusion to the crucifixion" (ibid., 1:390).

Effeminate and unjust, evil city, ill-fated above all.
Alas, city of the Latin land, unclean in all things,
Maenad [a frenzied woman],[59] rejoicing in vipers, as a widow you will sit
by the banks, and the river Tiber will weep for you, its consort.
You have a murderous heart and impious spirit.
Did you not know what God can do, what he devises?
But you said, "I alone am and no one will ravage me."
But now, God, who is forever, will destroy you and all your people,
and there will no longer be any sign of you in that land,
as there was formerly, when the great God found your honors.
Remain alone, lawless one. Mingled with burning fire,
inhabit the lawless nether region of Hades.[60]

This passage invokes God's curse upon Rome for its immoral, cruel and arro-gant behavior. Especially deserving of condemnation are the blatant sexual vices practiced by the "Latin land" (i.e., Italy, the Romans). The oracle also predicts everlasting, utter devastation at the hand of God.

Several observations about the literary features of this passage deserve mention. First, we detect allusions to, or unconscious phrasing from, Isa-iah 14 and 47 and Ezekiel 28. The prophetic oracles in Isaiah 14 and Ezek-iel 28 announce the death of a pagan tyrant and his mighty empire in the literary form of a "taunt song." The wording of these taunt songs seems to be reused and adapted in several lines by the author of this oracle against Rome (*Sib. Or.* 5:173; cf. Is 14:3; Ezek 28:2; *Sib. Or.* 5:177; cf. Is 14:15). In similar fashion, the author incorporates an idea from a prophetic judgment oracle against Babylon in Isaiah 47 (*Sib. Or.* 5:169-270; cf. Is 47:9; *Sib. Or.* 5:173-174; cf. Is 47:8). There are some clear instances in Jewish and Chris-tian sources where ancient Babylon serves as a code word for Rome (cf. 1 Pet 5:13; Rev 17:5; 18:1-24). For example, two lines of this oracle against Rome call to mind Revelation 18, a Christian judgment oracle likewise directed against Rome (*Sib. Or.* 5:169, 173; cf. Rev 18:7). The reference to "the nether region of Hades" also recalls a similar idea in 2 Peter 2:4 and Jude 13.[61]

Two other passages from *Sibylline Oracle* 5 further demonstrate Jewish loathing of Roman sexual vices and idolatry. Also noteworthy is the reference to Titus's burning of the Second Temple (*Sib. Or.* 5:399, 403-404, 411-413). One clearly senses a fervent hope for divine retribution upon the Romans, retribu-tion carried out by a messianic figure who will destroy the wicked and rule

---

[59]I have added the gloss to Collins's translation.
[60]Translation by Collins, "Sibylline Oracles," 1:397. Subsequent translations are also taken from Collins.
[61]For other points of contact between book 5 and the NT, see ibid., 1:392.

over the world. God himself will rebuild Jerusalem and its temple.[62]

Admonition to the Romans (lines 386-396)
Matricides, desist from boldness and evil daring,
you who formerly impiously catered for pederasty
and set up in houses prostitutes who were pure before,
with insults and punishment and toilsome disgrace.
For in you mother had intercourse with child unlawfully,
and daughter was joined with her begetter as bride.
In you also kings defiled their ill-fated mouths.
In you also evil men practiced bestiality.
Be silent, most lamentable evil city, which indulges in revelry.
For no longer in you will virgin maidens
tend the divine fire of sacred nourishing wood.[63]

Destruction of the temple (lines 397-413)
The desired Temple has long ago been extinguished by you,
When I saw the second Temple cast headlong,
soaked in fire by an impious hand,
the ever-flourishing, watchful Temple of God
made by holy people and hoped
by their soul and body to be always imperishable.
For among them no one carelessly praises a god
of insignificant clay, nor did a clever sculptor make one from rock,
nor worship ornament of gold, a deception of souls.
But they honored the great God, begetter of all
who have God-given breath, with holy sacrifices and hecatombs.
But now a certain insignificant and impious king
has gone up, cast it down, and left it in ruins
with a great horde and illustrious men.
He himself perished at immortal hands when he left the land,
and no such sign has yet been performed among men
that others should think to sack a great city.

The advent of a savior figure (lines 414-433)
For a blessed man came from the expanses of heaven
with a scepter in his hands which God gave him,
and he gained sway over all things well, and gave back the wealth
to all the good, which previous men had taken.
He destroyed every city from its foundations with much fire
and burned nations of mortals who were formerly evildoers.

---

[62]God seems to be the agent of re-creation in the passage (*Sib. Or.* 5:420-424), although it is possible that the messianic figure is the agent.

[63]Collins points out that this refers to the burning of the temple of Vesta in A.D. 64 ("Sibylline Oracles," 1:402).

And the city which God desired, this he made
more brilliant than stars and sun and moon,
and he provided ornament and made a holy temple,
exceedingly beautiful in its fair shrine, and he fashioned
a great and immense tower over many stadia
touching even the clouds and visible to all,
so that all faithful and all righteous people could see
the glory of eternal God, a form desired.
East and West sang out the glory of God.
For terrible things no longer happen to wretched mortals,
no adulteries or illicit love of boys,
no murder, or din of battle, but competition is fair among all.
It is the last time of holy people when God, who thunders on high,
founder of the greatest temple, accomplishes these things.

There is a Christian parallel to these judgment oracles, especially in Revelation 18. In a dirge, the saints celebrate the fall of Rome, symbolized by ancient Babylon. Echoing the taunt songs of several OT prophetic texts (Is 14; 23—24; 47; Jer 50—51; Ezek 26—27), this passage highlights the grievous sins of Rome, not least of which was "the blood of prophets and of saints" (Rev 18:24) that inevitably and rightly bring down God's wrath upon her. Revelation 19, like *Sybilline Oracle* 5:415-430, constitutes a counterpoise to the judgment oracle by describing the advent of the messianic figure, the one "called Faithful and True," "The Word of God," "the King of kings and Lord of lords" (Rev 19:11; 13, 16). This Messiah, clearly identified with the Lamb of God, destroys all the forces of the beast (i.e., antichrist) and casts him and his false prophet into the lake of fire (Rev 19:17-21). Out of the smoke of destruction, however, comes an entirely new earth with its centerpiece, the New Jerusalem in all its glory (Rev 21—22).

One might also usefully compare two Pauline texts that speak of retribution upon persecutors and opponents of the gospel (Phil 1:27-30; 2 Thess 1:5-10). These NT texts, however, manifest neither the personal venom expressed in the *Sibylline Oracles* toward the persecutors nor the anticipation of joy at their punishment and destruction.

As we have noted previously, in contrast to the Jewish hope for a rebuilt temple (cf. Ezek 40—48), Christian expectations for a New Jerusalem do *not* include a temple (Rev 21:22). Instead, God and the Lamb (Jesus Christ) are present with the redeemed in an unmediated presence, and thus the temple—and what it historically represented—is superseded by an experience of intimate communion and fellowship heretofore unrealized in redemptive history. Furthermore, the NT displays a realized eschatology whereby the new people of God, indwelt by the Holy Spirit, are already being raised up as God's temple (1 Cor 3:16-17; 6:19; 2 Cor 6:16; Eph 2:21; Heb 8—10; 1 Pet 2:5, 9).

For Further Discussion

1. How were the Jewish people able to cope with calamity on such a scale as we have read in this chapter? Is this different from the ways Christians have responded to tragedy over the centuries?

2. How is the expectation of the messianic kingdom in *2 Baruch* similar to and different from that found in NT literature?

3. What led to the Bar Kokhba revolt? How did its utter failure change Jews and Judaism?

4. What do the Babatha correspondence and the Bar Kokhba letters contribute to our understanding of this era?

5. What are some common ideas and themes that are found in the Jewish apocalyptic works read in this chapter and the book of Revelation in the NT?

For Further Reading

J. J. Collins, "Sibylline Oracles: A New Translation and Introduction," in *The Old Testament Pseudepigrapha,* ed. J. H. Charlesworth, 2 vols. (Garden City, N.Y.: Doubleday, 1983), 1:317-472.

————, "Sibylline Oracles," *DNTB,* pp. 1107-12.

————, "The Sibylline Oracles," in *Jewish Writings of the Second Temple Period: Apocrypha, Pseudepigrapha, Qumran Sectarian Writings, Philo, Josephus,* ed. Michael E. Stone, CRINT 2 (Assen: Van Gorcum; Philadelphia: Fortress, 1984), pp. 357-81.

C. A. Evans, "Simon ben Kosiba," *DNTB,* pp. 1112-16.

Joseph A. Fitzmyer, "The Bar Cochba Period," in *Essays on the Semitic Background of the New Testament,* SBLSBS 5 (Missoula, Mont.: Scholars Press, 1974), pp. 305-54.

I. Gafni, "Between the Wars: From Jerusalem to Yavneh," in *Jewish Writings of the Second Temple Period: Apocrypha, Pseudepigrapha, Qumran Sectarian Writings, Philo, Josephus,* ed. Michael E. Stone, CRINT 2 (Assen: Van Gorcum; Philadelphia: Fortress, 1984), pp. 27-31.

L. L. Grabbe, "Jewish History: Roman Period," *DNTB,* pp. 576-80.

————, "Jewish Wars with Rome," *DNTB,* pp. 584-88.

John H. Hayes and Sarah R. Mandell, *The Jewish People in Classical Antiquity* (Louisville: Westminster John Knox, 1998), pp. 207-15.

Ranon Katzoff, "Babatha," *EDSS* 1:73-75.

A. F. J. Klijn, "2 (Syriac Apocalypse of) Baruch," in *The Old Testament Pseudepigrapha,* ed. J. H. Charlesworth, 2 vols. (Garden City, N.Y.: Doubleday, 1983), 1:615-52.

Lee I. A. Levine, "Judaism from the Destruction of Jerusalem to the End of the Second Jewish Revolt: 70-135 C.E.," in *Christianity and Rabbinic Judaism: A Parallel History of Their Origins and Early Development,* ed. Hershel Shanks, Washington, D.C.: Biblical Archaeology Society, 1992), pp. 125-49.

Naphtali Lewis, Yigael Yadin and Jonas C. Greenfield, eds., *The Documents from the Bar Kokhba Period in the Cave of the Letters,* JDS (Jerusalem: Israel Exploration Society, 1989).

Doron Mendels, *The Rise and Fall of Jewish Nationalism* (Grand Rapids, Mich.: Eerdmans, 1992), pp. 385-93.

Frederick James Murphy, *The Structure and Meaning of Second Baruch,* SBLMS 78 (Atlanta: Scholars Press, 1985).

George W. E. Nickelsburg, "The Second Revolt," in *Jewish Literature Between the Bible and the Mishnah: A Historical and Literary Introduction* (Philadelphia: Fortress, 1981), pp. 311-18.

————, "Stories of Biblical and Early Post-Biblical Times," in *Jewish Writings of the Second Temple Period: Apocrypha, Pseudepigrapha, Qumran Sectarian Writings, Philo, Josephus,* ed. Michael E. Stone, CRINT 2 (Assen: Van Gorcum; Philadelphia: Fortress, 1984), pp. 72-75 *[Paraleipomena of Jeremiah].*

Aharon Oppenheimer, "Bar Kokhba, Shimʿon," *EDSS* 1:78-80.

————, "Bar Kokhba Revolt," *EDSS* 1:80-83.

S. E. Robinson, "4 Baruch," in *The Old Testament Pseudepigrapha,* ed. J. H. Charlesworth, 2 vols. (Garden City, N.Y.: Doubleday, 1983), 2:413-25 *[Paraleipomena of Jeremiah].*

M. E. Stone, "Apocalyptic Literature," in *Jewish Writings of the Second Temple Period: Apocrypha, Pseudepigrapha, Qumran Sectarian Writings, Philo, Josephus,* ed. Michael E. Stone, CRINT 2 (Assen: Van Gorcum; Philadelphia: Fortress, 1984), pp. 408-10 *[2 Baruch].*

J. E. Wright, "Baruch, Books of," *DNTB,* pp. 148-51.

Yigael Yadin, Jonas C. Greenfield, Ada Yardeni, Baruch A. Levine, eds., *The Documents from the Bar-Kokhba Period in the Cave of Letters: Hebrew, Aramaic and Nabatean-Aramaic Papyri,* Judean Desert Studies 3 (Jerusalem: Israel Exploration Society; Institute of Archaeology, Hebrew University; shrine of the book, Israel Museum, 2002).

Thirteen

The World of Mishnah

*F*or *the Mishnah, unless otherwise indicated, we will use the translation by Jacob Neusner,* The Mishnah: A New Translation *(New Haven, Conn.: Yale University Press, 1988). One may also consult the older standard work of H. Danby,* The Mishnah *(Oxford: Oxford University Press, 1933). For those who would like the Hebrew text with accompanying English translation, there is Philip Blackman, ed.,* Mishnayoth, *3d ed., 7 vols. (New York: Judaica, 1965). We will also draw upon the anthologies of C. K. Barrett,* The New Testament Background: Selected Documents, *rev. ed. (San Francisco: Harper & Row, 1987); and Lawrence H. Schiffman,* Texts and Traditions: A Source Reader for the Study of Second Temple and Rabbinic Judaism *(Hoboken, N.J.: Ktav, 1998).*

Introduction

This chapter focuses on the remarkable reconstruction of Judaism accomplished by the rabbis of Yavneh (Jamnia). At Yavneh, Rabbi Yohanan ben Zakkai and his colleagues gave impetus to a process, already begun around 50 B.C. by the two academies of Beth Shammai and Beth Hillel, that later generations of rabbis called the Tannaim (from the Aramaic verb $t^e n\bar{a}$', meaning "to repeat") brought to completion.[1] We break off our survey with the principal figure of the

---

[1]The period of the Tannaim covers approximately 20 B.C.-A.D. 200. The earlier date coincides with Hillel's appointment as Nasi (leader, prince, president) and the later with Rabbi Judah ha-Nasi (the Prince), who edited the Mishnah.

fourth generation, Rabbi Judah the Prince (A.D. 165-200), often referred to simply as "Rabbi." That process transformed Judaism into a nearly monolithic religion that would last until the Enlightenment. During this period Judaism left the era of diversity and entered a long era of uniformity—rabbinic Judaism.

Navigating the Mishnah

Our brief foray into the nearly impenetrable world of Mishnah illustrates how the rabbis transformed the Levitical purity laws. The home now became the hearth of the Second Temple. Biblical laws regulating the priesthood were transformed into an elaborate code of conduct regulating all of Jewish life. In some respects, the Protestant Reformation's notion of the "priesthood of the individual believer" was not an innovation; Judaism had already developed this notion long before the Reformation, when it came to grips with the destruction of the Second Temple. The rabbis created, through their halakic rulings, a consensus on the boundaries of ritual purity, a consensus that had not existed throughout most of the Second Temple period. In short, the end of the Second Temple was the dawning of a new day in Judaism and Jewish history.

Reading Mishnah presents considerable difficulties:

> How do you read a book that does not identify its author, tell you where it comes from, or explain why it was written—a book without a preface? And how do you identify a book with neither beginning nor end, lacking table of contents and title? The answer is you just begin and let the author of the book lead you by paying attention to the information that the author does give, to the signals that the writer sets out.[2]

So begins Jacob Neusner in his introduction to the Mishnah. My impression is that few of the untutored will persevere in Neusner's suggestion for learning Mishnah. Beginning on the first page of the Mishnah, a tractate called *Berakot* (Blessings), one is immediately thrust into the middle of a lengthy discussion and disputation about the proper time to recite the Shema, the central creed of Judaism. Here is how the tractate begins:

> From what time do they recite the *Shema* in the evening? From the time that priests enter their home to eat food in the status of priestly ration, "until the end of the first watch," the words of R. Eliezer. And sages say, "Until midnight." Rabban Gamaliel says, "Until the rise of dawn."[3]

After this come numerous questions concerning conditions under which it is

---

[2]Jacob Neusner, *The Mishnah: An Introduction* (Northvale, N.J.: Jason Aronson, 1989), p. 1.
[3]The translation used is by Jacob Neusner, *The Mishnah: A New Translation* (New Haven, Conn.: Yale University Press, 1988).

either permissible or prohibited to recite the Shema, locations where it may or may not be recited, various acceptable and unacceptable postures and other questions connected in some way with the recitation of this creed. Throughout the tractate we have opinions of various rabbis, some of which stand in direct opposition to each other.

Now we turn to the very last paragraph of the Mishnah, a tractate entitled *ʿUqṣin:*

> Honeycomb: from what point are they susceptible to uncleanness in the status of liquid? The House of Shammai say, "When one smokes out [the bees from the combs, so that one can get at the honey]." The House of Hillel say, "When one will actually have broken up [the honeycombs to remove the honey]."[4]

Most of the passages between the first and last paragraphs are similar in form or pattern. Thus the Mishnah in its entirety ranges over a daunting array of questions and problems related to the correct manner of observing Jewish law. But throughout there is no discernible argument or overarching thesis. It is not immediately apparent why one topic follows another. Paragraph after paragraph simply analyzes some aspect of halakah ("the way things are done"; from the Heb *hālak,* "to walk"). As Neusner aptly observes, "We begin nowhere, without a clear-cut purpose or proposition, in the middle of a conversation, and we end up in the middle of some other conversation."[5] Only a highly motivated reader, with a deep commitment to traditional or Orthodox Judaism, will likely plod through this mass of material, especially without teacher or fellow traveler.[6] No wonder, then, that Jews traditionally have not studied Mishnah individually but have banded together under the guidance of a teacher and paired up with another student for the arduous task. One does not read Mishnah as a novel; one reads, ponders, discusses and debates the meaning of each line and often each word.[7]

Given the traditional Jewish view that the Mishnah was directly revealed by God to Moses, nothing in the text is superfluous or without significance. The Mishnah is thus an elaborate casebook of religious law, custom and tradition. As such, it stands as a monument to the prodigious memories (some rabbis then and now memorize it completely!) and acute minds of those who had a hand in shaping its contents.

---

[4]I am indebted to Neusner for the idea of juxtaposing these two passages as an epitome of the content of the Mishnah (*Mishnah: An Introduction,* p. 2).

[5]Ibid.

[6]Though a good many Orthodox Jews do belong to groups who read a page of Talmud a day. Every seven years they hold a large public celebration commemorating the completion of reading through the entire Talmud.

[7]Readers who have viewed the movie *Yentl* will recall the scenes in which Jewish students are reading, discussing and arguing about the meaning of a passage of Mishnah or Talmud.

Composition and Date

How and when was the Mishnah written? The word *Mishnah* derives from the Hebrew verb *šānâ*, "to repeat." This emphasizes its didactic and oral nature. In Aramaic, a sister language widely spoken by Jews in Second Temple times, the word *tᵉnā'* ("to repeat, learn") was also applied to this material. Thus one learned authoritative explanations and interpretations of Torah by hearing it repeated over and over by masters of the tradition.

Mishnah may refer to a single halakah or to the entire collection of halakot (plural). Prior to the editorial work of Judah the Prince, the mishnayot (plural) of the various rabbis were not identical, as can readily be seen in the final work. To further complicate matters, not all Mishnah consists of halakah. Some passages are midrash (exposition of Scripture allowing for creative expansion and elaboration), and some are haggadah, that is, narratives best described as Jewish lore intended to reinforce or teach correct beliefs and attitudes. The Mishnah is thus a complex combination of genres and a comprehensive compilation of opinions.

The Oral Torah had its beginnings at least as early as the second century B.C., perhaps as early as Ezra (fifth century B.C.). This material was significantly augmented during the first and second Christian centuries. The Mishnah identifies about 150 rabbis as contributing opinions and sayings to the written corpus. These rabbis date from approximately 50 B.C. to A.D. 200. One may divide these rabbis into three different eras: those who lived prior to the destruction of the Second Temple in A.D. 70 (the Pharisaic period), those who belonged to or were associated with Yohanan ben Zakkai's academy (the Yavnean period) and those who lived after the Bar Kokhba revolt up to the publication of the Mishnah (the Ushan period).[8] These evolving mishnayot were finally committed to writing by Rabbi Judah the Prince at the beginning of the third century A.D. (ca. A.D. 200).[9]

Judah's publication of his redaction was probably necessitated by differing and competing mishnayot; his aim was to produce an authorized version for all Jews everywhere. Given the discouraging state of affairs among Jews generally at this time and the question of whether Judaism itself would survive in succeeding centuries, one may more readily appreciate his motivation for such an immense undertaking. This was not done without some controversy, however, as the genius of Mishnah lay in its oral nature and the reliance upon memory alone to preserve it.[10]

---

[8]See further Roger Brooks, "Mishnah," *ABD* 4:871-73.

[9]The plural form of *mishnah* in Hebrew refers here to the body of halakic traditions transmitted orally by specific rabbis prior to the work of Judah the Prince.

[10]On this issue, see further Ephraim Elimelech Urbach, "Mishnah," *EncJud* 12:93-105.

So what do we know about Judah the Prince, patriarch of Judea and redactor of the Mishnah? Judah's bloodlines were impeccable. As the son of Rabban Simeon ben Gamaliel II, he was the sixth (or seventh) descendant of the great Hillel, whose views so shaped first-century Pharisaism. According to tradition Judah was born on the day Rabbi Akiba was martyred during the Hadrianic persecutions (*b. Qidd.* 72b).

Judah established a yeshivah (an academy for the study of Torah) at Beth Shearim, a town near the western end of the Jezreel Valley, less than ten miles from the modern city of Haifa (*b. Sanh.* 32b). Later, on account of poor health, he moved to Sepphoris, just a few miles northwest of Nazareth, where he spent seventeen years (*b. Ketub.* 103b; cf. *y. Ketub.* 12:3 §35a).[11] Owing to his family, wealth and prodigious knowledge of the Oral Torah, Judah gained an enormous reputation among pious Jews, so much so that he was accorded a place with such towering figures as Simeon the Just, Mattathias the Hasmonean, Mordecai and Esther (*b. Meg.* 11a). Later Jewish tradition even accorded him the title *haqqādōš* ("the holy one"; *b. Šabb.* 118b).[12]

The Roman authorities acknowledged him as patriarch of the Jews, a position granting him considerable power over Jewish religious, social and economic life. He appears to have been on good terms with at least two of the Roman emperors (Septimius Severus [A.D. 193-211] and Antoninus Caracalla [A.D. 211-217]) and remained in their good graces, since he advocated civil obedience to Roman authority and squelched any moves likely to be viewed as seditious. Being patriarch also meant that Judah was over the *bêt dîn* (Jewish court), from which platform he was able to influence Jews not only in Galilee but also in the entire region as well as in the Diaspora. The preserved traditions about Judah suggest that he lived in regal splendor and did not hesitate to exercise his considerable authority (cf. *b. Ber.* 16b; *b. ʿErub.* 73a, 86a).

His enduring contribution, however, centers on Jewish law. He gathered around him students committed to the Oral Torah. Under his leadership the various mishnayot were edited and compiled. The upshot of his work was not a legal code per se but a canon, "a standard by which the remainder of the *mišnayot* were judged."[13] Those traditions not making it into Judah's canon became *baraitoth* (the singular *baraita* means "outside"), sayings or rulings outside the Mishnah of Judah ha-Nasi. Judah's work did not stop the further development of halakah, but it did provide a foundation for all subsequent

---

[11]For archaeological discoveries at Sepphoris, see articles in *BAR* 26/4 (2000).

[12]For arguments that this was later than the time of the Mishnah itself, wee Urbach, "Mishnah," 12:102-5.

[13]"Judah Ha-Nasi," *EncJud* 10:372.

endeavors. The result is a work that for Judaism is "second in significance and sanctity only to the Scriptures.[14]

Though we will not pursue the further development of the Talmud, we simply inform readers that the Mishnah itself was the subject of commentary and explanation, called Gemara. Finally, this combination of Mishnah and Gemara was also committed to writing, the end result being a massive work, the Talmud. The Jerusalem Talmud was composed about A.D. 400 and the more authoritative Babylonian Talmud in about A.D. 500.[15]

The Structure of the Mishnah

The Mishnah is divided into six main divisions called "orders" (see table 13.1). How large is this work? Neusner suggests that if the entire work were on one scroll, its length, if unrolled, would approximate that of a football field—300 feet.[16] This is indeed a formidable piece! Add to this the fact that the original text of the Mishnah had no chapter headings. So how may one tell when one topic concludes and another begins? The transitions are relatively easy to discern because of the topical arrangement of each tractate. The appearance of a new form or pattern of argumentation signals a new topic. On the other hand, why the various topics appear in the order they do is not explained by the editor of the Mishnah or by any other Jewish writing of the Second Temple period.

The Basis and Sources of the Mishnah

As noted above, the Mishnah is a compendium of the Oral Torah. The assumed substratum of the Mishnah consists of the various legal, cultic and ritual regulations found in the Pentateuch. Moses is the fountainhead of all Jewish religious tradition. The usual way of referring to Moses in rabbinical writings is "Moses our rabbi" *(Mōšeh rabbênû)*. Thus the Mishnah is, in part, exegetically founded on the Written Torah (called *miqrā'*, "that which is read"), following certain hermeneutical guidelines. These guidelines were gradually worked out and developed by successive sages. A passage from the Tosefta (supplements to the Mishnah) documents the earliest explanation of rabbinic exegetical method:

> Hillel the Elder expounded seven principles *(middoth)* before the elders of Petherah; *a minori ad maius*, analogy, a standard conclusion based on one passage (of scripture), a standard conclusion based on two passages, general and particular—particular and general, analogy with another passage, proof from the

[14]Ibid.
[15]See further H. Maccoby, "Rabbinic Literature: Talmud," *DNTB*, pp. 897-902.
[16]*Mishnah: An Introduction*, p. 11.

Table 13.1. The six "orders" (main divisions) of the Mishnah and their sixty-three "tractates" (subsections)

A. *Zeraʿim* (Agriculture, lit. Seeds)
  1. *Berakot* (Blessings)
  2. *Peʾah* (Corner of Field)
  3. *Demai* (Uncertain [Fruit])
  4. *Kilʾayim* (Mixtures)
  5. *Šebiʿit* (Sabbatical Year)
  6. *Terumot* (Wave Offering)
  7. *Maʿaśerot* (Tithes)
  8. *Maʿaśer Šeni* (Second Tithe)
  9. *Ḥallah* (Dough)
  10. *ʿOrlah* (Forbidden)
  11. *Bikkurim* (First Fruits)

B. *Moʾed* (Appointed Times or Festivals)
  12. *Šabbat* (Sabbath)
  13. *ʿErubin* (Incorporating)
  14. *Pesaḥim* (Passovers)
  15. *Šeqalim* (Shekels)
  16. *Yoma* (Day of Atonement)
  17. *Sukkah* (Booths/Tabernacles)
  18. *Beṣah (= Yom Ṭob)* (Egg [Holidays])
  19. *Roš Haššanah* (New Year)
  20. *Taʿanit* (Fasting)
  21. *Megillah* (Scroll [of Esther])
  22. *Moʾed Qaṭan* (Lesser Holidays)
  23. *Ḥagigah* (Festival Offering)

C. *Našim* (Women)
  24. *Yebamot* (Levirate Obligations)
  25. *Ketubbot* (Marriage Contracts)
  26. *Nedarim* (Vows)
  27. *Nazir* (Nazirite Vow)
  28. *Soṭah* (Defiled Woman)
  29. *Giṭṭin* (Bills of Divorce)
  30. *Qiddušin* (Engagements)

D. *Neziqin* (Damages)
  31. *Baba Qamma* (First Gate)

  32. *Baba Meṣiʿa* (Middle Gate)
  33. *Baba Batra* (Last Gate)
  34. *Sanhedrin* (Courts)
  35. *Makkot* (Lashes)
  36. *Šebuʿot* (Oaths)
  37. *ʿEduyyot* (Witnesses)
  38. *ʿAbodah Zarah* (Idolatry)
  39. *ʾAbot* (Fathers)
  40. *Horayot* (Judgments)

E. *Qodašim* (Holy Things)
  41. *Zebaḥim* (Sacrifices)
  42. *Menaḥot* (Offerings)
  43. *Ḥullin* (Unconsecrated)
  44. *Bekorot* (Firstborn)
  45. *ʿArakin* (Estimates)
  46. *Temurah* (Exchanges)
  47. *Kerithot* (Those Cast Out)
  48. *Meʿilah* (Trespasses)
  49. *Tamid* (Daily Offerings)
  50. *Middot* (Measurements)
  51. *Qinnim* (Nests [of birds])

F. *Teharot* (Purities)
  52. *Kelim* (Containers)
  53. *ʾOhalot* (Tents)

  54. *Negaʿim* (Leprosies)
  55. *Parah* (Heifer)
  56. *Teharot* (Purifications)
  57. *Miqwaʾot* (Ritual Baths)
  58. *Niddah* (Menstruation)
  59. *Makširin* (Preparations)
  60. *Zabim* (Secretions)
  61. *Tebul Yom* (Immersion)
  62. *Yadayim* (Hands)
  63. *ʿUqṣin* (Stalks of Fruit)

Table 13.2. New Testament employment of rabbinic hermeneutical principles

Rabbinic Principle	NT Example
qal wa-ḥomer (lit. "light and heavy"; i.e., *a minori ad maius*): What is true in an instance of lesser importance is surely true in one of more importance.	"Look at the birds of the air; they neither sow nor reap nor gather into barns, and yet your heavenly Father feeds them. Are you not of more value than they?" (Mt 6:26; cf. Lk 12:24; Jn 10:31-38; 2 Cor 3:6-11; Heb 9:13-14).
gezerah šawah (lit. "an equivalent regulation"; i.e., analogy): One passage is explained by another having similar words or phrases.	"Have you never read what David did when he and his companions were hungry and in need of food?" (Mk 2:25). Jesus likened his disciples' actions to that of David and his men (1 Sam 21:6; cf. also Rom 4:3-7; Heb 7:1-28; Jas 2:21-24).
binyan ʾab mikkatub ʾeḥad (lit. "constructing a father [principle] from one passage"; i.e., a standard conclusion based on one passage)	"And as for the dead being raised, have you not read in the book of Moses, in the story about the bush, how God said to him, 'I am the God of Abraham, the God of Isaac, and the God of Jacob'? He is God not of the dead, but of the living: you are quite wrong" (Mk 12:26-27). The Exodus text implies that Abraham will be resurrected. From this one may infer the general resurrection (cf. Jas 5:16-18).
binyan ʾab miššene ketubim (lit. "constructing a father [principle] from two passages")	"Take no gold, or silver, or copper in your belts, no bag for your journey, or two tunics, or sandals, or a staff; for laborers deserve their food" (Mt 10:9-10). This is based upon two passages: Deut 25:4, where oxen should be allowed to eat, and Deut 18:1-8, where priests are allowed to share the sacrifices (cf. 1 Cor 9:9, 13; 1 Tim 5:18).
kelal uperat uperat ukelal (lit. "general and particular, and particular and general")	" 'You shall love the Lord your God. . . . You shall love your neighbor as yourself.' There is no other commandment greater than these" (Mk 12:30-31). These two general laws sum up all the particular laws (cf. Rom 13:9-10).
kayoṣe bo mi-maqom ʾaher (lit. "as going forth to it from another place"; i.e., analogy with another passage)	"Jesus said, 'I am; and "you will see the Son of Man seated at the right hand of the Power," and "coming with the clouds of heaven" ' " (Mk 14:62). Jesus' statement implies that he understood himself to be the one who would sit on a throne before God (Dan 7:9), at God's right hand (Ps 110:1), and come on the clouds and judge his enemies (Dan 7:13-14; cf. Gal 3:8-16; Heb 4:7-9; 8:7-13).
dabar ha-lamed meʿinyano (lit. "word of instruction from context"; i.e., proof from context)	"They said to him, 'Why then did Moses command us to give a certificate of dismissal and to divorce her?' He said to them, 'It was because you were so hardhearted that Moses allowed you to divorce your wives, but from the beginning it was not so. And I say to you, whoever divorces his wife, except for unchastity, and marries another commits adultery' " (Mt 19:7-9). Jesus counters the Mosaic permission to divorce by the original divine intention that marriage be indissoluble as implied in Gen 1:27 and 2:24 (cf. Rom 4:10-11; Heb 11:1-13, 35-40).

context. These seven things did Hillel the Elder expound before the men of Petherah. (*t. Sanh.* 7:11)[17]

Examples of scriptural exegesis employing these hermeneutical principles appear in both haggadic and halakic material in the Mishnah. Rabbi Ishmael (first half of the second century) later expanded these seven principles to thirteen.[18] Interestingly, all seven of Hillel's principles of interpretation may be illustrated in NT literature, especially in the sayings of Jesus.[19] We include table 13.2 illustrating examples from the NT utilizing each of the seven principles. This demonstrates once again the importance of Judaism for understanding Christian exegesis and theology.

There are, however, many passages that are independent of and beyond the purview of the biblical text. The Mishnah displays a certain autonomy with regard to the biblical antecedents. While the Hebrew Bible is often appealed to as proof for an argument, the Mishnaic discussions are not fundamentally exegetical discourses but rather topical or thematic essays and disputations.

Close study of the Mishnaic text demonstrates stylistic differences within the tractates and chapters. These differences reflect the long evolution of halakah deriving from different rabbis at different times. Experts in Mishnaic Hebrew detect the presence of very old traditions, especially in tractates dealing with the temple rituals. Some passages testify to the eyewitness quality of the discussion. Later rabbis, called Amoraim (ca. A.D. 200-500), may now and then indicate that a certain saying was handed down by a *tanna* (a rabbi predating the publication of the Mishnah). Many rulings, particularly those dealing with priestly purity and genealogies, may well derive from priestly circles. Court rulings also seem to have been incorporated into the Mishnah.[20]

Purpose

Since the Mishnah nowhere states its aim, the internal structure and rhetori-

---

[17]Cited from C. K. Barrett, *The New Testament Background: Selected Documents,* rev. ed. (San Francisco: Harper & Row, 1987), p. 185. Barrett in turn uses the text found in J. Jocz, *The Jewish People and Jesus Christ* (London: SPCK, 1962), p. 427.

[18]For the text, see Lawrence H. Schiffman, *Texts and Traditions: A Source Reader for the Study of Second Temple and Rabbinic Judaism* (Hoboken, N.J.: Ktav, 1998), pp. 531-32.

[19]For examples, see Craig A. Evans, *Noncanonical Writings and New Testament Interpretation* (Peabody, Mass.: Hendrickson, 1992), pp. 117-18. See further Richard Longenecker, *Biblical Exegesis in the Apostolic Period* (Grand Rapids, Mich.: Eerdmans, 1975); and J. Julius Scott Jr., *Customs and Controversies: Intertestamental Jewish Background of the New Testament* (Grand Rapids, Mich.: Baker, 1995), pp. 127-33.

[20]The above paragraph is indebted to Urbach, "Mishnah."

cal patterns are all we have to go on. The most obvious response is that the Mishnah is a rulebook, a code of conduct intended to be normative for all Jews. Without doubt it functions as such, and as such it lies at the core of Judaism down to the present time. If one is to understand Judaism, one must have some understanding of the Mishnah.[21]

But more needs to be said than that. Let us review again the main divisions or orders of the Mishnah (see the structural outline above). The overriding issue in "Agriculture" concerns the manner in which Israelites make use of their land and its products in light of the fact that God owns it all. "Appointed Times" deals with the manner in which Israel responds to God's revelation of himself in history through mighty acts and providence. Set times throughout the calendar year commemorate and celebrate these moments of revelation, requiring certain rituals and actions. The "Division of Women" addresses issues relating to the basic sociological unit, the family. How do families reflect God's call to holiness? Of paramount importance are matters concerning women, since they are the "glue" that binds the family unit together. "Damages" addresses the implications of God's demand for equality among all the members of the house of Israel. These are spelled out in the areas of business, government and daily life. "Holy Things" concentrates upon the temple, the place where the holy God of Israel is worshiped in holiness. How is this done correctly? Finally, "Purities" elaborates on the manner in which the sanctification required for worship at the temple is applied and extended to everyday life. How does one maintain cultic purity in the home, in the field, in the marketplace, indeed, in all of life?

Is there an underlying assumption that provides coherence for these six divisions? I think there is. Each division speaks to some aspect of holiness. The demand for holiness from Israel in all of life arises out of the fundamental theological affirmation that the one holy God of the universe has chosen Israel for himself and has defined this relationship by a covenant. This relationship is maintained by obedience to the twofold Torah. "The Mishnah as a whole thus puts forward larger questions: What must a Jew do to reflect the special relationship between self and God? How does one cooperate in God's overall scheme? The answers lead us to the details of rabbinic law, expressed in individual rulings and disputes that make up the Mishnah's bulk.[22]

It is noteworthy that about two-thirds of the Mishnah deals with the temple and its rituals. Remember, this work was not written until about the

---

[21]See further discussion in Neusner, *Misnah: An Introduction,* pp. 37-38.
[22]Brooks, "Mishnah," *ABD* 4:872.

beginning of the third century A.D., so the Second Temple had been in ruins for over a century. This observation is surely significant, beyond the inference that the purity requirements of the Jerusalem temple were now binding on ordinary Jews who wished to be faithful to the twofold Torah of Moses. With its frequent discussions and debates about the temple rituals and worship practices, the Mishnah gives the impression that the temple is still standing, even though there are some explicit references to its destruction. In fact, there is a sort of timelessness in much of the discourse that unfolds in the Mishnah.[23]

What does this all mean? In light of our rehearsal of Jewish history, we recall that Jews were under Roman domination for almost three centuries (63 B.C.-A.D. 200). The destruction of Jerusalem and the Second Temple, followed by the futile revolts during Trajan's and Hadrian's reigns, were some of the darkest moments in Jewish history. Yet we have before us in the Mishnah an undistracted discussion about how Israel should live her life in covenant with the God of the patriarchs and Mount Sinai, with scarcely a concern about what the Romans have done to national and religious life. It is as if none of that had even happened! Do we not have a Jewish response to Roman imperial pretensions? Jewish prayers typically begin with this phrase: "Blessed art Thou, O Lord our God, King of the universe." Caesar, even though he was ignorant of the fact, was a mere subject of this High King of heaven. In the words of Roger Brooks: "Long-standing Roman domination over the Land of Israel conditioned the Mishnah's assertion that God alone rules sovereign over the Land and history. Under Roman imperial rule, the rabbis erected a framework of thought and practice on which to build Judaism's future.[24] And build they did. Today the Roman Empire is but a memory; Judaism, however, lives on as a robust religion and way of life.

Selections from the Mishnah
We include a few passages from the Mishnah in order to illustrate points made in the preceding discussion and to give the reader a feel for the forms and patterns found in it.[25]

---

[23]This is not to say that we agree with Neusner's contention that the Mishnah is an ahistorical or even antihistorical work. See E. P. Sanders's response in *Jewish Law: From Jesus to the Mishnah* (Philadelphia: Fortress, 1990), pp. 310-31; and Evans, *Noncanonical Writings,* pp. 141-43.

[24]"Mishnah," 4:872. He further says, "The Mishnah—and the rabbinic movement for which it serves as constitution—constitute the direct *literary* response to nearly 3 centuries of Roman occupation of the Jews' homeland" (italics his).

[25]Two useful works that help the beginning student get a feel for Mishnah are Barrett, *New Testament Background,* pp. 177-215; and Schiffman, *Texts and Traditions,* pp. 497-557, 671-748.

Mishnah 'Abot 1:1—2:8.

1:1   A. Moses received Torah at Sinai and handed it on to Joshua, Joshua to elders, and elders to prophets.

        B. And prophets handed it on to the men of the great assembly.

        C. They said three things:

           (1) "Be prudent in judgment.

           (2) "Raise up many disciples.

           (3) "Make a fence for the Torah."

1:2 II A. Simeon the Righteous was one of the last survivors of the great assembly.

        B. He would say: "On three things does the world stand:

           (1) "On the Torah,

           (2) "and on the Temple service,

           (3) "and on deeds of loving kindness."

1:3 III A. Antigonos of Sokho received [the Torah] from Simeon the Righteous.

1:4 I   A. Yose b. Yoezer of Seredah and Yose b. Yohanan of Jerusalem received [it] from them.

1:6 II A. Joshua b. Perahiah and Nittai the Arbelite received [it] from them.

1:8 III A. Judah b. Tabbai and Simeon b. Shatah received [it] from them.

1:10 IV A. Shemaiah and Abtalion received [it] from them.

1:12 V A. Hillel and Shammai received [it] from them.

1:16 I A. Rabban Gamaliel says,

           (1) "Set up a master for yourself.

           (2) "Avoid doubt.

           (3) "Don't tithe by too much guesswork."

2:1 I   A. Rabbi says, "What is the straight path which a person should choose for himself? Whatever is an ornament to the one who follows it, and an ornament in the view of others.

    II B. "Be meticulous in a small religious duty as in a large one, for you do not know what sort of reward is coming for any of the various religious duties.

        C. "And reckon with the loss [required] in carrying out a religious duty against the reward for doing it,

        D. "and the reward for committing a transgression against the loss for doing it.

    III E. "And keep your eye on three things, so you will not come into the clutches of transgression:

        F. "Know what is above you:

        G. "(1) An eye which sees, and (2) an ear which hears, and (3) all your actions are written down in a book."

2:8   A. Rabban Yohanan b. Zakkai received [it] from Hillel and Shammai.

        B. He would say, "(1) If you have learned much Torah, (2) do not puff yourself up on that account, (3) for it was for that purpose that you were created."

        C. He had five disciples, and these are they: R. Eliezer b. Hyrcanus, R. Joshua b. Hananiah, R. Yose the priest, R. Simeon b. Netanel, and R. Eleazar b. Arakh.

This passage is not typical of the style and format of most portions of the Mishnah, being a combination of historical narrative and wisdom sayings. We include it because it illustrates the alleged antiquity of the Oral Torah (Moses received it on Sinai) and the unbroken chain of transmission from Moses to the rabbis.[26] The "men of the great assembly" is traditionally equated with a body of 120 prophets and teachers during the time of Ezra (fifth century B.C.). But if Simeon the Just is the same individual who was high priest from 219 to 196 B.C. (cf. Sirach 50:1-21), then the great assembly more likely was a succession of teachers of whom Simeon the Just was the last. Tradition traces the founding of the Sadducees to Antigonos of Sokho. This then brings us to the "pairs" *(zûgôt)*, traditionally understood to be the president and vice president of the Sanhedrin (probably not actually the case but an idealized retrojection by the Tannaim). The "pairs" *(m. 'Abot* 1:4) were teachers and leaders of Pharisaism. Shemaiah and Abtalion most likely were the Pharisaic leaders during the time of Herod the Great, those whom Josephus names as Pollio and Sameas (cf. *Ant.* 9.4 §172; 15.10.4 §370). Hillel and Shammai flourished at the beginning of the Christian era and headed rival schools of Pharisaism. As indicated earlier, the NT probably alludes to one of the many disputes between these schools, the disagreement over what conditions permit a man to divorce his wife (Mt 19:1-12). Some scholars consider Hillel and Shammai to be the last of the Pharisees and their students to be the first of the Tannaim.[27] The NT, on the other hand, clearly identifies Rabban Gamaliel as a Pharisee (Acts 5:34). At any rate, Yohanan ben Zakkai was the one who picked up the pieces after the destruction of Jerusalem and the temple in A.D. 70 and established an academy at Yavneh. Judah the Prince is identified in the passage as simply "Rabbi." Thus the chain of transmission brings us down to the time of Judah the Prince and his contemporaries.

Especially important for grasping the ethos of rabbinic Judaism is the fol-

---

[26]This discussion is indebted to the notations of Barrett, *New Testament Background*, pp. 177-83.

[27]Schiffman, *Texts and Traditions*, p. 498.

lowing statement: "They said three things: 'Be prudent in judgment. Raise up many disciples. Make a fence for the Torah' " (*m. 'Abot* 1:1). The rabbis exercised authority much like the priests and prophets of biblical times. They conducted courts rendering verdicts on a wide range of religious, social and economic issues. The later Jerusalem Talmud ascribes the following saying to Judah the Prince: "the Holy One, blessed be He, left this crown to us that we may invest ourselves therewith" (*y. Demai* 2:1 §22c). Of course, the rabbis did not function as priests performing sacrificial rituals in a temple, nor did they lay claim to direct, divine inspiration for their teachings.[28] Rather, they established academies and circles of disciples in which the Oral Torah was memorized. Future leaders were groomed for their role as guardians of the religious traditions. In this way rabbinic Judaism achieved a uniformity of belief and practice hitherto unrealized in Jewish history.

These traditions functioned in part as a means of ensuring compliance with the written law of Moses, by promulgating other laws (the fence or hedge), laws designed to make even inadvertent transgression of the Written Torah less likely. For example, the third of the Ten Commandments states: "You shall not make wrongful use of the name of the LORD your God, for the LORD will not acquit anyone who misuses his name" (Ex 20:7). The rabbis ruled that one should not even pronounce the sacred name of the Lord, lest inadvertently one should say the name without proper respect or reverence. Only the high priest ever pronounced the Tetragrammaton (the four letters *y*, *h*, *w* and *h*, often vocalized today as Yahweh), and this was only done on the Day of Atonement when he was alone in the holy of holies. To this day observant Jews, when reading the biblical text, substitute Adonai (my Lord) for the sacred name. Texts written by modern, observant Jews display substitutions for the divine name or use abbreviations (such as G-d). Interestingly, the scribes at Qumran used Paleo-Hebrew letters for the personal name of God in one copy of Leviticus (1QpaleoLev [1Q3]). In texts and conversational speech, one reads and hears substitutions such as Hashem (the Name), Hamaqom (the place, i.e., heaven) and Hashamayim (heaven; cf. Lk 15:18).

---

[28]This is a moot point. Since Moses directly received the Written Torah from God on Mount Sinai and the same claim was made for the Oral Torah, it would follow that it too was divinely inspired. This is the view expressed by the Babylonian Talmud and Orthodox Judaism today. On the other hand, nowhere do the rabbis use biblical phraseology such as "Thus says the Lord." Furthermore, the mode of argumentation in the Mishnah highlights contradictions and divergences of opinion among the rabbis on a multitude of issues. These are characteristically harmonized by the latter Gemara (commentary on the Mishnah and included in the Talmuds). See further, Brooks, "Mishnah," 4:871-73.

Even the generic term *Elohim* (God) is pronounced Elokim in synagogue prayers. We could multiply examples, but this demonstrates how the Mosaic law was "fenced." The fence was given equal authority to the pentateuchal legislation by the conviction[29] that Moses also received the "fence" (the Oral Torah) on Mount Sinai and passed it along to Joshua and the elders and so forth.

Mishnah Šabbat 7:1; 23:1-2.

7:1		A.	A general rule did they state concerning the Sabbath:
	I	B.	Whoever forgets the basic principle of the Sabbath and performed many acts of labor on many different Sabbath days is liable only for a single sin offering.
	II	C.	He who knows the principle of the Sabbath and performed many acts of labor on many different Sabbaths is liable for the violation of each and every Sabbath.
	III	D.	He who knows that it is the Sabbath and performed many acts of labor on many different Sabbaths is liable for the violation of each and every generative category of labor.
		E.	He who performs many acts of labor of a single type is liable only for a single sin offering.
7:2		A.	The generative categories of acts of labor [prohibited on the Sabbath] are forty less one:
		B.	(1) he who sows, (2) ploughs, (3) reaps, (4) binds sheaves, (5) threshes, (6) winnows, (7) selects [fit from unfit produce or crops], (8) grinds, (9) sifts, (10) kneads, (11) bakes;
		C.	(12) he who shears wool, (13) washes it, (14) beats it, (15) dyes it;
		D.	(16) spins, (17) weaves,
		E.	(18) makes two loops, (19) weaves two threads, (20) separates two threads;
		F.	(21) ties, (22) unties,
		G.	(23) sews two stitches, (24) tears in order to sew two stitches;
		H.	(25) he who traps a deer, (26) slaughters it, (27) flays it, (28) salts it, (29) cures its hide, (30) scrapes it, and (31) cuts it up;
		I.	(32) he who writes two letters, (33) erases two letters in order to write two letters;
		J.	(34) he who builds, (35) tears down;
		K.	(36) he who puts out a fire, (37) kindles a fire;[30]

---

[29] Of course, modern scholars, not sharing a commitment to Orthodox Judaism, would substitute the word *fiction* here.

[30] In modern Orthodox Judaism, turning an electrical appliance on and off is considered the equivalent of kindling and putting out a fire. For a current illustration of complica-

L. (38) he who hits with a hammer; (39) he who transports an object from one domain to another—

M. lo, these are the forty generative acts of labor less one.

23:1 One may borrow jars of wine and jars of oil from his neighbor on the Sabbath, as long as he does not say, "Lend me." So too, a woman [may borrow] loaves of bread from her neighbor.[31] If [the lender] does not trust [the borrower], [the borrower] may leave his garment with him, and settle the account after the Sabbath. So too, in Jerusalem, when Passover eve is on the Sabbath, one may leave his garment with [the seller of sacrificial animals] and take his Passover lamb, and settle the account after the Festival.

23:2 One may count how many guests and how many delicacies, [only] by mouth, but not from a written document. One may cast lots among his children and the rest of his household for the [food on the] table, but only as long as he has not intended to make larger and smaller portions, for that would be like gambling with dice [on the Sabbath]. In the Temple, lots may be cast for sacrificial meat, but not for other portions.[32]

These two passages demonstrate how rabbis sought to answer questions not raised in the pentateuchal legislation. If one is not to work on sabbath (Ex 16:22-30; 20:8-11), what exactly qualifies as work? Are there any circumstances that qualify the general prohibition? If so, what are they? How may one fulfill the intent of the law and yet carry on with the necessities of life? Casuistry is raised to a fine art in the intricate discussions of the sages.

The Written Torah states that one should not light a fire on sabbath (Ex 35:3). Modern rabbis have ruled that electricity and the internal combustion

---

tions this may entail for observant Jews and how it may be resolved, we include the following story about Joseph Lieberman, the Democratic candidate for Vice President in the 2000 election in the United States: "Sen. Joseph Lieberman's first Friday in the U.S. Senate in 1988 ran late into the night, so he decided to sleep in a cot in his office rather than violate Shabbat and drive home. But his Senate colleague, Al Gore, instead offered his nearby parents' apartment. Lieberman was surprised to find that Gore had arranged for the bathroom lights to be turned on and the bedroom lights turned off. Lieberman later recounted, 'I may have had the most distinguished *Shabbos goy* in history'" (from the Jewish Telegraphic Agency website < http://www.jta.org/ >).

[31] My wife and I were on a trip to the Sinai in 1969 with a group of Israelis that included two observant Jews (*datiyyîm* in Hebrew). On Friday at sundown, we had not yet reached our destination. The two observant Jews decided to get out of the vehicle and walk the remaining distance to camp rather than ride and thus break the sabbath (the engine is a modern extension of lighting a fire on sabbath). The decision, however, was a bit of a dilemma, since they would also have to walk farther than is allowed on the sabbath. Later, when they arrived at our encampment for the night, they could not prepare food since the sabbath had begun. They did, however, just like the woman in the Mishnaic passage, accept food given them by members of our party.

[32] From Schiffman, *Texts and Traditions*, pp. 543-44.

engine are extensions of "lighting a fire." Thus turning electrical switches on or off, operating a motor vehicle or even using the elevator is the equivalent of lighting a fire. Needless to say, this leads to considerable complication for observant Jews. Observant Jewish homes generally have timer switches to help alleviate the difficulty, and meals are cooked ahead of time and nested in pots on the stove to keep them warm. On one occasion, an Orthodox woman whom my wife and I met while studying in Jerusalem invited us to a Shabbat (sabbath) meal. During our delightful visit, the phone rang. Our hostess debated about whether to answer; she didn't, even though the phone rang for what seemed like an interminably long time!

It is easy for Christians to lose patience with this sort of thing and dismiss it as meaningless legalism. But a moment's reflection reminds us that Christians have necessarily engaged in this enterprise as well. For example, have not Christian ethicists extended the NT prohibition against drunkenness (Eph 5:18) to include the use of addictive drugs for pleasure? Is not pornography on the Internet an extension of Jesus' prohibition about lustful thoughts (Mt 5:27-30)? Fundamentalists used to (and some still do) prohibit dancing because of the danger that it might lead to promiscuity, and card playing was banned because of its association with gambling.[33] We could multiply examples.

To be sure, Jesus severely castigated some Pharisees for a system that placed punctilious observance of minute laws above justice, mercy and faith (Mt 23:23), but he also told his disciples to "do whatever they teach you and follow it" (Mt 23:3). Furthermore, Jesus was not the only Jewish teacher who criticized Pharisaic deficiencies. The Essenes denounced the Pharisees more vehemently and with more vitriol than did Jesus, and even in the later Talmud one finds trenchant criticism directed at hypocritical Pharisees (*b. Soṭah* 22b).[34] Nor should we overlook the fact that Jesus gave his followers a code of conduct functioning, in some respects, like a Christian counterpart to halakah. Simply read through the Sermon on the Mount or scan the NT Epistles for proof. Jesus also reminded his disciples to be faithful in the little matters as well as the big (cf. Mt 5:17-20; 25:21, 23).

Strict adherence to a religious code of conduct was not the legalism that Jesus and the apostles resisted. Rather, the problem was relying upon meritorious works either for salvation or the maintenance of one's status among "the elect"

---

[33]Richard Quebedeaux has documented the shift in evangelical opinion on these matters in *The Worldly Evangelicals* (San Francisco: Harper & Row, 1978).

[34]David Flusser helpfully reminds us: "In general, Jesus' polemical sayings against the Pharisees were far meeker than the Essene attacks and not sharper than similar utterances in the talmudic sources. Jesus was sufficiently Pharisaic in general outlook to consider the Pharisees as true heirs and successors of Moses" ("Jesus," *EncJud* 10:10-14).

instead of having faith in God's gracious, saving activity revealed in Jesus Christ (cf. Rom 9:30-33; 14:1–15:6). Paul and James agree that saving faith is a faith that works (Gal 5:6; Eph 2:8-10; Jas 2:14-26). Jesus said, "If you love me, you will keep my commandments [note the plural]" (Jn 14:15; cf. 15:10-11; 1 Jn 5:2).

All of this to say, legalism is not unique to Judaism; it rears its ugly head among religious people of various persuasions. Evangelical Christians do well to remember that their religious tradition has been bedeviled by more than a little legalism. "Those who live in glass houses shouldn't throw stones."

Mishnah Ḥullin 8:1-4. Another example of how the Oral Torah reinterpreted the pentateuchal prohibitions relates to the enigmatic Exodus 23:19b: "You shall not boil a kid in its mother's milk" (cf. Ex 34:26; Deut 14:21). This was taken to be a requirement that meat and milk should be separated and never eaten together. This meaning is not obvious, and the precise meaning is uncertain.[35] Most commentators take it to be a reference to a Canaanite fertility ritual. At any rate, one may see in the following extract how this short text evolved into a rather complicated system.

8:1 A. Every [kind of] flesh [of cattle, wild beast, and fowl] is it prohibited to cook in milk,

B. except for the flesh of fish and locusts.

C. And it is prohibited to serve it up onto the table with cheese,

D. except for the flesh of fish and locusts.

E. He who vows [to abstain] from flesh is permitted [to make use of] the flesh of fish and locusts.

F. "Fowl goes up onto the table with cheese, but it is not eaten," the words of the House of Shammai.

G. And the House of Hillel say, "It does not go up, and it is not eaten."

H. Said R. Yose, "This is one of the lenient rulings of the House of Shammai and the strict rulings of the House of Hillel" [M. Ed. 4:1, 5:2].

I. Concerning what sort of table did they speak?

J. Concerning a table on which one eats. But as to a table on which one lays out cooking, one puts this beside that and does not scruple.

8:2 A. A man ties up meat and cheese in a single cloth,

B. provided that they do not touch one another.

C. Rabban Simeon b. Gamaliel says, "Two guests eat on one table, this one meat, and that one cheese, and they do not scruple."

---

[35]See John I. Durham, "Exodus," in *WBC on CD-ROM* (Logos Library System, version 2.0c, 1995, 1996).

8:3   A. A drop of milk which fell on a piece [of meat], if it is sufficient to impart flavor to that piece [of meat]—it is prohibited.

      B. [If] one stirred the pot, if there is in it sufficient [milk] to impart flavor to that [entire] pot's [contents], it [the contents of the pot] is prohibited.

      C. The udder:

      D. one cuts it open and takes out its milk.

      E. [If] he did not cut it open, he does not transgress on that account.

      F. The heart:

      G. One cuts it open and takes out its blood.

      H. [If] he did not cut it open, he does not transgress on that account.

      I. He who serves up fowl with cheese on the table does not transgress a negative commandment.

8:4   A. (1) The meat of clean cattle with the milk of a clean cattle—

      B. it is prohibited to cook [one with the other] or to derive benefit [therefrom].

      C. (2) The meat of clean cattle with the milk of an unclean cattle, (3) the meat of unclean cattle with the milk of clean cattle—

      D. it is permitted to cook and permitted to derive benefit [therefrom].

      E. R. Aqiba says, "A wild beast and fowl [are] not [prohibited to be mixed with milk] by the Torah.

      F. "For it is said, *You will not seethe a kid in its mother's milk* (Ex. 23:19, 34:26, Dt. 14:21)—three times, [for the purpose of] excluding [from the prohibition of milk and meat] (1) the wild beast, (2) the bird, (3) and unclean cattle [= C]."

      G. R. Yose the Galilean says, "It is said, *You will not eat any sort of carrion* (Dt. 14:21), and it is said, *You will not seethe the kid in its mother's* milk (Dt. 14:21)—

      H. "[The meaning is this:] What is prohibited on the grounds of carrion [also] is prohibited to be cooked in milk.

      I. "Fowl, which is prohibited on the grounds of carrion, is it possible that it is prohibited to be seethed in milk?

      J. "Scripture says, *In its mother's* milk—excluding fowl, the mother of which does not have milk."

Thus an obscure text in the Pentateuch becomes in time an essential plank in the kashrut system (kashrut means "what is suitable or acceptable"). Among other things, keeping kosher involves a complete separation between meat and dairy products. This ruling by the sages requires Jewish households to provide two sets of dishes and cooking ware: one for meat products and one for dairy. For modern, observant Jews, it even necessitates two refrigerators and two dishwashing machines.[36] Furthermore, one may not eat dairy products and meat at the same time. In the Orthodox tradition, up to six hours must pass before one may eat meat after eating a dairy product. The reverse order is less stringent. One may eat a dairy product after eating meat so long as the mouth is rinsed and a piece of bread is eaten first.[37]

Mishnah Qiddušin 1:1-2, 7-8; 2:1.

1:1 I   A.   A woman is acquired [as a wife] in three ways, and acquires [freedom for] herself [to be a free agent] in two ways.

            B.   She is acquired through money, a writ, and sexual intercourse.

            C.   Through money:

            D.   The House of Shammai say, "For a *denar* or what is worth a *denar*.

            E.   And the House of Hillel say, "For a *perutah* or what is worth a *perutah*.[38]

            F.   And how much is a *perutah?*

            G.   One eighth of an Italian *issar.*

            H.   And she acquires herself through a writ of divorce and through the husband's death.

     II   I.   The deceased childless brother's widow is acquired through an act of sexual relations.

            J.   And acquires [freedom for] herself through a rite of *halisah* and through the levir's death.[39]

1:2 III   A.   A Hebrew slave is acquired through money and a writ.

            B.   And he acquires himself through the passage of years, by the Jubilee year, and by deduction from the purchase price [redeeming himself at this outstanding value (Lev. 25:50–51)].

     IV   C.   The Hebrew slave girl has an advantage over him.

            D.   For she acquires herself [in addition] through the appearance of tokens [of puberty].

1:7 I   A.   For every commandment concerning the son to which the father is subject—men are liable, and women are exempt.

     II   B.   And for every commandment concerning the father to which the son is subject, men and women are equally liable.

     III   C.   For every positive commandment dependent upon the time [of

---

[36]Readers who are interested in how Jewish housewives maintain a kosher kitchen will enjoy reading Elizabeth Ehrlich, *Miryam's Kitchen: A Memoir* (New York: Viking, 1997).

[37]See Harry Rabinowicz, "Dietary Laws," *EncJud* 6:40.

[38]Note another dispute between the two branches of Pharisaism dominant between the last half of the first century B.C. and the first half of the first century A.D.

[39]This refers to the practice of Levirate marriage (see Deut 25:5-10).

year], men are liable, and women are exempt.

IV   D. And for every positive commandment not dependent upon the time, men and women are equally liable.

V   E. For every negative commandment, whether dependent upon the time or not dependent upon the time, men and women are equally liable,

F. except for *not marring the corners of the beard, not rounding the corners of the head* (Lev. 19:27), *and not becoming unclean because of the dead* (Lev. 21:1).

1:8   A. [The cultic rites of] laying on of hands, waving, drawing near, taking the handful, burning the incense, breaking the neck of a bird, sprinkling, and receiving [the blood]

B. apply to men and not to women,

C. except in the case of a meal offering of an accused wife and of a Nazirite girl, which they wave.

2:1 I   A. A man effects betrothal on his own or through his agent.

II   B. A woman becomes betrothed on her own or through her agent.

III   C. A man betrothes his daughter when she is a girl on his own or through his agent.

I   D. He who says to a woman, "Be betrothed to me for this date, be betrothed to me with this,"

E. if [either] one of them is of the value of a *perutah,* she is betrothed, and if not, she is not betrothed.

II   F. "By this, and by this, and by this"—

G. if all of them together are worth a *perutah,* she is betrothed, and if not, she is not betrothed.

III   H. [If] she was eating them one by one, she is not betrothed,

I. unless one of them is worth a *perutah.*"

2:2 I   A. "Be betrothed to me for this cup of wine," and it turns out to be honey

II   B. ". . . of honey," and it turns out to be of wine,

III   C. ". . . with this silver *denar,*" and it turns out to be gold,

IV   D. ". . . with this gold one," and it turns out to be silver,

V   E. ". . . on condition that I am rich," and he turns out to be poor,

VI   F. ". . . on condition that I am poor," and he turns out to be rich—

G. she is not betrothed.

H. R. Simeon says, "If he deceived her to [her] advantage, she is betrothed."

2:3 I   A. ". . . on condition that I am a priest," and he turns out to be a Levite,

B. ". . . on condition that I am a Levite," and he turns out to be a priest,

II   C. "... a *Netin*,"[40] and he turns out to be a *mamzer*,[41]

      D. "... a *mamzer*," and he turns out to be a *Netin*,

III   E. "... a town dweller," and he turns out to be a villager,

      F. "... a villager," and he turns out to be a town dweller,

IV   G. "... on condition that my house is near the bath," and it turns out
          to be far away,

      H. "... far," and it turns out to be near:

V   I. "... on condition that I have a daughter or a slave girl who is a
          hairdresser," and he has none,

      J. "... on condition that I have none," and he has one;

VI   K. "... on condition that I have no children," and he has;

      L. "... on condition that he has," and he has none—

      M. in the case of all of them, even though she says, "In my heart I
          wanted to become betrothed to him despite that fact," she is not
          betrothed.

      N. And so is the rule if she deceived him.

The above selections are of interest because they focus on the institution of
marriage and women's rights. Preservation of the Jewish family is a matter of
high priority in the Mishnah, and much space is devoted to discussion of its
many facets. An entire division is devoted to women *(Nashim)*, and tractates in
other divisions also take up issues related to women. For example, one of the
longest and most complex is *Niddah,* dealing with the problems of menstruation,
since this renders the woman ritually unclean for a time, which has important
ramifications for sexual relations between a husband and wife, not to mention
ordinary life in the household. The various Levitical laws concerning sexual
behavior (Lev 18) likewise receive considerable attention in the Mishnah.[42]

Note that women were not allowed full participation in worship. However,
it should also be noted that the ritual practices proscribed here deal with
priestly ritual as found in the Pentateuch (and adapted to the setting of the
Second Temple). How this should be applied in modern Judaism has proven
to be an explosive issue. Can women be rabbis and lead in public worship?
Orthodox Judaism has thus far steadfastly resisted this option, whereas
Reform Judaism ordained its first female rabbi in 1972 and permits full participation of women in worship services.[43] Other groups less liberal in their

---

[40]The man claims he is a citizen or member *(natin)* of the Jewish community. In fact, he is not.

[41]A *mamzer* is someone who is illegitimate.

[42]Attempts by some anti-Semites to use passages dealing with sexual issues in order to ster-
eotype Judaism and Jews generally as sexually depraved are scurrilous and uninformed.
A sad example of such a work is Theodore Winston Pike, *Israel: Our Duty . . . Our
Dilemma* (Oregon City, Ore.: Big Sky Press, 1984).

[43]This liberal movement arose in the nineteenth century and has dominated North Ameri-

theological stance, such as the Conservative and Reconstructionist movements, are of mixed opinion and practice on this issue. The Conservative
movement voted in the early 1980s to ordain women, but the vote was very
close and individual congregations remain divided over this issue. The debate
is sure to intensify in the days ahead.[44]

In *Qiddušin* 1:7-8, the exemptions granted women in regard to certain pentateuchal laws probably come down to practical matters: women must be
allowed to carry on the duties of daily life without undue encumbrance. Thus
the Pentateuch enjoins that all males appear at the sanctuary for the three
annual pilgrimage feasts (Ex 23:17; 34:23), but not females. The care of young
children no doubt was a major factor in this exemption.

As may be seen, women were afforded some protection from unscrupu-
lous suitors. In fact, deception by either the prospective bride or the groom
rendered the betrothal null and void.

One may profitably compare these Mishnaic rulings with the NT. In contrast generally to the role of Jewish women in the home, society and worship,
we detect significant participation on the part of Christian women in the public ministry of Jesus and of the apostles (Mk 15:40-41, 47; 16:1; Lk 8:1-3; Acts
1:14; 2:17; 21:9; Rom 16; 1 Cor 11:4-5; Phil 4:2-3). Some Christian women
hosted the house churches (1 Cor 1:11; Col 4:15), and one reads of women
who held office in the early church and were highly regarded. It is entirely
possible that besides the office of deacon, some women were also designated
as apostles (Rom 16:1-3, 6-7; 1 Tim 3:11). To be sure, a few Jewish women are
mentioned in Diaspora synagogue inscriptions as president or ruler, but these
were exceptional cases rather than the norm.[45] On the other hand, we also
encounter significant prohibitions concerning authoritative teaching and ruling by Christian women in some of Paul's letters (1 Cor 14:33b-36; 1 Tim 2:11-
12).[46] We can say, however, that in general early Christianity stood in some

---

can Judaism. See further David A. Rausch, *Building Bridges* (Chicago: Moody Press, 1988),
pp. 201-8.

[44]The participation of Jewish women in synagogue worship in Orthodox and Conservative congregations is a bitter issue. The novels of Naomi Ragan (*The Sacrifice of
Tamar, Jephthah's Daughter, Sotah*, and *The Ghost of Hannah Mendes*) and her
bimonthly column in the *Jerusalem Post* illuminate the conflict that rages over these
issues. Samuel G. Freedman documents the increased fragmentation within American Judaism in *Jew vs. Jew: The Struggle for the Soul of American Jewry* (New York:
Simon & Schuster, 2000).

[45]See B. Chilton and E. Yamauchi, "Synagogues," *DNTB*, pp. 1145-53, esp. p. 1146.

[46]These texts have generated enormous debate and disagreement, especially in evangelical
circles. To enter into this hermeneutical question takes us too far afield and should be
pursued elsewhere. As a starting point one may profitably consult C. S. Keener, "Man and
Woman," *DPL*, pp. 583-92 and the bibliography cited there.

contrast to rabbinic Judaism with regard to the role and participation of women in the cultic life of their respective communities.[47]

The standards of early Christians were stricter than Judaism in regard to divorce, though Christian women were allowed to separate from their spouses, and perhaps even to divorce them, under certain conditions (1 Cor 7:10-11, 15).[48] Admittedly, the NT, like rabbinic Judaism, envisions the home and family as the proper domain for women (1 Tim 5:9-16; Tit 2:3-5; 1 Pet 3:1-6). In this observation, cultural conditioning must be taken into account. Generally, however, women were more highly regarded in early Christianity than in rabbinic Judaism. Unfortunately, as Craig Keener observes, "Christianity in time began to reflect the more conservative values of the majority culture."[49]

Mishnah Yadayim 1:1-4.

1:1   A. [To render hands clean] a quarter-*log* of water do they pour for hands,
       B. for one,
       C. also for two.
       D. A half-*log* [is to be used] for three or four.
       E. A *log* [is to be used] for five and for ten and for a hundred.
       F. R. Yose says, "And on condition that for the last among them, there should not be less than a quarter-*log*."
       G. They add [to the water used] for the second [pouring], but they do not add [to the water used] for the first [pouring of water over the hands].
1:2   A. With all sorts of utensils do they pour [water] for hands,
       B. even with utensils made of dung, utensils made of stone, utensils made of [unbaked] clay.
       C. They do not pour [water] for hands either with the sides of [broken] utensils, or the bottom of a ladling jar, or with the plug of a barrel.
       D. Nor should a man pour [water] for his fellow with his cupped hands.
       E. For they draw, and they mix [water with the ash of the red cow], and they sprinkle purification water, and they pour [water] for hands only with a utensil.

---

[47]See further D. M. Scholer, "Women," *DJG,* pp. 880-87; Keener, "Man and Woman," pp. 583-92; C. C. Kroeger, "Women in the Early Church," *DLNTD,* pp. 1215-22; and Kroeger, "Women in Greco-Roman World and Judaism," *DNTB,* pp. 1276-80.
[48]See G. F. Hawthorne, "Marriage and Divorce, Adultery and Incest," *DPL,* pp. 594-601; and C. S. Keener, "Marriage, Divorce and Adultery," *DLNTD,* pp. 712-17.
[49]"Woman and Man," *DLNTD,* p. 1214.

      F. And only utensils afford protection with a tightly fitted cover, and nothing affords protection from the power of a clay utensil [in the Tent of a corpse] except utensils.

1:3   A. Water which was unfit for cattle to drink

      B. [When it is located] in utensils, is unfit.

      C. [When it is located] on the ground, it is fit.

      D. [If] there fell into it ink, gum, or copperas, and its color changed, it is unfit.

      E. [If] one did work with it,

      F. or if he soaked his bread in it,

      G. it is unfit.

      H. Simeon of Teman says, "Even if he intended to soak [bread] in this and it fell into the second, it [the second] is fit."

1:4   A. [If] he rinsed utensils in it,

      B. or scrubbed measures in it,

      C. it is unfit.

      D. [If] he rinsed in it vessels which had already been rinsed,

      E. or new [vessels],

      F. it is fit.

      G. R. Yose declares unfit in [the case of rinsing] new [vessels in it].

Regulations similar to the above for the ritual washing of hands and vessels were already in force during NT times. The Gospels include a pericope in which Jesus' laxity with regard to ritual washing becomes a bone of contention with the Pharisees (Mt 15:1-20; Mk 7:1-23; Lk 11:38). John's Gospel, in narrating Jesus' miracle of changing water to wine, mentions that the water was stored in six large jars, each holding some twenty to thirty gallons of water. These stone water jars—stone was less likely to convey impurity than clay—were probably employed for the ritual washing of the guests' hands and perhaps for various vessels used in the preparation of food (Jn 2:6). The minimal amount of water required to ritually wash one's hands according to *Yadayim* is about one third of a cup (a quarter *log*).

Selections from Mishnah Miqwa'ot. In order to get a feel for the kind of discourse found in large tracts of the Mishnah and to appreciate the exactitude and comprehensiveness of rabbinic rulings, we provide the following selections from the tractate *Miqwa'ot,* meaning, "immersion pools."

1:1   A. Six grades in gatherings [of water], this above that, and this above that:

1:4   B. All the same are (1) water of ponds, (2) water of cisterns, (3) water of ditches, (4) water of caverns, (5) water of rain drippings which have stopped, and (6) immersion pools which do not contain forty *seahs:*

C. during the rainy season, all are clean.

D. [When] the rain ends,

E. those that are near the village and the road are unclean.

F. And those that are far are clean,

G. until the larger numbers of people have passed by.

1:5   A. When is their purification?

B. The House of Shammai say, "After they have formed the greater part and overflowed."

C. And the House of Hillel say, "[If] they formed the greater part even though they did not overflow."

D. R. Simeon says, "[If] they overflowed, even though they did not form the greater part."

E. [When purified], they are suitable for *hallah* and for the washing of hands therefrom.

1:6   A. Above them:

II   B. Water of rain drippings which have not ceased.

1:7   A. Above them:

III   B. A pool of water which has forty *seahs,*

C. in which they immerse and dunk.

D. Above them:

IV   E. A spring, whose waters are sparse, and in which drawn water forms the greater part:

F. it is equivalent (1) to the pool,

G. to render clean by standing water;

H. and (2) to a fountain,

I. to dunk in it in any amount [of water] at all.

1:8   A. Above them:

V   B. Smitten [spring] water—

C. which render clean when they are flowing.

D. Above them:

VI   E. Living water—

F. in which [take place] immersion for *Zabim,*

G. and sprinkling for lepers;

H. and which is suitable to mix the purification water.

2:2   A. An immersion pool which was measured and found lacking [forty *seahs]*—

B. all things requiring cleanness which were made depending on it—

C. retroactively—

D. whether in private domain or whether in public domain—

E. are unclean.

F. Under what circumstances?

G. With reference to a major uncleanness.

H. But with reference to a minor uncleanness:

I. for example,

   (1) [if] one ate [a half-loaf of] unclean foods,

   (2) drank [a quarter-*qab* of] unclean liquids,

   (3) one's head and the greater part of one's body came into drawn water,

   (4) or three *logs* of drawn water fell on one's head and the greater part of one's body

J. and he went down to immerse—

K. it is a matter of doubt whether he immersed or did not immerse—

L. and even if he immersed, it is a matter of doubt whether there are forty *seahs* [of rainwater] in it or there are not [forty *seahs*] in it—

M. two immersion pools, in one of which there are forty *seahs*, and in one of which there are not—

N. one immersed in one of them and does not know in which one of them he immersed—

O. his matter of doubt is deemed clean.

P. R. Yose declares unclean.

Q. For R. Yose says, "Everything which is in the assumption of being unclean always remains in its unfitness until it will be known that it has been cleaned.

R. "But its matter of doubt, when it pertains to its becoming unclean and conveying uncleanness, is clean."

3:1 A. R. Yose says, "Two immersion pools which [respectively] do not contain forty *seahs*—

B. "and into this one fell a *log* and a half [of drawn water],

C. "and into that one [fell] a *log* and a half—

D. "and [then] they were mingled together—

E. "are fit,

F. "since the category of unfitness never applied to them.

G. "But: an immersion pool which does not contain forty *seahs* [of fit water]—

H. "and three *logs* of drawn water fell into it—

I. "and it was divided into two [parts]—

J. "is unfit,

K. "since the category of unfitness applied to it."

L. And R. Joshua declares fit.

M. For R. Joshua did say, "Any immersion pool which does not contain forty *seahs* [of fit water], and three *logs* of drawn water fell into it, and it lacks even so little in volume as a *qartob*—

N. "it is fit,

O. "because the [full] three *logs* are lacking in it."

P. And sages say, "It always remains in its unfitness, until there will go forth from it its fullness and more."

3:2   A. How so?

B. The cistern which is in the courtyard—

C. and three *logs* [of drawn water] fell into it—

D. it always remains in its state of unfitness,

E. until there will go forth from it its fullness and more.

F. Or:

G. until one will set up in the courtyard [another pool containing] forty *seahs,*

H. and the upper [water] will be cleaned by the lower one.

I. R. Eleazar b. Azariah declares unfit,

J. unless it ceases.

5:4   A. "All the seas are like an immersion pool, as it is said, *The gathering of the waters he called seas* (Gen. 1:10)," the words of R. Meir.

B. R. Judah says, "The great sea [the Mediterranean] is like an immersion pool. *Seas* is said only of something which contains many kinds of water."

C. R. Yose says, "All the seas purify when they are running [water], but are unfit for *Zabs*, lepers, and for mixing purification water therefrom."

5:5   A. Flowing water is like a spring.

B. And that which drips is like an immersion pool.

C. Testified R. Sadoq concerning flowing water which was more than dripping water [with which it was mixed] that it is fit.

D. "And dripping water which one made into flowing water,

E. "one sticks in even a staff, even a reed,

F. "even a *Zab* and a *Zabah,*

G. "one goes down and dips," the words of R. Judah.

H. R. Yose says, "Anything which receives uncleanness—they do not stop the flow of water therewith."

6:1   A. Any [pool of water] which is mingled with [water of] an immersion pool is [deemed to be as valid] as the immersion pool.

B. Holes of the cave and clefts of the cave—

C. one dunks in them as they are.

D. A pit of the cavern—they do not dunk in it unless it [the hole between the pit and the immersion pool] is as large as the spout of a waterskin.

E. Said R. Judah, "When? At the time that it stands by itself.

F. "But if it does not stand by itself,

G. "they dunk in it just as it is."

6:3   A. Three immersion pools—

B. in this one are twenty *seahs* [of fit water],

C. and in this one are twenty *seahs* [of fit water],

D. and in this one are twenty *seahs* of drawn water—

E. and [the one containing] drawn [water] is at the side—

F. and three people went down and dipped in them,

G. and it [the water in the three pools] was mingled together—

H. the immersion pools are clean.

I. And the people who immersed are clean.

J. [If] the one containing drawn [water] was in the middle,

K. and three people went down and immersed in them,

L. and they were mingled together—

M. the immersion pools are as they were.

N. And those who immersed are as they were.

6:7   A. The intermingling of immersion pools is through a hole the size of the spout of a waterskin,

B. in the thickness and capacity—

C. two fingers turned around in full.

D. [If there is] doubt whether it is the size of the spout of a waterskin or not the size of the spout of a waterskin,

E. it is unfit,

F. because it derives from the Torah.

G. And so:

H. the olive's bulk of a corpse, and the olive's bulk of carrion, and the lentil's bulk of a [dead] creeping thing.

I. Whatever stops up the spout of the waterskin diminishes it.

J. Rabban Simeon b. Gamaliel says, "[If it] is anything whatsoever that lives in the water—it is clean."

7:6   A. An immersion pool which contains exactly forty *seahs*—

B. two people went down and immersed in it, one after the other—

C. the first is clean, and the second is unclean.

D. R. Judah says, "If the feet of the first one were touching the water [as the second immersed], even the second person is clean."

E. [If] one immersed the thick mantle in it and brought it up, and part of it is touching the water,

F. it [the pool still] is clean.

G. The cushion or mattress of leather—

    H. once one has lifted their lips out of the water,
    I. the water in them is deemed drawn water.
    J. What should he do?
    K. He should immerse them and raise them by their bottoms.
8:1 A. The Land of Israel is clean, and its immersion pools are clean.
    B. The immersion pools of the peoples which are [located] outside
       of the Land are fit for those who have had a seminal issue,
    C. even though they have been filled with water from a swape well.
    D. Those which are in the Land of Israel which are outside the town
       gate are fit even for menstruating women.
    E. Those which are inside the town gate are fit for those who have
       had a seminal issue.
    F. And they are unfit for all [other] unclean people.
    G. R. Eleazar says, "Those which are near the town and the road are
       unclean,
    H. "because of laundry.
    I. "And those which are distant are clean."
9:1 A. These interpose on man:
       1. threads of wool,
       2. and threads of flax,
       3. and the ribbons which are on the heads of girls.
    B. R. Judah says, "Those of wool and those of hair do not interpose,
       because the water enters into them."
9:2 A. 4. the matted hair over the heart,
       5. and [on] the beard,
       6. and the woman's privy parts,
       7. the pus outside the eye,
       8. and the hardened pus outside the wound,
       9. and the bandage which is on it,
       10. and dried juice,
       11. and dried clots of excrement which are on his flesh,
       12. and dough which is under the fingernail,
       13. and sweat crumbs,
    B. 14. and miry clay,
       15. and potter's clay,
       16. and road clay.
    C. What is miry clay? This is clay of pits, as it is written, *And he
       brought me up out of a horrible pit, out of the miry clay* (Ps. 40:3).
    D. Potter's clay is in accord with its literal sense.
    E. R. Yose declares clean in the case of potter's [clay], and declares
       unclean in the case of that used for putty.

F. And road clay? The pegs by the roadsides—

G. In which they do not dip and in which they do not dunk.

H. And all other mud—they dunk in it when it is wet.

I. And one should not dip with the dust which is [still] on his feet.

J. And one should not dunk the kettle with soot, unless one scrapes.

9:3 A. These are [things] which do not interpose:

B. 1. the matted hair of the head,

2. and of the armpits,

3. and of the privy parts of a man.

C. R. Eliezer says, "All the same is the man and the woman:

D. "Whatever one takes note of interposes, and whatever one does not take note of does not interpose."

10:2 A. (1) The mattress and (2) the pillow of leather—lo, these require that the water come into them.

B. (1) The round pillow, and (2) the ball, and (3) the shoemaker's last, and (4) the amulet, and (5) the phylactery do not require that the water come into them.

C. This is the general principle: Whatever it is not the way to put in and take out—they immerse sealed up.

10:3 A. These [are objects] which do not require that the water enter into them:

B. 1. the knots of the poor man,

2. and the tassels,

3. and the knotted thong of the sandal,

4. and the phylactery of the head when it is fastened tightly,

5. and that of the arm when it does not move up and down,

6. and the handgrip of a waterskin,

7. and the handgrip of a shepherd's wallet.

10:4 A. These are [objects] which require that the water enter into them:

B. 1. the knot of undergarments which [is tied to] the shoulder,

2. and the hem of sheets (—it is necessary to unstitch—)

3. and the phylactery of the head when it is not fastened tightly,

4. and that of the arm when it moves up and down,

5. and the straps of a sandal.

C. And clothing which one immersed washed—[they must remain in the water merely] until they bulge.

D. If one immersed them dry, [they must remain in the water] until they will bulge and cease from bulging.

A regular feature of Second Temple Judaism, as well as modern Orthodox Judaism, concerns the necessity of immersion in water in order to remove ritual impurity. The origin of ritual immersion goes back to the Pentateuch, where it is enjoined for a variety of reasons: the cleansing of a leprous person (Lev 14); abnormal genital discharges (Lev 15:2-15, 25-30); normal seminal and menstrual discharges (Lev 15:16-24); eating of carcasses (Lev 17:15-16); and contact with a corpse (Num 19:10b-22).[50] In one instance, utensils captured from pagans were immersed before being used (Num 31:21-23). By Second Temple times proselytes to Judaism were also required to immerse themselves as part of the conversion process.[51] In modern Orthodox Judaism, its primary function is for women after their menstrual cycle, which, according to the pentateuchal laws, renders a woman unclean until seven days after her period. However, the many regulations and requirements for valid immersion, as seen in this passage, are later developments of the Oral Torah.[52] Virtually every possible circumstance that might affect the validity of ritual immersion is discussed in this tractate.

Today ritual immersion by Jewish men is generally not part of halakah,[53] although various groups (in particular, Hasidic Jews) continue to practice it as an aid to spirituality, especially before important religious times such as the sabbath and the Day of Atonement. Some Jews still observe the custom of immersing new vessels and utensils obtained from Gentiles.

The actual place of immersion was rigidly defined and called a *miqweh* (lit., "a collection [of water]"). The basic requirements were that it hold forty seahs (approximately 120 gallons), that the person totally immerse and that the water for the *miqweh* be fresh (the Hebrew word for fresh means literally "living"), that is, river, spring or rainwater. The water may not be drawn from a cistern.[54] Beyond this, the person or article to undergo ritual immersion must be clean (physically), with nothing adhering. The water must be allowed to

---

[50]On similar ancient Near Eastern practices, see Raphael Posner, "Ablution," *EncJud* 2:81-86.
[51]There is debate about precisely when proselyte baptism appeared in Judaism. For the two main views, see D. S. Dockery, "Baptism," *DJG*, p. 56.
[52]Once again we suggest that readers who are interested in knowing what it is like for Jewish women living under such a system should read the novels of Naomi Ragan mentioned above in note 44. Also interesting is Freedman's account of Anne Davis's conversion to Judaism, culminating in a threefold immersion in a *mikvah* (the name of the ritual immersion pool for women) (*Jew vs. Jew*, pp. 80-102).
[53]The reason given is because the ashes of the red heifer, indispensable for performing most acts of ritual cleansing, are unavailable. Technically speaking, then, all Jews are in a state of ritual impurity today. See further, Freedman, *Jew vs. Jew*.
[54]For further discussion and photographs of actual immersion pools, see the articles by Hanan Eshel and Eric Meyers in *BAR* 26, no. 4 (2000): 42-49, 61-62. For a technical discussion of the actual construction of a *miqweh*, see David Kotlar, "Mikveh," *EncJud* 11:1534-44.

touch the entire surface of the individual or object (cf. *m. Miqw.* 9:1-3; 10:2-4). *Miqwa'ot* prescribes only one act of immersion in order to effect purity, but it is customary today to perform three.[55]

So what is the relevance of *Miqwa'ot* for the study of the NT? Christian readers will already have thought of baptism. Is Christian baptism connected in any way to the ritual immersion practiced in Second Temple Judaism? We think there is indeed a connection, namely, that the baptism of John the Baptist was an adaptation of Jewish ritual immersion.[56]

The most obvious feature of ritual immersion in Judaism that parallels Christianity is proselyte baptism, in that it is performed only once and symbolizes a new beginning. We have already discussed this to some degree in our treatment of the Dead Sea Scrolls and the community at Qumran. Furthermore, modern NT scholars generally concede, regardless of denominational affiliation, that Christian baptism in NT times was by immersion, as it was and still is in Judaism. Not until the *Didache* (final form of the text ca. A.D. 100-150) do we read about the option of an alternative mode of baptism, namely, affusion, or pouring (*Did.* 7.1-4).

On the other hand, a distinctive of Christian baptism lies in its passive nature in contrast to self-administered baptism in Judaism, and its rationale and christological basis. In Romans 6 Paul argues that Christian baptism identifies the believer with the death, burial and resurrection of Jesus Christ. Thus its passive nature functions as an initiation rite into the new-covenant people of God. Baptism in a Christian context symbolizes union with Christ or, in other terms, a transfer from the old Adam into the new Adam.[57] This obviously, has no counterpart in Judaism.

But does the NT incorporate the notion of ritual impurity? One's answer must be carefully nuanced. What we can say is that the NT spiritualizes the concept of ritual impurity. Paul's letters give evidence that he resisted any imposition of the purity laws of first-century Pharisaism upon his Gentile converts. At the same time, he clearly stressed the ideal of both personal and corporate purity, now recast in moral and ethical terms.[58] Jewish Christians could, according to Paul, continue to observe the laws of ritual purity if they

---

[55]See also note 52.

[56]James D. G. Dunn puts it this way: "John's baptism itself is probably best understood as an adaptation of Jewish ritual washings, with some influence from Qumran in particular" ("Baptism," *NBD*, p. 122).

[57]See G. R. Beasley-Murray, "Baptism," *DPL*, pp. 60-66.

[58]See further Mark Reasoner, "Purity and Impurity," *DPL*, pp. 775-76. As a nice example of Paul's spiritual adaptation of halakic purity, see his pastoral directives and exhortation in 1 Cor 5:1-8. B. D. Chilton observes: "Early Christianity saw a shift in the understanding of the medium of impurity: no longer foods but moral intentions conveyed the danger of defilement" ("Purity," *DNTB*, p. 881).

Table 13.3. A sampling of points of contact between the Mishnah and the New Testament

Mishnah	NT
Criminal law, capital punishment, false witnesses, blasphemy (*m. Sanh.* 6:4; 7:5)	Throws light on the high priest's accusation of blasphemy (Mk 14:53-65). Jesus may have actually used the divine name Yahweh in his allusion to Dan 7:13-14 before the high priest Caiaphas. Also helps us understand why Jesus' body was not allowed to hang on the cross overnight (cf. Deut 21:23).
Ritual purity and sabbath laws dealing with (1) association with "sinners" (*m. Demai* 2:3); (2) fasting regulations (*m. ʾAbot* 1:2; 2:9); (3) types of work forbidden on sabbath (*m. Šabb.* 7:2, 4; 16:2; *m. Maʿaś.* 4:5; *m. Beṣah; m. Yoma* 5:2; 8:6); (4) things forbidden on sabbath (*m. Šabb.* 14:3-4; 19:1; *m. ʿErub.* 4:3; 10:13-14; *m. Yoma* 8:6-7; *m. Beṣah* 5:2; *m. Roš Haš.* 2:5; *m. ʿEd.* 2:5); (5) washing hands before eating (*m. Ber.* 1:1; 8:2; *m. Pesaḥ.* 5:5; *m. Yad.* 1:1-5; 2:2-3)	Demonstrates that the various criticisms leveled at Jesus and his disciples in the Gospels did indeed run counter to Mishnaic halakah: (1) association with "sinners," (Mk 2:15-17); (2) failing to fast (Mk 2:18-20); (3) gleaning on sabbath (Mk 2:23-27), (4) healing on sabbath (Mk 3:1-6); (5) eating with unwashed hands (Mk 7:1-13).
Passages in the Tosefta detail the shortcomings and vices of the last two generations of ruling priests in Jerusalem (*t. Menaḥ.* 13:18-22; cf. *t. Zebaḥ.* 11:16-17) and explain why the temple was destroyed, namely, the graft and violence of the ruling priests.	The Gospel narratives underscore the venality and violence of the priestly family. Jesus' cleansing of the temple, his prediction about its destruction, and his arrest and treatment by the high priest at his trial now come into clearer focus against the backdrop of the information provided by the Tosefta and later rabbinic writings and supplemented by Josephus. See Mk 11:15-17; 14:10-11, 43, 53-65. Cf. Mt 17:24-27 (implicit criticism of priestly handling of funds); Mk 12:1-12 (criticism of behavior and attitudes of priests and their scribes); Mk 13:1-2 (prediction of the temple's destruction).

so wished (cf. Rom 14:1-8), provided these rituals were not viewed as necessary to salvation and holy living (as Paul argues in Galatians). Gentile Christians, according to Paul and the majority at the Jerusalem Council (Acts 15), were not obligated to observe the ritual purity laws as a precondition for admission to the early Christian churches. They were, however, urged to be sensitive to Jewish-Christian sensibilities regarding this issue and by no means to act in such a way as to create a stumbling block.[59]

---

[59]For further discussion, see Reasoner, "Purity and Impurity"; M. B. Thompson, "Strong and Weak," *DPL*, pp. 916-18; Thompson, "Stumbling Block," *DPL*, pp. 918-19; Chilton, "Purity," pp. 874-82.

Summary

We have barely scratched the surface. The Mishnah is such an extensive corpus and there are so many passages that have possible relevance for interpreting the NT that we can only suggest in broad strokes some points of contact. In table 13.2 we give a few examples of the relevance of the Mishnah for the historical background of the NT.[60]

As to parallels between the specific teachings of Jesus and rabbinic sayings found in the Mishnah, the number is so great we would unnecessarily lengthen our discussion if we went into them. We simply recommend some specialized works that one may consult for particulars.[61] We offer only this word of counsel. Beware of falling into the extreme position of Joseph Klausner, who said: "Without any exception he [Jesus] is wholly explainable by the scriptural and Pharisaic Judaism of his time.[62] Better is the sage observation of Robert H. Stein:

> To say that there is nothing unique about a gold crown because that same gold is also found in a nearby mountain is to lose sight of the fact that in the mountain the gold is scattered and covered with dirt, rock, and vegetation. Certainly knowing where to find that gold, removing it from the dirt, rock, and vegetation, and then shaping it into a work of art require genius. In the similar way, Jesus showed his originality by his selection of what was essential and what was not from the mountain of commandments present in his day.[63]

For Further Discussion

1. What is the Mishnah, and what is its purpose?

2. How is the Mishnah arranged? How would you describe its characteristics?

3. Why did Jews feel a need for the Mishnah? Do Christians have a similar need?

4. Compare and contrast the Jewish mode of applying pentateuchal laws

---

[60]I am indebted to Evans, *Noncanonical Writings*, pp. 120-25, 139-41, for these examples.

[61]See the indices in such works as Bruce Chilton and Jacob Neusner, *Judaism in the New Testament: Practices and Beliefs* (New York: Routledge, 1995); David Daube, *The New Testament and Rabbinic Judaism* (Peabody, Mass.: Hendrickson, n.d. [1956]); Alfred Edersheim, *The Life and Times of Jesus the Messiah*, 2 vols. (New York; Longmans & Green, 1910); John Lightfoot, *Horae hebraicae et talmudicae: Hebrew and Talmudical Exercitations upon the Gospels, the Acts, Some Chapters of St. Paul's Epistle to the Romans, and the First Epistle to the Corinthians*, ed. Robert Gandell, 4 vols. (Grand Rapids, Mich.: Baker, 1979 [1859]); and Brad H. Young, *Jesus the Jewish Theologian* (Peabody, Mass.: Hendrickson, 1995). For those who can read German, there is the classic work of Hermann L. Strack and Paul Billerbeck, *Kommentar zum Neuen Testament aus Talmud und Midrasch*, 6 vols. (Munich: C. H. Beck, 1922-1961).

[62]*Jesus of Nazareth: His Life, Times, and Teaching* trans. Herbert Danby (New York: Macmillan, 1926), p. 414.

[63]*The Method and Message of Jesus' Teachings* (Philadelphia: Westminster Press, 1978), p. 110.

(especially Levitical purity laws) to post-Second Temple times with Christian application of Scripture to the contemporary world.

5. How is the Sermon on the Mount similar to halakah? How is it different?

6. Compare and contrast the status and role of women in the Mishnah and the NT.

7. Compare and contrast the Jewish idea of ritual immersion with the Christian concept of water baptism.

For Further Reading

Texts and Translations

C. K. Barrett, *The New Testament Background: Selected Documents,* rev. ed. (San Francisco: Harper & Row, 1987), pp. 177-215.

Philip Blackman, *Mishnayoth,* 2d ed., 7 vols. (New York: Judaica, 1964).

Herbert Danby, *The Mishnah* (Oxford: Oxford University Press, 1933).

Jacob Neusner, *The Mishnah: A New Translation* (New Haven, Conn.: Yale University Press, 1988).

Lawrence H. Schiffman, *Texts and Traditions: A Source Reader for the Study of Second Temple and Rabbinic Judaism* (Hoboken, N.J.: Ktav, 1998), pp. 497-557, 682-732.

Secondary Literature

Roger Brooks, "Mishnah," *ABD* 4:871-73.

Alfred Edersheim, *The Life and Times of Jesus the Messiah,* 2 vols. (New York; Longmans & Green, 1910). This work, by a Jewish-Christian scholar, is dated but still a helpful study in which there is constant reference to rabbinic sources as these throw light on Jesus' life and teachings.

Craig A. Evans, *Noncanonical Writings and New Testament Interpretation* (Peabody, Mass.: Hendrickson, 1992), pp. 114-22.

Charles R. Gianotti, *The New Testament and the Mishnah: A Cross-Reference Index* (Grand Rapids, Mich.: Baker, 1983).

John Lightfoot, *Horae hebraicae et talmudicae: Hebrew and Talmudical Exercitations upon the Gospels, the Acts, Some Chapters of St. Paul's Epistle to the Romans, and the First Epistle to the Corinthians,* ed. Robert Gandell, 4 vols. (Grand Rapids, Mich.: Baker, 1979 [1859]). An older work by a Christian scholar with a good working knowledge of rabbinic literature. It does, however, manifest here and there a less than desirable view of Jews and Judaism.

Jacob Neusner, *The Mishnah: An Introduction* (Northvale, N.J.: Jason Aronson, 1989).

————, "Rabbinic Literature: Mishnah and Tosefta," *DLNTD,* pp. 893-97.

Shmuel Safrai, ed., *The Literature of the Sages: Part 1: Oral Tora, Halakha, Mishna, Tosefta Talmud, External Tractates,* CRINT 2.3a (Assen: Van Gorcum; Philadelphia: Fortress, 1987).

Ephraim Elimelech Uhrbach, "Mishnah," *EncJud* 12:93-109.

Fourteen

The Partings of the Ways

*F*or the apostolic fathers we have used the edition by J. B. Lightfoot and J. R. Harmer, edited and revised by Michael W. Holmes, The Apostolic Fathers, 2d ed. (Grand Rapids, Mich.: Baker, 1992). One may also find the relevant texts in Alexander Roberts and James Donaldson, eds., The Ante-Nicene Fathers, 10 vols. (Grand Rapids, Mich.: Eerdmans, 1979); R. M. Grant, ed., The Apostolic Fathers: A New Translation and Commentary, 6 vols. (New York: Nelson, 1964-1968); C. C. Richardson, ed., Early Christian Fathers (New York: Macmillan, 1970 [1953]); and, with Greek text and facing English translation, K. Lake, ed. and trans., Apostolic Fathers, 2 vols., LCL (Cambridge, Mass.: Harvard University Press, 1912-1913). For texts from rabbinic Judaism we have made use of Lawrence H. Schiffman, Texts and Traditions: A Source Reader for the Study of Second Temple and Rabbinic Judaism (Hoboken, N.J.: Ktav, 1998).

We conclude our survey of the Jewish literature of the Second Temple on a sad note—the partings of the ways for the two surviving daughters of Second Temple Judaism. Only two Jewish sects really survived the collapse of the Second Temple: Pharisaism, which lived on in the modified form of rabbinic Judaism; and, of course, the Jesus movement, whose adherents were known variously as "the Way" (Acts 9:2; 19:9, 23; 22:4), "the sect of the Nazarenes" (Acts 24:5) and, later, "Christians" (Acts 11:26). These two monotheistic faiths competed for the designation of "the true Israel." Increasingly, the competition became bitter and hostile. When and under what circumstances did these two branches of the same root finally and mutually cut each other off from the tree called "Israel"? To change the analogy, what factors led at last to the partings of ways? A sampling of the apostolic church fathers and early rabbinical literature documents the mutual separation. Tragically, anti-Judaic attitudes steadily gained a foothold in Christian theology and continue to poison Christian-Jewish relationships.[1]

Introduction

As noted in our discussion of the Bar Kokhba revolt, antagonism between Christians and Jews became intense during this period. We have already mentioned the sporadic conflict between the two communities as witnessed by NT literature. As our point of departure, we contrast the attitude of the apostle Paul toward the Jewish people, in his magisterial letter to the Romans, to the sentiments about Jews found in the writings of the apostolic fathers. Clearly something happened to poison the well. The animosity ran both ways, of course, as we demonstrate from rabbinic sources.

We accept the view of Romans that sees several missionary-pastoral purposes behind its composition.[2] One of those was to help mend a growing rift between the Jewish Christian and Gentile Christian segments of the Roman church. This rift probably had its genesis in Claudius's decree to expel all Jews from Rome in A.D. 49 and was exacerbated by anti-Jewish sentiment in Roman society generally.[3] Whereas Paul forcefully defends his gospel against Judaism and Judaizers, he also directs remarks to Gentile Christians who seem disparaging and critical in their attitude toward Jewish Christians. Thus Paul wages a battle on at least two fronts in Romans.

One cannot sympathetically read Romans without sensing Paul's deep distress over his fellow Jews' rejection, for the most part, of the gospel of God concerning his son Jesus Christ (Rom 9:1-2). Paul was willing to suffer a divine curse if that would bring about an acceptance of Jesus as Messiah by the majority of Jews in his day (Rom 9:3; 10:1; cf. Ex 32:32). The theological question uppermost in Paul's mind in Romans 9—11 is, Can God be trusted? That is, having shown that God's saving activity revealed in Christ is available and unassailable (Rom 1—8), Paul must answer the question: Then why have

---

[1]See C. A. Evans, "Christianity and Judaism: Partings of the Ways," *DLNTD,* pp. 159-70.
[2]For a succinct statement of the issue, see James D. G. Dunn, "Romans, Letter to the," *DPL,* pp. 839-41.
[3]Ibid., pp. 838-39. According to Jerome Murphy-O'Connor, the decree of expulsion most likely affected only one synagogue (*Paul: A Critical Life* [Oxford: Oxford University Press, 1997], pp. 10-15, 333), but his view is based on nothing more than intuition.

not most Jews, the chosen people of God, responded to the gospel? If they have missed out, how can Gentile Christians be so sure that nothing "will be able to separate" *them* "from the love of God in Christ Jesus" (Rom 8:39)? His answer is crystal clear: "the gifts and the calling of God are irrevocable" (Rom 11:29). There has always been a believing remnant, a true Israel within the larger, empirical Israel. Furthermore, at the eschaton (the end of the present world order), all empirical Israel will be saved (Rom 11:26). Thus God may indeed be trusted because his saving plan has never failed nor will it ever.

Not to be missed in Paul's theological reflection upon the problem of Israel is his pastoral admonition to Gentile Christians (Rom 11:13). They must not adopt a haughty, superior attitude toward the people called Israel. On the contrary, they should remember that one's continuance in the true Israel (now consisting of both Jews and Gentiles on the same footing; cf. Eph 2:11-22) is conditioned upon faith in God's gracious promises ("you stand only through faith" [Rom 11:20]). Rather than indulge in self-congratulation, Gentile believers should "not become proud, but stand in awe" (Rom 11:20) and see to it that they continue in God's kindness (Rom 11:22). Furthermore, Gentile Christians need to be reminded that they have been incorporated into Israel, not the other way around. In Paul's famous analogy, Gentiles are wild olive branches that have been grafted into the natural olive tree, which is Israel (Rom 11:17-24). Gentiles should remember that "it is not you that support the root, but the root that supports you" (Rom 11:18). This brings into focus Paul's earlier comments on the advantages of the Jewish people (Rom 3:1-2; 9:4-5). The bottom line of Paul's argument appears to be this: Gentile Christians are deeply indebted to the Jewish people for the role they have played in salvation history. Furthermore, the drama of salvation history is not yet finished. Paul's ultimate optimism about Israel shines forth in the conclusion of Romans 11. Precisely when and how all this will happen is a "mystery" (Rom 11:25). What is certain is that it all will redound to God's glory in the end (Rom 11:36).

From Paul's remarks in Romans, we may safely infer that, were he to write an essay on how Christians should relate to Jews, it would be much more positive and affirming than Christian attitudes in general toward Jews have been down through the centuries. Paul does not write off, curse, castigate or vilify Jews. Nor is it possible to use him as support for doing so, even in the face of 1 Thessalonians 2:14-16, a text referring only to a limited number of Jewish religious leaders and opponents of Paul. While this is a hotly debated subject among NT scholars, I do not think the NT is anti-Semitic or anti-Judaic.[4] That is a post-NT phenomenon to which we now turn.

---

[4]For responses to the charge that the NT is anti-Semitic, see Graham Keith, *Hated Without A Cause? A Survey of Anti-Semitism* (London: Paternoster, 1997), chaps. 2-4; and Craig A.

Anti-Judaism in the Early Church

When we turn to the writings of the apostolic fathers, we sense that attitudes toward the Jewish people have changed, and that for the worse.[5] We preface our brief selections from these fathers by this general observation. During the latter part of the first century A.D. and throughout the second century A.D., church and synagogue often competed for converts from the pagan world and for recognition by the governing powers. As each movement defined more closely the parameters for who was "in" and who was "out," it was only natural that some hostility should arise. After all, they offered differing definitions of the true Israel. This hostility was abetted by long-standing anti-Judaic attitudes in the Greco-Roman world. Gentiles who converted to Christianity no doubt brought some of this baggage with them. Disappointingly, we see evidence of this cropping up in Christian writings after the NT era.

The Epistle of Barnabas

Our first selection dates to either the end of the first or the beginning of the second century A.D. The author is unknown, certainly not the Barnabas who accompanied the apostle Paul on his first missionary journey (Acts 13–14). The most likely place of composition is in Alexandria, Egypt, and the intended audience, Gentile Christians.[6] The work is a polemical essay of sorts that addresses two important questions for the nascent church: How should Christians interpret the Jewish Scriptures, and what relationship does Christianity have to Judaism? The author basically adopts the allegorical method with which we gained some familiarity in our earlier study of Philo. Thus at the same time the Tannaim were hammering out their understanding of what was canonical for Judaism, Christians were grappling with analogous questions. Here are a few excerpts from *Barnabas*.

> Moreover, I also ask you this, as one who is one of you and who in a special way loves all of you more than my own soul: be on your guard now, and do not be like certain people; that is, do not continue to pile up your sins while claiming that your covenant is irrevocably yours, because in fact those people lost it completely in the following way, when Moses had just received it. . . . But by turning to idols they lost it . . . and their covenant was broken in pieces, in order that the covenant of the beloved Jesus might be sealed in our heart, in hope inspired by faith in him. (*Barn.* 4.6, 8)

Evans and Donald A. Hagner, eds., *Anti-Semitism and Early Christianity* (Philadelphia: Fortress, 1993).
[5]For a survey of this literature, see Donald A. Hagner, "Apostolic Fathers," *DLNTD*, pp. 82-91.
[6]For particulars, see J. B. Lightfoot and J. R. Harmer, eds., *The Apostolic Fathers*, ed. and rev. Michael W. Holmes, 2d ed. (Grand Rapids, Mich.: Baker, 1992), pp. 271-72; and Holmes, "Barnabas, Epistle of," *DLNTD*, pp. 125-29.

Moreover, consider this as well, my brothers: when you see that after such extraordinary signs and wonders were done in Israel, even then they were abandoned. (*Barn.* 4.14).

Now let us see whether this people [the church] or the former people [the Jews] is the heir, and whether the covenant is for us or for them. (*Barn.* 13.1; two biblical passages, Rebecca consulting the Lord about the twins jostling in her womb [Gen 25:21-23] and the reversal of blessing by Jacob over Manasseh and Ephraim [Gen 48:8-20], are cited and interpreted allegorically)

Observe how by these means he has ordained that this people [the church] should be first, and heir of the covenant. (*Barn.* 13.6)

In the allegorical interpretation of *Barnabas,* the elder sons (Esau and Manasseh) represent Judaism, and the younger sons (Jacob and Ephraim) represent Christianity. Note the different spirit manifested from Paul's discussion in Romans 9—11. Our author here denies any continuing covenantal relationship between God and Israel. Paul, on the other hand, asks: "Have they stumbled so as to fall?" His answer is emphatic: "By no means!" (Rom 11:11). "As regards the gospel they are enemies of God for your sake; but as regards election they are beloved, for the sake of their ancestors; for the gifts and the calling of God are irrevocable" (Rom 11:28-29). *Barnabas* already displays a leading motif of post-NT Christian theology, namely, that Christians have displaced Jews as the true Israel. This displacement view, also designated supersessionism or triumphalism, affirms that the church inherits the blessings of the covenant, whereas Jews receive its curses because of their rejection of Jesus. Such defective theology would have drastic and tragic consequences for Christian-Jewish relations in succeeding centuries.

Another passage from *Barnabas* highlights an emerging Christian response to Jews and Judaism:

Finally, I will also speak to you about the temple, and how those wretched men went astray and set their hope on the building, as though it were God's house, and not on their God who created them. For they, almost like the heathen, consecrated him by means of the temple. . . . Furthermore, again he says: "Behold, those who tore down this temple will build it themselves." This is happening now. For because they went to war, it was torn down by their enemies, and now the very servants of their enemies will rebuild it. Again, it was revealed that the city and the temple and the people of Israel were destined to be handed over. . . . And it happened just as the Lord said.

But let us inquire whether there is in fact a temple of God. There is—where he himself says he is building and completing it! . . . This is the spiritual temple that is being built for the Lord. (*Barn.* 16.1-10).

The language with which *Barnabas* describes the Second Temple and the

Jews who worshiped there, although echoing some sayings of Jesus (cf. Mt 21:41-44) and developing ideas found in Paul (Rom 12:1; 1 Cor 3:16; 6:19; Eph 2:21), Hebrews (Heb 13:10, 15) and 1 Peter (1 Pet 2:4-9), has a decidedly sharper edge to it than the NT. We should also note that *Barnabas* was clearly written after the destruction of the Second Temple, and it shows how Christians used that tragedy in a polemical fashion. That is, the destruction confirms God's judgment upon Jews for rejecting Jesus.

Ignatius of Antioch

Ignatius, bishop of Antioch in Syria, wrote seven letters to various churches on his way to Rome as a prisoner. Most scholars place the composition of these letters, reminiscent of Paul's letters, in the period of Trajan's reign (A.D. 98-117).[7] Two of the letters refer to Judaism in a very negative way.

> Do not be deceived by strange doctrines or antiquated myths, since they are worthless. For if we continue to live in accordance with Judaism, we admit that we have not received grace. For the most godly prophets lived in accordance with Christ Jesus. This is why they were persecuted, being inspired as they were by his grace in order that those who are disobedient might be fully convinced that there is one God who revealed himself through Jesus Christ his Son. (Ign. *Magn.* 8.1-2).
>
> If, then, those who had lived in antiquated practices came to newness of hope, no longer keeping the Sabbath but living in accordance with the Lord's day . . . how can we possibly live without him, whom even the prophets, who were his disciples in the Spirit, were expecting as their teacher? (Ign. *Magn.* 9.1-2)
>
> It is utterly absurd to profess Jesus Christ and to practice Judaism. For Christianity did not believe in Judaism, but Judaism in Christianity, in which "every tongue" believed and "was brought together" to God. (Ign. *Magn.* 10.3)
>
> But if anyone expounds Judaism to you, do not listen to him. For it is better to hear about Christianity from a man who is circumcised than about Judaism from one who is not. But if either of them fail to speak about Jesus Christ, I look upon them as tombstones and graves of the dead, upon which only the names of men are inscribed. (Ign. *Phld.* 6.1)

The above extracts reflect an utter rejection of Judaism and Judaizers. One may infer that Jewish Christianity and Judaizing tendencies posed a real threat to the Syrian churches. The "otherness" with which Ignatius characterizes Judaism strikes a quite different note from the apostle Paul, with whom, ironically, Ignatius so much identifies. To Ignatius it is self-evident that the OT prophets had an understanding of Jesus Christ; indeed, they were his disciples even before his incarnation.

---

[7]See further M. W. Holmes, "Ignatius of Antioch," *DLNTD,* pp. 530-33.

The Didache

The *Didache*, an abbreviated title for a work known as *The Teaching of the Lord to the Gentiles by the Twelve Apostles,* is an early Christian manual of church order, thought to have reached its final, written form sometime between A.D. 100 and 150.[8] There is one passage that is relevant to our discussion:

> But do not let your fasts coincide with those of the hypocrites. They fast on Monday and Thursday, so you must fast on Wednesday and Friday. Nor should you pray like the hypocrites. Instead, "pray like this," just as the Lord commanded in his Gospel [the Lord's Prayer, following the form in Mt 6:9-13, is then quoted]. . . . Pray like this three times a day. (*Did.* 8.1-2)

Since Jews fasted on Monday and Thursday, continuing the practice of the Pharisees (*b. Taʿan.* 12a; *t. Taʿan.* 2:4), there can be little doubt that the "hypocrites" are understood as Jews or Judaizing Christians. To be sure, the *Didache* is simply following Matthean wording here, which in its own context was referring to a subset of Pharisees. Still, it is hard not to conclude that for the *Didache* the "hypocrites" are all Jews and those who adopt their customs. On the other hand, note that the Lord's Prayer was to be recited three times a day, a practice that seems to reflect the long-standing Jewish pattern of thrice daily prayers. We see a tension here between wanting to distinguish Christian from Jewish piety and yet the obvious indebtedness of Christian worship to its Jewish roots.

The Epistle to Diognetus

This work, really more of a tract than a letter, was addressed to nonbelievers and sought to answer various calumnies hurled at the early Christians. Even though in Lightfoot's opinion this work was "the noblest of early Christian writings,"[9] it unfortunately contains a very negative evaluation of Judaism. The author, date and location of the piece are all uncertain. Most would date it sometime between 150 and 225.[10] Sections three and four are the relevant passages.

> And next I suppose that you are especially anxious to hear why Christians do not worship in the same way as the Jews. The Jews indeed, insofar as they abstain from the kind of worship described above [pagans], rightly claim to worship the one God of the universe and to think of him as Master; but insofar as they offer this worship to him in the same way as those already described, they are altogether mistaken. For whereas the Greeks provide an example of their

---

[8]See M. W. Holmes, "Didache, The," *DLNTD,* pp. 300-302.
[9]Cited by Holmes in Lightfoot and Harmer, *Apostolic Fathers,* p. 529.
[10]See Lightfoot and Harmer, *Apostolic Fathers,* pp. 529-33; and T. H. Olbricht, "Apostolic Fathers," *DNTB,* p. 85.

stupidity by offering things to senseless and deaf images, the Jews, thinking that they are offering these things to God as if he were in need of them, could rightly consider it folly rather than worship. For he who made the heaven and the earth and all that is in them, and provides us all with what we need, cannot himself need any of the things that he himself provides to those who imagine that they are offering sacrifices to him by means of blood and fat and whole burnt offerings, and are honoring him with these tokens of respect do not seem to me to be the least bit different from those who show the same respect to deaf images; the latter make offerings to things unable to receive the honor, while the former think they offer it to the One who is in need of nothing.

But with regard to their qualms about meats, and superstition concerning the Sabbath, and pride in circumcision, and hypocrisy about fasting and new moons, I doubt that you need to learn from me that they are ridiculous and not worth discussing. For is it not unlawful to accept some of the things created by God for human use as created good but to refuse others as useless and superfluous? And is it not impious to slander God as though he forbids us to do any good thing on the Sabbath day? And is it not also ridiculous to take pride in the mutilation of the flesh as a sign of election, as though they were especially beloved by God because of this? And as for the way they watch the stars and the moon, so as to observe months and days, and to make distinctions between the changing seasons ordained by God, making some into feasts and others into times of mourning according to their own inclinations, who would regard this as an example of godliness and not much more of a lack of understanding? So then, I think you have been sufficiently instructed to realize that the Christians are right to keep their distance from the thoughtlessness and deceptions common to both groups and from the fussiness and pride of the Jews. But as for the mystery of the Christian's own religion, do not expect to be able to learn this from man. (*Diogn.* 3–4)

Our anonymous author obviously has little appreciation for Judaism, as he perceived it, and no acknowledgment of Christian indebtedness to Judaism. The only positive thing he can mention is that they are not as ignorant as the pagans. Especially puzzling is his assumption that Jews still sacrifice animals in their religious practices. This had not been the case since A.D. 70. His objections to dietary scruples and abhorrence of circumcision ("the mutilation of the flesh") reflect long-standing Gentile prejudices against Jews. Our author has no regard for any spiritual, ethical values that may have been involved in these ceremonies, nor does he even see any typological significance in them. We are, unfortunately, seeing the results of a Gentilization of the church.

Justin Martyr

Justin, a Gentile born in the pagan city of Neapolis, modern Nablus in the West Bank of Palestine, lived during the first half of the second century (c.

A.D. 100-165). One of his works, *Dialogue with Trypho,* purports to be a dialogue with a famous Mishnaic sage who escaped during the Bar Kokhba revolt and encountered Justin at Ephesus. Traditionally, Trypho has been equated with Rabbi Tarfon. This identification, however, seems improbable, since Tarfon is said to have served as a priest at Jerusalem before its destruction in A.D. 70. This would make him much too old to have debated Justin in about A.D. 135.[11] Most scholars accept that Trypho is a fictional character created to suit Justin's literary purpose. We select a few passages that reflect the growing hostility between Christians and Jews.

> Trypho then said . . . "Prove to us that Jesus Christ is the one about whom these prophecies were spoken."
>
> "At the proper time," I replied, "I will supply the proofs you wish, but for the present permit me to quote the following prophecies to show that the Holy Spirit by parable called Christ God, and Lord of hosts and of Jacob. God Himself calls your interpreters stupid (Jer. 4:22) because they claim that these prophecies were not spoken of Christ, but of Solomon. . . ."
>
> "It would be better for us," Trypho concluded, "to have obeyed our teachers who warned us not to listen to you Christians, or to converse with you on these subjects, for you have blasphemed many times in your attempt to convince us that this crucified man was with Moses and Aaron, and spoke with them in the pillar of the cloud: that He became man, was crucified, and ascended into Heaven, and will return again to this earth and that He should be worshipped."
>
> "I am aware," I replied," that, as the Word of God testifies, this great wisdom of Almighty God, the Creator of all, is concealed from you. It is, therefore, with feelings of pity that I exert every possible effort to help you understand our teachings, which to you seem paradoxical. . . .
>
> "It is small wonder," I continued, "that you Jews hate us Christians who have grasped the meaning of these truths, and take you to task for your stubborn prejudice. . . . Therefore, just as God did not show His anger on account of those seven thousand men [in the days of Elijah, 1 Kings 19], so now He has not yet exacted judgment of you, because He knows that every day some of you are forsaking your erroneous ways to become disciples in the name of Christ. . . ."
>
> "Don't you realize," interposed Trypho, "that you are out of your mind to say such things?"
>
> [Justin replies] . . . "we can show from the prophecies that you 'who are wise in your own eyes and prudent in your own sight' (Is 5:21), are in reality stupid, for you honor God and His Christ only with your lips. . . ."
>
> "Prove to us," interrupted Trypho," that this man who you claim was crucified, and ascended into Heaven, is the Christ of God. . . ."
>
> "My dear friends," I replied, "anyone with ears would know that I have already

---

[11]This is because priests were required to be thirty years of age before they could minister at the altar (cf. Num 4:1-4).

proved that very point, and it can be shown also from the facts which you your-selves have admitted." (*Dial.* 36, 38-39)[12]

Though Justin's dialogue does not vilify Jews, it does display a certain superiority and condescension not conducive to helpful dialogue. The passage highlights the main sticking point in Christian-Jewish dialogue, namely, the person of Jesus of Nazareth. Also interesting in the passage are the discernible contours of the Apostles' Creed, the *Dialogue with Trypho* being an early witness to the antiquity of this creedal statement. The relative civility of this debate will not, unfortunately, characterize later debates between Christians and Jews, some of which were little more than orations before a lynching.[13]

We summarize Justin's attitude toward Jews, as reflected in his writings, in this fashion.[14] He urges Christians to pray for Jews; thus they are not written off as beyond hope of conversion. On the other hand, according to Justin, Jews hate Christians, torture them and incite authorities against them. In this connection, Justin claims that the Jews urged Titus to punish Christians more severely than non-Christians. Justin also insists that Jews curse Christians in the synagogues, perhaps a reference to the insertion of the Twelfth Benediction into the Amidah (see below). He also makes the comment that "the Jews killed Christ more than ten times." In Justin's view, all Jews are guilty of crucifying Jesus. Essentially, then, Jews are mired in sin, sick, led by teachers who are ignorant and practice rites that are useless. Furthermore, Justin dismisses the notion of the restoration of Israel as absurd. In short, Justin Martyr displays a pronounced anti-Judaism that would only intensify in succeeding Christian theology.

Melito of Sardis

Melito was bishop of Sardis in Syria. Sometime in the latter part of the second century A.D. he wrote a sermon titled "On the Passover" *(Peri Pascha).*[15] Like the *Epistle of Barnabas*, this sermon highlights the rejection of Israel (the Jewish people) and the supersession of the church. Also, like *Barnabas,* Melito employed the allegorical method in order to make his point. Here is a sample:

---

[12]T. B. Falls, trans., *Writings of Justin Martyr* (New York: Christian Heritage, 1948), pp. 202, 204-8.

[13]This was especially so in the medieval period and the Inquisition.

[14]See further Clark M. Williamson, *Has God Rejected His People? Anti-Judaism in the Christian Church* (Nashville: Abingdon, 1982), pp. 94-95. This was also developed by Chuck Guth, "Anti-Judaism and the Apostolic Fathers" (paper delivered at the ETS Annual Meeting, November 15, 2000, Nashville, Tenn.).

[15]For background, see G. F. Hawthorne, "Melito of Sardis," *DLNTD,* pp. 731-33.

But when the church arose,
   and the gospel was shed abroad,
the type was rendered useless,
   yielding its power to the gospel.
Just as a pattern is left empty
   when its image is surrendered to reality,
and a parable is made useless
   when its interpretation is made known,
so also the law was finished
   when the gospel was revealed,
and the people was abandoned,
   when the church was established,
and the type was abolished
   when the Lord had appeared.[16]

Melito, however, introduced something even more destructive into Christian theologizing about the Jews. He is the first Christian writer that we know about who laid at the feet of the Jews the charge of deicide, that is, of killing God in the person of Jesus Christ. Here is his characterization of this event: "He who hung the earth was hung; he who affixed the heavens was affixed; he who sustained all was suspended on the tree; the master has been outraged; God has been murdered; the king of Israel slain by an Israelite hand."

Furthermore, the charge of deicide was embroidered in highly emotional and inflammatory language, as the following passage reveals:

You (i.e., Jews) brought both scourges for his body
   and thorns for his head;
and you bound his good hands,
   which formed you from earth;
and that good mouth of his which fed you with life
   you fed with gall.
And you killed your Lord at the great feast,
and you were making merry,
   while he was starving;
you had wine to drink and bread to eat,
   he had vinegar and gall;
your face was bright,
   his was downcast;
you were triumphant,
   he was afflicted;
you were making music,

---

[16]Richard C. White, trans., *Melito of Sardis Sermon "On the Passover": A New English Translation with Introduction and Commentary* (Lexington, Ky.: Lexington Theological Seminary Library, 1976).

> he was being judged;
>   you were giving the beat,
>   he was being nailed up;
>   you were dancing,
>   he was being buried;
>   you were reclining on a soft couch,
>   he in grave and coffin.

This kind of rhetoric set a precedent for anti-Jewish sentiment among Gentile Christians. Christian attitudes toward Jews down through the centuries have been so poisoned by this kind of characterization that a long-standing epithet hurled at Jews has been "Christ-killers." Nearly any adult Jew one might meet today could relate an incident in which he or she was derided as a Christ-killer. It became a standard Christian view that any suffering Jews might experience was entirely justified and divinely sanctioned. Indeed, the miseries of Jews served simply to reinforce the church's conviction that Jews had been rejected by God and lay under his terrible curse. No wonder that throughout medieval and even modern times Jews were violently assaulted by those who considered themselves Christians—and these attacks were deemed praiseworthy.[17]

At just about the same time as Judah the Prince was editing the Mishnah (ca. A.D. 200), Hippolytus of Rome wrote: "Hear my words and give heed thou Jew. Many a time dost thou boast thyself that thou didst condemn Jesus of Nazareth to death. . . . Of what retribution does Jesus speak? Manifestly of the misery which has now got hold of thee."[18] It must be constantly reiterated that such a view can only be branded as unchristian. The consequences of early Christian triumphalism and the Christ-killers charge by the church against Jews have been beyond calculation in terms of human misery. Rausch pointedly reminds Christians to reflect on a legacy of hatred:

> The foundation had been laid and the message was clear. The Jews were no longer God's chosen people. They had persecuted and killed Jesus Christ and Christians. The Jews deserved persecution and the loss of their land. The Christian church had inherited the covenant promises of God—the church was God's chosen people. The curses of the Bible were ascribed to the Jews; the blessings of the Bible to the Christians. This was religious anti-Semitism, and even Hitler would draw on this foundation.[19]

---

[17]For a survey of just a few episodes, see Williamson, *Has God Rejected His People?* pp. 89-122; David A. Rausch, *A Legacy of Hatred: Why Christian Must Not Forget the Holocaust* (Chicago: Moody Press, 1984), pp. 19-30; Marvin R. Wilson, *Our Father Abraham: Jewish Roots of the Christian Faith* (Grand Rapids, Mich.: Eerdmans; Dayton: Center for Judaic-Christian Studies, 1989), pp. 87-103; and Keith, *Hated Without A Cause?* pp. 91-210.

[18]J. H. Macmahon, trans., *Expository Treatise Against Jews,* ANF 5.1.

[19]*Legacy of Hatred,* p. 22.

The Synagogue Strikes Back

Of course the animosity was not one-way. As the fledgling Jesus movement spread beyond its Palestinian origins and followed the Roman roads to Rome and beyond, the Jewish community was forced to deal with this new competitor on the block. Both the Jewish community and the followers of Jesus claimed to be "the Israel of God." The Jewish community was not about to relinquish the title.

As the book of Acts testifies, early Christian missionaries such as the apostle Paul effectively spread the gospel along the network of Roman roads. In most Roman cities of any importance, a Jewish synagogue could be found. Paul's strategy typically involved three steps. First, he visited the local synagogue on the sabbath and was usually invited to preach. Using his knowledge of the Septuagint to great effect, he proclaimed the good news that Jesus of Nazareth was the fulfillment of Israel's messianic hopes. Second, after several sabbaths at most, a crisis would develop, and he would usually be asked to leave or be thrown out. He would take with him, however, the few Jewish converts and the not-so-few "God-fearers," that is, Gentiles who were attracted to Judaism but chose not to go all the way and convert. Third, with these converts as a core group, Paul would then establish house churches and aggressively pursue evangelism in the streets, marketplaces and public meeting halls of the city (Acts 13:44—14:7; 17:1-15; 18:1-11). Diaspora Jewish communities were understandably incensed by Paul's tactics and, according to the book of Acts, tried repeatedly to hinder him in this endeavor through various means, some subtle and others direct. One may assume that scenarios similar to this unfolded numerous times in the first two centuries A.D.

One of the subtle Jewish responses to Christian missionizing in synagogues consisted of the insertion of a benediction into the weekday prayer service (Amidah) that uttered a curse upon those who were followers of Jesus. This served as a "test benediction" and was a fairly effective means of discouraging Jewish (or Gentile) Christians from continuing to attend the services. It is called the *birkat hāminim* and is the twelfth of the Eighteen Benedictions (Shemoneh Esre). Here is the text thought to be close to the one introduced at the end of the first Christian century:

> For the apostates may there be no hope unless they return to Your Torah. As for the *notzrim* and the *minim,* may they perish immediately. Speedily may they be erased from the Book of Life and may they not be registered among the righteous. Blessed are you, O Lord, who subdues the wicked.[20]

---

[20]Translation by Lawrence H. Schiffman, *Texts and Traditions: A Source Reader for the Study of Second Temple and Rabbinic Judaism* (Hoboken, N.J.: Ktav, 1998), p. 415. For a slightly

The precise referent of the word *minim* ("heretics") is not certain. The term apparently was used as a cover term for a number of different Jewish heresies. In time, Jewish Christians were included in this designation. There is considerable scholarly debate about whether the reference to the Nazarenes (*nôṣrîm;* i.e., Christians) was original to the text or a later insertion. There is also debate on the origin of the "test benediction" itself. Although the Talmud traces its origin to Yavneh (*b. Ber.* 28b), many modern scholars doubt that it was prior to the Bar Kokhba revolt.[21]

Another measure that the Yavnean sage Yohanan ben Zakkai endorsed led to even more rivalry between church and synagogue. He decreed that the shofar could be blown in the synagogue on Rosh Hashanah, as had been done in the Second Temple (*m. Roš Haš.* 4:1-4). As Bruce Chilton and Edwin Yamauchi point out, "For those who saw Jesus as the true access to the sanctuary, any transfer of the temple's function to the synagogue necessitated the replacement of that institution; from that time, the attempt to replace the institutions of Judaism within Christianity became programmatic."[22] Very likely the harsh language of Revelation 2:9; 3:9, which speak of a "synagogue of Satan," reflects Christian reaction to the claim of Jews to be the true Israel, ritually and symbolically underscored by cultic acts drawn from the Second Temple.

A not-so-subtle approach, however, might also be employed against the followers of Jesus. The Gospel of John makes reference three times to Jews who believed in Jesus being "put out of the synagogue" (Jn 9:22; 12:42; 16:2). This too has generated scholarly debate. Many scholars, noting that the rest of the NT, the apostolic fathers and Tannaitic literature are silent about such excommunication, attribute the Johannine passages to anti-Judaic polemic on the part of the Evangelist or his community (i.e., they are not authentically connected to the time of Jesus' ministry). Given a precedent for excommunication already in the Persian period, however (Ezra 10:8; Neh 13:3; Is 66:5), and the undoubted practice in the Qumran community (1QS 6:24—7:25), we think a convincing case can be made for such measures by the synagogue during Jesus' day.[23]

---

different translation, see C. K. Barrett, *The New Testament Background: Selected Documents,* rev. ed. (San Francisco: Harper & Row, 1987), p. 211.

[21]For a judicious assessment of the origins of these terms, see Wilson, *Our Father Abraham,* pp. 66-69. See also Jack T. Sanders, *Schismatics, Sectarians, Dissidents, Deviants: The First One Hundred Years of Jewish-Christian Relations* (Valley Forge, Penn.: Trinity Press International, 1993), pp. 58-61; and J. D. G. Dunn, *The Partings of the Ways Between Christianity and Judaism* (London: SCM Press; Philadelphia: Trinity Press International, 1991). The Hebrew term *nôṣrîm* is still used in Israel as the designation for Christians.

[22]"Synagogues," *DNTB,* p. 1152.

[23]See Wilson, *Our Father Abraham,* pp. 69-71. Craig Evans thinks otherwise: "In three passages we find explicit reference to Christian expulsion from the synagogue (Jn 9:22;

Jewish religious leaders, of course, felt compelled to defend their tradition against the new challenger. This involved polemic for internal use as well as refutations aimed at the larger public. The following is a regulation from the Tosefta that had the effect of distancing Jews from Christians:

> If meat is found in the hand of a non-Jew, it is permitted to derive benefit from it. [If it is found] in the hand of a *min,* it is forbidden to derive benefit from it. That which comes forth from the house of a *min,* indeed it is the meat of sacrifices to the dead (idolatrous worship), for they said: The slaughtering of a *min* is idolatry; their bread is the bread of a Samaritan; their wine is the wine of [idolatrous] libation; their fruits are untithed; their books are the books of diviners, and their children are *mamzerim.* We do not sell to them, nor do we buy from them. We do not take from them, nor do we give to them, and we do not teach their sons a craft. We are not healed by them, neither healing of property nor healing of life. (*t. Ḥul.* 2:20-21)[24]

Another selection from the same tractate of the Tosefta indicates that there was interaction between the rabbis and Jewish Christians, but it was generally hostile:

> It happened that Rabbi Eliezer was arrested on charges of *minut* (heresy), and they brought him up to the platform to be tried. The governor said to him, "Does an elder like yourself busy himself with things like these?"
>
> He (Rabbi Eliezer) said to him (the governor), "The judge is reliable concerning me."
>
> The governor thought that he was referring to him, but he intended to refer to his Father Who is in Heaven.
>
> He (the governor) said to him (Rabbi Eliezer), "Since you have accepted me as reliable concerning yourself, thus I have said: It is possible that these gray hairs are in error concerning these charges. *Dimissus.* You are released."
>
> After he (Rabbi Eliezer) left the platform, he was troubled that he was arrested on charges of *minut.* His disciples came in to console him, but he would not take [consolation].
>
> Rabbi Akiva entered and said to him, "My teacher, may I say before you something so that perhaps you will not grieve?"
>
> He said to him, "Say [it]."
>
> He (Rabbi Akiva) said to him (Rabbi Eliezer), "Perhaps one of the *minim* said a word of *minut* which gave you pleasure?"
>
> He (Rabbi Eliezer) said, "By Heaven, you have reminded me. Once I was

---

12:42; 16:2). Although it is possible that such actions were taken in the time of Jesus, it is probable that these threats reflected the experience of the Johannine community sometime late in the first century, perhaps in the wake of the revision of the twelfth benediction of the *Amidah* . . . as part of a concerted effort to drive Christians out of the synagogue" ("Christianity and Judaism: Partings of the Ways," p. 166).

[24]Translation by Schiffman, *Texts and Traditions,* p. 416.

walking in the street of Sepphoris. I chanced upon Jacob of Kefar Siknin, and he said a word of *minut* in the name of Yeshua ben Pantira (Jesus), and it gave me pleasure. I was arrested on charges of *minut*, for I have transgressed the words of the Torah, "Keep your path far from her and do not draw near to the entrance of her house (Prov. 5:8), for she has brought down many victims [and numerous are those whom she has killed] (Prov. 7:26)."

For Rabbi Eliezer used to say: "Stay away from ugliness and from that which resembles ugliness." (*t. Hul.* 2:24)[25]

Recognizing that Sepphoris was but a few miles from Jesus' hometown of Nazareth, we are not surprised that Jewish Christians might be found there. The degree to which the rabbis sought to avoid Jewish Christians, however, is surprising. This reflects the elevated tension, at least in Palestine, between the respective religious communities by this time. Even casual conversation was problematic since one might, as rabbi Eliezer apparently did, assent to something uttered by a heretic. In this case it was a saying traced to Jesus himself.

The identity of ben Pantira in this passage is uncertain. The church father Epiphanius thought it an alternate name for Joseph (*Pan.* 3.78.7). But it may be that ben Pantira refers to a Roman soldier (*Panthera*) who, as some Jews alleged, had a secret affair with Mary and fathered Jesus.[26] It thus designates Jesus as a *mamzer*, that is, someone of illegitimate birth. Matthew's account of Jesus' birth almost certainly gives a Christian response to this Jewish allegation (Mt 1). John's Gospel may also allude to this early Jewish accusation about the paternity of Jesus ("We are not illegitimate children" [Jn 8:41]). The later Talmud contains a number of accusations of illegitimacy, idolatry, sorcery and heresy directed at Jesus.[27]

Conclusion

This ends our survey of Second Temple Judaism. The reader is encouraged to pursue further the respective stories of Christianity and Judaism. As each struggles to live out its respective faith, similarities and parallels surface time and again. These two faiths are, in some important respects, mirror images of each other.

Sadly, however, the two daughters of Second Temple Judaism mutually parted company and went their separate ways. The subsequent interaction between them has, for the most part, been hostile and distrustful. Christians need to do their homework and discover how hateful and vile many of the

[25]Ibid. This saying of Eliezer at the end of the passage reminds us of the apostle Paul's admonition, "Abstain from every form of evil" (1 Thess 5:22).
[26]For details, see David Flusser, "Jesus," *EncJud* 10:10-14.
[27]For references, see Evans, "Christianity and Judaism: Partings of the Ways," p. 167.

attitudes and actions of Christians toward Jews have been.[28] As David Rausch puts it, we need to build bridges back to our Jewish neighbors and not expect them to meet us halfway.[29] After so much water under the bridge, such an endeavor is not easy. It is my hope that this survey of the Jewish literature of the Second Temple will assist in the building of such a bridge. This "hope is built on nothing less" than a fundamental recognition: the NT is thoroughly Jewish and so was earliest Christianity.

Our primary purpose in writing this book has been to demonstrate the importance of the Jewish literature of the Second Temple period for a deeper understanding of the NT. The reader must judge whether we have accomplished this objective. We are convinced that the evidence speaks for itself. We do not mean to imply that the Greco-Roman world is unimportant for NT studies—quite the contrary. Much can be learned from that dimension of the NT world.[30] We do maintain, however, that the essential core of NT thought displays clear affinities with Second Temple Judaism, which itself is rooted in the Hebrew Scriptures.[31] We are also aware that much more could have been included from Second Temple Judaism for a more fully orbed perspective. But we are confident that enough has been examined so that the NT will never again be read in quite the same way.

For Further Discussion

1. In light of Paul's teaching in Romans, what attitude should Christians have toward Jews? What attitude should Christians have toward the modern State of Israel?

2. Detail the progression of Christian animosity toward Jews. Why did this happen?

---

[28]See further the works by Willliamson *(Has God Rejected His People?)*, Rausch *(Legacy of Hatred)* and Keith *(Hated Without A Cause?)*. Pope John Paul II's statements and actions during his papal visit in April 2000 to Yad Vashem and the Western Wall were a welcome step forward in the process of reconciliation between Catholics and Jews.

[29]See esp. *Building Bridges* (Chicago: Moody Press, 1988), pp. 232-33.

[30]Hans Dieter Betz writes, "The NT and other early Christian literature cannot be interpreted in a scholarly justifiable way unless it is understood in its relationships with the language, literature, religion, culture, and civilization of its Hellenistic (including the Jewish) environment" ("Hellenism," *ABD* 3:129). See also D. E. Aune, ed., *Greco-Roman Literature and the New Testament*, SBLSBS 21 (Atlanta: Scholars Press, 1988); M. E. Boring, K. Berger and C. Colpe, *Hellenistic Commentary to the New Testament* (Nashville: Abingdon, 1995); C. S. Keener, *The IVP Bible Background Commentary: New Testament* (Downers Grove, Ill.: InterVarsity Press, 1993); J. Paul Sampley, *Paul in the Greco-Roman World* (Harrisburg, Penn.: Trinity Press International, 2001); and Edwin Yamauchi, "Hellenism," *DPL*, pp. 383-88.

[31]Betz adds, "Consequently, the presence of the OT in the NT is not a direct but a mediated one: it is mediated through the Judaism at the time of Jesus and the early Church" ("Hellenism," 3:128).

3. What are some examples of anti-Semitism that you are aware of today? What reasons can you find for such attitudes?

4. What can be done by Christians to help build bridges to our Jewish neighbors?

For Further Reading

J. D. G. Dunn, *The Partings of the Ways* (London: SCM Press; Philadelphia: Trinity Press International, 1991).

Craig A. Evans, "Christianity and Judaism: Partings of The Ways," *DLNTD,* pp. 159-70.

————, "Judaism, Post-A.D. 70," *DLNTD,* pp. 605-11.

Craig A. Evans and Donald A. Hagner, eds., *Anti-Semitism and Early Christianity: Issues of Polemic and Faith* (Minneapolis: Fortress, 1993).

Donald A. Hagner, "Apostolic Fathers," *DLNTD,* pp. 82-91.

Sidney G. Hall III, *Christian Anti-Semitism and Paul's Theology* (Minneapolis: Fortress, 1993).

Graham Keith, *Hated Without A Cause? A Survey of Anti-Semitism* (London: Paternoster, 1997).

Judith Lieu, John North and Tessa Rajak, eds., *The Jews Among Pagans and Christians* (London: Routledge, 1992).

J. B. Lightfoot and J. R. Harmer, eds., *The Apostolic Fathers,* rev. and ed. by Michael W. Holmes, 2d ed. (Grand Rapids, Mich.: Baker, 1992), pp. 1-15, 274-327.

David A. Rausch, *Building Bridges* (Chicago: Moody Press, 1988), pp. 227-33.

————, *Fundamentalist Evangelicals and Anti-Semitism* (Valley Forge, Penn.: Trinity Press International, 1993).

————, *A Legacy of Hatred: Why Christians Must Not Forget the Holocaust* (Chicago: Moody Press, 1984), pp. 16-30, 204-9.

Clark M. Williamson, *Has God Rejected His People? Anti-Judaism in the Christian Church* (Nashville: Abingdon, 1982).

Marvin R. Wilson, *Our Father Abraham: Jewish Roots of the Christian Faith* (Grand Rapids, Mich.: Eerdmans and Center for Judaic-Christian Studies, 1989).

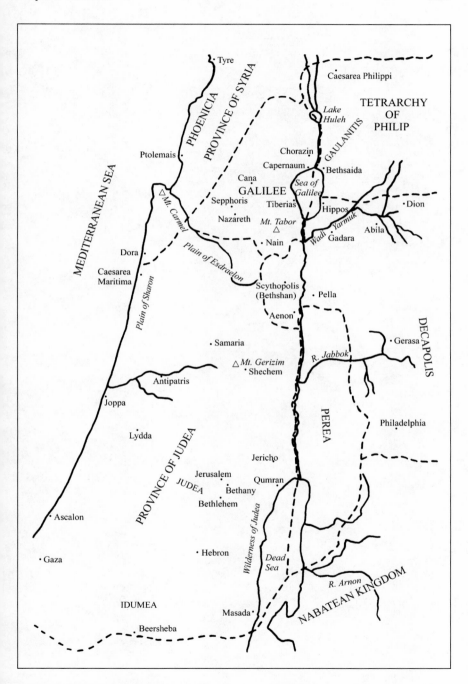

Palestine in the New Testament Era

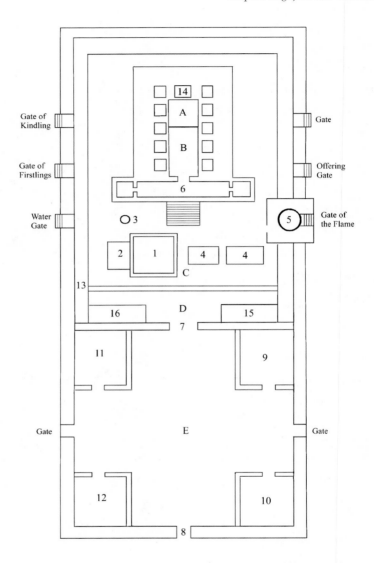

A	Holy of Holies	1	Altar	9	Chamber of Lepers
B	Sanctuary	2	Ramp	10	Chamber of Wood
C	Court of Priests	3	Laver	11	Chamber of Oil
D	Court of Israel	4	Slaughter Area	12	Chamber of Nazirites
E	Court of Women	5	Chamber of the Hearth	13	Chamber of Hewn Stone
		6	Porch	14	Chambers
		7	Nicanor Gate	15	Chamber of Vestments
		8	Beautiful Gate	16	Chamber of Baked Cakes

Plan of Herod's Temple

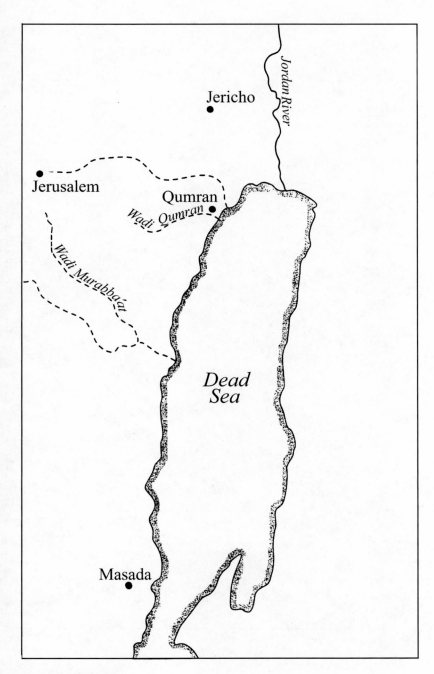

Location of Qumran

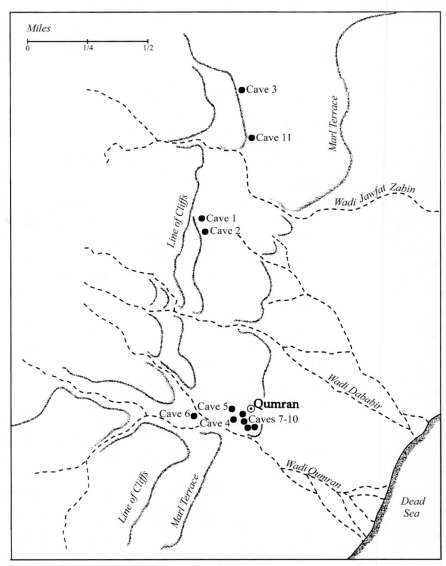

Location of Qumran Caves

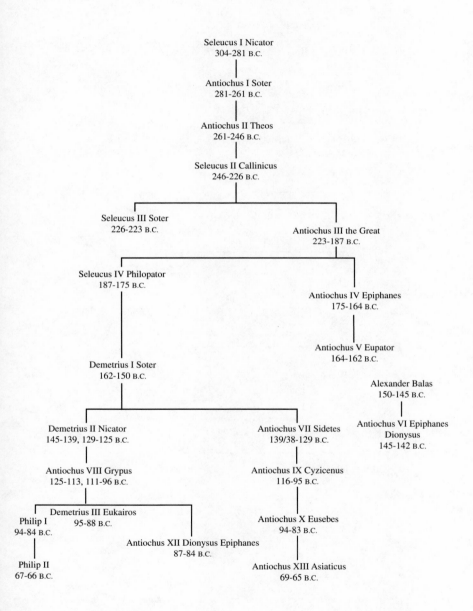

Seleucus I Nicator
304-281 B.C.

Antiochus I Soter
281-261 B.C.

Antiochus II Theos
261-246 B.C.

Seleucus II Callinicus
246-226 B.C.

Seleucus III Soter
226-223 B.C.

Antiochus III the Great
223-187 B.C.

Seleucus IV Philopator
187-175 B.C.

Antiochus IV Epiphanes
175-164 B.C.

Antiochus V Eupator
164-162 B.C.

Demetrius I Soter
162-150 B.C.

Alexander Balas
150-145 B.C.

Demetrius II Nicator
145-139, 129-125 B.C.

Antiochus VII Sidetes
139/38-129 B.C.

Antiochus VI Epiphanes
Dionysus
145-142 B.C.

Antiochus VIII Grypus
125-113, 111-96 B.C.

Antiochus IX Cyzicenus
116-95 B.C.

Philip I
94-84 B.C.

Demetrius III Eukairos
95-88 B.C.

Antiochus X Eusebes
94-83 B.C.

Antiochus XII Dionysus Epiphanes
87-84 B.C.

Philip II
67-66 B.C.

Antiochus XIII Asiaticus
69-65 B.C.

Seleucid Dynasty

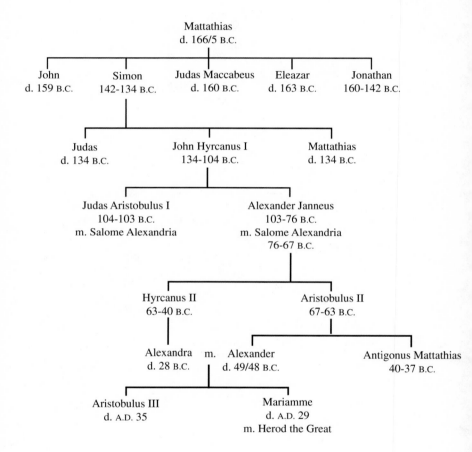

House of Hasmoneans

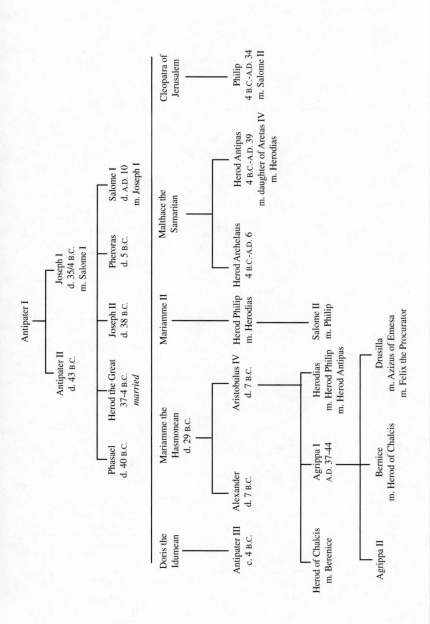

House of Herod

Index of Subjects

15:40-41, *471*
15:43, *68*
15:47, *471*
16:1, *471*
16:6, *263*
40, *59*
65, *205*

Luke
1--2, *173*
1:1-4, *285, 360*
1:3, *361*
1:3-4, *284*
1:5, *363*
1:16-17, *59*
1:19, *70, 87*
1:26, *70*
1:32, *391*
1:32-33, *59, 251*
1:71, *60*
1:74, *60*
2, *428*
2:1-3, *361*
2:22-38, *363*
2:25, *60*
2:32, *156*
2:38, *60*
2:41-50, *363*
3:1, *366*
3:1-2, *358*
3:1-3, *18*
3:2, *370*
3:7, *59*
3:7-9, *368*
3:15, *59*
3:19, *366*
3:20, *365*
3:21-22, *427*
4:1-13, *87, 144*
4:9-12, *363*
4:16-21, *239*
4:21, *239*
6:15, *155*
6:45, *90*
7:36-50, *173*
8:1-3, *471*
8:3, *366*
8:26-39, *131*
8:31, *89*
9:7-9, *366*
9:10-17, *61*
9:20-22, *61*
9:25, *429*
9:28-36, *59*
10:1, *285*
10:17, *285*
10:21-23, *205*
10:23, *392*
10:29-37, *156*
10:38, *105*
11:13, *90*
11:15, *71*
11:19, *71*
11:19-20, *89*
11:24-26, *89*
11:37-42, *372*
11:38, *473*
12, *429*

12:16-21, *104*
12:24, *456*
12:32, *205*
13:1-3, *367*
13:10-17, *173*
13:23-24, *397*
13:32, *366*
14:5, *208*
14:15, *391*
14:24, *391*
15:18, *73, 462*
16:4, *401*
16:9, *410*
16:10-31, *401*
16:14, *373*
16:18, *204*
16:22, *410*
16:23, *92*
16:26, *92*
17:11-19, *156*
18:9-14, *389*
18:11, *257*
18:22, *105*
18:35-43, *131*
19:1-10, *365*
19:12, *365*
19:45-48, *363, 374*
19:46, *374*
19:47, *363*
20:27-40, *164*
20:47, *207, 373*
21, *126, 134*
21:1-4, *364*
21:5, *364*
21:6, *364*
21:7-9, *427*
21:24, *73*
22:15-20, *206*
22:24, *62*
22:28-30, *235, 391*
22:35-38, *240*
22:37, *240*
22:63-70, *374*
23:1-5, *374*
23:1-25, *367*
23:4, *368*
23:6-12, *366*
23:8, *219*
23:13-16, *368*
23:13-25, *374*
23:22, *368*
23:35, *374*
23:45, *286, 364*
23:51, *68*
24:21, *60*
24:25, *241*
24:25-26, *60*
24:25-27, *297*
24:27, *201, 241*
24:44, *73, 259*
24:44-45, *103*
24:44-46, *201*
24:44-49, *297*

John
1--11, *241*
1:1, *299, 324, 328*
1:1-3, *324, 327*

1:1-5, *391*
1:1-14, *102*
1:3, *295, 299*
1:4, *295*
1:4-9, *219*
1:5, *89*
1:9, *443*
1:13, *92*
1:14, *328*
1:21-25, *219*
1:29, *138, 409*
1:49, *219*
2:6, *473*
2:13-22, *364*
2:19-21, *207*
2:20, *17*
3:16, *40*
3:19-21, *90, 219*
3:21, *73*
4:22, *202*
4:26, *61*
4:35-38, *222*
4:39-42, *156*
5:21, *67*
5:25-30, *263*
5:35, *219*
5:39, *202, 241*
5:39-47, *239*
5:46, *241*
6:1-15, *131*
6:14, *219*
6:15, *61*
6:15-21, *131*
6:27, *439*
6:41-51, *240*
6:45, *240*
7:14, *363*
7:28, *363*
7:40, *219*
7:42, *251*
8:12, *219*
8:41, *500*
8:44, *90*
8:46, *391*
9:22, *245, 498*
10:16, *139, 156*
10:22, *158*
10:22-23, *158*
10:24, *158*
10:25, *158*
10:31, *158*
10:31-38, *456*
11:41, *257*
11:48, *374*
11:49, *370, 374*
12:28, *427*
12:36, *219*
12:42, *245, 498*
12:48, *263*
13:12-20, *241*
13:18, *241, 262*
14:2, *383, 427*
14:6, *222*
14:15, *466*
14:30, *89*
15:18-25, *241*
15:21, *205*
15:25, *241*

15:27, *222*
16:2, *245, 498*
16:3, *205*
16:33, *412*
17:25, *205*
18:11, *153*
18:13, *370*
18:15, *370*
18:19, *370*
18:22, *370*
18:24, *370*
18:28--19:16, *367*
18:36, *61*
19:12, *367*
19:38-39, *68*
20:29, *393*
20:30, *157*
20:30-31, *202*
21:24-25, *202*
21:25, *157*

Acts
1:1, *360, 361*
1:1-2, *360*
1:3, *61, 241*
1:6, *60*
1:7-8, *72*
1:8, *383*
1:11-12, *443*
1:12, *208*
1:14, *471*
1:15-26, *154*
2, *238*
2:8-11, *58*
2:14-39, *88*
2:16, *238*
2:17, *471*
2:30, *251*
2:32, *238, 263, 383*
2:32-29, *411*
2:36, *263*
2:37-42, *220*
2:38-40, *238*
2:41, *220*
2:42, *220*
2:44-45, *209*
2:46, *364*
2:47, *220*
3:1, *171*
3:15, *383*
3:19-21, *61*
4:12, *222, 411*
4:25-28, *202*
4:27-28, *202*
5:12, *364*
5:17, *374*
5:19, *87*
5:21, *364*
5:21-39, *370*
5:34, *461*
5:34-39, *372*
5:36, *348*
5:36-37, *361*
5:37, *348*
5:38-39, *199*
5:42, *364*
6:5, *283*

6:7, *286*
7:2-53, *207*
7:38, *135*
8:26, *87*
9:2, *485*
9:36-42, *173*
10--15, *63*
10:1--11:18, *221*
10:3-22, *87*
11:26, *485*
12, *366*
12:1-17, *88*
12:3-11, *364*
12:7-11, *87*
12:15, *87, 88*
12:17, *369*
12:19-23, *347*
12:20-23, *366*
12:21-23, *315*
12:23, *87*
13--14, *488*
13:1, *366*
13:16-41, *207*
13:17-22, *242*
13:23, *242, 251, 391*
13:27-29, *242*
13:44--14:7, *497*
14:11, *64*
14:15, *64, 65*
15, *64, 221, 325, 482*
15:1-35, *221*
15:13-21, *369*
15:21, *64*
15:23-29, *155, 285*
16:13, *315*
16:20, *306*
16:22, *306*
17:1-15, *497*
17:7, *307*
17:16, *64*
17:25, *65*
17:29, *65*
17:32, *308*
18, *307*
18:1-11, *497*
18:12-17, *315*
18:14-16, *307, 368*
18:17, *307*
18:18-19, *221*
18:24, *300, 329*
18:24-28, *290*
19:9, *485*
19:13-14, *71*
19:21--28:31, *154*
19:23, *485*
19:23--20:1, *65*
19:23-41, *368*
19:32, *307*
19:33, *307*
19:34, *308*
21:9, *471*
21:18-25, *369*
21:20, *245*
21:20-26, *221*
21:27--23:31, *364*
21:38, *361*